FOURTH EDITION

Sociology
for the Twenty-First Century

Tim Curry
Robert Jiobu
Kent Schwirian
The Ohio State University

PEARSON
Prentice Hall

Upper Saddle River, New Jersey 07458

Library of Congress Cataloging-in-Publication Data

Curry, Timothy J. (Timothy Jon)
    Sociology for the twenty-first century / Tim Curry, Robert Jiobu, Kent Schwirian.—4th ed.
        p. cm.
    Includes bibliographical references and indexes.
    ISBN 0-13-185078-4
    1. Sociology. 2. Sociology—United States. 3. Social change. 4. Social change—United States.
    5. United States—Social conditions. I. Jiobu, Robert M. II. Schwirian, Kent P. III. Title.

HM586.C87 2004
301—dc22   2004009570

Publisher: Nancy Roberts
Executive Editor: Christopher DeJohn
Editorial Director: Leah Jewell
Director of Production and Manufacturing: Barbara Kittle
Editorial Liaison: Sharon Chambliss
Production Liaison: Rob DeGeorge
Copyeditor: Melissa Messina
Manufacturing Manager: Nick Sklitsis
Prepress and Manufacturing Buyer: Mary Ann Gloriande
Editorial/Production Supervision: Stacey Corbin/Interactive
    Composition Corp.
Creative Design Director: Leslie Osher
Art Director: Laura Gardner
Interior and Cover Design: Wanda España/
    Wee Design Group
Manager of Production Services: Guy Ruggiero
Electronic Art Creation: Mirella Signoretto

Director of Marketing: Beth Mejia
Senior Marketing Manager: Marissa Feliberty
Editorial Assistant: Kristin Haegele
Supplements Editor: Erin Katchmar
Media Editor: Kate Ramunda
Photo Researcher: Francelle Carapetyan
Image Permission Coordinator: Craig A. Jones
Cover Image Specialist: Karen Sanatar
Interior Image Specialist: Beth Brenzel
Manager, Rights and Permissions: Zina Arabia
Director, Image Resource Center: Melinda Reo
Cover Art: Rob Colvin/Stock Illustration Source, Inc.
Composition: Interactive Composition Corp.
Printer/Binder: Von Hoffmann Press, Inc.
Cover Printer: Coral Graphics
Text: 10.5/12 Goudy

Credits and acknowledgments borrowed from other sources and reproduced, with permission, in this textbook appear on appropriate page within text or, in the case of photographs, on p. 525.

Pearson Education LTD.
Pearson Education Singapore, Pte. Ltd
Pearson Education, Canada, Ltd
Pearson Education—Japan
Pearson Education Australia PTY, Limited

Pearson Education North Asia Ltd
Pearson Educación de Mexico, S.A. de C.V.
Pearson Education Malaysia, Pte. Ltd
Pearson Education, Upper Saddle River,
    New Jersey

10 9 8 7 6 5 4 3 2 1
ISBN 0-13-185078-4

Brief Contents

Contents

v

PART II   Social Inequality

CHAPTER 6   **Inequalities of Social Class** 158

CHAPTER 7   **Inequalities of Race and Ethnicity** 192

PART III   Social Institutions

Contents   **ix**

Box Features

Critical Thinking

Profiles

? What Do You Think?

Diversity

Social Change

Sociology Online

Preface

When we began *Sociology for the Twenty-First Century*, the new century was almost a decade away. Now we are in the new century, and we are pleased to continue our efforts with the fourth edition of our textbook. The events of the first half of the first decade of the new century have demonstrated the importance of understanding society and social change. Within the short period between our third and fourth editions, these recent events occurred: terrorism is now a concern of everyday life in the United States; global environmental problems have increased; managing the pace of immigration to the United States has become a significant political issue; white-collar and corporate crime have cost shareholders billions of dollars in losses and thousands of lost jobs; and the United States has launched a preemptive strike against Iraq, an action that angered many world leaders and made for difficult relations with the United Nations. On the positive side, nuclear war among the major powers has become even more remote, and science and technology continue to impress us with new discoveries in communication, medicine, and transportation. Now many of our students have cellphones and need to be reminded to turn them off during class!

This edition contains several significant updates, yet our teaching philosophy remains the same. We still argue that sociology is a good intellectual place to begin preparing for life in the new century because sociology directs our attention to both social stability and social change. We continue to believe that we are all social creatures, all linked to each other, and all responsible for the world in which we live. While other disciplines make similar claims, sociology does so from a unique perspective. This perspective is introduced in the first chapter of the book, and we believe that it will enable you to see the world in ways in which you have not before seen it.

Organization of the Book

This book contains four main sections. Part One introduces you to the basic concepts in sociology, fundamental approaches, theories, and methods. In our introduction to the discipline we stress the fact that sociology from its inception was interested in understanding social stability and social change. Part Two examines the topic of inequality, paying special attention to social stratification, racial–ethnic relations, and gender relations. Part Three covers the major institutions of society—the economy, political order, marriage and the family, education, religion, and medicine and health care. Whereas many shorter textbooks combine their examinations of various institutions into a single chapter, we do not. We devote a full chapter to each institution we cover. Part Four consists of the chapter on Population, Ecology, and Urbanization, and the chapter on Collective Social Action.

Features of the Book

Our text contains many features that encourage critical thinking about society and social change.

- We emphasis social change as a fundamental aspect of society, especially the shift from societies organized around personal relationships to those organized around impersonal relationships. We refer to this change as the Great Social Transformation. Beginning with Chapter 3, each chapter contains a section applying the concept of the Great Social Transformation to the subject matter under discussion.

■ We believe in analyzing the individual and society from different theoretical viewpoints. Accordingly, the viewpoints of functionalism, conflict theory, and symbolic interaction are introduced in Part One of the text and then systematically applied to each chapter in Parts Two and Three.

■ We reinforce this discussion with a chart comparing the three major theoretical perspectives. The first of these charts appears in Chapter 3, and the others appear in each chapter in Parts Two and Three. We believe these tables help students master more easily the sociological perspectives.

■ Critical thinking boxes entitled "What Do You Think?" These boxes are linked to the critical thinking model presented in Chapter 1 and systematically explore how the model can help us analyze current issues.

■ Society Today and World Today data tables that run in the margins of the text. These features present timely information on topics of current importance.

■ We end each chapter with a section on the future. In it, we extend the arguments made in the chapter, extrapolate data, and discuss informed predictions of what social life will be like in the future.

■ An important goal of any course is to improve the students' ability to engage in critical thinking. Consequently, we end each major section of each chapter with a segment on critical thinking. In it, we present a mini-summary of the section and a critical question for students to consider.

■ We include several additional types of educational materials:

1. In keeping with our emphasis on critical thinking, we provide boxed material profiling critical thinkers from sociology and other disciplines.

2. Diversity boxes introduce sociological material from other cultures or feature the contributions of people who might at one time have been marginalized in society.

3. Social Change boxes highlight important changes occurring in our own and other societies—changes that typically relate to the Great Social Transformation brought about by such trends as industrialization, urbanization, bureaucratization, rationalization, and globalization.

4. Illustrations and photographs provide examples, highlight contrasts, and expand on general points made in the text. Maps are included to pinpoint geographic localities and provide points of reference.

5. We provide a running glossary within the text so that students have the definitions of key terms immediately available.

6. We provide Sociology Online boxes in each chapter that suggest Internet sites where students can go to find additional information.

7. We provide end-of-chapter "What You Should Know" summaries and self-test items (multiple choice, true–false items, and matching).

We hope that you will find these materials as fascinating as we do, and that they will contribute to your understanding of society and the individual.

New Features for the Fourth Edition

■ Concepts maps have been added to the end-of-chapter materials. This is done to provide a visual scheme to indicate the relationships among the concepts in the chapter. Some students learn better if they see graphical representations of subject matter, and we believe these new enhancements to the text will be well received by many students and instructors.

- In-text study strategies have been created by Sarah Kravits, based on *Keys to Success, Fourth Edition,* © 2002, written by Carol Carter, Joyce Bishop, and Sarah Lyman Kravits. These strategies will help the students explore how they learn, understand how particular strategies may heighten their strengths and boost their weaknesses, and know when to use these strategies. The material also contains helpful study techniques. See *Learning Styles: An Important Part of Successful Studying* on page xx.

- The Deviance and Socialization chapter in the previous edition has been divided into two chapters in the Fourth Edition. One chapter now focuses on socialization and includes more extensive treatment of the life course, particularly the elderly. The second chapter focuses exclusively on deviance and crime. This chapter includes an expanded treatment of crime and crime rates and includes new material on the criminal justice system. We believe this new chapter is especially timely, given the increased attention to the crime problem in the United States.

- The text is now in two colors instead of four. This modification helps to reduce the net price of the book to the student without diminishing the substantive quality of the materials presented.

- Chapter openers now include photographs, and many of the photographs in the text are new and deal with recent events that give the book a contemporary look that connects more directly to student experiences.

- Statistical tables have in many cases been transformed into charts for greater student interest and comprehension.

- The Sociology Online sections have been updated and rewritten. These online sections now encourage the student to make use of Internet search engines to locate materials, enhancing the student's research experience.

Supplements

The supplements package to the text is of exceptional quality. Each component has been carefully selected to give the instructor all the aid and resources needed to teach a course in Introductory Sociology.

For the Instructor

Instructor's Resource and Testing Manual   Written by the authors, this essential instructor's tool includes detailed chapter outlines, teaching objectives, discussion questions, classroom activities, and additional instructors' resources. Also included are over 1,500 test questions *written* and *tested* by the authors. Each question is page-referenced to the text.

TestGEN-EQ   This computerized software allows instructors to create their own personalized exams, to edit any or all of the existing test questions and to add new questions. Other special features of this program include random generation of test questions, creation of alternate versions of the same test, scrambling question sequence, and test preview before printing.

Prentice Hall Film and Video Guide: Introductory Sociology, Seventh Edition
Keyed to the topics discussed in this textbook, this guide describes more than 300 films

and videos appropriate for classroom viewing. It also provides summaries, discussion questions, and rental sources for each film and video.

ABCNEWS **ABC News/Prentice Hall Video Library for Sociology** Prentice Hall and ABC News are working together to bring to you the best and most comprehensive video material available in the college market. Through its wide variety of award-winning programs—*Nightline, This Week, World News Tonight,* and *20/20*—ABC offers a resource for feature and documentary-style videos related to the chapters in *Sociology for the Twenty-First Century, Fourth Edition.* The programs have high production quality, present substantial content, and are hosted by well-versed, well-known anchors. In addition, an instructor's guide to the videos includes a synopsis of each video and discussion questions to help students focus on how concepts and theories apply to real-life situations.

Volume I: Social Stratification (0-13-466228-8)
Volume II: Marriage/Families (0-13-209537-8)
Volume III: Race/Ethnic Relations (0-13-458506-2)
Volume IV: Criminology (0-13-375163-5)
Volume V: Social Problems (0-13-437823-7)
Volume VI: Intro to Sociology I (0-13-095066-1)
Volume VII: Intro to Sociology II (0-13-095060-2)
Volume VIII: Intro to Sociology III (0-13-095773-9)
Volume IX: Social Problems (0-13-095774-7)
Volume X: Marriage/Families II (0-13-095775-5)
Volume XI: Race and Ethnic Relations II (0-13-021134-6)
Volume XII: Institutions (0-13-021133-8)
Volume XIII: Introductory Sociology IV (0-13-018507-8)
Volume XIV: Introductory Sociology V (0-13-018509-4)

Prentice Hall Introductory Sociology PowerPoint™ Transparencies These PowerPoint slides combine graphics and text in a colorful format to help you convey sociological principles in a new and exciting way. Created in PowerPoint™, an easy-to-use, widely available software program, this set contains slides keyed to each chapter in the text. For easy access, they are available on the Instructor Resource CD-ROM.

Prentice Hall Color Transparencies: Sociology Series VII Full-color illustrations, charts, and other visual materials from the text as well as outside sources have been selected to make up this useful in-class tool.

Instructor's Guide to Prentice Hall Color Transparencies: Sociology Series VII
This guide offers suggestions for effectively using each transparency in the classroom.

Census2000 Interactive CD-ROM Capturing the rich picture of our nation drawn by Census2000, this CD-ROM brings related Census data into your classroom in a rich, multimedia format. It uses files taken directly from the Census Bureau web site—even recently released Census Briefs—organizes them around your course, and offers teaching aids to support student learning. This updated CD-ROM is free when packaged with *Sociology for the Twenty-First Century, Fourth Edition.*

Distance Learning Solutions Prentice Hall is committed to providing our leading content to the growing number of courses being delivered over the Internet by developing relationships with the leading vendors. Please visit our technology solutions site at www.prenhall.com/demo.

For the Student

 **Research Navigator™** The easiest way for you to start a research assignment or research paper, *Research Navigator™* comes complete with extensive online documentation about the research process as well as four exclusive databases:

- *The New York Times* Search-by-Subject Archive
- *ContentSelect™* Academic Journal Database powered by EBSCO
- *Best of the Web* Link Library
- *Financial Times* Article Archive and Company Financials

Access to *Research Navigator™* is available via an access code that is found on the inside front cover of *The Prentice Hall Guide to Evaluating Online Resources with Research Navigator™: Sociology* guide. This supplementary book, along with the *Research Navigator™* access code, is free to students when packaged with the Fourth Edition. Please contact your Prentice Hall representative for more information.

The Prentice Hall Guide to Evaluating Online Resources with *Research Navigator™*: Sociology This guide focuses on developing the critical thinking skills necessary to evaluate and to use online sources. Encouraging students to become critical consumers of online sources, this guide walks students through the process of selecting and citing their online sources properly. It also includes a section on using *Research Navigator™*—Prentice Hall's own gateway to academically sound and current sources.

***TIME* Magazine Special Edition: Sociology** Prentice Hall and *TIME* magazine are pleased to offer you and your students a chance to examine today's most current and compelling issues in an exciting new way. *TIME Magazine Special Edition: Sociology* offers a selection of 20 *TIME* articles on today's most current issues and debates in Sociology. *TIME Magazine Special Edition* provides your students the full coverage, accessible writing, and bold photographs for which *TIME* is known. Free when packaged with *Sociology for the Twenty-First Century, Fourth Edition*, it is perfect for discussion groups, in-class debates, or research assignments. Please see your local Prentice Hall representative for more information.

10 Ways to Fight Hate Brochure (0-13-028146-8). Produced by the Southern Poverty Law Center, the leading hate-crime and crime-watch organization in the United States, this free supplement walks students through ten steps that they can take on their own campus or in their own neighborhood to fight hate every day.

Companion Website™ This online study guide provides unique support to help you with your studies in Sociology. Featuring a variety of interactive learning tools, including online quizzes with immediate feedback, this site is a comprehensive resource organized according to the chapters in *Sociology for the Twenty-First Century, Fourth Edition*. It can be found at www.prenhall.com/curry.

 The New York Times*/Prentice Hall *eThemes of the Times The *New York Times* and Prentice Hall are sponsoring *eThemes of the Times*, a program designed to enhance student access to current information relevant to the classroom. Through this program, the core subject matter provided in the text is supplemented by a collection of timely articles downloaded from one of the world's most distinguished newspapers, *The New York Times*. These articles demonstrate the vital, ongoing connection between what is learned in the classroom and what is happening in the world around us. Access to *The New York Times/ Prentice Hall eThemes of the Times* is available on the *Sociology for the Twenty-First Century, Fourth Edition Companion Website™*.

SocNotes A useful and exciting FREE student resource, SocNotes is Prentice Hall's one-stop resource for students studying sociology, and it is designed around the chapters in *Sociology for the Twenty-First Century, Fourth Edition* to help students keep their course notes and information in order.

Easy to use and portable, SocNotes includes the following for each chapter of this text:

- A short chapter summary.
- Learning objectives.
- Two to three key pieces of art from each chapter for classroom use.
- Perforated pages that provide space on each page for note taking.

SocNotes is FREE when packaged with this text. Please see your local Prentice Hall representative for more details.

Acknowledgments

We owe a debt of thanks to the many people who have been involved in supporting, encouraging, and critiquing our manuscript. Editorial assistance for the first edition was provided by Rochelle Diogenes and the staff of Prentice Hall. We would especially like to thank Nancy Roberts, Sharon Chambliss, and Bob Thoresen, who helped guide this book to completion.

Many of our colleagues generously consented to evaluate the various chapters as we wrote them, and some contributed original materials. Eddie Berry drafted material for the chapter on gender, Pat Schwirian developed material on aging and health, Jeff Jarosch tracked down statistics and researched information on socialization and deviance, and Pam Park-Curry provided material on careers for the chapter on the economy. Other reviewers who made comments on the Fourth Edition as well as on previous editions that were invariably helpful and on the mark were Jeffrey Sallaz, an honors student at Ohio State; Lee Braude, State University of New York at Fredonia; Brent Bruton, Iowa State University; Rhonda V. Carr, Tulane University; Sheying Chen, CUNY–College of State Island; Larry D. Crawford, Morehouse College; Walter M. Francis, Central Wyoming College; Robert H. Freymeyer, Presbyterian College; Robert Hassenger, SUNY–Empire State College; Robert Heiner, Plymouth State College; Gretchen J. Hill, Wichita State University; J. Selwyn Hollingsworth, University of Alabama at Tuscaloosa; Jeanne Humble, Lexington Community College; Audra Kallimanis, Mt. Olive College; David F. Krause, Lake Sumter Community College; James T. Minor, University of Nebraska; Dina B. Neal, Vernon College; David O'Donnell, Graceland College; Ronald A. Penton, Sr., Gulf Coast Community College; Joann Sloan, Gordon College; Thomas Soltis, Westmoreland County Community College; Kathleen A. Tiemann, University of North Dakota; A. Javier Trevino, Marquette University; Theodore C. Wagenaar, Miami University; Steve Weisner, Springfield Technical Community College; Debra Welkley, California State University at Sacramento; D.R. Wilson, Houston Baptist University; Sylvano S. Wueschner, William Penn College; and Norma Wilcox, Wright State University.

An Introduction to Learning Style

It happens in nearly every college course: Students listen to lectures throughout the semester. Each student hears the same words at the same time and completes the same assignments. However, after finals, student experiences will range from fulfillment and high grades to complete disconnection and low grades or withdrawals.

Many causes may be involved in this scenario—different levels of interest and effort, for example, or outside stresses. Another major factor is *learning style* (any of many particular ways to receive and process information). Say, for example, that a group of students is taking a freshman composition class that is often broken up into study groups. Students who are comfortable working with words or happy when engaged in discussion may do well in the course. Students who are more mathematical than verbal, or who prefer to work alone, might not do as well. Learning styles play a role.

There are many different and equally valuable ways to learn. The way each person learns is a unique blend of styles resulting from distinctive abilities, challenges, experiences, and training. In addition, how you learn is not set in stone; particular styles may develop or recede as your responsibilities and experiences lead you to work on different skills and tasks. The following assessment and study strategies will help you explore how you learn, understand how particular strategies may heighten your strengths and boost your weaknesses, and know when to use them.

Multiple Intelligences Theory

There is a saying, "It is not how smart you are, but how you are smart." In 1983, Howard Gardner, a Harvard University professor, changed the way people perceive intelligence and learning with his theory of Multiple Intelligences. This theory holds that there are at least eight distinct *intelligences* possessed by all people, and that every person has developed some intelligences more fully than others. (Gardner defines an "intelligence" as an ability to solve problems or fashion products that are useful in a particular cultural setting or community.) According to the Multiple Intelligences Theory, when you find a task or subject easy, you are probably using a more fully developed intelligence; when you have more trouble, you may be using a less developed intelligence.

In the table on the next page are descriptions of each of the intelligences, along with characteristic skills. The *Multiple Pathways to Learning* assessment, based on Gardner's work, will help you determine the levels to which your intelligences are developed. You will find the assessment on p. xxii.

Putting Assessments in Perspective

Before you complete *Multiple Pathways to Learning,* remember: no assessment has the final word on who you are and what you can and cannot do. An intriguing but imperfect tool, its results are affected by your ability to answer objectively, your mood that day, and other factors. Here's how to best use what this assessment, or any other, tells you:

Use assessments for reference Approach any assessment as a tool with which you can expand your idea of yourself. There are no "right" answers, no "best" set of scores. Think of it in the same way you would a set of eyeglasses for a person with blurred

Intelligences	Characteristic Skills
VERBAL/LINGUISTIC Ability to communicate through language through listening, reading, writing, and speaking.	■ Analyzing own use of language ■ Remembering terms easily ■ Explaining, teaching, learning, and using humor ■ Understanding syntax and meaning of words ■ Convincing someone to do something
LOGICAL/MATHEMATICAL Ability to understand logical reasoning and problem solving, particularly in math and science.	■ Recognizing abstract patterns and sequences ■ Reasoning inductively and deductively ■ Discerning relationships and connections ■ Performing complex calculations ■ Reasoning scientifically
VISUAL/SPATIAL Ability to understand spatial relationships and to perceive and create images.	■ Perceiving and forming objects accurately ■ Manipulating images for visual art or graphic design ■ Finding one's way in space (using charts and maps) ■ Representing something graphically ■ Recognizing relationships between objects
BODILY/KINESTHETIC Ability to use the physical body skillfully and to take in knowledge through bodily sensation	■ Connecting mind and body ■ Controlling movement ■ Improving body functions ■ Working with hands ■ Expanding body awareness to all senses ■ Coordinating body movement
INTRAPERSONAL Ability to understand one's own behavior and feelings.	■ Evaluating own thinking ■ Being aware of and expressing feelings ■ Taking independent action ■ Understanding self in relationship to others ■ Thinking and reasoning on higher levels
INTERPERSONAL Ability to relate to others, noticing their moods, motivations, and feelings.	■ Seeing things from others' perspectives ■ Cooperating within a group ■ Achieving goals with a team ■ Communicating verbally and nonverbally ■ Creating and maintaining relationships
MUSICAL/RHYTHMIC Ability to comprehend and create meaningful sound and recognize patterns.	■ Sensing tonal qualities ■ Creating or enjoying melodies and rhythms ■ Being sensitive to sounds and rhythms ■ Using "schemas" to hear music ■ Understanding the structure of music and other patterns
NATURALISTIC Ability to understand features of the environment.	■ Deep understanding of nature, environmental balance, and ecosystem ■ Appreciation of the delicate balance in nature ■ Feeling most comfortable when in nature ■ Ability to use nature to lower stress

vision. The glasses will not create new paths and possibilities, but will help you see more clearly the ones that already exist.

Use assessments for understanding   Understanding the level to which your intelligences seem to be developed will help prevent you from boxing yourself into categories that limit your life. Instead of saying "I'm no good in math," someone who is not a natural in math can make the subject easier by using appropriate strategies. For example, a learner who responds to visuals can learn better by drawing diagrams of math problems. The more you know yourself, the more you will be able to assess and adapt to any situation—in school, work, and life.

Face challenges realistically   Any assessment reveals areas of challenge as well as ability. Rather than dwelling on limitations (which often results in a negative self-image) or ignoring them (which often leads to unproductive choices), use what you know from the assessment to look at where you are and set goals that will help you reach where you want to be.

Following the assessment, you will see information about the typical traits of each intelligence, and more detailed study strategies geared toward the four intelligences most relevant for studying this text. During this course you should make a point to explore a large number of new study techniques, considering all of the different strategies presented here, not just the ones that apply to your strengths. Why?

Change   Because you have abilities in all areas, though some are more developed than others, you may encounter useful suggestions under any of the headings. Furthermore, your abilities and learning styles change as you learn, so you never know what might work for you.

Strategies help weaknesses as well as build strengths   Knowing learning styles is not only about guiding your life toward your strongest abilities; it is also about choosing strategies to use when you face challenges. Strategies for your weaker areas may help when what is required of you involves tasks and academic areas that you find difficult. For example, if you are not strong in logical-mathematical intelligence and have to take a math course, the suggestions geared toward logical-mathematical learners may help you build what skill you have.

As you complete the assessment, try to answer the questions objectively—in other words, answer the questions to best indicate who you are, not who you want to be (or who your parents or instructors want you to be). Then, enter your scores on p. xxiii. Don't be concerned if some of your scores are low—that is true for almost everyone.

Multiple Pathways to Learning

Rate each statement:

rarely = 1,   sometimes = 2,   often = 3,   almost always = 4

Write the number of your response on the line next to the statement and total each set of 6 questions.

1. _____ I enjoy physical activities.	7. _____ I use maps easily.
2. _____ I am uncomfortable sitting still.	8. _____ I draw pictures or diagrams when explaining ideas.
3. _____ I prefer to learn through doing rather than listening.	9. _____ I can assemble items easily from diagrams.
4. _____ I tend to move my legs or hands when I'm sitting.	10. _____ I enjoy drawing or taking photographs.
5. _____ I enjoy working with my hands.	11. _____ I do not like to read long paragraphs.
6. _____ I like to pace when I'm thinking or studying.	12. _____ I prefer a drawn map over written directions.
_____ **TOTAL for Bodily-Kinesthetic (B-K)**	_____ **TOTAL for Visual-Spatial (V-S)**

13. _____ I enjoy telling stories.
14. _____ I like to write.
15. _____ I like to read.
16. _____ I express myself clearly.
17. _____ I am good at negotiating.
18. _____ I like to discuss topics that interest me.

_____ **TOTAL for Verbal-Linguistic (V-L)**

19. _____ I like math.
20. _____ I like science.
21. _____ I problem-solve well.
22. _____ I question why things happen or how things work.
23. _____ I enjoy planning or designing something new.
24. _____ I am able to fix things.

_____ **TOTAL for Logical-Mathematical (L-M)**

25. _____ I listen to music.
26. _____ I move my fingers or feet when I hear music.
27. _____ I have good rhythm.
28. _____ I like to sing along with music.
29. _____ People have said I have musical talent.
30. _____ I like to express my ideas through music.

_____ **TOTAL for Musical (M)**

31. _____ I like doing a project with other people.
32. _____ People come to me to help them settle conflicts.
33. _____ I like to spend time with friends.
34. _____ I am good at understanding people.
35. _____ I am good at making people feel comfortable.
36. _____ I enjoy helping others.

_____ **TOTAL for Interpersonal (Inter)**

37. _____ I need quiet time to think.
38. _____ When I need to make a decision, I prefer to think about it before I talk about it.
39. _____ I am interested in self-improvement.
40. _____ I understand my thoughts, feelings, and behavior.
41. _____ I know what I want out of life.
42. _____ I prefer to work on projects alone.

_____ **TOTAL for Intrapersonal (Intra)**

43. _____ I enjoy being in nature whenever possible.
44. _____ I would enjoy a career involving nature.
45. _____ I enjoy studying plants, animals, forests, or oceans.
46. _____ I prefer to be outside whenever possible.
47. _____ When I was a child I liked bugs, ants, and leaves.
48. _____ When I experience stress I want to be out in nature.

_____ **TOTAL for Naturalist (N)**

Scoring the Assessment

Indicate your scores by shading the appropriate box below. A score of 20–24 indicates a high level of development in that particular type of intelligence, 14–19 a moderate level, and below 14 an underdeveloped intelligence.

	20–24 (Highly Developed)	14–19 (Moderately Developed)	Below 14 (Underdeveloped)
Bodily-Kinesthetic			
Visual-Spatial			
Verbal-Linguistic			
Logical-Mathematical			
Musical			
Interpersonal			
Intrapersonal			
Naturalist			

Study Strategies for Different Learning Styles

Finding what study strategies work best for you is almost always a long process of trial and error, often because there is no rhyme or reason to the search. If you explore strategies in the context of learning style, however, you give yourself a head start. Now that you have completed the *Multiple Pathways to Learning* assessment, you will be able to look at the following material with a more informed view of what may help you most.

The strategies presented here are linked to four intelligences, selected because they have the most relevance to your study in this course—Verbal/Linguistic, Logical/Mathematical, Visual/Spatial, and Interpersonal. Although they are written in the context of strength, remember that the strategies can also help you build up an area of weakness. Try strategies from all different areas and evaluate them. Do the ones that match your strengths work best for you? Do the ones that correspond to your weaker areas help you improve? Does a winning strategy come from an unexpected intelligence area? What might that help you learn about yourself?

Note Taking

Because it is virtually impossible to take notes on everything you hear or read, the act of note taking encourages you to evaluate what is worth writing down and remembering. Note taking keeps you actively involved with the material and helps organize your thinking. Knowing how you learn will help you decide how to take notes in class and from the textbook.

Learners with Verbal/Linguistic strength   Words are your thing, and notes are words, so you generally take comprehensive notes. In fact you may often overdo it by trying to write down everything that you hear. Your challenge is to be choosy, and organized, with what you write.

- Rewrite notes to cut out unnecessary material and focus on the important ideas.
- Summarize the main ideas and supporting points of chapters.
- Avoid writing out every word—use abbreviations and other "personal shorthand."

Learners with Logical/Mathematical strength   You prefer organized notes that flow logically. Unfortunately, not all classes and instructors make it possible for you to take the kind of notes you prefer. You often need time to convert your notes into a more structured format.

- On your own time, rewrite notes and organize the material logically.
- Write outlines of class notes or text material.
- Leave one or more blank spaces between points, in case making your notes more logical requires filling in missing information later.

Learners with Visual/Spatial strength   You retain best what is presented in some sort of graphic, visual format. Courses that primarily consist of lectures don't make the most of your abilities. Look for materials that tap into your strength—or create them when none exist.

- Take notes in a visual style—for example, use a "mind map" or "think link" that connects ideas and examples using shapes and lines; like the concept maps that have been provided at the end of each chapter.

- Use different colors—either during class or after—to organize your notes.
- Start a new page for a new topic.

Learners with Interpersonal strength Material stays with you best when you learn it and review it actively with others. Some classes give you the opportunity to interact—and some don't. Make your notes come alive by making interaction a part of your note taking experience.

- Go over notes with one or more fellow students, helping one another fill in the gaps.
- Solidify your understanding of your notes by teaching concepts to someone else.
- If you tend to talk with classmates and get distracted, try not to sit with your friends.

Reading

Research has shown that it is far more effective to break your reading into several steps than to spend the same amount of time going through the material once. SQ3R is a textbook reading technique that will help you grasp ideas quickly, remember more, and review effectively for tests. The symbols S-Q-3-R stand for *survey, question, read, recite,* and *review.* Following is a brief overview of SQ3R:

Survey *Surveying* refers to the process of previewing, or prereading, a book before you actually study it. When you survey, pay attention to frontmatter (table of contents and preface); chapter elements (title, outline or list of objectives, headings, tables and figures, quotes, summary, other features); and backmatter (glossary, index, bibliography).

Question *Questioning* means reading the chapter headings and/or objectives and, on a separate piece of paper or in the margins, writing questions linked to them. If your reading material has no headings, develop questions as you read. These questions focus your attention and increase your interest, helping you build comprehension and relate new ideas to what you already know.

Read Your questions give you a starting point for *reading,* the first R in SQ3R. Learning from textbooks requires that you read *actively*—engaging with the material through questioning, writing, note taking, and other activities. As you read, focus on your Q stage questions, look for important concepts, and make notations in your textbook (marginal notes, highlighting, circling key ideas). Read in segments and make sure you understand what you read as you go.

Recite Once you finish reading a topic, stop and answer the questions you raised in the Q stage of SQ3R. You may decide to *recite* each answer aloud, silently speak the answers to yourself, tell or teach the answers to another person, or write your ideas and answers in brief notes. Writing is often the most effective way to solidify what you have read because writing from memory checks your understanding.

Review *Review* soon after you finish a chapter. Reviewing, both immediately and periodically in the days and weeks after you read, solidifies your understanding. Reviewing techniques include rereading, answering study questions, summarizing, group discussion, quizzing yourself, and making flash cards. Reviewing in as many different ways as possible increases the likelihood of retention.

This text has features that fit into the SQ3R steps and reinforce your learning. The following table shows how you can use specific features as you move through the steps of SQ3R.

SQ3R Steps	Text Feature
Survey	Each chapter begins with a list of major topics and a "Chapter Preview" paragraph that gives an overview.
Question	Critical thinking questions appear after each major chapter heading and throughout the text beside photographs, tables, and figures.
Read	The text flows from topic to topic, with a "Pausing to Think" feature at the end of each section.
Recite	"What You Should Know" sections at the end of each chapter list and answer the chapter's significant points.
Review	A built-in study guide called "Test Your Knowledge" gives objective question quizzes at the end of each chapter.

Here are some reading tips geared toward the intelligences:

Learners with Verbal/Linguistic strength   You tend to function well as a reader. Set yourself up for success by being as critical as you can be when you read.

- As you read text, highlight no more than 10%.
- Mark up your text with marginal notes while you read.
- Recite information by rewriting important ideas and examples.

Learners with Logical/Mathematical strength   When reading material is organized and logical, you tend to do well. When it is not, you may run into trouble.

- Look for patterns and systems in your reading material.
- Read material in sequence.
- Think about the logical connections between what you are reading and the world at large.

Learners with Visual/Spatial strength   Textbooks with tables, figures, and other visuals help you to retain the concepts in your reading. You can make your own when there are few or none.

- As you read, take note of all visuals—photos, tables, figures, other visual aids.
- Reconstruct what you have read using a visual organizer (mind map, timeline, chart).
- Take time out to visualize concepts as you read.

Learners with Interpersonal strength   Since reading is solitary, not your strongest setting, you need to find group situations that can enhance your understanding of what you read.

- Start a study group that discusses assigned class readings.
- Have a joint reading session with a friend and take turns summarizing sections for each other.
- Teach someone else selected concepts from your reading.

Memory

In one theory, the human memory is compared to a computer, with an encoding stage, a storage stage (with three storage levels—sensory, short term, and long term), and a retrieval stage. Taking this view, memory improvement involves rehearsing information to move it form short-term to long-term memory. Another theory posits that there are different levels of processing information that lead to varying degrees of memory. From this perspective, improving your memory requires using increased effort when processing information.

Learners with Verbal/Linguistic strength   Use words to rehearse information.

- Write summaries of your text passages and notes.
- Rewrite notes, working to make them neater, more concise, easier to understand.
- Make up word-based mnemonics, such as acronyms.

Learners with Logical/Mathematical strength   Organizing your material will help you remember.

- Impose structure on information—write outlines, use grouping or chunking techniques.
- Put dates and events into timelines.
- Review systematically—for example, for 30 minutes at a particular time every day.

Learners with Visual/Spatial strength   Make your material visual.

- Draw mind maps and fill them in with important information.
- Turn information into charts or graphs.
- Use imagery—visualize items as you learn them.

Learners with Interpersonal strength   Reviewing with others helps you cement what you learn.

- Discuss material in a group; make quizzes for one another; teach one another.
- Work together to create mnemonic devices.
- Perform songs or poems for others that contain the information you need to remember.

Test Taking

Test taking is about learning. Tests are designed to show what you have learned and to help you figure out where you need to work harder. The best test takers understand that they train not just for the test but to achieve a solid level of competence. Using a learning styles-based approach to studying for and taking tests will boost your ability—if you learn the material in the way that suits you best, you will best be able to retain it and communicate it in a testing situation.

Learners with Verbal/Linguistic strength   Put your focus on words to good use.

- Think of and write out questions your instructor may ask on a test—and write answers.
- Pay attention to important words—directions that tell you how to answer, for example, or negatives that sway the meaning of a question ("Which of the following is *not* . . .").
- For math and science tests, do word problems first—and translate the words into formulas.

Learners with Logical/Mathematical strength   Find a sequential system.

- Devise and use a system that you prefer—going through the test in its exact order, for example, or doing all the simple problems first and then coming back to harder ones.

- Outline the key steps involved in topics on which you may be tested.
- If you don't know the right answer to a multiple-choice question, look for patterns that may lead to the right answer. For example, when there are two similar choices, one of them is usually correct.

Learners with Visual/Spatial strength   Do what you can to make the test appeal to the visual.

- Underline key words and phrases in the test questions.
- Make drawings to illustrate concepts you are being tested on.
- Create mind maps to organize your thoughts before completing an essay question.

Learners with Interpersonal strength   Testing, usually a solitary enterprise, rarely makes use of your strengths. Do what you can to prepare in settings that provide interaction.

- Study for tests in pairs and groups.
- In your group, come up with possible test questions and ask each other questions in an oral-exam type format.
- Debrief with others—talk about the test, how you answered questions, what you wish you had done differently, and what you will do differently next time.

Summing Up

Now that you have explored some possibilities of how to apply your learning styles knowledge to your study techniques, you can spend some time trying out strategies and finding what works best for you. As you read the text, watch for "Study Strategies" in the margins that offer specific strategies for mastering key concepts in the text. The "Study Strategies" are indicated with an icon, and look like this:

- For Verbal/Linguistic

- For Logical/Mathematical

- For Visual/Spatial

- For Interpersonal

Be strategic as you read, study, and learn, and you will find that your self-knowledge and your abilities can take you forward to a bright future in college and beyond.

These study tips are from *Keys to Success, Fourth Edition*, © 2002, written by Carol Carter, Joyce Bishop, and Sarah Lyman Kravits, and published by Prentice Hall.

About the Authors

TIM CURRY

Tim Curry is Associate Professor of Sociology at The Ohio State University. He has taught introductory sociology for more than 20 years at Ohio State, from large classes of 300 students to honors classes of 25 students. He currently serves as the department's chair of Instructional Development. In addition to teaching Introductory Sociology, Dr. Curry, who earned his doctorate from the University of Washington, teaches Sociology of Sport classes and a graduate seminar, Men in Society. Dr. Curry is a member of the Primary Care Research Institute at The Ohio State University and holds association memberships in the North American Society for the Sociology of Sport, the North Central Sociological Association, and the American Sociological Association. He has published more than 25 professional articles on the subjects of social psychology, sport and society, racial and gender depictions in mass media, and men's health issues, as well as three books: *Sports: A Social Perspective*; *Introducing Visual Sociology*; and *High Stakes: Big Time Sports and Downtown Redevelopment*. Dr. Curry is a past president of the International Visual Sociology Association, and the North American Society for the Sociology of Sport.

ROBERT JIOBU

Robert Jiobu has more than 30 years of teaching experience at several universities including California State University at Los Angeles, University of Southern California, and University of Wisconsin at Green Bay. He has taught introductory sociology to classes of 600 students and to honors classes of 25 students. In addition to teaching introductory sociology, he has taught racial and ethnic relations and statistical analysis at both undergraduate and graduate levels.

Dr. Jiobu, who earned a doctorate from the University of Southern California, has published more than 25 professional articles, mostly on racial and ethnic relations, as well as three monographs: *Sports: A Social Perspective*; *Ethnicity and Assimilation*; and *Ethnicity and Inequality*. He retired two years ago and is currently enjoying the outdoors and golf while writing a textbook on social problems.

KENT SCHWIRIAN

Kent Schwirian is Professor Emeritus of Sociology and a faculty member of the College of Medicine and Public Health's Primary Care Research Institute at The Ohio State University. Dr. Schwirian's broad experience as a teacher and researcher at Ohio State imbues this textbook with both scholarly expertise and a deep commitment to creating student appreciation for sociology. Dr. Schwirian, who earned his Doctorate of Philosophy in Sociology at the University of Iowa, is author and coauthor of numerous articles and research monographs on social statistics, population studies, and other topics. He has taught large classes on Introductory Sociology and smaller classes on Urban Sociology, Human Ecology, and the Community. He has published five books including *Beyond Edge Cities*; *Comparative Urban Structure: Studies in the Ecology of Cities*; and *Contemporary Topics in Urban Sociology*. Dr. Schwirian is a member of the American Sociological Association, the Population Association of America, and the American Association of University Professors, in addition to numerous other professional memberships.

1

What Is Sociology?

Chapter Outline

The American Sociological Association is the largest professional organization of sociologists in the world. The late James Coleman once served as its president. He began his 1992 presidential address to the association with the following story:

I recently took a canoe trip with two of my sons down the Wisconsin River and a portion of the Mississippi. We began the trip in a setting much like that experienced by Indians on the same river: Evidence of beavers abounded on the riverbanks; great blue herons, snowy egrets, and sandhill cranes flapped away as we approached; an American bald eagle soared overhead. We made our way down the river at three or four miles per hour. When we reached the Mississippi on the third day, nature retreated to the backwaters off the main channel. We saw barges traveling at maybe twice our speed, pushed by Mississippi river tugboats, descendants of the commercial riverboats that have plied that river for more than two centuries. River towns, electric power plants, and industrial cities interrupted the natural environment. As we progressed, we heard the whistles and clackety-clack of trains along the Iowa bank, moving past us at more than 10 times our speed. Power boats sped up, down, and across the river. Toward the end of our trip, a military jet took off nearby, screaming past us at nearly the speed of sound.

In this description, I draw attention to the changes in physical environment and in transportation my sons and I observed as we traveled: From the canoe at 3 or 4 miles per hour, to diesel-powered river traffic at 7 or 8 miles per hour, to a train at 50 miles per hour, to a jet at nearly the speed of sound. Accompanying this change was a change from beavers and great blue herons to the hustle and bustle of modern commercial, industrial, and leisure activity, all taking place with the aid of machines (Coleman 1993, p. 1).

In this brief excerpt, Coleman thinks about how technology has changed both our lives and the environment in which we live. For example, he first compares the speed of a canoe to the speed of a train, and then to the speed of a jet. He is fascinated by these examples because he knows that changes are always taking place, and as a professional sociologist, he is interested in how those changes affect our society and our individual lives. Of course, sociologists study many other topics as well, and Coleman is also well known for his research on education and social theory. In fact, sociology is such a broad field that no one could possibly master all of it in one course. Our goal, therefore, is not to cover everything in depth, but instead to introduce you to the fundamentals of sociology and to the ways that sociologists view the social world.

Chapter Preview

The first issue addressed in this chapter is the sociological viewpoint, or—to state it another way—what is sociology? After discussing the answer to that question, we examine the origins of the discipline and the ideas of three important sociologists: Karl Marx, Émile Durkheim, and Max Weber. We next discuss the functionalist and conflict perspectives, two major viewpoints in sociology. The last section of the chapter examines how sociologists go about doing research.

The Sociological Viewpoint

Each discipline within the social sciences has its own unique viewpoint. For example, economists take the view that people base their decisions on rational considerations, such as the monetary profit to be gained from selling or buying a home. In contrast, sociologists take a broad view, focusing on the social setting in which we live, on the interactions in which we engage, and on the way that social things change through time. These elements of the sociological perspective are reflected in the definition of **sociology** as the scientific study of social structure and social interaction and of the factors making for change in social structure and social interaction. This definition of sociology contains four key concepts, but the discussion here will be brief because we expand on each of them in subsequent chapters.

1. *Science* The term science refers to the body of knowledge produced by answering logical questions with evidence gathered through experimentation or systematic observation. In conducting research, sociologists follow the **scientific method**, an objective and judicious approach to empirical evidence. Scientists are objective because they do not allow their personal opinions to enter into their scientific work; and they are judicious because they require a substantial, if not overwhelming, body of objective evidence before arriving at a conclusion. In applying the scientific method, the sociologist begins by asking critical questions, such as, What happened? Why did it happen? How did it happen? Although posing the right question is crucially important, it is only the first step. The next step is to examine how other sociologists have answered the same question. These answers are found in sociological journals, books, monographs, newsletters, and, most recently, on e-mail bulletin boards. Out of this welter of past writings, coupled with the sociologist's own insight, the sociologist will devise a possible explanation for the question at hand. More formally, this explanation is called a **theory**: an explanation for the relationship between certain facts (Macionis 1996; Lieberson and Lynn 2002). The sociologist must then verify the theory by using random surveys, statistical analysis, in-depth interviews, participant observations, and other research techniques that we will discuss in the last section of this chapter.

2. *Social Structure* As individuals, we are part of a larger set of social units, such as family, school, and country. These units are examples of **social structure**: the relatively permanent components of our social environment. Because structure tends to be long-lasting, it imposes order and predictability on social life. To illustrate, our government and society existed before we were born and will presumably continue to exist long after we have departed. Thus, even though individuals come and go, the basic form of the family and the broad outline of their society will endure. Sociologists seek to understand how social structure is created, how it is changed, and how it shapes our lives.

3. *Social Interaction* If you act in some way toward another person, that person will, under normal circumstances, respond to your actions. These acts and responses constitute **social interaction**. Such interaction can be very informal and ordinary, such as chatting with a friend, or very formal and complicated, such as questioning a witness in a court of law. Social interaction can take place alone, as when a person has an imaginary conversation with a sibling who lives in a different city. It is even possible for an imaginary conversation to be carried on with someone who has passed away. These interactions, which are one of the most fundamental aspects of the human experience, are discussed in more detail in Chapters 3 and 4. Sociology seeks to understand the nature of social interaction and the way that relationships can work for good or ill within our lives.

4. *Social Change* In one way or another, sociologists are always studying change. They must do so, since nothing ever stays the same for long. Even though social life is structured, as we just discussed, it is still in continual flux. Consider an analogy. If you

Sociology ▲ The scientific study of social structure and social interaction and of the factors making for change in social structure and social interaction.

Scientific method ▲ An objective and judicious approach to empirical evidence. Scientists are objective because they do not allow their personal opinions to enter into their scientific work; and they are judicious because they require a substantial, if not overwhelming, body of objective evidence before arriving at a conclusion.

Theory ▲ An explanation for the relationship between certain facts.

Social structure ▲ The relatively permanent components of our social environment.

Social interaction ▲ The acts people perform toward one another and the responses they give in return.

stand in a river, the water that flows over your legs is always new, yet the form and appearance of the river will stay much the same from day to day. In a similar way, each day of your life is different from the previous day, yet the overall pattern does not change radically. Think of your own routine. In all likelihood, you get up at about the same time each weekday morning, take care of your personal needs, go to class, sit in the same seat you always sit in, and converse with the same people as you did the day before. By the end of the day, you will have gone through dozens of these little, routine episodes. Your routine will sometimes vary, of course, but over the school year, your life will take on a structure of its own and become highly predictable. This aspect of everyone's life is aptly expressed when someone asks, "How are you?" and the reply is "Same old, same old."

Over a long time period, however, your life may change dramatically. Hopefully, you will graduate and move on to another stage of your life, or perhaps you will fall in love, or perhaps war will break out and you will therefore join the military. Except for graduation, changes such as these are difficult to predict, yet we can be fairly sure that major changes will eventually come to pass. In short, the sociological viewpoint recognizes that both continuity and change are features of human social existence.

If sociology sounds vaguely familiar to you, that tendency might be so because everyone is, to some extent, a sociologist. We cannot help but observe the social world around us and at times ask "Why?" For example, we recognize the influence our parents have on us; we know that we sometimes cause other people to do certain things; and we realize that broader social structures, such as our government, can change the world against our will. These realizations constitute the beginning of a sociological awareness and make each of us a "natural" sociologist.

To think about society, social interaction, and social change in a casual way, however, does not do complete justice to the scope and complexity of the science of sociology. As we hope to show you throughout this book, understanding sociology will change your view of the world and, perhaps more important, will change your view of yourself. If you eventually forget every fact in this book, yet remember and appreciate the sociological viewpoint for the rest of your life, you will have learned something of immense value.

● ■ ▲ **Pausing to Think**   About the Sociological Viewpoint

As we have seen, sociology is the scientific study of social structure and social interaction and of the factors making for change in structure and interaction. What sets sociology apart from the other social and behavioral sciences is its unique viewpoint. The first element of the sociological viewpoint is science. Because sociology is a science, sociologists follow a prescribed set of research procedures in investigating social phenomena. Social structure is the second element of the sociological viewpoint. Society is structured, and this social structure consists of the relatively permanent components of our social environment such as the family, religion, and the state. Structure is long-lasting and imposes order and predictability on social life. The third element is social interaction. Individuals are, for the most part, involved with a large number of others with whom they interact regularly. Social change is the final element of the sociological viewpoint. Even though social life is structured, it is still in a state of flux, and sociologists recognize that both continuity and change are features of human social existence.

Throughout the text, we occasionally pause and ask you to answer a critical question. Doing this is our way of encouraging you to think about the material you have just read and of helping you to develop a richer sociological imagination. The box titled "What Is Critical Thinking?" explains more about this method. Here, then, is the first critical question:

 CQ   Most sociological observers believe that society is changing rapidly in many respects. ◆ What important changes have you observed in your lifetime?

✎ STUDY TIP

Describe yourself as a sociologist. Write freely for a page or so, in the style of a journal entry. What do you think about most in terms of your relationships with others and human relationships in general? What interests you, confuses you, frustrates you? What do you think needs to change? What makes you ask "Why do people do what they do?"

CQ In this text you will encounter critical questions, or CQ's, at the end of each major section. These CQ's are based on a model of critical thinking that we have used extensively in our own sociology classes—one that is derived from the contributions of a number of educators (Browne and Keeley 1998; Sociology Task Force 1991). What is critical thinking? Stated briefly, it is reflective skepticism about a given subject matter—in this case, sociology and society. The term "reflective skepticism" may sound somewhat pretentious, but it simply means that you ask some important questions before you accept a statement as true. For instance, if someone claims that the crime rate is rising, you might ask: "What makes you think that? Where did you get that information?" If you see an editorial in a newspaper with the headline "Welfare Robs People of Their Dignity," you might wonder, "How did the author come to that conclusion? What makes her or him think that?"

Critical Thinking, Personal Experiences, and Sociological Knowledge

Many social practices and problems have implications for our personal lives. For instance, if you have ever tried to add a class after the official enrollment period was over, you might have encountered someone in authority who would not let you do what you wanted to do, because of some silly rule. When you entered college, you may have wondered why so many forms had to be filled out before you were "officially enrolled," and why even more forms were required before you could obtain student housing or a loan. Max Weber, a central figure in the development of sociological theory, thought that such bureaucratic practices would become endemic in modern society—and he was right. Critically thinking about our own personal experience often leads us to important sociological questions.

The Process of Critical Thinking

The questions we ask about society and sociology determine the answers we get. Ask a good critical question, and you have pointed the search for an answer in the right direction. Ask a misleading question, and the answer, even if quickly and correctly discovered, is still misleading. Thus, the ability to frame the right question is an important component of critical inquiry. But how do you learn to ask the right question?

The first rule of critical thinking is to clarify the issue or assertion. An assertion is a statement that claims that something is true, whereas an issue is a statement that sets out what is to be discussed. For instance, if someone claims that critical thinking will make you a better student, that is an assertion that you could actually prove to be true or false. On the other hand, if someone claims to be discussing the issue of social class, you need to make sure he or she stays on track and presents material relevant to that issue and not some other one.

Once you have identified the assertion or issue, you can generally locate the key terms the author uses to explain his or her points. Are those key terms defined clearly? Has the author provided examples so that you can understand what the key terms mean? Throughout this text, we provide you with the key terms and definitions used in sociology. The key terms are always in boldface type. Learning these terms and definitions will greatly enhance your critical thinking skills in relation to social issues. In addition, we have placed the definitions of concepts central to critical thinking in the margins of the text. At the end of the chapter, we have an exercise that tests your knowledge of the key terms.

Some authors support their assertions with opinions or dramatic stories, whereas others use scientific evidence. As a critical thinker, you need to get in the habit of looking closely at the quality of the evidence before you make up your mind about an issue. Throughout the text, we will supply you with important tables and charts containing data about social trends. You will enhance your critical thinking skills by studying the sociological interpretation of the data included with the figures.

Sociology is a social science, and its findings are seldom neutral. Great inequality among social classes, for example, led Marx to call for a revolution. Also, much sociological insight can come from an understanding of social phenomena from the "inside out," that is, from the point of view of the individuals participating in the behavior under investigation. So at various points in the text, we will ask you to relate your personal experience to the issue being discussed; similarly, we will occasionally ask you to discuss personal or social implications of a sociological concept or finding.

The ultimate challenge of a critical thinker is to generate original assertions. You should not deny yourself the pleasure of making and defending assertions simply because you do not know everything there is to know about sociology. As a way of practicing this, we encourage you to think about the future, and we ask you to make sociological predictions about what society will be like. Because no one can be sure what the future holds, this activity stretches the sociological imagination and helps to develop critical thinking skills.

The Origins of Sociology and Three Central Figures: Karl Marx, Émile Durkheim, and Max Weber

STUDY TIP

Make a list of every significant person, related to the origins of sociology, mentioned or discussed in the chapter (include the figure on p. 9). Create a time line placing each person in time and listing a few significant points to remember. When one person is directly linked to another through work or theory, indicate that visually, perhaps with a line in a different color.

Although sociology is new compared with physics, biology, and other natural sciences, the discipline is actually over 100 years old. A century ago, traditional societies were changing in ways that no one could understand, because people did not have an intellectual tradition or viewpoint for dealing with society. As early observers and scholars struggled to understand these changes, their efforts gradually came together and formed the new science of sociology.

The major force that changed Europe during the nineteenth century was the Industrial Revolution. This revolution completely and forever rearranged society and changed the way people lived. For example, steam power was used to make new and extraordinarily powerful engines. With it, railroad locomotives could haul thousands of tons and hundreds of passengers to far-distant places. Steam engines freed ships from the vagaries of the wind and tide, and giant steam-driven turbines revolutionized mining, agriculture, and manufacturing. Centers of production sprang up and became home and workplace to millions of people. Rural communities withered, while cities, once mainly the hub of government and religion, became home to the masses of people who worked in the new factories. Because coal was the main source of energy, factories spewed out vast columns of smoke, turning day into dusk and coating buildings, streets, and people with black soot. These new cities were without effective police and fire protection, good sewers, clean running water, or efficient trash collection. Disease was normal; cholera routinely killed thousands of people every year.

As the social and industrial orders changed, so did the political order. A social class system with royalty and landed nobility at the top and almost everyone else at the bottom no longer made sense. Fortunes were being made in commerce, and through their new wealth, merchants and industrialists gained new power. Ordinary people began to believe that they, too, had a right to a voice in government and to "Liberty, Equality, and Fraternity"—the motto of the French Revolution. To attain these rights, some people fomented dissent and open revolution. Many of these revolutions are now celebrated as national holidays, such as Bastille Day in France and Independence Day in the United States.

It was against the backdrop of the Industrial Revolution that sociology first emerged. The new discipline represented an attempt to understand better the social forces that were sweeping through Europe and overturning the established order of society. Although Auguste Comte (1798–1857) is quite rightly regarded as the founder of sociology, it was the British scholar Harriet Martineau who translated and edited his most influential work, the *Positive Philosophy of Auguste Comte* (Comte 1896). In the process, Martineau clarified his ideas and brought his views to a wider audience. (The Profiles box titled "Harriet Martineau" discusses her life and work in greater detail.) Like Martineau, Comte believed that sociology was a science, or, in his terminology, a positive philosophy. As a science, he argued, sociology should study two fundamental aspects of society: why it changes, and why it does not change. The emphasis on science and social change are still important parts of the discipline today.

Although many other scholars played prominent roles in establishing sociology as a social science, three scholars—Karl Marx, Émile Durkheim, and Max Weber—were particularly important. They were concerned with the effects that the Industrial Revolution was having on how people related to each other. Although each scholar offered a different explanation for the same human experiences, their overall conclusions are broadly similar. As discussed in the next chapter, their ideas concerned the transformation of society from traditional to industrial; and as discussed here, their ideas contributed to the development of broad sociological perspectives (May 1996).

The French philosopher Auguste Comte (1798–1857) is considered the "father of sociology."

One of the pioneers of the new discipline of sociology was Harriet Martineau. Born in 1802 to an upper-class British family, she began to write at the age of 19, and by the time of her death in 1876, she was a well-known and respected author. Martineau lived during a time when women were viewed as appendages to their husbands, fathers, brothers, or other responsible men. Upper-class women such as Martineau were expected to fill domestic roles and bear children. They were not expected to work, lead causes, or become scholars, writers, or travelers. Thus, to succeed as Martineau did was to overcome great odds. In Martineau's case, the odds were even greater than for the average woman because she suffered from poor health and partial deafness.

Martineau believed that when the scientific laws governing human behavior were understood, they could be used to create a better world (Wheatley 1957). Following scientific procedures, Martineau carefully gathered evidence to support her beliefs. Although the process was costly, she refused government help because she feared that it would undermine her credibility. She chose, instead, to fund her research from royalties and commissions she earned from her writings.

One of Martineau's best-known works resulted from an extended research tour she took of the United States. In *Society in America*, she laid down ideas that have become a cornerstone of modern sociology (Lipset 1962). For instance, Martineau observed that the United States had a set of core values that concerned "human equality" and the "obligation of human justice." Starting with this observation, she came to a general conclusion: social strains are created when people behave in ways that are contrary to their core values. In time, these strains become the principal cause of social change. Today, many of her ideas about social change are embedded in modern "strain theory," discussed further in Chapter 3.

Harriet Martineau (1802–1876) was an early sociologist who helped found the discipline. She translated the works of French sociologist Auguste Comte, but of more importance, in the process of translation, she condensed, clarified, and sharpened many of his ideas. She also traveled extensively in the United States and analyzed American society from a sociological viewpoint. This contemporary cartoon shows her relaxing by a fire with her cat, heating water for tea.

Despite her originality, Martineau has been denied much of the credit she deserves. She is mainly remembered as the person who translated the work of Auguste Comte. Even so, it is important to note that before Harriet Martineau brought his work before a wider audience, Comte was not a particularly influential author, nor had he conducted any original research. In translating and abstracting Comte's works, Martineau used her considerable editing skills to reduce the essence of his six volumes down to two volumes. She also labored mightily to translate correctly and obtain verification of many unfamiliar scientific facts. Her abstraction was very successful; her two-volume edition of the *Positive Philosophy of Auguste Comte* was an immediate success and has been reprinted many times; Comte himself was extremely grateful for her editing. Because of her efforts, Comte's ideas were less likely to be misrepresented by critics, and his positive philosophy gained many new adherents in the English-speaking world. For instance, John Stuart Mill, an important British economist and philosopher, came to appreciate sociology through Martineau's translation. Today, to help credit Martineau as she deserves, the University of Massachusetts established a chair in sociology in her name.

CQ If Comte is revered as the "father of sociology" because he gave the discipline its name, should Martineau be equally revered as the "mother of sociology" because she brought Comte's work into a wider intellectual world?

SOURCE: Martineau, Harriet. 1802–1876. English novelist and economist. Steel engraving, 19th century/The Granger Collection. Also see: Hill and Hoecker Drysdale 2001.

Figure 1.1 on p. 9 shows some of the early twentieth-century American sociologists who built upon the theories of European sociologists.

Karl Marx (1818–1883)

A German philosopher of history, Marx received a doctorate from the University of Jena and worked as a journalist for a short time. *Das Kapital* (Capital) is his most important technical work, but it appealed mainly to scholars. In contrast, the *Communist Manifesto* was intended for public consumption, and it clearly lays out his political beliefs and his call for revolution.

William Graham Sumner (1840–1910). He studied at Oxford and was strongly influenced by the functionalist ideas of Herbert Spencer, a British sociologist. Sumner was a professor at Yale, where he had the distinction of teaching the first sociology course in the United States. Like Spencer, he viewed life as a struggle for existence in which only the fittest survive.

Lester F. Ward (1841–1913). A paleontologist with the United States Geological Survey, Ward nonetheless played a part in the development of theory in American sociology. He attempted to synthesize the ideas of Comte and Spencer. An important contribution Ward made was to create two subdivisions for sociology, terming them pure sociology and applied sociology. Pure sociology involves the effort to understand and explain society. Applied sociology, in contrast, uses sociological principles to improve society.

W. E. B. Dubois (1868–1963). He is known today as the father of African American sociology. He earned his undergraduate degree from Fisk and a doctorate from Harvard, and then studied sociology, history, and economics in postgraduate work at the University of Berlin under Max Weber. After returning to the United States, he created a sociological laboratory in Atlanta in 1897 for research on the African American experience.

Albion Small and the Chicago School. The first department of sociology in the United States was at the University of Chicago and was headed by Albion Small (1854–1926). As the first department, Chicago set the tone for much of the research training of graduate students. Many distinguished sociologists either taught or received their training at Chicago.

Robert Ezra Park (1864–1944). A journalist recruited by Albion Small for the new sociology department at Chicago, Park believed that the city of Chicago could be studied as a sociological laboratory, and he was interested in describing the everyday activities of people in different parts of the city.

Jane Addams (1860–1935). She cofounded Hull House in Chicago with Ellen Gates Starr in 1889. Hull House was a settlement house, an institution designed to serve the needs of people living in disorganized neighborhoods. Given the large numbers of immigrants who crowded into depressed urban slum areas of the time, settlement houses dealt with many urgent problems. Hull House provided a model for other settlement houses, and Jane Addams won the Nobel Peace Prize in 1931 for her outstanding achievements in public service.

FIGURE 1.1 Time Line of Early-Twentieth-Century American Sociology

American sociologists of the early twentieth century built on the theories of European sociologists but shaped those theories to fit American concerns. Social problems generated by massive immigration, rapid industrialization, and urbanization, along with upheavals brought on by the Great Depression and World War II, stimulated thought on many social issues. The people depicted in the time line are considered to be some of the key historical figures in American sociology between 1900 and 1940. The social turmoil of the 1960s and 1970s encouraged the establishment of many new sociology departments, and by the 1990s, sociology was taught at nearly every American university, with more than 1,500 universities having their own sociology department.

Marx believed that social scientists should work for a better society, and his personal goal was to liberate workers from the poverty and oppression brought on by industrialization. He saw revolution as the only way to do this—a view that deeply troubled many Americans, especially during the 1950s. Even today, many people incorrectly equate Marxism with old Soviet-style communism. However, if Marx had lived in the twentieth century, he would have been appalled by the bloody dictators who adopted his philosophy to justify their rule. One of the founders of the former

Trained in philosophy and history in Germany, Karl Marx (1818–1883) believed that the conflict between social classes was the driving force of change throughout history. With the arrival of the industrial era, he believed, this conflict became one between the capitalists and the working class. A major force in intellectual history, Marx's ideas continue to influence contemporary sociologists.

Soviet Union, Joseph Stalin, directly and indirectly murdered tens of millions of farmers and peasants, ostensibly to further communism. Yet nothing in Marx's philosophy suggests that he would have condoned mass murder (Dobriner 1969; see Chapter 9). Even during his lifetime, so many people were interpreting his writings to suit themselves that he once cried out: "I am not a Marxist!"

Marx lived during the nineteenth century, which was a time of unrestrained capitalism in Europe and the United States. Capitalism is a complex topic, but in brief, it allows private individuals to own production plants, steel mills, small businesses, and other aspects of commerce. These owners hire workers and compete with one another in a free marketplace to gain as much profit as possible (see Chapter 9). In Marxian terminology, production plants, steel mills, and the like are called the *means of production*, and the people who own them are called the *bourgeoisie*, or owners. Workers who sell their labor to the bourgeoisie are called the *proletariat*. Marx believed that any capitalist society will eventually be torn apart by the struggle between the bourgeoisie and the proletariat. The struggle is inevitable, and the final collapse of society cannot be avoided.

According to Marx, capitalism contains within itself the causes of its own destruction. This doomsday scenario unfolds roughly as follows: striving to earn as much profit as possible, the bourgeoisie drive down wages lower and lower until the proletariat are barely earning enough to survive. Marx predicted that individual workers living in misery would come to realize that their only hope was to unite and stage a revolution. Once in control, the proletariat would establish a new government and abolish privately owned property. The state would take over the means of production in the name of the people, and the society would then have a single class composed of the proletariat and the former bourgeoisie. In effect, a single, or classless, society would come into being. The armed insurrections of 1830 and 1848 in France and the German state strengthened Marx's belief that he was right in his analysis of class conflict.

Although the proletariat suffer the most under capitalism, Marx noted that the bourgeoisie were not living a life of ease. Economic competition forced them to concentrate relentlessly on increasing profits by outwitting their competitors. They had continually to seek new products, bigger markets, and cheaper labor. Marx concluded that neither the proletariat nor the bourgeoisie enjoyed life very much, nor did either class contribute to the betterment of the community. Capitalistic societies might be materially rich, Marx said, but they were socially impoverished.

Alienation   While Marx emphasized the class struggle, he believed that the nature of industrial labor would also contribute to the downfall of capitalism. He claimed that work was a distinct activity that separates humans from the lower animals. Whereas some animals build products, as when birds construct a nest, Marx argued that only humans could put imagination and creativity into their work and thus make their work meaningful (Coser and Rosenberg 1964). A cabinetmaker might spend long hours lovingly finishing a cabinet and might take great pride in what he had accomplished; or a farmer and his family might work their fields for weeks, and when the harvest was in, would feel fulfilled and proud of their work.

The tragedy of capitalism, Marx believed, lies in the way that the system transforms work from something that is meaningful to something that is meaningless. Because the system is relentlessly driven by profits, workers become mere machines in human form. This aspect of work is illustrated by a steelworker whom we (the authors) once knew:

> *Every morning, this man reported to work at a large pit behind the mill. The pit was filled with bundles of iron rods about four feet long. His job was to carry the bundles to a flatbed railroad car about 50 yards away. Although he dutifully performed this job for eight hours a day for two years, he was never told where the rods came from, what they were for, or where they were going.*

According to Marx, the essential qualities of this man's work—monotony, repetition, lack of meaning, and lack of control over the job—eventually produce **alienation**: a

Alienation ▲ A situation in which people are estranged from their social world and feel that life is meaningless.

situation in which people, having lost control over their lives, are estranged from their social world and feel that life is meaningless.

Even though Marx wrote his major works more than 100 years ago, his ideas are still important (McLennan 2001). In particular, he recognized a crucial weakness in industrial society: the impersonal, meaningless nature of work and the alienation that flows from it. We will return to this point in the next chapter when we discuss how society has changed (the Great Social Transformation), and we will examine many of Marx's other ideas when we discuss conflict theory in the next section and in Parts Two and Three of the text.

Mechanical solidarity ▲ Social solidarity based on shared values.

Émile Durkheim (1858–1917)

Durkheim was another thinker who greatly influenced the course of sociology. Born in Alsace, France, he attended French and German schools, where he studied law, philosophy, social science, folk psychology, and anthropology. He was both a theoretical sociologist and a practical educator. He was the first person to hold the title of professor of education and sociology; and as a high-ranking government official, he offered ideas about education that were taught throughout the secondary schools of France.

Whereas Marx emphasized conflict, Durkheim (1966/1893) focused on the unity of society. He distinguished between two types of social solidarity (or cohesiveness). Traditional societies, he said, are cohesive because everyone is much the same. The society is small, has a simple division of labor, and relies on uncomplicated technology. All hunters within a hunting and gathering society use the same type of weapons, for example, and all peasant farmers plant crops in the same way. Because everyone participates in the same social life within the same culture, they come to share the same values. It is these shared, nearly identical values that hold society together. Durkheim called this type of solidarity **mechanical solidarity**.

In industrial societies, on the other hand, people perform specialized tasks using complex tools, and they seldom interact directly. Although people share some values, they disagree on many others. Seemingly, industrial societies should have little to hold them together, yet they obviously do stay together. Why? In a brilliant insight, Durkheim pointed out that the differences among people make them interdependent. For example, the assembly-line workers at the Ford company in California do not interact with the accountants at Ford headquarters in Michigan. Yet they are interdependent. If the accountants do not perform their jobs, then the assembly-line workers

Émile Durkheim (1858–1917) *was an early sociologist whose ideas about social cohesion became the basis for important elements of contemporary sociological theory, notably functionalism.*

Max Weber (1864–1920), German political economist and sociologist, still very influential because of his ideas about rationalization, bureaucratization, religion, and social change.

 STUDY TIP

Gather in a group of three. Each person should study one of the three central figures of the origins of sociology: Karl Marx, Emile Durkheim, and Max Weber. Set a date to have a "sociology conversation" where the three of you "play" these three figures. Discuss sociological theory together, making sure that each person has a chance to present the primary views of the sociologist they represent.

Organic solidarity ▲ Social solidarity based on functional interdependence among people.

Anomie ▲ A social condition in which social norms are conflicting or entirely absent.

Rationalization ▲ The replacement of traditional thinking with rational thinking, or thinking that heavily emphasizes deliberate calculation, efficiency, and effectiveness in the accomplishment of explicit goals.

will not get paid; and if the assembly-line workers fall behind, then Ford will not meet its production schedules and the accountants might be out of work. In this way, if one fails, all fail; and if one succeeds, all succeed. Durkheim called this type of solidarity **organic solidarity**.

Anomie   Like Marx, Durkheim was disturbed by the industrial changes that were overwhelming Europe. He was especially concerned about the tendency of industrialism to produce **anomie**—a social condition in which societal norms are in conflict or entirely absent. According to Durkheim, anomie was an especially serious threat to morality. In the past, he noted, religion had been an important restraining force that taught people to dampen their desires and to seek rewards in spiritual accomplishments. Industrialization, however, had unleashed passions without establishing restraints. Without firm societal guidelines for behavior, Durkheim said, people are cast adrift from society without any sense of who they are. In short, they are anomic.

Durkheim believed that anomie was the cause of many social problems, and it was in this area that he produced one of his best-known works, *Suicide* (1966/1897). In this study, Durkheim examined suicide under various conditions and in various countries. For instance, he found that suicide rates were lower for people engaged in agriculture than for people working in industrial occupations. This trend was true in France, Italy, Prussia, and several other European countries. The reason, he said, is that people in agriculture are protected from the destructive effects of anomie. They follow the practices of their traditional communities and are caught up in a tightly knit moral world that has existed for generations. They have realistic expectations, which are largely forced on them by crop failures, floods, and other natural disasters. Even though their lives may not be very glamorous, in the long run they benefit from stability and from the absence of anomie.

Whereas Marx warned of alienation, Durkheim warned of a related possibility: anomie. As we discuss in the next chapter, both ideas help us to understand the state of contemporary society. In addition, Durkheim's work is regarded as the classical foundation for the functionalist school of sociology, which is discussed later in this chapter (Collins 1994; Emirbayer 1996; Thompson 2002).

Max Weber (1864–1920)

Max Weber was another thinker who had an enormous impact on the development of sociology. He was born in Erfurt, Prussia, and his family moved to Berlin when he was quite young. Weber was a passionate scholar who studied a wide variety of subjects, including law, economics, history, religion, and philosophy. He held important academic posts at a number of German universities during his career and was a well-known figure among politicians of his time (Gerth and Mills 1958). Weber devoted a significant part of his professional life to attacking Marx's ideas, yet both thinkers arrived at related conclusions about life under industrial capitalism. Whereas Marx emphasized alienation, Weber emphasized **rationalization**: the replacement of traditional thinking with thinking that heavily emphasizes deliberate calculation, efficiency, self-control, and effectiveness in the accomplishment of explicit goals.

Weber believed that as tradition faded and was replaced by rationality, Europe industrialized and adopted a capitalistic economy. The new way of life was very different from what had gone before, and nowhere was this difference clearer than in the impersonal, goal-directed activities of government agencies, large businesses, and other bureaucracies. For example, in a traditional society, a farmer who gets sick might ask a neighbor for help, but in an industrial society, a worker who gets sick might have no one to turn to except a bureaucratic government agency.

Weber conceded that rationality made for greater efficiency, but he also thought that the price was high. The strength and warmth of an extended family could not be replaced by cold calculation; nor could the bonds of mutual obligation be supplanted by a government bureaucracy.

Marx, Durkheim, and Weber Compared

In a far-reaching argument, Marx laid the foundation for analyzing contemporary society in terms of conflict and alienation. He believed that industrial capitalism was an oppressive system that would fail, in part because it produced alienation. Weber approached the same issue but from a different viewpoint. He concluded that under industrial capitalism, society was becoming excessively rational and calculating. As a consequence, social vitality was lost, and life was lacking in spontaneity. Like Weber, Durkheim stressed the importance of shared values (Giddens 1971). When common values are absent, anomie prevails, and people suffer from the anxiety of not being attached to society. Very often, Durkheim feared, social pathologies are the result. The contrast among the three concepts may be illustrated by imagining how different people would answer the simple question, "How's life treating you?"

ALIENATED PERSON: I really don't care (because I am detached from my work and from other people).

ANOMIC PERSON: I'm distressed by it (because there are no common values or norms to guide me).

RATIONAL PERSON: Let me think about it, and I'll get back to you later (because I need to make some calculations before I know the answer).

● ■ ▲ **Pausing to Think** **About the Origins of Sociology and the Three Central Figures**

There are many important figures in the development of sociology; however, the three central figures are Karl Marx, Émile Durkheim, and Max Weber. Each of them made important contributions to our understanding of social structure, social relationships, and social change. Although Marx, Durkheim, and Weber each selected a different aspect of society to emphasize, they all agreed that a new social and economic order was emerging as the Industrial Revolution swept across Europe and, later, across the United States. Émile Durkheim saw this transformation as a change from one base of social solidarity to another, from the mechanical to the organic, and from nonanomic to anomic. In contrast, Karl Marx saw the Industrial Revolution as an economic transformation that would temporarily produce order but that would contribute to alienation and, eventually, revolution. Finally, Max Weber saw the transformation as a fundamental shift away from traditional ways of thinking to a highly rationalized way of thinking that emphasized deliberate calculation, efficiency, and effectiveness in goal attainment. Weber feared that we would all become imprisoned in an iron cage of rationality, surrounded by rules and regulations, overly cautious, and unwilling to act without authority. The ideas of these central figures were important in the development of American sociology (Morgan 1997).

CQ Can you supply examples of the problems of alienation, anomie, and imprisonment in the iron cage of rationality from your own life? ◆ Do these terms have meaning to today's college students?

Perspectives within Sociology

As we discussed in the opening of the chapter, sociology has a unique viewpoint that distinguishes it from other sciences. We also mentioned that within sociology itself, different sociologists emphasize different aspects of social structure and social interaction. These viewpoints are generally referred to as **perspectives**: consistent ways of looking at some aspect of the world. Some sociologists rely on a perspective called structural-functionalism or functionalism and pay particular attention to the social

Perspectives ▲ Our mental pictures of the relative importance of things.

Bank failure was common during the depression. This photograph, which was made on December 11, 1930, shows bewildered and irate customers in front of the locked doors of the Bank of the United States in New York City.

CQ *From a functional perspective, how did the failure of the banks disrupt the equilibrium of society?*

mechanisms that hold society together. Other sociologists emphasize social conflict and concentrate on the changes and disputes that could tear society apart. Both functionalism and conflict theory are general perspectives that will be applied to many topics throughout the book; a third general perspective, symbolic interaction, is introduced in Chapter 3.

The Functionalist Perspective

The functionalist perspective within sociology traces its roots to the work of Émile Durkheim. Although he was not the first *structural-functionalist*, his version of functionalism is still popular among many sociologists (Collins 1994). We have already discussed his ideas about social solidarity and anomie, but we have not discussed his view of society as a whole.

Durkheim assumed that society, like a plant or an animal, consists of systems that act together to maintain the life of the organism. Contemporary functionalists no longer rely on this assumption, but they do say that the parts of a social system work together to maintain the cohesion of the system. For instance, each of the six institutions covered in this book—the economy, politics, family, education, religion, and medicine—deals with an important aspect of social life. If these institutions work well, then the broader society also works well. If they work poorly, then the broader society encounters difficulties and, in a worst-case scenario, might collapse. Consider what happened during the Great Depression of the 1930s. Banks failed, farmers went bankrupt, jobs vanished, families disintegrated, people lost their homes, and hoboes wandered the country. The United States was tottering on the brink of a social and an economic collapse, which fortunately did not occur. From the functionalist perspective, American society was failing because its various parts—the economy, government, family, and other institutions—were no longer working together. The failure of one part had set off a chain reaction of failures that caused the total system to begin breaking down.

Functionalist theorists also assume that society maintains itself in a state of equilibrium (balance) that permits it to operate efficiently. The equilibrium may be upset, however, for any number of reasons. External circumstances such as war, trade imbalances, or catastrophes of nature can cause the equilibrium to falter and then to fail entirely. Internal threats to equilibrium also exist. For example, as industrialization advanced, the family lost its economic role, and domestic life was thrown into chaos for a time (see Chapter 10).

Functionalist theorists further believe that societal cohesion derives from consensus and common values. People in the United States, to illustrate, believe strongly in the values of individual effort and hard work. These common values strengthen the cohesion of American society because people of different ethnic groups, religions, and regions are drawn together in common beliefs that outweigh their differences.

In discussing society and the individual, functionalist theorists use a special vocabulary. **Functions** are actions that have positive consequences for the social system, and **dysfunctions** are actions that have negative consequences for the social system. **Manifest functions** are those intended or recognized by others, whereas **latent functions** are unintended. To illustrate these terms, consider the school system. Its manifest function is to teach children reading, math, history, and other academic subjects. In the course of teaching these and other topics, the school also serves several latent functions. It teaches students to be polite, to respect authority, and to believe in capitalism and the American way of life (see Chapter 11). Although most school activities are functional in the sense that they result in positive outcomes for society, some activities are dysfunctional. A few bad experiences in the classroom, for instance, might teach children to dislike learning; or perhaps their school friends might teach them to drink and smoke—activities that are dysfunctional for their health. Almost certainly, a system as large and complex as the school system will produce manifest and latent functions, and manifest and latent dysfunctions.

Functions ▲ Actions that have positive consequences for society.

Dysfunctions ▲ Actions that have negative consequences for society.

Manifest functions ▲ Functions that are intended or recognized by others.

Latent functions ▲ Functions that are unintended or unrecognized by others.

In sum, functionalist theory emphasizes the articulation of social parts, functions, and social equilibrium. When things are going well, therefore, society continues to run smoothly, and people interact harmoniously. However, when things are not going well, another viewpoint—conflict theory—may be more useful.

The Conflict Perspective

In contrast to functionalists, conflict theorists view society as a collection of parts held together by **social power**—the ability to control the behavior of others against their will. To conflict theorists, power is the tool that enables some groups to dominate others. Dominance, in turn, sets in motion the potential for conflict between those who receive the benefits of power and those who do not. For example, whites have historically dominated nonwhites, and men have dominated women. In each case, the dominant group has used its power to gain benefits at the expense of the subordinate group. Thus, whites have the most political influence, and men typically have higher-paying jobs than women (see Collins 1994; Coser 1956; Dahrendorf 1959).

Conflict theorists further recognize that conflict takes place among organizations. Organizations, in other words, try to use their power for their own benefit. The tobacco industry is a case in point. Tobacco companies maintain powerful lobbies in Congress, and they have, until recently, easily fought off attempts to regulate nicotine as an addictive drug. Even though medical opinion overwhelmingly links smoking with heart disease, cancer, breathing disorders, and other afflictions, these companies have resisted attempts to ban smoking. Despite a settlement proposed in 1997 under which tobacco companies would agree to reimburse states for the costs incurred in treating tobacco-related diseases, the tobacco industry continued to maintain that smoking was a matter of individual choice rather than a harmful addiction. When asked if he thought that smoking was addictive, the president of one large tobacco company said that "most people" that want to kick the habit succeed (Candiotti 2000). In short, the tobacco industry continually engages in strife with the medical establishment, consumer advocacy groups, and others who argue that smoking is a public danger.

According to conflict theorists, social change is a regular feature of social life. Those categories of people with fewer privileges will periodically attempt to change their status, whereas the dominant categories will try to maintain their positions of

Social power ▲ The ability to get others to conform to one's wishes even against their own desires.

According to conflict theory, power ultimately determines the outcome of a dispute. Each group in this photograph of protesters for and against abortion will doubtlessly attempt to mobilize resources, including economic and political power, to overwhelm the other group.

power. Examples of these conflicts are the struggle of women to gain the vote, the struggle of labor to gain the right to unionize, the fight to obtain civil rights, and more recently, the fight to gain women's equality (see Chapter16). To the extent that these movements succeeded, the status quo of American society was upset, and a new status quo came into being.

Although the process is not self-evident, conflict theorists believe that conflict holds society together. In a way, this belief contradicts common sense, for if society is a hotbed of many conflicts, how is cohesion possible? One answer is through power. To illustrate, Native Americans were driven from their lands for the benefit of settlers; African Americans were enslaved for the benefit of plantation owners; and thousands of immigrants toiled in sweatshops to make profits for the owners of the means of production. Obviously, the subordinate group suffers, but as long as the dominant group has power, there is little that the subordinate group can do about it.

The second way in which conflict produces cohesion is through shifting alliances. You might join one group for a given purpose but then might join another group to achieve another purpose. For instance, the American Civil Liberties Union (ACLU), an organization that staunchly defends free speech, has supported the right of the Ku Klux Klan to hold marches and to put up its displays in public places. While opposed to the racism and violence associated with the Klan, the ACLU argues that everyone has the right to free speech. Hence, an alliance on a specific issue can emerge between two parties that disagree on everything else.

Contemporary conflict theory originated in the thinking of Karl Marx. His ideas about the dominance of the bourgeoisie and the exploitation of the proletariat are clear instances of how power is used for the benefit of some people at the expense of other people. As with functionalism, we will be returning to conflict theory throughout this book.

● ■ ▲ **Pausing to Think**   **About Viewpoints within Sociology**

Functionalism and social conflict are two fundamental sociological perspectives. Functionalism views society as a system of parts that work together to maintain the cohesion of the whole system. In doing so, society maintains itself in a state of equilibrium that permits it to operate efficiently. Functionalists view social change as the movement of society from one equilibrium state to another. Social conflict theory stresses the role of power and dominance in social relations and in the organization of society. Fundamentally, power is the ability to control others against their will. Conflict theorists see many sources of conflict in society. Conflict occurs, for instance, between social classes, between dominant and subordinate ethnic and racial groups, between men and women, between religious groups, and elsewhere when people's goals or interests differ. Conflict holds society together through the sheer power of some groups to control others and through the shifting alliances that groups make with one another as they pursue their goals.

CQ How would a functionalist and a social conflict theorist differ in their interpretation of the enslavement of Africans for the plantation system of America's South?

Sociological Research and Research Methods

Sociology is a science, and sociologists therefore must know how to perform scientific research. In fact, a major portion of graduate training in sociology is devoted to learning the techniques, practices, and ethics involved in gaining new knowledge. Some sociologists even specialize in studying research methods, whereas others specialize in statistical techniques.

Sociological research is the systematic investigation of society that is designed to develop or contribute to a generalized knowledge of social life. Research may be either inductive or deductive. Inductive research begins with making empirical observations with the aim of developing a hypothesis or theory that accounts for the observations. Deductive research starts with a hypothesis or theory, and then makes systematic empirical observations that help in the evaluation of the hypothesis or theory. A **hypothesis** is a specific statement of expected relationship between two variables. For example, it is hypothesized that *one's education level affects one's income level*. A theory is a more general statement of causation such as *social strain is created when people behave in ways that are at a variance with their core values*.

Research methods may be divided into two types: qualitative and quantitative. Each type is especially well suited for a particular kind of inquiry; hence both are important. We will first discuss qualitative methods and then move on to quantitative methods.

Qualitative Methods

Many sociologists depend heavily on **qualitative methods**: research techniques designed to obtain the subjective understanding, interpretation, and meaning of social behavior. An important goal of qualitative research is to obtain a deep understanding of what people are doing, and to interpret their behavior in ways that make sense to the people themselves. Consequently, qualitative research endeavors to capture the feel, texture, and meaning of behavior and the broader context within which it takes place. To obtain such understanding, qualitative researchers rely on three basic techniques: historical records, interviews, and participant observation.

Historical Records   Historical analysis is usually based on old letters, diaries, baptismal records, official chronicles and publications, and similar materials. The historical method is valuable because it provides both detailed information and broad explanations. It also provides a sense of where we have been and helps us to understand our place in the world.

In interpreting historical events, it is important to consider the time in which they took place. Behavior that might seem to be peculiar or irrational can take on an entirely new meaning when viewed from the perspective of the subject's own historical time. For example, our own conception of deviance is different from the conception held by the early settlers of New England. They believed that some forms of deviance were caused by demons or by Satan. Marvin Harris, a cultural anthropologist, studied the witchcraft trials that took place in Salem, Massachusetts, during the sixteenth century. He noted that the imprisonment and hanging of suspected witches occurred during a period when Salem was undergoing rapid changes that threatened the stability of the community. He concluded that the persecution of suspected witches strengthened the power of the state by striking fear into the populace and, at the same time, reinforced the boundaries of acceptable behavior (see Chapter 13; Harris 1975). Thus, what strikes us as irrational and "stupid" behavior actually stemmed from the social conditions that existed at the time the witch trials took place.

Performing historical research can be difficult because records are often inaccurate, incomplete, or biased. The lives of powerful people are usually well documented, whereas the lives of the poor and powerless are ignored. Thus, much is known about white men—who traditionally have wielded the most power in the United States—whereas less is known about women and minorities. During the Civil War, African Americans made up some 10 percent of the Union army, and women were responsible for providing medical care. Yet most historical accounts give the impression that the war was fought exclusively by white men.

Interviews and Life Histories   Many sociologists are primarily interested in problems that involve meaning, symbolism, or some other aspect of social behavior that is

123 STUDY TIP

Create a Research Methods outline with two major segments—Qualitative Methods and Quantitative Methods. Outline the details of each method category in the indented material below the primary headings of the outline. Use formal (letters and numbers) or informal (dashes and indentations) structure according to what you prefer.

Sociological research ▲ The systematic investigation of society that is designed to develop or contribute to a generalized knowledge of social life.

Hypothesis ▲ A specific statement of expected relationship between two variables.

Research methods ▲ The techniques, practices, and ethics involved in gaining new knowledge.

Qualitative methods ▲ Research techniques designed to obtain the subjective understanding, interpretation, and meaning of social behavior.

difficult to translate into numerical responses. For example, a sociologist might investigate why people are attracted to certain recreational activities, or how people develop their sense of identity during the course of their lifetimes. For these broader, more interpretive issues, the researcher might turn to a **structured interview**: a procedure in which the researcher asks the respondent a series of questions and then records the answers, usually by writing them down word for word, or by checking off responses on a list of possible answers, or by recording answers on tape to be transcribed later.

Another qualitative technique that is occasionally used is called a **life history**. This is a long interview, or series of interviews, in which the researcher attempts to discover the essential features, decisive moments, or turning points in a respondent's life. Doing this requires the researcher to spend many hours scattered over several days talking to the respondent in great depth. The researcher usually asks general questions and then gently prods the respondent to fill in the details. Successful use of this method requires a great deal of skill and much patience on the part of the researcher. This method, as you might suspect, is practical only when used on one respondent or a few respondents.

Participant Observation   The goal of a participant observation study is to obtain in-depth understanding from a highly detailed and sometimes intimate knowledge of the people being studied. To achieve this goal, researchers sometimes participate in the activities of the unit under study. When they do this undertaking, the research method is called **participant observation**. On the other hand, if researchers observe but do not participate, the research method is simply called observation.

To illustrate participant observation, consider William Foote Whyte's classic study of "Street Corner Society" (Whyte 1943, 1984). As a junior fellow at Harvard University, Whyte had four years' worth of funding available to him and so decided to study a street gang in Boston. Although Whyte participated in many social activities with the gang, only a few gang leaders knew that he was actually conducting research. In one part of the study, Whyte described a hierarchy of authority, or pecking order, that accounted for much of the group's stability. He observed that when the gang members went bowling together, the gang leader, a man called Doc, usually won even though he was not the best bowler. At first Whyte was puzzled by this anomaly, but after many hours of participating in and observing the bowling games, he was able to arrive at an explanation. Gang members unconsciously knew that if Doc lost, the authority structure of the gang would be undermined. To maintain the authority structure, therefore, gang members unconsciously helped Doc to win. They did so by heckling, insulting, and physically intimidating anyone who stood a chance to beat Doc, thus ensuring that he won (Homans 1950; Whyte 1943). Of course, gang members would not have described their behavior in the language that Whyte used, nor were they aware of why they intimidated anyone who threatened Doc's standing.

Participant and nonparticipant observational studies have both strengths and weaknesses. By actually being there when the activity takes place, the sociologist can describe and explain both the behavior and its context. A good observer, such as William Whyte, will see the significance of supposedly insignificant behaviors, words, and gestures. These observations then become the basis for interpreting the social dynamics and deep feelings that are part of group life. In addition, as the researcher develops trust among the group members, the members may reveal behaviors that are normally hidden from public view. Researchers conducting observational studies are often able to get at the meaning of social behavior and to understand the motives of the participants.

On the negative side, the most serious criticism of observational research concerns generalization. In this case, generalization refers to the extent to which the results of a study can be enlarged to a broader population of people. Because no two cases are ever completely identical, the observation of a single case always leaves doubts about generalizability (Boelen 1992). For example, Whyte's study was conducted in a particular place at a particular time in history and on a particular group of young men. Thus, the study does not easily generalize to another gang in another place at another time.

Structured interview ▲ A procedure in which respondents are asked the same series of questions and the answers are recorded in a standard format.

Life history ▲ A long interview, or series of interviews, in which the researcher attempts to discover the essential features, decisive moments, or turning points in a respondent's life.

Participant observation ▲ Type of observation in which the researcher participates in the activities of the group to obtain an in-depth and intimate understanding of it.

Quantitative Methods

Quantitative methods rely heavily on statistical and mathematical techniques to answer questions about social behavior (Babbie 2001). Although the vast majority of sociologists trained before World War II relied mainly on qualitative methods, over the last 50 years, quantitative methods have increasingly come to the fore. Sociologists now perform more quantitative research than any other kind.

To illustrate quantitative methods, consider the assertion, "The more you study, the higher your grades will be." To address this statement quantitatively, we might ask a sample of students how many hours they typically spend studying for an examination. At the same time, we could also ask them for their grade point average. If the assertion is correct, then the grade point averages of students who study the most should be higher than the grade point averages of students who study the least. In other words, we determine how the variation in one variable, hours studied, produces a change (variation) in another variable, grade point average.

Survey   The **survey** is probably the most widespread method for gathering quantitative information or data. The method is so popular that most people have at one time or another been targeted for a survey of some kind. You might, for instance, have been telephoned by a company interested in what you watch on television, or you might have been stopped while walking to class and asked whom you plan to vote for in the next student body election, or you might have walked past a booth in a shopping mall and been asked to sample two soft drinks and indicate which you liked the best. As these examples suggest, surveys are common, and, unfortunately, widely abused. As a general rule, unless a survey is conducted scientifically, you should not place much faith in the results.

A scientific survey is directed at a **population**. As used in science, population refers to any group that the researcher is studying, such as all the students in a class, all the inmates in a prison, or all the women in a society. As a practical matter, it is usually impossible to survey every member of a population, especially if you are studying a country such as China, with over a billion people, or the United States, with some 290 million. And even if every person in the population could be located and persuaded to cooperate, the cost would be prohibitive. Researchers therefore **sample** a small number of cases and use them to represent the entire population.

Rather than striving for a large sample, quantitative researchers emphasize the importance of a representative sample. A **representative sample** of the United States

Quantitative methods ▲ Research techniques designed to produce numerical estimates of human behavior.

Survey ▲ A systematic procedure for gathering information, usually through the application of standardized interviews or questionnaires.

Population ▲ In the context of a research project, any group that the researcher is studying, such as all the students in a class, all the inmates in a prison, or all the women in a society.

Sample ▲ A small number of cases selected to represent the entire population.

Representative sample ▲ A sample that in its characteristics mirrors the population from which it comes.

This photograph shows a social worker taking notes as she interviews her client in her office at a family service center. Interviewing is an important skill in sociology and much research has been done on how to word questions so as to avoid misunderstandings and miscommunication.

would, for example, have about the same proportion of women in it as the proportion in the nation, about the same proportion of African Americans as in the nation, and so on. Because the representative sample is a small mirror of the population, it can serve as the basis for generalization: outcomes that are true of a representative sample should be true of the population. For instance, if a representative sample of the United States finds that 66 percent of the respondents favor abolishing welfare, then 66 percent of the population should feel the same way. With correct procedures, a surprisingly small sample can yield results that mirror the population. To illustrate, a properly drawn sample of some 1,500 respondents can provide an accurate estimate of how some 290 million Americans feel about a given political issue.

The best way to obtain generalization is to use **random sampling**—a sampling procedure in which everyone in the population has an equal chance of being selected as a respondent. For instance, if you are sampling your class for a term paper and want to select randomly 10 out of 30 students, a simple but effective random sampling procedure would be to write each student's name on a slip of paper, place the slips in a hat, shake the hat until the slips are mixed, and then blindly draw 10 slips. If these procedures are followed, then every slip (person) has about the same chance of being selected as every other slip. In short, you have a random sample, and what is true of the 10 students in the sample should also be true of the 30 students in the class (population).

Obviously, drawing slips from a hat is not practical with larger groups. To sample large units randomly—businesses, schools, cities, or states—sociologists have developed complex sampling schemes. In one scheme, a number is assigned to every member of a population, and a computer is used to select randomly the sample from the numbers. Election pollsters often use this technique and randomly select respondents from lists of registered voters.

If an improperly drawn or biased sample is used, the situation is much different. No matter how large, data from a biased sample are invariably misleading. A classic instance of a large but misleading sample occurred in 1936, before sampling techniques were well understood. In that year, the *Literary Digest* surveyed approximately 2 million people and predicted that in the 1936 presidential election the Republican candidate, Alfred Landon, would defeat the Democratic candidate, Franklin Roosevelt. In fact, Roosevelt won by a landslide. Why did the *Digest* go so far wrong? The problem was the sample. *Digest* researchers drew the names of respondents from telephone directories and automobile registration lists. The lists were biased, because in 1936, amidst the Great Depression, only the prosperous could afford telephones and automobiles. Excluded from the survey were people with low and modest incomes, the very people who favored Roosevelt. It is interesting to note that two years later, the *Literary Digest* went out of business, in part because it lost so much credibility by mispredicting the 1936 presidential election.

Controlled Experiment   An **experiment** is a method for studying the relation between two or more variables under highly controlled conditions. To illustrate a typical experiment in the social sciences, suppose that a researcher at a large business firm wishes to assess the effectiveness of a training film intended to raise the morale of employees. Further, suppose that the researcher decides to evaluate the film by conducting an experiment. She might proceed in three steps. First, she would select a sample of employees and measure their level of morale, perhaps by administering a questionnaire. This measurement is called the pretest. Second, she would randomly divide the subjects into two groups. The **experimental group** receives the "treatment"—in this case, they see the training film. The other half of the sample, the **control group,** does not receive the treatment; that is, they do not see the film. Instead, they engage in their regular activities. Third, after the experimental group has seen the film, the researcher would again measure morale. This measurement is called the posttest. If the film had the intended effect, then the morale of employees in the experimental group should be higher after seeing the film than before seeing it, and the morale of

Random sampling ▲ A sampling procedure in which everyone in the population has an equal chance of being selected as a respondent.

Experiment ▲ A method for studying the relation between two or more variables under highly controlled conditions.

Experimental group ▲ In an experiment, the group to whom the experimental stimulus is administered.

Control group ▲ In an experiment, the group not exposed to the experimental stimulus but used as a comparison with the experimental group.

employees in the control group should remain unchanged (cf. Stouffer 1950). If that outcome occurs, then the researcher would conclude that the film did, in fact, raise morale, and she could be highly confident in her conclusion.

Although the controlled experiment is well suited for linking cause to effect, sociologists seldom use it. The main reason is that experiments are best conducted in a laboratory; however, most sociologists want to study behavior as it occurs in the real world. A partial exception to this consideration concerns small groups, which are discussed in Chapter 5.

Quantitative and Qualitative Methods Compared

The debate over qualitative and quantitative research was foreshadowed very early in the history of sociology. Both Comte and Martineau believed in "positive philosophy"—the faith that sociology would eventually develop into a science with clearly known laws of behavior. Durkheim followed this same path and used it to analyze suicide. Although agreeing that sociology should strive to be a quantitative science, Weber argued that human behavior did not occur in isolated bits. To understand it truly, he said, we must take into account the situation and environment in which the behavior occurs. Weber developed a method for obtaining a rich description and empathetic perception of behavior; he called his method "Verstehen" (the German word for understanding).

During the 1960s, a period known for controversy, the virtues and drawbacks of the two methods were hotly debated. Proponents of qualitative methods referred to quantitative researchers as "numbers crunchers" and "crass empiricists." Quantitative researchers called qualitative researchers "soft sociologists" and accused them of being "poets instead of scientists." Today, such passions have cooled, and most sociologists agree that the debate produced a clearer understanding of different research techniques. Each method, when properly understood and used, can provide knowledge that the other method cannot. The result is a richer, deeper understanding of social structure and social interaction.

Ethics and Research

By historical standards, the concern for ethics in research is a recent development. It began after World War II when it became widely known that some scientists had used their expertise to help the Nazis murder and torture millions of Jews, Gypsies, Poles, and others. In the United States, the issue of scientific ethics struck home with special force when several prominent scientists began to question their role in building the atomic bomb and in testing the effects of radiation on naive sailors and soldiers and innocent civilians. From these early beginnings, the issue has expanded to include not only a concern for the role of the scientist but also a concern for not harming the people who participate in a study. Harm goes beyond physical damage; it includes mental and emotional distress and violations of privacy (Emanuel, Wendler, and Grady 2000). Both qualitative and quantitative research methods require good ethical judgment on the part of sociologists.

Sometimes seemingly innocent and inoffensive questions may cause severe embarrassment or damage. Respondents might not want to divulge information about their sexual lives or income, for instance, or they might hesitate to reveal their opinions about their boss because they fear reprisals if the information were to become public. To avoid these problems, sociologists take great care in framing their questions and go to great lengths to guarantee that their respondent will remain anonymous.

Whereas surveys and observational studies can raise ethical issues, experimental studies often pose more of a threat. In an experiment, the researcher has almost complete control over the situation and thus can expose subjects to great risk. For example, Philip Zimbardo, a social psychologist at Stanford University, conducted an

Society Today ● ■ ▲

Is Everybody Happy?

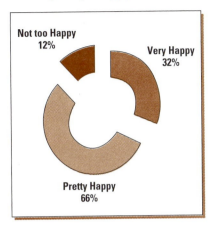

Despite the personal issues and social problems that beset us, in the United States most people say they are "pretty happy." This finding may or may not contradict your previous opinion. However, the point we wish to make is that survey findings—to be valid—must be based on random samples. In this case, they were. Survey researchers contacted a random sample of 2,806 adults (General Social Survey 1999). The relatively small size of the sample might surprise you. However, the critical issue is not absolute size, but randomness. Even a small random sample will produce results that may be generalized to the population. However, if the sample is not random, then no matter how large it is, the results cannot be generalized. In short, a small random sample is infinitely better than a large nonrandom sample.

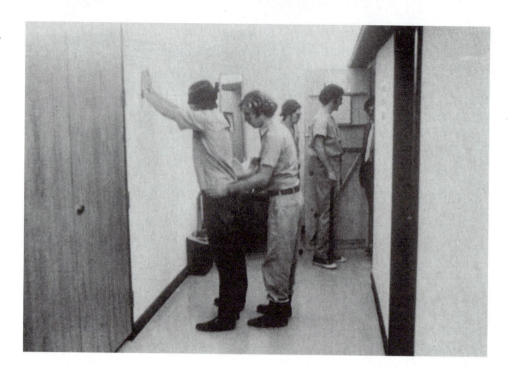

"Prisoners" and "guards" in Zimbardo's experiment. So thoroughly did the participants internalize their roles that Zimbardo had to terminate the experiment.

experiment on the interaction between jail prisoners and their guards. As part of his experiment, he built an artificial jail in the basement of a campus building. The jail had drab walls, locked entrances and exits, and cells for prisoners. He then recruited 21 subjects for a study of "prison life." They were college-age men, middle-class, and carefully screened for emotional maturity, respect for law, and physical health. The subjects then were randomly selected to play the role of guard or prisoner. Neither group was told how to behave, but within a few days, both groups were actively playing their roles. The guards became nasty, tough, unyielding, and even brutal. After six days of harsh treatment, the prisoners became clinically depressed and showed signs of emotional distress. At this point, Zimbardo concluded that he had unleashed unforeseen forces that could cause serious psychological harm. He therefore terminated the experiment (Zimbardo et al. 1973; Zimbardo, Ebbesen, and Maslach 1977).

The major professional association for sociologists in North America, the American Sociological Association, has prepared a set of guidelines to protect people involved in research (American Sociological Association 1997; see the Sociology Online box). Under the guidelines, the respondents must be completely anonymous

Sociology Online

www

The largest organization of sociologists in the United States is the American Sociological Association, or the ASA. To learn about this organization, we suggest that you visit the homepage of the ASA.

Using your favorite Internet search engine, search for American Sociological Association. You know you will have reached the correct site when you find the name of the organization listed on the top of the home page. As you look at the ASA's site, note that they have provided a special section with information for students. Looking through this information, see if you can find details about the following:

- What information does the ASA provide about putting together an undergraduate major in sociology?

- How can the sociology major be used as preparation for a career in business and other professional organizations?
- How well do sociologists compete in the job market with other liberal arts majors?

After you have answered these questions, write a brief report that describes the occupational prospects for undergraduates with a degree in sociology.

CQ Of course, the ASA provides a lot of additional information on its web page. What information about important social problems or issues is on the site? Write down the names of three or four publications that the ASA lists that might be useful in studying current social problems or issues.

and may quit whenever they wish. They must be told the researcher's institutional affiliation and the purpose of the research. In addition to the guidelines of the American Sociological Association, in most universities any research involving human subjects (whether supported by the government or not) must first be approved by a Human Subjects committee. This committee makes certain that in each research project, the participants are fully informed as to the nature of the study and of their role in it, and that they give their free consent for their participation.

●■▲ Pausing to Think   About Research Methods

Sociological research methods may be divided into two types, qualitative and quantitative. Each type is especially well suited for a particular kind of inquiry. Qualitative research techniques are designed to obtain the subjective understanding, interpretation, and meaning of social behavior. To obtain such understanding, qualitative researchers rely on such techniques as historical records, including old letters, diaries, baptismal records, and the like; life histories and in-depth interviews; and participant observation. Quantitative methods rely heavily on statistical and mathematical techniques to answer questions about social behavior. The survey and the controlled experiment are two basic quantitative research approaches.

Today researchers are more concerned than in the past about the well-being of people who participate as respondents. In most universities, research studies involving human participants must be approved by a Human Subjects committee.

CQ Have you ever participated in a research project as a subject, respondent, or informant? ◆ Were you fully informed as to the purpose of the research? ◆ Was your participation voluntary?

Sociology and the Twenty-First Century

Throughout this book, each chapter concludes with a section on the future. We include this section because change is continually taking place and has implications for the future of society and for our future as individuals. As individuals, moreover, each of us lives today with anticipations about tomorrow, next week, the following month, or another future time period. This tendency to try to anticipate the future is an essential feature of human existence, and it is built into "symbolic interaction," a theory we discuss in Chapter 3.

FIGURE 1.2 What Can You Do with a Sociology Degree?

Many students, after taking the basic course in sociology, decide that they would like to major in sociology. When they make this decision, they are often asked by their parents and friends—and they often ask themselves—"What can you do with a degree in sociology?" To answer that question, one sociology department surveyed its graduates to find out exactly what they were doing for a living. This figure shows the job titles of graduates of the sociology department of Ohio State University. As you can see, sociology graduates go on to a wide range of careers in the professions, human services, communications, and business and industry.

CQ *What do you want from this course—information? ◆ Course credit? ◆ Meeting a graduation requirement? ◆ Finding an interesting major? ◆ All of the above*

Society Today ● ■ ▲

Television in Our Lives

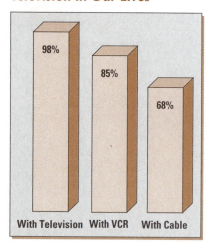

The term television was coined in 1900; however it first became widely available after World War II. When introduced, a television set was a novelty for the wealthy, but then the medium quickly spread throughout the nation and world. Although your grandparents might recall a time before television, anyone born after World War II can hardly imagine life without it. Today, television is the dominant medium of communication, and various forms, such as cable, are becoming standard.

SOURCE: U.S. Bureau of the Census, 2002; members.aol.com/jeff560; *A U.S. Television Chronology, 1975–1990;* accessed August 6, 2003.

WHAT CAN YOU DO WITH A SOCIOLOGY DEGREE?

WRITER/COLUMNIST
PROFESSOR* POLICE Teacher
City Sales Representative Grants OFFICER
Planner* Investigator Mgt. OPERATIONS COORD. SUPERVISOR
FINANCIAL Asst. PRINTER Registered Public Strategic
PLANNER Branch Claim Nurse* Inquiries Project
Manager Captain Director Asst. Manager
Probation Sales Specialist Psychologist* Health
Officer Representative PRODUCTION MANAGER Director Service
Account Pastor Inspector Stockbroker BOOKKEEPER Worker
Executive Customer Serv. Coord.
Underwriting Social Dept. Head PROTECTIVE COMPUTER
Manager Worker* Branch Manager FLOOR PLAN MANAGER SERVICE SPECIALIST Manager
PHYSICIAN* WORKER Project Director
DIRECTOR SUPERVISOR
OF RESEARCH Program Evaluator* Bank Officer/Financial Manager
PERSONAL Coordinator Research Human DIRECTOR
SERVICE Claims Branch Manager Assoc. Resources CAREER
WORKER CASE MANAGER DIRECTOR Asst. SERVICES*
Mitigation Specialist
Social/Researcher Correctional Counselor
Requires Additional Education

The most common way to anticipate the future is to examine trends that are currently taking place. Unfortunately, many well-publicized reports of trends are based more on commonsense assumptions or myths than on facts, yet they are believed as if they were true. Here is an example:

■ Social change is thought to be happening at a faster and faster rate. This belief is difficult to evaluate statistically, but a historical comparison of different generations can shed light on it. Let us compare the generation born in 1890 with the generation born in 1960.

■ By the time they reached age 30, people born in 1890 had witnessed the adoption of the automobile, airplane, motorcycle, outboard motor, personal camera, motion picture, phonograph, radio, electricity, vacuum cleaner, central heating, washing machine, toaster, typewriter, skyscraper, and synthetic fabric. The generation born in 1960, by the time they reached age 30, had experienced the personal computer, video recorder, space travel, civil rights legislation, women's liberation, legal abortion, AIDS, organ transplant, industrial robots, lasers, and shopping malls. Although the two lists are not complete, we would hesitate to conclude that the pace of change has dramatically increased in recent times. If anything, it seems to have slowed (Caplow 1991; see Television in Our Lives).

As this example illustrates, very often what we believe to be true about the future is questionable or not true. One of the great values of sociology, then, is that it forces us to identify our myths, beliefs, and assumptions. Once we identify them, we can then subject them to examination and scientific testing. Quite often, we will discover that the obvious is subtle and that common sense is wrong.

Because of its great appeal through its study of social life, sociology is one of the most popular majors on college campuses. For those of you who find yourselves attracted to sociology, you might ask, "What does one do with a degree in sociology?" Figure 1.2 shows a selection of actual jobs held by sociology graduates. Another good source of ideas is *Careers in Sociology*, published by the American Sociological Association (1995).

CONCEPT WEB What Is Sociology?

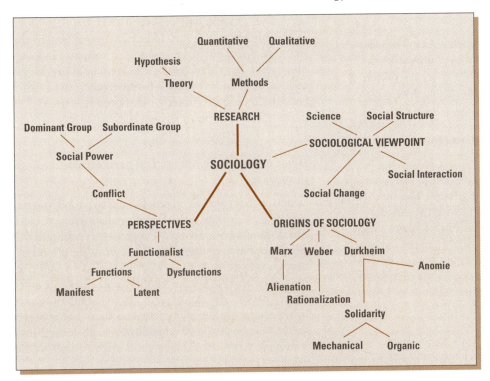

A concept web is a graphic way of organizing and presenting a series of related concepts. The links between the concepts show which concepts are directly related. For example, this chapter describes sociology as a *viewpoint*, as an *area of research*, as a *set of perspectives*, and as a *history of ideas and people*. The web shows *sociology* directly connected to those concepts. The web shows other connections as well. For example, sociological research is shown to connect to the concepts of *theory* and *methods*. In turn, *theory* is linked to *hypothesis* and *methods* is linked to *quantitative* and *qualitative*. The web may be expanded in two ways. The first is by adding concepts and connections to the concepts already present in the web, such as adding *experiment* to *quantitative methods*. The second way the web may be expanded is by adding links not already present. For example, we could link *Marx* to *conflict perspective*s since his theoretical arguments stressed the role of conflict in social life.

Critical thinkers find webs useful for organizing information and for identifying additional links that need to be made among concepts. In addition, students whose learning skills favor spatial relationships find concept webs particularly helpful in organizing information and in identifying linkages among concepts and ideas.

One way to draw a web is to first organize the material in an outline form. The major headings of the outline become the central concepts. The secondary headings are then connected graphically to the major headings.

- Using the discussions of research methods in this chapter, add additional concepts and connections among concepts.
- Add August Comte and Harriet Martineau to the web. Would you draw a direct connection between them? Why or why not?

Looking Ahead

The next chapter presents three of the central topics of sociology. These topics are culture, society, and social change.

WHAT YOU SHOULD KNOW ●■▲

1. What is sociology, and what is the sociological point of view?

Sociology is one of the social and behavioral sciences, but it is set apart from the others by a unique viewpoint. This viewpoint includes the notions of science, social structure, social interaction, and social change.

2. How did Karl Marx view the impact of the Industrial Revolution on society?

Karl Marx saw the Industrial Revolution as one stage in the social evolution of human societies. The Industrial Revolution went hand in hand with the development of capitalism. Under capitalism, workers and capitalists are separated by the ownership of the means of production. Production processes are broken down into repetitive tasks; workers are depersonalized, lack control over their work, and become alienated. Ultimately, Marx foresaw a revolution and the creation of a classless society.

3. What contribution did Émile Durkheim make to our understanding of the impact of the Industrial Revolution on society?

Émile Durkheim argued that traditional societies are cohesive because everyone participates in the same social life within the same culture and comes to share the same values. In industrial society, people are held together because they are functionally interdependent—they each perform different and specialized tasks and, thus, must rely on one another. Durkheim argued that industrialization had swept away traditional society but had not replaced it with anything of similar substance. Consequently, industrial societies risked becoming anomic.

4. How did Max Weber expand our understanding of the effects of the Industrial Revolution on society?

According to Weber, in traditional societies, life revolves around what has gone before. With industrialization comes rationalization: thinking that heavily emphasizes deliberate calculation, efficiency, and effectiveness in the accomplishment of explicit goals. Weber thought that rationalization was taken to the extreme in the workings of government agencies and other large bureaucracies. People living in industrialized and bureaucratic societies, he further thought, would eventually find themselves trapped in a situation of depersonalized and oppressive regulations and unvarying routine.

5. What are the basic theoretical perspectives in sociology?

Functionalism and social conflict are two fundamental sociological perspectives. Functionalism views society as a system of parts that work together to maintain the whole system in a state of equilibrium. When the equilibrium is disturbed, a set of activities is set in motion that aims to restore the equilibrium. Social conflict theory stresses the role of power in social relations and in the organization of society. Conflict theory views society as consisting of conflicting groups locked into a struggle to control their own destiny as well as the destiny of other groups.

6. What are the typical research methods used by sociologists?

Sociological research methods may be divided into two types, qualitative and quantitative. Qualitative research techniques are designed to obtain the subjective understanding, interpretation, and meaning of social behavior. To obtain such understanding, qualitative researchers rely on such techniques as studying historical records, life histories, in-depth interviews, and participant observation. Quantitative methods rely heavily on statistical and mathematical techniques to answer questions about social behavior. The survey and the controlled experiment are two basic quantitative research approaches.

7. How are human subjects' rights protected by social researchers today?

The American Sociological Association has prepared a set of guidelines to protect people involved in research, and academic research supported by the federal government has to be reviewed by a Human Subjects committee. In most universities, all research studies involving human participants must be approved by a committee that safeguards the rights, health, and social welfare of subjects and respondents.

8. What can sociology tell us about the future?

One of the great values of sociology is that it forces us to identify our myths, beliefs, and assumptions. Quite often, we discover that the obvious is subtle and that common sense is wrong.

TEST YOUR KNOWLEDGE ●■▲

Key Terms Matching

Match each of these key terms with the best definition or example from the numbered items that follow. Write the letter(s) preceding the key term in the blank before the definition that you choose.

a. alienation
b. anomie
c. control group
d. dysfunctions
e. experiment
f. experimental group
g. functions
h. latent functions
i. life history
j. manifest functions
k. mechanical solidarity .
l. organic solidarity
m. participant observation
n. perspectives
o. population
p. qualitative methods
q. quantitative methods
r. random sampling
s. rationalization
t. representative sample
u. research methods
v. sample
w. scientific method
x. social interaction
y. social power
z. social structure
aa. sociology
bb. structured interview
cc. survey
dd. theory

___aa___ 1. The scientific study of social structure and social interaction and of the factors making for change in social structure and social interaction.

___f___ 2. In the context of a research project, any group that the researcher is studying.

_____ 3. The relatively permanent components of our social environment.

___o___ 4. The term Marx used to refer to a situation in which people are estranged from their social world and feel that life is meaningless.

___j___ 5. Functions that are intended or recognized by others.

_____ 6. The term Durkheim used to refer to a social condition in which societal norms are conflicting or entirely absent.

___t___ 7. A small number of cases selected to represent the entire population.

___d___ 8. Actions that have negative consequences for the social system.

___k___ 9. Social solidarity based on shared values.

___N___ 10. Our mental pictures of the relative importance of things.

___i___ 11. A long interview, or series of interviews, in which the researcher attempts to discover the essential features, decisive moments, or turning points in a respondent's life.

___s___ 12. The replacement of traditional thinking with thinking that heavily emphasizes deliberate calculation, efficiency, and effectiveness in the accomplishment of explicit goals.

___dd___ 13. An explanation for the relationship between certain facts.

_____ 14. An objective and judicious approach to empirical evidence.

_____ **15.** The acts people perform toward one another and the responses they give in return, which may consist of spoken words, subtle gestures, visual images, or even electronically transmitted digits.

_____ **16.** In an experiment, the group to whom the experimental stimulus is administered.

_____ **17.** The ability to get others to conform to one's wishes even against their own desires.

_____ **18.** A sample that in its characteristics mirrors the population from which it comes.

_____ **19.** Research techniques designed to obtain the subjective understanding, interpretation, and meaning of social behavior.

_____ **20.** Actions that have positive consequences for the social system.

_____ **21.** Research techniques designed to produce numerical estimates of human behavior.

_____ **22.** In an experiment, the group not exposed to the experimental stimulus but used as a comparison with the experimental group.

_____ **23.** A procedure in which respondents are asked the same series of questions and the answers are recorded in standard format.

_____ **24.** Type of observation in which the researcher participates in the activities of the group to obtain an in-depth and intimate understanding of it.

_____ **25.** Functions that are unintended or unrecognized by others.

_____ **26.** A systematic procedure for gathering information, usually through the application of standardized interviews or questionnaires.

_____ **27.** A sampling procedure in which everyone in the population has an equal chance of being selected as a respondent.

_____ **28.** Social solidarity based on a functional interdependence among people.

_____ **29.** The techniques, practices, and ethics involved in gaining new knowledge.

_____ **30.** A method for studying the relations between two or more variables under highly controlled conditions.

Multiple Choice

Circle the letter of your choice.

1. Which is NOT of concern to sociology?
   a. social structure
   b. social interaction
   c. sociological point of view
   d. all of the above are of concern to sociology

2. The relatively permanent components of our social environment which impose order and predictability are known as
   a. social change.
   b. social structure.
   c. social interaction.
   d. sociological imagination.

3. The term natural sociologist refers to the idea that
   a. sociologists study social interaction with the same methods that natural scientists study the natural world.
   b. sociologists are concerned with natural causal ordering.
   c. each of us practices sociology informally to make sense of our world.
   d. none of the above.

4. Which is NOT a component of critical thinking?
   a. identifying the issue or assertion
   b. determining whether key terms are clearly defined
   c. disagreeing with existing assertions
   d. generating new assertions

5. Which sociologist contributed the idea that social strains emerge when people behave in ways that conflict with their core values?
   a. Karl Mark
   b. Émile Durkheim
   c. Max Weber
   d. Harriet Martineau

6. According to Marx, which of the following is the potential product of repetition, monotony, lack of meaning, and lack of control in the workplace?
   a. mechanical solidarity
   b. alienation
   c. anomie
   d. Verstehen

7. In small farming villages, the division of labor is simple, and the residents have identical values. This arrangement is an example of
   a. mechanical solidarity.
   b. anomie.
   c. organic solidarity.
   d. Verstehen.

8. A situation in which societal norms are in conflict or entirely missing is known as
   a. alienation.
   b. anomie.
   c. dysfunction.
   d. hostility.

9. Yolanda is an accountant who lives in a complex industrial society. When her car breaks down, she seeks the help of a mechanic, and when she is sick, she visits the doctor. What links Yolanda to the other members of her society?
   a. mechanical solidarity
   b. anomie
   c. organic solidarity
   d. Verstehen

10. The replacement of traditional-mindedness with thinking based on self-control, efficiency, and deliberate calculation is
    a. rationalization.
    b. industrialization.
    c. bureaucratization.
    d. politicization.

11. Which sociologist emphasized the role in modern society of rationalization?
    a. Émile Durkheim
    b. August Comte
    c. Max Weber
    d. Karl Marx

12. Which group of theorists would argue that, like an organism, components of a social system work together for the cohesion of the whole system?
    a. interactionists
    b. functionalists
    c. conflict theorists
    d. Marxists

13. Professor Singh assigned a group project to his introductory sociology class. As a result of the interaction within a work group, two students met, began dating, and eventually married. This circumstance is an example of
    a. mechanical solidarity.
    b. latent consequences.
    c. organic solidarity.
    d. manifest consequences.

14. Qualitative research techniques are designed to attain which of the following?
    a. subjective understanding of behavior
    b. interpretation of behavior
    c. meaning of social behavior
    d. all of the above

15. The assertions that whites have historically used their domination over nonwhites to gain benefits at the expense of nonwhites and that men have historically used their domination over women to gain benefits at the expense of women reflect which sociological viewpoint?
    a. conflict
    b. interactionist
    c. functionalist
    d. organic

16. The ability to get others to conform to one's wishes even against their own desires is called
    a. muscle.
    b. coercion.
    c. social power.
    d. social control.

17. In the context of a research project, any group that the researcher is studying is referred to as the
    a. sample.
    b. cases.
    c. population.
    d. subjects.

18. In which of the following sampling techniques does everyone in the population have an equal chance of selection?
    a. random
    b. representative
    c. controlled
    d. selected

19. Dr. Torres designs an experiment to test the effect of taking a women's studies class on attitudes toward women. He divides participants into two groups, one group that takes the class and one that does not. The group that takes the class is called the

    a. random sample.
    b. control group.
    c. representative group.
    d. experimental group.

20. A sample that mirrors the characteristics of the population from which it comes is a

    a. uniform sample.
    b. representative sample.
    c. random sample.
    d. purposive sample.

True-False

Indicate your response to each of the following statements by circling T for true or F for false.

T   F   1. Sociology's emphasis on answering logical questions with evidence obtained from experiments and systematic observation defines sociology as a science.

T   F   2. In order for social interaction to occur, the actors must be in close physical proximity to each other.

T   F   3. Critical thinking involves studying a subject skeptically.

T   F   4. Weber is known as the founder of sociology.

T   F   5. Alienation describes a situation in which one feels estranged from his or her social world and feels that life is meaningless.

T   F   6. Dysfunctions are actions that have negative consequences for the social system.

T   F   7. Research techniques of participant observation, interviewing, and historical analysis are used in qualitative analysis.

T   F   8. Quantitative analysis relies heavily on statistical and mathematical techniques.

T   F   9. If constructed correctly, random samples will yield representative samples.

T   F   10. Quantitative analysis is often the best way to describe and explain both behavior and its context.

T   F   11. Bob has been asked to participate in a study of how people make up their minds to vote or not to vote for a particular political candidate. The group to which he is assigned is called the experimental group since it is to receive exposure to media material that the other group in the study will not.

T   F   12. Tina has been asked to participate in a study that consists of a lengthy interview by which the researcher attempts to discover the essential features, decisive moments, or turning points in her life. This type of study is called a life history.

T   F   13. Juan grew up in a rural isolated section of central Mexico. In his village it seemed that everyone was the same in habits, language, values, and in the course of their lives. In addition, the social bonds that held the people together were very strong. The social theorist Émile Durkheim called this type of solidarity mechanical solidarity.

T   F   14. Shari not only wants to study gang behavior but she also wants to come to a subjective understanding of gang behavior and its meaning to the gang members themselves. To do this she will employ qualitative research methods.

T   F   15. Rhonda thought that she might like to major in sociology. In talking with the undergraduate advisor she correctly learned that sociology is the scientific study of social structure and social interaction and of the factors making for change in both social structure and social interaction.

NOTE: The answers to these exercises are at the end of the book.

For additional practice tests and other resources please visit the companion web site at http://www.prenhall.com/curry.

Essay

1. Why is sociology called a science? How is it similar to other sciences studies in college?

2. Compare the concepts of mechanical solidarity and organic solidarity. Which is characteristic of traditional societies? Which of industrial societies?

3. What are the basic assertions of functionalism and of conflict theory? Within functionalism, contrast functions, dysfunctions, manifest functions, and latent functions.

4. What is the relationship between work and alienation? What work experiences have you or your friends had that have produced alienation?

5. What are four of the ethical guidelines prepared by the American Sociological Association for sociologists to follow when conducting research?

2

Culture, Society, and Social Change

Chapter Outline

The Kwakiutl Indians live in the Pacific Northwest area of Canada. This area has an abundance of natural resources, and the Kwakiutl have developed a culture in which that abundance plays a key role. In fact, food, furs, and items obtained through trade are so abundant that the Kwakiutl can afford to destroy them in a ceremonial feast called a potlatch.

Periodically, a wealthy male Kwakiutl will host a potlatch. At this feast, he will lavish gifts of food, blankets, and other valuable property on his guests. In doing so, the host is not trying to help others less fortunate than himself; rather, he is being generous because the more he gives, the greater his prestige. According to anthropologist Ruth Benedict (1934), in some potlatches the host would actually destroy his own boats, kill slaves, and burn an entire village to the ground. Such magnificent feats of gift-giving and destruction of property would earn the host supremely high prestige, and his potlatch would be long remembered.

At one time, the Canadian government tried to end potlatches by declaring them illegal. The effort failed, and today potlatches are still being given in secluded areas away from the prying eyes of the police. Although not as magnificent as in the past, the modern potlatch still bestows honor upon the host who can afford to give away or destroy the most property. As the Kwakiutl illustrate, humans adapt to their environment in specific ways. The Kwakiutl had so much wealth that they could afford to destroy it to gain social honor. Groups living in other circumstances, however, have had to adopt a different pattern of living. For instance, the Jigalong, described on p. 40, live in the barren, inhospitable desert of Australia and have developed a belief system consistent with that environment. According to their beliefs, the survival of the group is guaranteed only by performing certain rituals that cause the gods to provide them with food, water, and shelter. As a result, the Jigalong devote a considerable portion of their time to making sure that these rituals are performed in the proper manner (Cowan 1992; Tonkinson 1974).

Chapter Preview

This chapter continues introducing the major ideas that are the building blocks of sociology. The first section introduces culture and society, two of the broadest and most fundamental of all concepts in sociology. We continue the discussion by focusing on the major types of societies in the world, and then we introduce the Great Social Transformation. This transformation, as we shall see throughout the book, influenced the nature of contemporary society and the quality of our individual lives. Theories of change and development are discussed next, and then we describe specific catalysts or sources of change. In the last section, as is our practice throughout the book, we address the major topics of the chapter in relation to the future.

Culture and Society

Culture and society are broad concepts that are the foundations for understanding social existence. Without them, in fact, it is difficult to imagine what life would be like. Let us consider culture first.

To understand better the lifestyle of various peoples, including ourselves, sociologists often use the concept of culture: the mutually shared products, knowledge, and beliefs of a human group or society. This concept, you should note, is not limited to art, literature, classical music, and other "high" elements. Instead, sociologists consider culture to include all aspects of life within a given society. There is so much culture, in fact, that sociologists divide it into two basic types: (1) *material culture*, which consists of the physical objects used by people to accomplish goals, such as the tools and machinery used in construction, or the computers and calculators used to analyze mathematical problems; and (2) *nonmaterial culture*, which consists of values, art, language, worldviews, and other symbolic representations of the social and physical world. Examples of nonmaterial culture would be fairy tales we learn as children, or complex legal codes, music, and ideas we learn as adults.

Everything we know is part of our culture, but it is society that provides us with an overarching social structure. All human groupings must live within some given territory. Those groupings that also obey a central authority (government) and share a common culture constitute a **society**. Very often the boundaries of a nation-state coincide with societal boundaries. For that reason, we can speak of American, Canadian, or Mexican society. The opposite, however, is not always true. The Kwakiutl have a culture and a government, and they live in a specific territory. They are therefore a society but not a nation-state separate from Canada.

Although a few social scientists use the terms culture and society interchangeably, we do not. Instead, we reserve *culture* for the products created by humans, and *society* for the entity that divides humankind into a particular kind of grouping. Our usage enables us to speak of the culture of African Americans, for example, even though African Americans do not constitute a society separate from the United States. Similarly, the phrase "cultural diversity" refers to the many distinct cultures that exist within a large, heterogeneous society such as the United States.

All societies face many broadly similar problems. The cultural solutions to these problems are called **cultural universals** (Murdock 1937). For instance, all people get sick at times, and therefore all societies must develop a solution to the problem of illness. Some societies rely on complex institutions and sophisticated technology to handle the problem, whereas other societies rely on a single person, a shaman, who offers prayers and performs rituals for the sick person (see Chapter 14). Similarly, all societies must confront the issue of human origins and mortality. Where did we come

Society ▲ A grouping that consists of people who share a common culture, obey the same political authority, and occupy a given territory.

Cultural universals ▲ Similar cultural solutions in different societies for similar problems of survival.

St. Paul Island, the Pribilofs, Alaska: Aleut boys and girls with traditional skin drums celebrate the end-of-subsistence seal harvest. The community shares the meat, still an important source of protein.

from, and where are we going after death? Because these questions are universal, all societies have myths, beliefs, legends, and religions that answer these questions (see Chapter 13). Other cultural universals are reproduction, rearing children, obtaining sustenance, and maintaining order in society.

Values and Norms

Each society has its own set of values and norms. **Values** are the preferences people share about what is good or bad, right or wrong, desirable or undesirable. As part of culture, these values influence behavior, emotion, and thought. For instance, a society that values individualism will develop laws limiting the power of government; people who value learning will work hard in school; and people who value democracy may become angry if their views are not taken into account by elected officials.

Sociologist Robin Williams (1970) says that American culture stresses values such as personal achievement, hard work, equality, and democracy (see the What Do You Think? box). Other sociologists have added to the list and include such things as romantic love and the traditional family as deeply ingrained American values. One way to infer the relative importance of different values is to note those qualities that parents feel are most important to instill in their children. Some of these are presented in Chapter 3.

Although some values are widely held, that tendency does not mean that everyone holds them. Most Americans believe in some of the values mentioned by Williams, but a few Americans might not believe in any of them. Moreover, the content of these values can change even though the outward form remains the same. For example, what is now meant by equality is certainly different from what was meant 50 years ago when racial segregation and gender discrimination were widely accepted practices; and what was meant 50 years ago was different from what the signers of the U.S. Constitution meant when slavery was legal and men legally owned their wives' property.

Whereas values are general guidelines for behavior, **norms** are specific expectations about how people behave in a given situation. Norms provide us with a pool or reservoir of behavioral guidelines that we can draw on as the situation demands. For instance, you draw on the norms of classroom decorum when sitting in class and on another set of norms when attending a party. To mismatch norms and setting is a social blunder. You do not want to wear your party clothes to class, nor do you want to bring your classroom decorum to a party.

Values ▲ The preferences people share about what is good or bad, right or wrong, desirable or undesirable.

Norms ▲ The specific expectations about how people behave in a given situation.

What Do You Think? ●■▲ American Values　[?]

In his study of the United States, sociologist Robin Williams identified several major value orientations: complex patterns of belief that are passionately held by many people in a society. Some value orientations are in the list that follows.

AMERICAN VALUE	ORIENTATIONS
Personal Achievement	Efficiency and Practicality
Activity and Work	Science and Rationality
Material Comfort	Nationalism and Patriotism
Morality	Equality
Humanitarianism	Freedom
Individuality	Democracy
Conformity	Progress and the Future

Key Terms:*

To Robin Williams, the values listed here are key terms or concepts. How would you define these terms? Do you see any contradiction between certain concepts and other concepts?

*To answer these critical questions, review the box titled "What Is Critical Thinking?" in Chapter 1, and pay special attention to the discussion of key terms.

SOURCE: Robin M. Williams, Jr., *American Society: A Sociological Interpretation,* Third Edition (New York: Alfred A. Knopf, 1970).

Not knowing the appropriate norms can lead to feelings of intense anxiety. New college students often feel uneasy or scared because they do not know what is expected of them in the classroom, nor do they know how they are supposed to act as college students: what should I say, what should I do, what should I wear? When new students learn the correct answers to these and to hundreds of other questions regarding college life, their anxiety disappears.

Norms vary in importance. Those concerning relatively unimportant matters are called **folkways**. For example, we should say hello to our friends on meeting them for the first time each day and say goodbye on leaving them at night. We expect other people to say that they are sorry if they bump into us in the hallway, and we expect to wait our turn at the end of the checkout line in a supermarket. All of these expectations are norms, but violating them results only in mild punishment. In contrast to folkways, **mores** are norms concerning very serious matters. Mores frequently deal with the welfare and continued existence of the society. To illustrate, expectations such as "do not kill or steal" are mores that, if violated, bring down heavy sanctions on the violator. Finally, **taboos** are norms about things that are so serious as to be almost beyond comprehension. In American culture, eating another human or having sexual relations with animals would constitute taboos. Violating taboos typically will result in extreme punishment and ostracism.

Symbols and Language

Although a great deal of communication takes place through words, either written or spoken, a large amount also takes place through **symbols**, or representations that stand for something else. Under the right conditions, almost anything can be a symbol. A smile or frown symbolizes happiness or anger. A picture of a mushroom cloud represents a nuclear explosion, whereas a screaming siren warns of an impending tornado. Some symbols, moreover, represent important cultural values and take on political importance. For instance, "The Star-Spangled Banner" stands for the United States, and when television star Roseanne Barr deliberately sang it in a screechy voice at a baseball game, she was booed by fans and criticized by the media. In contrast, Whitney Houston was highly praised when she sang the same song respectfully and emotionally at a Super Bowl. In fact, her performance is often replayed on television and sold on videocassette.

Of all of the symbols used to communicate meaning, language is the most powerful and complex. A **language** consists of words that are symbols standing for ideas or objects, and of rules for combining words into longer, more complex ideas. In effect, language consists of a vocabulary and a grammar. Although many animal species might use some form of language, human language is undoubtedly the most complex and most sophisticated. It is so complex that most people spend a considerable portion of their lives learning how to use it correctly.

Language is such a powerful system of symbols that it might even shape our perception of the world (see Chapter 3). This possibility is called the "Sapir-Whorf hypothesis," named after the two linguists who formulated it (Whorf 1956). According to them, we have little choice but to interpret the world in terms of the words and grammar of our native language. To illustrate this idea, consider the behavior and language of the original Navajo, or Diné, people. They were, according to early European observers, rather docile, and their language contained no active verbs. Sapir and Whorf would say that without words to express ideas such as "attack," "fight," or "repel," the Navajo could not conceive of such actions, and therefore appeared to be a rather passive people. In their later writings, Sapir and Whorf softened their views. They said that language merely predisposes people to see reality in certain ways and also that some languages are so flexible that they allow people to generate novel ideas and to express themselves in a variety of actions (Popenoe 2000).

Currently, the world's stock of languages is rapidly being depleted. Of the thousands of languages now in use, perhaps only a few hundred are spoken by enough

Folkways ▲ Norms concerning relatively unimportant matters.

Mores ▲ Norms concerning very serious matters.

Taboos ▲ Norms about matters that are so serious as to be almost beyond comprehension.

Symbol ▲ A representation that stands for something else.

Language ▲ Words that are symbols and rules for conveying complex ideas.

people to remain secure in the immediate future. Many of the languages of indigenous peoples of the world have already disappeared, lost when the cultures that created them were swept away by more powerful nations. Entrenched languages of science, commerce, and diplomacy, such as English, Spanish, German, and French, are in no danger of disappearing, nor are the languages spoken by millions of people, such as Japanese, Chinese, Hindi, and Russian. But as the world becomes a smaller place, more and more people speak fewer and fewer languages. Sadly, when a language disappears, so does the accumulated experience of the culture that produced it (Diamond 1991; Maybury-Lewis 1992).

Ethnocentrism and Cultural Relativity

Most people are reared exclusively within a single culture and as adults seldom venture outside it. It is not surprising, therefore, to find that they know their own culture best and view other cultures with a mixture of curiosity, acceptance, and loathing. These mixed feelings are the basis for **ethnocentrism**: the tendency to judge other cultures by the standards of our own culture. Put simply, ethnocentrism is the belief that our culture is superior to all other cultures.

The tendency to be ethnocentric was recognized around the early part of the twentieth century by sociologist William Graham Sumner (1959 [1906]). Sumner thought that ethnocentrism was an erroneous way of thinking. To illustrate the errors of ethnocentric thinking, consider the following: some people in our society are disgusted when they learn that people from other cultures eat dog meat. The mere fact of eating a dog disgusts them, and they think anybody who would eat a dog must be a degenerate. On the other hand, we, who eat baby sheep and baby cows, consider ourselves normal. In the same vein, people who pierce their noses with sharp bones and make sounds on wooden flutes are considered strange, whereas we, who pierce our ears with needles and make deafening noises on metal guitars, feel we are behaving properly. Our behavior feels right to us—but it does not follow that people who behave differently are abnormal, weird, or inferior.

To some extent, ethnocentrism is the result of prizing the familiar over the unknown. But extreme ethnocentrism is a problem, especially in a global society. For example, as Japan and the United States become more intertwined economically, it will be impossible for them to work together if Americans and Japanese view each other as dumb, odd, or untrustworthy. Many American commentators assume that no matter what the Japanese say, they will cheat on trade practices. In turn, many Japanese counterargue that Americans would do better to work harder and complain less (Samuelson 1990a). In this way, misunderstandings brought about by ethnocentric thinking harm both countries (Friedman 1994).

To avoid the great harm caused by ethnocentric thinking, people need to adopt an open mind and an eager acceptance of different cultures and peoples. This view, called **cultural relativism**, recognizes that each culture is unique and valid. It was strongly advocated during the 1920s by social scientists doing cross-cultural research. Anthropologist Ruth Benedict, for instance, expressed the hope that cultural relativism would be embraced worldwide and that intolerance, bigotry, and prejudice would end (Benedict 1959; orig. 1934).

The idea of multiculturalism is closely related to cultural relativism, but the two ideas have different origins. Whereas cultural relativism began in anthropology during the early part of the twentieth century, multiculturalism began in education during the 1960s and has gained currency over the last decade (Eldering 1996; Grin 1996). Formally, **multiculturalism** may be defined as the belief that cultures should be viewed from the perspective of different groups.

One goal of multicultural education is to incorporate other cultural viewpoints into the curriculum. For example, rather than teach history exclusively through the eyes of white Europeans (a Eurocentric view), multicultural educators try to teach minority viewpoints as well. To illustrate this goal, consider how schools commonly

 STUDY TIP

Choose a particular culture that is represented in the American print media (newspapers and magazines). Create a collage that you feel displays key elements of that culture. Be sure to include symbols that typify the culture.

Ethnocentrism ▲ The belief that one's own culture is superior to all other cultures.

Cultural relativism ▲ The belief that each culture is unique and must be analyzed and judged on its own terms.

Multiculturalism ▲ The belief that culture should be viewed from the perspective of different groups.

New Haven, Connecticut. International Day in 2001 at the Hooker Public Elementary School celebrates the diversity of cultures in this community. Here fourth graders wait to perform a Hindu dance. The gold paper balls symbolize gold in the dancer's story. Many Yale University professors and graduate students live in the Hooker district and support multicultural education.

teach that the discovery of the "New World" by Christopher Columbus opened the way for European expansion. Although seemingly harmless, this teaching, as multicultural educators quickly point out, has several Eurocentric features: (1) In all probability, Nordic seafarers, not Christopher Columbus, were the first Europeans to set foot on North America; (2) Columbus did not discover the American continent; he accidentally bumped into it while trying to reach India; (3) The so-called New World was new to Europeans but not to the several million Native Americans already living there; and (4) European expansion was, from the viewpoint of Native Americans, a European conquest in which they lost their land, their rights, and frequently their lives (Banks 1979; Grant 1978; Stannard 1992). By teaching how both the powerful and the powerless react to events, multicultural educators hope to produce both a more complete picture of society and greater tolerance for diversity. As we point out in Chapter 7, the United States is becoming increasingly diverse, and maintaining harmony among different cultures will probably become a central issue of the twenty-first century.

●■▲ Pausing to Think   About Culture and Society

Culture provides us with the tools and understanding necessary for social life, whereas society provides us with the overarching social structure that shapes our relationships with others. Values provide us with guidelines about what is good or bad, whereas norms translate values into specific guidelines for behavior.

People interact with one another through the use of symbols, the most important of which is language. Language is a powerful cultural element because it transmits information to others and shapes our perception of the world. Because our language and culture differ from those of other societies, we tend to be ethnocentric: to judge other cultures by our own. A solution to ethnocentrism is to develop an attitude of cultural relativism that recognizes that each culture is unique and valid.

CQ Suppose you were describing American culture to a recently arrived exchange student from Moscow University. Where would you begin, and what would you tell him or her about life in your city?

Types of Societies

By definition, a society consists of people who share a common culture, but obviously no two societies are identical. They differ in geographic location, degree of isolation from competing societies, available technology, environmental resources, and in many other respects. These and other differences shape the culture of a society and determine its **mode of subsistence**: how it obtains the basic materials necessary to sustain itself. The mode of subsistence is perhaps the most basic feature of a society. From it flows much of its economy, social organization, political structure, and lifestyle. Because it is so fundamental, sociologists use it to divide societies into the following types.

Hunting and Gathering Societies

The **hunting and gathering society** obtains its sustenance primarily through hunting game animals and gathering nuts, berries, and other wild plants. Hunting and gathering societies are held together by kinship ties and by a simple division of labor based on age and gender. Adult men engage primarily in hunting, and young boys help around the camp. Adult women gather and prepare food, while young girls help their mothers and care for the very young. Although life can sometimes be very harsh for hunters and gatherers, most of the time they live comfortably. They devote about three hours a day to hunting and gathering food, and they have more leisure time than the people in any other type of society.

The strategy of hunting and gathering works well, provided that people are nomadic and collect together in small bands of 50 to 100. No matter how plentiful the environment, long-term hunting and gathering will eventually deplete it. Therefore, hunters and gatherers are constantly on the move, do not accumulate bulky goods, and do not erect permanent housing.

For much of human history, hunting and gathering was the most common way of life, and it still exists. Current hunting and gathering societies include the aboriginal Australians, the Mbuti and other pygmies of Africa's Ituri forest, and the Cree of Canada's Moose River Basin (George 1995; Scupin 1992; see the Diversity box, The Jigalong). Numerically, however, there are only a few thousand hunters and gatherers left in the world, and sometime during this century they could disappear entirely.

Mode of subsistence ▲ The manner in which a society obtains the basic materials necessary to sustain itself; the most basic feature of a society.

Hunting and gathering societies ▲ Societies that obtain their sustenance primarily through hunting game animals and gathering nuts, berries, and other wild plants and that are held together by kinship ties and by a simple division of labor based on age and gender.

A Mbuti hunter in the Ituri forest. The Mbuti pygmies are among the few remaining hunting and gathering societies in the world.

The Jigalong are an aboriginal people living in the deserts of Western Australia. Much of their culture has been shaped by this environment, especially by the threat of drought. To ensure an abundant water supply, each year the Jigalong engage in a ritual directed to the "rainmaking beings." This rainmaking ceremony is the most complex such ritual on record. During one small but important part of it, Jigalong men retreat to an area away from the main camp and set up two rainmaking piles. These piles consist of sacred stones, hair string, and pearl shells. The Jigalong pierce their arms and sprinkle blood on the piles to symbolize rain, and they cover the piles with feathers to symbolize clouds. They believe that rain snakes grow in the piles and that when the rituals have been performed correctly, their gods will bring them rain (Cowan 1992; Tonkinson 1974).

In addition to ensuring that they will have enough water, the rainmaking ceremony reaffirms the Jigalongs' rich set of cultural beliefs about their past. They believe that they were created by their ancestral gods during "the dreamtime." At that time, the gods took the shape of animals and walked the desert, leaving behind caves for shelter, watering holes, tools, and other implements helpful for survival. Then the gods became spirits and transformed themselves into stars in the heavens. When the Jigalong dream at night, they enter the dreamtime and communicate with the gods. These dreams are so real that the Jigalong are convinced that they can travel great distances, returning to the sacred sites in the desert. Although we might use the word "dream" to mean a fantasy or an illusion, the Jigalong sincerely believe that their dreams are real.

At one time, aboriginal people such as the Jigalong were considered simple or primitive, but now they are recognized as having an intricate and sophisticated spiritual life. Such people, moreover, have a deep knowledge of their environment and can survive where so-called modern people would perish. Although the Jigalong have followed their traditional way of life for hundreds of years, they are now being contacted by the outside world. Missionaries, for instance, are trying to convert the Jigalong to Christianity, and the traditional Jigalong way of life might soon disappear. If it does, we will have lost a unique culture and the opportunity to learn from it.

CQ What role does the rainmaking ritual play in the life of the Jigalong?

Horticultural and Pastoral Societies

Some 10,000 to 13,000 years ago, both horticultural and pastoral societies began to develop. In **horticultural societies**, the cultivation of domestic plants satisfies most needs for food. In a sense, horticulture is gardening, but on a much larger scale. Horticulture was made possible by the invention of the hoe, a simple digging tool that enabled people to turn over the earth. Without a hoe, cultivating plants is tiring, tedious, and time-consuming. Today, horticultural societies are most typically found in the tropical areas of Africa, Central America, and Southeast Asia (Campbell 1995).

Although horticulture requires people to remain near their crops to take care of them, they must occasionally move if the soil becomes depleted. Depletion occurs because many horticulturalists use "slash and burn" techniques: they clear a section of land, burn the vegetation to produce fertilizer, plant and harvest crops, and then move on as the soil becomes exhausted.

Horticultural people develop relatively permanent housing and form large social groups. Several families may be linked through common ancestry into larger kin groups, or clans. These clans become autonomous and powerful political units that may unite to deal with common problems.

Even though crops are subject to droughts, famine, and insects, horticulture is more efficient and reliable than hunting and gathering. In fact, horticulture usually produces more food than the population can immediately consume, thus creating a surplus that becomes a source of wealth and inequality. In turn, wealth and inequality necessitate some form of permanent government that can ensure the safety of its people and the continuity of the society. For these reasons, then, horticulture encourages people to settle in a single place and to develop a culture suited to permanent residence.

In many arid parts of the world, poor soil and bad weather make horticulture impossible. In these places, a different type of society called a pastoral society emerged. **Pastoral societies** derive most of their sustenance from grazing domestic animals. Pastoralists who follow their herds as they migrate from place to place are called

Horticultural societies ▲ Societies in which the cultivation of domestic plants satisfies most needs for food.

Pastoral societies ▲ Societies that derive most of their sustenance from raising domesticated animals.

nomads (Kradin 2002). Current examples of pastoral societies are the Lapps, or Sami, of northern Scandinavia, the Tungus and Chukchee of Siberia, the Tuareg of the Sahara Desert, and the Masai of East Africa.

Agrarian Societies

About 6,000 years ago, **agrarian societies** began to appear. The invention of the plow allowed farmers to cultivate the land intensively, using draft animals to supply pulling power. Irrigation and fertilization further increased the efficiency of production and the amount of land that could be cultivated. The resulting large output created food surpluses that could be used to support even larger populations and permanent settlements. Cities emerged and became political powers, which then subdued the less powerful horticultural societies in their region. Increased production per farmer, moreover, helped to bring about the specialization of labor by freeing farmworkers for other occupations. There was enough wealth being produced to support toolmakers, government administrators, religious leaders, and other nonagricultural specialists.

Agrarian societies sometimes grow very large, often including several million inhabitants. They also become complex and stratified. Power becomes centralized in the hands of a nobility, and clear social classes develop. Because the nobility own the land, they can monopolize the wealth created by the peasants and rise to the top of the class system. Religion becomes an institutionalized part of the society and often shares power with the nobility. Intricate doctrines become the basis for religious belief, and religious authority becomes centralized in the hands of a small group of selected leaders. Because agrarian societies produce considerable wealth, an economy develops that supports elaborate markets for trade. Money becomes the medium of exchange, and buying and selling with money replaces bartering and trading for goods and services. The feudal system of medieval Europe is an example of a developed agrarian society. Today, Vietnam is still predominantly an agrarian society, with most of its citizens involved in growing rice or other crops.

Industrial Societies

Whereas horticultural and agrarian societies rely on agriculture, **industrial societies** rely on technology and mechanization as the main source of sustenance. In contrast

Agrarian societies ▲ Societies whose technology of food production is such that annual food surpluses are used to support larger populations and permanent settlements.

Industrial societies ▲ Societies that rely on technology and mechanization as the main source of sustenance.

Prior to the mechanization of agriculture, human and animal power provided the energy required to plant and harvest crops. In the days of horse-drawn farm equipment, farming was a labor-intensive industry, and many people found employment as farmers and farmhands. In the industrial era, large tractors do the work. This wide-angle view of a tractor cultivating a soybean field gives some idea of the efficiency of agriculture in the United States today. With such machinery, fewer people are needed, and farm employment has declined greatly as a result.

The emergence of an industrial, manufacturing society was a key feature of the Great Social Transformation.

to preindustrial societies, industrial societies institutionalize innovation (Lauer 1991). For instance, they invest in research and education, and they use government to create and foster commerce. New technology facilitates contacts between people, thereby speeding up transactions and stimulating further economic growth. Some industrial societies maintain a large military establishment that requires heavy investments in defense technology. Sometimes this technology is transferred to the civilian industrial sector and stimulates further changes. Industrial societies have values that prize innovation and that motivate change in all areas of life. Later in this chapter, we return to the Industrial Revolution and the nature of industrial society.

Postindustrial Societies

Beginning in the mid-1970s, sociologists began to recognize an emerging type of society that they called **postindustrial** (Bell 1973; Gershuny 2000). Whereas an industrial society is based primarily on manufacturing, a postindustrial society is based primarily on the creation and transmittal of specialized knowledge. Lawyers, professors, and accountants, for instance, earn their livelihood by what they know rather than by what they can do physically. These jobs can also be thought of as service occupations—for example, a physician offers specialized knowledge to a patient, but at the same time, also offers a service. For this reason, some sociologists and many economists define postindustrialism according to the size of the service sector of the economy.

As yet, sociologists do not completely understand how and why societies change from industrial to postindustrial, but education seems to be important. Most jobs that require a college education are concerned mainly with information. For instance, professors of dentistry teach their students knowledge and the manual skills necessary to care for teeth; attorneys advise their clients about the law; and technologists and technicians of all kinds rely on their skills and knowledge to earn a livelihood.

According to some measures, the United States was the first society to pass from industrial to postindustrial. Today, more than half of all American jobs are in the service sector of the economy, in fields such as food service, repair work, education,

Postindustrial societies ▲
Societies based primarily on the creation and transmitting of specialized knowledge.

government, counseling, banking, investments, sales, law, and mass media (Chapter 10). For that reason, some sociologists consider the United States to be a postindustrial society. Others, however, believe that it is still mainly industrial. Other emerging postindustrial societies are Japan, most of Western Europe, Australia, and New Zealand.

Some people believe that service workers produce nothing and therefore are not as important as workers who produce material goods. For instance, an old American saying is "Those who can, do, and those who can't, teach"—implying that teachers are unable to produce anything very practical or useful. If the term to produce is taken to mean "to create material products," then they are correct. However, other observers note that produce can also refer to creating knowledge and inventing skills. These are valuable outputs, too, and from that viewpoint, teachers and researchers are some of the most productive members of the postindustrial society.

Transitional Societies

Most societies of the world do not fit neatly into one of the types mentioned before. In fact, most societies are **transitional**: they are somewhere between agrarian and industrial and have elements of both types. For example, China is largely agrarian; about 80 percent of its people obtain their livelihood from farming small plots of land, mainly to support themselves. At the same time, China is heavily industrialized, with the capacity to produce jet aircraft, automobiles, television sets, and thousands of other products that we typically associate with an industrial nation (Goldstone 1996). China also has some of the world's largest cities, with many of the same cosmopolitan features found elsewhere in the world (Zhou et al. 1997). Since the death of Chairman Mao in 1971, China has begun to develop a limited market economy and a more open social class system (Dirlik 2001; Bian 2002). India is another example of a transitional society, as are many countries in South America, Africa, and Asia. In fact, the vast majority (81 percent) of the people on earth live in transitional societies (Chapter 15; Population Reference Bureau 2003).

Most of the people in transitional societies are peasants—farmers who rely mainly on their own labor to raise crops. Peasants are poor and are caught in a trap that prevents them from gaining wealth. They typically do not own their own land and therefore must rent it from wealthy landowners. The rents are so high that the peasants cannot accumulate enough wealth to buy land for themselves. To supplement their meager earnings, peasants often work temporarily on the estates of the rich, or they migrate to nearby cities for whatever jobs they can get. As we discuss further in

Transitional societies ▲ Societies that are partly agrarian and partly industrial and whose population members are largely peasants.

In many transitional societies, industrialization creates new wealth, but that wealth is insufficient to raise the living standards of everyone. Here in New Delhi, the capital of India, a beggar with an injured child in her arms pleads for money at a traffic light. The passengers in the taxi avoid her beseeching look.

Chapter 15, the migration of millions of peasants the world over has created enormous problems in maintaining city services and in providing even minimal shelter for the new arrivals.

● ■ ▲ Pausing to Think   About Types of Societies

Societies differ in many respects, such as geographic location, degree of isolation from competing societies, available technology, and environmental resources. From its mode of subsistence flows much of a society's economy, social organization, political structure, and lifestyle. Societies can be placed into categories according to their modes of subsistence: hunting and gathering, horticultural and pastoral, agrarian, industrial, and postindustrial. Most societies in the world today are transitional.

CQ   Was the United States ever an agrarian society? ◆ If so, when? ◆ What aspects of our agrarian heritage are still evident in our culture? ◆ For instance, how are our agrarian roots evident in the song "America the Beautiful"?

The Great Social Transformation

Contemporary life in an industrial society such as the United States is obviously different from life in agrarian, horticultural, or other types of societies. Some sociologists describe these differences using the terms traditional and preindustrial on the one hand, and modern and industrial on the other. However, no set of terms is accepted by everyone, and we have chosen the terms communal and associational to describe these contrasts (Weber 1947). Communal societies are characterized by rich personal relationships. The main social units are family, kin, and community. In contrast, associational societies are often highly impersonal, and the main social units are organizations, corporations, and bureaucracies. Life in these two contrasting types of society is, as we discuss throughout the book, quite different (Caplow 1991; Didsbury 1989; Knapp 1994; see also Bellah et al. 1991). The change from a culture and society that emphasizes communal relationships to one that emphasizes associational relationships is called the **Great Social Transformation (GST)**.

Communal Relationships

Imagine life in a preindustrial, traditional society. For instance, suppose you had lived in the United States before the Civil War. If you had lived during that bygone era, your daily routine would have been saturated with personal relationships. In all probability, you would have been a member of an extended family living on a small farm. Because the death rate was high and few social services existed, your family might also include orphans or widowed relatives. You would eat with your family, work with your family, and play games with your family. Sometimes neighbors might drop in—probably people you would have known for your entire life. At other times, you might accompany a family member into town. There you might shop in stores that had been run by the same people for many years—perhaps they even knew you as a child. You would personally know everyone in town, including the mayor, the pastor, the sheriff, and council members. And everyone would know you, and your family too.

If by chance you had lived in one of the few large urban areas in the United States, you would still be immersed in communal activities. You would know your neighbors, and if you lived in a boardinghouse, you would eat your meals with the other boarders. If new people moved into your building or into the neighborhood,

Great Social Transformation (GST) ▲ The profound change in social relationships from communal to associational brought about by industrialization, urbanization, bureaucratization, rationalization, and globalization.

they would not be strangers for very long. Surprisingly, much of your urban environment would not be greatly different from that of cities that existed over 1,500 years ago. For instance, prior to 1850 American cities, like those of ancient Rome, were lit at night by candles and oil lamps, and warmth was obtained from stoves and fireplaces. Few buildings were over four stories tall; obviously, there was no telephone, and person-to-person communication was the rule (Didsbury 1989).

As these examples imply, life in **communal society** consists of personalized relationships. Life is anchored in the family, kin, and community—small-scale social units that foster closeness and intimacy. Consequently, people know each other as individuals with unique personalities and histories. Personalized relationships extend throughout the community. Everyone knows everyone else personally, and for that reason, banking, law enforcement, and politics take place mostly on an informal level. Tradition is also important. The old religion is still the dominant religion, and the old holidays are still the best holidays. The level of technology is low, and the division of labor is simple; and if Marx, Weber, and Durkheim are correct, then people in communal societies do not suffer from the ills of alienation, rationalization, and anomie.

Associational Relationships

Associational relationships are the opposite of communal relationships. In an **associational society**, such as the United States today, social relationships are often highly impersonal. Rather than knowing many people as friends, we know many people as casual acquaintances. And when we do interact with them, we treat them as role-players rather than as individuals. Our physician, for instance, knows us in the role of patient rather than as an individual, and in turn, we know our physician in the role of a medical doctor rather than as a unique person (Chapter 5). While the family, kin, and community remain important social units, other large-scale social units also have prominent, if not dominant, roles. The manufacturing corporation, the governmental agency, and the superstore replace the small shop, the local magistrate, and the general store. Traditions remain but lose much of their force. People are freer to experiment with new beliefs and no longer respect the past as a guideline for the present. The industrial base of the society is highly sophisticated, spawning a demand for specialists and creating great wealth, most of which is unequally distributed.

As you might suspect, there is a relationship between societal type and communal and associational relationships. Hunting and gathering, horticultural, and agrarian societies are largely communal, whereas industrial and postindustrial societies are largely associational. Transitional societies are a mixture of both types. Table 2.1 summarizes some of the features of communal and associational societies.

The Great Social Transformation and This Text

As we shall see in the remainder of the book, contemporary life has been directly and indirectly shaped by the Great Social Transformation—the transition from communal to associational relations. Because the transformation has such widespread impact, we relate the subject matter of each chapter to it, first as a brief section near the beginning of each chapter, and then wherever it applies in the chapter. For example, in Chapter 3, we examine the relationship between the Great Social Transformation and socialization. In Chapter 4, we look at deviance and crime in modern society; in Chapter 5, we show how bureaucracy has altered social relationships.

Part Two focuses on social inequality, and so in Chapters 6 through 8 we examine inequalities of class, race, and gender. In each case, we find that the transformation from communal to associational relationships has affected some aspect of inequality.

Communal society ▲ A society characterized by rich personalized relationships and in which the main social units are family, kin, and community.

Associational society ▲ A society in which social relationships are often highly impersonal and the main social units are organizations, corporations, and bureaucracies.

TABLE 2.1 • *The contrasts between communal and associational societies are far-reaching and involve many aspects of social organization and social interaction.*

Characteristics of Communal and Associational Societies

CHARACTERISTICS OF COMMUNAL SOCIETIES	CHARACTERISTICS OF ASSOCIATIONAL SOCIETIES
1. Limited division of labor	1. Complex division of labor in all activities
2. Family, clan, tribe, and village basic social units	2. Associations, organizations, and corporations basic units
3. Personalized relationships	3. Relationships formalized, transitory, less personal
4. Economy based on commodities in nearby habitat	4. Economy based on manufacturing and related activities
5. Overall level of technology is low	5. Level of technology is high
6. Political institutions nonbureaucratic	6. Political institutions complex and bureaucratic
7. Limited system of social stratification	7. Complex social stratification—large middle class
8. Rich ceremonial life	8. Rationality prized, diminished role of spirituality
9. Limited contact with other societies	9. Society part of a global network of societies

10. Life in communal societies is
  a. Less complex
  b. Less diverse
  c. More traditional
  d. More personal
	10. Life in associational societies is
	  a. More complex
	  b. More diverse
	  c. Less traditional
	  d. More impersonal

123 STUDY TIP

Using Table 2.1 as your guide, create a detailed description of two specific societies. Choose one communal society and one associational society. For each, find and list examples that broaden your understanding of each of the ten points in the two table lists.

Part Three deals with institutions. In Chapters 9 through 14 we show how the Great Social Transformation has changed the economy, the family, religion, and other major institutions of contemporary society. Finally, Part Four, Population, Ecology, and Urbanization, and Collective Social Action, concludes the book. Figure 2.1 illustrates some of the connections made in the text.

FIGURE 2.1 The Great Social Transformation

Throughout the text, we emphasize how life has been changed by the Great Social Transformation, or GST.

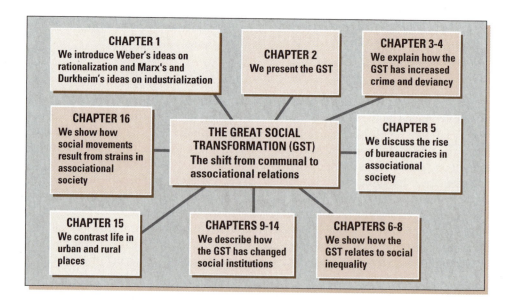

Pausing to Think About the Great Social Transformation

In the past, most societies relied on communal relationships, whereas today industrial societies rely on associational relationships. Life in communal societies is characterized by rich personalized relationships, and the main social units are family, kin, and community. In associational society, social relationships are often highly impersonal, and the main social units are large-scale organizations, corporations, and bureaucracies.

CQ What does the concept "communal" mean to you? ◆ Which relationships of yours are primarily communal, and which are primarily associational?

Theories of Change and Development

Social Change and the Credit Card

There are 173 million people in the United States who hold a total of 1.6 billion credit cards. They annually spend about 2 trillion dollars on them (U.S. Bureau of the Census 2002). If you are like the typical college student, you already have at least one card, and you probably have several. Nationwide, some two-thirds of all college and university students have a credit card, and those who do not are flooded with offers to sign up for one (*USA Today*, May 31, 2002:B3).

Society Today ● ■ ▲

Family Use of Credit Cards

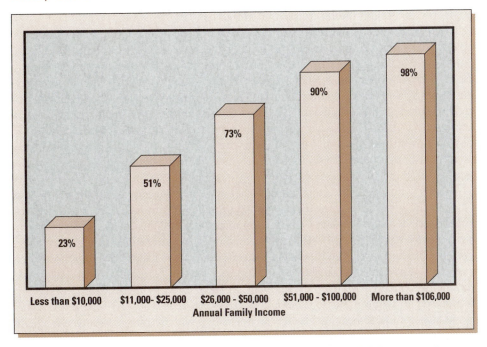

Even though credit cards are commonplace, wealthy people are more likely use one than poor people. For instance, the graph shows that of families with less than $10,000 annual income, 23 percent have a credit card; but virtually all families with annual incomes exceeding $100,000 have a card.

 Why do you think so many companies urge college students to adopt one of their credit cards?

Although we now take credit cards for granted, they are actually rather new. The credit card was invented in the 1920s, but did not become widespread until the 1950s. At that time, Diner's Club became the first card to be widely used. Other cards followed soon thereafter: American Express in the late 1950s, Visa and MasterCard in the 1960s and 1970s, and the Discovery card in the 1980s. Today, thousands of organizations, from the National Rifle Association to the American Sociological Association, offer their members various inducements to use one of their cards. Even your school soon might be offering you a card, if it has not done so already.

At one time, credit was difficult to obtain. An applicant would have to approach a bank, submit a detailed life history, and provide cosigners and character witnesses. Today, sophisticated technology and effortless communication have made credit easy and quick to obtain. Some cards simply appear in your mail preapproved, and some "virtual" credits appear in your e-mail. Using a card is even simpler: swipe it through a machine, and you can instantly purchase whatever you wish or convert your wish to cash (up to your credit limit, of course). If you have more than one card, you have even more credit at your disposal. For instance, a *New York Times* reporter at the University of Texas (Austin) doing a story on credit cards quickly turned up the following students: a 19-year-old freshman with five cards and $2,000 worth of debt; a 22-year-old senior with eight cards and $8,000 worth of debt; and a 26-year-old senior with eight cards and $9,000 worth of debt (*New York Times*, April 30, 1995:F11). Or consider Pete and Pam Ward, both out of school. Over the course of two years, Pete accumulated 25 credit cards and a debt of over $35,000. Only when Pam discovered a stack of unpaid bills did Pete face up to his financial obligations and begin systematically to reduce his debt and economize on his lifestyle.

The credit card industry illustrates many aspects of contemporary society, including how fast things change. Assuming you progress through school at a reasonable rate, by the time you graduate, credit cards will be even more widespread, and banking as we now know it will be on the decline. Virtually all banking transactions will be handled at a "money machine," and you probably will have to pay an extra fee to interact with a human teller inside a building.

The rapid spread of credit cards also illustrates the problems created when technology changes faster than the cultural values and guidelines associated with it. Technology now makes credit easy and instantaneous, but we have few norms for how to use it. Without norms, many people like Pete Ward succumb to the temptation of buying anything they want. And rather than encouraging moderation, the credit card industry induces us to buy now and pay later. But should we use a credit card to pay for new party clothes? To take a vacation? To purchase a car? To pay a medical bill? To finance tuition? As yet, our culture has few answers for us, and as a result we have no standard or customary responses to these questions (Ritzer 2000; *New York Times*, December 28, 1995:C1, C16).

Credit cards are just one example of change in contemporary times, and they illustrate how developments in technology often outpace developments in values, norms, and ideology. William Ogburn, a pioneering sociologist, called this phenomenon *cultural lag* (Ogburn 1950). Another example of cultural lag concerns advances in medicine that now make it possible to keep people alive for prolonged periods. This possibility is not an unmixed blessing. Suppose you have terminal cancer and are experiencing horrible, racking pain that cannot be relieved by medication. Should you be allowed to commit suicide? Should a physician help you die? These and other moral questions arise because changes in our values have not kept up with changes in technology (Morganthau, Barrett, and Washington 1993).

Sociologists have always been interested in explaining social change. We already know from Chapter 1 that sociology emerged during the Industrial Revolution of the nineteenth century. You may recall that Harriet Martineau and August Comte defined sociology in terms of change, whereas Karl Marx, Émile Durkheim, and Max Weber laid the foundation for analyzing the Great Social Transformation. The topic of change, however, is broader and deeper than what we have examined thus far.

STUDY TIP

With two or three other students, discuss the phenomenon of "cultural lag." Talk about the two examples given in the text and together brainstorm as many more examples as you can. Discuss the consequences of technological change that outpaces change in norms and values.

Cultural lag ▲ The tendency for elements of material culture to change more rapidly than elements of nonmaterial culture.

Consequently, in this section we will explain several current theories of change and development.

Social Evolution

Some early theories of social change and development drew their inspiration from Charles Darwin's theory of evolution. These evolutionary theories assert that societies are shaped by the forces of social evolution. Social evolutionists believed that, just as relentless biological competition selects the fittest animals for survival, so too does social competition select the fittest society for survival. Furthermore, just as life began as a simple form and evolved into complex organisms, human society begins as a simple entity and evolves into a complex society. For instance, social evolutionists would argue that a hunting and gathering society represents a relatively simple form of existence, whereas an industrial society is an example of a complex form.

Early evolutionary theorists believed that social evolution was unilinear; that is, all societies followed a single path of development from simple to complex. They also believed that social evolution was a form of progress that ended with the survival of a superior society. These beliefs are no longer accepted by contemporary sociologists. Critics point out that social evolutionists were ethnocentric in the extreme and often confused personal beliefs with sociological theory.

In many ways, the notion of social evolution served the interests of European powers as they expanded their colonial empires. During the nineteenth century, Germany, Belgium, Great Britain, France, and other European nations actively carved out huge portions of the world for themselves. The theory of social evolution was then used to justify the belief that Western civilization and the white race were at the top of the evolutionary scale. Hence, the "primitive" societies of Africa, the "degenerate" societies of Asia, and the "backward" societies of the Americas were lumped together into one broad category: inferior. Carrying this line of thought further, Western Europeans took on the duty of performing the necessary but unappreciated task of bringing civilization to these people. It would be necessary, of course, to dominate their government, change their culture, and extract their wealth. In short, social evolution became a rationale for European expansion and oppression.

Functionalism and Social Evolution

As we discussed in Chapter 1, functionalist theory attempts to explain how social systems achieve and remain in equilibrium or balance. Because change and development upset the balance, functionalism has difficulty explaining those processes. To solve this problem, some functionalists have introduced an updated version of social evolution into their theory. The leading proponent of this approach was also the leading proponent of functionalism: Talcott Parsons (1902–1979).

Viewing society as a social system at equilibrium, Parsons argued that change moves the equilibrium from one state to another state. To illustrate this idea, consider the price of oil. A sudden rise in the price of oil will cause the price of gasoline to increase and the amount of driving to decrease. As a result of less driving, many gasoline stations, motels, and other businesses dependent on travel will lose customers and possibly will fail. And because the price of oil affects the cost of all transportation, prices throughout the economy will rise, causing a general decline in consumer spending. If oil prices remain high for a prolonged period, these and other changes will work their way through society. According to functionalist theory, we will eventually adjust to less driving and higher prices, and a new equilibrium will come into being.

Like evolutionary theorists before him, Parsons assumed that society evolves from simple to complex and that the task of the theorist is to explain how this transformation takes place (Parsons 1966). For this purpose, Parsons introduced the concept of differentiation: the division of a single social unit into units that are independent but related to one another. For example, communal societies are relatively simple and depend on a few social units to accomplish many different tasks. A famous story about

The electronic calculator has become part of the global culture; here it is being used by Maori children dressed in their ceremonial costume. The children live in the village of Te Kahn, New Zealand. Technology is a powerful force that is changing traditional societies throughout the world.

Abraham Lincoln's childhood describes how he learned to read the family Bible by the light of the fireplace after the day's farmwork was done. Had Lincoln been a child today, he probably would have learned to read in a bureaucratically organized school while his parents were busy working at jobs away from home. The functions of the family, in other words, have been differentiated into school and work.

Unlike early evolutionary theorists, contemporary theorists recognize that development occurs in different ways in different societies; that is, they recognize that social evolution must be multilineal. These theorists also acknowledge that evolution is not the same as progress and that industrial societies are not superior to traditional societies. Finally, contemporary theorists believe that societies may remain stable for long periods, regress in development, or even become extinct (Caplow 1991).

Functionalism in partnership with evolutionary theory provides a broad perspective that emphasizes the role of social systems and the tendency for societies to achieve balance. Nevertheless, the joining of these two perspectives has not been entirely successful. The perspective still is a better explanation of why systems remain in equilibrium than of why they change. Nor does the theory take into account political actions. Japan, Korea, and other nations have made a deliberate choice to industrialize, whereas other nations have had industrialization forced on them. In either case, the gradual processes of evolution have been bypassed altogether. Finally, the basic analogy to biological evolution eventually breaks down. Unlike plants and animals, we humans have the ability to think and to anticipate. We can choose our future, choose to cooperate rather than to compete, and thus we do not have to rely blindly on social evolution to run its course for us.

Modernization Theory

In everyday language, "modernization" means streamlining or updating, but when used in explanations of social change, modernization refers to a specific theory. According to modernization theory, traditional societies will eventually take on the characteristics of an industrial society. In particular, manufacturing and related activities will become the basic means of sustenance, and jobs will become highly specialized. Urban areas will expand as people move to be near their places of employment. Both private organizations and government will grow in size and scope, and will become increasingly bureaucratic. Although the wealth of industrializing societies may increase, the increase will not be shared equally. The gap between rich and poor, or between working-class, middle-class, and upper-class people, will actually grow larger.

According to modernization theory, many places in Africa, South America, and Asia have not developed because they lack Western attitudes and values. For example, if people do not strive to compete with one another and do not value technology, efficiency, profits, and rationality, then they are not likely to value an industrialized, capitalist society (Inkeles and Smith 1974). Modernization, moreover, requires an educated workforce and a stable government. Eventually, modernization theorists predict, all societies will converge on a single type and become much like the United States.

The driving force for modernization comes from both internal and external sources. Of critical importance is technology, which passes from the so-called modern societies to traditional societies. Once in place, technology will begin producing the many characteristics of a modern society. Internal forces also play a role. The government, for instance, might adopt a policy of modernization and might actively seek technology from industrialized nations. To illustrate, Saudi Arabia is now upgrading its national telephone system by contracting with American firms to install new equipment and computer software. The technical personnel necessary to perform the installation are also part of the arrangement, as are the managers who direct the hundreds of specific projects necessary to accomplish the overall task.

Modernization theory rests on several assumptions. One such assumption is that the benefits of industrialization outweigh its disadvantages and that therefore traditional societies will benefit from modernization. This assumption is disputable, of course. The discussions of Marx, Durkheim, and Weber have already suggested that alienation, anomie, and excessive rationalization may go hand in hand with industrialization. Modernization theory further assumes that the history of traditional societies will be like the history of the United States and other industrialized nations. This assumption is simply untrue, particularly in the case of the United States. The United States was historically shaped by Protestantism and has a more traditional value system than have other advanced industrial societies (see Chapter 13; Inglehart and Baker 2000). Modernization theory also assumes that traditional societies have stagnant cultures and would benefit from Western values, political beliefs, and technology. These assumption are dubious, at best.

Conflict Theory and Change: World Systems

Conflict theorists assume that change is universal and ongoing (Dahrendorf 1959). They further assume that power is an essential ingredient of life and that power provides the structure for social relationships. Over the past 20 years or so, these assumptions have been incorporated into a general explanation of change and development called world systems theory (Sanderson 1995; Sklair 1995; Wallerstein 2000).

According to this theory, all nations are part of a world system. The system consists of *core nations*, which are highly industrialized and powerful; *periphery nations*, which are poor and economically dependent on the core nations; and *semiperiphery nations*, which are emerging from the periphery of the world system and receive more benefits from that relationship than do the periphery nations. This system was established over the last 200 years as Western powers scrambled to colonize Africa, Asia, and South America. Their goal was to obtain new markets and new sources of raw materials and cheap labor. As we mentioned in the previous section, the philosophy of social evolution provided the Western powers with a ready-made idealistic justification for their actions.

Most of the world system was initially established through military force. Economic power was also used as large businesses established branches in periphery countries and took over their economies while colonial powers assumed control over local government. Although domination still remains, over the last several years, its form has changed. The old colonial powers no longer strive for political and military control over their former colonies; rather, they strive for control over markets, for sites of lower production costs, and for cheap sources of raw materials. Some scholars refer to this new situation as neocolonialism.

Under the contemporary world system, core nations hold periphery nations in economic bondage for two reasons. First, international corporations now play a major role in economic development. Most of these companies are headquartered in the United States, Europe, Japan, and a few other countries. Although periphery nations often welcome them because they provide employment, most of the benefits go to the ruling class of the periphery nation rather than to the average person, and most profits go to the international corporation rather than to the local government. Second, during the colonial period, core nations often changed the basic economic structure of periphery nations. Agricultural production, for instance, was revamped to emphasize specialized crops that the core nations demanded, such as tea, coffee, hemp, and even opium. In other cases, the local economy was reorganized to provide for the extraction of raw materials, such as lumber, copper, gold, or diamonds. As the economy was transformed, native peoples were driven from their traditional pursuits to become wage laborers, often crowded into unfamiliar urban areas or forced to live in settlement camps without their families. As a result, local patterns of culture were disrupted or destroyed and have never been reestablished.

Overall, the stratification of nations into a world system of unequal economic relationships produces an unequal sharing of the earth's resources and wealth. Core nations use their greater power to benefit themselves at the expense of periphery nations. According to world systems theory, this imbalance will be righted only if periphery nations can reassert control over their own destinies. For more about conflict and modernization, see the Sociology Online box.

We suggest that you begin your exploration of web destinations with the official site of the United States Agency for International Development (USAid). The mission of this agency is to provide economic and humanitarian assistance for impoverished or needy countries.

Using your favorite Internet search engine, search for USAID. You know you will have reached the correct site when you find a mission statement similar to that provided above. As you look at the site, make a list of half a dozen or so societies where the United States is focusing its aid. Then for each of these countries, answer the following questions.

- What are the problems that USAid identifies for this society?
- What are the economic and humanitarian programs that USAid has begun in the country?

- What success stories does USAid report for its involvement in the society?

After you have answered these questions for several countries, examine the site for information about the HIV/Aids programs. It represents an especially large expenditure of funds. Then write a brief report that describes the role of USAid as an agent of social change in the world today.

CQ Does USAid seem to be most heavily involved in societies where the United States has intervened militarily such as in Afghanistan, Iraq, and Haiti? Or is USAid's involvement broader than that?

 Pausing to Think About Theories of Change and Development

According to evolutionary theory, societies compete among themselves, and the survivors of this competition are those societies that are best adapted to their circumstances. Functionalist theory argues that societies move from one equilibrium to another, whereas modernization theory assumes that all societies eventually become industrial. World systems theory, which is a branch of conflict theory, argues that the nations of the world are dominated by a small core of nations and that these core nations use their power for their own benefit. See Table 2.2 for a comparison of the major theoretical perspectives on change and development.

CQ Is change and development always a good thing? ◆ How would a modernization theorist respond to that question? ◆ A world systems theorist?

TABLE 2.2 • This table compares four major theoretical perspectives on change and development.

Comparison of Theoretical Perspectives on Change and Development

PERSPECTIVE	VIEW OF CHANGE AND DEVELOPMENT	KEY CONCEPTS AND PROCESSES
Evolutionary theory	Sees societal change as progressing from simple to complex forms	Competition Survival of the fittest Unilinear evolution
Functionalism	Sees societal change as a way to increase efficiency of society	Differentiation Equilibrium Multilinear evolution
Modernization	Sees societal change as inevitable because of benefits of industrialization and advanced technology	Modernization Industrialization
World systems	Sees development and change as a contest of power between industrialized and less-developed nations	Core, periphery, and semiperiphery nations Neocolonialism

Catalysts for Change

General perspectives and theories of change and development are concerned with the broad social forces that affect society over time. There are, however, many catalysts (causes or sources) of change that lie outside the scope of any given theory. Because there are so many, we will discuss them as general categories.

Human Agency: Individual and Collective

Perhaps the source of change that comes to mind most immediately concerns people, or **human agency** (Emirbayer 1996). For instance, if President Lyndon Johnson had not ordered American troops to enter the war in Vietnam, over 50,000 American soldiers and over 200,000 South Vietnamese soldiers would not have died, not to mention the hundreds of thousands of civilian dead on both sides. The peace movement would not have arisen, protests would not have broken out on college campuses throughout the nation, and the students killed by the National Guard during an anti-war protest at Kent State University would probably still be alive (Chapter 16). Not tainted by the war, President Johnson would probably have run for the presidency again and won. Richard Nixon would not have become president, and the Watergate scandal would not have occurred. In fact, the whole course of modern American history would have been different—but obviously, we cannot go back in time and redo history to find out for sure. The inability to conduct experiments with history also makes it impossible to know, with certainty, what effect the so-called "great people" have on social change. Would radium have been discovered if Madame Curie had not lived? Would millions of lives have been spared if Hitler had been declared insane and had been imprisoned by German authorities? Would the United States have invaded Iraq if Al Gore were elected president rather than George W. Bush? (see Tripp 2002).

Although great people influence world events, sociologists generally prefer other explanations of change. Instead of creating social change, sociologists argue, great people direct change along the lines already established by the social forces embedded in society. Thus, sociologists would say that because science was already well established at the turn of the century, if Madame Curie had not isolated radium, then some other scientist would have. In a similar vein, the Germany of the 1920s and 1930s was suffering from immense economic problems and already had a deeply ingrained hostility toward Jews. Hitler seized on these issues and rode them to power, but he did not create them.

Human agency is not confined to a single person. Very often, change is caused by the organized efforts of individuals and groups working for or against a goal—that is, by a social movement. An important aspect of a social movement is its **ideology**: beliefs that support and justify a particular social arrangement. The ideology may be complicated and formulated in writing, such as the works of Lenin that were used to justify communism in Russia. Because of its complexity, an ideology is sometimes summarized in a slogan. For instance, World War I was fought to "make the world safe for democracy"; and during the Vietnam War, antiwar protesters chanted, "Hell no, we won't go."

Revolution and War

Revolution and war also can produce major changes. For example, the Mexican Revolution of 1910 resulted in Mexico's enacting major land reform programs, changing the relationship between church and state, developing major education programs for the people, and initiating other economic and political changes. Warfare also produces huge social changes. New governments and entirely new nations are established by war. After World War II, the governments of Japan and Germany changed form, and the nations of North and South Korea came into existence. War also speeds up the pace of innovation. World War II speeded the development of the computer and jet engine, for instance, and the cold war with the former Soviet Union triggered the race to the moon and the development of rocket-powered flight.

Senior man holding a sign that reads "Fight Terrorism By Making Friends Not War" participates in anti-war protest.

CQ *What do you think? Do you suppose he has protested other wars, too?*

Human agency ▲ The activities of individuals or groups aimed at attaining a goal or end.

Ideology ▲ The pattern of beliefs that legitimizes or justifies a particular societal arrangement.

Cultural Processes

Change may also be introduced through the cultural processes of invention, discovery, and diffusion. **Invention** involves combining known cultural elements in a novel manner to produce a new product. Although we tend to think that inventions are always highly complicated, such as the microprocessor or the laser disk, many of the most powerful inventions in human history have been relatively simple. As mentioned before, the invention of the hoe opened the way for horticulture, whereas the invention of the plow made agriculture possible. Because inventions are created by combining existing cultural elements, the rate of invention depends on the size of the cultural storehouse. The more knowledge, tools, and technology a society possesses, the more likely it is that some of those elements will be recombined into a new product. For this reason, traditional cultures produce relatively noncomplex inventions. A hunting and gathering society, for example, might invent a throwing stick, spear, or perhaps the bow and arrow, but it could not invent a gasoline engine because the cultural storehouse is simply too small to permit it.

The importance of invention in industrial and postindustrial society is indicated by the complex legal structure for protecting the ownership rights of inventors. Patents are issued to give them the exclusive right further to develop and market their inventions for profit. Because many inventions have enormous practical consequences, American culture glorifies invention and the inventor. Thomas Edison, for instance, is an American hero. His invention of the motion picture, light bulb, and record player have transformed American society.

Occasionally, someone suddenly notices something that has not been noticed before. Such an observation is an instance of **discovery**. Because the natural and social world are so vast and complicated, discovery is a major preoccupation of scientists. Some examples are the discovery of the law of gravity, of the principle of the screw, or of the role of germs in disease. Even today, discoveries are being made about the physical principles that explain the universe and about the anatomy of the human body.

Inventions and discovery do not occur randomly (Lauer 1991). Unless the existing culture is ready, inventions and discoveries may lie dormant for centuries. Gunpowder was known in China long before it was known in Europe, but in China it was used mainly for fireworks. Why? Chinese culture at the time venerated the past, and the Chinese saw no need to improve on their existing weapons of war. Just the reverse was true in Europe. Once gunpowder was introduced, it was immediately used to fire mortars and cannon that revolutionized warfare.

Inventions and discoveries that depart too radically from current ways of thinking are usually rejected. For example, Gregor Mendel's work with plant genetics in the nineteenth century was mostly ignored until a growing interest in evolutionary theory led to a renewed interest in his experiments. In a manner of speaking, Mendel was simply ahead of his time.

Another cultural process that leads to change is **diffusion**, or the transmission of a cultural element from one group or society to another (see Figure 2.2). The element may be physical, such as a tool, or social, such as a custom, an idea, or a belief. Diffusion can involve an entire society. The Polynesians of the South Pacific migrated thousands of miles in open canoes to other islands and established themselves as new societies. Since most items in a given society are there because of diffusion, some anthropologists argue that diffusion is the main source of social change. When a cultural element diffuses, it often is modified to meet the requirements of the receiving society. Native Americans used tobacco in religious rituals, for instance, but when tobacco was taken to Europe, it lost its religious significance.

Population

Shifts in population often trigger massive social changes. Demographers—scholars who study population—are mainly interested in three topics: birth, mortality, and migration. Changes in any of these processes may produce substantial changes in

Invention ▲ A new material or nonmaterial product resulting from the combination of known cultural elements in a novel manner.

Discovery ▲ Noticing something that has not been noticed before.

Diffusion ▲ The transmission of a cultural element from one group or society to another.

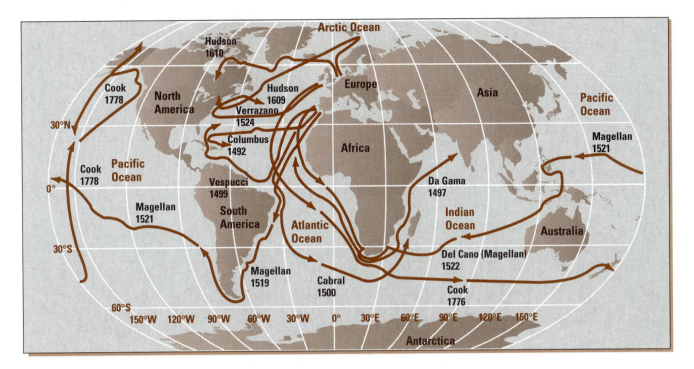

FIGURE 2.2 Global Map of the European Voyages of Contact

The European voyages of exploration and conquest, begun in the fifteenth century, diffused European culture throughout the world. Europeans also brought back to their home nations many new discoveries from their voyages, and Europe became a clearinghouse of world information and products. After the final voyage of British explorer Captain James Cook, Europeans could map fairly accurately all the world's continents and islands, and global interconnectedness became a possibility.

SOURCE: Edward F. Bergman and Tom L. McKnight, *Introduction to Geography*, © 1993. Reprinted by permission of Prentice Hall, Inc., Upper Saddle River, NJ.

society. For instance, immigration of Europeans to North America wiped out huge portions of the Native American population through disease, warfare, and social dislocation. Currently, the immigration of Asians and Hispanics is transforming the social landscape. As people of color have gained political power, their advances may have triggered a backlash. Many people, for example, advocate legislation that denies illegal immigrants certain social services.

Changes in birthrates and death rates also produce change. The unprecedented increase in the birthrate after World War II produced the baby boom generation that is now entering middle age and assuming power. Bill Clinton is a baby boomer, the first of his generation to be elected president. Changes in the death rate also affect the course of population growth. As more and more infants survive into school age and more elders survive to become very old, society must shift its resources to support the young and the elderly. With fewer workers and more retired persons, economic growth may be slowed, and people may become more concerned about health issues (see Chapter 15 and Figure 2.3).

Throughout history humans have been engaged in a deadly war with the microbe world. For example, the fourteenth-century plague known as the Black Death killed one-third of Europe's population in four years. The sheer size and rapidity of the population loss ruined Europe's economy, destabilized politics, and set back Europe's Age of Exploration for decades (McNeill 1976; Weiss 2002). The microbe war continues today. In the last 25 years, scientists have discovered 30 previously unknown and potentially deadly diseases including AIDS, SARS, and Marburg disease. For most of these newly discovered diseases there are no known cures. In the same period, 20 previously known major diseases have reemerged in new, more deadly, and drug-resistant

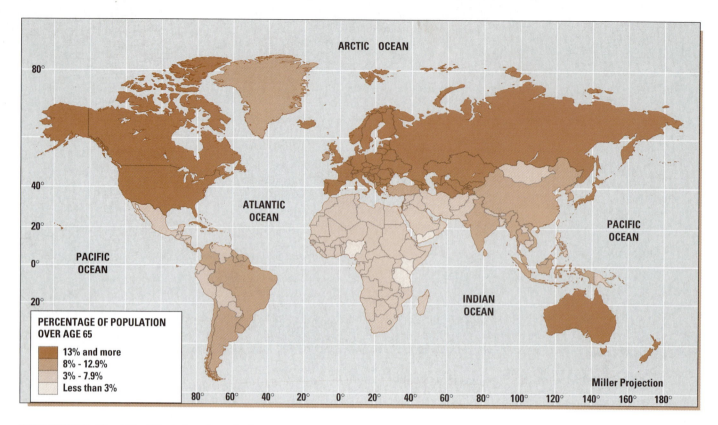

FIGURE 2.3 **The World's Aging Population**

This map projects the percentages of the world's population that will be aged 65 or older in the year 2025. What changes in society are caused by an aging population?

SOURCE: Edward F. Bergman, *Human Geography: Cultures, Connections, and Landscapes* (Upper Saddle River, NJ: Prentice Hall Inc., 1995).

forms. In addition to the human toll of suffering these diseases cause, they have serious economic impact. For example, the SARS epidemic of 2002–2003 cost the world's economy over $50 billion (Newcomb 2003).

Natural Catastrophes

Sometimes, dramatic social changes are triggered by natural catastrophes, such as earthquakes in Los Angeles and Kobe, Japan; floods along the Mississippi River; and hurricanes in Florida. Other natural events might be less common but still have major effects on society. For example, prolonged drought in the Midwest and plains states led to huge dust storms in 1935, forcing thousands of people to flee. Many people abandoned their homes and farms and migrated to the West.

Although there is little we can do to prevent some natural events from occurring, we can prepare for them. Disaster research is a small but significant area of sociology that is devoted to studying the social factors associated with disaster. In general, it has been found that people initially respond to disaster with poise, courage, and teamwork, but later turn to bickering and complaining. For instance, when a flood or hurricane forces people to flee from their homes, the victims quickly develop a sense of camaraderie, and social interactions take on a personal tone. If the dislocation drags on, however, people enter a period of frustration and conflict. In part, their frustration is caused by government officials who offer aid but then insist that to get it, the victims must fill out detailed forms, stand in line, and go through official channels.

Technology

As we already know, technology is a major source of change. The impact of technology, however, is based on cultural factors. To illustrate: although most people agree

Society Today ● ■ ▲

A Surge in Creativity

A patent is a government protection issued to an inventor that gives the inventor the exclusive right to the use of the invention and the income derived from it for a number of years. The number of patents issued by the federal government per year between 1980 and 1997 increased by 81 percent.

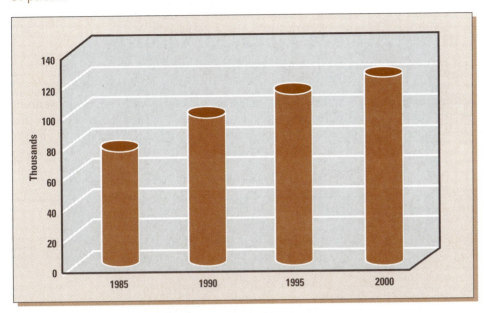

SOURCE: U.S. Bureau of the Census 2000, *Statistical Abstract of the United States.*

CQ Can you think of any social forces that help explain the increase in patients? [Hint: what effect does the increase in population have?]

that the computer is a wonderful and powerful invention, widespread acceptance of the computer came only in halting steps. Computers were not widely accepted until they were repackaged as word processors and then touted as a powerful replacement for the typewriter. Because the typewriter was already taken for granted, people quickly learned to appreciate the added power of the word processor. Once the word processor gained acceptance, the next incremental step was to introduce the general-purpose desktop computer that we commonly see today. Now, with the development of the Internet, the computer is being used for entertainment, chats, and e-mail, along with a multitude of different tasks.

As with invention, few technological developments are entirely new; most build on the technology, science, and inventions that already exist. The vast power of the computer, for example, comes from the ability of the machine to manipulate binary (0 and 1) digits at a fantastically high rate of speed. Yet the theory of binary digits has long been known, and primitive machines to manipulate them have existed for over a century. Without this earlier base of knowledge to build on, the modern computer would never have come into existence when it did. When new technologies interact with existing technologies, frequently the result is an increase in discoveries (see the Society Today box, A Surge in Creativity).

● ■ ▲ Pausing to Think   About Catalysts for Change

Many catalysts for change are not included within a specific sociological theory of change. These catalysts involve the acts of individual people (that is, human agency); revolution and war; cultural processes such as invention, discovery, and diffusion; changes in the population; the occurrence of natural catastrophes; and changes in technology.

CQ One reason that change is continuous in contemporary society is that we have a large cultural warehouse of items to use in creating new arrangements. Can you think of any recent "new" and "improved" inventions or discoveries that were really a recombination of existing cultural elements? ◆ What about the cellular telephone?

Culture, Society, and Social Change in the Twenty-First Century

Although we may not realize it, the processes of social change are homogenizing culture. That is, local differences are being replaced by a standard culture that comes from the major urban centers of industrial nations. For example, in the

CONCEPT WEB Culture, Society, and Social Change

This concept web places the concept of the Great Social Transformation at the center of the web. The concept of the Great Social Transformation is emphasized throughout the book. We show how the GST is reflected in all of the major topics we cover. Ongoing social change has become a permanent feature of life in human societies. It is important for students today to realize that all aspects of our lives are affected by the GST. Through that realization, we may become proactive in attempting to influence social change so that its outcomes are humane and positive for all people. In Chapter 16 we describe how such actions may be undertaken.

CQ How would you redraw the concept web to make theories of change the central concept?

United States about 100 years ago, the rural areas of Minnesota reflected the Scandinavian culture that the early settlers had brought with them; and parts of rural Ohio and Pennsylvania were so heavily Germanic that German was the language of instruction in the public schools. Today, these variations in culture no longer exist. They have been replaced by the more standard, homogeneous culture of the United States.

The homogenization of culture is, in part, due to the diffusion of technology, as illustrated by the nomadic herders of Mongolia. In most respects, they live in much the same way their ancestors did. When they camp for the night amid their flocks, they set up tents made of animal skins and cook over fires in the center of the floor. But now there is a difference. They also start up their portable generators, and as they eat, they watch their portable televisions, which pick up broadcasts from a passing satellite. These Mongol herders know who Madonna is, what chic women are wearing in Paris, and whether the president of Russia is in political trouble. If these herders continue adopting technology for a long enough time, their local uniqueness will eventually vanish and be replaced by a homogeneous world culture.

Cultural homogenization is also being created by multinational organizations that view the entire world as their marketplace but no particular nation as their home. These companies emphasize the standardization of materials, of production processes, and of consumer tastes. The reason they do so is that it is more efficient to sell the same product worldwide than to sell a specific product in a local market. As the world becomes a smaller place, it seems likely that the processes of cultural homogenization will continue unabated.

Looking Ahead

Up to now, our attention has been focused on discussing change and the nature of contemporary society. In the next two chapters, we change our focus and introduce two fundamental issues: why do we conform to the norms of society, and why do we deviate from them? These topics will add to our understanding of why culture changes more slowly in some areas than in others.

WHAT YOU SHOULD KNOW ●■▲

1. *What do sociologists mean by the term culture?*

   Culture consists of the mutually shared products, knowledge, and beliefs of a human group or society. There are two types of culture: material and nonmaterial. There is a tendency for the material elements of culture to change before the nonmaterial elements do, and this tendency is called cultural lag.

2. *In which ways are all cultures alike?*

   Societies develop certain common solutions to common problems; at the same time, each culture is suited to its particular environment. Every culture has core elements called values and norms. More important norms are called mores, and less important norms are called folkways.

3. *What is the symbolic content of culture?*

   Some symbols are extremely powerful because they represent important cultural values. Language is the most fully developed system of symbols, and it plays a role in shaping people's perception of the world.

4. *How does ethnocentrism affect us?*

   Within a culture it is common for people to experience some ethnocentrism, but extreme ethnocentrism can be harmful to social relations. An alternative to ethnocentrism is cultural relativity, or the belief that each culture is unique and must be analyzed and judged on its own terms.

5. *What types of societies are there?*

Different societies rely on different modes of subsistence. Hunting and gathering societies rely on hunting wild game and gathering wild plants. Pastoral societies rely on grazing animals, whereas horticultural societies satisfy most food needs by cultivating plants. Agrarian societies, using draft animals, intensively cultivate large parcels of land. Industrial societies obtain sustenance through manufacturing and trade; postindustrial societies rely on the creation and transmission of specialized knowledge.

6. *How has social life changed?*

In the past, life in most societies was characterized by communal relationships. Today, some societies are still largely communal, but many other societies have developed an industrial mode of subsistence. Life in industrial societies is largely associational in nature. This textbook calls the shift from communal to associational the Great Social Transformation.

7. *What are the basic theories of social change?*

According to evolutionary theory, societies compete among themselves, and the survivors are those societies best adapted to their circumstances. The course of change is seen as moving from the simple to the complex. Functionalist theory argues that changes move through a society and disrupt it. However, over time the society readjusts and settles on a new equilibrium. Modernization theory assumes that all societies will eventually become industrial, much like the United States. World systems theory, which is a branch of conflict theory, argues that the nations of the world are dominated by a small core of nations. Nations trapped in this power relation, called periphery and semiperiphery nations, are exploited by core nations for their own benefit.

8. *What are the catalysts for social change?*

Many sources of change exist but are not part of a specific sociological theory. These catalysts for change can be grouped into broad categories. Some changes are caused by human agency or the acts of individual people. Revolution and war are other catalysts with major consequences. Cultural processes such as invention, discovery, and diffusion cause further change. A major catalyst is any change to the population, such as a change in birthrate. The occurrence of natural catastrophes can cause cataclysmic changes to a society or can even destroy it. Finally, a catalyst that receives a great deal of publicity today is technology.

9. *How will culture and society change in the future?*

Cultural homogenization is under way, and a continued erosion of cultural differences can be expected as the influence of multinational organizations spreads throughout the world. Satellite television and global economic networks also are making the world a smaller place and contributing to cultural homogenization.

TEST YOUR KNOWLEDGE ●■▲

Key Terms Matching

Match each of these key terms with the best definition or example from the numbered items that follow. Write the letter(s) preceding the key term in the blank before the definition that you choose.

a. agrarian societies
b. associational society
c. communal society
d. cultural lag
e. cultural relativism
f. cultural universals
g. culture
h. discovery
i. ethnocentrism
j. folkways

_____ 1. Norms concerning relatively unimportant matters.

_____ 2. Societies that are held together by kinship ties and by a simple division of labor based on age and gender; sustenance is based on game animals, nuts, berries, and other wild plants.

_____ 3. A grouping that consists of people who share a common culture, obey the same political authority (government), and occupy a given territory.

_____ 4. The profound change in social relationships from communal to associational brought about by industrialization, urbanization, bureaucratization, rationalization, and globalization.

_____ 5. Norms about matters that are so serious as to be almost beyond comprehension.

k. horticultural societies

l. human agency

m. hunting and gathering societies

n. ideology

o. industrial societies

p. invention

q. language

r. mode of subsistence

s. mores

t. multiculturalism

u. norms

v. pastoral societies

w. postindustrial societies

x. society

y. symbol

z. taboos

aa. Great Social Transformation (GST)

bb. transitional societies

cc. values

_____ 6. A society that is characterized by rich personalized relationships and in which the main social units are family, kin, and community.

_____ 7. The manner in which a society obtains the basic materials necessary to sustain itself; the most basic feature of a society.

_____ 8. The pattern of beliefs that legitimizes or justifies a particular societal arrangement.

_____ 9. Societies whose technology of food production is such that annual food surpluses are used to support larger populations and permanent settlements.

_____ 10. The belief that culture should be viewed from the perspective of different groups.

_____ 11. A new material or nonmaterial product resulting from the combination of known cultural elements in a novel manner.

_____ 12. Similar cultural solutions in different societies for similar problems of survival.

_____ 13. The specific expectations about how people behave in a given situation.

_____ 14. The activities of individuals or groups aimed at attaining a goal or an end.

_____ 15. A society in which social relationships are often highly impersonal and the main social units are organizations, corporations, and bureaucracies.

_____ 16. A representation that stands for something else.

_____ 17. Societies that derive most of their sustenance from raising domesticated animals.

_____ 18. Words that are symbols and rules for conveying complex ideas.

_____ 19. Noticing something that has not been noticed before.

_____ 20. Societies that are partly agrarian and partly industrial and whose populations members are largely peasants.

_____ 21. Norms concerning very serious matters.

_____ 22. Societies that rely on technology and mechanization as the main source of sustenance.

_____ 23. Societies in which the cultivation of domestic plants satisfies most needs for food.

_____ 24. The belief that each culture is unique and must be analyzed and judged on its own terms.

_____ 25. The preferences that people share about what is good or bad, right or wrong, desirable or undesirable.

_____ 26. The tendency for elements of material culture to change more rapidly than elements of nonmaterial culture.

_____ 27. Societies based primarily on the creation and transmitting of specialized knowledge.

_____ 28. The belief that one's own culture is superior to all other cultures.

_____ 29. The mutually shared products, knowledge, and beliefs of a human group or society.

Multiple Choice

Circle the letter of your choice.

1. Computer software is an example of
   a. nonmaterial culture.
   b. norms.
   c. material culture.
   d. values.

2. Within a large and socially heterogeneous society such as the United States, there are many distinct cultures. The term that describes this situation is
   a. cultural plurality.
   b. cultural diversity.
   c. cultural universality.
   d. multiculturalism.

3. All societies must confront the issue of rearing children. This fact is one example of
   a. material culture.
   b. folkways.
   c. cultural diversity.
   d. cultural universals.

4. Language is such a powerful system of symbols that, according to the Sapir-Whorf hypothesis,

   a. we have little choice but to interpret the world in terms of the words and grammar of our native language.
   b. only a few hundred languages are spoken by enough people to remain secure in the immediate future.
   c. English, Spanish, German, and French are in no danger of disappearing.
   d. nonverbal communication is as important as verbal communication.

5. The five interlocking rings of the Olympics is an example of a/an

   a. expression.
   b. symbol.
   c. value.
   d. nonmaterial culture.

6. World systems theory with the concepts of core nations, periphery nations, and semiperiphery nations is a branch of what theory?

   a. functionalism
   b. dysfunctionalism
   c. conflict
   d. multiculturalism

7. Which is the goal of multiculturalism?

   a. to incorporate the minority point of view into the curriculum
   b. to produce a more complete picture of society
   c. to create greater tolerance for diversity
   d. all of the above are goals of multiculturalism

8. Agrarian societies

   a. were made possible by the invention of the plow.
   b. were characterized by the emergence of cities.
   c. had enough wealth to support toolmakers, administrators, and other nonagricultural specialists.
   d. all of the above.

9. Through time within a society,

   a. the content of values remains the same.
   b. the content of values may change even though their outward form remains the same.
   c. the outward form of values may change even though their content remains the same.
   d. the content of values and their outward form remain the same.

10. Industrial societies

   a. rely on technology and mechanization as the main source of sustenance.
   b. institutionalize innovation.
   c. often invest heavily in defense technology.
   d. all of the above.

11. Which is characteristic of associational societies?

   a. complex stratification
   b. the valuing of rationality
   c. the complexity and diversity of life
   d. all of the above are characteristics of associational societies

12. The scientific ability to genetically alter plants and animals (including humans) has progressed faster than the ability to develop norms and values surrounding that ability. This situation is an example of

   a. material culture.
   b. cultural lag.
   c. culture shock.
   d. nonmaterial culture.

13. What sociological perspective has integrated aspects of social evolution theory into its discussion of change, emphasizing the tendencies for societies to achieve and remain in equilibrium?

   a. functionalist
   b. conflict
   c. postmodernist
   d. world systems

14. Which theory of social change argues that traditional societies will eventually take on the characteristics of industrial societies?

   a. cyclical
   b. social evolution
   c. modernization
   d. world systems

15. What type of catalyst for change was illustrated by President Johnson's ordering of American troops into Vietnam?

   a. human agency
   b. revolution and war
   c. cultural processes
   d. natural catastrophes

True-False

Indicate your response to each of the following statements by circling T for true or F for false.

T F 1. The Kwakiutl Indians' cultural practice of potlatch was unrelated to their physical environment.

T F 2. The sanctions for violation of taboos are generally more severe than the sanctions for violation of mores.

T F 3. Language is the most powerful and complex type of symbol.

T F **4.** Most of the world's population lives in industrial societies.

T F **5.** The diffusion of technology and the actions of multinational corporations are contributing to the homogenization of cultures.

T F **6.** In the United States, people tend to have more communal relationships than associational relationships.

T F **7.** The United Kingdom is an example of a core nation.

T F **8.** According to world systems theory, nations that are highly industrialized and powerful, and also that control the world system, are called modernized.

T F **9.** Noticing that something has not been noticed before is called diffusion.

T F **10.** Folkways, mores, and taboos are all norms, yet they vary in importance.

T F **11.** The fourteenth-century plague known as the Black Death killed one-quarter of Europe's population.

T F **12.** The notion of social evolution served the interests of European powers as they expanded their colonial empires.

T F **13.** As societies change, there is a tendency for material cultural elements to change more quickly than nonmaterial cultural elements.

T F **14.** According to Marx, Weber, and Durkheim, people in communal societies suffer from the ills of alienation, rationalization, and anomie.

T F **15.** Few technological developments are entirely new; most build on existing science, technology, and inventions.

NOTE: The answers to these exercises are at the end of the book.

For additional practice tests and other resources please visit the companion web site at http://www.prenhall.com/curry.

Essay

1. What are some of the predominant values of American society? Can you think of norms that are associated with those values?

2. What are the characteristics of communal societies? Of associational societies?

3. What are the major difference between industrial and postindustrial society.

4. Explain the difference between society and culture.

5. What does the Sapier-Whorf hypothesis say about language?

3

Socialization

Chapter Outline

What does it take to become a Supreme Court justice, a successful executive, a talented musician, or a professional athlete? How much is due to luck? How much to training? Can a person of superior ability be taught greatness?

In many different fields, a surprising number of children *seem* to inherit the talents and abilities of their parents or other family members. For instance, of the 91 Supreme Court justices appointed from 1789 to 1957, the majority came from judicial or political families. Within industry, many businesses are family owned, and frequently the children seem to have a knack for the family business. To illustrate, the Du Pont family turned a gunpowder business into a vast chemical company—many of their offspring were not only good at business but also great chemists. In the world of music, both sons of former Beatle Ringo Starr became drummers. Similarly, Enrique Iglesias, the son of world-famous Julio Iglesias, followed in his father's footsteps and sold over 14 million records by the time he was 24.

In athletics, star quarterback Peyton Manning in the National Football League (NFL) is the son of retired NFL star Archie Manning. Similarly, in Major League Baseball, outfielder Barry Bonds is the son of Bobby Bonds and the godson of Willie Mays. The top ranked woman tennis player in 2003, Kim Clijsters, came from a very sports-minded family. Her father, Leo, was a soccer star in Belgium, and her mother, Els, was a national champion in gymnastics.

In studying incidents of children achieving success in similar careers as their parents, social critic Adam Bellow (2003) points to many factors. He notes that growing up around a business or vocation often means absorbing how it works, and getting to know the people in it. This knowledge creates a powerful advantage for the child who later competes in the same field. Bellow's study raises many interesting questions about **socialization**: the process by which people learn the skills, knowledge, norms, and values of their society, and by which they develop their social identity.

Chapter Preview

In this chapter, we first discuss the basic aspects of socialization in contemporary society. We then describe how socialization is structured through the life course. Next, we discuss symbolic interaction as a perspective for interpreting socialization. After that, we turn to moral socialization and examine the views of different theorists. Following that, we discuss resocialization in total institutions. We conclude with a consideration of the future of socialization.

The Great Social Transformation and Socialization

Socialization is a complex, intricate task, and its success is by no means guaranteed. It is probable, however, that the shift from communal to associational society has made successful socialization even more difficult. In communal societies, virtually all members of society receive much the same socialization—the major differences are distinctions made for gender and age. Moreover, most of what is learned comes from people who share a common outlook on life and who have strong personal ties to the person being socialized. Parents and relatives, for instance, teach children almost everything they will ever learn as young people. For this reason, socialization tends to be a conservative force within traditional society. Parents teach their children how things worked for their generation, and in that way, they prepare the children for the here and now but not for a new world that the parents are unable to anticipate or expect. But in an associational society, the schools, peer groups, and the mass media all teach norms, values, and beliefs that may or may not be in agreement with the norms, values, and beliefs held by family members. Nor do all members of an associational society receive the same socialization experiences. In fact, a substantial number of people do not receive sufficient socialization to become fully responsible and respected members of society.

Socialization and the Life Course

Through socialization we learn the language, values, rules, and knowledge of the culture in which we are born. We also develop a sense of who we are, and we form a social identity. Because society deems it important that people learn certain essentials, socialization is not left to chance; rather, it is an integral part of our **life course**: the stages into which our life span is divided, such as adolescence and middle age.

At each stage of the life course, we acquire new knowledge and learn social skills appropriate for that stage. Although the number, length, and content of each stage vary from one society to another, all societies regard socialization as progressive and cumulative. That is, what we learn at one stage becomes the foundation for the socialization of the next stage. In the United States, for instance, we learn elementary reading, writing, and arithmetic during childhood, and from that point on, other people simply assume that we have those skills.

The early stages of the life course are devoted to **primary socialization**, which stresses the basic knowledge and values of the society. Primary socialization is followed by **secondary socialization**, which emphasizes synthesis, creativity, logic, emotional control, and advanced knowledge. Secondary socialization also emphasizes reality and practicality (Mortimer and Simmons 1978). Primary socialization largely takes place within the family, whereas secondary socialization usually takes place in the institutions, groups, and organizations of the wider world.

Socialization and Stages of the Life Course

In industrial societies, the life course is typically divided into several stages: childhood, adolescence, adulthood, old age, and death and dying.

Childhood   This stage is typically romanticized as a time for playful innocence. Adults believe that children should not be exposed to topics such as sex, death, alcohol, and violence. Adults therefore censor the films and language that young children are exposed to and will not discuss certain topics or use certain words in their presence. To further protect children from exposure to taboo material, adults confine them to a specialized social world. Children attend age-segregated schools, compete in special athletic leagues, and wear distinctive clothing. They visit physicians and dentists who specialize in treating their problems, and they are exempt from legal, social, and economic responsibilities.

By the end of childhood, the elementary aspects of formal learning have been completed, and most children have developed enough maturity and self-esteem to cope with the routines of family, peer groups, and school. They also have developed

Socialization ▲ The process by which people learn the skills, knowledge, norms, and values of their society, and by which they develop their social identity.

Life course ▲ Consists of the stages into which our life span is divided, such as adolescence or middle age.

Primary socialization ▲ Early socialization that stresses the basic knowledge and values of the society.

Secondary socialization ▲ Socialization following primary socialization that emphasizes synthesis, creativity, logic, emotional control, and advanced knowledge.

"cultural common sense": they know how to cross the street safely, to work a vending machine, to make purchases at the store, and in general to participate in everyday activities with only limited adult supervision.

The period of childhood, while roughly between birth and adolescence, is not precisely the same for everyone. Ethnicity and class make a difference. Compared with whites, African Americans and Hispanic Americans traditionally socialize their children to become more independent at earlier ages and to assume more responsibility for the welfare of the family. Older children spend a great deal of time caring for their younger brothers and sisters while their parents work; and older children with jobs are expected to use their pay for family support. To some extent, working-class white families may engage in similar practices.

Adolescence Adolescence became a separate stage in the life course during the latter part of the nineteenth century when the forces of industrialization created a surplus of workers (Campbell 1969; Skolnick 1986). Whereas the cultural image of teenagers used to include physical grace and economic independence, the new image emphasized awkwardness, immaturity, and poor qualifications for entering the adult world (Kett 1984). The insertion of adolescence into the life course provided an opportunity for more socialization, but it also created a tempestuous period of life: a jarring mixture of norms regarding freedom and subordination.

Adolescents are now recognized as physically mature, but they are expected to limit or abstain from sexual activity. They are old enough to drive a car, but only if their parents permit it. The saying that teenagers are old enough to serve in the armed forces and die for their country but not old enough to drink legally, summarizes the dilemma of being treated as an adult while being regarded simultaneously as a dependent. As described in this chapter's Profiles box, Margaret Mead's study of adolescence in Polynesia focused attention on whether cultural values in a communal society would moderate this often conflicted period.

A new stage in the life course may be emerging. Sandwiched between adolescence and full adulthood is youth: a period in which people are no longer adolescents but are not full participants in the world of established adulthood. This period includes people in their late teens and early twenties who have not yet settled into a conventional adult role involving a career and an independent family (Chudacoff 1999; Skolnick 1986). For these people, youth is the ideal time to engage in leisurely

New York, New York: High School students having a conversation during lunch break. Young people spend a lot of time with their friends, making the peer group of great importance in their socialization.

Margaret Mead (1901–1978) was a 23-year-old graduate student from Columbia University when she arrived in Samoa to gather materials for her doctoral research in 1925. One can only imagine her feelings. At that time, female researchers were rare. Lone females did not undertake fieldwork in remote, unstudied, and exotic cultures. Her faculty advisor and mentor, Franz Boas, had tried to convince her to study American Indians; instead, she convinced him that it was more important to undertake the long journey to Polynesia to gather firsthand evidence on a remote civilization. In those days, Samoa could be reached only by ship, and the journey took six weeks to complete.

On the advice of Professor Boas, Mead wanted to research how culture shaped the behavior of adolescent Samoan girls. Boas was interested in several questions in particular: How did young girls in Samoa react to the restraints of culture—did they manifest the strong rebellious spirit that seemed typical of American teenagers? Also, what was the place of romantic love in Polynesian society? Were sexual relations controlled and were marriages imposed, and if so, what was the reaction of the girls? In short, to what extent are the troubles of adolescents dependent on the attitudes of a culture, and to what extent are they due to biological aspects inherent in the adolescent stage of development?

While in Samoa, Mead gathered case histories and made observations of village life. She argued that adolescent girls in Samoa were free from the turbulence and conflict that characterized American adolescence, and she felt that a major reason for this state of affairs was that Samoan culture treated sexual matters forthrightly. Her emphasis on the importance of an open, relaxed view of sex was especially relevant during the 1920s, because the discussion of sex was then even more restricted than it is today. Far ahead of her time, Mead analyzed her data from the

Margaret Mead's research in Samoa increased our knowledge of the effects of culture on human behavior.

female point of view and argued that human behavior was readily modified through socialization.

Mead's work resulted in a startlingly popular book, *Coming of Age in Samoa* (1928). In the decades since it was first published, it has been reprinted many times and quoted in thousands of textbooks, professional journals, and popular magazines. It has been the subject of debate within the field of anthropology and has withstood attacks by many of its critics (Freeman 1983; Grant 1995; Holmes 1986). Clearly, it established the reputation of Margaret Mead, who quite likely will be remembered as the most famous female social scientist of the twentieth century. Later, she conducted other important studies in New Guinea and in other South Sea cultures that provided further evidence that human behavior is learned and shaped by cultural practices (Mead 1935). Nowadays, social scientists are more likely to debate the importance of culture as compared with biology rather than debating whether culture has any impact at all.

Of interest is that Margaret Mead accepted this research topic partly because she felt that it would be the least likely to offend senior male researchers in anthropology. Although both her mother and her paternal grandmother had been professional women who had imbued her with an enthusiasm for combining career goals with the traditional marriage and family expectations, she felt it was wise not to compete directly with "men in male fields, but instead to concentrate on the kinds of work that are better done by women" (Mead 1972:100). In the case of her field research in Samoa, she felt she would have a particular advantage in working with teenage girls: men attempting such research might be resented by the girls' fathers and by other important men of that traditional society.

recreational pursuits, travel, volunteer work, contemplation—and college (J. R. Kelly 1990). It is also a period of adjustment, as "twentysomethings" try to leave childhood behind and meet the challenges of adult life, (Robbins and Wilner 2001; see the What Do You Think box, Quarterlife Crisis).

Adulthood   The period between the mid-twenties and the mid-sixties is reserved for adulthood. Because adult socialization builds heavily on primary socialization, the pace of learning becomes slower. Rather than being a time for new learning, adulthood is the time to put previous learning into practice. All the skills, talent, and education acquired earlier are applied at this stage (Bush and Simmons 1990).

During early adulthood until about age 40, many of life's initial tasks are achieved. For example, young adults loosen the bonds with their parents, redefine their lives

Everyone has heard of the midlife crisis. We have stereotypes regarding who goes through this crisis and how they behave. Alexandra Robbins and Abby Wilner have recently suggested that another life crisis exists, not for the middle-aged, but for those who are just beginning adult life. Robbins and Wilner call these people "twentysomethings," and they call this crisis the quarterlife crisis.

People going through a midlife crisis have a few questions that they might ask themselves: Have I done anything significant with my life? Have I spent my adult life wisely? Am I too old to have any more major accomplishments? Did I complete the goals that I had for myself when I was younger? In their book, *Quarterlife Crisis: The Unique Challenges of Life in Your Twenties,* Robins and Wilner identify several question that people face as they leave childhood and enter adult life. These create a crisis and a sense of doubt similar to the midlife crisis but different in substance. The major questions faced by

twentysomethings are: Who am I and what do I want to do with my life? Am I ready to leave my childhood behind and be an adult? Who do I want to spend my life with and how do I find them? (Robbins and Wilner 2001). These questions are brought on by abrupt changes in life following graduation from college. After college, twentysomethings must find sometimes difficult solutions to problems that did not exist before. For instance, twentysomethings must figure out what to do with their time, how to find and make friends and romantic interests after college, how to live on their own, and often, how to get a job (Robbins and Wilner 2001).

CQ Have you ever asked yourself any of the questions that are associated with the quarterlife crisis? Do you now wonder what you want to do with your life or worry about leaving childhood behind? Has this ever filled you with an uncertainty that you would describe as a crisis?

around their own families, and assume responsibility for their own economic and social welfare. Young adults must also learn to satisfy the expectations associated with being a spouse, an employee, a parent, and a responsible member of the community.

Men and women may face sharply different expectations about their work careers during early adulthood. American culture traditionally assigns domestic duties to women and makes little allowance for women who work full-time with an eye to establishing an identity outside the home (Blumstein and Schwartz 1983; Rindfuss, Brewster, and Kavee 1996; Chapter 9). In addition, expectations about the timing of careers create substantial disadvantages for women. The years between 25 and 35 are the period when women are most likely to leave the labor force to have children, but those are the same years in which men are acquiring key promotions, skills, and seniority that will ensure success in later adulthood (Thurow 1987).

During middle age (about age 40 to age 60), careers peak, and the physical charms of youth, long taken for granted, now become problematic. This fact strikes especially hard at those who have internalized the standards of youthful beauty (Gelman 1990; Lasch 1995). Although the societal expectations of adulthood can challenge even the strongest person, meeting the challenges successfully produces a profound sense of accomplishment. Most adults view this period of life as very satisfying (Crosby 1987; Palmore 1981).

At the beginning of adulthood, people emphasize new relationships and egoistic accomplishments. By middle age, they begin emphasizing closeness and compassion in social relationships. For example, 80 to 90 percent of the American population believes that middle age is the time for drawing closer to family and friends. The willingness to help others also increases with age (Midlarsky 1994). Unfortunately for some individuals, their interest in strengthening social bonds comes just when their children and spouses may be seeking greater independence (Gilligan 1993; Levinson 1978).

Old Age   As people grow older in the United States, they confront the need to withdraw from long-held roles and to be socialized into new positions. Elders must learn to be retirees rather than workers, to be grandparents rather than parents, and to give advice rather than orders. Patterns of personal interaction also must change as spouses long used to being apart during the day must adjust to being together most of the time. Health takes on greater importance; thus, elders must learn about new diets, about medical insurance, and about the way to live on their retirement incomes. Some elders must learn new forms of recreation: walking rather than running, fishing rather than mountain climbing. The loss of driving skills may be especially confining when there is no reasonable alternative to the automobile (see the Sociology Online box, The AARP).

As living conditions and medical treatment have improved, the human life span has slowly but steadily grown longer (Chapter 15). Because increasing numbers of people are living into their eighties, a new category of elder has recently been recognized: the very old (or old old). Although many people in this category begin to show the symptoms of physical and mental decline, many others remain vigorous and active. Very old age is the most rapidly growing segment of the life course, and in the future, it will account for an increasingly important proportion of the population.

Gerontology, the study of the aging and the elderly, has become an important area of study. A central question of this field is, What explains successful aging? Researchers have developed some interesting approaches to this question, known as disengagement and activity theory.

Disengagement theory. Disengagement theory emphasizes how society prevents disruptions from occurring when elders leave—or disengage—from their current positions. This theory was first presented by Elaine Cumming and William Henry (1961; Cumming 1976) and was based on their six-year study of 275 older adults in Kansas City. Even though the sample was small and did not represent the entire United States, many sociologists found the theory intriguing and it quickly gained a wide following.

According to this theory, disengagement takes place at two levels. At the societal level, norms, values, and laws encourage and sometimes force elders to vacate their positions at a certain time. The net result of disengagement is that younger people move up to replace older people, and that an orderly transfer of authority takes place.

Disengagement also occurs at an individual level, that is, in the lives of the people who are disengaging. People socialized into American culture accept, unthinkingly, that life progresses though stages and that one stage is retirement. For example, an executive nearing age 65 may gradually give her assistant more and more responsibilities. At the same time, she may begin to withdraw from an active role in her church and start to encourage her married children to make more decisions over family matters. This woman, in other words, has started to disengage from the world of work, community, and family.

Disengagement from different roles takes place at different times. A business might suddenly decide to downsize, and with little warning, many older workers will be forced to retire early. The day after these workers retire, they will have no jobs to go to and will soon lose contact with their colleagues at work. On the other hand,

Gerontology ▲ The study of aging and the elderly.

Disengagement theory ▲ A theory of aging that emphasizes the importance of the elderly gradually disengaging from their roles in society.

these workers will continue to interact with their family, perhaps more than before because they have more time. Although it is possible for people to disengage and then change their minds and return to work, in practice disengagement is usually permanent. Once people begin to disengage, they continue the process.

Disengagement theory is widely accepted, but not uncritically. A recent study found that inactivity or disengagement does not heighten perceived quality of life (Khullar and Reynolds 1990). Some sociologists believe that it is a biased theory because it assumes that elders are not productive. In fact, these critics argue, elders exchange old roles for new roles, and these new roles are just as valuable as the old ones. Disengagement theory also assumes that elders cannot keep up with a rapid pace of change. While this assumption may be correct for some elders, it does not apply to all. For example President Reagan was 69 when inaugurated; and the writer, producer, and novelist Sydney Sheldon was well into his eighties and continued to produce best-selling books and hit television dramas.

Activity theory. Disengagement theory assumes that withdrawal leads to satisfaction, but activity theory assumes the opposite (Maddox 1964; Havighurst, Neugarten, and Tobin 1968). According to activity theory, elders have essentially the same psychological and social needs as the middle-aged, and therefore elders benefit from maintaining a high level of activity in a wide range of roles. According to this theory, rather than sitting back passively and watching television all day, elders should exercise, participate in community affairs, engage in volunteer work, go to school, and otherwise live actively. Such activity seems to be correlated with a sense of well-being and health. For example, when asked what they do to keep healthy, a group of robust elders answered (Schwirian 1991/1992):

I keep doing my own housework.

I walk as much as I can every day.

I stay active.

I keep up with my painting and friends who paint.

Unlike these elders, unfortunately, many have little to do and are isolated and lonely. According to activity theory, isolation and loneliness occur mainly because other people withhold opportunities from elders. Thus a retiree may not be offered the

Activity theory ▲ A theory of aging that argues that the elderly should participate actively in society.

Fishkill, New York: Retired man in second career as a greeter in a Wal-Mart store.

CQ *What do you think? Is this an example of activity theory, disengagement theory, or continuity theory?*

opportunity head up the church fund drive because the church board feels that he is "too old," or children might assume that their parents or grandparents are too frail to go hiking with them.

Although activity theory recognizes that elders can remain active, it also assumes that elders prefer activity. This assumption is not always correct. Some elders thrive on activity while others want a quieter, sedentary lifestyle. The theory, also, does not apply very well to elders who cannot remain active because they suffer from poor health, or live in social isolation through no fault of their own.

A problem with both disengagement and activity theory concerns the assumption that people change dramatically when they enter old age. In fact, according to *continuity* theorists, people do not change much, if at all. These theorists say that deep-seated traits such as personality, disposition, and identity tend to remain the same regardless of age. For example, if you have a negative outlook on life when you are young, continuity theory predicts that you will have a negative outlook when you are old. Successful aging, therefore, depends on maintaining a similar level of engagement into later adulthood (Havighurst et al. 1968).

Death and Dying

In contemporary society, most people do not expect to die young. This is due to the simple fact that most people in the United States are living longer than previous generations—over 85 percent die after the age of 55 (National Center for Health Statistics, 1995). To illustrate further, only 90 years ago (a short time historically), most people in the United States worked almost until the day they died. Now the average American man will spend more than 20 percent of his life in retirement and the average American woman will spend 40 percent. In other words, Americans expect to die *after* they have raised their families and experienced the pleasures and pains of the other stages in the life course, including a long retirement. With so many people dying later in life, personal and social arrangements for death and dying are important. Married couples are wise to prepare for the death of a spouse with legal and financial planning, and families with aging parents must consider the possibility of financing an illness over an extended period.

Modern medicine cannot prevent death, but it can prolong the dying process. Elisabeth Kübler-Ross, a well-known physician and researcher on death and dying, has dedicated herself to educating health care professionals and clergy about the needs and fears of terminally ill patients and their families. Based on her many years of observation of adults and children as they deal with impending death, she outlined the major emotional reactions of patients, family, and sometimes even hospital staff. (Kübler-Ross 1987, 1968; Kübler-Ross and Kessler 2000). She discovered five typical stages of dying. Although people do not necessarily go through these stages in the same order, many patients in different societies experience all five stages. The first stage is *denial and isolation*—the person rejects the prospect of dying and isolates themselves from others. The second stage is *anger*—the person sees the approaching of death as unfair. The next stage is *bargaining*, as the person tries to avoid death by striking a bargain with God. The fourth stage is *depression*, when the person realizes that negotiation has failed. *Acceptance* is the final stage, when the person realizes that their life is ending. This stage can be a blessing, as the person uses whatever time remains to them to make preparations for death.

In her more recent research, Kübler-Ross worked with AIDS patients. This disease is unusual in that it has afflicted millions of young people. These 20- to 30-year-old patients do not have the resources necessary to pay for extended hospital stays and in many cases they are unwilling to tell their families they are sick because of the stigma attached to the disease. Health care systems were initially unprepared to care for young patients who might keep on living for months and perhaps years even while they were terribly debilitated. Kübler-Ross's research helped others to accept the fact

Continuity theory ▲ A theory of aging that states that successful aging is a matter of maintaining the same level of engagement experienced as an adult.

that AIDS is a life-threatening illness that involves millions of people and will decimate large portions of the human population (Kübler-Ross 1987, see Chapter 14). Since Kübler-Ross published her book, attitudes toward AIDS have changed and new medicines have become available, significantly extending the life span of people with the disease.

Agents of Socialization

Every society has individuals, groups, organizations, and institutions that provide substantial amounts of socialization during the life course. These are called **agents of socialization**. Although many agents do not consider socialization to be their primary duty, they nevertheless socialize individuals by passing on knowledge, acting as role models, rewarding compliance, and punishing noncompliance. Some of the important agents are discussed in the following sections.

Family   Of all the agents of socialization, the family is arguably the most important. Although the form of the family differs from place to place (see Chapter 11), in all societies, the family bears the main responsibility for socializing the child from birth through independent adulthood. Within the family, the child first develops physical skills, such as walking, and the intellectual skills of counting and naming things. The family is also important because it gives the child a social location within society. A child born to an upper-class family will be socialized into wealth, power, and social acceptance, whereas a child born to an impoverished family will learn about day-to-day survival, low pay, and social rejection. Families also provide a social context for learning values. Table 3.1, for instance, shows what qualities that parents in the United States believe are important for their children to learn.

School   The school is the agent of socialization responsible for teaching formal cognitive skills, such as reading, writing, math, and history. In industrial and postindustrial societies, the state is responsible for the school system, largely because such societies require an educated workforce. The school is usually the child's first introduction to a formal agent of socialization. Whereas the family regards the child as a unique individual, the school regards the child as a student who is expected to meet objective standards, abide by standard rules, and behave like everyone else.

Although the formal curriculum of the school emphasizes the development of cognitive skills, the informal life of the school subtly reinforces values that are central to the society. In the United States, for instance, children learn that outdoing their friends to receive an A grade is rewarding, whereas being outdone is punishing; that

Agents of socialization ▲ The individuals, groups, organizations, and institutions that provide substantial amounts of socialization during the life course.

What Things Do Parents Believe Are Most Important for a Child to Learn to Prepare Him or Her for Life	
ITEMS	**PERCENT WHO BELIEVE THAT THIS ITEM IS MOST IMPORTANT**
To think for himself or herself	53
To obey	18
To work hard	15
To help others when they need help	13
To be well liked or popular	0

SOURCE: The National Opinion Research Center (NORC) (1994).

TABLE 3.1 • *What do parents believe are the important things for their children to learn to prepare them for life? This table shows that the majority of parents value the quality of thinking for oneself as the most important of the five choices listed in the table. Being popular was considered the least important of the five. Learning to think for oneself is an important characteristic of critical thinkers, and we are glad to see that in this national survey, parents value this quality in their children.*

CQ *Which of these values do you believe are most important for children to learn in today's world? Why those?*

San Benito, Texas. Children from low-income families throughout the Rio Grande Valley attend daily classes at the La Gallina Head Start facility north of Brownsville, Texas. The Head Start program was part of the Great Society programs created by President Lyndon Johnson in the 1960s. Although highly successful, funding for such programs is not guaranteed.

is, they learn to compete. The school is also a place for sharing informal knowledge. Simply listening to students as they talk over lunch will reveal the importance placed on movies, sex, sports, popular songs, proper dress, and who likes whom.

All societies control what is taught in the school, usually to support the position of the dominant group. Despite the recent emphasis on multiculturalism, American history is still viewed mainly through the eyes of white men and ignores the importance of women and ethnic minorities. History textbooks seldom mention the fact that African Americans made up 10 percent of the Union army during the Civil War, or that Chinese made up 50 percent of gold miners during the California gold rush. Neither do textbooks mention the part played by women in settling the frontier or the leadership of black women in the civil rights movement (Giddings 1996; Takaki 1994).

Peer Group   How important to you are your friends? Have you ever done anything that they have totally disagreed with? Sociologists have found that the peer group, which consists of friends who are approximately the same age and have approximately the same social status, is very influential in shaping the child's values and behaviors (Pugh and Hart 1999). Because children spend so much time with their peers, the peer group provides a great deal of informal socialization. The influence of the peer group increases with age, peaking during adolescence. Teenagers are in the process of forging their own identities and participating in a distinctive, youth-oriented culture that helps them gain independence from their parents and other adults. The peer group also provides a social setting within which adult roles can be tried. Dating, for instance, is an opportunity for each partner to try out new social interactions and to practice adult roles in public situations, such as dining at a fancy restaurant on prom night.

Mass Media   The term *mass media* refers to communications that are disseminated to large audiences without direct feedback or other interpersonal contacts between the senders and the receivers. Although films, radio, newspapers, and books are part of the media, television is the dominant medium, by far. To illustrate, more than 98 percent of American households have at least one television set, and in 1999, the average adult American watched approximately 1,600 hours of broadcast television and

800 hours of basic cable television. In contrast, in the same year, the average adult listened to only 300 hours of recorded music (U.S. Bureau of the Census 2000).

Because the media are so pervasive, many observers worry that both children and adults will be socialized into a world that does not exist. They say that the media are so simplistic, overly selective, and distorting that a true picture of society never appears. For instance, television news concentrates on airplane crashes, sex scandals, celebrity murders, and other events that are lurid or visually exciting. Drama and comedy programs portray women as sex objects and ethnic minorities as criminals or incompetents (Kimball 1986; Vande-Berg and Streckfuss 1992; Wilson and Gutiérrez 1995a; Lauzen and Dozier 2002).

The amount of violence shown on television causes further concern. By the time children reach adolescence, they will have witnessed thousands of fictional murders, rapes, armed robberies, and assaults (Lometti 1995). For example, an average of 150 acts of violence and 15 murders occur each week on prime-time television dramas (Gerbner 1995). This deluge of fictional violence could, conceivably, encourage viewers to become violent themselves (National Institute of Mental Health 1982; Institute for Social Research 1994). Current research has tended to support the contention that television violence contributes to aggressive behavior by children. For example, a unique study compared the aggressiveness of children in two Canadian towns similar in size, race, and social class. One of the towns had television, whereas the other did not. Children from the town without television were less physically and verbally aggressive than were the children from the town with television. Two years later, after the town without television acquired it, the aggression level of the town's children had come to equal that of the children in the town that had had television all along (Williams 1986).

Although the mass media are easily criticized, pinpointing their impact on behavior is not easy. We do not simply absorb everything we see or hear. Instead, we choose the medium and the message to suit our own purposes, and we seek out programs that resonate with our experience. Nor do we make choices in isolation. As voters, for instance, we gather information from the media and then discuss our choices with other people. In short, human behavior takes place in a social setting, and it is the combination of the setting and the media that influences beliefs and actions (Alteide and Snow 1991; Cantor and Cantor 1992; Tuchman 1988).

Socialization takes place throughout life. Every society divides life into stages, and within stages, certain expectations about socialization are imposed. Within contemporary associational society, the stages are childhood, adolescence, adulthood, old age, and death and dying. Although humans absorb knowledge and skills from many sources, the agents of socialization are especially important sources. In contemporary society, the most important agents are family, school, peers, and the mass media. The importance of any specific agent varies from individual to individual, however, and no two people in contemporary associational society receive identical socialization experiences.

CQ Many critics feel that the mass media, particularly television, offers little to enhance a child's primary socialization. Do you agree? ◆ Which shows that are currently on television do you think are positive socialization experiences for children? ◆ Which are negative? ◆ What about the commercials?

Socialization and the Self

We, as humans, have the ability to think about ourselves and to form opinions, attitudes, and feelings about who we are. As early as age two, we understand that we have a unique existence that is different from that of other children and adults. As we mature, our sense of uniqueness grows, but we also learn to recognize that other people have their own needs, views, and perceptions. Over the life course, in other words, we develop a sense of **self**: a perception of being a distinct personality with a unique identity. The works of two sociologists, Charles Horton Cooley and George Herbert Mead, laid the foundation for explaining how the self develops.

Cooley: The Looking Glass Self

Charles Horton Cooley originated a famous metaphor—the **looking glass self**—or the process through which we imaginatively assume the reactions of other people (Cooley 1902). According to him, the self emerges in the following three-step sequence:

1. *The image of your own appearance*   First, you form an image of how you appear to other people. This image might include physical appearance, personality, social characteristics, and behaviors. Do you, for instance, think that you are witty, intelligent, and the life of the party? Do you display that side of your personality in public?

2. *The image of how others judge you*   Next, you imagine how other people judge this image of you. Do others enjoy your wit, invite you to their parties, and want to hear your jokes? This image of how others perceive and judge you is the image you see in the looking glass (mirror). It shows the responses of other individuals and of the broader society.

3. *Your response to the imagined reactions of others*   If you like what you see in the looking glass, your self-esteem will be bolstered, and you may develop that side of your self even more. For instance, you might pay close attention to witty stories that you hear on television and retell them later. Conversely, if you detect negative reactions from other people, your self-esteem will be challenged, and you may try to change. You could conclude that other people perceive you as obnoxious, and you might therefore decide to behave more conservatively.

The looking glass self has proven to be a powerful metaphor that emphasized the importance of the self. However, it was proposed almost a century ago, and since that time, sociologists have learned a great deal about self-perceptions. One difficulty with the theory is that different people respond to what they see in the looking glass in

Self ▲ A perception of being a distinct personality with a unique identity.

Looking glass self ▲ The process through which people imaginatively assume the reactions of people.

different ways. When faced with apparent disapproval, some people will discredit the evidence, especially if they question the qualifications of the person making the judgment. Others may become acutely self-conscious and even develop stage fright when they have to appear before others (Lindesmith, Strauss, and Denzin 1999). In addition, people do not consult the looking glass to determine all aspects of their selves. Some people rely on the looking glass to judge their personal attractiveness but rely on standardized test scores to judge their intelligence (Felson 1985). Finally, as Cooley recognized, culture changes, and new values make old images obsolete. Although these criticisms point to shortcomings of the looking glass self, Cooley's work remains an insightful explanation of how the self emerges from social interaction. It remains true that, to some extent at least, we judge ourselves by our perception of how other people judge us.

Mead: Role Taking

As adults, we all too often regard children's play as a frivolous activity that should not interfere with learning, work, and other serious matters. Even though this opinion is based in American culture, George Herbert Mead (1934) would totally disagree with

Mekong Delta, Vietnam: Mother teaching child how to use chopsticks. Children learn how to use the utensils for eating in their culture by watching others. Mead termed this the imitation stage of development.

it. Although children's play might be fun, he said, it has serious consequences. Without play, normal socialization and the development of the self will not occur.

The process of socialization takes place over our lifetime, Mead said, and it begins in childhood. As children play, they learn **role taking**: assuming the role of another person and then judging themselves from the viewpoint of that other person. For example, a child might ask himself, "If I cheat on my homework, what will my teacher think of me?"; or another child might imagine that if she rides her bicycle on a busy street, her father will be angry. In each case, the child is judging what he or she might do, not from their own points of view, but from the viewpoint of another person.

Children do not take just any role, according to Mead; instead, they eventually distinguish between specific roles and abstract roles. They begin by taking the role of specific others, or individuals who are important to them, such as parents, peers, and teachers. This type of role taking is commonly observed when children play house, pretend to be jet pilots, or momentarily imagine themselves as rock-and-roll superstars. Although children assume such roles for fun, their play is affecting their self-development. They are learning the values, norms, and behaviors associated with those roles. And they are vicariously experiencing what it is like actually to have such a role, if only for a few moments. Over the course of a few years, children will take the role of hundreds or thousands of specific others. Their ability to take roles will increase until they learn to take the role of an abstract entity, such as a peer group, school, community, and eventually, society as a whole. Mead called this the *role of the generalized other*.

The ability to take the role of the generalized other is a mark of full social development. Without it, we would have to be continually supervised by a specific person. With it, we can responsibly carry on with our lives because we are guided by the values and norms of society.

Mead said that the ability to take the role of the generalized other develops over the course of childhood in three stages. Briefly, these stages are as follows:

1. *Imitation*   Up to about age 3, children do not have an independent identity and are not capable of taking any roles. Instead, they imitate the behavior of other people without fully understanding what they are doing.

2. *Play*   From about 3 to about 6, children spend a good deal of time pretending to be someone else. That is, they play by taking the role of specific others.

Role taking ▲ Assuming the role of another person and then judging oneself from the viewpoint of that person.

3. Game After age 6, the nature of play changes significantly. Children now play at activities requiring multiple roles and complex behaviors determined by what other children do. These features are typically found in games. In a game, rules must be followed, and roles must be coordinated. All players must therefore know their own roles as well as the roles of other players.

Mead recognized two aspects of the self: the *I* and the *Me*. The I consists of the spontaneous acts of the self, or the self as subject. Thus, a student might say, I aced that exam, or I went to a movie. In contrast, the Me is the deliberate aspect of the self, or the self as object. The professor flunked me, the student might say, or she asked me to explain why I went to the movies instead of studying. Although the I and Me are separate concepts, there is only one self. The Me is the part of the self that evaluates the ongoing thought and action of the I. The Me surfaces whenever an individual faces problems that require thoughtful responses, whereas the I dominates whenever more spontaneous behavior is involved (McCall and Simmons 1978).

Blumer: The Symbolic Interactionist Perspective

Herbert Blumer studied under Mead and broadened the latter's approach to make it a general theory of society. Blumer called the theory symbolic interaction, and it became popular because it emphasized the fact that human interaction is fundamentally symbolic rather than a mechanical pattern of stimulus and response (Blumer 1986; Wallace and Wolf 1998). Formally, *symbolic interaction* is a theory based on the idea that individuals construct the nature of their social world through social interaction. The theory assumes that social life is possible only because humans can communicate through symbols. As we discussed in Chapter 2, a symbol is something that stands for something else, as when the motion of an upturned thumb signifies that everything is all right, or when a red light signifies "stop." Of all the symbols that humans use, though, language is the most important because it enables people to construct their own version of reality. In short, symbolic interaction theory stresses the importance of symbols and meanings in social relationships and social interactions.

Following Mead and Cooley, symbolic interactionists also argue that we can perceive ourselves as objects; that is, we have a self-concept that allows us to think about our own actions. Because we interpret the world through symbols and because we can stand back and think of ourselves as objects, symbolic interactionists further believe that human behavior is ultimately subjective. This assumption is very powerful because it leads to the conclusion that if we "define situations as real, they are real in their consequences" (Thomas 1923). For instance, children who believe in Santa Claus act as though Santa is coming to their house on Christmas Eve, and they sometimes leave cookies and milk for him. Because these children have built their beliefs around Santa, they will be disappointed and perhaps angry when they suddenly learn that he is a mythical figure. In another example illustrating the power of defining the situation, suppose a friend of yours lacks self-confidence and believes that he cannot possibly succeed in passing calculus. Because he perceives himself as incapable, he decides that it is useless to study any more. Once he stops studying, failure is virtually guaranteed. In short, because your friend perceives himself as incapable, he follows a course of action that guarantees that the consequences of his perception will come true.

Symbolic interaction, because it emphasizes the importance of subjectivity and meaning, is especially useful for understanding socialization. The perspective stresses the importance of the meaning that objects and situations have for us. We build meanings by observing what other people do, by imitating them, and by following their instructions. A person who serves as an especially important reference point for our thoughts and behavior is called a **role model**. Very often, we adopt our parents and teachers as role models, especially during the early years of socialization. These processes are far from uniform, however, and no two of us ever learn exactly the same things (Shibutani 1986; Musolf 1996).

⊙ **STUDY TIP**

Create a visual way—perhaps through a drawing or icons—to lay out and understand the elements of George Herbert Mead's role taking theory (specific and generalized others, the stages of the development of the ability to take the role of the generalized other, and the two aspects of self).

Role model ▲ A person who serves as an especially important reference point for our thoughts and actions.

	Comparison of Three Theoretical Perspectives	
PERSPECTIVE[a]	**VIEW OF SOCIETY AND PROCESSES**	**KEY CONCEPTS**
Functionalism	Sees society as a system of parts that work together to maintain the cohesion of the whole system	Manifest functions Latent functions Dysfunctions Anomie
Conflict Theory	Sees society as a collection of parts held together by social power	Conflict Dominance Inequality Alienation
Symbolic Interaction	Sees society as socially constructed by everyday encounters between people	Symbols Meaning Significant others Definition of the situation

STUDY TIP

In your own words, summarize Herbert Blumer's theory of symbolic interaction. Highlight or bold the important terms in your summary.

In this chapter, we have introduced the fundamentals of symbolic interaction theory. Along with the functionalist and social conflict perspectives introduced in the first chapter, it provides a broad approach to the sociological analysis of inequality and social institutions discussed in Parts Two and Three of the text. Table 3.2 compares these perspectives.

● ■ ▲ **Pausing to Think**   About Socialization and the Self

We become what we are and who we are by interacting with other people. Cooley referred to the sense of self that is developed through our imagining the reactions of others as the looking glass self. Mead stressed the importance of role taking, of specific and generalized others, and of the imitation, play, and games stages in human development. Blumer further developed and systematized Mead's thought into a general theory and gave it the name of symbolic interaction. Symbolic interaction is very useful for studying socialization because it emphasizes the importance of language, self, subjectivity, and meaning for understanding human behavior and the choices people make.

CQ From a sociological viewpoint, could your self-concept exist apart from the reactions of other people? ◆ How does your unique sense of self reflect the various experiences you have had in groups, such as your family, religious groups, sports teams, and the like?

Moral Socialization

All societies have value systems that specify what is good, right, and desirable; that is, they have a moral code. Sociologists have long recognized the importance of morality and have tried to explain **moral socialization**: how people come to acquire a sense of right and wrong. In this section, we will review the work of five prominent thinkers in this area: Sigmund Freud, Eric Erickson, Jean Piaget, Lawrence Kohlberg, and Carol Gilligan.

Moral socialization ▲
Socialization to the "moral" values of society.

Sigmund Freud

Sigmund Freud (1856–1939) based his view of human behavior on the idea that the mind (psyche) has both *conscious* and *unconscious* elements. Freud believed that the unconscious mind could influence a patient's feelings and behavior, sometimes resulting in apparently irrational behavior. Freuds' discovery of the workings of the unconscious mind came from his interest in hypnosis, then a new and relatively untried technique (Giovacchini 1977). Trained as a physician, Freud specialized in neurology, and made his living in a private clinical practice in Vienna. Freud kept careful case records, and from these cases came his theory of psychoanalysis (Freud 1961, 1957).

Freud is most famous for his model of personality that incorporates the id, ego, and superego. The **id** (the Latin word for "it") represents the basic drives of the unconscious, which are present at birth. The **ego** (the Latin word for "I") is the term Freud used to represent a person's conscious efforts to balance the drives of id with the demands of society. Through the ego, a person maintains a hold on reality. Freud's term for the cultural values and norms internalized by an individual is the **superego** (Latin for "above or beyond the ego"). In Freud's scheme, the superego is our conscience, telling us why we must limit our demands.

In a well-adjusted person, the ego manages the opposing forces of the id and superego. However, Freud's patients for the most part were not well adjusted. In examining case histories, he thought that most maladjustment problems stem from childhood. Conflicts between the id and the superego that are not resolved during childhood frequently surface as personality disorders many years later. In some cases the problems stem from **repression**, the maintenance of what is and what is not appropriately retained in the conscious mind. The ego is charged with the task of repressing inappropriate urges, pushing them back to the level of the unconscious. Freud recognized that the ability to repress inappropriate behavior is of fundamental importance to gaining acceptance in society.

Repression, however, is not without its costs. Repressed urges and conflicts have the potential to cause anxiety and guilt. Repression itself requires energy, and the person may be spending much psychic energy fighting off desires from the id that might be put to better purposes. To illustrate, in Freud's time few people were willing to accept sex as a basic drive. Thoughts about sex outside of marriage were scandalous, and talk about sex was considered inappropriate. People were supposed to repress their inappropriate sexual urges and to sublimate their sexual desires until marriage. In analyzing cases where his patients were not able to resolve the conflict between societal expectations and their inner sexual drives, Freud stressed that childhood experiences can have a lasting impact on adult personalities. Understanding the repression might help the person release repressed urges and memories.

Freud has had a lasing impact on the study of moral socialization even though many sociologists are critical of his interpretations of his cases (Fisher and Greenberg 1977). Freud's concepts of the id, ego, and superego are well known and still influential. Freud, however, may have overstated the negative qualities of human personality. Wilson (1993), for instance, points out that humans in virtually every society have a seemingly innate moral sense that favors such qualities as sympathy, fairness, self-control, and duty. He believes that conscience arises not out of repression, but out of the human desire for affiliation. Similarly, Jones (1999) believes that Freud's framework for studying guilt is inappropriate for those cases where guilt is often a valid emotional response to wrongdoing that lacks any excuse or justification.

Erik Erikson

Erik Erikson (1902–1994) was initially interested in a career as an artist and came into contact with Freud's method of psychoanalysis while he was teaching art at an experimental school in Vienna. Erikson gained a certificate from the Vienna Psychoanalytic Society, and he moved to the United States when the Nazis came into power. He taught at Harvard Medical School, Yale, and the University of California at Berkeley.

Id ▲ Freud's term for the basic drives of humans.

Ego ▲ Freud's term for the part of the psyche that is conscious and in touch with reality.

Superego ▲ Freud's term for the cultural values and norms internalized by an individual.

Repression ▲ Freud's term for the process of maintaining appropriate thoughts in the conscious mind.

While at Berkeley, he conducted studies of life among the Lakota and Yurok tribes of Native Americans. Erikson's theory views personality formation as a lifelong process. It is based on Freudian thinking but extends past childhood and adolescence into adult life (Erikson 1963, 1968).

Erikson formulated the **epigenic principle**. This principle states that humans develop through a biologically predetermined unfolding of personality through eight stages. Each stage involves certain developmental tasks that are psychosocial in nature. Each task is referred to by two opposing terms, because a balance must be found within each task for healthy development to continue. Each stage has a certain optimal time—parents cannot rush their children into adulthood nor can they prevent the child from becoming an adolescent. If people manage a stage well, they carry a certain *virtue* or psychological strength for the rest of their lives.

Stage 1—First year of life. Infants face the challenge of *trust* (versus *mistrust*). Between birth and about 18 months, infants face the first of life's challenges: to gain a sense of trust that their world is a predictable and safe place. Family members play a key role in how any infant meets this challenge. Too little trust and the infant will become overly fearful—too much trust and the infant may endanger itself.

Stage 2—Second and third years. Toddlers face the challenge of *autonomy* (versus *shame* and *doubt*). The challenge is to learn skills to cope with the world in a confident way. Failure to gain self-control leads children to doubt their abilities—too much autonomy and the child is overconfident.

Stage 3—Fourth and fifth years. Early childhood—the challenge of *initiative* (versus *guilt*). Preschoolers begin to ask "Am I good or am I bad?" as they engage their surroundings. They experience guilt when they fail to meet the expectations of parents and others. In Erikson's scheme, successful socialization requires a balance of initiative *and* appropriate feelings of guilt.

Stage 4—Ages 6 through 11. Middle childhood—now the challenge is *industriousness* (versus *inferiority*). As children enter school, and develop wider circles of friends, they wonder "Am I competent or am I worthless?" Again, a balance is sought between the two extremes.

Stage 5—Ages 12 through 20. Puberty and adolescence—the challenge of gaining *identity* (versus *confusion*). During the teenage years, questions of "Who am I and where am I going?" emerge. Almost all teens experience some confusion as they struggle to establish an identity, and this challenge can be very stressful.

Stage 6—Ages 20 through 24. Early adulthood—the challenge of *intimacy* (versus *isolation*). The challenge here is to form and keep intimate relationships with others—"Shall I share my life with another or live alone?" Romantic attachment and close friendship are balanced against the need to have a separate identity.

Stage 7—Ages 25 through 65. Middle adulthood—the challenge of *generativity* (versus *self-absorption*). By generativity Erikson means the challenge to contribute to the lives of others versus becoming stagnant, trapped, or totally self-absorbed in one's own limited concerns.

Stage 8—Ages 65 and older. Late adulthood—the challenge of *integrity* (versus *despair*). Near the end of their lives, people begin to question whether they have lived a full life. Meeting this challenge successfully results in a sense of integrity and satisfaction. But for those who have been self-absorbed, missed opportunities bring a sense of despair.

While Erikson was successful in broadening Freud's psychoanalytic theory beyond childhood and in introducing other crises beyond repression and sexuality that typically confront people as they age, he did rely on a biological clock as the determining

Epigenic principle ▲ Erik Erikson's formulation which states that humans develop through a biologically predetermined unfolding of personality through eight stages.

factor for entry and exit from these eight stages. Sociologists are more likely to stress cultural and social factors in the emergence of the stages (Corsini 1977). In addition, not everyone will confront these challenges within the exact periods specified by Erikson, and it is not clear that a failure to meet a challenge at one stage of life dooms one to fail later on. Even so, Jackson and Finney (2002) find that younger college students are more likely than older students to be angry or hostile, because they lack psychological resources of maturity and experience or they adapted ineffective coping strategies. Research on mixed-ancestry adolescents indicates that identity conflict may result in increased suicidal tendencies among young people (Olivera 2001; Phinney 1991, 1989). In sum, Erikson's model helps us make sense of shifting demands of socialization through the life course and how biological factors may intertwine with sociological and cultural factors in important ways (see the Society Today box, Thoughts of Suicide and Adolescence).

Jean Piaget and Lawrence Kohlberg

Jean Piaget is a famous researcher in moral socialization. To understand better the mental processes behind the ethical judgments of children, Piaget used "moral dilemmas"— little stories that revolve around an ethically ambiguous situation. Piaget would relate a moral dilemma to a child and then would ask the child to discuss the behavior of each character (Piaget 1932). On the basis of these studies, Piaget concluded that morality develops in two stages. The first is the *heteronomous* stage ("heteronomous" means subject to the laws of other people). This stage lasts up to approximately age 12. During this period, children, in the main, simply accept the rules laid down by adults. Sometimes they disobey, to be sure, but even when disobeying, they are not challenging the right of adults to make the rules. Morality thus is reduced either to following the orders given by adults, or if they disobey those orders, to not getting caught. The second stage, according to Piaget, is the *autonomic* stage ("autonomic" means being subject to one's own laws). During this stage, children learn that rules may be flexible. A child therefore will negotiate the time when he or she should be home from school and will question the parents' right to impose punishments.

Piaget mainly studied children; he had little to say about adolescents and adults. To fill this gap, Lawrence Kohlberg expanded on Piaget's ideas and applied them to older people (Kohlberg 1975; Schrader and Damon 1990; Rest et al. 1999). The following is one of Kohlberg's most widely known dilemmas (reported in Brown 1965):

> In Europe, a woman was near death from a special kind of cancer. There was one drug that the doctors thought might save her. It was a form of radium that a druggist in the same town had recently discovered. The drug was expensive to make, but the druggist was charging ten times what the drug cost him to make. He paid $200 for the radium and charged $2,000 for a small dose of the drug. The sick woman's husband, Heinz, went to everyone he knew to borrow the money, but he could only get together about $1,000, which is half of what it cost. He told the druggist that his wife was dying, and asked him to sell it cheaper or let him pay later. But the druggist said, "No, I discovered the drug and I'm going to make money from it." So Heinz got desperate and broke into the man's store to steal the drug for his wife.

Was Heinz right to steal the drug? Would you have done the same thing? Note that the case of Heinz pits the duty to preserve human life against the duty to abide by the law. Does one of these duties take precedence over the other? How does one decide? This is a complicated moral issue; it is not surprising that most people have difficulty resolving it. On the basis of his research with this and other dilemmas, Kohlberg concluded that morality develops over three main stages extending from childhood through adulthood.

1. The earliest stage of morality is the *preconventional*, in which people obey laws and social expectations only to avoid punishments or to gain benefits. This type of

Society Today ● ■ ▲

Thoughts of Suicide and Adolescence

What unique crises concerning identity do teenagers face? Are you surprised that people at this age think about suicide? This table shows the percentage of males and females in 9th, 10th, 11th, and 12th grades who considered suicide. Females are much more likely than males to consider suicide.

GRADE	MALES	FEMALES
9th	14.7	23.6
10th	13.8	26.2
11th	14.1	24.1
12th	13.7	23.6
Total	14.2	18.9

SOURCE: Centers for Disease Control and Prevention, National Center for Chronic Disease Prevention and Health Promotion, National Youth Risk Behavior Survey, 2003.

STUDY TIP

Assign one of Kohlberg's three stages of moral socialization to each member of a group of three. Take five minutes for each group member, working alone, to come up with examples of people and/or situations that illustrate his or her particular stage. Then gather together and share your examples. Discuss how people in each stage might solve the dilemma about Heinz and his wife.

morality characterizes most children under age 9 and some adolescents. Later in this stage, children develop a sense of exchange, a kind of tit-for-tat morality: the right thing is to do something good for another person, but only if that person will do something good in return. Similarly, if someone does you wrong, you must respond in kind. Although preconventional morality applies mainly to children, some people continue to think in preconventional terms even as adults. For example, Timothy McVeigh, the young man found responsible for the bombing of the federal building in Oklahoma City on April 19, 1995, had a self-centered worldview and a philosophy of "dirty for dirty" as he expressed it (Gibbs 2003). Angry at the federal government for enforcing gun control laws and other issues, he "got even" by killing 168 innocent men, women, and children.

2. The next stage is the *conventional*, in which people incorporate societal rules and expectations into their own value system. Many adolescents and most adults are at this stage of moral development. They obey rules not only because they wish to win approval or to gain rewards but also because they feel obligated to do the right thing. Loyalty becomes an important value, and some people believe that it takes precedence over all other commitments.

3. The *postconventional* stage is the highest level of moral development. At this point, people use broad ethical principles to guide their behavior, such as respect for human dignity and equality, and, more recently, concern for the environment and for the rights of animals. Even though postconventional morality is based on a particular set of ethical principles, it does not follow that everyone holds to the same principles. Kohlberg studied the stages of human moral development, not what constitutes morality itself (Kohlberg 1975).

In general, people do not reach postconventional morality before the age of 20, and many never reach it. Kohlberg estimates that fewer than one-quarter of the people in the United States are at the postconventional stage, in part because American society does not routinely socialize people to question authority and explore alternative ethics.

People at the postconventional stage of morality often are instigators of social change and are in the forefront of social movements. To illustrate, in 1963 in Birmingham, Alabama, Martin Luther King and his followers ignored a court order and staged a protest march. Dr. King struggled with the morality of this tactic, but he concluded that racial equality was a higher principle than obeying a court order (Bell 1993).

Carol Gilligan: Morality and Gender

Over the past several years, it has become increasingly obvious that a gender bias runs through much of science, including research on morality. Social scientist Carol Gilligan argues that theorists such as Piaget and Kohlberg defined morality from a masculine viewpoint and assumed that the moral reasoning of women was inferior to that of men (Gilligan 1993).

Rather than relegating women's morality to a lower level, Gilligan argues that women approach morality from a different perspective. Whereas men define morality in terms of justice, women define it in terms of responsibility. According to the justice approach that men routinely learn, morality is determined by the logical application of preset rules, laws, and regulations. The goal is to reach a decision that can be judged as either right or wrong. Women, on the other hand, view morality in terms of an obligation to exercise care, to satisfy needs, and to avoid hurting people—ethical principles that are distinctly different from those of men. Kohlberg's failure to recognize these differences, Gilligan claims, led to a systematic bias in his results.

As part of her research, Gilligan conducted interviews with male and female children, asking them to interpret the story of Heinz mentioned earlier. To illustrate

The bombed-out front of the Alfred Murrah Federal Building in Oklahoma City stands littered with debris and charred cars after a truck bomb set on April 19, 1995, by Timothy McVeigh exploded killing 168 innocent people and injuring more than 500. McVeigh's tit-for-tat motive was to get even with the federal government for its conduct in several situations that McVeigh found offensive.

 **CQ** What Stage 1 morality is characterized by tit-for-tat motives according to Kohlberg?

her findings, consider how Jake (an 11-year-old boy) and Amy (an 11-year-old girl) interpreted the Heinz dilemma. Jake's interpretation emphasized the conflict between the laws of property and the value of a human life. Jake remarked, "For one thing, a human life is worth more than money, and if the druggist only makes $1,000, he is still going to live, but if Heinz doesn't steal the drug, his wife is going to die." When asked about breaking the law, Jake responded, "The laws have mistakes, and you can't go writing up a law for everything that you can imagine."

Amy had a much different interpretation of the Heinz dilemma. She said, "There might be other ways besides stealing the drug, like if he could borrow the money or make a loan or something, but he really shouldn't steal the drug but his wife shouldn't die either." When asked why Heinz should not steal, she emphasized the effect of stealing on the social relationships between Heinz and his wife. "If he stole the drug, he might save his wife then, but if he did, he might have to go to jail, and then his wife might get sicker again, and he couldn't get more of the drug, and it might not be good." Amy is confident that if Heinz and the druggist "had talked it out long enough," they could have come to a solution. Thus, rather than viewing morality as a problem to be solved by applying preestablished criteria, she saw it as a problem of maintaining delicate social balances and arriving at a mutually satisfying outcome.

Although Gilligan's work has drawn both a large following and a vocal body of critics, even her severest detractors recognize the importance of broadening the interpretation of morality. Gender differences in socialization do affect how boys and girls come to interpret rules and perform moral reasoning. As children, Gilligan points out, girls are socialized to become mothers and caretakers, whereas boys are socialized to become economic providers (see Chapter 8; Prose 1990).

Timothy McVeigh is lead out of the Noble County Courthouse by state and federal law enforcement officials. He was tried, found guilty, and executed for his crimes.

●■▲ Pausing to Think   About Moral Socialization

All societies have value systems that specify what is good, right, and desirable behavior. Freud viewed moral socialization in terms of the impulses of id being monitored and control by the ego. Erikson developed a model based on Freud's ideas that involved the whole life course. Erikson believed that moral socialization was matter of overcoming different crises at eight stages of development. Piaget and Kohlberg viewed morality as interpretive skills that develop through socialization. More recently, Gilligan has emphasized the importance of gender. She believes that women see morality in terms of social relationships, whereas men see it in terms of preset rules.

CQ Have you ever faced a moral dilemma? ◆ If so, how did you resolve it? ◆ Did you consider the reactions of others, or did you rely on preset rules? ◆ Or did you find some other way?

Resocialization and Total Institutions

Sociologist Erving Goffman studied a mental hospital using an ethnographic technique—he had himself admitted as a patient (1961, see also Chapter 5). He discovered that life in a mental institution has some distinctive characteristics that are shared by similar institutions. For instance, the staff closely supervises the daily life of the patients including where they eat, sleep, and work. The environment of the institution is highly standardized and nearly everybody shares a similar set of activities, eats the same food, and wears the same uniforms. The patients or "inmates" as

Goffman termed them are required to follow schedules set by the administration and abide by rules that dictate how they perform their daily routines. Goffman refers to such places as **total institutions**, settings in which people are isolated from the rest of society and controlled by an administrative staff. Other examples of total institutions include prisons, slave plantations, monasteries, cloisters, nursing homes, and boarding schools.

The purpose of such institutions is frequently aimed at **resocialization**, radically changing an inmate's behavior, values, or attitudes by carefully controlling the environment. By manipulating rewards and punishments and reducing or eliminating potentially conflicting influences from outside the institution, the staff hopes to produce lasting change—or at least obedience—in the inmate.

Once inside the walls of the institution, the inmate soon learns that his former identity no longer carries much weight. To achieve change the staff tries to break down a new inmate's existing identity using what Goffman (1961:14) describes as "abasements, degradations, humiliations, and profanations of self." Once the old identity is destroyed, the staff may try to build a new self in the inmate. In fact, the length of incarceration may depend on how well the inmate cooperates with the staff in this endeavor. In Goffman's study, for instance, inmates could not leave the asylum until the staff declared them to be "cured." Inmates who wanted to get out learned to tell the staff what they wanted to hear. In some cases, this meant that an inmate would have to confess to having been crazy or mentally ill in order to be released.

Total institutions have frequently been used as educational systems. For example, researchers studying boarding schools for female and male youth from wealthy families in nineteenth century France discovered that these students were rigidly controlled and constantly supervised. Vacations home were restricted, and uncompromising authority structures permeated the entire system. The boys received particularly harsh treatment. Teachers routinely ridiculed and humiliated them. They forced the boys to adhere to a stringent work environment, and severely punished those boys who disobeyed rules. The aim was to force the boys to acquire the substantive knowledge, mental skills, and character that would allow them to become the next generation of French leaders. As a result, the boys became hostile, aggressive, and cruel—mimicking the environment of the total institution. The girls were treated with more compassion. Their environment was designed to prepare them to assume domestic, supportive roles in adult life. Their curriculum was not as academically rigorous. They had a greater emphasis on Biblical studies, and were also taught domestic skills such as music, dance, writing, sewing, and keeping household budgets. When they left the institution, they either returned to live with their parents or relatives or began an arranged marriage. They were not expected to live alone (Knottnerus and Poel-Knottnerus 1999).

The U.S. military attempted a different approach to educational resocialization during World War II. Toward the end of the war, the army was capturing many German soldiers. Keeping these soldiers in camps near the combat zone was difficult and potentially dangerous, since the prisoners might escape and return to the battle. Instead, the prisoners of war (POWs) were shipped back to the United States and confined in some 500 POW camps.

Since the military was planning on eventually returning these troops to their home countries, the task of resocializing the soldiers was considered. No one wanted to return to war-torn Europe over 300,000 enemy troops who still maintained the extremist ideology of Nazi Germany. Professors from liberal arts colleges were recruited by the military to teach the POWs new ways of thinking. The administrators of the camps let the prisoners organize themselves into familiar military style-units, and take care of their own discipline problems. Meanwhile, the professors planned intensive schedules of classes, readings, and films that tried to reeducate the POWs as to why democracy had failed in Germany but succeeded in the United States. The POWs were required to attend these classes and activities and were forced to learn a totally

Total institution ▲ A setting in which people are isolated from the rest of society and controlled by an administrative staff.

Resocialization ▲ A process that aims at reforming or altering an inmate's personality through manipulation and control of the environment.

different perspective for the reasons for the war. Upon departure from the camps, the POWs were asked to complete a questionnaire about their ideas about the war and German history. Unfortunately, no pretest was done, so the analysis of the results could not address the extent to which the POWs actually changed their attitudes. However, careful analysis of the questionnaire items revealed a telling pattern. The majority of the POWs simply answered the questions the way they believed that the administrators of the camps wished. They were willing to state that the United States had a superior form of democracy, because they had been socialized as soldiers to obey authority. The resocialization effort had been in vain, because the POWs looked upon it as propaganda (Robin 1995).

 Pausing to Think   About Resocialization and Total Institutions

Resocialization is an unpredictable process. While total institutions can restrict freedom, they affect people in different ways. While some inmates seem to improve or reform, others may change little and still others may become hostile. Some inmates may even lose their desire or capacity for independent living after a long period of institutionalization. Nonetheless, society relies on total institutions to control inmates who are considered as problems or who are thought to be in need of resocialization under supervision.

CQ To what extent is the educational institution you attend similar to a total institution? In what ways is it different?

Socialization in the Twenty-First Century

Tomorrow's Lesson: Learn or Perish

> *Time* (Special issue, fall 1992, p. 59)

This quotation is the title of an article that appeared in a special issue of *Time* magazine more than a decade ago. The issue concerned the future, and *Time* predicted that the twenty-first century would place an unprecedented emphasis on learning and relearning throughout the life course. So far, the article has proved to be correct. Technical knowledge already changes so rapidly that the lessons of today's classrooms are obsolete within a short time after graduation, if not before. In the future, technical knowledge will become obsolete even faster and will necessitate a different type of teaching. Far less time will be devoted to acquiring specific knowledge and far more time to teaching students how to learn on their own. Values will also change, although less rapidly, and people will have to learn general principles that can be used in a variety of situations. Rather than being socialized into a single career, people will have multiple careers, and education will become a lifelong process. Socialization for domestic roles will become a more drawn-out process. In the future, some people will be parents, grandparents, and great-grandparents all at the same time. With the lines between generations blurring and family roles overlapping, people will simultaneously play multiple family roles. Although not anticipated by the *Time* article, the United States has launched a War on Terrorism after the events of September 11, 2001. Americans have had to learn about living with terrorism on a daily basis since then. This includes adopting a more watchful stance at airports, being more alert to governmental warnings about travel in the United States and abroad, and even learning how to identify dangerous biological and chemical agents.

CONCEPT WEB Socialization

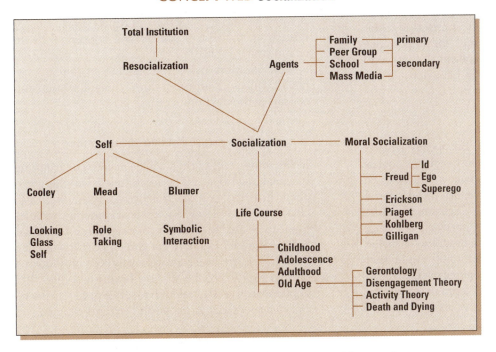

This is a concept web for socialization. What argument would you make to support connecting *Resocialization* to *Agents of Socialization*? What argument could be made to support connecting *Childhood* to *Mass Media*?

Looking Ahead

The next chapter focuses on deviance and crime. Here we present the major theories that explain why people do not conform to the norms of society and the workings of the criminal justice system.

WHAT YOU SHOULD KNOW ●■▲

1. How is socialization related to the Great Social Transformation?

Socialization takes place throughout life. The shift from communal to associational society has made successful socialization more difficult. In communal societies, all members of society receive much the same socialization, share a common outlook on life, and have strong personal ties to the person being socialized. But in an associational society, much of what is learned comes from schools, peer groups, the mass media, and other impersonal sources.

2. What does the life course have to do with socialization?

Every society divides life into stages and imposes certain expectations within these stages. Within contemporary associational society, the stages are childhood, adolescence, adulthood, old age, and very old age.

Although humans absorb knowledge and skills from many sources, the agents of socialization are especially important sources at each stage of the life cycle.

3. What do gerontologists say about successful aging?

Continuity theorists argue that successful aging results when people maintain the same level of activity in old age as they did during their adult years. Activity theory assumes that being active is desirable for nearly all of the elderly. Disengagement theory stresses the value to society of retiring elderly people from social positions. Acceptance of death is the final step.

4. How does the self develop?

Cooley argued that the self develops through our imagining the reactions of others. Mead stressed the importance of role taking; specific and generalized others; and the imitation, play, and games stages in human development. Blumer further developed and systematized Mead's thought into a general theory, and he gave it the name of symbolic interaction. Symbolic interaction theory emphasizes the importance of language, self, subjectivity, significant others, and meaning for understanding human behavior and the choices people make.

5. How do people become moral?

All societies have value systems that specify what is good, right, and desirable behavior. People are socialized to these values and are, therefore, socialized to be moral and to develop a sense of morality. Freud saw the id, ego, and superego as key terms in discussing morality. Erikson drew upon Freud and developed an eight-stage model, with morality issues beginning at Stage 3. Piaget and Kohlberg viewed morality as interpretive skills that develop through socialization. More recently, Gilligan argues that women see morality in terms of social relationships, whereas men see it in terms of preset rules.

6. What is the purpose of a total institution?

A total institution is a setting in which people are isolated from the rest of society and controlled by an administrative staff. The purpose of a total institution is resocialization, radically changing an inmate's behavior, values, or attitudes through manipulation and control of the environment.

7. What does the future hold for socialization?

In the future, far less time will be devoted to acquiring specific knowledge and far more time to teaching students how to learn on their own. Values will also change, and people will have to learn general principles that can be used in a variety of situations. Rather than being socialized into a single career, people will have multiple careers, and education will become a lifelong process. Politically, the War on Terrorism, begun after September 11, 2001, has increased the need for Americans to learn about terrorism and terrorist activity.

TEST YOUR KNOWLEDGE ●■▲

Key Terms Matching

Match each of these key terms with the best definition or example from the numbered items that follow. Write the letter preceding the key term in the blank before the definition that you choose.

a. agents of socialization

b. ego

c. epigenic principle

d. id

e. total institutions

f. repression

g. life course

h. looking glass self

i. moral socialization

j. primary socialization

k. resocialization

l. superego

m. role model

n. secondary socialization

o. self

p. socialization

_____ 1. Settings in which people are isolated from the rest of society and controlled by an administrative staff.

_____ 2. The process through which people imaginatively assume the reactions of people.

_____ 3. The individuals, groups, organizations, and institutions that provide substantial amounts of socialization during the life course.

_____ 4. The cultural values and norms internalized by an individual.

_____ 5. A perception of being a distinct personality with a unique identity.

_____ 6. The basic drives of the unconscious which are present at birth.

_____ 7. The maintenance of what is and what is not appropriately retained in the conscious mind.

_____ 8. Socialization to the "moral" values of society.

_____ 9. Humans develop through a biologically predetermined unfolding of personality through eight stages.

_____ 10. The process by which people learn the skills, knowledge, norms, and values of their society, and by which they develop their social identity.

_____ 11. A person who serves as an especially important reference point for our thoughts and behavior.

_____ 12. A person's conscious efforts to balance basic drives with the demands of society.

_____ 13. Socialization following primary socialization that emphasizes synthesis, creativity, logic, emotional control, and advanced knowledge.

_____ 14. Radically changing someone's behavior, values, or attitudes by carefully controlling their environment.

_____ 15. Consists of the stages into which our life span is divided, such as adolescence or middle age.

_____ 16. Early socialization that stresses the basic knowledge and values of the society.

Multiple Choice

Circle the letter of your choice.

1. Which of the following is true of childhood?
   a. Childhood is a period romanticized as a time of playful innocence.
   b. By childhood's end, the elementary aspects of formal learning have been completed.
   c. Ethnicity, race, and class make a difference in the course of childhood.
   d. All of the above are aspects of childhood.

2. Adolescence became a separate stage of the life course in American society
   a. when World War II required that a decision be reached at the draft age.
   b. when in the nineteenth century the forces of industrialization created a surplus of workers.
   c. because in the 1950s, Dr. Spock argued that the developmental tasks of the teenager were different from those of the subteens.
   d. because of local laws requiring mandatory education until the age of 16 years.

3. Which of the following is NOT true of adulthood in the United States?
   a. The pace of learning quickens in adulthood in comparison with that in adolescence and childhood.
   b. Most people find adulthood a satisfying time of life.
   c. Adulthood occurs from the mid-twenties through the mid-sixties.
   d. The willingness to help others increases in this stage.

4. Usually a child's first experience with a formal agent of socialization takes place in the
   a. family.
   b. school.
   c. mass media.
   d. peer group.

5. Which agent of socialization becomes more important during adolescence and less important during adulthood?
   a. family
   b. school
   c. mass media
   d. peer group

6. According to Mead, which of the following is an example of the generalized other?
   a. brother
   b. teacher
   c. supervisor
   d. peer group

7. In which of Mead's stages do children play at activities requiring multiple roles and complex behaviors that are determined by what other children do?
   a. play
   b. imitation
   c. game
   d. postconventional

8. Symbolic interaction theory stresses the importance of
   a. our innate biological constitution as a source of motivation for our behavior.
   b. symbols and meanings in relationships and social interactions.
   c. human behavior as objective rather than subjective.
   d. symbols that are grounded in our biology.

9. In which of Piaget's stages of moral development does a child simply accept the rules as set by adults?
   a. heteronomous
   b. preconventional
   c. autonomic
   d. postconventional

10. According to Kohlberg, Martin Luther King Jr. reached which stage of development?

    a. heteronomous
    b. preconventional
    c. autonomic
    d. postconventional

11. In studying the moral development of men and women, Carol Gilligan argues that

    a. women approach morality as an obligation to exercise care, to satisfy needs, and to avoid hurting other people.
    b. women and men approach morality from different perspectives.
    c. men view morality as governed by preset rules and laws.
    d. all of the above are true.

12. Why has gerontology recently become an important field?

    a. because sociologists have recently realized that older people matter
    b. because older people have a lot of voting power
    c. because the very old make up the fastest growing segment of society
    d. because sociologists have gotten older

13. Which of the following is a logical extension of disengagement theory?

    a. We do not need to worry about older people.
    b. Older people are more likely to be active in the church than younger people.
    c. Older people are as active as younger people.
    d. It is normal and acceptable for older people to become less involved in society.

14. Which of the following is associated with Erikson's stage of initiative (versus guilt)?

    a. "Am I good or bad?"
    b. The challenge is to learn skills to cope with the world in a confident way.
    c. Family members play an intimate role in how an infant meets this challenge.
    d. "Shall I share my life with another, or live alone?"

15. Which of the following is not a total institution?

    a. a prison
    b. a political party
    c. a mental institution
    d. a monastery

True-False

Indicate your response to each of the following statements by circling T for true or F for false.

T F 1. Margaret Mead studied Samoan girls and found that the openness of Samoan society with regard to sexual matters increased the girls' turbulence and conflict.

T F 2. Very old age is a relatively new stage in the life course.

T F 3. In all societies, the family is responsible for socializing children from birth through independent adulthood.

T F 4. In role taking, we assume the role of another person and then judge ourselves from the viewpoint of that other person.

T F 5. The main feature of Mead's game stage is that children spend a great deal of time pretending to be someone else.

T F 6. Symbolic interactionists argue that "If we define situations as real, they are real in their consequences."

T F 7. In Kohlberg's preconventional stage of moral development, people incorporate societal rules into their own value systems.

T F 8. Freud believed that most problems stem from a series of crises that individuals face in life.

T F 9. According to activity theory, older people must remain very active.

T F 10. Resocialization is a normal process that everyone goes through.

T F 11. The id is Freud's term for the basic drives of humans.

T F 12. According to disengagement theory, disengagement from different roles usually happens at the same time.

T F 13. The looking glass self is a process through which we imaginatively assume the reactions of other people.

T F 14. According to Mead, without play normal socialization and development of self will not occur in children.

T F 15. According to Gilligan, women and men approach morality from the same perspective.

NOTE: The answers to these exercises are at the end of the book.

For additional practice tests and other resources please visit the companion web site at http://www.prenhall.com/curry.

Essay

1. How is socialization connected to the Great Social Transformation?

2. How does the self develop?

3. What contribution did Carol Gilligan make to the study of moral socialization?

4. How do people age successfully?

5. How do total institutions function as socializing agents?

4 Deviance and Crime

Chapter Outline

Criminologists Patrick Anderson and Donald Newman were curious about the variety of crime stories reported in newspapers. Looking at stories for just one day in November, they found a considerable diversity. In one case, an infanticide, a teenage couple from the middle class was arrested for the murder of their baby. The couple had beaten the baby to death and then thrown his body in a dumpster. They had never been in trouble with the police before. Apparently, they did not want their parents to know about the baby, and had panicked after the child's birth.

On the same day, the Central Intelligence Agency (CIA) reported a case of espionage. The FBI had arrested a CIA agent at Dulles Airport outside of Washington, D.C. The agent had been selling secrets to the Russian government. The agent was considered a successful employee with a bright future. He had given the Russians information for over two years about CIA activity in Eastern Europe in return for about $120,000. He had made no effort to hide his illegal income, and had spent it to travel, buy a car, and pay off his debts.

Fraud was reported on that same day in Polk County, Florida. Here a former minister was appealing his conviction for defrauding elderly citizens by selling them nonexistent mortgages. This man was promising his victims a high rate of return on these "investments," and invoking the name of God while he stole their life savings.

Anderson and Newman also found an unusual report about a robbery. In Houston, Texas, police were searching for a gang of young men who had been reported for robbing motorists stopped at a traffic signal. The young men surrounded cars stopped at the signal and threaten to harm the drivers unless they gave them money and jewelry.

In examining these cases, Anderson and Newman point out that the behaviors involved in infanticide, espionage, fraud, and robbery have little in common. They ask, to create a criminal justice system that can effectively prevent or respond to behavior such as this, how important is it to understand the motivation, the causes for these behaviors? Can any single explanation account for such diverse behavior or are a number of explanations necessary? (Anderson and Newman 1998: 59, 82).

Chapter Preview

As the opening for the chapter implies, sociologists and criminologists have found that multiple explanations for deviance and crime are necessary, and in this chapter we present several of the leading explanations for deviance and crime. But first some definitions are in order, and so we define what is meant by deviance and crime. We follow that discussion with some data on crime rates, and then present the sociological explanations. We follow that discussion with an outline of the criminal justice system, and conclude with a consideration of how policies might evolve toward deviance and crime in the future.

The Great Social Transformation and Deviance and Crime

Deviance and crime are universal. All societies have deviance and crime, because people are not machines. They are humans and their behavior is subject to interpretation and evaluations by others. Even so, communal societies are often thought to be characterized by low levels of deviance. This is so because people in communal societies are socialized into long-standing traditions and develop strong internal controls. Communal societies are, moreover, relatively simple and therefore require fewer rules than associational societies. In a hunting and gathering society, for instance, most everyone agrees on how food should be shared, and no one has to worry about paying taxes on capital gains or exceeding speed limits. However, if you look below the surface of a communal society you will find instances of deviance. Indeed, some communal societies have higher rates of murder and rape than those in the big cities of advanced industrial states (Edgerton 1979). When it comes to punishing those who deviate, communal societies often use **restitution** *rationale* to determine a suitable punishment. Here the effort is to make the victim and the community "whole again" by restoring things to how they were before the deviance or crime occurred. In some cases this means that the offender pays money to the victim or his or her relatives in compensation for losses. Communal societies that use restitution hope to rid themselves of any grudges victims and their relatives hold toward the offender (Reichel 2002).

Deviance in associational societies presents a much different situation. Because associational societies are impersonal, tradition and informal rules are not always adequate to prevent deviance. In addition, associational societies require many **laws**: bodies of rules governing the affairs of a community that are enforced by a political authority, usually the state. Many associational societies are diverse, and the mix of ethnicities, languages, and regional differences requires coordination, which in turn requires even more laws. Punishments in associational society tend to focus on the offender, rather than the victim. Detention or imprisonment in jail is used as a way to protect society from the offender, along with such punishments as fines and community service.

Deviance and Crime

While most people will admit to breaking the law sometimes during their lives, almost all of us oppose serious violations. And while our everyday life may be orderly, there are times when life is less orderly—when murder, scandal, and other normative violations take place. In fact, these violations occur often enough that deviance and crime have become fields of specialization practiced by sociologists and criminologists.

What is deviance? Technically, **deviance** is any violation of a widely held norm. In practice, however, most deviance is ignored, mildly punished, regarded as amusing, or even supported. It is one thing to mug a person and quite another to wear cutoff blue jeans to a formal banquet. All deviance involves violating norms, but some norms attract the attention of the authorities. An act that has been declared illegal by some authority is called a **crime**. The authority might be the formal government of an industrial society or a group of elders who, through long tradition, govern a hunting and gathering society. Regardless of the societal type, however, authorities tend to criminalize acts that severely upset societal order and that cannot be easily controlled through internal controls.

Not all crimes are deviant acts, and not all deviant acts are crimes. Murder and incest are both deviant and criminal, whereas piercing your eyebrows to insert a ring,

Restitution ▲ A policy of attempting to restore things, as much as possible, to the way they were before a crime was committed.

Laws ▲ A body of rules governing the affairs of a community that are enforced by a political authority, usually the state.

Deviance ▲ Any violation of a widely held norm.

Crime ▲ An act that has been declared illegal by some authority.

though not criminal, is mildly deviant in most American communities (cf. Meyer 1992). However, since body piercing is becoming more popular in the United States, within the near future perhaps only the most extreme forms of it will be considered deviant. Scalping—illegally selling tickets to an event—is a crime in some localities, but the practice is so common that in most places, it is not considered to be deviant. Similarly, driving a few miles per hour over the speed limit posted on an interstate highway is technically a crime, but the police usually give drivers some leeway before pulling them over.

Like judgments about culture, judgments about deviance and crime are relative. What was deviant at one time might be nondeviant now, and what is a crime in one place might be legal somewhere else. Wearing animal fur was normal for both men and women in the United States during the 1950s but would be considered by some as less appropriate today. In fact, many animal rights activists feel strongly about the issue and have attacked people who are wearing furs. Similarly, many animal species that were once abundant sources of furs have become nearly extinct, and hunting these animals for their pelts is now a crime.

Because deviance is disruptive to social life, all societies develop some means of controlling it. Mechanisms that monitor behavior and penalize the violation of norms are called **social controls**. These mechanisms vary from mild rebukes such as "Don't do that!" to execution by the state. Because there are so many different kinds of mechanisms for controlling deviance, sociologists divide them into two kinds. The first, **internal social controls**, are located within the individual and are learned through socialization. No behavior is inherently deviant; rather, we are taught that certain behaviors are normal and other behaviors are not. This socialization runs deep; we actually come to like or love nondeviant behavior and to dislike or hate deviant behavior. Consequently, no external pressures are required to ensure conformity. For example, most people do not steal, not because they fear punishment but because they have internalized the belief that stealing is morally wrong. Many parents try to instill internal social controls in their children. Sometimes they try very hard, and still fail (see the What do You Think? box, Can Parents Push Too Hard?).

In contrast to internal controls, **external controls** rely on societal mechanisms to prevent deviance. Examples are the police, the Internal Revenue Service, the peer group, or any other societal mechanism that monitors our behavior and rewards us for compliance and punishes us for noncompliance. External controls are brought into play whenever internal controls cannot be relied on or whenever the slightest amount of deviance will disrupt an important social process. For instance, almost half of all American taxpayers "fudge" on their annual income tax returns. Without the Internal Revenue Service—an external control—we can only speculate on what the rate of cheating would be. In this case, internal controls are not strong enough to ensure a high rate of compliance; hence, the IRS must swing into action with its selective audits, computer checks, and human agents. Similarly, internal controls are insufficient to prevent people from speeding on the highway; hence, the police must constantly patrol and give tickets for speeding. And, of course, internal controls fail, sadly, for some students during exams; hence, the need for proctors to monitor the classroom when an examination is being given.

Occasionally, we hear of people who commit wanton murder or serial killings over a long period of time. For reasons not well understood, such people apparently have no internal controls at all. They know that murder is against the law, and they can articulate principles of morality at great length. These same people, however, have not internalized the conventional norms against murder and other deviant behaviors. Without internal controls, they are free to engage in acts that most people find abhorrent (Stratton 1996). Fortunately for the rest of society, such individuals are few in number. They are called **sociopaths**, and the discipline within sociology that studies them is called sociopathy.

Johnny Cash (1932–2003) was the youngest person ever elected to the Country Music Hall of Fame. During his career he sold over 50 million albums. He was famous and well respected for using his music to bring attention to the plight of poor and downtrodden people in society. Here he is shown giving a free concert to inmates at a prison. Cash believed that even prisoners deserved a little fun in their lives and refused to stigmatize them as unworthy individuals.

Social controls ▲ Mechanisms that monitor behavior and sanction the violation of norms.

Internal social controls ▲ Social controls seated within the individual that are learned through socialization.

External social controls ▲ The societal mechanisms external to the individual that prevent deviance.

Sociopaths ▲ People who commit wanton murder or serial killings apparently because they lack any internal social controls.

Todd Marinovich was clearly a gifted athlete, but even before anyone knew that he had innate talent, he was undergoing a training regime like no other player in history. Todd's father, Marv, took over his son's life at birth and began the long, arduous task of making him a professional player. When Todd was an infant in a crib, Marv started him on a daily exercise routine. Marv also encouraged Todd to play with balls and unlike most parents, Marv wanted Todd to crawl rather than walk to better develop the infant's hand-eye coordination. As a result, Baby Todd was doing push-ups and crawling along a balance beam before he could walk. In addition to physical training, Marv strictly controlled the child's diet, allowing him to eat only eggs, fresh fruits, and vegetables. Although Marv permitted small amounts of red meat, he did not allow him to eat processed foods and white sugar. Rather than break his diet, young Todd would take his own sugarless ice cream and carrot sticks to other children's birthday parties. Realizing that he did not know everything about football, Marv brought in professional trainers to help with Todd's development. At one time or another, thirteen specialists coached Todd on the fine points of the game and helped to develop his physical skills. The training regime produced results. As a high school quarterback, Todd set national passing records and maintained good grades. Upon graduation he was besieged with scholarship offers and chose to attend the University of Southern California, his parents' alma mater. Even though Todd immediately led the Trojans to a conference championship and an appearance in the Rose Bowl, his coaches were displeased with his attitude (Looney 1988). They felt he was not trying hard enough and he seemed to lack interest in the team. In his sophomore year, Todd began experimenting with drugs and missing team meetings and classes. Generally unhappy with college life, he dropped out of school to play professional football. He joined the Los Angeles Raiders and quickly became their starting quarterback, signing a three-year contract worth over $2 million. In achieving this position, Todd accomplished a very difficult feat. Only 250 or so rookies are added to the National Football league (NFL) each year, and many never get a chance to start in a game (Leonard 1988). But continuing drug problems ended his NFL career the next season. He next played some professional football in the Canadian Football League and then in the Arena League in 2000 and 2001, but had reoccurring problems with drugs. He spent time in jail for growing marijuana in 1998, and was ordered into a drug treatment program in the same year for violating probation on another drug-related charge. His many ups and downs were reported in over 300 stories in *USA Today,* and many people were fascinated by his repeated downfalls and attempted comebacks (Ruibal 2001).

Marv Marinovich is not the only parent who ever attempted to rear his child along narrow lines of achievement. Many young athletes, for example, experience similar regimented lifestyles (Curry 1993). Their parents are so anxious for them to become star athletes that they willingly stunt their children's growth in other areas. Like Marv Marinovich, they tell their children when to go to bed and when to get up; when and how to work out. Becoming an athlete becomes the whole focus of the child's life, and parents may involve themselves to such an extent that they lose their objectivity. Sport sociologist Jay Coakley (1998) refers to this process as an "identity tunnel," where all other identities are removed but that of being an athlete. Coakley feels that kids may experience "burnout" from sports in their late teens because they grow tired of the discipline and are anxious to experience other activities. To some extent, this is what happened to Todd.

The case of Todd Marinovich reveals an important aspect of deviancy. Many parents feel that it is important that their children turn out to be successes in life, and are willing to go to great length and considerable cost to socialize their children in a fashion that will guarantee their success (Mannon 1990). Despite the best efforts of the parents, however, socialization is unpredictable, complex, and subtle. No parent gets exactly what he or she had in mind no matter how hard he or she tries.

CQ What do you think? Did Todd's father push too hard? ◆ Is there any way a parent can ensure that their child will develop strong internal controls to prevent deviancy?

 Pausing to Think About Deviance and Crime

Deviance addresses the possibility of societal disintegration, for deviants do not abide by shared norms. Crime and criminals exist because a formal authority has declared certain behaviors to be illegal. Social controls are mechanisms for controlling deviance and crime. They include both internal and external social control. Internal social controls are located within the individual and leaned through socialization. External controls rely on societal mechanisms such as the police to prevent deviance. Sociopaths have few internal controls.

CQ Can a society rely purely on internal social control? ◆ Purely on external controls?

Crime Rates

The facts of crime and crime rates in the United States are compelling. In this section we briefly describe some of the major types of crime in the United States and show how the rates of crimes have fluctuated in recent years. We begin with a simple question, How much crime is there? This simple question is surprisingly difficult to answer. The most frequently cited figures come from the Federal Bureau of Investigation (FBI). This agency compiles information gathered from thousands of local police departments and then reports the data to the public. The reports have been published annually since 1930 as the Uniform Crime Report (UCR).

The FBI pays special attention to eight crimes in the UCR. These eight are termed **index crimes**. The crimes that make up the index crimes are homicide, robbery, aggravated assault, forcible rape, burglary, larceny-theft, auto theft, and arson. The first four of these crimes are known as **crimes against the person**, and the second four are **crimes against property**. The use of the index crimes gives the FBI a convenient way of statistically describing the rate of crime in the United States and changes in the rate from year to year. To illustrate, Figures 4.1 and 4.2 summarize trends for the UCR index crimes between 1983 and 2002. Definitions of the Index Crimes are listed in Table 4.1.

The UCR data are useful but have some problems. The problems come from several sources. Although most police departments cooperate with the FBI, a few do not. Human error also plays a role. Since there are thousands of reports to sift through, misprints, misinterpretations, and carelessness creep into the data and render them less than perfect. However, the major reason for inaccuracy in the figures is underreporting by the victims of crime. Only about half of all crimes are reported to the police. People are reluctant to report minor crimes, such as having a backpack or an umbrella stolen. Furthermore, the police often regard minor violations as a time-consuming nuisance and discourage people from reporting them. Even serious crimes can go unreported, particularly if the crime involves a **stigma**, or social marker that brings shame on a person. For example, rape victims sometimes fear being stigmatized and will not contact the police. The stigma is so powerful that they would rather bear their victimization in silence than seek justice under the law.

Given the problems in compiling the data, official UCR statistics should not be regarded as hard facts but as rough estimates. The statistical details of even our most serious crime—murder—are not fully known. For example, 30 years ago, the police solved over 90 percent of all homicides, largely because the murderers personally knew their victims—spouses, lovers, friends, or family members. This is not true today (Shannon 1995; U.S. Federal Bureau of Investigation 2002; see Figure 4.3.)

Sociologists have developed ways to study crimes that are underreported to the police. The National Crime Victimization Survey (NCVS), begun in 1972, is based on interviews conducted with a random sample of American households. People living in the sampled households aged 12 and over are asked about their crime victimization over the past six months. The survey includes six of the eight index crimes, but leaves out arson and homicide. While the NCVS provides information on many crimes that were not reported to the police, it still has its problems. For instance, the people interviewed may still underreport stigmatized crimes, and often they have difficulty applying official definitions to their experiences (Biderman and Lynch 1991; see Table 4.2).

In addition, other crime goes unreported even to the NCVS. Child and spouse abuse have been social issues for many years, but only recently has abuse of the elderly been recognized as a major problem. It came to light during the 1980s, and much more research will be required before a complete picture of the problem can be drawn. Research has shown, however, that some one-half to two-and-one-half million cases of elder abuse occur each year. Possibly, (the data are not perfectly clear)

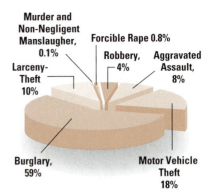

FIGURE 4.1 Types of Crimes Committed

This chart shows the various type of crime tabulated by the Federal Bureau of Investigation. The two most violent and feared crimes—murder and rape—account for about 1 percent of all crimes committed. Most crimes are burglaries.

Index crimes ▲ Eight crimes given special attention in the Uniform Crime Reports published by the Federal Bureau of Investigation.

Crimes against the person ▲ Violent crimes or the threat of violence directed against people.

Crimes against property ▲ Crimes that involve theft or destruction of property belonging to others.

Stigma ▲ A social marker that brings shame on a person.

FIGURE 4.2

NOTE: The FBI reports crime rates per 100,000 persons in the United States. The charts show the rates after they have been standardized for comparison.

SOURCE: U.S. Federal Bureau of Investigation, *Crime in the United States,* 2002.

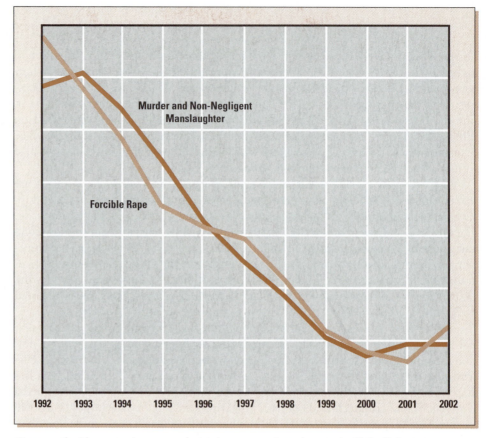

Compared with most crimes, murder and rape occur at a low and still declining rate.

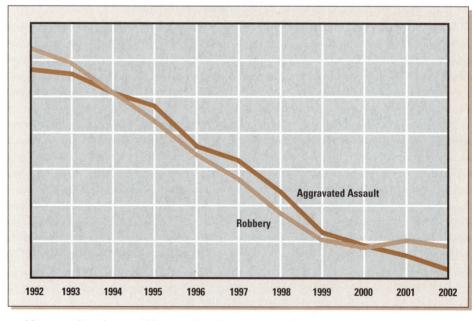

Robbery involves the use of force and so does aggravated assault. These rates are declining.

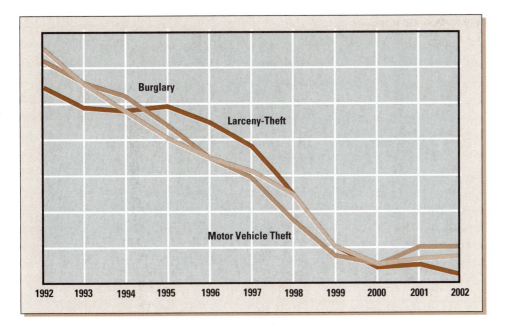

FIGURE 4.2 (*continued*)

The most common crimes involve property, and they have declined the most.

one out of every ten elders living with their families are abused in some way, from outright physical harm to violation of their legal rights. In an effort to begin tracking this form of crime, the National Center on Elder Abuse recently conducted a survey of Adult Protection Services in the United States. Information from 40 states indicated that the most frequently occurring substantiated allegation of maltreatment involved self-neglect (42%), followed by physical abuse (20%), and caregiver neglect/abandonment (13%). Other forms of maltreatment were noted. These included financial exploitation (including stealing), emotional/verbal abuse, and sexual abuse. Women, especially the very old, are the most likely victims of abuse (Teaster 2000).

Most sociologists, even after making due allowances for the inadequacies of the data and the falling rates, believe that the United States is one of the most crime-ridden societies in the world, particularly for violent crime. Rough comparisons show that the homicide rate for the United States is eight to ten times that of Japan and most of the Western European nations (Fairchild and Dammer 2000). Major urban centers such as New York, Chicago, Houston, and Los Angeles have more homicides in a single year than Great Britain and Japan have in a decade. In recent years, the crime rate has decreased (see Figure 4.2). Even though the crime rate has decreased, it is still at a high level. Although it is difficult to measure with statistics, it also appears that the viciousness of crime has also escalated. For instance, so many children have been killed by being thrown from the windows of a high-rise apartment building in Chicago that authorities have placed bars on the windows (LeBlanc 1995).

With such a high crime rate, many people are personally affected by crime or know of someone who has been victimized. Victims are more likely to be found in neighborhoods with high crime rates, and in the United States, African Americans are likely to live in such neighborhoods. To illustrate, in the case of homicide, African Americans are almost six times more likely to die from that crime as white Americans (Murphy 2000; see the Diversity box, Who Are the Victims of Crime?). As for why crime rates are high in African American communities, experts cite several reasons. Some believe that black youth are more likely to turn to crime

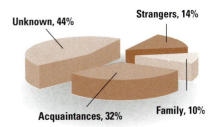

FIGURE 4.3

Most murders occur between family, friends and acquaintances. Murder between strangers is relatively uncommon (14 percent). However, in most cases (44 percent) the police know nothing about the relationship between murderers and their victims.

Definitions of the Index Crimes

CRIME	DEFINITION
Arson	To unlawfully and intentionally damage or attempt to damage any real or personal property by fire or incendiary device.
Aggravated Assault	An unlawful attack by one person upon another wherein the offender uses a weapon or displays it in a threatening manner, or the victim suffers obvious severe or aggravated bodily injury involving apparent broken bones, loss of teeth, possible internal injury, severe laceration, or loss of consciousness. Note: Aggravated Assault also includes assault with disease (as in cases when the offender is aware that he/she is infected with a deadly disease and deliberately attempts to inflict the disease by biting, spitting, etc.). This usually includes offenses such as Pointing and Presenting a Firearm, Brandishing a Firearm, etc. A severe laceration is one that should receive medical attention. A loss of consciousness must be the direct result of force inflicted on the victim by the offender.
Burglary	The unlawful entry into a building or other structure with the intent to commit a felony or a theft.
Murder and Nonnegligent Manslaughter	The willful (nonnegligent) killing of one human being by another.
Larceny/Theft	The unlawful taking, carrying, leading, or riding away of property from the possession or constructive possession of another person.
Motor Vehicle Theft	The theft of a motor vehicle.
Robbery	The taking or attempting to take anything of value under confrontational circumstances from the control, custody, or care of another person by force or threat of force or violence and/or by putting the victim in fear of immediate harm.
Forcible Rape	The carnal knowledge of a person, forcibly and/or against that person's will or not forcibly or against the person's will in instances where the victim is incapable of giving consent because of his/her temporary or permanent mental or physical incapacity.

because of the lack of opportunities in their communities, and, with a high poverty rate within the black family, no one should be surprised at that outcome (Chapter 7). Others believe that white police may be prejudiced, and more likely to arrest black people (Covington 1995). Others point to family structure, and note that two-thirds of non-Hispanic black children are born to single mothers, which may mean less adult supervision for the children (U.S. Bureau of the Census 2003;

TABLE 4.2

Comparison of Crime Rates as Reported by the UCR and the NCVS in 2001

	UCR	NCVS
Forcible Rape	31.8	40.0
Robbery	148.5	190.0
Aggravated Assault	318.6	530.0
Larceny Theft	2,485.7	12,480.0

NOTE: Rates are per 100,000 people.

SOURCE: U.S. Federal Bureau of Investigation, *Crime in the United States,* 2002; U.S. Department of Justice, 2001.

Chapter 11). Lastly, the United States has become so individualistic that communities have difficulties enforcing their laws. Acts of violence seem to have become routine, especially in poor urban areas with abundant drugs and firearms (Derber 2004; Chapter 15).

A violent crime that many people find particularly loathsome is the **hate crime**. These are crimes motivated by prejudice or other biases against a person. Race is typically the most common bias, but these crimes are also based on religion, sexual orientation, ethnic ancestry, even physical disability (see Figure 4.4). Hate crimes are recorded by the federal government, and thousands occur each year. Supporters of hate crime legislation are gratified that the federal government and 43 states have increased penalties for crimes motivated by hate, but there is controversy on this issue. Some argue that increasing penalties for a hate crime is punishing people for politically incorrect attitudes. They do not believe it is wise to allow the government to criminalize bigotry, because this might encourage state and federal authorities to control the minds of citizens (Greenhouse 1993).

In contrast, **organized crime** is that conducted by businesses supplying illegal goods or services and that routinely use corruption and violence to gain their ends. Organized crime typically moves in where there is strong and sustained demand for illegal goods or service. For instance, during Prohibition in the United States (1920–1933), many organized crime syndicates thrived by supplying alcohol to local and national markets. More recently, harsh drug laws have created many opportunities for

STUDY TIP

Devise visual icons for the different types of crimes, including the eight index crimes. Make sure these icons are easy to draw, and use them to identify different crimes in your notes.

Hate crime ▲ A crime motivated by racial prejudice or other biases against a person or a person's property.

Organized crime ▲ Crime conducted by businesses supplying illegal goods or services and that routinely use corruption and violence to gain their ends.

Diversity ●■▲ Who Are the Victims of Crime?

Do you think the following statements are true or false?

T or F   Younger people are more likely than older people to be victims of violent crime.

T or F   People aged 65 and older are more likely than other age groups to be victims of property crime.

T or F   Blacks are more likely to be victims of violent crime and property crime than are people of other races.

T or F   Males are more likely to be the victim of violent crime than are females.

T or F   People who had an annual household income under $50,000 in 2002 were more likely to be the victim of rape/sexual assault.

T or F   People who have never married are more likely to be the victim of violent crime than are people who are married, widowed, or divorced.

NOTE: All of these statements are true.

SOURCE: U.S. Department of Justice: Bureau of Justice Statistics. 2003. Victim Characteristics. Retrieved online on December 9, 2003 at <http://www.ojp.sdoj. gov/bjs/cvict_v.htm>.

FIGURE 4.4

The Federal Bureau of Investigation attempts to tabulate so-called hate crimes, but many police jurisdictions do not keep track of them. Of the hate crimes known to the FBI, half were motivated by race.

SOURCE: U.S. Federal Bureau of Investigation, *Crime in the United States,* 2002.

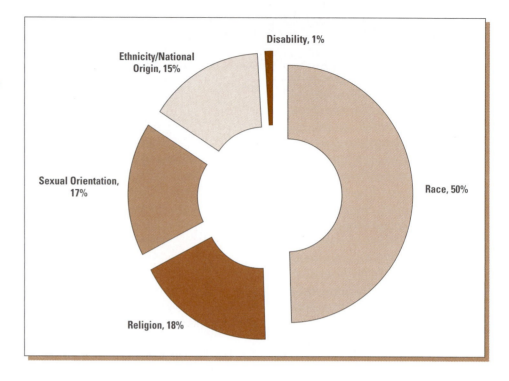

Disability, 1%

Ethnicity/National Origin, 15%

Sexual Orientation, 17%

Religion, 18%

Race, 50%

organized crime, and efforts to control illegal immigration has created a market for false identification papers in the United States (Valdez, 1997).

Organized crime may spread across national boundaries easily. With the opening of new markets in Eastern Europe, organized crime has become an important influence. Drug and arms trafficking frequently involve the coordination of many people located in different countries, and a network of organizations. These networks are expanding to include other illicit goods and service, such as female and child prostitution, stolen works of art, illegal emigration from many areas of the world, and selling of fraudulent documents (Reichel 2002). The United Nations tries to bring attention to these activities through research publications, because it believes that international organized crime can undermine the democratic process in developing countries through bribing and corruption of public officials. One such publication describes the activities of 40 organized crime groups in 16 countries (United Nations 2002). Each group is profiled based on a survey conducted by the United Nations with correspondents in the country (see the World Today box, International Organized Crime).

This photograph shows some of the people who attended a Ku Klux Klan and neo-Nazi rally in Boca Ratan, Florida. Children attending such events are apt to learn white-supremacist views from their parents. As differential association theory points out, deviancy is often learned through interaction with others.

In this section we introduced a variety of surveys used to keep track of crime. These included the Uniform Crime Reports gathered by the Federal Bureau of Investigation from police departments on the major index crimes, including both personal or violent crimes, and property crimes. We also provided some information on the National Crime Victimization Survey, a survey of people aged 12 and over about their own experiences with crime. Statewide data on elder abuse is obtained by Adult Protection Services, data on hate crimes is obtained by the federal government, and the United Nations conducts surveys designed to track international organized crime.

CQ What is your impression of crime in the United States after considering these different sources of data? ◆ Is crime a bigger problem than you thought, about the same as you thought, or less of a problem than you thought?

Explanations for Deviance and Crime

Deviance is one of the most intriguing topics in sociology, partly because it is easier to understand why people conform than why they deviate. We will now discuss several explanations for deviance and crime. We present these explanations in four categories, functionalist, symbolic interactionist, conflict, and demographic.

Functionalist Explanations

Émile Durkheim, introduced in Chapter 1, thought that some deviance is functional for society in that it helps to clarify moral boundaries. The deviant provides an opportunity to examine what is unacceptable, and thereby assists people in knowing right from wrong. For instance, if everyone cheated on their income taxes, soon the government would be bankrupt. The Internal Revenue Service, by targeting some cases of taxpayer fraud, helps to remind people that there are limits to what may be deducted. Occasionally, deviance affirms cultural values in that the community rejoices when a criminal is brought to justice. Deviance can also be a force for social change. Many fashions began as statements of a deviant identity, yet were eventually absorbed by the mainstream culture. For instance, the drug culture of the 1970s produced tie-dyed shirts and rock and roll music that insulted the establishment. Today, these items seem almost quaint.

Strain Theory Durkheim was particularly concerned about anomie, a condition in which norms and values are weak, in serious conflict, or absent. During the 1960s, Robert Merton built upon Durkheim's insights and offered a formal theory of deviance based on the concepts of structural strain and anomie. This theory is called *strain theory*.

Merton argued that in an anomic, changing situation, a structural strain develops between the culturally prescribed goals of the social system and the socially approved means of attaining the goals. According to Merton, this structural strain produces a large amount of deviance. Merton said that individuals respond to the strain in one of five ways. Only the first way is not deviant; the rest are deviant.

1. *Conformity* A conformist accepts both the conventional goals of society and the conventional means to obtain them. For instance, conformists who aspire to prestige through sports success will spend many years practicing and improving their skills until they are able to perform and succeed at the highest levels.

2. *Innovation* An innovator accepts the goals of society but rejects the socially approved means and thus opts for deviance to attain those goals. Members of organized crime are considered innovators because they accept society's goal of materialistic

World Today ● ■ ▲

Organized Crime in the World

The United Nations has recently completed a study of 40 organized crime groups in 16 countries. They examined the activities, customs, and organization of these groups. One particular group, "The Cock Group," operates mainly in Western Lithuania and is made up of Lithuanian and Russian men.

Organized crime groups are often involved in both legitimate and illegitimate activities and may be formed in response to historical and social changes. This is the case with The Cock Group that formed as state property in Lithuania was being privatized. This group has established a large influence over these economic institutions as well as over public enterprises such as customs, police, and law enforcement through violence and intimidation. They are engaged in such crimes as counterfeiting, forgery, bank fraud, armed robbery, trafficking in women and children for the sex industry, smuggling of firearms, and illegal gambling schemes.

The majority of members of The Cock Group are former prison inmates. A single leader is in charge, and he has two deputies who oversee smuggling and drug trafficking. Another group of members are responsible for the leader's personal protection. The UN refers to this as a standard hierarchy, a formation that is used by organized criminals all over the world to recruit and organize group members.

CQ What sociological explanations would you use to explain the formation of this group?

SOURCE: United Nations Office on Drugs and Crime. 2002. Global Programme Against Transnational Organized Crime: Results of a Pilot Survey of Forty Selected Organized Criminal Groups in Sixteen Countries. Retrieved online on December 10, 2003 at <http://www.unodc.org/pdf/crime/publications/Pilot_survey.pdf>.

success, but instead of following the legitimate means to acquire wealth, they substitute deviant means such as drug dealing.

3. **Ritualism**   A ritualist has no interest in the conventional goals of society, yet goes through the motions by following the prescribed rules and behaviors. By rejecting the conventional goals, the ritualist is a deviant. Merton's example was of a cautious bureaucrat who compulsively follows all the regulations and forgets the goals that the regulations were meant to achieve.

4. **Retreatism**   A retreatist rejects both the means and the goals of society but does not replace them with anything that the society regards as worthwhile. Some retreatists find solace in chemical dependencies, whereas others might live as hermits in an isolated part of the country.

5. **Rebellion**   The rebel rejects the goals and means of society and replaces them with new goals and means. A rebel might reject education as a means of obtaining wealth and prestige, for example, and substitute meditation to achieve inner peace and enlightenment.

Over the years, many sociologists have found Merton's logic compelling, and strain theory has been a widely cited explanation for deviance (Vowell and May 2000). Its major strength lies in where it places the origins of deviance. According to Merton, deviance begins in the broader social setting, in a culture that does not allow everyone equal access to the legitimate means of acquiring legitimate ends. Ironically, the major weakness of strain theory also concerns means and ends. It assumes that the means and ends provided by society are legitimate and ignores the broader issue of who has the power to define goals and means as legitimate. Are rebels, innovators, ritualists, and retreatists really deviant, or are they simply deviant in the eyes of some powerful group? Certainly, most of these people view themselves as legitimate and regard the broader society as the deviant party because it limits their opportunity for success.

Symbolic Interactionist Explanations

There are several explanations for deviance and crime that involve elements of symbolic interaction. The first of these is social bond theory.

Social Bond Theory   This theory sometimes is called "social control theory," but because that term also refers to "deterrence theory," we use the term "social bond theory." According to social bond theory, the key to understanding deviance is not to focus on why people commit deviant acts but rather to understand why people conform to conventional norms, values, and laws. Instead of asking "Why do people do it?" social bond theorists ask, "Why don't they do it?" (Bartollas and Dinitz 1989:205). The answer may be found in the social bonds that connect individuals to their family, friends, community, and society. The important social bonds are as follows (Hirschi 1969):

Interpersonal Attachment–Involvement   When people have strong relationships with their families, with community-based organizations such as the Chamber of Commerce, and with other legitimate communal structures, they tend to accept the prevailing norms, values, and laws. In contrast, when people are unattached and uninvolved, they are free to engage in whatever behaviors they choose, and many of their choices will be deviant.

Commitment-Belief   People who are strongly committed to nondeviant activities, such as at work or in church, tend not be deviant. This tendency is further strengthened if they also believe in the conventional morality and in the justice of the prevailing laws.

To illustrate how social bonds affect deviance, consider the typical readers of this book—college students. To begin with, they are attached to their schools, and thereby to the broader and accepted institution of education. Most college students are involved in college life and committed to earning a degree and entering a career.

They also believe that the conventional morality is, for the most part, a good thing. In other words, most college students have established social bonds with the individuals, groups, and institutions of the broader, conventional society; and these bonds prevent them from entering a life of deviance.

Research has generally supported social bond theory, making it a very promising line of inquiry and explanation. Nevertheless, the theory does have weaknesses. It applies best to deviance that is regarded as less serious, such as vandalism and graffiti writing. It does not do a very good job of explaining murder and other very serious crimes. In addition, the theory does not lay out the precise steps involved in creating and breaking social bonds. Why do some people develop strong bonds, whereas others do not? This question remains unanswered.

Cultural Transmission and Differential Association　Cultural transmission theory claims that deviance is learned through the same fundamental processes as conformity: that is, through socialization. Accordingly, a child reared by thieves in a community of thieves will become a thief; and furthermore, the child will internalize the norms of thievery and come to like stealing and to despise working.

The empirical foundation for cultural transmission theory begins with the early research of Clifford Shaw and his associates (1929). They found that even though several different ethnic groups had inhabited certain Chicago neighborhoods over a period of time, the crime rates in those neighborhoods remained high. This persistence, they concluded, meant that deviance had become a part of the neighborhood's local culture. As different people moved into the area, new arrivals learned the culture of deviance from older residents. After the new residents had been there for a time, they became the established group and then passed on the culture of deviance to the next batch of new arrivals.

Although Shaw and McKay established the framework for understanding deviance as a normal response to a deviant cultural setting, their work left several loose ends. In particular, cultural transmission theory simply assumed that socialization would take place. The work of Edwin Sutherland helped to fill in this assumption. He suggested the concept of *differential association*: people learn conformity or deviance from the people with whom they associate (Heimer and Matsueda 1994; Sutherland and Cressey 1978).

Viewed simplistically, differential association is nothing more than a fancy restatement of the saying "birds of a feather flock together." That is, peers are a strong influence, especially over young people who have not yet developed a firm sense of self. Sutherland had more in mind than deviant peers, however, and went on to specify how socialization into deviant behavior takes place. He outlined four points, as follows:

1. Like behavior in general, deviant behavior is learned through interaction with others, but the most influential learning comes from small, intimate groups.

2. Learning deviant behavior consists of acquiring techniques, motives, drives, and attitudes appropriate for such behavior.

3. An individual learns "definitions" (mind-sets or attitudes) that are favorable or unfavorable to prevailing norms. People then become deviant when they learn to accept more unfavorable definitions than favorable definitions.

4. The frequency, length, and intensity of a person's associations determine the impact of associations on the person. Infrequent contacts of limited duration will have less impact than frequent, intense contact (Sutherland and Cressey 1978:80–83).

Cultural transmission theory and differential association have been frequently used to explain urban youth gangs. Youths are attracted to gangs, according to these theories, because the gang provides social support, recreational opportunities, group identity, and physical protection. They may also provide economic opportunities not available in the legitimate community. In exchange, gang members must conform to the gang's culture, which includes petty deviance, violence, and crime. The social benefits from gang membership are a powerful attraction to many youths, and the gang is beginning to replace the family and the school as the most significant source of adolescent socialization, particularly in neighborhoods in which broken homes and single-parent households predominate and children have few positive adult role models (Moore 1991; Howell 1999).

The theories of cultural transmission and differential association provide a basis for understanding why attempts to resocialize or rehabilitate deviants so often fail. Releasing convicts back into their former community places them in the cultural and social networks that taught them crime in the first place. With nothing else changed, the processes of cultural transmission and differential association will quickly erase the impact of any rehabilitation efforts, and life will revert to old, deviant ways.

Although cultural transmission and differential association are insightful explanations, they fail to address two major issues. First, most youths who encounter deviant cultures do not become deviant, and most people living in high-crime areas are not criminals. Second, the theories explain how deviance is transmitted, but they do not address the more basic question of why a given culture is defined as deviant.

Labeling Theory   To some extent, the omissions of cultural transmission and differential association theory are taken up by labeling theory. **Labeling** is the process through which a definition is attached to an individual. The theory of labeling examines how labels are applied, the consequences of the label for the individual, and the power of some people to attach labels to others.

According to labeling theorists, deviance resides in the reactions of other people to a behavior. The English language has plenty of labels: con, queer, dope fiend, nut, crazy, slut, weirdo, cuckoo, grunge, nerd, and many others. These words make convenient labels that, if attached to you by other people, define you as that particular kind of person (Link and Cullen 1990). Thus, labeling is not just the process of naming or identifying deviance; instead, labeling is the process that actually creates deviance.

How do labels create deviance? The answer is through the narrowing of options and the internalization of a definition supported by significant others. The process is fairly straightforward. Once you are labeled, other people treat you as a deviant. They are suspicious of you; they do not want to be around you; and they will not help you. Being constantly subjected to such treatment, you may soon define yourself in terms of the label and thus behave in deviant ways. Eventually, feeling isolated, you might even seek the company of other deviants, who will then reinforce your perception of yourself as a deviant, and the prophecy of the label will have fulfilled itself (Heimer and Matsueda 1994; Lemert et al. 2000).

Soon after labeling theory appeared, many sociologists quickly pointed out that power is an important factor in the process. Invariably, they said, it is people with status and power, such as physicians, lawyers, and clergy—most of whom are white males—who have the power to label other people as deviant. For that reason, lower-class nonwhite offenders may be defined as more serious threats to the community than middle-class white offenders. And issues pertaining to women will be trivialized, whereas issues pertaining to men will be taken seriously.

Labeling theory provides a plausible explanation for how deviance can be created through social interaction. The theory, nevertheless, has gaps. It fails to account for crimes of passion that suddenly erupt without time for labeling to occur, and it ignores the possibility that some people self-consciously choose to engage in deviance on their own. Finally, the application of a label might not be a self-fulfilling prophecy for everyone. Some people are so threatened by a label, or by the mere threat of being labeled, that they abruptly change their behavior. Rather than causing deviance, in these instances, labeling causes conformity.

Conflict Theory

Conflict theorists stress that that laws of any society reflect the interest of the powerful. Karl Marx (Chapter 1) argued that law, as do the other major social institutions of

Labeling ▲ The process by which a definition is attached to an individual.

society, supports the interests of the rich and that those who threaten the wealthy are defined as outlaws, radicals, and political outsiders. Quinney (1977) notes that most people do not reflect enough upon whether the laws are inherently unfair to poorer people and accept the idea that laws are applied equally. For instance, who is likely to be charged with vagrancy, a rich person or a poor person? Conflict theorists are also likely to note that most everyday concepts of deviants are aimed at the relatively powerless members of society. The typical criminal in prison is likely to have come from an impoverished background. Moreover, when someone who is powerful breaks the law and is challenged by the legal system, they can afford the full use of the many safeguards provided by the system. A classic case of this was the "dream team" of expensive lawyers hired by O.J. Simpson to defend him against charges of murder of his former wife and an acquaintance of hers on June 12, 1994 (Bugliosi, 1996, Chapter 7). Poorer defendants must rely on court-appointed defense attorneys who may be more anxious to settle a case and move on. Conflict theorists also point out the social consequences of inequalities in our society. For instance, Eitzen and Zinn (2003) write that the United States leads the world in spending for advanced military technology, military exports, gross domestic product, number of millionaires and billionaires, but is last in the world in protecting children from gun violence.

Illegal drugs are seen as a threat to society by the federal government, and the official policy is to punish those who use drugs and those who provide them unlawfully. But conflict theorists point out that while whites are more likely to use drugs, African Americans are more likely to be imprisoned for drug offenses. Federal authorities have concentrated their efforts on enforcement of crack cocaine laws in minority neighborhoods—as a result, about 96% of the defendants in crack cases are nonwhite. Moreover, there is a tendency for the courts to administer medical treatments for white drug users, while black users face the brunt of the criminal justice system. All in all, conflict theorist see the punishments dealt out on drugs as having a strong race and class bias (Eitzen and Zinn, 2003; see also Chapters 6 and 7).

Conflict theorists are quick to point out that while common street crime appears frequently on the front pages of newspaper, deviance that takes place among organizations is reported less frequently. This is called **corporate** or **white-collar crime** and it costs the United States billions of dollars. Corporate crime is the illegal actions of a corporation or people acting on behalf of a corporation, while white collar refers to crime committed by people of high social status in the course of their occupation. To illustrate, in 2002, 570 corporations were accused of corporate fraud. Many of the practices uncovered in the subsequent investigations revealed a desire for higher earnings in the stock markets and personal greed on the part of managers. Executives at Enron, WorldCom, Quest, Global Crossings, Inclone, Kmart, Adelphi, Tyco, Cendant, and Martha Stewart Enterprises were indicted for fraud, insider dealing, or similar charges. Even worse, employees at Arthur Andersen, one of the largest accounting firms in the United States, helped to shred tons of documents and hundreds of computer files that might have provided evidence on the Enron fraud. The Justice Department brought criminal charges against Arthur Andersen. Its creditability ruined, Arthur Andersen was forced into bankruptcy, and thousands of innocent people who worked for the company lost their jobs. In spite of these cases and other involving massive fraud, important politicians in Washington, D.C. did not call for a "War on White Collar Crime," but instead said that the problem was just a case of a few bad apples. Politicians protect the corporate world, conflict theorists claim, because of the many large contributions corporations make to political campaigns (Derber 2004; Chapter 10; see also Table 4.3, "Comparison of Three Theoretical Perspectives on Deviance and Crime").

Demographics

Although we discuss demography later in the text, two demographic characteristics are relevant to understanding crime and deviance. The first characteristic is age. **Aging-out** is a term used by criminologists and sociologists to refer to the fact that

This photograph shows a young man shoplifting CDs. Such crimes raise the cost of doing business to stores, and stores pass these costs on to consumers. Even more costly are the unseen "white collar" crimes that cost consumers billions of dollars.

123 **STUDY TIP**

Outline the essential characteristics of the four categories of explanation for crime—functionalist, symbolic interactionist, conflict, and demographic—and include the stated weaknesses. Then, focus your analysis on the weaknesses. Which weaknesses do you think are more significant, and why? Based on your opinion, which theory do you find to be the strongest?

Corporate crime ▲ Illegal actions of a corporation or people acting on behalf of a corporation.

White-collar crime ▲ Crime committed by people of high social status in the course of their occupation.

Aging out ▲ Refers to the fact that most crime declines sharply after people reach their mid-thirties.

TABLE 4.3

Comparison of Three Theoretical Perspectives on Deviance and Crime		
PERSPECTIVE	**VIEW OF DEVIANCE**	**KEY CONCEPTS AND THEORY**
Functionalism	Sees deviance as a threat to the social system, reactions to deviance help define and strengthen the moral foundation of society	Anomie Strain theory
Conflict Theory	Sees laws as reflecting interests of the wealthy and punishments unfairly influenced by race and class	White-collar crime Corporate crime Power and inequality
Symbolic Interaction	Sees deviance as socially constructed by everyday encounters between people	Labeling theory Cultural transmission Differential association Social bonds

most crime declines sharply after people reach their mid-thirties. To illustrate, about half of the people arrested for violent crime and about two-thirds of the people arrested for property crime are aged 16 through 25. Because this age group accounts for so much crime, the crime rate rises or falls as the proportion of people in this age category rises or falls. However, as we discuss in Chapter 15, the American population is aging, and the crime-prone age category is shrinking.

Gender is the second demographic characteristic relevant to crime and deviance. Men constitute about 90 percent of people arrested for violent crimes and about 75 percent of people arrested for property crimes (U.S. Federal Bureau of Investigation 1999). Clearly, crime is mostly a male activity. Why are men, especially young men, so prone to crime? Although sociologists have not yet arrived at a conclusive answer to this question, part of the answer seems to lie in the intersections of race, class, and gender socialization (see Chapter 8). Frequently, men are taught to be tough, unemotional, knowledgeable about violence, and not shy about using it. These traits are especially emphasized among the less educated and less wealthy segments of American society. Thus, most muggings, armed robberies, and murders are committed by uneducated men rather than by women or by highly educated men. As to why crime is a youth activity, sociologists suspect that the answer concerns the nature of criminal activity and the increasing neglect of children (see Chapter 11). Many youthful offenders have been brought up in "no-parent homes." Without proper supervision and with few elders around to temper their behavior, youth gangs may develop a culture of extreme violence (Shakur 1993). Moreover, although it is not often mentioned, violent and dangerous crime is stressful work. The threat of being caught induces some stress, and the danger of being wounded, shot, or killed induces even more. Like anyone else, criminals can tolerate only so much stress. Over time, they begin to "burn out" and eventually they give up crime for other activities. Thus, as youthful criminals age, they become less of a menace to society.

● ■ ▲ **Pausing to Think** About Explanations for Deviance and Crime

The functionalist perspective is represented by strain theory, which places the origins of deviance in the broader social setting and the way it provides or denies people access to the culturally approved goals and means. Symbolic interactionist theory concerns social psychological motivations for deviance and crime, and emphasizes such processes as

STUDY TIP

Before you meet in a group of three, have each group member focus on a type of criminal justice system—common law, civil law, and religious law. Then gather and start with the assumption that a person has been arrested and charged with a crime. Each person then describes in detail what would happen under his or her assigned system. Talk further about the pros and cons of each system, including whether some systems might work better for particular crimes or particular societies.

social bonding, cultural transmission, differential association, and labeling. Conflict theory stresses the fact that the laws are generally written by and for the wealthy, and that white-collar crime causes great economic losses to society. The demographic perspective stresses age and gender.

 Do these different perspectives compete with each other or do they actually explain different aspects of deviancy and crime?

The Criminal Justice System

The social system of police, courts, and prison officials that responds to violations of the law is known as the **criminal justice system**. Criminal justice systems vary, and we discuss three types that are based on common laws traditions, civil law traditions, and religious law traditions. The United States follows the English **common law** tradition. Here the defendant is presumed innocent until proven guilty, and evidence is presented following the **adversarial principle**: a legal tradition where guilt or innocence is determined by a contest between the prosecution and the defender. Legal principles are based on customs some of which may be centuries old. When making a ruling, a judge relies on rulings made by other judges on similar cases in the past.

In contrast, many societies follow a **civil law** tradition. Here, the law or code is written down and imposed on society by a ruler, legislature, or judicial panel. The code Napoleon, drawn up in France in 1804, serves as a source of civil law for most European nations, and it, in turn, was based upon ancient Roman law (Reichel 2002). The role of the judge in this case is to establish the truth, and the judge may insist that considerable effort is made to gather evidence before charges are brought. It is the judge who calls and questions the witnesses. **Religious law** is a third major type of legal system, and it is common in many communal and transitional societies. Here the source of the law is believed to be divine will. The legal system of Iran, for instance, is based on sacred writings in the Qur'an (Chapter 13). Persons who commit serious

Criminal justice system ▲ The social system of police, courts, and prisons officials that responds to violations of the law.

Common law ▲ Law that is developed over time by the accumulation of many cases.

Adversarial principle ▲ A legal tradition where guilt or innocence is determined by a contest between the prosecution and the defense.

Civil law ▲ Law that is imposed on society from above by civil authority.

Religious law ▲ Law that is believed to stem from divine authority.

"Not guilty."

This photograph shows an attorney questioning a witness during a civil trial in Texas. It captures the essence of the adversarial system.

offenses may face mandatory penalties that include amputation of the hands and stoning to death. Even so, the Qur'an also urges forgiveness, and offenders may be set free if they provide restitution to those victimized by their crimes (Reichel 2002). Judges in this type of system seek to interpret general religious principles to specific situations. Iranian officials sometimes assert that divine law overrides international law and view some western standards of human rights as undesirable and possibly corrupting to Iranian society (Entessar 1988).

The Police

The United States has an extremely decentralized police force as compared with other societies. In fact, with as many as 17,000 state and local law enforcement agencies the United States has more separate police forces than any other country in the world (Maguire et al. 1998). The reasons for the decentralization are the historical traditions that state and federal governments share power, and that the power for policing is vested primarily at the local level. The U.S. Constitution mentions only two federal crimes—counterfeiting and treason—and does not provide for a national police force to enforce federal laws (Johnson 1981). As federal and state bureaucracies grow in number and take on additional tasks, however, they also assume more law enforcement responsibilities. Even so, these responsibilities tend to be narrowly defined as enforcement of only those laws relevant to the jurisdiction of the department in question. For example, the U.S. Department of Agriculture now employs agents that enforce legislation concerning food stamps while the Federal Bureau of Investigation (FBI) investigates crimes falling under the jurisdiction of the Department of Justice. These cases include robbery of federally insured banks, interstate racketeering, transporting stolen property across state lines, and so forth (Reichel 2002). With an increased concern with international terrorism, the United States is attempting to better coordinate its many policing functions through the new Department of Homeland Security, created in 2002. The department's mission is to protect the American homeland by coordinating state and local governments and the resources they have at hand.

The public sees police as central to law and order, and hiring more police is almost always a politically popular anticrime measure. Even so, in 2001 the United States had about 660,000 full-time police—not very many considering the population at that time was over 280 million (Macionis 2004). With so few police per capita, many police departments emphasize *community policing*, a model that is based on people in

Sociology Online
www

We suggest that you begin your exploration of the Web destinations with the official site of the Federal Bureau of Investigation (FBI). You may locate this site by searching for the FBI or the Federal Bureau of Investigation.

You know that you have arrived at the correct homepage when the graphic for the FBI shield appears on the screen. From the menu of choices, select Uniform Crime Reports. Read through the report, and then answer the following questions:

Was the rate of violent crime in the nation higher or lower than in the previous year?

Has the rate of violent crime in the nation's largest cities increased or decreased from the previous year?

Examine the rates for geographical regions. Which region shows the greatest percentage change from a year ago?

Now locate a city near your college or university. Does it show a higher or lower percentage change than the rate for the region it is in?

After you have answered these questions, go back to the menu and explore other places that interest you within the FBI site. For example, you might wonder about what major investigations are under way and how many of those involve white-collar or organizational crime.

CQ Now that you know where to find many of the official statistics on crime, what research questions come to mind? ◆ What assertions about crime could you investigate with this information?

the community exercising informal social control in their neighborhoods. Under this approach, police serve as a backup to the community's own internal control mechanism (Brown 1990; Wilson and Kelling 1982).

While the image of the police on television is dramatic, much of the actual routine of police work consists of such everyday activities as directing traffic, controlling crowds, dealing with the intoxicated and other public nuisances, and filling out paperwork. Only 20% of police time is actually spent in crime control (Siegel 2000). Even so, police work is stressful, and police officers typically have high rates of marital violence and divorce, as well as suicide and alcoholism (Wilson 1983).

Much attention has been directed to the question of how police decide which situations warrant their attention. One study of police behavior in five cities found six factors that influence decisions (Smith and Visher 1981).

1. The more serious the situation, the more likely they are to make an arrest.

2. Police take into account the victim's wishes in deciding whether to make an arrest.

3. The odds of arrest go up the more uncooperative a suspect is.

4. Police are more likely to take into custody someone they have arrested before, presumably because this suggests guilt.

5. The presence of observers prompts police to take stronger control of a situation, if only to move the encounter from the streets (the suspect's turf) to the police department (where the officers have the edge).

6. Police are more likely to arrest people of color, perceiving people of African or Latino descent as more dangerous or more likely to be guilty.

The Courts

Through much of its history, the United States relied on private citizens to press charges against offenders. However, in 1874 the state of Pennsylvania began the practice of employing public prosecutors as officers of the state. Now public prosecutors have significant discretion in deciding what the charges will be in a case, and whether a case will be brought to trial or handled in some other way. The public prosecutors office is, like the police, an independent law enforcement agency. Because of the latitude

This photograph is a scene from the television series, The Shield. Television police shows are popular adult entertainment. A person watching these shows will get the impression that police work involves constant violence. Fortunately, that is not true. Police file paperwork more often that they fire bullets.

CQ *Do you watch a lot of police shows on television? ◆ If so, have those shows affected your views of the police?*

the public prosecutor has in deciding how to handle a case, he or she is thought to be one of the most influential persons in the community in terms of the power he or she has over the lives of the citizens.

The functions of the courts are to determine guilt or innocence. However, not all cases have the same probability of being brought to trial. Friedman and Percival (1981) indicate that there are four fundamentally different types of crimes as far as the courts are concerned, and each of these is treated somewhat differently.

Celebrated Cases. These cases are prosecuted in a fully adversial fashion. Sometimes the prosecutors wish to make an example of a particular case, and bring it to trial to create publicity. To illustrate, in 2003 Martha Stewart was prosecuted on several charges steming from insider trading for a relatively minor amount while others on Wall Street escaped prosecution.

Serious Felonies. These cases are also handled adversarially, though somewhat less so than the celebrated cases. Crimes such as murder, forcible rape, and burglary are typically brought to trial, especially if they were crimes committed by strangers to the victims.

Minor Felonies or Misdemeanors. Crimes like simple assault, theft, or vandalism, especially when the victim knows the perpetuator, are frequently resolved without the expense of a trial. The judge, prosecutor, and defense attorney work together rather than as adversaries. Their goal is to ensure that defendants, who are in practice assumed to be guilty, receive a sentence similar to the sentences given to similar defendants.

The primary means by which these agreements are reached is the **plea bargain.** Plea bargaining is a system by which defendants plead guilty to a lesser charge rather than go to formal trial (Schulhofer 1984). There is little doubt that if it were not for plea bargains, the American court system would become overloaded. But it is also apparent that innocent defendants have sometimes been pressured to accept a plea bargain.

Punishment and Corrections

Prisons have several functions. Some see confinement in prison as a form of **retribution,** an act of vengeance by which society inflicts on the offender suffering comparable to that caused by the offense. Some hope that the mere threat of imprisonment will deter people from committing crimes. **Deterrence** is the formal term for the use of punishment to discourage crime, and many people favor the death penalty for its possible deterrence effects (see the What Do You Think? box, Of Crimes and Punishment). Another primary purpose of prisons is **incapacitation.** This concept refers keeping the most dangerous criminals locked away where they cannot hurt innocent people. Another function is **rehabilitation**—the use of education and other programs to reform offenders to prevent future offenses. Here the effort is to resocialize criminals so that their behavior is modified.

These different functions are seldom stressed to the same extent during any one historical period. In the period following the Civil War, for instance, the popular idea was to have criminals work, partly as a form of retribution. In the South, prisoners were forced to provide labor in agriculture, mining, on railroads, and to cut timber. Later in the nineteenth century, many prison officials believed that a greater emphasis should be placed on education, and inmates were provided more opportunities for education in the hopes that they would reform themselves and reintegrate into society after their release. In some cases, rehabilitation did make more sense, particularly for first-time or youthful offenders. But in other cases, people convicted of crimes commit subsequent offenses when released, a serious problem known as **criminal recidivism.**

Plea bargaining ▲ A commonly used procedure whereby defendants agree to plead guilty to a lesser charge rather than to proceed to a formal trial.

Retribution ▲ An act of vengeance by which society inflicts on the offender suffering comparable to that caused by the offense.

Deterrence ▲ The use of punishment to discourage crime.

Incapacitation ▲ Refers to keeping the most dangerous criminals locked away.

Rehabilitation ▲ The use of education and other programs to reform offenders to prevent future offenses.

Criminal recidivism ▲ When people convicted of crimes commit subsequent offenses.

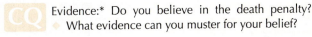

All societies have crime of some kind, and therefore all societies must control it. One way is to apply deterrence: the idea that punishment will prevent criminals from committing further crimes, and more importantly, that the publicity about crime and punishment will prevent other people from committing crimes in the first place. The idea of deterrence is very old. It goes back at least to the seventeenth century, when it was most forcefully voiced by Cesare Beccaria, who wrote *Of Crimes and Punishment*. Beccaria said that in order for punishment to be effective, the punishment must have the following three characteristics:

1. Celerity (swiftness): The punishment must follow closely upon the criminal act.
2. Sureness: The punishment must be administered whenever the crime is committed.
3. Severity: The punishment must be harsh enough to make the criminal stop.

Today, many of Beccaria's ideas are incorporated in the demand to "get tough" on crime. People who believe in getting tough usually believe that crime is a major threat to American society; that punishment is the right tool for deterring crime; that punishment should be severe; and that criminals deserve the punishment they get. The "get tough" proponents also favor the death penalty. If belief in the death penalty is an indication, then the chart suggests that the majority of people in the United States believe in getting tough on crime.

Of course, there are differences among groups. According to the chart, on the whole, men believe in the death penalty more than women, whites believe in it more than African Americans, and people without a college degree believe in it more than people with a college degree. Nevertheless, a majority of people in every category of gender, race, and education believe that the proper punishment for a convicted murderer is death.

CQ Evidence:* Do you believe in the death penalty? What evidence can you muster for your belief?

*To answer these critical questions, review the box titled "What Is Critical Thinking?" in Chapter 1, and pay special attention to the discussion of evidence.

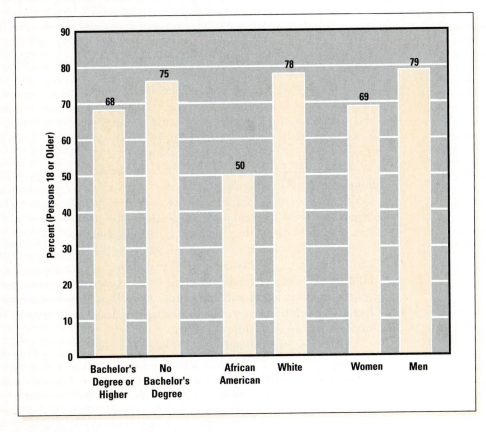

Favor Death for a Convicted Murderer

SOURCE: Courtesy of NORC, Chicago, IL, 1996.

Prisons in the United States are filled to capacity, and many are over-crowded. This photograph shows the Deuel Vocational Institution auditorium in Tracy, California. It has been converted into a dormitory to house prisoners.

CQ *Are there alternatives we should consider to long prison sentences?*

Some claim today that the very idea of rehabilitation excuses criminals from responsibility for their acts, and in recent years incapacitation has been a favored strategy (Melossi and Lettiere 1998; Methvin 1997). One reason for this is that research has shown that some offenders commit many crimes. For instance, Inciardi (1992) studied 254 juvenile cocaine users in Miami and found that each had committed hundreds of crimes, including 37 major felonies in the past year. Clearly, these persons are a threat to society, and locking them up is a way to remove that threat. Others point out that any attempt to rehabilitate first-time or youthful offenders in the midst of a population of offenders is especially difficult because of the many negative and antisocial attitudes prevalent within the population. They claim that 60 to 75 percent of all offenders commit new crimes within three years after they are released from correctional institutions (Wilson 1983).

Given the threat posed to society by dangerous offenders, some suggest making more space available in prison for those convicted of serious crimes against persons by reducing sentences of those involved in recreational drug use and other **victimless crimes**, violations of the law in which there are no obvious victims. For instance, if some currently illegal drugs such as marijuana were made legally available to adults but prohibited to children, there more space available for dangerous offenders. In addition, money could be generated by taxing the sale of marijuana, much like alcohol and tobacco are taxed now. This money could be spent on educational and therapeutic programs (Rydell and Everingham 1994). Those opposed to this policy fear that decriminalization of marijuana and other drugs will only encourage more crime by weakening the moral fabric of society.

Although crime rates have increased over the long run until recently, the fear of crime remains a leading social issue. Despite the fact that the United States already is a world leader in incarceration, the political solution has been to impose even more severe punishment. For example, the U.S. incarceration rate is approximately 450 per 100,000 people as compared with Canada's rate of 110 per 100,000 people and Japan's rate of 40 per 100,000 people. The cost of following a "get tough" policy is staggering: In the United States in 2000, states alone spent $32 billion for the construction of prisons and for the maintenance of inmates (Justice Policy Institute 2003). Many observers wonder whether it would be more cost-effective to prevent young people from becoming criminals in the first place rather than keeping them locked up after they have committed a crime, (see the Society Today box, Increases in State Spending on Corrections).

Victimless crimes ▲ Violations of law in which there are no obvious victims.

Society Today ● ■ ▲

Increases in State Spending on Corrections, 1985–2000

These numbers are the percent increases in state spending on corrections between 1985 and 2000. Notice that most states increased their spending on corrections by more than 100%. Where does your state stand?

STATE	PERCENT INCREASE IN STATE SPENDING ON CORRECTIONS	STATE	PERCENT INCREASE IN STATE SPENDING ON CORRECTIONS
AL	107	NV	107
AK	45	NH	138
AR	188	NJ	137
AZ	191	NM	48
CA	184	NY	137
CO	366	NC	149
CT	262	ND	250
DE	156	OH	211
FL	217	OK	128
GA	234	OR	314
HI	164	PA	413
ID	424	RI	188
IL	110	SC	113
IN	214	SD	214
IA	107	TN	74
KS	192	TX	346
KY	164	UT	195
LA	13	VT	179
ME	75	VA	76
MD	29	WA	138
MA	273	WV	139
MI	227	WI	274
MN	148	WY	110
MS	185		
MO	236	Average Percent Change	175
MT	181		
NE	148		

SOURCE: Justice Policy Institute 2002. Cellblocks or Classrooms: The Funding of Higher Education and Its Impact on African American Men. Retrieved online December 17, 2003 at <http://www.justicepolicy.org/article.php?id=3>.

● ■ ▲ Pausing to Think   About the Criminal Justice System

The criminal justice system in the United States is based on common law and the adversarial principle. The United States has an extensive set of policing agencies and vests great powers among public prosecutors. The prosecutors do not bring all cases to trial, but instead rely on plea bargaining. Prisons serve many functions, and the current climate of opinion in the United States favors harsh punishment for deviants and long prison sentences for criminals. However, to imprison all deviants would stifle the freedom of many people and cost taxpayers additional billions of dollars. In time, greater efforts to rehabilitate criminals may once again gain favor.

 Freedom requires the toleration of deviance. ◆ In what ways is this true? ◆ In what ways is it false?

Deviance and Crime in the Twenty-First Century

Criminologist Elliott Currie believes that the United States is reaching a turning point in the development of criminological thought and social policy toward crime (Currie 1989). He states "the big job for the twenty-first century criminologists—and for twenty-first century social policy generally—will be to place the integrity of the social environment firmly at the top of the political and intellectual agenda, and to keep it there" (Currie 1989, p. 23). By this, he means that efforts to reduce the high level of deviancy and crime in the United States must go beyond the "get tough" policy that dominated thought during the later part of the twentieth century. More attention should be paid to controlling the social and economic forces that place individuals, families, and communities at risk. For instance, he thinks that more focus must be directed to alleviating the disintegration of communities caused by shrinking adult labor markets, the flood of hard drugs, and declines in social and health services. He also suggests that more funding needs to be spent on successful early education programs that improve the social functioning of parents as well as children. An important idea, he argues, is to make the connection between interpersonal violence and the economic and social deprivation brought on by vast inequality within the United States.

Other criminologists echo this theme, and stress that the current policies are devastating the urban African American male population and throwing into jail ever-larger sections of the American citizenry. From their view, the U.S. prison system seems to be overly committed to prisons as warehouses whose only missions are incapacitation and deterrence, and it's time for new ideas and solutions (Melossi and Lettiere 1998).

CONCEPT WEB Deviance and Crime

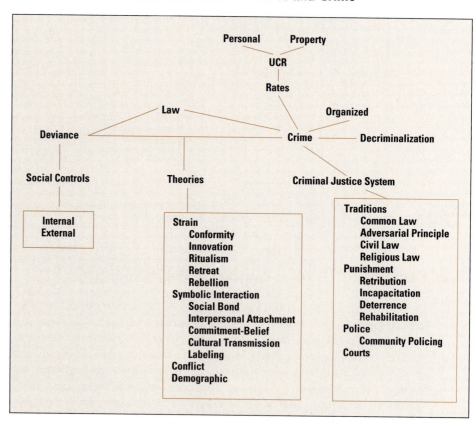

Here is a concept web for deviance and crime. Try this. Where would you place *hate crimes* in this web? Where would you place *sociopaths*? Where would you place *stigma*? Redraw the web to include these three concepts.

Looking Ahead

Additional important basic concepts are introduced in the following chapter. Groups, organizations, and interactions are the fundamental building blocks of sociological analysis. The Great Social Transformation has also influenced them.

WHAT YOU SHOULD KNOW ●■▲

1. *How are deviance and crime related to the Great Social Transformation?*

In communal societies, there are comparatively few rules to violate, and people are socialized into long-standing traditions. Because associational societies are complex, they require many laws and rules; because they are impersonal, tradition is not adequate to prevent deviance. Moreover, many associational societies are diverse, and the mix of ethnicities, languages, and regional differences requires coordination, which in turn requires laws and rules. Associational societies usually focus on the offender when determining suitable punishment, while communal societies pay more attention to the victim. That is why communal societies are more likely to use a restorative rationale in determining punishment.

2. *How is crime related to deviance?*

In all societies, authorities criminalize acts that upset the social order. Deviance is any violation of a widely held norm, but not all crimes are deviant acts, and not all deviant acts are crimes. Internal social controls are located within the individual and are learned through socialization. External social controls rely on social mechanism to prevent deviance. External social controls are relied upon whenever internal social controls cannot be relied upon.

3. *What are the major sources of data on crime rates?*

The Federal Bureau of Investigation collects data from police departments in the United States, and these are compiled into the Uniform Crime Report (UCR). The UCR tracks eight Index crimes that include personal or violent crimes, and property crimes. Another source of data is the National Crime Victimization Survey (NCVS) that is based on interviews conducted with a random sample of American households. Comparing victimization rates in the NCVS with the UCR indicates that the UCR probably underreports certain types of crimes. The federal government collects data on hate crimes and there are thousands of these types of crimes each year. Elder abuse is becoming an important issue, and the National Center on Elder Abuse gathers data from states on that that important topic. The United Nations supplies some data on international organized crime.

4. *What are the functionalist and conflict perspectives on crime and deviance?*

Durkheim suggested that crime has some positive functions in society in that it helps to clarify moral behavior. The major contemporary functional approach is strain theory, which places the origins of deviance in the broader social setting and the way it provides or denies people access to the culturally approved goals and means. Conflict theory stresses the fact that the laws are generally written by and for the wealthy, and that white-collar crime causes the greater economic losses to society. Conflict theory also sees the punishments dealt out on drug users and suppliers as having a strong race and class bias.

5. *What is the symbolic interactionist perspective on deviance and crime?*

The symbolic interaction perspective includes cultural transmission theory, differential association, labeling, and social bond theory. Cultural transmission theory argues that deviance is learned through socialization; differential association theory asserts that people learn conformity or deviance from people with whom they associate; labeling theory examines how labels such as "crook" come to be applied to people, the consequences of the label for the labeled individual, and the power of some people to attach labels to others; and social bond theory emphasizes the strength of the connections between individuals and their friends, family, and community.

6. *What are the demographic explanations for crime and deviance?*

The first characteristic is age. Aging out is a term used by criminologists and sociologists to refer to the fact that for most offenders crime declines sharply after the mid-thirties. The second characteristic is gender. For various reasons, crime is mostly a male activity, especially violent crime.

7. *What is the criminal justice system?*

The criminal justice system in the United States consists of police, courts, and prisons officials that respond to violations of the law. The criminal justice system is based on common law and an adversarial principle: a legal tradition where guilt or innocence is determined by a contest between the prosecution and the defender.

8. What are the functions of prisons?

The functions of prisons include retribution, deterrence, incapacitation, and rehabilitation. Punishing people by sending them to prisons may be thought as retribution, but it can also have deterrence effects. Retribution is defined as an act of vengeance by which society inflicts on the offender suffering comparable to that caused by the offense, while deterrence means the use of punishment to discourage crime. Some believe that the main purpose of a prison is incapacitation—keeping the most dangerous criminals locked away where they cannot hurt innocent people—while others believe that prison should be a place for rehabilitation, especially for younger prisoners.

9. What does the future hold for deviance and crime?

In the future, the integrity of the social environment needs to be given higher priority, according to Elliott Currie. For instance, more attention must be paid to controlling the social and economic forces that place individuals, families, and communities at risk. Current policies are too harsh, and prisons have become warehouses for millions of people—its time for new ideas and solutions.

TEST YOUR KNOWLEDGE ●■▲

Key Terms Matching

Match each of these key terms with the best definition or example from the numbered items that follow. Write the letter preceding the key term in the blank before the definition that you choose.

a. hate crime
b. organized crime
c. crime
d. deviance
e. plea bargaining
f. rehabilitation
g. internal social controls
h. restitution
i. laws
j. aging out
k. common law
l. external social controls
m. retribution
n. white-collar crimes
o. civil law
p. criminal justice system
q. adversarial principle
r. labeling
s. crimes against the person
t. social controls
u. incapacitation
v. crimes against property
w. deterrence
x. criminal recidivism
y. stigma
z. corporate crime
aa. victimless crimes
bb. religious law
cc. index crimes
dd. sociopaths

_____ 1. Social controls seated within the individual that are learned through socialization.

_____ 2. Any violation of a widely held norm.

_____ 3. Law that is developed over time by the accumulation of many cases.

_____ 4. Refers to the fact that most crime declines sharply after people reach their mid-thirties.

_____ 5. Crime committed by people of high social status in the course of their occupation.

_____ 6. Violations of law in which there are no obvious victims.

_____ 7. The process by which a definition is attached to an individual.

_____ 8. An act that has been declared illegal by some authority.

_____ 9. Law that is imposed on society from above by civil authority.

_____ 10. The use of punishment to discourage crime.

_____ 11. People who commit wanton murder or serial killings apparently because they lack any internal social controls.

_____ 12. A legal tradition where guilt or innocence is determined by a contest between the prosecution and the defense.

_____ 13. Mechanisms that monitor behavior and sanction the violation of norms.

_____ 14. Violent crimes or the threat of violence directed against people.

_____ 15. A crime motivated by racial prejudice or other biases against a person or a person's property.

_____ 16. Illegal actions of a corporation or people acting on behalf of a corporation.

_____ 17. An act of vengeance by which society inflicts on the offender suffering comparable to that caused by the offense.

_____ 18. A social marker that brings shame on a person.

_____ 19. A policy of attempting to restore things, as much as possible, to the way they were before a crime was committed.

_____ 20. Crimes that involve theft or destruction of property belonging to others.

_____ 21. A body of rules governing the affairs of a community that are enforced by a political authority, usually the state.

_____ 22. The societal mechanisms external to the individual that prevent deviance.

_____ 23. The social system of police, courts, and prisons officials that responds to violations of the law.

_____ 24. Crime conducted by businesses supplying illegal goods or services and that routinely use corruption and violence to gain their ends.

_____ 25. The use of education and other programs to reform offenders to prevent future offenses.

_____ 26. Law that is believed to stem from divine authority.

_____ 27. Refers to keeping the most dangerous criminals locked away.

_____ 28. A commonly used procedure whereby defendants agree to plead guilty to a lesser charge rather than to proceed to a formal trial.

_____ 29. Eight crimes given special attention in the Uniform Crime Reports published by the Federal Bureau of Investigation.

_____ 30. When people convicted of crimes commit subsequent offenses.

Multiple Choice

Circle the letter of your choice.

1. According to strain theory, which of the following would be an example of an innovator?
   a. organized crime member
   b. a bank teller
   c. a professional athlete
   d. a terrorist

2. Which of the following does not deter people from committing crimes?
   a. internal social controls
   b. aging out
   c. external social controls
   d. stigma

3. Which of the following groups are least likely to experience violent crime?
   a. young people
   b. blacks
   c. men
   d. the elderly

4. Cultural transmission could explain which of the following ideas?
   a. Young people are more likely to be the victims of violent crime than older people.
   b. People who have parents or siblings in prison are more likely to end up in prison themselves.
   c. Parents pass criminal tendencies to their children through their DNA.
   d. Men are more likely to commit murder than women.

5. Conflict theorists often dislike the war on drugs. Which of the following is a reason for this?
   a. They like to take drugs.
   b. They do not think that drugs cause social problems.
   c. Whites are more likely to use drugs, but blacks are more likely to go to jail for drug offenses.
   d. It costs the United States a lot of money to keep drug offenders in jail.

6. Communal societies are characterized by low levels of deviance because
   a. people in these societies are naturally better than people in other societies.
   b. there are fewer possibilities for deviant behavior in communal societies.
   c. these societies are more likely to exercise capital punishment.
   d. people in communal societies develop strong internal controls.

7. Which of the following is not a reason that people fail to report crimes to the police?
   a. They think the crime is too small or insignificant to be important.
   b. They do not want to bother the police.
   c. They are embarrassed that they were the victim of a crime.
   d. All of the above are reasons that people do not report crimes to the police.

8. Which of the following functions of prisons is not meant to make society safer?

   a. deterrence
   b. rehabilitation
   c. incapacitation
   d. retribution

9. How does labeling create deviance?

   a. through the narrowing of options and the internalization of a definition supported by others
   b. by making others suspicious of the actions of someone who has a specific label
   c. by defining the behavior of labeled individuals as deviant
   d. all of the above

10. Which concept in strain theory refers to a person who rejects both the goals and the means of society?

    a. retreatism
    b. rebellion
    c. innovation
    d. ritualism

11. Émile Durkheim suggested that some deviance in society might not be bad. Which of the following did he give as a reason for this?

    a. If there were no deviant people to put in jail, prison guards would face massive unemployment.
    b. Deviance is entertaining for the rest of society.
    c. Deviance affirms cultural values because the community rejoices when a criminal is brought to justice.
    d. None of the above.

12. Punishments for norm violations in communal societies are often

    a. aimed at restoring group harmony.
    b. deferred until the violator has an opportunity to make restitution.
    c. swift, harsh, and to the point.
    d. based on an ancient system of formal laws and social controls.

13. Which is NOT a reason why crime is underreported in the United States?

    a. A few police departments will not cooperate with the FBI in order to compile accurate crime data.
    b. Most crime in rural areas goes unreported.
    c. People are reluctant to report minor crimes such as the theft of a backpack.
    d. Some victims are reluctant to report a crime if they think they will be stigmatized.

14. Which of the following is NOT a part of differential association theory?

    a. People acquire techniques, motives, and attitudes for deviant behavior from generalized others.
    b. Deviant behavior is learned through interaction with others, especially small intimate groups.
    c. An individual learns definitions that are favorable or unfavorable to prevailing norms.
    d. A person who has frequent, intense contact will be influenced more than if he or she had infrequent contacts of limited duration.

15. Which theory argues that if people define a person as deviant, that person may internalize the definition and behave accordingly?

    a. differential association
    b. cultural transmission
    c. labeling
    d. strain

True-False

Indicate your response to each of the following statements by circling T for true or F for false.

T   F   1. Organized crime has not been a problem in the world for several years.

T   F   2. Nearly all crime is reported to the police.

T   F   3. All deviant activities are crimes.

T   F   4. Nearly all murders are committed by the victim's spouse or significant other.

T   F   5. The Internal Revenue Service is an example of an internal social control.

T   F   6. All societies have deviance and crime.

T   F   7. Compared with other countries, the United States has relatively little crime.

T   F   8. Feeling guilt at the mere thought of stealing is an external control mechanism.

T   F   9. Cultural transmission theory fails to explain why people who live in high crime areas do not become criminals.

T   F   10. Instead of asking, "Why do people commit crimes and deviant acts?" social bond theory asks, "Why don't people commit crimes and deviant acts?"

T   F   11. According to strain theory, a person who rejects both the goals and means of society is called a ritualist.

T · F 12. Age-out is a term used by criminologists to refer to the fact that for most offenders crime declines sharply after their mid-thirties.

T F 13. The criminal justice system of the United States is based on common law and the adversarial principle.

T F 14. When punishing a deviant, communal societies often use a restitutive rationale.

T F 15. The UCR is a principal source of crime statistics.

NOTE: The answers to these exercises are at the end of the book.

For additional practice tests and other resources please visit the companion web site at http://www.prenhall.com/curry.

Essay

1. According to Sutherland's differential association theory, how does socialization into deviant behavior take place?

2. What is labeling and how is it used to explain deviance?

3. What are the functions of punishment in the criminal justice system?

4. How do civil law and religious law differ from the adversarial principle as legal systems?

5. Criminologist Elliot Curry believes that the United States is reaching a turning point in the development of criminological thought and social policy toward crime. Explain.

5

Interaction, Groups, and Organizations

Chapter Outline

The South American rugby team and other passengers aboard a chartered airliner were flying through the Andes Mountains. All was going well and everyone was in high spirits when, without warning, the airplane crashed into a mountain. Of the 42 passengers and crew aboard the plane, 28 survived the initial crash. No distress call had been made, and the entire flight crew was dead. Now, at 11,500 feet in the snowy mountains, with meager supplies and only the plane's broken fuselage for shelter, the survivors would have to fight for their lives.

Although the group lacked equipment, it did have some social resources. The captain of the rugby team, Marcelo, was well respected and immediately assumed leadership. He organized the survivors into work squads and, without realizing it, created a division of labor. For instance, a medical student became the acting doctor, while other people specialized in food preparation, melting snow for water, and keeping the cabin clean. New roles emerged. Some team members became "inventors" and fashioned snowshoes and water-melting devices from the debris. The strongest of the group became "explorers" and scoured the mountainside for anything useful. Liana, one of the few women to survive the crash, took charge of the children.

On the 17th day after the crash, disaster struck again. An avalanche swept through the cabin of the downed airliner and suffocated eight more people, including Marcelo and Liana. A new leadership clique emerged and was supported by three other group members. Now faced with starvation, the group decided to eat the frozen bodies of the dead and in that way survived from one day to the next. When warmer weather approached, two members managed to hike down the mountain and return by helicopter to save their 14 friends (Read 1974).

When thinking about how people survive under extreme conditions, we naturally focus on food, medical care, and shelter. These aspects are vitally important, but social considerations are often equally important. Even under extreme conditions, people must interact and create social patterns that guide their behavior. For instance, the Andes crash survivors created a social organization when they selected leaders, established a division of labor, and assigned roles. Without this organization, their ability to survive would have been impaired, perhaps fatally. What was extraordinary was their ability to create quickly a workable social organization, before the cold, starvation, and exposure killed them all (Forsyth 1994; see Figure 5.1).

While the Andes episode was very dramatic, the importance of social organization for survival has been recognized for a long time—but not highly publicized. For example, many of the survivors of the 9/11 attack on New York's Twin Towers owe their lives to social organization. The news reported that one group of trapped people were milling about when a group member assumed the leadership role. He quieted everyone and ordered them to link hands. He then led them down a pitch-black stairwell. As they slowly felt their way in the darkness, he ordered each person say something out loud to encourage others. In this manner, they worked their way to the ground floor and safety. In another episode, the explosion trapped three men in an elevator. One happened to be a window washer who was familiar with the layout of the building. The three men quickly devised a way to force their way out with the window washer's tools. But when they climbed out, they found themselves in an area with no ready exit. The window washer recognized where they were, and knew that a stairwell ran behind a wall panel. They quickly devised another plan. Using the same tools, they worked together and punched a hole through the panel; and from there they managed to get out. Although these two episodes of survival took place in a much different situation from the Andes, they further suggest how important social organization can be.

CQ Have you ever been in an emergency that required a group of people immediately to organize themselves for action? ◆ If so, how did the group respond to the challenge?

FIGURE 5.1 Social Organization of the Survivors

After the avalanche, the group formed a centralized authority structure with a simple division of labor.

SOURCE: From *Group Dynamics,* 2nd edition by D. R. Forsyth. Copyright © 1990, by D. R. Forsyth. Reprinted with permission of Wadsworth, an imprint of the Wadsworth Group, a division of Thomson Learning: *www.thomsonrights.com.* Fax 800 730-2215.

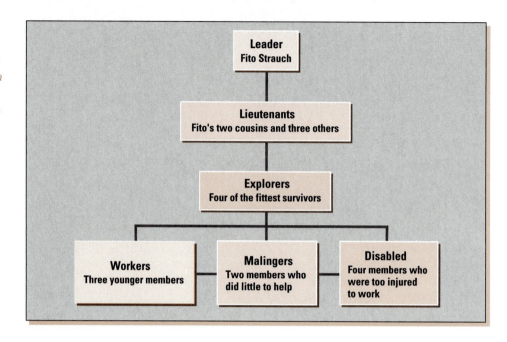

Chapter Preview

In this chapter, we discuss three fundamental topics in sociology. The first is social interaction. This topic is of crucial importance to understanding social life because we spend much of our time interacting with other people. The second topic is groups, which form out of the interactions we have with others. The last topic concerns a special type of group—the organization—that has come to be especially important in industrial and postindustrial societies.

The Great Social Transformation and Interaction, Groups, and Organizations

In communal societies, social interaction revolves around personal relationships, and people typically interact with the same group of people for their entire lifetimes. Interactions within associational society are much more diverse, involving many different groups and organizations. To epitomize this distinction, consider the following story. An anthropologist encountered a remote tribe of hunters and gatherers in the jungles of Brazil. After being introduced to the tribal leader, the anthropologist innocently inquired the name of the leader's daughter, a young girl. Immediately, much discussion took place between the leader and his wives and other kinfolk. The anthropologist became alarmed, because he had no idea why such a question would raise a fuss. As it turned out, the tribe he was studying, the Xerente people, do not give names to their children until they are 6 or 7 years old. There is no need to, because Xerente children seldom venture far from the village, and everyone in the village knows who they are. They are referred to as "daughter," "son," "niece," "nephew," or other relational terms. When children do occasionally meet strangers, they are referred to as "boy" or "girl" (Maybury-Lewis 1992).

In contrast to life among the Xerente, in industrial and postindustrial societies, babies are required to have names at the moment of birth in order for the hospital to complete their birth certificates. By the age of 5, many children have Social Security numbers, which will be part of them for the rest of their lives. These names and numbers are essential, because in associational society, groups and organizations keep track of people through records rather than through personal contact.

The groups we establish in associational society, whether in the classroom, dormitory, workplace, neighborhood, or other setting, often provide some communal relationships that buffer us against the impersonal forces of a highly mechanized society. As we will discuss in this chapter, sociologists know a great deal about the way these groups are formed and the effects they have on the individuals within them.

Social Interaction

If you wrote down everything you did during an ordinary day in your life, you would find that, like most students, you spent a considerable portion of your time talking and listening to other people. You would also find that much of your time was devoted to thinking about other people and about how you would respond to them in real life. In other words, during a typical day, you engaged in a great deal of **social interaction**. This term refers to the acts people perform toward one another and the responses they give in return (see Chapter 1).

Types of Interaction

Social interaction necessarily involves communication and may consist of spoken words, subtle gestures, visual images, or even electronically transmitted digits. Virtually all human behavior is involved: a parent talking to a child, friends laughing at a joke, two people sharing a silent moment together over a cup of coffee in the morning, ethnic gangs yelling racial slurs at each other, or an American soldier firing at an Iraqi soldier during the Gulf War. Because social interaction includes so much behavior, sociologists have organized it into five types, as follows:

1. **Exchange**   is the process in which people transfer goods, services, and other items with one another. Although we usually think of exchange as an economic activity involving money, most exchange is social. In everyday life, exchange may be quite straightforward: a child exchanges good behavior for a cookie; a friend gives you a compliment and receives one in return; you say "thank you," and the store clerk says, "you're welcome." In each case a social behavior was exchanged for a social reward of roughly equal value.

2. **Cooperation**   is the process in which people work together to achieve shared goals. A group of students helping each other prepare for an examination is one example, and a physician and nurse working together to save a patient's life is another. Sometimes, people must set aside their personal goals to achieve the goals of the group. For instance, the rugby team in the Andes would not have survived without cooperating to share their limited resources.

3. **Competition**   is the process in which two or more parties attempt to obtain the same goal. People in the United States are quite familiar with competition, because American culture hails it as the best way to determine social outcomes. Through competition the best player rises to the top, the most qualified worker gets the promotion, and the hardest-working student gets the A. Sometimes the dividing line between competition and conflict is very thin.

4. **Conflict**   is the process in which people attempt to physically or socially vanquish one another. War is perhaps the most obvious form of conflict, one in which the goal is physically to eliminate the enemy. Many conflicts, however, aim to vanquish

Social interaction ▲ Acts people perform toward one another and the response they give in return.

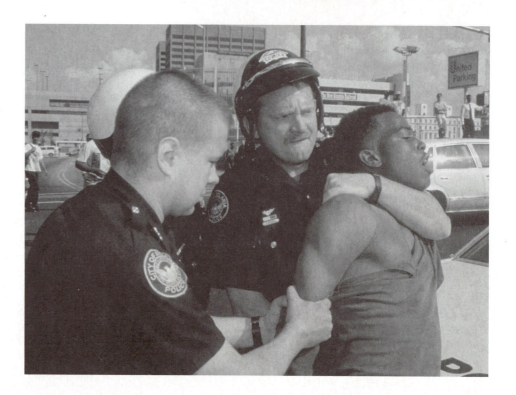

Coercion is a form of interaction that depends on force. Most societies regard coercion as extremely disruptive and therefore restrict the right to use this tactic to the police, military, and other state officials. When white police officers use coercion on members of minority groups, questions regarding abuse of power often arise.

the opposition socially, as in political campaigns. By "smearing the opposition," a political candidate increases his or her own chances of election, while ruining the reputation of the opponent.

5. Coercion is the process in which people compel other people to do something against their will. It is based, ultimately, on force. Most societies regard coercion as extremely disruptive and therefore reserve its use for the police, the military, and other officials of the state. Private individuals, if they have any right to use force, may do so only under very limited conditions (see Chapter 10). Thus, if a friend breaks a promise, you may not legally use force to gain compliance, no matter how angry you may be. An interesting partial exception to the ban on coercion involves parents. Traditionally, they may spank, paddle, shake, or cuff their children to teach them a lesson, provided the force does not get out of hand and become abusive.

In practice, we use all five types of interaction and freely mix them in the same social episode. A father trying to get his young child to behave might at one moment plead for cooperation, then offer a reward, and then threaten a spanking. Or you might, in an effort to outcompete other students for a good grade, offer a friend in the class a set of lecture notes in return for an outline of a chapter. You will probably not try coercion, however, because it violates the norms, values, and laws of society.

Components of Interaction

Contrary to what people may believe, their social interactions are not always a matter of conscious choice. Each of us is linked to society, and whether we realize it or not, these linkages can determine how we interact with others. One of the most important linkages is status. As used by sociologists, the term **status** means a position in society. To illustrate, American society has thousands of statuses: president of the United States, governor, teacher, nurse, parent, career criminal, and so on (Schooler 1996; DeLisi 2002). Because so many statuses exist, especially in an industrial society, a person will have several at the same time—for instance, student, daughter, aunt, friend, worker, and group leader. For any individual, the collection of statuses that the person occupies at any one time is called that person's **status set** (see Figure 5.2).

Status ▲ A position within society.

Status set ▲ The collection of statuses a person occupies at any one time.

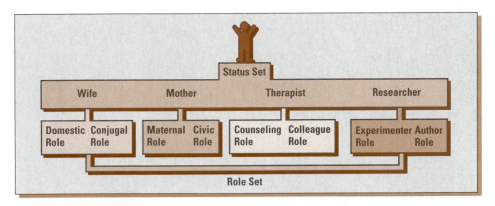

FIGURE 5.2 **Status Set and Role Set**

This figure shows the status set and role set for a woman whose statuses are wife, mother, therapist, and researcher. As a wife she plays both domestic and conjugal roles. As a mother she plays both a maternal role and a civic role. As a therapist she plays both the counseling role and the colleague role. As a researcher she plays two roles, one as a laboratory researcher and the other as an author of research-based publications. These statuses are achieved. In addition to these, she has ascribed statuses that are no doubt important in her life—as a woman, as a daughter, and as an African American. Of all of these, which is her master status? To answer that question, we would have to conduct an extensive personal interview with her.

 What types of role stress and role strain do you think she experiences?

To a certain extent, statuses determine how people interact. Peers are casual with each other; managers and workers are formal; and two lovers are deeply intimate. To use the wrong interaction with a given status is a major breach of propriety. Thus, a worker would not share intimacies with his manager, nor would peers address each other as Mister or Ms.

Sociologists frequently distinguish between two types of statuses: ascribed and achieved. An **ascribed status** is one that cannot be changed by individual effort; we have it whether we want it or not. To illustrate, race, sex, and old age are ascribed because we cannot choose our race, sex, or age. Religion and social class are also ascribed because we acquire them from our parents when we are too young to have any choice in the matter. Even though we may change when we become older, in practice, most people maintain the religion and class of their parents (see Chapter 6).

In contrast to ascribed statuses, an **achieved status** is one that can be obtained through individual effort. Our occupation and amount of education, for instance, can be attained through some combination of effort, ability, and luck. Competitive industrial societies such as the United States place great importance on achieved statuses and use some of them as measures of worth. When people become college graduates, for example, they reach an achieved status that is honored by other people and signified by a diploma. For this reason, physicians, engineers, and many other professionals prominently display their degrees on their office wall.

In some instances, achieved and ascribed statuses are related. Many institutions in society provide greater opportunities for men (an ascribed status) to reach a high position (an achieved status) than they do for women. For instance, professional male athletes may participate in football, baseball, hockey, basketball, golf, tennis, and auto racing, but professional female athletes have mainly tennis, golf, and recently basketball and soccer as outlets (Coakley and Donnelly 1999). In addition, the mass media typically depict men and women athletes differently. Men tend to be portrayed as more athletic and committed than are women (Billings and Eastman 2002). A woman's sex, in other words, can prevent her from achieving certain outcomes. Ethnicity, another ascribed status, sometimes combines with sex to produce a

Ascribed status ▲ A status assigned to people whether they wish to have it or not.

Achieved status ▲ A status over which people can exert at least some control.

Obtaining an advanced degree confers an important status in society. The number of years of education that you receive are less important than the fact that you graduate. The ascribed characteristics of race, class, and sex all influence the probability of achieving a college degree in the United States.

complex pattern of achievement. For example, to obtain a college degree in engineering (an achieved status), an African American woman (an ascribed status) will have to overcome more obstacles than a white, Anglo-Saxon man and more than a white, Anglo-Saxon woman. Because engineering is a male-dominated profession, a female student will have few role models to inspire her imagination and few mentors to encourage her on a day-to-day basis. The black female student, however, will find even fewer role models and mentors, because engineering, in addition to being male dominated, is white dominated. As we discuss in Part Two of this book, inequality in an industrial society rests largely on ascription. Ascribed statuses such as race, sex, social class, and age are the focal points of conflicts leading to vast disparities in wealth and power.

Among all the statuses that people hold, a few or even one status will be more important than the others. Such a status is called a **master status**, and it is so important that people organize their lives and identities around it. A master status may be ascribed, such as belonging to a certain family, or it may be achieved, such as becoming a teacher. For example, "slackers" are students who remain in school so long that the status of college student becomes their main social identity and their entire way of life. Although many people view slackers as deviants, slackers see themselves as students who have yet to find themselves.

Role

We spend much of our lives trying to meet expectations—to get good grades, to be a decent person, to act kindly toward those less fortunate than ourselves, and so forth. These expectations or norms concern so many aspects of our lives that sociologists organize them into roles. A **role** is defined as the expected behavior associated with a status. Thus, an elementary schoolteacher (a status) is expected to be on time, know pupils by name, and engage in other behaviors appropriate to teaching. As a student, you are expected to attend class, study, pass your courses and, at appropriate times, party. In other words, to say that you are playing the role of a college student means that you are following the behaviors expected of a typical college student.

In principle, role expectations are so powerful that each of us should play the same role in the same way. In fact, we each play the same role somewhat differently. Diverging too far from role expectations, however, will result in criticism and other

Master status ▲ A status, ascribed or achieved, that is so important that a person organizes his or her life and social identity around it.

Role ▲ The expected behavior associated with a status.

social punishments. Thus, if you party every night, cut your classes regularly, and fail your courses, you can expect quick reprimands and punishments from other people.

For the most part, our roles mesh neatly together and allow us to engage in pleasant and productive social interactions. But sometimes one or more of our roles will interfere with our other roles. This situation is called **role conflict**—the incompatibility of the different roles played by a single person (Turner 1990). Many role conflicts pose difficult moral choices. Should a priest (a role) who is a friend (another role) of a criminal turn in the criminal to the police? Should the personnel manager of a business (a role) fulfill a personal obligation by hiring a friend? None of these dilemmas has an easy answer, and the priest and the personnel manager will spend many restless nights suffering from **role stress**—the anxiety produced by being unable to meet all role requirements at the same time (Aneshensel 1992).

Related to role stress is another possibility that also produces anxiety. Sometimes people find themselves trying to meet incompatible expectations within a single role, a situation called **role strain**. High school principal is a single role, but it includes norms about administration, teaching, community service, counseling students, and counseling parents. Each of these audiences demands that the principal give priority to its problem, something that is obviously impossible to do. Sooner or later, therefore, every principal will experience some role strain. In general, the complexity of modern roles virtually guarantees that, at some point, we will all encounter conflicting expectations and be subjected to role strain and role conflict.

The nature of society has a large effect on the amount of role strain and stress that people encounter. As societies undergo the transformation from traditional to industrial, roles increase in number and complexity. To take but one instance: women used to be responsible mainly for housework and child rearing. But today women have all their old roles plus the additional roles of economic provider, civic leader, family head, and others. Many of these roles conflict with one another. The demands of work and child care, or of housework and civic duty, require a woman to split her time and energy in ways that may be impossible. The result is role conflict, stress, and strain (Roscow 1994; Frisco and Williams 2003).

Although life may be more difficult than it used to be, contemporary industrial society is not all bad. According to sociologist Rose Coser (1991), complexity might frustrate us, but it also can liberate us. Rather than becoming mired in routine roles, we acquire new statuses and new roles that provide opportunities for growth and creativity. The challenge is to make room for those roles that intrigue us and to have the courage to embark on new endeavors. For instance, by having a number of different roles to play, we become less dependent on any one role. If one role turns sour, we can still find other relationships that provide meaning. And if resources are needed to solve complex problems, the person with many role partners can draw on these partners for the information and resources necessary to solve the problem. For example, in comparison with industrial society, Coser believes traditional societies are too inward looking. People in traditional societies always turn to family and relatives for emotional support and for information, assistance, and resources. This inward-looking view often works well, but on occasion it does not. She illustrates her point with a newspaper story that she translated about a family in Pakistan:

> *Twelve members of one Pakistan family were asphyxiated in a water-well last Monday. This family drama took place in a village a hundred kilometers west of Rawalpindi. The first victim had gone down into the well in order to fix a broken pump. When he did not come up again, a second family member went to look. He didn't come back either. This went on until the twelfth family member had gone down into the well. Then a fellow villager hit on the idea that the motor might be exuding toxic gases. He alerted the police.*
>
> *This story contrasts with one printed that same year in the* New York Times *(December 15, 1979), according to which an eight-year-old boy in Illinois responded to his four-year-old brother's fall into a 40-foot well by throwing two life*

STUDY TIP

Using lines, symbols, and/or words, make a drawing that illustrates your own roles you play in your social interactions. Make up a "code" of colors to note where role stress, role strain, and role conflict occur.

Role conflict ▲ The incompatibility of different roles played by a single person.

Role stress ▲ The anxiety produced by being unable to meet all role requirements at the same time.

Role strain ▲ The incompatibility of expectations within a single role.

Day-care centers have become a routine feature of everyday life for working parents. Here a three-year-old hugs her mom goodbye. Role stress and role strain often accompany the mix of career and homemaker roles, especially for women.

CQ Did you spend much time in a day-care center as a youngster? ◆ Do you think that situation helped or hurt your family life?

preservers into the well, calling the telephone operator for help, and then running for assistance. Through his quick action, his brother's life was saved. (Coser 1991:76; slightly edited)

These examples illustrate the point that people in communal societies rarely look outside their families for help in times of need, whereas people in associational societies share a general understanding that there is social support outside the family. Whereas in a communal society it might never occur to someone to seek help from people playing specialized roles outside the family such as the police or the rescue squad, in an associational society, such people are often called before anyone else (Hurlbert, Hains, and Beggs 2000).

Networks of Social Relationships   Each of us is part of a network that links us to other people, groups, and organizations. Our network also includes secondary units, such as the friend of our friend, or the governing association of our church. The network might also include a few tertiary units (a friend of a friend of a friend), but at some point the linkages become weak and the network reaches its outer boundary. Some of our networks may consist of long-distance relationships involving people who live thousands of miles away. Electronic linkages, such as the telephone and, increasingly, the computer, can provide us with information and support from people we would never meet face-to-face (Wellman et al. 1996; Wellman and Haythornthwaite 2002).

In industrial society, the number of units in the network of a single person is surprisingly large. Including slight acquaintances, the number usually ranges from 500 to 2,500 (Milgram 1967). The large number arises because each unit in a network also has a network of its own, and each unit within that network has a network of its own, and so on. If we take all of the networks into account, each of us has literally millions of direct and indirect linkages to other social units. Put another way, contemporary society is crisscrossed with networks that link everyone to a huge number of other persons, groups, and organizations. This fact helps to explain the often-occurring "small-world" phenomenon. For example, we are delightfully surprised when we visit another city and bump into a friend at a downtown restaurant, or meet a stranger and find that we know someone in common. We are likely to say, "It's a small world!"; but in fact, such occurrences are readily explained by the extensive networks that connect us to our society.

As the small-world phenomenon suggests, networks also place us in close social proximity to everyone else in our society, including people in very high places. For example, the typical college student is only three handshakes away from the president of the United States: you shake the hand of the president of your college or university, your president shakes the hand of the governor of the state, and the governor shakes the hand of the president. Thus, even in a large, industrial, and impersonal society such as the United States, people may be close to one another socially even though they are far apart physically.

Because networks link us to so many others, some people make it a practice conscientiously to attend parties, banquets, weddings, funerals, and other gatherings. Their goal is to make the right contacts with the right people in the right networks. This practice—called networking—often produces valuable results. For example, some business opportunities and jobs are available only through the "old boys' network"—a network consisting of influential men, almost all of whom are white. Although this network helps some people, it hurts women, ethnic minorities, and others who cannot become one of the "old boys." Social position also affects the ability to network successfully. Whereas a working-class person might belong to a softball league, an upper-class person might belong to the chamber of commerce, a professional association, and the board of the local museum or orchestra—networks that have considerable prestige and power. Hence, people high in the social structure can use their networks to exert great influence, often on their own behalf (cf. Coser 1991).

Sociological Analysis of Interaction

All the world's a stage,
And all the men and women merely players:
They have their exits and their entrances;
And one man in his time plays many parts.

Shakespeare, *As You Like It*

Life's but a walking shadow, a poor player,
That struts and frets his hour upon the stage,
And then is heard no more.

Shakespeare, *Macbeth*

The Dramaturgical Approach   In *As You Like It* and *Macbeth*, William Shakespeare drew an analogy between the stage and human life. This analogy was adopted, more or less intact, by the late Erving Goffman. He developed an approach called dramaturgy (Goffman 1959, 1961, 1971, 1986; Denzin 2002).

Goffman believed that in real life, we play out social scenes following a "script" written by society. These scripts are usually unstated, yet they are understood by everyone and become the rules that make orderly social interaction possible. One illustration is the way, on entering an upscale restaurant, we immediately begin following a certain script—a set of rules—that governs how we eat in public when surrounded by strangers. A few of the rules are as follows: talk quietly, do not make large gestures or body movements, avoid eye contact with diners at other tables, do not slouch or lean on the table, do not talk with food in your mouth, and so forth. Surely, if this script were not followed, dining out would be a very different, and possibly less pleasant, experience for everyone.

Carrying the stage analogy further, Goffman also claimed that our role performances are judged in the same way the performance of an actor is judged by a drama critic. If we act the role poorly, other people will criticize us; but if we act the role well, the same people will praise us and encourage us to continue our performance. Sometimes other people will also help us perform our roles by, paradoxically, ignoring our shortcomings and errors. Rather than call attention to a mistake, they pretend not to notice, thereby permitting us to carry on without embarrassment. Goffman called this studied nonobservance, or pretending not to notice a mistake in a role performance. For instance, if while dining out we dribble water down our chin, other diners and the waiter will probably ignore our little accident, and dinner can continue as scripted.

The dramaturgy approach also takes an audience into account (Coates 1999). In life, just as in the theater, we have a front region where we play a role before one audience and a back region where we play a different role before a different audience. Consider teachers. In the classroom they are in the front region, acting out the teacher role before their students. However, when teachers join other teachers in the lounge, they enter a backstage area where they perform roles appropriate to their peers. They might talk about their spouses, gripe about the principal, prepare for their classes, or discuss the behavior of their students.

Many organizations consciously manipulate the front and back regions by providing lounges, clubs, and dining areas that are reserved for certain members. Hospitals have "doctors only" lounges that shield them from patients; colleges have "faculty only" dining areas where professors can play collegial roles before other professors; and business organizations have "officers only" restrooms where managers can speak freely about matters that might have an adverse effect on workers.

Finally, Goffman argued that people engage in **impression management**: the conscious manipulation of props, scenery, costumes, and behavior in an attempt to present a particular image to other people. For instance, a recent college graduate interviewing for a job with the Federal Bureau of Investigation, an agency noted for

Impression management ▲ The conscious manipulation of props, scenery, costumes, and behavior in an attempt to present a particular image to other people.

A candidate at a job interview tries to present a positive image to a potential employer.

CQ *What would you wear to an important job interview?* ◆ What impression management issues might disabled people face in job interviews that could put them at a disadvantage?

its formality, would do well to wear the appropriate costume (a suit and tie) and to carry the appropriate props (perhaps a leather planner or fountain pen). In contrast, the same attire would not be appropriate if the graduate were interviewing for a job at The Gap, a clothing store noted for its informality. In both cases, of course, the graduate should be careful to display the appropriate behaviors: laughing at the correct time, addressing the interviewer politely, and showing enthusiasm for the job.

Goffman's dramaturgical approach draws strength from its roots in everyday life and from Goffman's skill in describing behavior, almost as a novelist would. As a result, the approach sheds light on commonplace occurrences and suggests how social meaning arises from social interaction. On the negative side, the approach has been criticized for being overly cynical. The choice of terms—impression management, role playing, back region, and front region—implies that people are actors who are out to fool other people by playing roles and managing impressions (Douglas et al. 1980). However, even assuming that people wish to fool others, only a few people have the skill to assume a role and to play it convincingly. Finally, Goffman does not provide any quantitative evidence to support his theory. Without such evidence, some sociologists will not accept dramaturgy as anything more than an insightful metaphor for everyday life.

Ethnomethodology The approach to social interaction known as **ethnomethodology** is linked to dramaturgy on the one hand and to the classical sociologists Durkheim and Weber on the other. Nevertheless, it is unique because it focuses on the very basic assumptions that underlie everyday life (Lynch 1999, Lynch 2002). These assumptions are so fundamental that we rarely think of them or even know that they exist. For instance, we assume that everyone shares our view of reality, and we rarely question the assumptions behind our social interaction. In discussing our pet dog, we do not stop and define "dog" because we assume that everyone else knows what a dog is. But is our assumption valid? Does everyone know what a dog is? And if so, how do we know that everyone else's idea of a dog is the same as our idea?

Such questions are appropriate for ethnomethodology. *Ethno* means *folk* in Greek, and thus ethnomethodology is the methodology for studying the common understanding of everyday life. Sociologist Harold Garfinkel developed ethnomethodology from his original interest in jury deliberations (1967). He believed that we come to share a sense of reality with other people by following social rules. These rules are

Ethnomethodology ▲ The methodology for studying the common understanding of everyday life.

unspoken and are so deeply embedded in our culture that we are not usually aware of their existence. The goal of ethnomethodology is to bring these rules to the surface and then to determine what effect they have on our behavior.

Garfinkel once demonstrated the power of these unstated rules by conducting a simple experiment. He had his students pretend to be boarders in their own homes, but without informing their parents of what they were doing. In playing this role, the students were to address their parents in formal terms such as "Sir" or "Madam" and to request explanations for common assumptions. They were supposed to play this role for 15 minutes to an hour, but very few could sustain it over even the shorter time period (Garfinkel 1967). A conversation between a parent and a student often went as follows:

PARENT: How was school?

STUDENT: What do you mean, "How was school?"

PARENT: You know what I mean.

STUDENT: I really don't know what you mean. Can you explain what you mean to me?

PARENT: Why are you being so difficult?

STUDENT: What do you mean, difficult?

It is surprising, that parents were first puzzled by the students' behavior and that then they became frustrated or angry. Some parents accused the students of being mean, inconsiderate, or selfish. One parent asked, "Are you out of your mind or are you just stupid?"

Garfinkel also used another technique for discovering the unstated rules of interaction, a breaching experiment—a procedure whereby the experimenter violates a suspected rule and observes people's reaction to the violation. The power of this experiment comes from its very simplicity. We (the authors) have occasionally asked our students to conduct a breaching experiment as part of their course work. A common experiment concerns elevator behavior in a high-rise dormitory. Normally, people enter an elevator and immediately turn to face the door. To breach this rule of behavior, we ask a group of students to ride the elevator normally, but facing the rear. When the door opens and entering students see their backs instead of their faces, the entering students are surprised, shocked, and puzzled. They always immediately ask "What is going on?" "What are you doing?" A few students will think that the situation is so bizarre that they will not enter the elevator.

Ethnomethodology has been on the scene for more than three decades, yet many sociologists still consider it to be novel but suspect. Some sociologists even dismiss ethnomethodology as lacking in scientific merit; yet it has established a major point: orderly social interaction is possible only if we abide by social rules that we rarely, if ever, notice.

Exchange Theory   Of the five types of social interaction mentioned at the beginning of the chapter, exchange theory singles out exchange as the most important (Homans 1958, 1993). As mentioned, in many cases, exchange involves money; but in most cases, the currency is social, and in some cases, it is emotional: for example, gratitude, friendship, and love (Blau 1986; Curry and Emerson 1971; Levinger 1979; Lovaglia 1999; Sprecher 2001).

Many cultures contain a strong norm that says that if you do something for a person, then that person must do something of approximately equal social value in return. This is the **norm of reciprocity**. For example, you might lend a friend a book, and although you never mention it, you expect a similar favor in return. Sometimes the reciprocity is very casual. You hold a door open for a stranger, and the stranger reciprocates by saying "thanks." Even though social reciprocities are informal obligations, people still keep a rather close account of the rewards they owe others and that others owe them. If someone consistently fails to reciprocate, the exchange relationship

123 **STUDY TIP**

Describe the different ways to analyze social interaction. Summarize by giving your own analysis of the effectiveness of each and which is overall most useful (if you feel one is superior).

Norm of reciprocity ▲ A strong norm that says that if you do something for a person, then that person must do something of approximately equal social value in return.

will be discontinued. Thus, if you do not send a Christmas card to a particular person who sends you a card, after a few Christmases, that person will drop you. If you stop reciprocating when people do you favors, then after a time, no one will do you any favors.

From the exchange perspective, social life is an intricate web of reciprocal relationships, as illustrated by a study of an automobile mechanic in upstate New York. Sometimes the mechanic's customers could not pay for his services and would do him favors instead or would give him old pieces of machinery that he might later use or salvage. If a customer reneged on a promised favor, the mechanic did not say anything but would not do repair work for that person anymore. Because of the many favors he did for others, the mechanic was respected by everyone and exerted considerable influence over community matters. In effect, the mechanic rose to prominence by engaging in mutually satisfying exchange relationships (Harper 1987).

Exchange theory is useful because it recognizes that self-interest and social rewards motivate people to interact. However, the argument that all social life is based on exchange is not accepted by all sociologists. If people never do anything for free, then there is little or no room in life for true charity or altruism. Yet people die for others or devote their lives to lost causes—and in neither case do the rewards seem to be commensurate with the sacrifice. Also, it is often difficult to be precise on what is rewarding to people. Sometimes people do what they do out of sheer habit, rather than in pursuit of self-interest or social rewards.

● ■ ▲ **Pausing to Think**   **About Social Interaction**

Human beings are social creatures who create their social world from their interactions. As we have seen, there are five types of social interaction: exchange, cooperation, competition, conflict, and coercion. Each of us is linked to others through our statuses and roles. In fact, our lives and our very identity are organized around our master status. As we play the roles linked to our statuses, we often confront role conflict, role stress, and role strain. As society changed from communal to associational, role conflicts, stresses, and strains increased, as did the size of social networks. The process of social interaction is not random, however, and in going about our daily life, we unconsciously follow a social script and abide by unstated rules. The dramaturgical approach helps us to understand this aspect of relationships. Ethnomethodologists, moreover, tell us that many of the rules we follow are unspoken and are so deeply embedded in our culture that we are often unaware of their existence. A much different approach is exchange theory. It emphasizes the role of mutual obligations and reciprocity in everyday life.

CQ In modern society, is role stress inevitable? ◆ Do you think your life as a college student is more stressful than the lives of college students 20 or 30 years ago? ◆ Why, or why not?

Groups

Human life is social life—this is a simple dictum but one with profound implications. It implies, among other things, that we go through life in the presence of other people and that we constantly take them into account. At times, we are directly involved with them, and our activities could not go forward without them. At other times, they are present only in our imagination, yet their imaginary presence influences our current behavior (see the section Socialization and the Self, Chapter 3).

Types of Groups

Although social interaction must involve other people, we do not always interact only with a particular individual. Instead, we band together with others to form a **group**: a

Group ▲ A collection of people who take each other's behavior into account as they interact, and who develop a sense of togetherness.

collection of people who take each other's behavior into account as they interact and who develop a sense of togetherness. When the same interactions are carried on routinely over time, they become the accepted way of doing things. Eventually, each group develops its own norms and values as well as its own roles and statuses. In effect, a group culture and a group structure emerge from the interactions among the group's members.

The sense of togetherness that characterizes a group is sometimes called a sense of we-ness. That is, members develop a collective identity as a group and come to view the group as transcending their individual identity. Consider a possible conversation among a group of friends after class:

JANE: What do you guys want to do now?

HARRY: Why don't we go get something to eat?

JANE: Well, I'm not too hungry right now, but I could get some coffee.

MARY: We should do something else, like maybe go to the library and study.

HARRY: I just had an exam, but I'll go if you all want to go.

In this brief conversation, members refer to the group as we, which implies that the group is the reference point for their behavior. They also are willing to subordinate their individual goal to the group goal. Even though Jane and Harry would prefer to do otherwise, they are willing to do what the group wants to do.

A group of friends is also an illustration of an informal group, or one without a rigid social structure. In contrast, a group with a rigid social structure is a *formal group*. Such a group has a well-defined set of roles and statuses, and sometimes it has written rules and regulations. For instance, the zoology department of a college or university is a formal group, because it is governed by carefully drawn-up rules and it has official positions, such as chair, executive assistant to the chair, graduate research assistant, and undergraduate student.

Another distinction between groups concerns the feelings we have about belonging to a group. An **in-group** is a group to which people feel they belong, whereas an **out-group** is a group to which people feel they do not belong. The distinction between in-groups and out-groups is useful for describing group structure and interaction. For instance, you could probably describe much of the interaction that took place in your high school in terms of in-groups and out-groups (students sometimes call an in-group a "clique"). In the adolescent world of the typical American high school, membership in the "right" clique or in-group brings with it high status and many social honors. Everyone in the school (including teachers) knows that athletes tend to hang out together and form a clique; that the "smart" students have another clique; and that some students seem not to fit in with any clique at all.

The sociological concept of a group differs from that of a **category**, or a cluster of people who share a social trait such as age, sex, or race. Members of a category do not interact, do not share a culture, and are not organized into a social system. A group also differs from a *collection*: two or more people who gather together at a specific place without developing a sense of togetherness. If these people interact at all, their interactions are superficial. For example, strangers waiting at a bus stop seldom speak to one another, but if they do, they restrict their conversation to the weather, bus schedules, and other polite topics.

Although sociologists categorize groups in several ways, the most basic distinction is between primary and secondary. **Primary groups** are characterized by intimate, warm, cooperative, and face-to-face relationships. Members of a primary group are concerned about one another's well-being, and they treat each other as valued ends rather than as means to other ends. Groups of family members and friends are the two most common examples of a primary group.

Primary groups tend to be small, perhaps made up of no more than a dozen members, because intimate relations are difficult to maintain among a larger number of

In-group ▲ Group to which people feel that they belong.

Out-group ▲ Group to which people feel that they do not belong.

Category ▲ A cluster of people who share a social trait such as age, sex, or race.

Primary group ▲ Group characterized by intimate, warm, cooperative, and face-to-face relationships.

TABLE 5.1 • *This table presents a summary of the basic characteristics of primary and secondary groups in terms of the kind of relationships within each group, the typical length of relationships, the scope of the relationships, and the purpose of the relationships. The table identifies the family and close friendship groups as examples of primary groups, and coworkers and political organizations as examples of secondary groups. In communal societies, a person's life is conducted largely within primary-group contexts. In associational societies, a person's life is divided between primary- and secondary-group contexts.*

 What other examples can you give of primary and secondary groups?

Primary and Secondary Group Characteristics

RELATIONSHIP	KIND	LENGTH	SCOPE	PURPOSE	TYPICAL EXAMPLES
Primary Group	Personal orientation	Usually long-term	Broad; usually involving many activities	As an end in itself	Families; close friendships
Secondary Group	Goal orientation	Variable; often short-term	Narrow; usually involving few activities	As a means to an end	Coworkers; political organizations

people. Although many larger groupings, such as the extended family, military unit, or athletic team, may appear to be primary groups, they actually consist of several smaller groupings, cliques, or factions. In turn, each of these might or might not constitute a primary group.

In contrast to primary groups, **secondary groups** are characterized by limited participation and by impersonal and formal relationships (see Table 5.1). People join secondary groups to accomplish explicit goals; hence, the members are not much concerned about the personal well-being of other members. Instead, they view group membership as a means to an end. Examples are the types of groups we frequently encounter in associational society—work groups, most classrooms, political organizations, labor unions, businesses, and so forth.

Although secondary groups are impersonal, they can be the setting for the development of primary groups. For instance, a class of 50 or so new students would be a secondary group, but as the year progresses, a few students might strike up a mutual friendship and develop into a primary group. A very large secondary group, such as a business corporation or college, will contain hundreds, or even thousands, of primary groups within it.

In communal societies, most requirements of daily living can be satisfied in the context of the family and peer group; hence, relatively few secondary groupings are required. However, when societies shift from communal to associational, the situation is quite different. The size and complexity of contemporary society require us to interact with people in limited ways and to confine our interactions to specific ends. Even those interactions that have the veneer of primary relations are actually secondary in nature. We interact with our hairdresser as a friend, but then we do not recognize her when we meet her face-to-face in the supermarket. We join a labor union to protect our rights as workers but make no effort to know other members intimately. We have an extended family, but we barely know our cousins or aunts and uncles living in another state.

The simplest and smallest human group is a dyad: a group with two members. A dyad is unique because the interaction between the two members constitutes just one social relationship. You and your best friend, for instance, are a dyad and have just one

Secondary group ▲ Group characterized by limited participation and impersonal and formal relationships.

social relationship between you. If either of you refuses to interact anymore, your group then vanishes. On the other hand, because each member of a dyad can focus exclusively on the other, dyadic relationships are often intimate, emotional, and deep. Thus, two friends, two lovers, two sisters, or two brothers may form exceptionally strong social bonds that last a lifetime.

When the number of group members extends beyond two to three or more, the complex characteristics of a social group begin to appear. Whereas a dyad has only one social relationship, a three-person group, or triad, has three possible social relationships. If you consider a triad to be a dyad plus one other person, then this characteristic becomes clear. For instance, in a three-person family, the mother and father might unite to oppose the child's demands for a new toy; or the child and father might unite and plead for a new toy that the mother opposes; or the child and mother might unite to argue against the father. As this example indicates, in a triad, coalitions form and shift easily, and with every shift, the "odd person" can become the target of group pressures (Simmel 1950, orig. 1902).

Although groups vary in size from two to some large number, sociologists have been mainly concerned with small groups. How many members can a small group have? This easily asked question is not easily answered. In principle, a small group is one that permits members to interact as individuals. However, the precise size of such a group will vary depending on the group's activities and its setting. For example, a peer group meets for personal satisfaction, whereas a work group meets to accomplish an objective goal. As a consequence, work groups are often larger than peer groups, are more formal, and meet on a regular basis. Although there is no hard-and-fast number that divides a small group from a large group, when group size increases beyond 12 or so members, personal interactions become difficult to maintain. At this point, the group becomes more formal, and several smaller groups will usually form within it.

Although we commonly belong to many groups, we do not have to be a member of every group that is important to us. Even though we do not belong to it, a group could have values, norms, and beliefs that serve as a standard for our own behavior. Such a group is called a **reference group**. Examples of reference groups, which we might or might not join, are political parties, professional associations, religious orders, or even sport teams. For instance, the individual may respect a political party's position on political issues and may vote the way the party suggests. Similarly, professional

Reference group ▲ Group whose values, norms, and beliefs come to serve as a standard for one's own behavior.

groups often influence their members' values and beliefs by suggesting appropriate behavior or serving as a normative guide. For example, many sociologists may not be members of the American Sociological Association (ASA), yet they may attend the annual meeting as part of their vacation time. They go to sessions on various sociological topics, lunch with their fellow sociologists, peruse new books on display, discuss the careers of the people they knew as graduate students, and so forth. After the meeting, they may subscribe to journals published by the association. All of these activities help make the association an important reference group for sociologists, whether they actually belong to the ASA.

Group Dynamics

Groups tend to exert powerful and active influences on their members, and they tend toward change. In search of a word that captured the essence of the processes that occur in groups, Kurt Lewin, a famous researcher of groups, came up with the term *group dynamics*. This term refers to the scientific study of the powerful processes that operate in groups (Forsyth 1998). Well over 10,000 studies on group dynamics have been reported, and three of the most frequently studied areas are leadership, cohesiveness, and conformity. We start the discussion with leadership.

Leadership   Groups are almost always directed or guided to some extent. That is, all groups have a **leader**—a person who can consistently influence the behavior of group members and the outcomes of the group. In some cases, the leader is formally designated, whereas in other cases, the leader emerges informally out of group interaction. Peer groups have informal leaders, for instance, whereas work groups have formally appointed managers. A group could, of course, have both types of leaders at the same time. If it does, the two leaders may compete for the loyalty of the group's members and thereby create splits and conflicts within the group.

Another distinction among group leaders is based on outcomes. An **instrumental leader** is concerned with attaining group goals, whereas an **expressive leader** is concerned with promoting group solidarity, cohesion, and morale. For example, the instrumental leader of a work group will drive the group toward meeting production goals on time, whereas the expressive leader will look after the group's morale. Without the instrumental leader, the group will lack direction, and without the expressive leader, some group members may become so unhappy that they quit. Either way, the group fails. Thus both types of leadership are important.

For many years it was thought that leaders had personalities that set them apart from group members. Although research did show that leaders were somewhat brighter and more talkative than followers, and perhaps even physically larger, the research could not identify a unique "leadership personality" (see Stogdill 1974). Research has shown, however, that leaders have styles that affect group outcomes (e.g., Forsyth 1998; Gibson and Marcodides 1995; Lewin, Lippett, and White 1939; White and Lippett 1960). A classic study identified three styles of leadership: authoritarian, democratic, and laissez-faire.

1. Authoritarian   In the authoritarian style, communication flows from the top down; the leader retains authority and responsibility for group actions, assigns members to clearly defined activities, and closely monitors their behavior. In effect, the role of the leader is to give orders, and the role of group members is to take them. The benefit of authoritarian leadership is the prompt, orderly, and predictable performance of tasks. However, these outcomes may be achieved at the expense of individual initiative and creativity. To see an authoritarian leader at work, suppose you are in a group of students that is trying to raise student awareness of sexual harassment on campus. The authoritarian leader would gather the group together and assign activities to them with little in the way of consultation about what the students did or did not want to do. This leader would set work schedules and task loads and would push

Leader ▲ A person who can consistently influence the behavior of group members and the outcomes of the group.

Instrumental leader ▲ A group leader whose activities are aimed at accomplishing the group's tasks.

Expressive leader ▲ A group leader whose activities are aimed at promoting group solidarity, cohesion, and morale.

the students hard to complete their tasks on time. The authoritarian leader would view the other students in the group simply as inputs into the programs that he or she designed.

2. **Democratic** In the democratic style, communication flows from members to the leader, and from the leader to members. The leader delegates authority and responsibility, discusses matters with group members, and encourages them to divide tasks among themselves. Democratic leadership promotes commitment to group goals and is well liked by participants. To include everyone in the democratic process, however, requires considerable time and raises the possibility that group cohesiveness will weaken if members begin to wrangle among themselves. In the example of sexual harassment, the democratic leader would begin by conducting several sessions with the other students in the group, getting their input into what specifically they want to attain and in which activities they should engage. After these decisions were made, the leader would ask students to sign up for the activities they would like to work on and give them a great deal of latitude in carrying out their tasks.

3. **Laissez-faire** A laissez-faire leader might be described as "laid back" and "chilled out." Such a leader exercises authority sparingly and functions mainly as a source of knowledge, skill, and experience that the group can draw on as it sees fit. In effect, the laissez-faire leader guides group behavior by forcing members to assume leadership tasks for themselves. This type of leadership encourages members to be creative and to exercise initiative, but if no members with these abilities are present, the group may drift aimlessly. With regard to the students working to eliminate sexual harassment, they would find little direction from the laissez-faire leader. Instead, the leader would urge them to do things on their own. The laissez-faire leader would also act as a resource person, give encouragement, and provide broad ideas. If no students step up to assume an active leadership role, however, the group will not succeed.

As you might suspect, no single style of leadership is best for all situations. In situations requiring quickness and decisiveness, such as combat or rescue work, authoritarian leadership works best because there is no time for debate or for individual creativity. For this reason, armies, police forces, rescue squads, airline crews, and emergency rooms in hospitals rely on authoritarian leadership.

Democratic leadership works best in situations that require participation and commitment to group goals. Boards of professional associations, for instance, are democratically led because everyone assumes that everyone else is equally competent. Friendship groups also have democratic leadership because everyone is a peer.

Laissez-faire leadership is relatively rare because it applies to very few situations. It is, however, fairly common in the research departments of formal organizations and in the academic departments of universities—units that are concerned with the production of new ideas and original research. Because no leader can force group members to think creatively, department chairs and managers of research units often define their jobs as providing resources, inspiration, and work conditions that encourage originality among researchers.

There are distinct cultural preferences in leadership styles. Most people in the United States prefer democratic leadership because it fits well with American norms and values. However, people in many societies prefer authoritarian leadership. For example, North and South Korea have different political systems, yet in both countries, authoritarian leadership styles predominate. Apparently, that style is more compatible with Korean culture, which emphasizes the unquestioned right of leaders to direct their followers.

Whereas these three styles of leadership are found in industrial societies, in traditional societies they are irrelevant because the leadership role is dictated by custom and long tradition. Thus, the tribal chief, the council of elders, and the shaman lead because they have always led, and it is assumed they always will lead (see Chapter 10; Weber 1946).

Group Cohesiveness   Consider a group of friends who gather every Christmas Day to celebrate and exchange gifts. As they mature and have families, their children will join the annual gathering. As their children have children, the grandchildren will join, but many original members will pass away. In everyday language, this group might be described as strong, tight, solid, or firm; but technically, sociologists would describe it as cohesive, since it is a group consisting of members who are strongly attracted to it (Forsyth 1998; Kleinfield 1996).

Few groups were more cohesive than the world-famous rock-and-roll group of the 1960s, the Beatles (Stokes 1980). Early in their career, when they were trying to hone their techniques, the group members fought over musical styles, the group's appearance, and who should be the lead guitarist and who should be the drummer. Eventually the group stabilized around four members: Paul McCartney, John Lennon, George Harrison, and Ringo Starr. These four young men spent virtually all their time together as they tried to develop a successful band. At first they were only marginally successful, playing their music in small clubs and beer joints. The Beatles finally came together after a prolonged stay in a foreign city. Isolated from family and friends, they developed confidence in themselves and took on an outward uniformity of appearance. They went on to overwhelming financial success, world tours, and international fame. The group broke up in the 1970s, when Paul McCartney decided to leave (Forsyth 1998). The murder of John Lennon by a deranged individual ended the possibility of a reunion of the full group. Nevertheless, the fame of the Beatles has long outlived the existence of the group.

As the example of the Beatles indicates, if members interact frequently, cohesion usually increases. The process is circular in that frequent interaction increases the attractiveness of the group to its members, and in turn, attractiveness causes the members to interact. All else being equal, therefore, a group that meets once a week will be more cohesive than a group that meets once a month.

Events and people outside the group also affect cohesion. If outsiders define a group positively, cohesion will increase. As the Beatles example indicates, being alone in a foreign city helped create cohesion, because the band members were forced to rely on themselves. In extreme situations, such as survival under drastic circumstances or in military combat, group members develop extraordinarily strong bonds of commitment to each other, and sometimes they even lay down their lives to meet those commitments.

Finally, changes in membership affect cohesion. Old members are most comfortable with the social relationships they have developed among themselves. To some extent, new members will invariably disrupt these relationships, and cohesion will suffer until a different pattern emerges. In addition, if the new arrivals increase the size of the group, cohesion will decline because personal interaction will then be more difficult. The departure of old members will also lessen cohesion, but if their departure reduces the size of the group, then personal interactions will be easier and cohesion might increase.

Group Conformity   As we know from Chapter 3, conformity is usually rewarded, whereas deviance is usually punished. In a small group, if the pressures to conform are so strong that no dissension or critical questioning is allowed, the state is called **groupthink** (Flippen 1999). Two classic experiments demonstrated group pressures. The first was conducted by Muzafer Sherif (1936, 1937; C. W. Sherif 1976). In this experiment, Sherif made clever use of the "autokinetic effect": when a fixed point of light is shown against a dark background, the light will appear to wander around even though it is actually stationary (if you have ever stared at a star in the night sky, you might have noticed the autokinetic effect without knowing it). Because people differ in their visual acuity, no two individuals perceive exactly the same amount of movement.

Sherif placed a number of participants in a dark room that had a fixed pinpoint of light shining on the wall. He then instructed each participant to stare at the light and

Groupthink ▲ Intense social pressure within a group for individuals to conform to group norms and abandon individual and critical thinking.

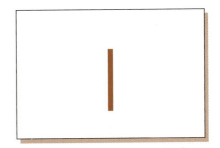

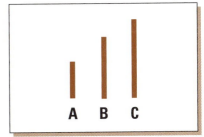

then silently to estimate how much the light moved. Next, Sherif assigned each participant to a small group and repeated the procedure, except that now the participants took turns stating their estimates out loud. As Sherif predicted, individuals modified their private estimates to match more closely the estimates they heard from other participants. Soon everyone had converged on a single, group estimate. Finally, the participants were again tested separately. Even though they were no longer in the presence of others, they continued to use the group estimate as their own. Sherif concluded that in unstructured situations, group norms quickly develop, and from that point on, individuals will follow those norms even when they are alone (Pollis, Montgomery, and Smith 1975).

The second classic experiment on conformity was conducted by Solomon Asch on groups of college students (1952, 1955). In one part of his study, he instructed participants to look at a picture of three unequal vertical lines that were projected on a screen. He then had the participants match one of the three lines with a fourth vertical line. The task was very easy, as demonstrated by a preliminary study in which participants correctly matched the lines over 99 percent of the time.

Asch then assigned each participant to a group with seven other "participants." Unknown to the real participant, the seven others were Asch's secret accomplices. Asch showed the lines as before but had each participant answer out loud. In some trials, the seven accomplices, by prearrangement, all gave correct answers, whereas in other trials, they all gave the same answer but one that was clearly wrong. In the latter case, the real participant became a minority of one in the midst of a unanimous majority of seven. Asch repeated the experiment many times, and he found that one-third of the real participants rejected their own judgment and went along with the decision of the group—even when the group was clearly incorrect (see Figure 5.3).

After the trials were over, Asch interviewed the conforming participants and found that most of them actually believed that the group was incorrect and that they were right. Why, then, did they conform to the group decision? In the main, they conformed because they did not want to be deviant, even though conforming meant being wrong. Even though Asch's findings may be hard to believe at first, they have been replicated many times and in different cultures (Neto 1995).

FIGURE 5.3 Samuel Asch's Experiment

These are examples of the types of cards used by Samuel Asch in his famous experiment. Many participants deliberately gave false responses to conform with other members of their group.

What Do You Think? ●■▲ Social Loafing   ?

How would you answer this question:

Do people work harder when they are

1. working together as a member of a group, or
2. working alone?

Although common sense and your personal experience might suggest otherwise, answer 2 is correct: people work less hard when they are working together. This phenomenon is called social loafing. Researchers have known about it for a long time (Latané and Harkins 1979).

To illustrate social loafing, suppose that you and two other students are assigned to do a joint term project for your English literature class. Specifically, your group is assigned *Hamlet* and required to turn in a 15-page paper on why Hamlet's character is so indecisive about avenging his father's death. All three of you will receive the same grade for the project. Under these circumstances, social loafing is likely to occur (not by you, of course, but by the other two members).

Why does social loafing occur? The answer to this question involves several social processes: (1) individuals in a group may slack off because they feel that they are not getting their fair share of the rewards; (2) individuals may feel that the other members of the group will make up for their lack of effort; and (3) individuals may think that they can hide in the group and that their loafing will go unnoticed.

CQ Suppose you are assigned to do a group project with three classmates, what can you do to prevent social loafing?

*To answer these critical questions, review the box What Is Critical Thinking? in Chapter 1, and pay special attention to the discussion of implications and assertions.

SOURCE: Adapted from Bibb Latané, K. Williams, and S. Harkins, "Many Hands Make Light the Work: The Causes and Consequences of Social Loafing." *Journal of Personality and Social Psychology* 37 (1979):822–832. Copyright © 1979. Adapted with permission of American Psychological Association.

As we discussed in Chapter 1, experiments are powerful but lack realism. The conditions present in these experiments would hardly happen in everyday life. Moreover, there is some question as to whether the groups formed by Sherif and Asch were groups in the sociological sense of the concept. At least in the beginning, the participants who gathered in the laboratory were mostly strangers and probably lacked a sense of togetherness.

On the other hand, if the processes revealed by Asch and Sherif do take place in everyday life, then groups and collections of individuals have an almost frightening hold over each member. To illustrate, suppose one member of a jury believes the defendant to be innocent, whereas the other 11 jurors believe the defendant to be guilty. In the light of Asch's and Sherif's research, we would expect the one member to go along with the majority and vote guilty about a third of the time. Or consider the crash survivors described at the opening of this chapter. Once the group decided to engage in cannibalism, any individual who opposed the idea would still feel pressure to yield to the group decision and to eat human flesh, too.

●■▲ Pausing to Think About Groups

As social creatures, humans spend a huge amount of time interacting with other humans. In some cases, these humans clump together, form bonds among themselves, and develop into a group. Once formed, a group has a vitality and identity above and beyond the individuals within it. Groups differ in how formally organized they are—some are informal and have little in the way of a rigid structure, whereas others are more formal, with a well-defined set of roles and statuses. In communal societies, most daily living takes place in the context of primary groups, but in associational societies, a large portion of time is spent in secondary groups. All groups have leaders, but they differ greatly in leadership style. Some leaders are authoritarian, others are democratic, and some are laissez-faire. Some groups are more cohesive than others. The most cohesive groups are those whose members interact frequently, define the group as attractive, are seen by outsiders as attractive, and have stable memberships. Groups can bring great pressure to bear on their members to conform to group norms.

CQ Sociologists assert that teenagers and young adults are often subject to strong group pressures to conform. ◆ Have you ever felt such group pressure? ◆ If so, how did you react?

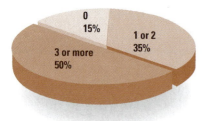
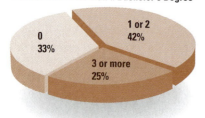
Organizations

In communal societies, life is conducted through personal social relationships and small groups. The opposite is true in associational societies, in which personal relationships give way to formal relationships and the small group gives way to the formal organization. Personal relationships continue to exist and remain important, to be sure, but the main affairs of an associational society are conducted through its organizations (Coleman 1982).

The importance of organizations to an associational society and to the lives of its members can be illustrated by considering the following: We are born and die in hospitals, are socialized in schools, work in corporations, play in athletic clubs, visit elders in rest homes, and lastly, are memorialized in funeral homes. Even in our private lives, when we obtain our meals from fast-food restaurants, buy ready-made clothes off the rack, and watch programs on television, we are relying on organizations to supply these goods and services. Modern society is, in other words, an organizational society (Ritzer 2000; see the Sociology Online box for Internet examples).

Organizations have found it useful to develop web sites to tell their stories. Both public and private organizations spend millions in creating and maintaining their sites. Go online and find a web site for a utilitarian organization such as the federal or state government or a corporation such as IBM or Xerox. Compare the site's content with that of a voluntary organization such as the Girl Scouts or Young Democrats or Young Republicans. How are the web sites similar? How are they different?

What do sociologists mean by the term organization? An **organization** may be defined as a group with three characteristics:

1. It is deliberately constructed; that is, someone or some group of people decided to create the organization for some purpose.

2. It is structured, with well-defined roles and positions. Typically, the roles differ in prestige and power.

3. It has rules, and it has sanctions for violations of those rules.

Types of Organizations

In the United States, there are perhaps 10 million organizations serving various purposes. Most of these organizations are small. For example, the majority of businesses employ fewer than 100 people; voluntary associations have, on average, 50 or fewer members; and the typical elementary school has about 25 teachers. There are, of course, large organizations. The federal government employs over 3 million people, and corporations such as General Motors employ in excess of 200,000 people worldwide.

Organizations serve many purposes. Sociologists studying the functions of organizations often classify groups by the purposes they serve. For instance, some organizations provide recreation, enjoyment, and the satisfaction of participating in a common endeavor with other people. These are called voluntary organizations because members can enter and leave them freely. Examples are political clubs such as the Young Democrats and Young Republicans, youth organizations such as the Girl Scouts, and civic associations such as the Rotary Club. In contrast to free entry and exit, some organizations restrain people within well-defined boundaries. These are called *coercive organizations*, because they take in and keep members against their will. Obvious examples are prisons and mental hospitals. It is interesting that many organizations we normally think of as voluntary in fact are coercive. For example, children must attend school whether they want to or not. And once there, they cannot leave until the school dismisses them. Lastly, some organizations are concerned with matters of everyday life. These are called *utilitarian organizations* because people join them to gain objective ends. Examples are businesses, government agencies, and labor unions (Etzioni 1975).

Bureaucracies

As an organization grows, it changes, and at some point, the old ways of doing things cease to work very well. Primary relationships between employees and supervisors break down, lines of responsibility and authority become blurred, and vital records get lost or are not kept. In fact, the organization might become so large and complex that its old form must be replaced by an entirely new one. Almost always, that replacement is a **bureaucracy**: a form of organization based on explicit rules with a clear, impersonal, and hierarchical authority structure. Almost any large organization you might

Organization ▲ A group that is deliberately constructed, with well-defined roles and positions that differ in prestige and power, and has rules and sanctions for violation of those rules.

Bureaucracy ▲ A form of organization based on explicit rules, with a clear, impersonal, and hierarchical authority structure.

think of is a bureaucracy, including your school, government, and local library (cf. Blau and Meyer 1987).

Weber's Analysis Max Weber, who was introduced in Chapter 1, recognized the importance of bureaucratic organizations and developed a widely used framework for studying them. This framework begins with the concept of an **ideal type**: a composite of characteristics based on many specific examples. According to Weber, an ideal type of bureaucracy would have the following characteristics:

1. A complex division of labor among its members with each person having specialized duties and responsibilities.

2. A hierarchy of authority with a few people at the top, many people in the middle, and even more people at the bottom. Managers are held responsible for the performance of those under them in the chain of command.

3. Explicit rules and procedures that govern all aspects of the organization, down to the tiniest details. When these rules and procedures are followed, a common and predictable outcome is obtained.

4. A system that rewards people on the basis of performance rather than on family ties, friendships, or other primary relationships. Competence in skills may be determined by tests, past experiences, or formal training. Rewards, salary advances, and promotions are based on job performance.

5. Extensive written records of the organization's activities and detailed dossiers on every member of the organization. A paper flow is generated within the organization and, in total, comes to be the official history of the organization.

As an ideal type, the bureaucracy is the very picture of a well-oiled social machine that accomplishes a great deal of work evenhandedly and with a high degree of efficiency. Weber of course knew that no real bureaucracy could actually meet all five criteria completely. His goal in developing the ideal type was to identify the essential features of a bureaucracy, and he provided a model by means of which organizations might be compared. In real life, many small businesses, social clubs, and even a few large organizations do not very well fit Weber's ideal type, but a government agency and many big businesses come very close to meeting all five criteria completely (see the Sociology Online box).

The Negative Consequences of Bureaucracy Bureaucracies have evolved socially over literally thousands of years, and in the course of their evolution, they have become better at handling complex problems. Nevertheless, they are not perfect, and sociologists have identified several problems with them, as follows:

1. *"Service without a smile"* (Hummel 1994). Because a bureaucracy is an impersonal organization, all clients of the organization are treated in the same way. All too frequently, they are also treated with indifference or even contempt. For example, people seeking unemployment compensation often must wait for hours to fill out a form and then perhaps wait for days or months before finding out the results of their request. Or college students planning to graduate in June might receive a short, blunt notice in the mail informing them that they have not met all requirements and therefore cannot graduate as planned. As a result of such treatment, clients often become alienated from the organization that was originally designed to serve them.

2. *"Rules are rules."* Although rules are the essence of a bureaucracy, a blind devotion to rules may interfere with the achievement of organizational goals. The tendency for bureaucrats mechanically to follow rules rather than use their imagination is called trained incapacity (Veblen 1921; Hummel 1994).

People volunteering to build housing for the poor are an example of a voluntary organization. In contrast, prisoners working in chains are an example of a coercive organization.

CQ *What other types of voluntary and coercive organizations can you think of?*

Ideal type ▲ A composite of characteristics based on many specific examples.

3. **"Goal displacement."** This term refers to the process by which the original goals of the organization—to make a profit, to serve a clientele, or to provide a service—are replaced by goals that serve the personal interest of the bureaucrat. To illustrate, it is not unusual for charitable organizations to devote more money to the salaries of the bureaucrats who run the organization than to the people they hope to help.

4. **"Work expands to fill the time available."** This cynical statement is known as Parkinson's Law, named after the person who first wrote about it. According to Parkinson, even if there is no work to be done, employees will find busywork to do; and if there is not enough busywork, they will create work for one another. In this way, the amount of work to be done expands to fill the workday. Of course, at the end of the day, nothing of much value will have been accomplished.

5. **"Bureaucrats rise to the level of their incompetence."** According to Lawrence Peter, competent bureaucrats are rewarded with a promotion to a higher-level job demanding greater ability. This process of rewarding success at one level with a promotion to a higher level will continue until the bureaucrats reach a level that is beyond their ability. At this point, they will have risen to their level of incompetence. Moreover, because demotion is rare, every position in the organization eventually comes to be filled by an incompetent bureaucrat.

6. **"Iron Law of Oligarchy"** (Michels 1966, orig. 1911). According to Robert Michels, every bureaucracy is controlled by an **oligarchy**: a small clique of people who rule the organization for their own benefit. These few people can easily dominate because they control the organization's funds, records, and plans; and in addition, they control the flow of information within the organization and can fire people who oppose them. Michels pessimistically concluded that oligarchy is inevitable (Lipset 1996).

7. **"Invisible woman."** Even though most bureaucracies supposedly follow a policy of equal opportunity, the men and women in an organization are seldom equal. In addition to the problems that will be discussed in Chapter 8, women are subjected to many sexist ploys (Benokraitis and Feagin 1994; Thorne 1993). Some of these are as follows:

- Condescending chivalry—when a woman's supervisor protects her from criticism, even though she might benefit from it.
- Supportive discouragement—when a woman's coworkers discourage her from competing for a challenging position because she might not get it.
- Benevolent exploitation—when a woman is assigned the detailed, tedious work of a job but a male superior takes credit for the final product.

The end result of these ploys is to undermine a woman's reputation for competence. She will then become less of a threat to competitors in the workplace and hardly visible to her supervisors (Lorber 1995).

Anyone who has ever stood in line for hours to change a class schedule or apply for an automobile tag can easily appreciate the negative aspects of a bureaucracy. Many people have difficulty filling out the paperwork required by large bureaucracies. In addition, as more and more organizations seek efficiency, bureaucracy spreads into more and more aspects of our lives. It becomes increasingly difficult to avoid being treated like a number or to find a place where rationality and efficiency do not outweigh other human considerations. The sociologist George Ritzer refers to this tendency as the "McDonaldization of Society." Ritzer warns that habitual use of McDonaldized systems is destructive to our mental health and to society because it eliminates variety and spontaneity (Ritzer 2000). To avoid being McDonaldized, Ritzer suggests that we all seek out and occasionally use nonbureaucratic, inefficient organizations. For instance, he suggests that we should cook our own dinner at least once a week, avoid all national store chains, use cash instead of credit cards, and send back to the post office all the mail we receive addressed to "occupant."

STUDY TIP

Make a set of flash cards to illustrate the seven negative consequences of bureaucracy. On one side, write the consequence; on the other, write a definition in your own words and come up with an example not given in the text.

Oligarchy ▲ A small clique of people who rule an organization for their own benefit.

Some corporate brand names have become fixtures in the American city. Here, people are entering and leaving a Barnes & Noble bookstore next to Starbucks Coffee shop. Successful corporations market themselves carefully because they have much to lose if their corporate image becomes tarnished.

The Corporation

In associational society, the **corporation** is a familiar type of bureaucratic organization. It is becoming a major factor in the global economy (Chapter 9), and, as Ritzer warns, is becoming an almost inescapable part of our daily routine. Although we think nothing of seeing the word "Inc." or "Incorporated" attached to the name of a company, the concept of a corporation is rather unique.

By definition, a corporation is a group that, through the legal process of incorporation, has been given the status of a separate and real social entity. A corporation thus has rights that are separate from those of the people within it. The distinction between the corporation and the individual is important. It means, among other things, that a corporation may be held responsible for the acts of its officers but that its officers may not be held responsible for the acts of the corporation (Cahill and Cahill 1999). If a passenger airline crashes, to illustrate, the corporation may be sued, but its officers are immune from liability. This aspect of the corporation—limited liability—helps to explain why it is the most common organizational form among large businesses. Even so, corporate executives have been held legally liable for fraud and other crimes they committed to amass personal fortunes at the expense of stockholders and the general public (Berman and Latour 2003; Hays 2003; see Chapter 4).

The corporation as we know it is a fairly recent social invention, but its seeds were planted centuries ago in feudal Europe (Coleman 1993). At that time, the major organizational units of society were based on primary relationships, such as the clan, manor, guild, church, and family. Even a peasant had a personal relationship with the lord of the manor, who in turn had a personal relationship with the local nobility. As time went on, however, a new type of organization began to develop. In 1243, Pope Innocent IV provided a metaphor for the new organization when he designated it a *persona ficta* ("fictitious person") and proclaimed that it had the same legal standing as a natural person. This fictitious person was the forerunner of the modern corporation.

By the seventeenth century, the corporation had come to control European commerce. Companies such as the Dutch West India Company and the English

Corporation ▲ A group that, through the legal process of incorporation, has been given the status of a separate and real social entity.

East India Company were given monopolies over commerce in certain areas of the world, and they flourished. In the eighteenth and nineteenth centuries, this form of organization—the corporation—became the most popular organizational form throughout the industrializing world. Today, of course, corporations are part of our everyday life, and we take them for granted. Corporate names such as IBM, Pepsi Cola, Xerox, and Levi Strauss are part of our everyday vocabulary and are known the world over.

●■▲ Pausing to Think   About Organizations

In communal societies, life is conducted through personal social relationships and small groups. The opposite is true in associational societies. There, personal relationships give way to formal relationships, and the small group gives way to the formal organization. Personal relationships continue to exist and remain important, to be sure, but the main affairs of an associational society are conducted through its organizations. Organizations serve many purposes and as a result may be classified as voluntary, coercive, or utilitarian. As organizations grow and expand their range of activity, they tend to become bureaucracies. Bureaucracy as a form of organization gained prominence with the rise of industrial societies, and today bureaucracies dominate life. Paradoxically, bureaucracies make it possible to achieve collective goals, but, at the same time, they often subvert the goals they were meant to achieve and subordinate the individual to the organization. The bureaucratic organization known as the corporation is a relatively recent human invention. In most associational societies, the corporation has the same standing before the law as a natural person.

CQ What aspects of bureaucracies do you find especially frustrating? ◆ Are these the same aspects that create greater efficiency for society?

Interaction, Groups, and Organizations in the Twenty-First Century

Futurist Alvin Toffler believes that this century will see an increasing division between *fast* and *slow* societies. The major distinction between fast and slow societies is the speed at which their economies operate. In fast societies, advanced technology speeds the entire business cycle, from the rapid movement of investment capital to the delivery of the final product to customers (Toffler 1990). Obviously, to have a fast society, one needs fast groups, fast organizations, and fast interaction. Toffler believes that extensive use of computers in fast societies will create new ways of organizing society, new ways of interacting, and the formation of many new groups all dedicated to increasing speed and efficiency. Current trends already reflect this tendency.

To illustrate, rapid technological change has placed a premium on information in the financial capitals of the world. Linked by computers, satellites, fiber-optic cables, and high-speed electronic transfers, global markets are developing that conduct business around the clock. Financial transactions are picked up in one center when another one shuts down for the night, and trading in these markets goes on 24 hours a day, bouncing from one major exchange to another (Kennedy 1993; Cohen and Kennedy 2000; Chapter 8).

Companies have found that they need to develop strategic partnerships with other companies if they are to keep abreast of this rapidly changing business world. Rather than attempting to develop more hierarchies and larger bureaucracies, many corporations have reconstituted themselves into smaller, more efficient organizations

Society Today ● ■ ▲

Telephones and the Great Social Transformation

The number of telephones in a society indicates its level of development (Caplow 1991). Telephones also index the associational and communal characteristics of a society. Rapid and convenient communication encourages trade, scientific development, innovation, political activity, and international linkages—all aspects of associational societies.

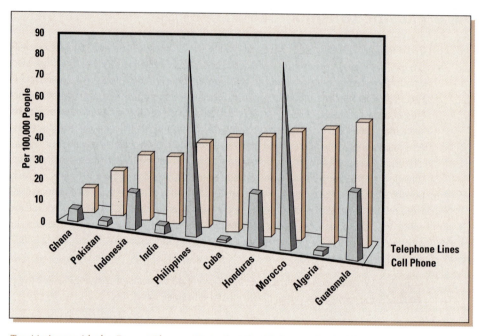

Ten Nations with the Fewest Phones: Note that the highest value is 80.

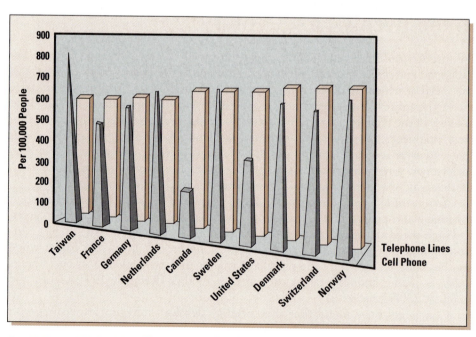

Ten Nations with the Most Phones: Note that the highest value is 800.

Countries on the first chart—"ten nations with the fewest phones"—tend to be less developed economically. They have few phones, and the phones they have are concentrated in urban centers. These societies tend to be communal in nature. In contrast, countries on the second chart—"ten nations with the most phones"—are economically well developed and are characterized by associational relationships.

Recently cell phones have become popular, and as the charts show, in some countries cell phones probably carry more conversations than conventional phones. Soon, we suspect that walkie-talkies, satellite phones, and tiny portable computers with electronic mail services will become increasingly popular. In your lifetime, you will probably witness the demise of the conventional telephone.

that are linked to other organizations. For instance, Corning Glass Works maintains joint ventures or partnerships with 15 other companies. These companies are spread over 13 countries, giving Corning a global network of strategic alliances that provides vital information quickly on what its competitors are doing (Hage and Powers 1992).

Similar developments are occurring in nonprofit organizations, such as government and public service agencies. For example, many libraries have become electronically networked to allow for nearly instantaneous communication between branches and a speedier exchange of books, magazines, and other materials. This arrangement means faster service to customers and less cost to the libraries, since they may share a larger number of books between them. Even the federal government has gotten into the act. The Library of Congress, along with most federal agencies, the Pentagon, Congress, and the White House, has become linked to the Internet, a vast electronic communications system. In 1995 that system consisted of approximately 13.5 million people on 3.5 million computers (Associated Press 1995b). Since then, it has grown by uncounted millions of people. Individuals with computers linked to the Internet can even send messages to the president by e-mail with the simple address president@whitehouse.gov.

The restructuring of society from large, unwieldy organizations dependent on layers and layers of hierarchy to smaller, more efficient, faster organizations has important implications for social roles, interaction, and interpersonal relations. For instance, people who take on jobs in "downsized" organizations will find that their role is complex. Rather than learning to perform a simple, routine job that seldom changes, their jobs in the organization are likely to be very dynamic, changing as a result of external forces in far-off places. They are likely to find less bureaucracy in their work, but more uncertainty. They will need to be able to respond more quickly to change and to learn how to report to multiple bosses (Kennedy 1993; Cohen and Kennedy 2000). No doubt their work will become more exciting and stressful as more corporations develop global networks, requiring employees to adjust to different languages and to other cultural differences. Employees may be expected to relocate frequently, perhaps even moving to a corporate office in a different society, to learn how the work gets done there. Such relocations may help efficiency, but they are likely to place more stress on the family.

In contrast, societies with slow economies are likely to have a slower pace of life, in which bureaucracies and organizations are less efficient, people are less willing to move, friendships are more stable, and marriages are more permanent. In other words, being in the fast lane has its disadvantages as well as its advantages.

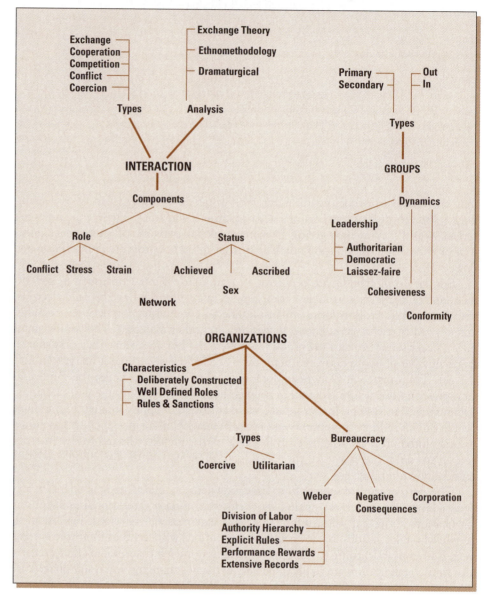

There are three concept webs for this chapter. However, they may be expanded. For example, the negative consequences of bureaucracy are not listed in the web. For practice in drawing concept webs, add them to the web.

Looking Ahead

The next chapter begins the section on inequality. Social class and stratification are central features of society and are important factors in determining an individual's opportunity for participating in society. Over the years, sociologists have devised many ways of studying stratification and have put forth several important theories.

WHAT YOU SHOULD KNOW ●■▲

1. What forms does social interaction take?

Interaction involves a wide variety of communication forms including spoken words, subtle gestures, visual images, and electronically transmitted information. There are five types of social interaction: exchange, cooperation, competition, conflict, and coercion.

2. How are roles and statuses linked to the Great Social Transformation?

Individuals are linked to other individuals through statuses and roles. A status may be either ascribed or achieved. As people play out their roles, they often confront role conflict, role stress, and role strain. Associational societies tend to be characterized by more role conflicts, stresses, and strains than are communal societies.

3. How do sociologists analyze social interaction?

According to the dramaturgical approach, all people unthinkingly follow a social script and abide by unstated rules while going about their daily lives. According to ethnomethodology, many of the rules people follow are deeply embedded in their culture, and people rarely know that the rules exist and guide their behavior. Exchange theory suggests that social interaction often is based on the expectation of reciprocity.

4. How are groups connected to the Great Social Transformation?

A group has a vitality and identity above and beyond the individuals within it. Groups differ in how formally organized they are, while in-groups and out-groups help define group structure and interaction. In communal societies, most daily living takes place in the context of primary groups, whereas in associational societies, a much larger portion takes place in secondary groups.

5. What types of group leaders are there?

Group leaders may be classified as instrumental or expressive. Another way to classify group leaders is by style: authoritarian, democratic, or laissez-faire.

6. What holds groups together, and how does this characteristic affect individual behavior?

The most cohesive groups are those whose members interact frequently, define the group as attractive, are seen by outsiders as attractive, and have stable membership. Groups can bring great pressure to bear on their members to conform to group norms. Groupthink may suppress critical thinking among the members.

7. How has the role of organizations changed with the Great Social Transformation?

In traditional, communal societies, life is conducted through primary social relations and small groups. In associational, industrial societies, primary relationships give way to secondary relationships, and the small group gives way to the formal organization. Primary relationships continue to exist and remain important, but the main affairs of an industrial society are conducted through its organizations.

8. What type of organization is a bureaucracy, and when did it develop?

As organizations grow and expand, they tend to become bureaucracies. Bureaucracies gained prominence with the rise of industrial societies, and today bureaucracies dominate modern life. Paradoxically, bureaucracies make it possible to achieve collective goals, but, at the same time, they often subvert the goals they were meant to achieve and subordinate the individual to the organization. A special type of bureaucracy is the corporation.

9. What does the future hold for interaction, groups, and organizations?

Futurist Alvin Toffler believes that this century will see an increasing division between fast and slow societies. Fast societies place a premium on the speed with which their economies operate, and they require fast interaction and efficient organizations. Slow societies have a more leisurely pace to their economies, and they place fewer demands on people and organizations to be quick and efficient.

TEST YOUR KNOWLEDGE ●■▲

Key Terms Matching

Match each of these key terms with the best definition or example from the numbered items that follow. Write the letter(s) preceding the key term in the blank before the definition that you choose.

a. achieved status

b. ascribed status

c. bureaucracy

d. coercion

e. competition

f. conflict

g. cooperation

h. corporation

i. ethnomethodology

j. exchange

k. expressive leader

l. group

m. groupthink

n. impression management

o. in-groups

p. instrumental leader

q. leader

r. master status

s. norm of reciprocity

t. oligarchy

u. organization

v. out-groups

w. primary groups

x. reference group

y. role

z. role conflict

aa. role strain

bb. role stress

cc. secondary groups

dd. social interaction

ee. status

ff. status set

_____ 1. The process through which two or more parties attempt to obtain the same goals.

_____ 2. The process through which people transfer goods, services, and other items with each other.

_____ 3. A person who can consistently influence the behavior of group members and the outcomes of the group.

_____ 4. A strong norm that says that if you do something for a person, then that person must do something of approximately equal social value in return.

_____ 5. A form of interaction in which the parties attempt physically or socially to vanquish each other.

_____ 6. The expected behavior associated with a status.

_____ 7. The collection of statuses a person occupies at any one time.

_____ 8. The incompatibility of different roles played by a single person.

_____ 9. The methodology for studying the common understanding of everyday life.

_____ 10. Groups to which people feel that they belong.

_____ 11. Intense social pressure within a group for individuals to conform to group norms and abandon individual and critical thinking.

_____ 12. Groups characterized by limited participation and by impersonal and formal relationships.

_____ 13. A form of organization based on explicit rules, with a clear, impersonal, and hierarchical authority structure.

_____ 14. A small clique of people who rule an organization for their own benefit.

_____ 15. The process of compelling others to do something against their will.

_____ 16. Groups to which individuals feel that they do not belong.

_____ 17. A group that, through the legal process of incorporation, has been given the status of a separate and real social entity.

_____ 18. A status, ascribed or achieved, that is so important that a person organizes his or her life and social identity around it.

_____ 19. A collection of people who take each other's behavior into account as they interact and who develop a sense of togetherness.

_____ 20. Status over which people can exert at least some control.

_____ 21. Groups characterized by intimate, warm, co-operative, and face-to-face relationships.

_____ 22. A group leader whose activities are aimed at accomplishing the group's tasks.

_____ 23. A position within society.

_____ 24. The incompatibility of expectations within a single role.

_____ 25. A status assigned to people whether they wish to have it or not.

_____ 26. A group whose values, norms, and beliefs come to serve as a standard for one's own behavior.

_____ 27. The anxiety produced by being unable to meet all role requirements at the same time.

_____ 28. A group that is deliberately constructed, with well-defined roles and positions that differ in prestige and power and that has rules and sanctions for violation of those rules.

_____ 29. The conscious manipulation of props, scenery, costumes, and behavior in an attempt to present a particular image to other people.

_____ 30. A group leader whose activities are aimed at promoting group solidarity, cohesion, and morale.

_____ 31. The process in which people work together to achieve shared goals.

_____ 32. The acts that people perform toward one another and the responses that they give in return.

Multiple Choice

Circle the letter of your choice.

1. According to sociologist Rose Coser, one advantage to the complexity of contemporary society is that
   a. roles are actually less complex, leading to less role stress, strain, and conflict.
   b. the network of social interactions is less.
   c. there are more opportunities for growth and creativity.
   d. participation in primary groups outnumbers that in secondary groups.

2. Which type of social interaction is largely limited to the police or other officials of the state?
   a. coercion
   b. exchange
   c. conflict
   d. competition

3. Terrence is a single father with two children. He is also a chef. When his responsibilities as a parent and as an employee cause him to feel as if he cannot handle all his role requirements, he is experiencing
   a. master status.
   b. role set.
   c. role strain.
   d. stress.

4. Which of the following best describes the situation of teachers interacting in the teachers' lounge?
   a. They are engaging in impression management.
   b. They are exhibiting dramaturgy.
   c. They are acting in the front region.
   d. They are acting in the back region.

5. If you dress professionally as you prepare for a job interview, you are engaging in
   a. ethnomethodology.
   b. impression management.
   c. dramaturgy.
   d. studied nonobservance.

6. Rekha pretended to be a guest in her parents' home to discover the unstated rules of interaction. Harold Garfinkel called this activity
   a. the back region.
   b. a breaching experiment.
   c. exchange theory.
   d. dramaturgy.

7. Professor Lee is not a member of the American Sociological Association (ASA), but she uses the organization as a standard for her research. In this case, the ASA, including its members, is a
   a. primary group.
   b. reference group.
   c. secondary group.
   d. democratic group.

8. Which type of leader provides the group with his or her knowledge and skill but forces the members to assume leadership tasks for themselves?
   a. authoritarian
   b. democratic
   c. laissez-faire
   d. none of the above

9. Which is NOT a characteristic of organizations?
   a. They are constructed for a purpose.
   b. They reward people on the basis of kinship relations.
   c. They have well-defined roles and positions.
   d. They have rules and sanctions for rule violations.

10. Robert Michels's Iron Law of Oligarchy states that
    a. work expands to fill the available time.
    b. bureaucrats rise to their level of incompetence.
    c. rule by a few people is inevitable.
    d. there can be only one leader in a group.

11. Which is NOT a characteristic of bureaucracies?
    a. hierarchical authority structure
    b. clear rules
    c. written records
    d. simple division of labor

12. The tendency for bureaucrats mechanically to follow the rules rather than to use their imaginations is called
    a. Iron Law of Oligarchy.
    b. trained incapacity.
    c. goal displacement.
    d. supportive discouragement.

13. What term is used to describe a situation in which a woman's male supervisor protects her from criticism, even though she might benefit from it?
    a. supportive discouragement
    b. goal displacement
    c. benevolent exploitation
    d. condescending chivalry

14. A corporation is a distinct type of organization in that
    a. it has rights that are separate from the people within it.
    b. it is not responsible for the actions of its officers.
    c. people who work in a corporation are held responsible for its actions.
    d. it has a hierarchical authority structure.

15. Sociologists would define "mother" as a
    a. role.
    b. status.
    c. master status.
    d. cultural universal.

True-False

Indicate your response to each of the following statements by circling T for true or F for false.

T F 1. Sometimes a person's ascribed status will affect her or his achieved status.

T F 2. The social network of a member of an industrial society has more units than that of a member of a preindustrial society.

T F 3. Pretending not to notice a mistake in a role performance is called studied nonobservance.

T F 4. Primary groups often develop within secondary groups.

T F 5. An in-group is a well-liked popular group whether or not you are a member of that group.

T F 6. As societies undergo the transformation from traditional to industrial, roles decrease in number and complexity.

T F 7. When compared with communal societies, social interaction in associational societies is more diverse, involving many different groups and organizations.

T F 8. Membership turnover tends to disrupt group cohesiveness, at least temporarily.

T F 9. Weber's concept "ideal type" means that something is the best it can be.

T F 10. In the future, the use of technology may cause an increased division between fast and slow societies based on the speed at which their economies operate.

T F 11. Ethnomethodology singles out exchanges as the most important type of social interaction.

T F 12. "Service without a smile" refers to the tendency of bureaucrats to rise to their level of incompetence.

T F 13. A corporation is an organization that has been given the status of a separate and real social entity.

T F 14. Organizations have rules and sanctions for violating the rules.

T F 15. Utilitarian organizations include businesses, government agencies, and labor unions.

NOTE: The answers to these exercises are at the end of the book.

For additional practice tests and other resources please visit the companion web site at http://www.prenhall.com/curry.

Essay

1. Discuss what the "theater" and Goffman's dramaturgical approach have in common.

2. Contrast primary and secondary groups and give examples of each.

3. Discuss two classic experiments that demonstrate group pressure on individuals.

4. According to Weber, what are the five characteristics of a bureaucracy?

5. What are seven negative consequences of bureaucracies? Give examples of each that you have observed.

6

Inequalities of Social Class

Chapter Outline

In 1912 the *Titanic* was the pride of the British White Star Line. Four city blocks long and 11 stories high from the bottom of her keel to the top of her masts, the *Titanic* could make 25 knots in good weather. The designers and builders of the *Titanic* believed her to be unsinkable, because she incorporated the latest in maritime design. On April 10, 1912, the *Titanic* left Southampton, England, on her maiden voyage to New York. On the night of April 14, the *Titanic* struck an iceberg and sank. More than 70 percent of her 2,207 passengers died (Caren and Goldman 1998).

The *Titanic* carried three classes of passengers. First-class passengers were wealthy and stayed in deluxe cabins, whereas third-class passengers were mainly poor immigrants, many of whom could not speak English. Because they were housed in barrackslike dormitories far down in the ship's hold, they were called "steerage" passengers. The social standing of second-class passengers was midway between these extremes.

An intriguing social pattern can be seen in the records of the disaster. All of the children in first and second class survived, but one-third of the children in third class perished. Overall, the losses were 40 percent of the first-class passengers, 64 percent of the second-class passengers, and 76 percent of the third-class passengers.

Why did so many third-class passengers perish and so many first- and second-class passengers survive? One part of the explanation concerns location. First-class cabins were on the upper decks near the lifeboats; second-class passengers were on the lower decks farther away from the boats; and third-class passengers were in steerage, farthest away of all. As steerage passengers climbed up from the lower decks, some crew members actually prevented them from reaching the lifeboats, saying that the boats were off-limits to third-class passengers (Lord 1955).

The *Titanic* sank some 80 years ago, but the last survivor who actually witnessed the ship go down passed away in 1996, the same year that yet another book examined the *Titanic* from a variety of historical viewpoints (*New York Times*, February 16, 1996:A15; Biel 1996). A love story set on the doomed ocean liner became one of the most popular films of all time, and the sound track became an enduring musical piece.

Although the *Titanic*'s disastrous voyage might seem remote in time, the lesson that social standing affects virtually every aspect of our lives is still relevant. More recently, to illustrate further, three-fourths of the American soldiers who served in Vietnam came from lower-middle-class or working-class families, and one-fourth came from families below the poverty level (Summers 1983). And even more recently, when a devastating earthquake hit the city of Kobe, Japan, in 1994, the poor suffered the most. A larger proportion of their homes were destroyed than were the homes of the middle and upper classes.

Like the risks of drowning on a luxury liner and the risks of war, the risks of being hurt by a natural disaster—or of virtually any other aspect of life—are not shared equally among all classes. Every society, in other words, is arranged into a series of layers or strata that form a hierarchy. The stratum or group at the top has the most resources, whereas the stratum at the bottom has the least. Stated another way, all societies have some form of **social stratification**.

Chapter Preview

We begin our analysis of social class inequality with a look at the relationship between inequality and the Great Social Transformation. Next, we take up a fundamental distinction between systems of social stratification—caste systems versus class systems. A description of socioeconomic status and class in the United States is next, followed by a discussion of both the myth and the reality of social mobility in the United States. Poverty in America is the next topic of discussion, and this is followed by the sociological analysis of stratification from the standpoints of functionalism, conflict theory, distributive systems theory, and symbolic interaction. The chapter closes with a discussion of social stratification in the future.

The Great Social Transformation and the Inequalities of Social Class

Agrarian societies usually have a small, elite upper class dominating a mass of peasant laborers, whereas industrial societies usually consist of three main strata: a small upper class, a larger middle class, and a sizable lower class. Many gradations exist within each class, however, such as upper-lower class and lower-lower class.

With the Great Social Transformation, social stratification systems changed greatly. Traditional hunting and gathering societies have little in the way of social stratification. As wealth accumulates in horticultural and agrarian societies, the social class system becomes more developed. With industrialization, the intensity of the system lessens somewhat as the system becomes less rigid, permitting some social mobility.

Caste and Class

All societies are stratified, but not necessarily in the same way. One of the most important differences among them concerns individual social mobility: the possibility that an individual can change her or his position in the stratification system. Depending on how much individual mobility is possible, societies may be classified as either caste systems or class systems.

Caste Systems

A **caste system** consists of a fixed arrangement of strata from the most to the least privileged, with a person's position determined unalterably at birth. The boundaries between castes are discrete—that is, they are distinct and sharply drawn (Matras 1984). As a result of these characteristics, mobility between castes is extremely rare, if not impossible.

In large part, the boundaries between castes are maintained by regulating who marries whom. If such restrictions did not exist, a marriage across caste lines would confuse the position of the spouses. Would the wife enter her husband's caste, or would the husband enter that of his wife? Moreover, to which caste do the offspring of such a marriage belong? There are no easy answers to such issues, and to prevent them from arising in the first place, caste societies prohibit sexual relations and marriages between members of different castes. Thus, neither partner can acquire mobility through marriage or sexual relations, and children always belong to the same caste as their parents.

The most extensive contemporary example of a caste system is found in India. There, caste distinctions permeate all aspects of life, especially in rural areas.

Social stratification ▲ The arrangement of society into a series of layers or strata on the basis of an unequal distribution of societal resources, prestige, or power, such that the stratum at the top has the most resources.

Caste system ▲ A fixed arrangement of strata from the most to the least privileged, with a person's position determined unalterably at birth.

Although discrimination based on caste is illegal, it still exists, and it determines where people live and work, whom they marry, and even from which well they draw water. In addition, just as American newspapers routinely mention people's occupations in news items to indicate their social standing, when Indian newspapers report people's names, they also indicate their castes.

There are four main castes in India, called varnas. The highest caste, the Brahmans, are mostly priests and scholars. Warriors, rulers, and large landholders make up the next highest caste, the Kshatriyas. They are followed by merchants, farmers, and skilled artisans, or Vaishyas. The lowest caste, the Shudras, are laborers and unskilled artisans. Beneath the Shudras are the Harijans, or "untouchables." They are ranked so low that, technically, they are outside the caste system itself (Matras 1984). Within these broad castes are several hundred specific subcastes based on occupation. Some Harijan, for example, work as scavengers and leather workers, and they marry other Harijan who perform the same work. Their children, in turn, follow in their parents' footsteps.

Caste boundaries in India are reinforced further by the practice of ritual pollution or ritual avoidance. Physical contact between members of different castes, or even simply being close together, might bring shame and revulsion on the higher-caste individual. To purge the shame, the polluted person must undergo a ritual cleansing of the body and clothes. The Harijan are considered to be especially polluted. For this reason, up until 1973 some untouchables were permitted in the streets only during the morning or evening, while other untouchables could go out only at night (Leonard 1994; Srinivas 1971). Whereas the caste system serves to separate people into discrete social levels, within each caste, gender makes a difference. Women typically have much less education and fewer economic opportunities than men (Dunn 1993; Narasimhan 2002).

A caste system may be based on many ethnic and cultural factors (Scheffel 1999). European imperial powers in Africa, for instance, imposed a caste system based on skin color: all whites were in a higher position or caste than all nonwhites. With regard to India, the situation is changing. Modern communication and transportation encourage traveling, congregating, and intermingling, all of which make it difficult to maintain the norms of ritual pollution. At the same time, India has become more industrialized and has developed links to the global economy. These developments have dramatically increased the size of the middle class, which now cuts across the boundaries of the traditional caste system. According to some estimates, 20 to 25 percent of the Indian population is now or soon will be middle class (Desmond 1989). The Indian value system, moreover, has become more democratic. Now a few members of low-ranking castes hold high political office, and the legitimacy of the caste system itself is under attack. These changes have come about because the lower-ranking castes have mobilized their voting power, thereby forcing politicians to take their numbers and influence into account (Pratap 1994). Lastly, former untouchables have been provided with specific benefits and resources, including seats in the national legislature.

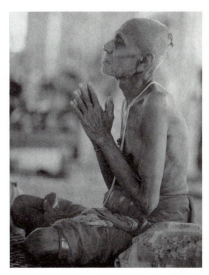

Brahman priests, like the one shown here, are at the top of the caste system in India.

Class Systems

In contrast to a caste system, in a **class system**, social standing is determined by factors over which people can exert some control, such as their educational attainment, their income, and their work experience. In practice, the amount of control might be very slight, but at least in principle you might change your class standing by acquiring more education or by obtaining a better-paying job (see Tumin 1953a, b). Because some mobility does take place in a class system, the boundaries between the strata are continuous: they merge into each other without a clear distinction between them. The lower-middle class merges gradually with the upper-middle class, which merges with the lower-upper class, and so on.

Class systems also exhibit a fairly high amount of **class consistency**. This concept refers to the similarity among the characteristics that define class strata (Lenski 1954,

Class system ▲ A system in which social standing is determined by factors over which people can exert some control, such as their educational attainment, their income, and their work experience.

Class consistency ▲ The similarity among the characteristics that define class strata.

A middle-class family and a lower-class family, both from Brazil.

CQ *How do you explain the persistence of class differences in modern societies?*

1956). In many European societies, for example, the upper classes are highly consistent because political power, prestigious family background, and high education all coincide in the upper stratum (Bourdieu 1986a). Stratification in the United States, on the other hand, is less consistent, because people from humble social backgrounds occasionally accumulate great wealth, and people with little education sometimes acquire immense power. Harry S. Truman, for instance, worked as a tailor and did not finish college, yet he became president of the United States.

Great Britain provides an interesting illustration of a class system. Currently, that nation has an upper class making up 1 to 5 percent of the population and a working, or lower, class composed of approximately 50 percent of the population. Between these two classes lies the middle class. The upper portion of the middle class consists of fairly wealthy individuals, such as physicians and business executives, who have achieved their position through work and education. The lower portion consists of clerks, small entrepreneurs, and other white-collar workers.

The British upper class displays a great deal of class consistency. Its members enjoy wealth, high prestige, and considerable influence over politics and economics. Upper-class dominance is self-perpetuating, in large part because the British educational system is a self-perpetuating, elitist system. Starting from childhood, upper-class children attend exclusive boarding schools, where they meet other upper-class children and form relationships that last a lifetime. Oxford and Cambridge, two of the most prestigious universities in the world, draw approximately half of their students from the British upper class. Graduates of these two schools dominate British humanities, sciences, law, medicine, and politics. For instance, at least 18 of Britain's prime ministers have been Oxford graduates (Sampson 1983).

Above the British upper class stands the monarchy. Although the monarchy now has little political power, the royal family represents Britain at ceremonial occasions, sets the tone for British social life, and grants titles and honors that help perpetuate class distinctions. Members of the royal family are famous throughout the world, and the press reports every detail of their behavior (Pye 1989). The news media still cover the story of the late Princess Diana, and the song dedicated to her, "Candle in the Wind," is the largest-selling single record in history. Another symbol of the British class system is the upper branch of Parliament, the House of Lords. A person becomes a lord through heredity. Like the monarchy, the House of Lords has relatively little political power, but its very existence symbolically perpetuates the position of the British upper class.

British class distinctions are far more prominent than those in the United States. Because the British working class is so large and the upper class is so small, the gap between the classes is wide, and people are very conscious of social standing. There are major class differences in the consumption of economic goods, lifestyles, and speech patterns (Tomlinson 2003). One common way to identify a stranger's class is through speech (Goldthorpe 1980)—for example, a Cockney accent identifies the speaker as being of lower-class origin. For many years, British actors and actresses with Cockney accents could not obtain leading roles and were confined to playing minor characters of lower-class standing. George Bernard Shaw's play *Pygmalion* (from which the musical and the film *My Fair Lady* were adapted) rests on the premise of a lower-class Englishwoman passing as an aristocrat. In a well-known scene, the woman is drilled endlessly to say, with perfect upper-class diction and trilling R's, "The rain in Spain falls mainly on the plain."

The British economy has been undergoing fundamental changes, and those changes may be affecting the class system. During the 1980s, industrialism seemed to be losing ground, and continued high unemployment seemingly trapped more and more people in permanent poverty. Radical measures were taken to increase productivity and investment, and some of these measures may have encouraged growth in recent years (Morris 1993; Robinson and Gregson 1992; Chapter 9).

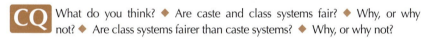

●■▲ Pausing to Think   About Caste and Class

Caste systems have well-defined boundaries between castes, and there is little mobility from one caste to another. In contrast, class systems have less clear boundaries between social classes and offer more opportunities for social mobility. India is an example of a society with a traditional caste system. Great Britain, on the other hand, has a class system in which the distinctions among the classes are far more prominent than they are in the United States.

CQ What do you think? ◆ Are caste and class systems fair? ◆ Why, or why not? ◆ Are class systems fairer than caste systems? ◆ Why, or why not?

Socioeconomic Status and Class in the United States

The United States prides itself on being an egalitarian society. Children are taught that everyone has an equal right to life, liberty, and the pursuit of happiness, that all people are born equal, and that anyone can be president. These are lofty ideals, but unfortunately, the reality is much different. This fact becomes evident when we examine socioeconomic status and class in the United States.

Determinants of Socioeconomic Status

Max Weber argued that social standing consists of three parts or dimensions: class, which he regarded as determined mainly by economic standing or wealth; party, which was equivalent to political power; and status, or social prestige and honor (Weber 1958). Weber observed that these three dimensions are related to each other with "extraordinary regularity" (Gerth and Mills 1958:187). Thus, most people are **status consistent**: that is, they have a similiar ranking along the various dimensions of **socioeconomic status**. For example, medical doctors have high job prestige, earn a substantial amount of money, and are influential in politics. Following Weber's lead, contemporary sociologists often use the broader concept of socioeconomic status to refer to a person's ranking along several social dimensions, particularly education, occupational prestige, and wealth (Collins 1986; Wright 1979). We will discuss each of these in turn.

Status consistent ▲ Having a similar ranking along the various dimensions of socioeconomic status.

Socioeconomic status ▲ A person's ranking along several social dimensions, particularly education, occupational prestige, and income.

STUDY TIP

Write a summary of socioeconomic status. Include discussions of its three primary components.

Education Education is valuable because it raises income. For example, a woman who has completed four years of college will earn 73 percent more during her lifetime than a woman who has completed only four years of high school. The comparable figure for men is 83 percent (U.S. Bureau of the Census 1994). Although education is valuable for many reasons, clearly economic gain is a major reason for going to school. More than ever, students are going to school to raise their material standard of living and thus raise their socioeconomic standing (Higher Education Research Institute 1989; Chapter 12).

Although education is one of the most profitable investments you can make in yourself, the benefits are not shared equally by everyone. Race and ethnicity make a difference. For example, African American high school graduates experience about twice the rate of unemployment as white high school graduates. Gender also plays a role. On average, women earn 30 to 40 percent less than men of equal education. As these statistics suggest, education is important, but it is not the only factor involved in acquiring economic rewards (see Chapters 7 and 8).

Wealth Sociologists divide total wealth into two kinds: assets, such as real estate, stocks, and jewels; and income, such as wages, salaries, interest received, and stock dividends. Both types of wealth influence social standing and indicate existing inequality, especially in a capitalist society. To illustrate, in the United States a few thousand individuals are near the top of the pyramid of wealth: Approximately 0.3 percent of the population have $1 million or more in assets. Even higher on the pyramid and fewer in number are the very wealthy. There are about 100 individuals or families in the United States with a net worth of $1 billion or more (Seneker 1992). Inequality is also apparent when measured in terms of income. For instance, over 47 percent of the total family income in the United States goes to those 20 percent of families with the highest incomes, whereas about 4 percent goes to the 20 percent of families with the lowest incomes (Morris and Western 1999; U.S. Bureau of the Census 2000). Over the last 30 years, income inequality has increased, with the result that there is a growing gap between the rich and the poor.

Figures such as these represent enormous economic disparities, but the disparities are even greater than the figures suggest. Wealthy people own assets that often increase in value, such as stocks, bonds, and real estate, whereas poor people typically own assets that decrease in value, such as household furnishings. Moreover, the incomes of wealthy people typically rise as they mature, whereas the incomes of poor people typically decline with age. Thus, the felt gap between the wealthy and the poor tends to increase over people's life spans.

Occupation and Prestige The federal government has identified over 20,000 separate occupations, ranging from such well-known ones as schoolteacher and lawyer to obscure ones such as chick sexor (a person who sorts newly born chicks into male and female) (U.S. Department of Labor 1986). Because this number is too large for most purposes, sociologists categorize occupations into a smaller number. The following scheme is commonly used (Gilbert and Kahl 1997):

White-Collar Occupations

- Professional, manager, and administrator
- Technical
- Clerical

Blue-Collar Occupations

- Craft, precision production, and repair
- Operative
- Labor (excluding farm)
- Farmworker

Occupations of High and Low Prestige

TEN OCCUPATIONS WITH HIGH PRESTIGE	TEN OCCUPATIONS WITH LOW PRESTIGE
1. Physician (86)	1. Barber/Hairdresser (36)
2. Lawyer (75)	2. Construction laborer (36)
3. College professor (74)	3. Truck driver (30)
4. Computer analyst (74)	4. Taxicab driver (28)
5. Architect (73)	5. Waiter/Waitress (28)
6. Dentist (72)	6. Garbage collector (28)
7. Chief executive (70)	7. Gas station attendant (27)
8. Clergy (69)	8. Bill collector (24)
9. Laboratory technologist (68)	9. Janitor (22)
10. High school teacher (66)	10. Messenger (22)

SOURCE: Courtesy of NORC, Chicago, IL, 1996.

TABLE 6.1 • *Sociologists have long studied the prestige of various occupations, both in the United States and throughout the world. The first of these studies was conducted in 1947, and ever since then, sociologists have conducted them on a regular basis. The rankings have changed very little over time, and they are much the same in all societies. The ratings scores, shown in parentheses, are for 1989 and are reported in the* General Social Survey, 1996.

Occasionally even this scheme is too unwieldy, and sociologists divide occupations into only two categories: white collar and blue collar. Whereas blue-collar work involves mostly physical labor carried out under close supervision, white-collar work emphasizes mental activity and usually takes place indoors amid pleasant surroundings, with little direct supervision. Sometimes another type of occupational category is discussed: the pink-collar occupation. This category reflects the segregation of women into certain occupations, such as kindergarten teachers, secretaries, file clerks, waitresses, nurses, librarians, and even pet groomers. These highly feminized occupations are characterized by relatively low pay and low prestige. We discuss gender inequality in greater depth in Chapter 8.

Occupations with the highest prestige typically require long training, at least a college education and often much more, and that elusive attribute called ability (see Table 6.1). Conversely, low-prestige occupations require no special abilities and little or no training or education. Although high incomes usually are associated with high-prestige occupations, there are exceptions. The clergy, for instance, enjoy high prestige but are not particularly well paid. Successful professional athletes, on the other hand, have moderate prestige and multimillion-dollar salaries. In view of their celebrity, the prestige of successful professional athletes might seem implausibly low. However, a distinction should be drawn between the individual and that individual's occupation. To capture this distinction, sociologists sometimes use the term **prestige** to mean the honor associated with an occupation or other position in the social system, and **esteem** to mean the honor that accrues to the individual filling the position. For example, an award-winning actress such as the late Jessica Tandy was highly esteemed but nevertheless belonged to an occupation with midlevel prestige. Conversely, Richard Nixon held the most prestigious job in the nation—the presidency—but was held in low esteem when forced from office under the cloud of the Watergate scandal. Before he died, Nixon attempted to regain esteem by assuming the role of an "elder statesman" or diplomat (Chapter 9; Morganthau 1994).

The Class System of the United States

As we mentioned in the previous section, in a class system some mobility is possible. To measure social class standing, sociologists have developed three main methods. The first is the *objective* method, which ranks individuals into classes on the basis of measures such as education, income, and occupational prestige. The second is the

Prestige ▲ The honor associated with an occupation or other position in a social system.

Esteem ▲ The honor that accrues to the individual filling a position in a social system.

John D. Rockefeller founded the Standard Oil Company. When he died at the age of 98 in 1937, he was thought to be the richest man in the world. The son of a country doctor, he received little formal education. Because wealth is passed on from one generation to the next, members of the Rockefeller family are still very wealthy and influential in the United States.

reputational method, which places people into various social classes on the basis of reputation in the community (Warner 1960). This method is best suited to small communities where people have detailed information about one another. The third method, *self-identification*, allows people to place themselves in a social class. Although people can readily place themselves in a class, the results are often difficult to interpret. People might be hesitant to call themselves upper class for fear of appearing snobbish, but at the same time they might be reluctant to call themselves lower class for fear of being stigmatized. The net result is that the method of self-identification substantially overestimates the middle portion of the class system.

Description of the American Classes

What is it like to belong to a given class? What is the lifestyle? How do people in that class think and behave? To answer these questions, the following section describes the social classes of the United States. We present the six classes first identified by sociologist W. Lloyd Warner (1960) and now in widespread use. The descriptions necessarily are broad, and exceptions to them exist, but they are based on research. Each description starts with a profile of a fictitious couple who have many of the characteristics of their class.

The Upper Classes   The Gerald and Ellen Eatons are a middle-aged couple who live on the outskirts of Boston, not far from where they were born. They were married in their late twenties after he graduated from Princeton and she from Yale. Two years later they became the parents of twin girls, and a year later, of a boy. Before the children arrived, Mrs. Eaton worked briefly as an assistant book editor, but now she devotes her time to charitable causes and to supervising the household, which includes a governess for the children, a housekeeper, and a handyman to take care of the grounds. Mr. Eaton manages the bond investment section of the banking empire that was originally established by his great-grandfather. Both have a deep interest in political and civic causes, but they view their role as providing behind-the-scenes support rather than running for public office. They are Episcopalian and attend church fairly regularly. They often mingle with other wealthy people at fund-raisers and social events. Some of these acquaintances are actually wealthier than they are. However, the Eatons have "old wealth" and trace their genealogy back to two wealthy British families that settled in the colonies before the American Revolution. By and large, the Eatons confine their close social relationships to other families with similar old wealth.

The Eatons illustrate a family that stands at the very top of the American stratification system. They are members of a group called the *elite*, the *ruling* or *dominant class*, or the *upper-upper class*. Generally, elite status is ascribed: to be a member of the elite, one must be born into an elite family. Numbering no more than 3 percent of the population at most, this group possesses 25 to 30 percent of the private wealth in the United States, owns 60 to 70 percent of all corporate wealth, and receives 20 to 25 percent of all yearly income (Domhoff 1974; Rossides 1990; Wehr 1994). For example, the du Pont family controls ten billion-dollar corporations and has a net worth of over $8 billion, while the Rockefeller family has a substantial interest in 5 of the 12 largest oil companies and in 4 of the largest banks in the world, and has a net worth of over $5 billion (Seneker 1992). In short, these families are extraordinarily wealthy, and if any group dominates the economic system of the United States, they do.

As a group, the elite are rather close-knit. Many of its members share friendships dating back to their youth when they went to a select boarding school such as Choate or Hotchkiss—schools that most people have never heard of. Although less than 1 percent of the high school population attends such boarding schools, some of them draw half of their students from elite families. In their halls, elite youths forge friendships and connections that will serve them all their lives, whether in private business or in government service. Equally important, they are socialized into an upper-class

Thorstein Veblen (1857–1929) was born on a small farm in Manitowoc County, Wisconsin. His parents were Norwegian immigrants who greatly valued education. Veblen learned Latin, German, and Norwegian before he entered Carleton College, a small preparatory school in Minnesota. At Carleton, Veblen studied a broad range of topics: English, philology (literature), natural history, philosophy, and economics. After graduation, he continued his education at Johns Hopkins University and then at Yale University, where he studied with the noted sociologist William Graham Sumner. After earning a Ph.D. in philosophy, Veblen pursued an academic career and taught at the University of Chicago (1892–1906), Stanford University (1906–1909), the University of Missouri (1911–1918), and the New School for Social Research (1919).

During his academic career, Veblen became a noted figure. A creative and brilliant writer, he crafted some of the sharpest, most cynical criticisms of economics and of American business that have ever been written. Consistent with his broad background, he combined diverse strains of thought from psychology, sociology, anthropology, economics, and history.

Today sociologists remember Veblen for introducing the phrase "conspicuous consumption." Seeking a dynamic set of principles for economic behavior, Veblen (1899) argued that people continually strive for esteem and status. He concluded that spending on things that served no useful purpose was the best way to earn status, because it demonstrated a person's unlimited financial resources.

Veblen was writing at a time when there were few restraints on acquiring wealth. Those who could gain control of a large corporation or an industry could amass a huge fortune quickly. To show that they had arrived, many of the nineteenth century's nouveau riche spent lavishly on their homes. For instance, the homes of the Vanderbilts, Goulds, Harrimans, and other members of the upper class were glittering palaces. Even their summer vacation homes were built to lavish scale, containing huge dining rooms, many guest rooms, and extensive servants' quarters. Used only a few months during the year, these summer homes nonetheless were filled with fine furnishings, elaborate decorations, and expensive artwork.

Veblen believed that conspicuous consumption was not limited to the wealthy. Rather, he said that each class tries to emulate the class above it. To gain status, for instance, the middle class demonstrates its wealth by furnishing their homes with whatever luxuries they can afford. No honor or esteem comes to those who live as simply as they can, he said, and those who consume only the necessities of life are scorned.

Conspicuous consumption is still with us today. In Medina, a suburb of Seattle, Microsoft billionaire Bill Gates has recently completed construction of a huge house that is filled with electronic gadgets—at a cost of more than $50 million. Expensive automobiles parked in the driveway are another way to display a luxurious style of life—a Rolls-Royce costs more than $200,000 and suggests great wealth. Toyota Land Cruisers are currently popular among the upper-middle class—and some list at $60,000. Another way to consume conspicuously is to keep up with the latest fashion in designer clothing and accessories (Solomon 1987). A Rolex watch encrusted with diamonds tells time no more accurately than an inexpensive Timex, but it does suggest that the wearer is a person of means. Although college students may not be able to spend conspicuously, many students are willing to spend the extra dollars for the hottest pair of running shoes and the trendiest sunglasses.

world in which only they know the "rules of the game" that characterize elite standing (Cookson and Persell 1985; see also the Profiles box on Thorstein Veblen). As adults they continue to move in the same circles of social activities, community service, and work, and so their cliques remain tightly knit (Rossides 1990).

Although we often hear about the "idle rich" or the "jet set," not all members of the elite are idle or frivolous (Lewis 1995). To be sure, they do not have to worry about their paychecks; yet some seek work with abiding social importance. Many participate in finance, education, the arts, and government. The ruling class also controls much of the nation's political apparatus, either through direct participation or through influence behind the scenes. Examples are the Roosevelt family, which has produced two presidents; the Rockefeller family, which has produced three state governors, a senator, and a vice president; and the Bush family, which includes two presidents, a former senator, and the governor of Florida. The Kennedy family is also important, producing two senators, one of who became president, along with other elected officials. An example of upper-class, behind-the-scenes influence is provided by the Wolfe family of Columbus, Ohio. This family owns (among other holdings) the largest newspaper in central Ohio, a major television and radio station in Columbus, Ohio, and a national financial chain. Even though no member of the family holds public office, the family's position enables it to influence those who do (*Columbus Monthly* 1989; Mills 1956; also see the Sociology Online box for this chapter).

Sociology Online

Who are the rich? Go on the Web and find the Forbes Top 400 Rich List, which contains short biographies of the richest people in the United States. When you have arrived there, you are presented with a choice of the list sorted by Worth or by Names. In addition to being rich, what do the top ten have in common? In what ways are they different? After you find those selections, you may search for the rich people who live in your state or for the names of persons who have become very successful in certain industries. When you have browsed the list, answer the following questions:

Do most of the very wealthy seem to have earned their money on their own, or have they inherited their fortune?

What evidence is there that the very wealthy engage in politics or make large contributions to political parties?

Do the very wealthy live lavishly and engage in conspicuous consumption?

Do the very wealthy contribute to charities?

How do women become very wealthy?

What assets do the wealthy control that guarantee them high incomes?

Ranking below the elite is the lower-upper class. Perhaps 4 percent of the population falls into this group. These are people who have recently achieved success and wealth, such as Les Wexner, who founded The Limited clothing company; Helen Gurley Brown, the former advertising executive, best-selling author, and successful editor of *Cosmopolitan* magazine; Wally Amos, the founder of Famous Amos Cookies; Lee Iacocca, automobile executive; and Ted Turner, owner of television networks and the Atlanta Braves. Some members of the lower-upper class actually may have more wealth than many of the upper-upper class, but the lack of an established family name and of close social ties to the elite may preclude them from full acceptance into the upper-upper class. Over time, the children of the lower-upper class may become the next generation of the elite. For example, Joseph Kennedy was denied full membership in the upper-upper class because his wealth had been acquired too recently; perhaps, too, his Catholicism was unacceptable at that time. His children, however, became full-fledged members of the elite.

The Middle Classes   William Allen and Sarah Blackwell are an African American couple; each prefers to keep his or her family name. They are in their middle thirties and live in a well-to-do suburb of Los Angeles. He is a lawyer with a midsized law firm that specializes in real-estate and financial law. He works 50 to 60 hours per week and has established a promising list of clients. Sarah works full-time as an architect for a large construction firm, a job that gives her deep satisfaction. William and Sarah are quite goal oriented, and they fret that their 12-year-old daughter, who is about to enter the local junior high school, might not develop into an adult capable of expressing her individuality and of achieving her own goals. They also worry that as an African American woman, she will encounter discrimination.

The Allen-Blackwells' combined income enables them to live very comfortably. For example, their house is valued at almost $500,000; he drives a BMW sedan, and she drives a Volvo station wagon. They are both Baptists, but neither attends church regularly because of a lack of time. William and Sarah met while studying at the University of California at Berkeley. Even though Berkeley is a state-supported school, both had to work part-time because they came from a lower-middle-class background. His father was an insurance claims adjuster; because her father had passed away, her mother, a librarian, had to struggle to make ends meet.

The Allen-Blackwell family exemplifies an upper-middle-class family with roots in the lower-middle class. When the upper-middle and the lower-middle classes are combined into a single group, the middle class, they account for half of the American population. In that sense, the United States is a middle-class nation. As a point of comparison, the American middle class makes up approximately the same proportion of society as the British lower class. In general, middle-class people define themselves as embodying all that is good about the United States: hard work, success on the job, and individual freedom.

The upper portion of the middle class forms the *upper-middle class*. This group consists mostly of professionals and others with well-paying, respected occupations. Their work typically takes a large part of their time, even after hours, and is a major source of their identity. Members of the upper-middle class are overwhelmingly college educated, but usually they have not attended the same exclusive boarding schools and private colleges as the upper-upper class. Very often both spouses work; their dual income enables them to afford fine homes in the suburbs, to take expensive vacations, and generally to enjoy a pleasant lifestyle.

The political influence of the upper-middle class is not as great as that of the upper classes. Although the upper-middle class collectively exerts power because its members participate in political affairs and support various causes, they do not have as much direct access to powerful individuals, nor do they have the time and the wealth for extensive political activity. For example, the cost of running for the U.S. Senate now exceeds several million dollars, a sum far beyond the reach of most members of the upper-middle class.

Lower-middle-class people typically earn a middle-range income and enjoy a middle-range lifestyle. This category includes teachers, small-scale entrepreneurs, and middle-level managers. The members of this class are usually less educated than members of the upper-middle class. Those who did finish college typically attended local public institutions rather than the private and more prestigious schools attended by members of the upper-middle class. Because they have relatively few assets, persons in the lower-middle class depend heavily on their earnings to maintain their lifestyle; thus, job security is as important as income.

Whereas the upper-middle class emphasizes career achievement, interpersonal skills, and creativity, the lower-middle class emphasizes respectability, proper behavior, and reliability. These differences in values reflect the different career lines followed by each class. Upper-middle-class people achieve success through occupations demanding social sophistication and originality, whereas lower-middle-class people work at midrange jobs that emphasize conformity to established patterns and rules (Kohn and Schooler 1983).

The Lower Classes   Harry and Jane Wider and their three children live in Chicago, not too far from the downtown area. Although many of the apartments near them are expensive remodeled units, their apartment is modest and small. The baby sleeps in a crib in the living room, while the two older boys share a bedroom. Harry works in the construction industry as a "jack of all trades," a job that involves moving heavy building materials, digging ditches for pipes, and other manual labor. He has a slight limp, the result of having been accidentally struck on the knee by a falling beam. Harry is often unemployed, especially during the winter when construction slows down. Jane mostly stays at home but will take a temporary job as a waitress if Harry is unemployed for a prolonged period. They blame themselves for not having graduated from high school, and they hope that their children will at least attend vocational school. Because they are concerned that their children learn respect for authority, when the boys act up, Harry swats them with an old tennis shoe that he keeps in the closet for that purpose. Both the Widers are Catholic, and although they are highly respectful of the church, they are not especially religious in their daily lives. The Widers do not consider themselves to be well off, but they see many other people who are less well off than they are—people without jobs, and parents whose children have fallen into delinquency and drug abuse.

The Widers illustrate the upper portion of the lower class—that is, the *upper-lower class*. This group, also called the *working class*, consists of service personnel, tradespeople, semiskilled operatives, and other blue-collar workers. Many popular myths hold that plumbers, automobile mechanics, and construction workers earn more than many professionals. In large part, this myth arises because people fail to distinguish between income and hourly rates or shop charges. For example, automobile mechanics may

There have always been homeless people in the United States, but since 1970 the number of homeless has increased more than threefold. Several factors account for the rise in the number of the homeless (Barak 1991; Jencks 1994; Nussbaum 2000; O'Hare 1996; Rossi 1989; Wagner 1993; Wolch and Dean 1993):

1. Shortages of housing for the poor. There have been major cutbacks in the construction of public housing combined with the demolition of older public housing in the dilapidated sections of our cities.

2. Joblessness or low wages. Contrary to the images shown on television, however, many homeless people actually work. For example, 54 percent of the homeless in San Antonio, 40 percent of the homeless in Atlanta, and 30 percent in Chicago held part-time or day-work jobs. Sadly, these jobs do not pay enough to lift these people out of homelessness.

3. Deinstitutionalization of the mentally ill. Most communities have not been able to provide the outpatient care and supervision required by these people. As a result, many of the mentally ill have drifted into joblessness and homelessness.

4. Displaced families. Most of these families are headed by young women faced with the task of raising their children by themselves. Many of the mothers purposely stay out of public sight because they fear that they may be arrested for vagrancy or have their children taken from them by the courts.

5. Substance abuse. A large number of the homeless are addicted to various kinds of substances.

6. AIDS. Having lost their jobs and unable to find new jobs, many AIDS victims are forced to take to the streets and seek shelter where they can.

As America loses manufacturing jobs to other countries, many factory workers have been thrown into poverty and worse. Forty-year-old Ron Gardner was laid off from his factory job in Lima, Ohio. He had to give up his mobile home because he could no longer afford the rent. He sold his car because he no longer had payment money. He packed what belongings he could and hitchhiked 122 miles to Cincinnati in hopes of finding something better. He slept under bridges there, ate at soup kitchens, and showered at drop-in shelters for the homeless. Eventually, he found a low-wage job driving a fork-lift and was provided housing by Goodwill Industries. Ron's future is uncertain, and so is that of other factory workers that share his fate (Kelley 2003).

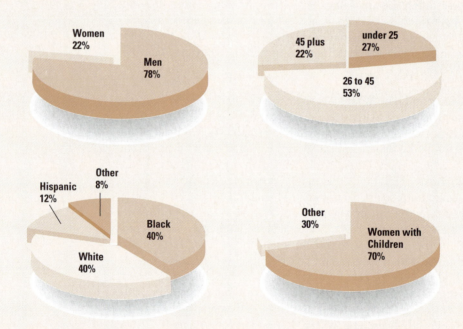

This chart shows information for both homeless individuals and homeless families. Most homeless individuals are men in their mid-20s to mid-40s. They are equally split between white Americans and African Americans. However, since African Americans constitute a much smaller proportion of the United States population than whites, African Americans are greatly overrepresented among the homeless. Most poor families consist of a single woman and her children.

SOURCE: Wright, Kelly. 2002. *Homeless in America: How Could it Happen Here?* Detroit: Gale Group.

charge $35 to $45 an hour for labor, but only rarely does the entire amount go to the mechanic. The garage owner withholds part of the amount to pay for overhead and to make a profit. Meanwhile, the mechanic must use part of his or her share to cover the cost of tools, clothing, and other items. Likewise, construction work is seasonal, and construction workers are often laid off. On the whole, members of the working class earn approximately $10,000 per year less than middle-class people (Beeghley 1999).

Working-class people usually do not earn enough to accumulate substantial savings and other assets. They have difficulty purchasing a home and financing their children's education. They earn too little to afford college for their children but too much to receive financial aid from the federal government. They are extremely vulnerable to disruptions in their income; temporary layoffs or unemployment can have immediate and devastating consequences. Although the voting power of the working class could be substantial, its members tend to be sporadic participants in the political process and lack the ability to control their own destiny as a class.

The lower-lower class is made up of people who lack education and skills and who therefore lack steady employment at well-paying jobs. They often live in the most dilapidated sections of the community and in substandard housing. Most of the people in this class have little interest in politics and have almost no control over their own fate (see the Diversity box, Who Are the Homeless?).

The *lower-lower class* may be divided into two subgroups. The working poor are lower-lower-class people who have jobs but who simply cannot earn an adequate income. Day laborers, migrant workers, and some blue-collar workers are in this position. The second subgroup is now called the chronically poor. Most of these people are unemployed or work only occasionally. Many are involved in crime. Although a few might earn a considerable income from deviant behaviors, such as dealing in drugs, most street criminals actually earn less than the hourly minimum wage. A youth working as a runner or a lookout for a drug dealer may earn only a few dollars for a 12-hour stint (Dinitz 1989).

Class, Race, and Gender Social class is just one form of stratification. Other fundamental forms of stratification systems are based on race and gender (Brewer, Conrad, and King 2002). Although we discuss each of these systems of stratification in a separate chapter, it is worth pointing out here that the systems work together to create a person's place in society. For instance, an upper-middle-class African American couple will share many of the values of the African American community, but they will also have a social class position higher than that of most other members of that community. Similarly, an upper-class woman will have much in common with women in the middle class, but she will retain distinct class advantages. In the United States, a great deal of power is concentrated in the hands of middle- and upper-class white males. Women and people of color, even if equal to white males in social class and similar in age, do not always receive equal treatment. Thus, a clerk at a department store might ignore an African American lawyer wearing an expensive, conservative business suit and might attend to the needs of a white man or a white woman immediately; and a white woman of equal class standing next to a white man may feel that her gender carries a stigma and thus subjects her to unfair treatment when she goes to buy a new automobile (Lorber 1995; Chapter 8). In sum, as these examples indicate, race, class, and gender combined determine our place in society, the manner in which we are treated, and our self-identity.

● ■ ▲ **Pausing to Think** About Socioeconomic Status and Class in the United States

In the United States, the upper class is made up of the upper-upper class and the lower-upper class; the middle class is made up of the upper-middle class and the lower-middle class; and the lower class is made up of the upper-lower class, or working class, and the lower-lower class, which consists of the working poor and the chronically poor. Another way to divide society into layers is by socioeconomic status, usually some combination of wealth, education, and occupational prestige. Social-class standing is often measured by one of three methods: objective, reputational, or self-identification.

CQ What social class do you belong to? ◆ Do you think that people are really the same, regardless of their social-class position? ◆ Why, or why not? ◆ What answer is a sociologist likely to give to this question?

The Myth and the Reality of Mobility in the United States

One of the enduring myths in American culture is the rags-to-riches story: the saga of a poor youth of good character who works hard, acquires an education, has a respected career, amasses a fortune, and raises a fine family (Wohl 1966). Surveys consistently show that the overwhelming majority of people in the United States believe in this story. They have been socialized to think that hard work is the most important ingredient for getting ahead in life and that the United States is the land of unlimited opportunity (NORC 1994). In a few cases, this rags-to-riches saga has come true. An example is John D. Rockefeller, who began life poor but eventually became one of the wealthiest people in the United States. Because individual cases of extraordinary success draw so much attention, they seem to confirm the American belief that anyone can rise to the top. The reality, however, is that many people experience no mobility at all. We now turn to this point.

Amount of Mobility

How much mobility takes place in the United States? The specific answer to this question depends on how mobility is defined. Sociologists frequently focus on the **intergenerational mobility** of individuals: upward and downward movements in socioeconomic status measured by the standing of children compared with that of their parents. A classic study by Peter Blau and Otis Duncan (1967) found that 26 percent of the sons of managers, 43 percent of the sons of clerical workers, and 84 percent of the sons of laborers had occupations that ranked higher than their fathers' occupations. These numbers suggest that a fair-to-moderate amount of upward mobility took place. Of course, not all mobility is upward. Approximately 80 percent of the sons of self-employed professionals and slightly more than 50 percent of the sons of clerical workers had occupations that ranked lower than their fathers' occupations (Blau and Duncan 1967). Subsequent studies have revealed similar rates of upward and downward mobility. Although the United States has strong values that promote striving for success, American mobility is not exceptionally high. For example, Switzerland, France, and Japan have more upward mobility than has the United States, and Sweden and Germany have only slightly less (Featherman and Hauser 1978; Grusky and Hauser 1984; Lipset and Bendix 1967; see Chapter 8 regarding women).

Determinants of Mobility

Intergenerational mobility ▲
Upward and downward mobility in socioeconomic status measured by the standing of children compared with that of their parents.

What accounts for the comparatively modest rates of upward mobility in the United States? The answer to this question involves several factors. One is the lack of room at the top. American society has room for only so many heart surgeons, Wall Street bankers, and real estate tycoons. Out of a labor force of some 142 million people, only one person can be president of the country, only 435 persons can be congressional

representatives, and only 49,000 (0.04 percent) can be presidents of banks. In other words, the socioeconomic pyramid is very steep, with the result that there are not enough high-status jobs to satisfy everyone—regardless of how hard one works.

Another impediment to upward mobility is related to where you start your climb up the socioeconomic ladder. Some people begin closer to the top than others. Using the Blau and Duncan study (1967), the rate of mobility from laborer to service operator—a relatively short climb—turns out to be 37 percent. A much longer climb is that from laborer to professional, which occurs at a rate of 6 percent. And the longest climb, from laborer to self-employed professional, occurs at a rate of less than 0.1 percent. Even though these rates are low, for women and racial-ethnic minorities, the rates are even lower.

Paradoxically, even though the odds against making a long or moderate climb are formidably large, most Americans have risen slightly higher than their parents because of **structural mobility**: the movement of entire categories of people caused by changes in society itself. The distance from the bottom to the top of the stratification ladder is now filled with many rungs spaced very close together. Consequently, individuals can achieve small amounts of upward mobility while remaining within their original stratum. The upward mobility produced by these changes depends less on an individual's achievements than on the expansion of the labor market, especially in the middle range of the class system. The long post–World War II economic expansion, for instance, created millions of white-collar jobs, thus allowing many people to move from blue-collar backgrounds to the lower echelons of the middle class (Archer and Blau 1994). Currently, however, we may be seeing a reversal of this trend. The restructuring of the American economy during the 1970s and 1980s resulted in the loss of many white- and blue-collar jobs, greatly diminishing the economic prospects for young people and generally depressing the salaries of many working- and middle-class people (O'Hare 1996; see also Chapter 8).

Ideological Support for Inequality

Although American culture strongly values equality of opportunity, it does not follow from those values that everyone is equal. As we have just discussed, American society is actually characterized by a great deal of social inequality. This arrangement is justified by an **ideology**, or pattern of beliefs, that legitimizes or justifies a particular societal arrangement. Currently the most prominent analysis of class ideology derives

Structural mobility ▲ The movement of entire categories of people caused by changes in society itself.

Ideology ▲ The pattern of beliefs that legitimizes or justifies a particular societal arrangement.

This figure shows the argument of Marx that the subordinate class of industrial society provides the labor for the organizations of economic production owned by the ruling class. The ruling class exploits the subordinate class because the ruling class does not return to the subordinate class just rewards for its labor. In addition, the ruling class, because of its social power, is able to create an ideology that justifies its exploiting behavior. This ideology is accepted by the subordinate class, and so it cooperates in its own exploitation.

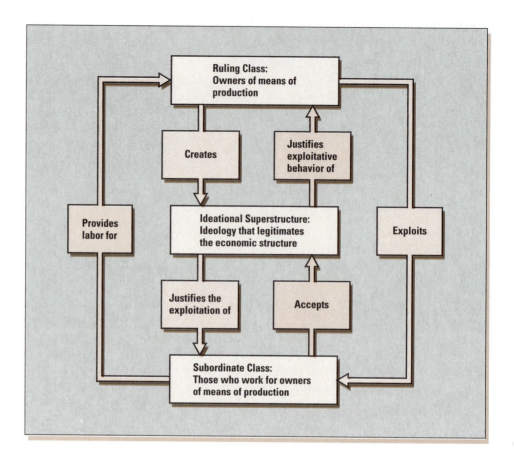

from the ideas of Karl Marx, a figure we have studied previously in this text. Marx stated his argument succinctly, writing that "the ruling ideas of each age have ever been the ideas of its ruling class" (Marx and Engels 1967/1848). By this statement, Marx meant that the class in power imposes its ideology on the entire society, thereby bending the culture and the individual to suit its own ends (see Figure 6.1).

It is not difficult to understand why the upper class would support an ideology that justifies its dominant position. More difficult to understand is why other classes would endorse the same ideology. Such a situation—a class's acceptance of an ideology that is contrary to the best interests of that class—is called **false consciousness**. It prevails, for instance, if lower-class people believe that their plight is caused by their own inadequacies rather than by the economic control of the ruling class.

Marx argued that false consciousness will exist until the exploited stratum develops a sense of **class consciousness**: an awareness that it is, in fact, being oppressed and that membership in the class dooms everyone to the same fate. When class consciousness forms, the stratum will become a true social class and will begin challenging the ruling class (Ossowski 1983).

Although Marx's ideas were developed in the last century, they remain vital to this day. Consistent with his notion of false consciousness, 50 percent or more of the people in the United States—including the poor—agree that social inequality is right, just, and proper (Johnson 1989). The most common justification is the belief that the rich provide a goal for people who are not rich. Thus, two-thirds of all Americans agree that large differences in income are necessary "to get people to work hard" (NORC 1994). Such beliefs represent a state of false consciousness in the sense that failure is attributed to a lack of hard work or to poor character, whereas success is attributed to hard work and the openness of the system. Meanwhile, the position of the lower classes remains largely unchanged, and the position of the ruling class remains largely unchallenged.

False consciousness ▲ A class's acceptance of an ideology that is contrary to the best interests of the class.

Class consciousness ▲ An awareness by members of a social class that it is being oppressed and that membership in the class dooms everyone to the same fate.

● ■ ▲ **Pausing to Think** About the Myth and the Reality of Mobility in the United States

American culture contains many stories about people who have achieved great upward mobility. Although the degree of actual individual mobility in the United States is not particularly high, most people have moved upward through structural mobility. American ideology justifies inequality, but Karl Marx believed that lower-class people suffer from false consciousness.

CQ Which element most affects mobility in the United States: (a) hard work, (b) expansion of the opportunity system, (c) luck, (d) family background?

◆ What role do these elements play in your life and career plans?

Poverty in the Land of Riches

Throughout history there have always been a large number of poor, and that is still the case. During the Great Depression of the 1930s, half of all the people in the United States were poor, and even when the United States became the preeminent economic power in the world after World War II, approximately one person out of three was still poor. Since that time, however, the poverty rate generally has declined. During the 1960s, President Lyndon Johnson launched the War on Poverty—an effort to marshal government resources, develop programs, and provide money to assist poor people in developing their job and leadership skills (Raspberry 1995). By the early 1970s, the poverty rate had fallen to 11 percent, only to rise again to its current level of about 13 percent (U.S. Bureau of the Census 2000). This figure translates into 36 million individuals—roughly equivalent to all of the people living in California, Oregon, and the state of Washington. In short, although poverty has fallen from its levels of 50 or 60 years ago, there are still large numbers of poor people in the United States, and even larger numbers throughout the world (see Figure 6.2).

Poverty does not strike everyone equally (see the Society Today box). For example, poverty is now increasing among the young but decreasing among the elderly

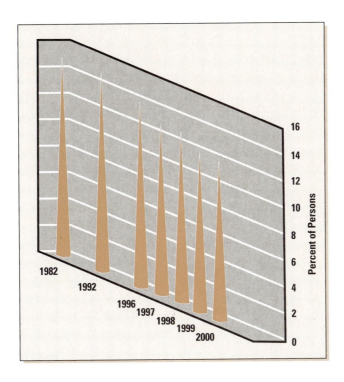

FIGURE 6.2 Poverty in the United States

Since the early 1980s, the poverty rate has hovered around 12 to 14 percent.

SOURCE: U.S. Bureau of the Census, 2001.

Society Today ● ■ ▲

Poverty Threshold for a Family of Four

The poverty line has changed over the years, mainly to keep up with increases in the price of housing, food, clothing, and other items. Note that these figures are for a family of four persons.

YEAR	THRESHOLD
1960	$3,000
1970	$4,000
1980	$8,400
1990	$13,400
2000	$17,600

SOURCE: U.S. Bureau of the Census, *Statistical Abstract of the United States,* 2002.

Who Are the Poor? [Selected Poverty Rates]

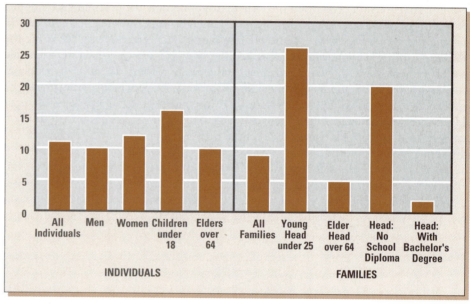

SOURCE: U.S. Bureau of the Census, 2002.

Percentage of Children Below Poverty Level by Race or Ethnic Group, 1997

There are large differences among racial and ethnic groups in the extent to which children are in poverty. The figures show that black and Hispanic children on the whole have a poorer start in life than do white children.

GROUP	PERCENT
All groups	16
White	12
Black	30
Asian and Pacific Islander	14
Hispanic*	27

*May be of any race.

SOURCE: U.S. Bureau of the Census, *Statistical Abstract of the United States,* 2000.

(O'Hare 1996; Scripps Howard News Service 1994; U.S. Bureau of the Census 1994). Increasingly, poverty is a more serious problem for women in single-parent households than it is for women in two-parent households (Bianchi 1999). Moreover, because some people are falling into poverty while others are climbing out, at some point in their lives, one-fourth of all people in the United States will be poor. In the case of a prolonged economic slump in the United States, half of the adults between 25 and 75 years of age likely will experience at least one year below the poverty line (Rank and Hirschl 2001). Given that the United States is one of the richest nations in history, why does so much poverty exist? This is a profoundly disturbing question that has no simple answer. A part of the answer, however, lies in the way in which poverty is defined.

What Is Poverty?

Poverty may be defined in either of two ways. According to the idea of **relative poverty**, people are poor only in comparison with others. For example, the poor might be defined as people with the least wealth, perhaps the lowest 10 percent of the population. Although another number could be substituted (say, the lowest 5 percent), relative poverty always involves comparing one group with another group. One implication of this approach is that poverty will never vanish. Regardless of how wealthy the society becomes, there will always be some group at the bottom of the hierarchy.

An alternative approach is to say that poverty is the inability of people to maintain a certain standard of living, a condition known as **absolute poverty**. According to this idea, people who cannot afford some minimum of food, clothing, shelter, and other necessities are considered poor regardless of how they compare with other people. Following this approach, everyone in a society could have the minimum necessities, and no one has to be poor. In practice, unfortunately, that happy state has never existed, and it seems very unlikely that it will come about in the near future.

In the United States, absolute poverty is usually measured with an index developed by economist Mollie Orshansky of the Social Security Administration (Hershey 1989). She first estimated the cost of an adequate but economical food plan and then tripled that amount to cover other expenses such as housing, clothing, and transportation. The resulting figure is called the "poverty index." The exact value of the index is revised yearly to account for changes in the cost of living (U.S. Department of Health, Education, and Welfare 1976).

Relative poverty ▲ Poverty determined only by comparison with others.

Absolute poverty ▲ The poverty of people who cannot afford some minimum of food, clothing, shelter, and other necessities regardless of how they compare with other people.

Diversity ●■▲ Myths and Misinformation about the Poor

Public perceptions regarding the poor, welfare programs, and welfare recipients are frequently shaped by misinformation. For instance, which of the following five statements do you think are false?

1. The vast majority of the poor are Blacks or Hispanics.
2. The poor get welfare, and the middle class pay the bills.
3. Poor families are trapped in a cycle of poverty that few escape.
4. The majority of the poor live in inner-city neighborhoods.
5. Most of the poor are single mothers and their children.

Answers: Research indicates that all of the preceding statements are false.

1. Non-Hispanic whites are the most numerous welfare recipients.

2. About three times as much federal money is spent on Social Security and Medicare, programs that mainly benefit the middle class, as is spent on welfare.
3. Some 90 percent of the people classified as poor move out of poverty within five years.
4. Over half of the poor live in the suburbs and in rural areas.
5. Female-headed households account for about one-third of the poor; the remaining two-thirds are accounted for by other family types.

SOURCE: William P. O'Hare, "A New Look at Poverty in America." *Population Bulletin* 51(2)(1996):11.

According to the 2000 poverty index, a family of four with a total income of $17,600 per year or less was considered poor (U.S. Bureau of the Census 2002). It is important to realize what this figure means in terms of an individual's lifestyle. Suppose you are married, have two children, and work full-time earning $5 per hour. Your annual family income would then be $10,000, a figure well below the poverty line. Moreover, if your family spends one-third of its income on food—the amount the government estimates—you would have $3,330 per year to feed four people. If you eat three meals a day (but no between-meal snacks), that amount would permit you to spend 75 cents per person per meal—hardly enough for each person to have a peanut butter sandwich and a glass of milk. As this example indicates, the poor do not live well even if they are working full-time.

Whether poverty is defined as relative or absolute, it can be a temporary condition for an individual but a permanent feature of society. Approximately one-third of the poor rise above poverty each year, only to be replaced by others who fall into poverty. Thus, even though upward mobility takes place constantly, the percentage of the population that is poor can remain much the same from year to year.

Because the poor in the United States are a very heterogeneous group, it is difficult to make general statements about them. We explore the topics of racially based poverty in the next chapter and the feminization of poverty in Chapters 8 and 11.

The Truly Disadvantaged

Recently, a new concept for analyzing poverty—the **truly disadvantaged**—has been developed to analyze urban poverty. The truly disadvantaged consists of people who live predominantly in the inner city and who are trapped in a cycle of joblessness, deviance, crime, welfare dependency, and unstable family life. In total, this group might number 5 to 10 million people (Wilson 1987, 1997; Small and Newman 2001).

Sociologist William Julius Wilson argues that poor economic conditions are the main problems facing the truly disadvantaged. Changes in the economy have wiped out many unskilled jobs that use to absorb a large portion of the people living in urban core areas. Given this fact, the economic condition of the truly disadvantaged will not improve until the economy of the urban core is revitalized. Other sociologists assert that to rely only on economic solutions ignores the complexity of the problem (Lawson 1992). They agree that economics are important but note that not everyone drifts into a life of dependency or deviance because they cannot find work. Many others have chosen to leave economically depressed areas and seek jobs or training elsewhere. In addition, they note that many of the truly disadvantaged are people who are involved in a cultural system that leads them to disavow mainstream values such as education, work, and conventional family life. Solving the problems of this group will require both economic assistance and programs aimed at changing cultural values and expectations. Finally, it has been pointed out that if unemployment does become a permanent feature of people's lives, many of the disadvantaged will find themselves locked into an undercaste which they and their children can never leave (Gans 1996).

The Culture of Poverty

Although the poor participate in mainstream culture, they have, like all groups, evolved a culture that helps them to cope with the realities of their situation. Accordingly, the term **culture of poverty** refers to the set of norms and values that helps the poor to adapt to their situation (Banfield 1974; Lewis 1968). For example, the poor often spend their money as quickly as they obtain it. This behavior strikes middle-class people as irresponsible, but because the poor lack faith in the future, they have no reason to delay gratification. The poor also feel that they are marginal to society, helpless, inferior, and at the mercy of others. These feelings, when coupled with a belief that life will not improve, leads them to discount the value of education and to ignore the work ethic. Completing the circle, the children of the poor are socialized to conform to the culture of poverty, and when they reach adulthood, they will pass on the culture of poverty to their children.

Truly disadvantaged ▲ People who live predominantly in the inner city and who are trapped in a cycle of joblessness, deviance, crime, welfare dependency, and unstable family life.

Culture of poverty ▲ The set of norms and values that helps the poor to adapt to their situation.

Society Today ● ■ ▲

Children Below the Poverty Line

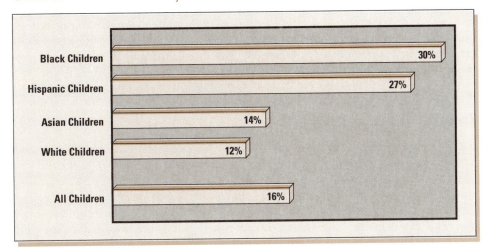

Black Children	30%
Hispanic Children	27%
Asian Children	14%
White Children	12%
All Children	16%

On the whole, 16 percent of all children are poor. However, that varies considerably by race and ethnicity. More Black and Hispanic children live in poverty than white or Asian children. Poverty tends to be self perpetuating from one generation to the next. Children are poor because their parents are poor. These children grow up poor and their children, in turn, are poor.

CQ One of the long standing questions in American society is, "How can the cycle of poverty be broken?" Can you think of any anti-poverty programs that help break the cycle? Why?

SOURCE: U.S. Bureau of Census, 2000.

Ever since the concept was introduced, the culture of poverty has been a controversial topic. Characterizing the poor as shortsighted is inaccurate, many sociologists argue, because middle-class and upper-class people also have doubts about the future and live for the moment. Unlike the poor, however, wealthier people have savings, homes, investments, credit, relatives with money, and other resources to draw on in times of need. Consequently, if their shortsightedness causes them problems, wealthier people can recover, whereas the poor cannot.

Another criticism comes from a different angle. It asserts that the culture of poverty "blames the poor" for their plight when, in fact, the causes of poverty lie in society. The lack of opportunity to gain a good education, the shortage of jobs that pay more than the minimum wage, and racism, sexism, and ageism are examples of how poverty is caused by society rather than by the characteristics of the poor. From this view, the unwillingness of the poor to defer gratification is not the cause of their poverty; instead, it is the result of living in a society that systematically shuts them out of the mainstream (Ryan 1976).

●■▲ Pausing to Think About Poverty

The United States is a wealthy nation, yet poverty remains a persistent problem, especially among the truly disadvantaged. Some sociologists argue that the poverty is caused by structural conditions, whereas others argue that cultural factors are also important. Most sociologists, however, criticize the idea that a culture of poverty explains the inability of the poor to gain upward mobility.

CQ For the sake of argument, suppose you had the power to make the United States a country without poverty. Would you do it? ◆ Why, or why not? ◆ What are your reasons?

Poverty in the United States affects many children. Here a homeless family with two children sits on street corner as dad holds a sign asking for help.

CQ *Does the experience of seeing such poverty motivate other people to achieve more?* ◆ *Does it motive people to become more generous in helping others? What do you think?*

Sociological Analysis of Stratification and Class

In this section, we will discuss four attempts to explain the existence of stratification and class. Three of these attempts we have encountered before: functionalism, conflict theory, and symbolic interaction. The other attempt—distributive systems theory—is unique to the study of stratification.

The Functionalist Perspective

Functionalist theorists note that all societies have positions that must be filled but that vary in attractiveness, pay, and prestige. Obviously, people will, if they have a choice, opt for the most rewarding position they can obtain. The net result is a social stratification system in which some people have more wealth and prestige than others. From the functionalist perspective, this type of stratification system has two major benefits. First, it benefits individuals by ensuring that they are rewarded for their talents and qualifications; and second, it benefits society by ensuring that positions are filled by qualified persons (Davis 1953; Davis and Moore 1945).

During the 1960s and 1970s, functionalist theorists expanded the argument to explain seemingly nonfunctional aspects of society. For instance, they pointed out that even though poverty appears to drag a society down, in fact, poverty produces some benefits. First, the poor constitute a pool of inexpensive laborers ready to do work such as collecting trash, cleaning floors, picking fruit, and the like. Second, because the poor earn low wages, they help hold down prices. The garment industry, for example, relies on workers who live in or close to poverty. If their wages were higher, clothing prices would be higher for everyone. Third, a "trickle-up" effect is associated with fighting poverty (Beeghley 1999). Approximately one-third of all antipoverty funds, for instance, go to the middle-class workers who staff the governmental bureaucracies that service the poor. And fourth, the poor act as a buffer that protects the middle class against economic changes. During the 1970s, for example, fiscal policy turned from encouraging economic growth to holding down prices. The poor took the brunt of the resulting unemployment that helped to keep prices low (Gans 1993; Ryan 1976).

Although the functionalist explanation initially was received enthusiastically, the approach eventually came under heavy criticism. One criticism concerned the link between the importance of a position and its financial rewards. Some positions offer high financial rewards but are of questionable societal importance. Major film stars earn anywhere from $3 million to $40 million per motion picture, which is thousands of times more than what schoolteachers earn. Do film stars contribute more to society than teachers? Most people would say no. Moreover, consider the same schoolteacher in comparison with the typical physician, who now earns around $200,000 per year. Is the physician more important than the teacher? Most people would again say no, pointing out that education is as vital to society as health care. The fact is, salaries are frequently arbitrary and vary by industry (Davis 1953; Samuelson and Nordhaus 1998; Stinchcombe 1963; Tumin 1953a). Prestige, rather than income, might be the most reliable indicator of the social importance of a position.

Another criticism of the functionalist argument centers on the role of rewards in motivating individuals (Wesotowski 1962). For instance, a violinist will devote years of practice and study to music for the sheer joy of the art. A physician may derive great satisfaction from healing and might practice medicine even if she earned considerably less than she actually does earn. Finally, critics note that the functionalist explanation implicitly assumes that society is equally open for everyone. In reality, of course, discrimination often prevents women and members of ethnic minorities from finding positions commensurate with their qualifications.

This photograph depicts some of the material benefits of success. A father, a mother, and their two young children are shown with expensive cars and toy automobiles in an upscale cobblestone driveway. Automobiles have long been seen as status symbols in the United States.

CQ *What do you think? Are the kids being taught to value things that will enrich their lives, or do material possessions actually mean little in the pursuit of happiness?*

The Conflict Perspective

Conflict theorists are strongly influenced by Marx's ideas of class (see Chapter 1). As you may recall, Marx believed that a person's class position is determined by the ownership of property. The capitalistic class, or bourgeoisie, own the means of production, whereas the working class, the proletariat, own only their own labor. The proletariat have no choice but to work for the bourgeoisie, and the bourgeoisie exploit the labor of the proletariat by keeping wages low. Marx also believed that once the proletariat become aware of their true class interest, they will be transformed from a disorganized mass of individuals into a disciplined social class that will rise in revolution and overthrow the bourgeoisie. Once in power, the proletariat will install a classless, socialist society in which the means of production will be owned by the state for the benefit of all.

Marx did not envision a significant role for the middle class in industrial society. He assumed that the bourgeoisie would crush the middle class and force it into the proletariat. Yet contrary to his prediction, the middle class has grown steadily over the years. The U.S. middle class has increased from 18 percent of the population in 1900 to 55 percent today (Beeghley 1999). These middle-class people sit at desks, sometimes supervise others, and earn good salaries. They maintain a professional orientation and identify with management and the company rather than with the worker and the union. The middle class thus has acted as a buffer that mediates conflicts between proletariat and bourgeoisie (Mills 1951).

Whereas the middle class has increased since Marx's time, the working class has decreased. In 1900, some 80 percent of the U.S. population belonged to the working class, but now the figure is about 35 percent. Of equal importance, the modern blue-collar worker does not fit the Marxian mold. Rather than feeling alienated and oppressed, many blue-collar workers derive great satisfaction from their jobs and take pride in having helped to construct a bridge, a house, or a fine piece of machinery. These people are not the alienated, impoverished masses that Marx envisioned.

Because of these developments, modern-day conflict theorists are developing alternatives to Marx's view of stratification. Some are attempting to incorporate Weber's ideas of stratification within a Marxian framework. For example, whereas Marx was concerned with only one form of capital, the French sociologist Pierre Bourdieu believes that stratification in society is due to inequalities in the distribution

This photograph shows a homeless woman, Mardie Andrews, carrying a sign in the first annual Los Angeles Homeless Parade in 1999. She is confronting a national problem.

STUDY TIP

In a group of three or four, discuss the four types of capital that Pierre Bourdieu believes are at the heart of stratification. Come with up a list of examples for each type of capital. Then, name and compare the effects of in-equalities in each, and whether you agree that these inequalities cause stratification.

of four types of capital: (1) economic capital—money or material objects that can be used to produce goods and services; (2) social capital—positions and relations in social networks that can be used to create economic capital; (3) cultural capital—interpersonal skills, habits, educational credentials, and the like that can be used to advantage in society; (4) symbolic capital—the ability to use symbols to legitimate the possession of varying levels of the other three levels of capital. The classes are, according to Bourdieu's argument, now locked in a struggle that revolves around manipulating symbols to make a particular pattern of social, cultural, and economic resources seem appropriate (Turner and Turner 1997). Bourdieu finds evidence for his views in France, where the cultural elite gather in Paris, attend many of the same schools, and help each other obtain privileged positions in society. The elite defend their privileged positions in society by claiming superior education and training.

Distributive Systems Theory

Although the functionalist and conflict perspectives appear to be totally different, sociologists have begun the task of synthesizing the two approaches into a unified theory. Gerhard Lenski has made the most notable attempt to date, and his ideas go under the name of distributive systems theory (Haas 1993; Lenski 1966; Nolan and Lenski 1999).

According to Lenski, societal resources consist of two types: necessities (such as food and shelter) and surplus (resources above and beyond the necessities, or luxuries). Each type plays a different role in producing stratification. With regard to necessities, Lenski argues that people will share what they have only as long as it is in their own interest to do so. In hunting and gathering societies, for example, group survival depends heavily on everyone's contributions to the common good. Successful hunters therefore share their kill with other members of the group, perhaps taking only a choice cut as an individual reward. Sharing in this manner reduces inequality and, at the same time, contributes to the survival of the individual and of the society. This line of reasoning is consistent with the functionalist perspective.

A far different situation occurs with regard to surplus. Lenski argues that people do not benefit from sharing surplus because it is not needed for group survival. Individuals thus are free to acquire as much surplus as possible, and those with the most power accumulate the most surplus. This outcome is consistent with the conflict perspective (see Beeghley 1999; Matras 1984).

Because the necessities must be shared more or less equally to ensure individual and societal survival, inequality can occur only when a surplus exists. For example, hunting and gathering societies lack the technology to obtain a vast surplus of food; hence, even the most honored individuals do not eat appreciably better than the average person. In contrast, agrarian societies can generate enormous surpluses, and so a rigid stratification system develops. A few members of the landed aristocracy control the society's wealth and use their power to protect their position and holdings. Status becomes a matter of inheritance, mobility into the aristocracy is all but eliminated, and the right to rule the country is reserved for the aristocracy and the monarchy.

In industrial societies, stratification follows a more complex course of development. During the early stages of industrialization, the bourgeoisie extract the bulk of the society's wealth, thereby creating a vast gulf between themselves and the proletariat. As industrialization progresses, however, inequality declines because productivity increases so much that a small elite can no longer monopolize all of the wealth. At the same time, a growing middle class forces the government to become responsive to its demands. In the course of these developments, a sophisticated ideology develops about the use of power. As Lenski puts it, "the rule of might" changes into "the rule of right." Although Lenski's theory suggests that industrialization and ideology eventually will cause inequality to disappear, he stops short of predicting that it will completely vanish. As long as any surplus exists, he argues, the struggle over it will produce at least some inequality.

Distributive systems theory is most noteworthy for combining the functionalist and conflict perspectives in an insightful way—by distinguishing between necessities and surplus. This distinction is reasonable in many cases. Basic food and shelter are clearly necessary for survival, whereas caviar and country estates are not. Beyond extreme contrasts, however, the distinction between necessity and surplus may be fuzzy. Items that some people consider necessities, other people consider surplus. At what point does housing change from a shelter to a luxury? When does clothing change from a necessity that provides warmth to a display of conspicuous consumption? To date, these distinctions have not been fully drawn out.

The Symbolic Interactionist Perspective

Stratification inevitably produces inequality that, in turn, produces deprivation, misery, and poverty. Why do Americans tolerate inequality? How do they learn to cope with it? Symbolic interactionists assert that just like any other aspect of society, inequality is sustained and created through interaction and definitions of the situation (Hewitt 1999). Formal and informal socialization plays a major role in this process (Chapter 3). From birth we are socialized to accept inequality in virtually every realm of life. For example, schoolchildren are encouraged to compete for high grades to distinguish themselves from their peers. Those who do not "measure up" must accept lower grades and fewer rewards (Chapter 12). These same children learn to differentiate people according to their power and wealth, and they further learn to obey and defer to some adults and authorities more than to others (Goffman 1977, 1979; Mead 1934).

Another factor that produces toleration for inequality is the self-fulfilling consequences of class discrimination (Della Fave 1980). People who occupy subordinate class positions sometimes adopt the value system of those above them and come to view themselves as unworthy. Consider John Coleman, a college president who spent ten days impersonating a homeless person in New York City. After the first few days, he found himself walking the streets slowly, not hurrying to beat traffic lights because he had no appointments to keep and no particular place to go. Other pedestrians, as if

STUDY TIP

Design a visual representation for *distributive systems theory*. You can use lines, shapes, words, drawings of objects, anything that you believe illustrates the concept clearly and shows the relationship between the two perspectives (functionalist and conflict).

In 1996 Congress passed a welfare act that is officially known as the Personal Responsibility and Work Opportunity Reconciliation Act. It totally revamped the welfare system. The act had these three fundamental goals:

1. Reduce spending for welfare.
2. Give states more power over welfare rules and regulations.
3. Curb some types of assistance.

The reasoning that led to the act seems to be fairly clear. It is premised on two widespread beliefs:

People are poor because they will not work.

People who work will not be poor.

If these two beliefs are correct, then it seems reasonable to conclude that the only way to get people out of poverty is to force them to work. Many provisions of the 1996 reform act are attempts to accomplish just that. For example, the act specifies that healthy adults cannot receive cash benefits for longer than two years unless they get a job; it limits food stamps for unemployed persons to a three-month period within a given year; and it allows states to drop unwed teenage mothers and their children from the welfare roles unless the mothers attend school and live with an adult.

Evidence:* Have the results of these changes to the welfare program had the desired effect? What evidence can you find reported in journals, books, or newspapers that indicates that the revamping of the welfare system has reduced poverty and encouraged better work habits among the poor?

*To answer these critical questions, review the box "What Is Critical Thinking?" in Chapter 1, and pay special attention to the discussion of evidence.
SOURCE: William O'Hare, "A New Look at Poverty in America," *Population Bulletin* 51(2)(1996).

---

fearing ritual pollution, gave him a wide berth or walked past him as if he were invisible. Store clerks treated him indifferently or rudely. When making small purchases, he frequently was asked to show his money before anyone would wait on him. Coleman realized that if his impersonation had continued longer, his self-respect would have sunk so low that he would have interpreted any rebuff as further proof of his own unworthiness (Coleman 1983).

Finally, inequality is tolerated because many derogatory stereotypes suggest that the poor are lazy, dumb, and pampered by the welfare system. Such stereotyping has effectively painted a false perception of the poor and of welfare. For instance, some 84 percent of people in the United States agree with the statement that welfare "makes people work less" (NORC 1994). The facts, however, suggest a different conclusion: only one-third of the poor receive public assistance, half of all impoverished families contain at least one full-time worker, and one-fifth contain two full-time workers (O'Hare 1996; Rank 1994). Half of the poor, moreover, receive no aid for food, and the half who do receive it get an average of 50 cents per meal (Brown 1987). In any event, most people get themselves off welfare after a short time—by working. Clearly, the poor are not being treated generously by government aid, but, as symbolic interactionists assert, "events defined as real are real in their consequences" (see the What Do You Think? box).

●■▲ Pausing to Think   About the Sociological Analysis of Stratification and Class

The conflict and functionalist perspectives rest on different assumptions, yet each is valuable for understanding different aspects of inequality. Conflict theory readily addresses such issues as why some people benefit from inequality, why the interests of one group differ from those of another, and how one group comes to dominate another. Functionalism, on the other hand, raises questions as to how positions are filled, how individual needs are brought into harmony with societal needs, and why society as a whole remains stable in spite of great inequality. Distributive systems theory attempts to blend aspects of conflict and functionalist thought. Finally, the symbolic interactionist perspective explains why people tolerate inequality and how disdain for the poor becomes internalized through the

TABLE 6.2

[a]The functionalist and conflict perspectives were introduced in Chapters 1 and 2, and symbolic interaction was discussed in Chapter 3.

Comparison of Three Theoretical Perspectives on Stratification and Class

PERSPECTIVE[a]	VIEW OF STRATIFICATION	KEY CONCEPTS AND PROCESSES
Functionalism	Sees stratification as necessary for efficient operation of society	Social positions Functions Prestige and rewards
Conflict Theory	Sees stratification as a process of exploitation and dominance	Bourgeoisie Proletariat Economic, social, cultural, and symbolic capital
Symbolic Interaction	Sees stratification as created and sustained through social interaction and shared meanings	Informal and formal socialization Self-definitions Stereotypes

process of socialization and interaction. For a summary of the functionalist, conflict, and symbolic interactionist perspectives, see Table 6.2.

 How does each of the perspectives presented in this section explain the persistence of social class? ◆ Which perspective makes the most sense to you?

Social Class Inequality in the Twenty-First Century

The stratification system is always changing, and the future holds both great promise and great danger. One danger in particular has been a subject of speculation and controversy: will today's young people be better off or worse off than their parents? This controversy has arisen because the American middle class seems to be shrinking (Sheak and Dabelko 1993).

If the trend continues long enough, the United States will come to have only two main classes: a large dominant class, which will possess most of the nation's economic wealth, and another large group of people who are just scraping by. As Figure 6.3 shows, the very rich are taking home a very large portion of total household income, almost as large as they did before World War II (Hacker 1998).

Many signs of a troubled middle class are visible in the lifestyle of the baby boom generation. As one recent headline in the *New York Times* stated, "Working Families Strain to Live Middle-Class Lives" (Uchitelle 2000). For example, housing prices have increased faster than the earnings of baby boom men, yet home ownership among young couples is now at a historically high level. This anomalous situation has come about because of the two-income family. In the future, however, families will not be able to expand their incomes by adding more workers to the family unit, and a middle-class lifestyle will become increasingly difficult to attain. Many two-income families today work much harder than their parents did, and yet they feel that they are on a financial treadmill (Solomon, Annin, and Kandell 1995). In addition, family types are changing, and the single-parent household is becoming more common. Single parents, especially single mothers who face gender discrimination, may find it increasingly difficult to raise children and stay in the middle class (see Chapter 11).

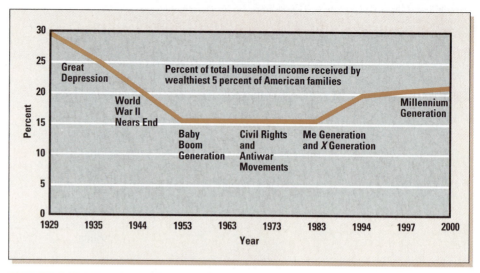

FIGURE 6.3 What Is the Future of Inequality?

A common way to measure the amount of inequality in a society such as the United States is to calculate the percentage of all household income received by the wealthiest families in the nation. To take a hypothetical example, suppose the nation of Lilliput had 100 families and generated $1,000 of total household income in 1929. If the wealthiest 5 percent of families received 30 percent of the income, then the 5 wealthiest Lilliputian families would split $300 among themselves, for a share of $60 each (30 percent of $1,000 divided by 5 families). The remaining 95 families would split $700 among themselves, for a share of $7.36 each—clearly a top-heavy distribution of income.

In the case of the United States, the figure shows that in 1929 the distribution of household income was much like that in Lilliput: the wealthiest 5 percent of American families received 30 percent of all the household income generated in that year. Today, the wealthiest 5 percent receive 21 percent, which is less than in 1929 but more than the percentages for the 30-year period beginning in 1953 and ending in 1983. Moreover, the percentage received by the wealthiest families seems to be increasing at the present time.

SOURCE: Andrew Hacker, "Who They Are," *New York Times Magazine*, November 19, 1995:70–71; U.S. Bureau of the Census, *Statistical Abstract of the United States*, 2000.

What is causing the middle class to dwindle? Many analysts believe that the long-term downward trend in heavy industries, such as steel, automobiles, and durable goods, is now beginning to take its toll throughout society (see Chapter 9). Plant closings and layoffs have occurred repeatedly throughout manufacturing industries, thus causing the number of people with middle-range incomes to decline (Myles and Turegun 1994; Uchitelle 1991). Also, many middle-range jobs are lost when large companies relocate overseas. To be sure, some of the loss has been made up by growth in the service sector, but service jobs pay low wages and involve long hours (Uchitelle 2000). Others point to the loss of earning potential of a high school diploma relative to that of a college degree (Chapter 12; Campbell 2000). Finally, taxpayer rebellions, by preventing local governments from raising taxes, have contributed to the demise of many programs meant to improve the life chances of the middle class and of the poor.

Some social scientists believe, however, that fears of a shrinking middle class are unfounded. They point out that the baby boom generation is so large that when it entered the workforce during the 1960s, the number of people with low-paying jobs increased dramatically. This development caused the middle class to become smaller, but only temporarily. As the baby boomers mature, they will assume higher-paying positions, and the size of the middle class then will rebound. Moreover, when the baby boomers retire, many new positions for the next generation will open up (Linden 1986). If this argument is true, then the decline of the middle class is a transient phenomenon, a shadow cast by the immense size of the baby boom generation.

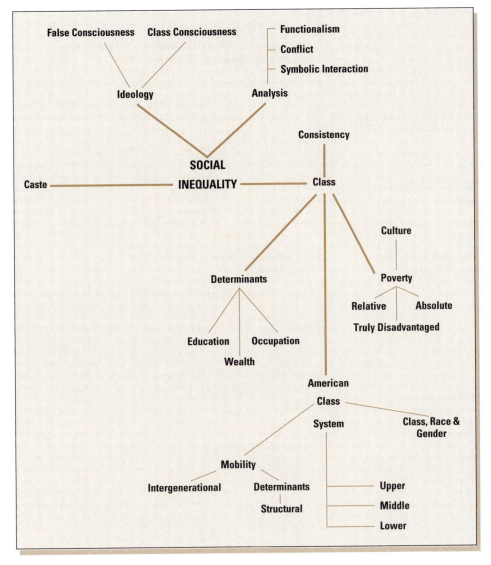

This is a concept web for social inequality. Add homelessness to the web.

Other critics point out that the American economy is still the most productive and efficient in the world. Productivity reached an all-time high in the late 1990s, suggesting that American commerce is still a vibrant, driving force capable of creating well-paying jobs. In the future, some critics suggest, the United States will be even stronger, and the standard of living will continue to rise during the twenty-first century.

Looking Ahead

Inequality caused by caste, class, and socioeconomic status affects everyone within a given society, but it is not the only form of stratification. All societies are stratified by gender, and many societies are also stratified by race and ethnicity. Accordingly, the next chapter continues the discussion of inequality by focusing on race and ethnicity.

WHAT YOU SHOULD KNOW ●■▲

1. How is social inequality manifested in human societies?

All societies are characterized by social inequality, which is the unequal distribution of societal resources, prestige, and power. Within every society, people may be grouped into general layers or strata in terms of the amount of resources, prestige, and power that they have.

2. How did social stratification systems change with the Great Social Transformation?

Hunting and gathering societies are not very stratified. Horticultural, pastoral, and agrarian societies have more complex, rigid stratification systems, whereas industrial societies tend to have systems that are less rigid.

3. How is social mobility related to social stratification?

Societies differ in the amount of social mobility that is possible within the system. Caste systems permit very little or no social mobility, whereas a class system provides opportunities for social mobility.

4. How is one's social standing determined?

Max Weber argued that social stratification occurs along three dimensions: class, status, and party. Weber also argued that a person's position in society is determined by where she or he stands on the three dimensions. Following Weber, sociologists emphasize the importance of education, wealth, and occupational prestige in determining socioeconomic status.

5. What are America's social classes, and what methods are used to determine social class?

Researchers often recognize the following social classes in American society: the upper-upper and the lower-upper class; the middle class, divided into the upper-middle class and the lower-middle class; and the lower class, divided into the upper-lower class and the lower-lower class, which is in turn divided into the working poor and the chronically poor. Sociologists may use one of three methods to determine social class: the objective method, the reputational method, and self-identification.

6. How much social mobility is there in the United States, and is it consistent with America's mythology about mobility?

Overall, the amount of upward intergenerational mobility in American society is not large. Impediments to upward social mobility include the limited number of high-prestige occupations; the great length of the climb for those at the bottom of the social ladder; and racial, ethnic, and gender discrimination. The myths supporting America as the land of opportunity do not fit the reality of mobility in the United States.

7. What is the nature of poverty in America?

In the United States, people who cannot afford a minimum of food, clothing, shelter, and other necessities are considered to be poor regardless of how they compare with others. Some sociologists have argued that the poor construct a culture of poverty, but other sociologists argue that such a culture of poverty does not really exist and that it is incorrect to blame the poor for their own plight.

8. How do functionalists view social stratification?

According to functionalists, stratification is beneficial because it means that people will be rewarded for their qualifications and ensures that all social positions are filled by qualified individuals. The poor perform the less desirable tasks in a society and help to lower prices for consumers. Poverty further helps the middle class because a large percentage of antipoverty funds goes to middle-class workers who staff the programs for the poor.

9. How is social stratification viewed from the conflict perspective?

Conflict theorists draw on Karl Marx's argument that society is divided into two main classes: workers and the owners of the means of production. Bourdieu, a modern conflict theorist, recognizes four types of capital: economic, social, cultural, and symbolic. The dominant class maintains its position through possession and manipulation of all four types.

10. *What has distributive systems theory added to the analysis of social stratification?*

Distributive systems theory attempts to bridge the functionalist and conflict views of social stratification. Gerhard Lenski has said that people will share necessities but that the most powerful members of society will accumulate any surplus that is available. In the early stages of industrialization, the bourgeoisie extract the bulk of society's wealth, but as industrialization proceeds, inequality declines.

11. *How does symbolic interaction theory view social stratification?*

According to the symbolic interaction perspective, many people accept inequality because they are social-

ized to do so, because they believe in equal opportunity but not in equal outcomes, and because they accept the derogatory stereotypes of the poor.

12. *What is the future of social class inequalities?*

Some researchers say that the middle class is shrinking, and they fear a polarization of the American class system. Other researchers argue that as the baby boom generation works its way through the occupational system and eventually retires, many new positions will open up, and the middle class will expand.

TEST YOUR KNOWLEDGE ●■▲

Key Terms Matching

Match each of these key terms with the best definition or example from the numbered items that follow. Write the letter preceding the key term in the blank before the definition that you choose.

a. absolute poverty

b. caste system

c. class consciousness

d. class consistency

e. class system

f. culture of poverty

g. esteem

h. false consciousness

i. ideology

j. intergenerational mobility

k. prestige

l. relative poverty

m. social stratification

n. socioeconomic status

o. status consistent

p. structural mobility

q. truly disadvantaged

_____ **1.** The set of norms and values that helps the poor to adapt to their situation.

_____ **2.** The poverty of people who cannot afford some minimum of food, clothing, shelter, and other necessities regardless of how they compare with other people.

_____ **3.** The honor associated with an occupation or other position in a social system.

_____ **4.** An awareness by members of a social class that it is being oppressed and that membership in the class dooms everyone to the same fate.

_____ **5.** A person's ranking along several social dimensions, particularly education, occupational prestige, and income.

_____ **6.** The pattern of beliefs that legitimizes or justifies a particular societal arrangement.

_____ **7.** The honor that accrues to the individual filling a position in a social system.

_____ **8.** A fixed arrangement of strata from the most to the least privileged, with a person's position determined unalterably at birth.

_____ **9.** People who live predominantly in the inner city and who are trapped in a cycle of joblessness, deviance, crime, welfare dependency, and unstable family life.

_____ **10.** The movement of entire categories of people caused by changes in society itself.

_____ 11. Poverty determined only by comparison with others.

_____ 12. The similarity among the characteristics that define class strata.

_____ 13. Having a similar ranking along the various dimensions of socioeconomic status.

_____ 14. The arrangement of society into a series of layers or strata on the basis of an unequal distribution of societal resources, prestige, or power, such that the stratum at the top has the most resources.

_____ 15. Upward and downward movements in socioeconomic status measured by the standing of children compared with that of their parents.

_____ 16. A class's acceptance of an ideology that is contrary to the best interests of that class.

_____ 17. A system in which social standing is determined by factors over which people can exert some control, such as their educational attainment, their income, and their work experience.

Multiple Choice

Circle the letter of your choice.

1. Which type of society permits the greatest social mobility, therefore lessening the intensity of the social class system?
   a. hunting and gathering
   b. horticultural
   c. agrarian
   d. industrial

2. Which is NOT one of the components of socioeconomic status?
   a. occupational prestige
   b. education
   c. lifestyle
   d. wealth

3. Professor Jackson developed a survey with which she measured social class by asking the respondents to list their levels of education, income, and occupation. Which method of determining social class was she using?
   a. reputational
   b. objective
   c. self-identification
   d. subjective

4. A major difference between the upper-middle class and the lower-middle class is that the
   a. upper-middle class emphasize career achievement, interpersonal skills, and creativity, whereas the lower-middle class emphasize respectability and reliability.
   b. lower-middle class is more interested in sports.
   c. upper-middle class marry only among themselves.
   d. lower-middle class is downwardly mobile.

5. The working class
   a. do not earn enough to accumulate substantial savings.
   b. are extremely vulnerable to disruptions in income through temporary layoffs or unemployment.
   c. earn too little to afford college for their children but too much to receive financial aid.
   d. all of the above.

6. What term did Thorstein Veblen use to refer to spending money on useless things to gain esteem and status?
   a. conspicuous consumption
   b. class consciousness
   c. false consciousness
   d. structural mobility

7. Which is NOT a factor in the increase in the number of the homeless?
   a. Most of the homeless are families headed by young women with young children.
   b. Many of the homeless are substance abusers.
   c. It is difficult for the poor to find jobs that pay enough to lift them out of homelessness.
   d. There is an abundant supply of public housing for the poor.

8. Which age group has the largest number of poor?
   a. under 18 years
   b. 18 to 24 years
   c. 25 to 60 years
   d. over 60 years

9. Which type of capital consists of interpersonal skills, habits, and educational credentials that can be used to gain advantage in society?
   a. economic capital
   b. social capital
   c. cultural capital
   d. symbolic capital

10. Which theory argues that people are willing to share only when it is in their best interests to do so and that because the necessities must be shared more or less equally to ensure individual and societal survival, inequality can occur only when a surplus exists?
    a. conflict
    b. functionalist
    c. distributive systems
    d. interactionist

Identifying Sociological Perspectives on Social Class

For each of the following statements, identify the sociological perspective associated with the statement by writing F for functionalist, C for conflict, SI for symbolic interactionist in the appropriate blank.

_____ 1. Stratification in society is due to inequalities in the distribution of economic, social, cultural, and symbolic capital.

_____ 2. A social stratification system in which some people have more wealth and prestige than others benefits individuals by ensuring that they are rewarded for their talents and qualifications; and it benefits society by ensuring that positions are filled by qualified people.

_____ 3. Toleration for inequality is the self-fulfilling consequence of class discrimination, that is, people who occupy subordinate class positions sometimes adopt the value system of those above them, and come to view themselves as unworthy.

_____ 4. Poverty produces some benefits such as having a pool of inexpensive laborers to do undesirable work; also, the low wages that the poor earn help to hold down prices.

_____ 5. Inequality is tolerated because stereotyping has effectively painted a false perception of the poor and of welfare.

_____ 6. The proletariat have no choice but to work for the bourgeoisie, and the bourgeoisie exploit the labor of the proletariat by keeping wages low.

_____ 7. Poverty helps society by employing middle-class people in occupations associated with fighting poverty, and poverty acts as a buffer that protects the middle class against economic changes.

_____ 8. People tolerate inequality and cope with it because, just like any other aspect of society, inequality is sustained and created through definitions of the situation learned through formal and informal socialization.

True-False

Indicate your response to each of the following statements by circling T for true or F for false.

T F 1. Horticultural societies have the least intense stratification systems.

T F 2. Castes are based on achieved statuses.

T F 3. Boundaries between castes are maintained by controlling who marries whom.

T F 4. The boundaries between classes are continuous.

T F 5. Your paycheck is a component of your wealth.

T F 6. The term pink-collar refers to women who work in male-dominated fields.

T F 7. As a group, the elite, or upper-upper class, are a close-knit group.

T F 8. The deinstitutionalization of the mentally ill contributed to an increase in homelessness.

T F 9. Marx did not envision a significant role for the middle class in industrial society because he assumed that the bourgeoisie would crush it.

T F 10. All social scientists agree that the middle class in America is shrinking.

T F 11. In the United States intergenerational social mobility is large.

T F 12. Max Weber argued that social stratification occurs along two dimensions: class and status.

T F 13. Stratification inevitability produces inequality that, in turn, produces deprivation, misery, and poverty.

T F 14. Lenski argued that social inequality occurs only when a surplus of resources exists.

T F 15. Many critics argue that the concept of "culture of poverty" blames the poor for their plight when, in fact, the causes of poverty lie in society.

NOTE: The answers to these exercises are at the end of the book.

For additional practice tests and other resources please visit the companion web site at http://www.prenhall.com/curry.

Essay

1. Describe the concept of the "culture of poverty."
2. Discuss the signs that the middle class may be shrinking and what impact that may have in the future.
3. What was Thorsten Veblen's contribution to the sociological understanding of class behavior?
4. What is the relationship between Marx's bourgeoisie and proletariat? Does that distinction still hold today?
5. What factors have contributed to homelessness?

7

Inequalities of Race and Ethnicity

In 1932 the U.S. Public Health Service began a study of syphilis that was to last more than 40 years. The purpose of the study was to observe the course of the disease, especially during its advanced stages. The study took place near Tuskegee, Alabama, and was based on a sample of 399 adult males who had syphilis and 201 who did not have it. All of the men were poor, uneducated, rural, and African American.

Although an effective treatment for syphilis was developed not too long after the study began, no effort was made to treat the infected men. Thus, by 1962 some 100 of them had died from syphilis or from its complications. As planned, the investigators compiled many findings from autopsies.

This study later became known as the "Tuskegee Study," and when its existence became public knowledge, a storm of controversy erupted. The basic issue was simple: how could reputable medical researchers, sponsored by the federal government, allow men to die of syphilis just to observe the stages of the disease? Although this question has never been completely answered, a large part of any answer must take into account the racial beliefs that were prevalent at the time of the study.

All of the principal investigators were white, and like much of white society at the time, they believed that African Americans were an inferior race. By thus defining health problems in racial terms, white physicians could absolve themselves of any responsibility for what happened to African American patients. A few white physicians even suggested that syphilis was a justified retribution for the sexual promiscuity that they believed was rampant among African Americans. One investigator who examined the Tuskegee Study concluded that "whether by accident or design, physicians had come dangerously close to depicting the syphilitic black as the representative black" (Jones 1981:28).

The Tuskegee Study ended, but that was not the end of the story. A $1.8 billion lawsuit was later filed on behalf of the survivors and their heirs. Tracking down these people proved to be a difficult and tedious task that involved hundreds of claims and counterclaims. Although the case was eventually settled out of court, by that time, only 120 verified survivors could be found (Parker 1997). Finally, in 1996 President Clinton, in a White House ceremony, offered an apology for the Tuskegee Study.

The Tuskegee Study was initiated several decades ago, yet race continues to play a major role in American life. To illustrate the contemporary importance of race, consider the Los Angeles riot of 1992. More than 3,000 fires broke out and there was unchecked looting when four white police officers were acquitted of beating an African American motorist, Rodney King (Takaki 1994). Then there are the cases of everyday discrimination on a more private scale, such as an incident that involved an African American professor at a private college on the West Coast. The professor, who was being considered for promotion, one day accidentally overheard the promotion committee discussing his case. Committee members were making comments such as "I don't know how I would feel working with a black man" and "Us white people have rights, too." The professor claimed that he was being discriminated against, took his case to court, and won (McCurdy 1990). Another example is O. J. Simpson, a famous African American football star and actor, who stood trial for the murder of his former wife and an acquaintance of hers. Whatever role race might have played in the jury's decision, it was clear that race made a difference to the public. The majority of African Americans believed that Simpson was innocent, whereas the majority of whites believed that he was guilty (ABC 1995). Although racial incidents such as these occur with distressing frequency in the United States, other nations experience racial hostilities too. For instance, German neo-Nazis have firebombed the homes of immigrants, and Brazilian settlers have devastated vast sections of the Amazon rain forest, thereby directly and indirectly killing thousands of Indian inhabitants.

As these examples show, the racial and ethnic differences among people are often more important than the similarities. And sometimes, as these examples further show, racial and ethnic differences are used to justify the mistreatment of one group by another group.

Sociologists have long been interested in incidents such as these and have accumulated a considerable body of knowledge about race and ethnicity. In this chapter, we examine the major findings and conclusions about racial and ethnic relations.

Chapter Preview

In this chapter we first explain the concepts of race and ethnicity and the nature of prejudice and discrimination. We then discuss the typical patterns of interaction among different racial and ethnic groups. Next, we present descriptions of the major American racial and ethnic groups, and we follow these descriptions with a sociological analysis of ethnic and racial inequality. Finally, we make some predictions for racial and ethnic relations in the future.

The Great Social Transformation and Racial and Ethnic Inequality

Ethnic and racial ties are among the most basic communal relationships that bind people together. To illustrate this point, consider the former Soviet Union. While it was intact, the communist government ruled the nation with an iron hand. Every individual and every ethnic group was subordinate to the central government, and no ethnic quarrels were permitted. However, once the central government crumbled, various ethnic groups began demanding more autonomy and, in some cases, outright independence. The national identity evaporated and was replaced by stronger racial and ethnic ties. In times of disorganization and stress, it would seem, people turn to their ethnic group to find security and social support. They cling to their ethnicity to establish a community, and they rally around their ethnicity to make demands and to defend themselves from others (Bremmer and Taras 1996; Reitz 1980).

In contemporary associational societies, the situation is much different. The ties that hold society together are not the bonds of racial and ethnic identity nor those of a powerful central government, but other kinds of links—economic ties, a uniform set of laws, similar values and culture, public education, shared currency and language, interdependence through a sophisticated division of labor, and so on. Race and ethnicity become badges that distinguish one group from another, and in the competition for wealth and political power, some groups come to dominate others.

Race and Ethnicity

In everyday speech, the terms race and ethnicity often are used interchangeably, but sociologists give the terms specific, technical meanings, which we now discuss.

Race

Several schemes have been proposed for classifying people into races. The best-known scheme uses three categories: (1) Caucasoid, people with fair skin and hair ranging from light to dark; (2) Negroid, people with dark skin and curly hair; and (3) Mongoloid, people with yellow skin and distinctive folds on the eyelids (Simpson and Yinger 1985). Although this scheme is widely known, it is not very useful. One problem is inaccuracy. For instance, some Caucasoids are darker than some Negroids, and some Negroids have fair hair. The Negroid aborigines of Australia sometimes have blond hair, and the Caucasians of southern India have darker skin than many African Americans. In addition, humans have migrated over the earth for thousands of years and have produced so much genetic intermixture that no pure race exists. Instead, humans vary along a biological continuum, with different societies dividing the continuum in different ways. For example, in Brazil the continuum of skin color varies from dark to light with several categories in between, such as mulatto or moreno. In the United States, in contrast, people are defined as either black or white with little attention being paid to the middle portion of the continuum. Thus, an individual might be considered black in the United States but mulatto or moreno in Brazil. Because of these problems, sociologists have stopped trying to define race in terms of biological characteristics.

If race cannot be defined biologically, then how can it be defined? The answer is that race is a social construction in the sense that biological traits may be endowed—however arbitrarily—with social meaning. If fair-skinned people believe that dark skin indicates inferiority, then fair-skinned people will act on their belief. They may deny education to dark-skinned people and refuse to hire them for well-paying jobs. In this way, beliefs about skin color rather than any substantial biological differences will cause the two groups to become distinct and unequal. In sum, therefore, a **race** may be defined as a group of people who have been singled out on the basis of real or alleged physical characteristics (Feagin and Feagin 1998; Sahlins 1978). It is important to consider what this definition does not say: that biological characteristics are important or that some races of people are superior or inferior to others. As we will discuss later in the chapter, such statements are dubious at best and form the basis for stereotyping, prejudice, discrimination, and institutional racism.

Ethnicity

Whereas race refers to the social construction of a category based on so-called biological characteristics, **ethnicity** refers to people who have common cultural characteristics, such as the same language, place of origin, dress, food, and values. People who share these cultural features are said to be members of the same **ethnic group**.

In addition to sharing a unique culture, members of an ethnic group share a unique **ethnic identity**; that is, they have internalized ethnic roles as part of their self-concept (see Chapter 3). Ethnic identity forms early in life, and by adolescence, individuals are fully aware of it.

Because they share a common culture and a common identity, members of an ethnic group are drawn toward one another and feel a strong sense of "oneness," unity, and shared fate. Marriage across ethnic lines, although not uncommon, is not typical. The practice of marrying within the group is a result of both ethnic hostility and preference. As long as a group marries within itself, the ethnicity of the group will be preserved and passed on to subsequent generations (Petersen 1971; Phinney and Tarver 1988; Thernstrom 1980; Van den Berge 1967).

Sometimes race and ethnicity overlap. For example, Vietnamese Americans are considered to be a race (in the sociological sense) as well as an ethnic group. So too are African, Chinese, and Japanese Americans. This overlap sometimes causes confusion, as illustrated by the experiences of Caribbean Hispanics living in the United States. In the Caribbean, race is defined by a continuum of skin color—some people

Race ▲ A group of people who have been singled out on the basis of real or alleged physical characteristics.

Ethnicity ▲ Common cultural characteristics people share, such as the same language, place of origin, dress, food, and values.

Ethnic group ▲ People who share basic cultural features such as language, place of origin, dress, food, and values.

Ethnic identity ▲ The internalization of ethnic roles as part of a person's self-concept.

are light-skinned, others are darker, and others are darker still (Torres and Whitten 1998). As we noted earlier, in the United States, the racial division is basically black and white; and so when Caribbean Hispanics immigrate, they are tugged in different directions. They are accepted as neighbors by white Hispanics on the basis of ethnicity but are rejected by non-Hispanic whites on the basis of race (Denton and Massey 1989).

Minority

The concepts of race and ethnicity stem from social and cultural characteristics. It is also possible, however, to classify groups according to power. Thus, a **minority** is a group that has less power than the dominant group. Minority groups usually are poorer than the majority, have less prestige, and suffer from discrimination.

The sociological meaning of minority, you might note, does not refer to the numerical size of a group. However, many racial or ethnic groups in the United States are minorities both in numbers and in power. Mexican Americans, for instance, are a small percentage of the population and lack power as well. The same is true of African Americans, Asian Americans, Native Americans, and other groups commonly studied by sociologists.

●■▲ **Pausing to Think**   About Race and Ethnicity

From the sociologist's perspective, race and ethnicity are considered to be categories created by the interplay of social forces. Foremost among these forces is the power of one group to impose a racial or ethnic category on another. A racial or ethnic group may be a minority group even though it may be larger in size than other racial and ethnic groups in the society. Minority status is based on the relative social power of a group.

CQ Does the assertion that race is a social fact mean that there are no physical differences between one race and another?

Prejudice and Discrimination

Sociologists explain persisting inequality between groups by the key concepts of discrimination and prejudice. Although the words prejudice and discrimination often are used as synonyms in everyday language, sociologists distinguish between them. Sociologically, a **prejudice** is an attitude that predisposes an individual to prejudge entire categories of people unfairly. This attitude is rigid, emotionally loaded, and resistant to change. It usually involves selective perception: only those facts and beliefs that fit the prejudice are given credence. Contradictory arguments and evidence are ignored, are not believed, are dismissed as illogical, or sometimes are not even perceived. Consequently, the forces of logic and evidence are seldom strong enough to change an entrenched prejudice.

Prejudice can be directed toward any social category. Women and the poor, for instance, often are the targets of prejudice, as are animals and even inanimate objects. Because of their association with Germany during World War I, many people in the United States in those years were prejudiced against both German shepherd dogs and sauerkraut. To lessen these prejudices, the German shepherd was renamed the Alsatian (a name that is still used in Great Britain), and sauerkraut was called "victory cabbage." Likewise, when France did not support the United States' attempt to gain United Nations support for the 2003 invasion of Iraq, many Americans boycotted French wines, and in some eateries french fries were renamed "victory fries."

Minority ▲ A group that has less power than the dominant group.

Prejudice ▲ An attitude that predisposes an individual to prejudge entire categories of people unfairly.

	Does Not Discriminate	Discriminates
Unprejudiced	1. Unprejudiced Nondiscriminator. (All-weather Liberal)	2. Unprejudiced discriminator. (Fair-weather Liberal)
Prejudiced	3. Prejudiced Nondiscriminator. (Timid Bigot)	4. Prejudiced Discriminator. (All-weather Bigot)

FIGURE 7.1 Patterns of Prejudice and Discrimination

This figure shows that attitudes and behavior do not always match. Not all prejudiced people discriminate against minorities, and not all discrimination toward minorities is done by prejudiced individuals. Active bigots discriminate and are prejudiced. Timid bigots are prejudiced but do not discriminate. Fair-weather liberals are not prejudiced but do discriminate, and all-weather liberals neither are prejudiced nor engage in discriminatory behavior.

Sociologists distinguish between prejudice, which is an attitude, and discrimination, which is a behavior. Following this distinction, **discrimination** is defined as the unfair and harmful treatment of people based on their group membership (see Figure 7.1). For example, when an employer refuses to hire well-qualified Asian or African Americans because of their ethnic and racial membership, that practice is discrimination. Similarly, when a teacher assumes that Puerto Rican children have less intellectual ability than white children and as a result does not encourage Puerto Ricans to excel academically, that treatment is also discrimination.

During the early 1930s, a classic study showed the importance of distinguishing between prejudice and discrimination. Social scientist Richard LaPiere traveled around the United States with a Chinese couple. Six months after their trip, LaPiere wrote to each restaurant and hotel they had visited and asked whether it would serve Chinese patrons. Some 90 percent of the respondents said that Chinese patrons were not welcomed, yet only one restaurant actually had refused to serve the couple. Thus, even though restaurant and hotel managers were prejudiced against the Chinese, as indicated by their responses to LaPiere's letter, they did not engage in discrimination when they met the Chinese couple face to face. Perhaps this behavior was due to the upper-class appearance of the couple, who arrived at the hotel well-dressed, in their own car, accompanied by a white male (LaPiere 1934).

Prejudice often takes a major psychological toll on the individuals and groups that are the objects of prejudice. Being an object of prejudice adversely affects a person's emotional state. It makes people who are the object of the prejudice feel negative about those who feel prejudice toward them. When people feel that others are prejudiced toward them, they want to avoid interaction with the prejudiced (Tropp 2003). Such feelings can adversely complicate a person's life, as in the case of a student who feels that a teacher is prejudiced against the student's racial group, and therefore, does not seek needed help from the teacher.

Hate crimes are an extreme form of discrimination (Levin and Rabrenovic 2001). They are crimes that are racially motivated. African Americans are most often the objects of hate crimes. Since 1992 there has been a 52 percent increase in hate crimes against African Americans. To a large extent, this increase reflects a growing acceptance of racial prejudice among some elements of white society (Torres 1999).

Sociologists believe that human thought, attitudes, and conduct are molded by society. Accordingly, sociologists define **racism** as the belief that race determines human ability and that as a result, certain races deserve to be treated as inferior, whereas other races deserve to be treated as superior. If people are socialized into a culture that promotes racism, then in all likelihood they will be prejudiced and will freely discriminate. Conversely, if society opposes racism, then people

Discrimination ▲ The unfair and harmful treatment of people based on their group membership.

Racism ▲ The belief that race determines human ability and that, as a result, certain races deserve to be treated as superior.

socialized into that culture will hold egalitarian values and will treat individuals of other races and ethnic groups as equals (Deutscher 1973; Feagin and Feagin 1998; Hacker 1995a).

Stereotypes

Racism does not exist in a vacuum; it is supported by other features of society and culture. One of these features is **stereotypes**: rigid and inaccurate images that summarize a belief. Because stereotypes reflect beliefs rather than facts, they are illogical and self-serving. Consider the following examples. When Chinese people congregate with their families, they may be stereotyped as "clannish," but when Swedes engage in the same behavior, they may be described as "showing strong family solidarity." Scots are stereotyped as "stingy," but the same behavior by the British is described as "thrifty." Germans might be stereotyped as "hard-working," but when the Japanese work equally hard, they are criticized for engaging in "unfair competition" (Katz and Braley 1933; Merton 1968). Thus, the same characteristic may be interpreted positively when performed by one group but negatively when performed by another.

If stereotypes are factually incorrect and illogical, why do they persist? Why do people continue to accept them uncritically? One reason is that stereotyping elevates the status of the group that engages in it. A poor white racist might take comfort in believing that he or she is superior, simply because of skin color, to any member of another racial or ethnic group (Hacker 1995b). A second reason is that stereotypes simplify thinking and reduce guilt. If a person believes that all members of a group are inferior, then he or she does not have to accept any responsibility for their situation. A third reason for the popularity of stereotypes is ignorance. Most people have limited contacts with members of other ethnic and racial groups and therefore cannot verify the inaccuracy of the stereotype. When a prejudiced person does encounter a member of a group who contradicts the stereotype, the prejudiced person may simply assume that that person is the "exception that proves the rule" (Simpson and Yinger 1985; Travis and Velasco 1994).

Although racial and ethnic minorities face prejudice and discrimination, individuals can overcome those hurdles. For example, Lauro F. Cavazos, a Hispanic, became secretary of education during the administrations of presidents Reagan and Bush; and an African American, Bill Cosby, has become one of the wealthiest and most influential entertainers in the world. Success, however, does not totally insulate such people from discrimination. To illustrate, Alberto Cisneros was a Mexican American student at the University of Washington. Imagine how he must have felt at an academic awards banquet where he was about to receive recognition for his outstanding academic accomplishments. As reported by the *Chronicle of Higher Education* (May 23, 1990:23), the president of the university, while addressing the group, commented that Mr. Cisneros, upon arriving in Southern California from Mexico, had been fascinated with how the freeway system enabled huge numbers of cars to travel together at speeds of over 70 miles per hour. The president then ad-libbed that Mr. Cisneros "was probably traveling on the freeway late at night and driving that fast to avoid immigration authorities." The president's comments clearly played on the stereotype of Mexicans as illegal aliens, and rather than laughing, Mr. Cisneros could only feel embarrassed and insulted.

Institutional Racism

Racist practices often become part of the social practices and institutions of a society. When that happens, **institutional racism** is said to exist (Hamilton and Carmichael 1967; Jalata 2002; Jones and Carter 1996; Lopez 1996). A long-standing example of institutional racism is housing segregation. In 1990, the latest year for which this type of data is available, 70 to 80 percent of all African Americans living in major metropolitan areas would have had to move to achieve a nonsegregated

123 STUDY TIP

Clarify the relationship between prejudice and discrimination by coming up with three situations where a prejudicial attitude has led to a discriminatory practice. Analyzing each situation, identify one or more stereotypes that may have been a factor.

Stereotypes ▲ Rigid and inaccurate images that summarize a belief.

Institutional racism ▲ A situation in which racist practices become part of the social practices and institutions of society.

pattern of housing. The same is true of 60 to 80 percent of all Hispanics and 40 to 60 percent of all Asians. In other words, these groups are concentrated into ghettos, barrios, Koreatowns, Chinatowns, and so forth (also, Denton and Massey 1989; Jiobu 1988). Even in Honolulu, a city long idealized as a haven of multicultural harmony, Chinese, Filipinos, and Japanese live in predominantly segregated areas (Jiobu and Nishigaya 1985).

Institutional racism is so deeply entrenched in everyday life that we often fail to notice it. For instance, some banks refuse to provide mortgage loans to African Americans who live in low-income areas of a city. This practice is called redlining. Although the bank will defend redlining as good business, the practice discriminates against low-income groups. It especially affects African Americans because many of them live within redlined areas (Hewitt 1999). Another example of institutional racism concerns the Scholastic Aptitude Test (SAT), which is commonly used to screen college applicants. The scores on this test vary among racial and ethnic groups. For example, African Americans and Mexican Americans typically score lower than whites, whereas Asian Americans outdo whites in the mathematical portion of the examination but lag behind in the verbal portion. These differences are, according to many sociologists, the product of a cultural bias built into the SAT test itself. For example, many questions on the test assume knowledge of white middle-class culture, an assumption that penalizes anyone who comes from a different background. Even though cultural bias might not account for all of the differences among groups, the fact that more than 1 million students take the SAT each year means that even a small bias will translate into a substantial amount of institutional racism. Hopefully, recent revisions to the SAT will alleviate these problems (Celis 1990; National Commission on Testing and Public Policy 1990).

●■▲ Pausing to Think   About Prejudice and Discrimination

Prejudice refers to the attitudes underlying racism, whereas discrimination refers to actual behavior. However, institutional racism may persist even when prejudice is not present.

Malcolm X, a black leader of the 1960s, said "Racism is a human problem and a crime that is absolutely so ghastly that a person who is fighting racism is well within his rights to fight against it by any means necessary until it is eliminated."

CQ What did Malcolm X mean? ◆ Do you agree? ◆ Should racism be fought by any means necessary? ◆ Why, or why not?

Patterns of Racial and Ethnic Interaction

When different racial and ethnic groups live in the same society, the various groups can relate to each other in different ways. Many of these interactions form broad patterns, and we now turn to a discussion of them (Simpson and Yinger 1985).

Assimilation

The term **assimilation** refers to the blending of the culture and structure of one racial or ethnic group with the culture and structure of another group. If assimilation takes place over a long period, the distinction between the groups disappears. For example, the Normans and the Saxons were once distinct groups, but after several hundred years of assimilation, they blended into a single group now called the British or English.

Assimilation is not unilinear in the sense of proceeding along one fixed path and producing a certain outcome. There are, instead, several possible outcomes. One is

Assimilation ▲ The blending of the culture and structure of one racial or ethnic group with the culture and structure of society.

Assimilation takes place over time and affects each generation differently. The Japanese women in the photograph on the right immigrated to the United States in 1916. Many came as "picture brides" of Japanese men who were already working in the United States. This first generation of immigrants usually lived in Japanese American communities and did not interact very much with the dominant society. The photograph below right shows a fully assimilated Japanese American couple paying bills. Many years separate this couple from the original immigrant generation.

that the majority group remains the same, whereas the minority changes and becomes like the majority group. In the United States, this outcome is called *Anglo conformity* or **Americanization**. Alternatively, both the minority and the majority might change, and a new, blended grouping then emerges that combines some features of both groups. This outcome is called melting-pot assimilation, named after a line in an early twentieth-century stage play: "America is God's Crucible, the great **melting-pot** where all races of Europe are melting and reforming" (Zangwill 1909/1921). Although the media and politicians routinely pay homage to "America, the melting pot," most assimilation has occurred among white ethnic groups, and Anglo conformity has been the result.

A convenient and insightful approach to understanding assimilation is to divide it into two dimensions: culture and structure (Gordon 1964). To use Chinese Americans as an illustration, the overwhelming majority of third- and fourth-generation Chinese Americans are culturally assimilated. They have, for example, adopted American dress, foods, customs, values, norms, and language, and in these respects, they are virtually indistinguishable from the majority. At the same time, however, most of these Chinese are not highly assimilated structurally. For the most part, they interact socially with other Chinese, tend to marry other Chinese, and often work in Chinese-owned businesses. Even Chinese professionals who have moved out of ethnic neighborhoods might continue to interact mainly with other Chinese people after working hours (Daniels and Harry 1994; Kitano and Yeung 1982). In short, Chinese Americans are much more assimilated culturally than structurally.

Assimilation takes place over time and affects each generation differently. To illustrate, consider the case of Japanese women who immigrated to the United States. The first generation of women arrived during the years 1908 to 1920. Many came as "picture brides" of Japanese men who were already working in the United States. The social world in which these women lived was rather isolated and permitted very little cultural or structural assimilation. The daughters of these immigrants were born in the United States between 1915 and 1940. Citizens by birth, they were culturally assimilated—in large measure through their experiences in the public schools. For this second generation of women, the family still had high priority, but many of them took jobs outside the Japanese American community. The daughters of the second generation were born in the United States between 1940 and 1960, and they experienced even more cultural assimilation than did their mothers. This third generation also attained a significant degree of structural assimilation, because they took jobs in the majority economy and often participated in majority organizations such as churches and recreational groups. Many of them intermarried with whites to create multicultural families, an act that represents the highest possible level of structural assimilation (Gordon 1964; Yukawa 1992).

Pluralism

Whereas assimilation refers to the possibility that different racial and ethnic groups will blend, the opposite is also possible (Gill 2000). In that case, separate racial and ethnic groups will maintain their distinctiveness even though they may have approximately equal social standing. This state of affairs is called **pluralism**. The concept of pluralism implies that ethnic diversity is a desirable social goal and that group distinctiveness is voluntary rather than forced on any group by another group (Kallen 1924).

Throughout the world, pluralism is now common (Williams 1994). For example, only 9 percent of the world's nations are ethnically homogeneous, and 40 percent have populations that are divided into five or more ethnic groups (Connor 1972; Smith 1981). The United States, with more than 100 distinct ethnic and racial groups, is especially pluralistic. That number includes well-known groups such as African Americans, Hispanics, and Asians, as well as little-known groups such as Abyssinians (Thernstrom 1980).

STUDY TIP

Draw a picture to represent your view of America's racial and ethnic diversity. Is it a melting pot? A mosaic? Something else? Write a brief explanation of your drawing, noting what image you have chosen and why it seems appropriate for the United States.

Americanization ▲ The process within American society in which minority group members change their behavior and in doing so become more like the majority group.

Melting pot ▲ A situation in which the culture and social structure of both the minority and the majority change in such a way that a new, blended grouping emerges that combines some features of both groups.

Pluralism ▲ A situation in which separate racial and ethnic groups maintain their distinctiveness even though they may have approximately equal standing.

Seemingly, pluralism should undermine the stability and cohesiveness of a society, for how can highly diverse groups ever get along harmoniously and act together for the common good? This question is often asked, and Horace Kallen, the person who first developed the concept of pluralism, provides an answer. He argues that pluralistic societies are stable for two reasons. First, even though the various groups are distinct, they share a common cultural core. They follow the law of the land and abide by many customs of the larger society. These groups eventually master the predominant language and participate in many key institutions, such as education and commerce. Second, all groups are ruled by the same government, and this government provides avenues for resolving disputes. For instance, Cubans living in Miami sometimes come into conflict with African Americans. If Kallen is correct, then both groups should accept the principles of American democracy and resolve their disputes through the courts or through participating in political life. Thus, if diverse groups participate in government democratically, societal cohesion will be preserved (Kallen 1924).

Currently, race and ethnicity are reemerging as salient issues in American life. This new interest has given rise to the phenomenon known as **ethnic revival**: a situation in which racial and ethnic groups clamor for political autonomy and sometimes demand independence. In the United States, ethnic revival has not generated a widespread movement to divide the country among the various American ethnic groups. Many groups, however, are experiencing renewed interest in their ethnicity. Groups such as African Americans, Chicanos, and Native Americans are reviving their ethnic identities to create a greater sense of community and belonging (Reitz 1980). This process may also be observed among white ethnic groups, which now are reemphasizing their ethnic ancestry (Waters 1990). For minority groups facing discrimination, the goal of the revival is to replace a sense of being inferior with a sense of group pride. For example, some educators argue that American history should be taught from an Afrocentric viewpoint, or one that emphasizes the cultural achievements of African civilizations and the links between black cultural roots and contemporary African Americans (Anderson and Frideres 1981; Smith 1981; Stebbins 1987).

Related to ethnic revival is another concept that mainly affects the third and later generations of a racial or ethnic group. This concept is voluntary or **symbolic ethnicity**: an attempt to preserve and participate in disappearing ethnic roles and culture (Gans 1979). To illustrate, consider the fact that Irish Americans celebrate St. Patrick's Day with parties, parades, and green-colored beer. They take pride in Irish culture, are highly interested in the political problems besetting Ireland, and try to visit Ireland whenever possible. By engaging in these and other voluntary behaviors, Irish Americans are both learning about Irish culture and voluntarily reaffirming their ethnicity.

Expulsion and Annihilation

Assimilation represents a pattern of accommodation in which the racial or ethnic minority is incorporated into the society. In many cases, however, the opposite pattern has been adopted: racial and ethnic prejudice has resulted in the forceful **expulsion** of the minority (Bell-Fialkoff 1996). For this tactic to be successful, one group must possess enough political and military power to force the other group to leave. This pattern has been commonly seen throughout history, as suggested by these examples:

- In 1492, Spanish Jews were given the choice of converting to Catholicism or leaving Spain; most left.
- In the winter of 1838, the United States government forced 16,000 Cherokee Indians to march from their homelands in the Carolinas and Georgia to a reservation in Oklahoma. Along the way, one-quarter of them died.
- When India became independent from Great Britain in 1947, the country of Pakistan was created, and Muslims throughout India were encouraged or forced to move there amid great turmoil and much bloodshed.

Ethnic revival ▲ A situation in which racial and ethnic groups clamor for political autonomy and sometimes demand independence.

Symbolic ethnicity ▲ An attempt to preserve and participate in disappearing ethnic roles and culture.

Expulsion ▲ The forceful exclusion of a racial or ethnic group from a society.

- In 1972, the entire Asian Indian population of Uganda was suddenly ordered to leave.
- Anti-Armenian violence in Azerbaijan, a former republic of the Soviet Union, created thousand of refugees with no place to go (*Newsweek*, March 19, 1990:30).
- In the former Yugoslavia, Croats, Bosnian Serbs, and Muslims attempted to drive out members of the other two groups and to establish territories inhabited by only one group. In the process, thousands of civilians were killed, raped, injured, and made homeless (Watson et al. 1992). A fragile peace was eventually put in place, but the United States had to guarantee order by sending armed troops into the area.

Whereas expulsion represents an extreme and often a violent response to a racial or ethnic minority, there is a still more violent alternative: **annihilation**, or the process by which one group exterminates another group (Ferrarotti 2002). This can be done by rounding up all the members of a particular group and then executing them or incarcerating them under such brutal conditions that they slowly perish. These tactics were used by the Nazis during World War II to kill 6 million European Jews. Another tactic is to spread disease among a group or to allow its members to perish for lack of food, shelter, and medicine. Practicing an early form of germ warfare, the United States cavalry sometimes left clothes infested with the smallpox virus among Native Americans. Whether this tactic was widely used or not is difficult to document, but it is known that through European diseases, forced relocation, warfare, and mistreatment, the Native American population was decimated and rendered defenseless (Josephy 1994).

Annihilation is an extreme reaction, but one that has been fairly common throughout the world. In Tasmania, British settlers literally hunted the natives for sport and wiped them out. The Dutch did the same to the Hottentots of Africa. In 1915, more than 1 million Armenians perished at Turkish hands. And during the 1970s, the communist Khmer Rouge government of Cambodia killed 2 million of its fellow Cambodians for supposedly representing capitalist culture. Included in this group were teachers, bureaucrats, lawyers, officials, and anyone who spoke English (Hinton 1998; Kinloch 2002).

● ■ ▲ **Pausing to Think**   About Racial and Ethnic Interaction

For many years, assimilation was the major approach to handling the millions of immigrants to the United States, but today cultural pluralism seems to be gaining favor. Race and ethnicity are social constructs, and nothing in their construction requires groups to be hostile to one another. Nonetheless, in practice, hostility is a common group response.

CQ Are you in favor of cultural pluralism as a general approach to maintaining peaceful racial and ethnic interactions? ◆ What are the advantages and disadvantages of maintaining racial and ethnic diversity? ◆ If you are not in favor of pluralism, what nonviolent alternatives do you see?

Racial and Ethnic Groups in the United States

We became not a melting pot but a beautiful mosaic. Different people, different beliefs, different yearnings, different hopes, different dreams.

President Jimmy Carter, in a speech in Pittsburgh, Pennsylvania, October 27, 1976

Annihilation ▲ The process by which one ethnic or racial group exterminates another group.

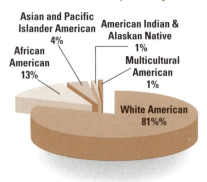

U.S. Population: Self Identified Racial Groups
(U.S. Bureau of the Census 2002)

This pie chart shows how people in the United States identified themselves in terms of racial categories. In the census of 2000, the Census Bureau allowed multiple racial categories. For instance, people could list their racial category as "African American and white." This was done to recognize the increasing diversity of the country. As a consequence, though, racial data for the 2000 census cannot be directly compared to the racial data of earlier censuses.

CQ Recently, sociologists have begun using the term "ethnicity" rather than "race." Do you think that is a good idea? ◆ Why or why not?

More than 25 years ago, President Carter described the United States as a mosaic composed of many racial and ethnic groups. As we have just discussed, the United States is a diverse country. According to American cultural values, this diversity is a blessing, for out of it flow strength of character and nationhood. The degree to which American society has succeeded or failed in its embrace of diversity can be seen in the background and current standing of major ethnic and racial groups (see the Society Today box, U.S. Population by Self-Identified Ancestry Group).

White Americans

In the United States, whites are both a numerical majority and the dominant group. However, to believe that all whites are alike is as much a stereotype as to believe that all Asians or Hispanics are alike. The category of white American includes many different groups, of which white Anglo-Saxon Protestants are the most dominant.

White Anglo-Saxon Protestant   The most powerful group in the United States consists of a diverse grouping of whites of English descent, as well as whites of Canadian, Scottish, Australian, and Northern European descent.

This group originally composed the majority of free immigrants to the United States, and not until the nineteenth century did substantial numbers of other groups begin arriving. Up to then, the United States had followed a policy of open immigration: anyone could come and leave as each one wished. But with the arrival of immigrants from Eastern Europe and Asia, this policy came under fire and led to the adoption of an immigration policy based on quotas. These quotas were written into the Immigration Act of 1924 and were a thinly disguised way to exclude African Americans, Hispanics, Asians, and Eastern Europeans. Although the 1965 immigration law replaced racial-ethnic quotas with a system based on occupation and other qualifications, white Anglo-Saxon Protestants remain the most powerful group in the United States.

White Ethnics   The term *white ethnic* refers to white European groups that are not Anglo-Saxon Protestants. Among them are people of Italian, Irish, French, Polish, Czech, and Russian origin. With the exception of Russian immigrants, who are mostly Jewish, these groups are predominantly Catholic (Rosenthal 1975).

White Catholics encountered a storm of prejudice and discrimination during the nineteenth century. For instance, Italians were sometimes lynched; the Irish were forced into the lowest occupations for meager wages and were stereotyped as being the "missing link" between lower animal forms and humans. A political party, the "Know-Nothings," ran and elected many politicians on an explicitly antiforeign, anti-Catholic platform.

Hostility toward white ethnics continued into the twentieth century. In one of the most sensational trials in American history, two Italian American workers—Nicola Sacco and Bartolomeo Vanzetti—were accused of killing a paymaster at a shoe factory in Massachusetts. Objective observers overwhelmingly agreed that the evidence presented at their trial proved them innocent, yet because of anti-Italian prejudice and hostility toward their radical political views, both were found guilty and executed in 1927 (Davidson and Lytle 1982).

Will white ethnic groups remain distinct in a pluralistic mode, or will they assimilate and become indistinguishable from the dominant group? For a time, many sociologists believed that white ethnics would eventually assimilate and disappear. This belief has waned, however, as many white ethnic groups continue to maintain ethnically identifiable neighborhoods, businesses, social clubs, and churches (Greeley 1981). It is true, however, that white ethnics have assimilated to a substantial degree.

The Irish are possibly the most assimilated of the white ethnic groups today, for several reasons. They came from an English-speaking homeland, and they arrived when demand for manual labor was high. Over time, they moved into local politics, thereby enabling them to control the apparatus of local government to their own

This photograph shows an extended family of Navajo Indians in Monument Valley, Arizona. It is sheep-shearing time on the reservation, and the family is having a lunch break. The Navajo struggle with many of the problems of reservation life and try to be self-sufficient in a beautiful but dry and barren land.

CQ What images come to mind when you think of Native Americans? ◆ What do these images imply about Native Americans?

benefit (Blessing 1980; Ignatiev 1995). In contrast, Greek Americans are an example of how a white, non-Anglo-Saxon Protestant group has maintained strong ethnic institutions. Among them, the Greek Orthodox Church, the Greek-language press, national Greek social organizations, and concentrated ethnic neighborhoods permit Greek Americans to spend a large part of their daily lives in close contact with their cultural roots (Georgakas 1987).

Native Americans

No one knows for sure how many Native Americans lived in North America when European settlers first began arriving—one estimate puts the number as high as 40 million, divided among 500 tribes (Josephy 1994). By the middle of the nineteenth century, nevertheless, diseases brought by European settlers, along with dislocation, warfare, genocide, and impoverishment, had reduced the original Indian population to approximately 250,000 individuals. Only recently has the Native American population begun to recover. Between 1970 and 1990, the number of people claiming Native American origins rose from about 800,000 to 1.8 million. Today, 2.7 million people list themselves in that category (U.S. Bureau of the Census 2002). A principal reason for this increase was that many people reclaimed their native origins (Hacker 1995a). Currently, Native Americans are divided into some 170 tribes. About one-third of them live in cities, whereas the remainder live in or very close to 267 government reservations, mostly located in the West. Native Americans are one of the most disadvantaged groups in the United States. Anywhere from 50 to 80 percent are unemployed, over half drop out of school before the eighth grade, their suicide rate is twice the national average, and their alcoholism rate is eight times the average.

Policies set by the federal government largely determined the fate of Native Americans. These policies evolved through several stages, which can be summarized as follows (Spicer 1981).

The first stage was *separation*. The British originated this policy during the 1600s, and under it, the Indian tribes were treated as nations. Britain laid claim to all lands east of the Appalachian Mountains and by default ceded all western lands to Native Americans. With the American Revolution and the establishment of the United States, a new policy emerged. Friction between settlers and Cherokee Indians led the Cherokee tribe to sue the state of Georgia, asking for recognition of the boundaries

Society Today ● ■ ▲

Largest Native American Tribes

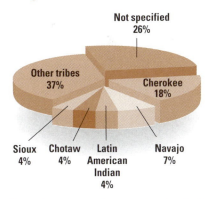

Not specified 26%

Other tribes 37%

Cherokee 18%

Sioux 4% Chotaw 4% Latin American Indian 4% Navajo 7%

This chart shows that one-fourth of all Native Americans are either Cherokee or Navajo. The chart also shows that about one-fourth of all Native Americans do not affiliate with a specific tribe.

CQ Can you list three social processes that explain why so many Native Americans do not affiliate with a tribe?

SOURCE: U.S. Bureau of the Census, *Statistical Abstract of the United States*, 2002.

In what has become known as the Trail of Tears, thousands of Cherokee Indians were forced to move from their traditional homelands to new lands in Oklahoma in 1838. Nearly one-fourth of the Indians died along the way. The Trail of Tears is an example of the policy of expulsion that was practiced by the government during the nineteenth century.

between the state and the Indian nation. The Supreme Court refused their claims, but that decision established the legal principle of allowing Native Americans to keep jurisdiction over matters within their defined territories.

The second stage was *expulsion* and *extermination*. Under congressional approval granted in 1830, the federal government removed all Indians from the East Coast. Originally, this relocation was to be accomplished by making treaties with the Indian nations, but in practice, it was a forced, brutal migration. For example, of the 70,000 Indians removed from the Southeast, 20,000 died in the journey to their new homes. By 1850, Native Americans were being forcibly moved to territories west of the Mississippi River. Today, as a result, almost 90 percent of Indians reside in the West.

By the 1880s, the policy of relocation-extermination gave way to *forced assimilation*. Largely inspired by religious groups, assimilation took place along two fronts. One front involved redistribution of land, with the hope that Native Americans would enter the white economic system. This hope was never realized on a large scale. The other involved a dissolution of Indian social structure and culture. For the next half-century, Indian tribal customs, institutions, and culture came under attack, becoming lost, forgotten, or destroyed. During the 1930s, government policy changed again. The new federal policy was tribal *restoration*. Under it, Native Americans were encouraged to restore their cultural roots, if they wished. Tribes were also urged to incorporate legally, to adopt a modified form of constitutional government, and to establish business enterprises. Currently, the view that Native Americans are wards of the government may be giving way to the view that they can be *self-sufficient*, independent groups. With this emerging definition, some observers say that Native Americans should be treated the same as any other racial-ethnic group and that through assimilation they will melt into the American mainstream. An opposing view claims that Native Americans have been rendered so disadvantaged that they will not assimilate in the foreseeable future (Nagel 1996).

African Americans

African Americans are among the oldest racial-ethnic groups in the United States. In 2000 there were 34 million African Americans in the United States. In 1619 the first group was brought to Virginia as slaves. In the United States, slavery evolved into an institution under which African slaves had virtually no rights whatsoever (Stinchcombe 1994). At the peak of the slave trade, between 1740 and 1760, five thousand slaves per year were being imported into the United States, most directly from Africa, with a few coming from the Caribbean.

By contemporary standards, the slave trade was one of the cruelest economic institutions ever developed. People were captured by slave-trading kingdoms in the interior of Africa and transported to holding camps on the Atlantic coast. There they were sold to white slave traders, who brought them to the United States in chains, packed tightly in the holds of ships. Once ashore, they quickly become the property of the highest bidder at a slave auction. Although the United States made the slave trade illegal in 1807, slavery itself remained until the end of the Civil War (1865).

Because slaves were gathered from various tribes and regions of Africa, they had little in common—other than their status as slaves. Most of their original African culture vanished and was replaced by a slave culture that emerged in the new environment. A well-known cultural feature that survived from Africa was music. African American musical forms eventually developed into ragtime, blues, jazz, rhythm and blues, and rock and roll.

The Civil War ended American slavery but not the subordination of African Americans. After the Reconstruction period, during which the federal government attempted to ensure the equality of the newly emancipated slaves, Southern whites regained control of major political and economic institutions. White supremacist groups openly lynched and whipped African Americans and thereby made it dangerous or impossible for them to exercise their right to vote (see the Profiles box on Ida B. Wells-Barnett). At the same time, the institution of "Jim Crow" emerged. Jim Crow is the name given to a set of discriminatory practices, sanctioned by law and tradition, that lasted into the 1960s and in some places still exists in modified form. Under Jim Crow, African Americans and whites had separate restrooms, water fountains, schools, work environments, and dining places. African Americans could not stay at white hotels, play in white parks, or go to white movie theaters, and, of course, they could not live in white neighborhoods.

Although the decade of the 1960s is remembered as the era of civil rights activity, two major related events occurred during the 1950s. In 1954, the Supreme Court ruled in *Brown* v. *Board of Education* that segregated public schools were illegal, a decision that forever changed the nature of education in the United States and that continues to be contested to this day. And in 1955 in Montgomery, Alabama, an African American woman refused to surrender her seat in the black section of a bus to a white man who could not find a place in the white section. The woman, Rosa Parks, was subsequently arrested for refusing to yield her seat. When the incident became public knowledge, it triggered a massive bus boycott by African Americans. Under a new leader, Dr. Martin Luther King, Jr., the boycott lasted over a year and did not end until the buses in Montgomery were finally desegregated (Chapter 16).

Groups held in a subordinate position for prolonged periods sometimes adopt the value system of the dominant group and come to view themselves as unworthy. In effect, a minority group turns against itself, and in so doing, it reinforces the dominance of the majority. For this reason, African Americans have had to struggle against the notion that white culture is superior to African culture and that white people are superior to African people. To combat these false ideas, movements aimed at revitalizing African American culture and "black pride" emerged during the 1960s. Whereas African Americans once were tempted to mimic whites by, for instance, straightening their hair and even applying lotions that supposedly lighten the skin, the black pride movement emphasized the desirability of African features. Buoyed by an assertive ethnic pride, many African American leaders called for a racial social order based on pluralism rather than assimilation. In their view, African Americans should stand alongside white Americans as equals, and each group should maintain its racial and cultural distinctiveness.

Mistrust by African Americans of white authority dates back many decades in American history. The life of Ida Wells-Barnett (1862–1931) illuminates some of the reasons for this mistrust, and it also illustrates how the majority has used stereotypes to justify mistreatment of the minority.

Lynching—mob violence that often involves mutilation, burning, and hanging—used to be commonplace in the South. Between 1882 and 1930, 2,041 lynchings occurred in the Deep South; 90 percent of the victims were black (Beck and Tolnay 1990). Although lynching was illegal, the police often colluded with the lynch mob, making it impossible for victims to receive protection.

In a society presumably based on laws and equal rights, how could lynching be justified? Although no single response may be sufficient to answer this question, an important consideration was the negative stereotype of African Americans. Black men were portrayed as driven by uncontrollable sexual lusts, hence posing a threat to white women. This stereotype was applied even to middle-class African American professionals like teachers, ministers, and legislators. In a bizarre twist of logic, middle-class African Americans were believed to be especially threatening because they aspired to social equality and were not awed by white superiority. The negative stereotype was so widespread that the entire nation seemed to take it for granted that lynching was necessary to control the African American population (Giddings 1996).

Ida Wells-Barnett, born a slave during the Civil War, was a driving force behind the campaign to end lynching. Her father was a skilled carpenter; after the war he became an independent craftsman. In 1878, Wells-Barnett's parents and baby brother died in a yellow fever epidemic. Neighbors wanted to parcel out the surviving family members to different homes, but she insisted that they remain together. Subsequently, she became a country schoolteacher and supported the family until her brothers were old enough to work, and the younger ones took up residence with an aunt.

Wells-Barnett enjoyed writing and often wrote columns for African American newspapers throughout the country. Her reputation as a columnist and as an advocate of civil rights grew steadily; soon she was able to support herself as part owner and editor of an African American newspaper in Memphis. As a result of an incident that occurred in a black grocery store in Memphis, she became passionately opposed to lynching.

The principal owner of the store, a postal worker, was a family man with a wife, a child, and an unborn baby. He managed the store at night while his partners took care of the business during the day. The trouble began with a quarrel among white and African American children over a game of marbles. What should have been a minor children's disagreement erupted into a black-white confrontation when the father of one white boy beat a victorious African American child. The conflict escalated and soon involved several white and African American adults (Duster 1970). Subsequently, three armed white men were wounded while attempting to break into the black-owned store. The local police then arrested more than 100 African Americans on charges of conspiracy.

Three days later a white mob entered the jail with help from the local authorities. The mob removed the postal worker and two other African American men and lynched them. On a note of complete finality, another white mob looted the black grocery store, and its creditors foreclosed on the property. No one was ever charged with any crime; the local newspapers claimed falsely that the acts were justified because the store was a place frequented by criminals.

This incident might have been remembered as just another lynching had it not been for Ida Wells-Barnett. Like many other people who knew of lynching only through newspapers and gossip, she accepted the idea that sometimes lynching was necessary to control unruly and violent elements of society. However, because she knew the reputations of the victims of this lynching, she suspected that the newspaper accounts were not accurate. Wanting more information, she began systematically to study the circumstances surrounding this incident. When she found that the newspaper accounts were indeed false, she broadened her study to include reports of lynching nationwide. She sifted through newspaper accounts, visited the scenes where lynchings had occurred, and interviewed eyewitnesses.

Wells-Barnett found that contrary to common belief, only a minority of African American victims had even been accused of rape, let alone been found guilty. Most had been lynched for being perceived as troublemakers—"quarreling with whites," "making threats," and "incendiarism" (Giddings 1984:28). Also contrary to common belief, women and children often were lynched. Wells-Barnett's report eventually was published and became the definitive document on lynching.

Wells-Barnett launched herself into an antilynching campaign. She lectured in the United States and in Great Britain, and she formed antilynching organizations to help fight for the rights of African Americans. Slowly she convinced people that lynching was a means used by whites to preserve their own status and socioeconomic position. Lynching worked by intimidating African Americans, thus preventing them from challenging white supremacy. On a broader scale, Wells-Barnett argued that lynching threatened both blacks and whites because it threatened law and order itself. Without a public trial and the safeguards of due process, anyone who was perceived as a threat to the establishment could be taken out and lynched by a mob. Although the great majority of victims were African Americans, whites occasionally were lynched as well. Thus, as long as lynching was an accepted part of the social order, no one was safe from mob rule.

Wells-Barnett's daughter summed up her mother's life as follows:

> The most remarkable thing about Ida B. Wells-Barnett is not that she fought lynching and other forms of barbarianism. It is rather that she fought a lonely and almost single-handed fight, with the single-mindedness of a crusader, long before men or women of any race entered the arena; and the measure of success she achieved goes far beyond the credit she has been given in the history of the country. (Duster, 1970:xxxii)

CQ Ida B. Wells-Barnett argued that lynching threatened law and order itself. Do you agree or disagree with her?

Rosa Parks was arrested in Montgomery in 1955 for refusing to give up her seat on a bus. Her arrest led to a boycott of city buses by African Americans.

CQ *Can you think of any current laws that you would be willing to break in order to change American society?*

As this portrait of an African American McDonald's owner wearing a suit and standing at the restaurant counter suggests, success in business is a matter of great personal pride. Society needs to ensure that members of all racial and ethic groups have equal opportunities for success through fair lending practices.

In view of the upheavals that occurred during the 1960s and 1970s, a reasonable question is whether the condition of African Americans has improved. Whereas some sociologists argue that race is no longer the major barrier to achievement that it once was, other sociologists claim that it remains a formidable barrier to equality (Blake and Darling 1994; Hacker 1995b; Wilson 1980, 1987). To illustrate this debate, consider that for the first time in American history, a sizable African American

Although almost everyone in American society recognizes that some racial discrimination takes place, African Americans and whites do not see eye-to-eye on the issue. African Americans see a considerable amount of racially based discrimination, whereas whites see very little, as this table suggests.

Answers to the question: "Are blacks treated less fairly than whites [in the following situations]?"

CQ African Americans perceive more anti-black discrimination than white Americans. Do you think this is

because African Americans perceive discrimination where none exists, or do you think that white Americans knowingly and unknowingly discriminate?

SOURCE: From "Are Blacks Treated Less Fairly than Whites [in the following situations]?" from *USA Today,* June 16, 1997:18a. Reprinted by permission.

	AFRICAN AMERICANS SAYING YES	WHITES SAYING YES
At work	45%	14%
In malls	46%	19%
In restaurants	42%	16%
By the police	60%	30%

middle class is emerging. In fact, one-third of all African American households earn a middle-class income, and one-fourth of all African American families live in the suburbs (Lacayo 1989). The same numbers, however, also suggest that a great deal of inequality remains. To say that one-third of African Americans are middle class is to say that two-thirds are not; in fact, most African Americans are working class. African Americans are 14 percent more likely to be working class than are whites (Horton et al. 2000). To say that one-fourth of African Americans live in the suburbs is to say that three-fourths live elsewhere, mainly in the urban core or in impoverished rural areas of the South (Pattillo 2003). There are other indicators of inequality. Babies of low birth weight (5.5 pounds or less) are born to African American mothers about twice as often as to white mothers; among African American youths, the leading cause of death is homicide; one African American male youth in four is in jail, on probation, or on parole, but only one in five is in college (see Collins and David 1990; Johnson 1990; Krivo and Peterson 2000). The overwhelming majority of African Americans still live in segregated neighborhoods, and most attend predominantly black schools (Charles 2003). Clearly, a great deal of inequality coexists with some equality, and the situation is far from perfect (see Chapter 6; Cottingham 1982; Jiobu 1990; Taylor, Casten, and Flickinger 1994; Wilson 1987; see the What Do You Think? box).

Hispanic Americans

The term *Hispanic Americans* refers to Mexicans, Puerto Ricans, Cubans, and other groups who have a Spanish heritage. There is considerable diversity within the Spanish category, but Mexicans are, by far, the largest Hispanic group (approximately 21 million), followed by Puerto Ricans (3 million), and Cubans (1 million). Another ten million are classified as other Hispanic.

Mexican Americans Currently, Mexican Americans are the second-largest racial or ethnic minority in the United States, but by early in this century, they will be the largest group. Their numbers will swell as a result of continual immigration from Mexico and the relatively high Mexican birthrate. Mexican Americans are one of the oldest racial-ethnic groups in the United States. Under the terms of the treaty ending the Mexican-American War in 1848, Mexicans living in territories acquired by the United States could remain there and were to be treated as American citizens. Those that did stay became known as "Californios," "Tejanos," or "Hispanos."

Mexican Americans are overwhelmingly Roman Catholic and have a strong family orientation. At one time they worked predominantly as manual laborers on railways and as farmhands, but today over 80 percent of them reside in urban areas, usually in ethnic neighborhoods known as **barrios**. This settlement pattern, coupled with the close proximity of Mexico to the Southwestern part of the United States, has encouraged Mexican Americans to retain much of their culture (Williams and Alverez 2002). In the Los Angeles barrio, for instance, signs, posters, newspapers, magazines, television programs, and movies are all in Spanish. Stores, shops, garages, service stations, restaurants, and other stores all feature Mexican goods and services oriented toward Mexican shoppers. Immigrant store-owners service immigrant shoppers and employ immigrant workers, thus playing a central role in the economic adaptation of Mexican immigrants (Hansen and Cardenas 1988).

Mexican Americans face considerable prejudice and discrimination. Films frequently stereotype Mexicans as being uneducated, stupid, cowardly, lazy, and cruel. Socioeconomically, Mexican Americans are near the bottom of the income scale. They earn about 70 percent of what whites earn, and almost one-third live in poverty. A high dropout rate from school combined with a high adult illiteracy rate in English compounds the difficulties encountered by many Mexican Americans (Jasinski 2000; Livingston and Kahn 2002).

Illegal immigrants from Mexico face an even more precarious existence. Frequently afraid to seek the protection of the law, they are at the mercy of employers who pay extremely low wages and impose substandard working conditions. In many cities of the Southwest and West, Mexican Americans have recently made political gains by electing Mexican Americans to local and state political office (Takaki 1993).

Puerto Rican Americans The island of Puerto Rico became a part of the United States as a result of the Spanish-American War of 1898 and has the status of a U.S. commonwealth. Puerto Ricans were granted citizenship in 1917. Puerto Rican Americans can therefore travel freely from the island to the mainland and anywhere in the 50 states, and they are eligible to serve in the U.S. military. They cannot, however, vote in federal elections, nor do they pay federal taxes.

Puerto Ricans have immigrated to the mainland in large numbers and have settled mostly in the Northeast. In particular, more than half of all Puerto Ricans on the mainland live in New York City. Small pockets of Puerto Ricans also live on the West Coast; a few were brought to Hawaii to work in the fields; and one significant pocket lives in Lorraine, Ohio (Fitzpatrick 1980). Puerto Rican immigration is a result of several factors, including rapid population growth in Puerto Rico, limited economic opportunities on the island as compared with those on the mainland, the lack of legal and political restrictions on migration because Puerto Ricans are United States citizens, and comparatively inexpensive air transportation between San Juan and the cities of the mainland's East Coast.

Even though Puerto Ricans come from an American commonwealth, they face the same obstacles that most highly urbanized immigrant groups face: lack of education, high rate of poverty, little job opportunity, poor housing, and discrimination (Moore and Pachon 1985). Many Puerto Ricans are dark-skinned, and when they immigrate to the mainland United States, they are treated as African Americans

Barrios ▲ Ethnic residential neighborhoods primarily made up of Mexican Americans.

The term Hispanic refers to a category of people that are quite diverse. This photograph shows four Hispanic teenage girls with Cuban ancestry at carnival in Florida. They would doubtlessly have different tastes in music and food from teenagers from Mexico, who would also be considered Hispanic.

(Landale and Oropesa 2002). Hence, they are discriminated against both because of their ethnicity and because of their skin color. As members of one of the poorest minorities in the United States, Puerto Ricans in New York City have a median family income 22 percent lower than that of African Americans and 42 percent lower than that of whites (Grosfoguel 1999).

The future of Puerto Rican migration to the mainland is unclear. Puerto Ricans have not assimilated to a significant degree. One reason is that their place of origin is near at hand; another is that high residential segregation has compacted them into homogeneous Puerto Rican neighborhoods and isolated them from many white contacts.

Puerto Rico is an advanced transitional society whose economic and political fate has been tied closely to that of the United States. However, at some point, Puerto Ricans will have to decide whether they want to maintain their current relationship with the United States, become the 51st state of the union, or become an independent nation. Opinion is divided on this for the present, and many Puerto Ricans prefer the status quo.

Cuban Americans Cubans have lived in the United States for generations, but large-scale emigration did not occur until the communist government of Fidel Castro assumed power in 1959 (Chapter 10). Since that time there have been periods when Cubans could leave Cuba and apply for political asylum in the United States.

Most Cuban American immigrants have settled in Miami. Some Cubans are black and, like dark-skinned Puerto Ricans, encounter the double discrimination of color and culture. It is interesting that about 2 percent of the immigrants from Cuba are Chinese. This tiny minority-within-a-minority has long played an important business role in the Cuban community.

A major surge of immigration occurred in 1990, when 125,000 Cubans were permitted to leave Cuba. These people are called "Mariel" immigrants (named after the Cuban port from which they departed). Although the media portrayed the Mariel immigrants as consisting mostly of criminals and mental patients, in fact some 95 percent of them were political refugees whose social backgrounds resembled those of earlier Cuban exiles (Portes, Clark, and Manning 1985).

On average, Cuban Americans have done well. They have the highest family income of any Hispanic group, almost equaling that of whites. Cuban Americans also are well educated: more than 50 percent have completed four years of high school, and 15 percent have college degrees. The Cubans' economic success is due largely to two factors. First, many early Cuban immigrants were middle class or well-to-do and had considerable experience in commerce and government. With remarkable quickness, they managed to establish a network of vibrant small businesses. Second, the Cuban community of Miami is culturally homogeneous, is fairly large, and is now active in politics (Portes and Bach 1985). Although Cuban Americans are undeniably successful as a group, analysts point out that the success of some Cubans has created an inaccurate picture of all Cuban Americans. For instance, statistics on average income mask the fact that most Cuban Americans hold clerical and semiskilled jobs, and many fall below the poverty line.

The visible success of the Cubans in Miami has created an uneasy relationship with Miami's African American community. Many African Americans regard Cuban Americans as foreign competitors for jobs; in 1988 rioting broke out, inspired in part by Cuban-black hostility. In addition to competing for jobs, Cuban Americans have exerted increasing political influence in local elections, which has led to the charge that Cuban politicians, public servants, and police officers discriminate against blacks. Although on logical grounds it would appear that Cuban Americans and African Americans would benefit by uniting to promote their common interests, that step seems unlikely to happen in the near future. The cultural, social, and structural gaps between the two groups are too wide to bridge at present.

Asian Americans

Asian Americans are one of the fastest-growing minorities in the United States, but numerically they still represent only about 4 percent of the population (see Figure 7.2). The influx of consumer products from Asia, the establishment of Asian manufacturing plants in the United States, the growing political influence of Asian countries, and—perhaps most important—three wars (World War II, Korean War,

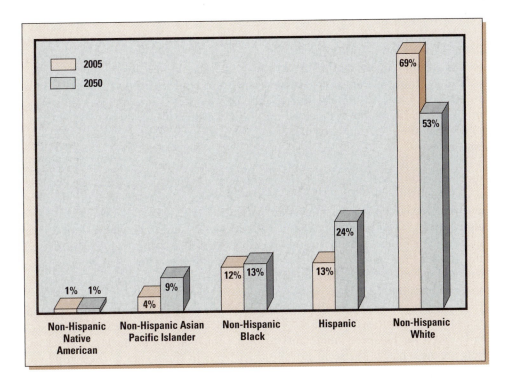

FIGURE 7.2 **U.S. Population by Race and Ethnicity, 2005–2050**

Immigration and relatively high fertility rates among most minority groups will result in a substantial increase in U.S. minority populations by the year 2050. Asians and Hispanics are the fastest-growing groups. By the year 2050, Hispanics are expected to become the largest minority group.

Note: Hispanics may be of any race.

SOURCE: U.S. Bureau of the Census 2002.

and Vietnam War) have focused public attention on Asian Americans and have molded their history (Lai and Arguelles 2003).

Chinese Americans   The earliest Asian arrivals to the United States were the Chinese, who began immigrating to California during the gold rush of 1849. At one time, almost half of all gold miners were Chinese, and like other prospectors, the Chinese dreamed of making a fortune and then returning home rich and respected (Jiobu 1988). This goal is reflected in the Chinese nickname for the United States: the "Mountain of Gold." In addition to mining, the Chinese were also employed on the railroad that was then being built across the United States. Although work on the railroad was strenuous and dangerous, it was very attractive to immigrants. A Chinese laborer who might earn three to five dollars a month in China could earn thirty dollars a month working for the railroads in California. Seeking the higher wages paid by the railroads, hundreds of thousands of Chinese men left their families and immigrated to the United States (Takaki 1993).

Once the gold mines were played out and the railroads had been completed, the demand for Chinese labor vanished. Now viewed as competitors for scarce jobs, the Chinese quickly became targets of discrimination, protest, and violence. Possibly the most virulent anti-Chinese riot occurred in Los Angeles, where mobs looted Chinese businesses and residences and lynched Chinese men, women, and children from street poles. As a result of this hostility, the Chinese American community turned inward and became a highly urbanized, segregated, isolated population. Wherever significant numbers of Chinese lived, they formed a neighborhood of their own. During the late nineteenth century, labor leaders and politicians began calling for an end to Chinese immigration, a call that resulted in the Chinese Exclusion Act of 1882. This was the first of a series of laws aimed at excluding immigrants on the basis of race alone.

Despite many obstacles, Chinese Americans have succeeded to a significant extent. Their success is partly due to the Chinese cultural emphasis on education and to a strong work ethic. In addition, Chinese Americans created many self-help organizations composed of immigrants from the same area of China. These organizations provided their members with social and welfare services, furnished economic resources, resolved disputes, and dispensed justice.

Currently, the Chinese American population is undergoing major changes. Whereas early Chinese immigrants came mainly from southern China, today many are coming from Taiwan and Hong Kong. In addition, criminal gangs, with the cooperation of corrupt Chinese government officials, have developed a flourishing trade of smuggling Chinese into the U.S. (Chin 2001). These more recent immigrants, both legal and illegal, have increased the cultural diversity within the Chinese community, but they have also contributed to outbreaks of violence among Chinese youth gangs.

Japanese Americans   Just as Chinese exclusion was going into effect, the demand for cheap labor on the West Coast began to increase. The newly arriving Japanese were welcomed to fill this brief demand, but when it was over, an anti-Japanese campaign erupted. The campaign was especially strong in California, where most of the Japanese immigrants to the mainland United States were settling. In 1908 the United States entered into a series of diplomatic accords with Japan known as the "Gentlemen's Agreement." Under these accords, Japan agreed to end further immigration to the United States.

The Japanese who were already in the United States moved into farming, and their success brought swift reactions. The state of California passed several laws making it illegal for Japanese immigrants to own farmland. To circumvent these laws, many Japanese placed the legal titles to their farms in the names of their children, who were citizens by birth, or formed corporations with whites.

The National Association for the Advancement of Colored People (NAACP) is the largest and strongest civil rights organization in the United States. The NAACP was founded in 1909 in New York City by a group of both black and white citizens committed to social justice. Locate the web site of the NAACP.

As you explore the NAACP's web site, answer the following questions:

What is the principal objective of the NAACP?

Who were the NAACP's founders?

What current programs does the NAACP support?

 CQ On the Web you will note that in addition to the sites for the national NAACP, there are sites for chapters in several cities. Check some out. What material do they contain that is not contained in the site for the national NAACP?

Despite these legal barriers, the California Japanese achieved considerable success in agriculture, for three reasons. First, Japanese American farmers were willing to toil for long, hard hours on marginal lands, raising labor-intensive crops such as strawberries. Second, they established wholesale and some retail outlets for these crops—outlets that afforded them protection from discrimination in the workplace. Finally, they were growing so much produce that white retailers had no choice but to deal with them (Jiobu 1988).

At the onset of World War II, two-thirds of Japanese Americans were American citizens by birth; most had never been to Japan; and most could hardly speak Japanese. Nevertheless, all Japanese Americans on the West Coast were rounded up and sent to incarceration centers throughout the West. A total of 120,000 men, women, and children were imprisoned, and in the process, they lost their homes, belongings, and businesses. In effect, an entire category of people identified solely by race was arrested and imprisoned without being charged with any crime and (as was revealed later) without any evidence (Takaki 1993; see the Sociology Online box).

In one of the most unusual stories to emerge from World War II, the United States government formed an army unit composed of Japanese American soldiers but led mostly by white officers. This unit, which fought in France and Italy, became the most highly decorated unit in the army. Japanese American interpreters also served in the Pacific theater, at great personal risk. As Japanese, they faced the possibility of being attacked by American troops. As Americans, they faced the possibility of being attacked by the enemy Japanese. Almost 50 years after the end of World War II, the United States government finally recognized the injustices of the incarceration and made amends. Each living survivor of the incarceration received $20,000 in compensation. Although this was a token amount in view of the losses incurred, it symbolically ended a bitter memory. Currently, Japanese Americans are doing well. Their income and educational levels exceed white levels, and they have dispersed throughout the economy (Jiobu 1988). Oddly enough, the best-known Japanese American is Judge Lance Ito, who presided over the murder trial of O. J. Simpson. Ito's fame, of course, came about because the trial was the focus of an extraordinary amount of television coverage.

New Asian Groups After the Vietnam War, many new Asian groups came to the United States as political and economic refugees. Coming in the aftermath of the war, these immigrants have had a much different experience than previous emigrants from Asia. The Vietnamese, for instance, were initially housed in refugee camps and supported by the U.S. government. Although the government dispersed the Vietnamese throughout the country, most of them eventually migrated to Southern California and formed an ethnic community of their own.

The immigration of another Asian group—Koreans—was not related to the Vietnam War. They came on their own to find a better life and have become well known for establishing small retail outlets. Filipinos have also immigrated to the

STUDY TIP

Develop a mnemonic device (an acronym, song, rhyme, etc.) to help you remember all of the major racial and ethnic groups in the United States, including subgroups.

Life Chances: 1900–2000					
	WHITE	**BLACK**	**HISPANIC**	**ASIAN**	**NATIVE AMERICAN**
Education: % with college degree	26	16	11	44	9
Poverty: % below poverty line	9	22	21	14	31
Birth: % low birth weight	6	13	6	7	7
Death: Rate per 1,000 (age adjusted)	853	1,225	NA	502	698

SOURCE: U.S. Bureau of the Census 1994, 2000, 2002.

TABLE 7.1 • *Your racial or ethnic group greatly affects your life chances, as this table shows. Perhaps the most important life chance is the opportunity to obtain a college degree. Low birth weight is important because it is associated with poor health later in life. The death rate is important for many reasons, but as a life chance, it indicates the overall well-being of a group.*

United States in fairly large numbers. Even though the Philippines were once an American possession, Filipinos were not permitted to immigrate freely to the United States. Currently, they seem to be doing moderately well and are one of the largest Asian groups in the United States (Espiritu 1996).

Another group that is doing well consists of people from India. They are called Asian Indians. In 1917 Congress barred further immigration from India, but under the 1965 immigration act, almost 1 million Asian Indians have settled in the United States. This group is remarkably well educated: more than 50 percent have a college degree, and approximately 14 percent have a professional degree or a doctorate. Interestingly, a large number of Asian Indians run motels, and in some parts of the United States, they dominate that business.

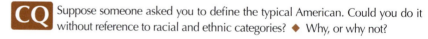 **Pausing to Think**   **About Racial and Ethnic Groups in the United States**

The United States is a pluralistic society with several large racial and ethnic groups, including WASPs, white ethnics, Native Americans, African Americans, Hispanic Americans (a group that includes Mexican Americans, Puerto Rican Americans, Cuban Americans, and others), Chinese Americans, Japanese Americans, and several new Asian groups. Most racial and ethnic minorities have experienced gradual gains in wealth, power, and social standing over the course of this century. This gain does not mean, of course, that they have achieved full equality (see Table 7.1). Differences in culture and physical features often are regarded as badges of inferiority, while social relationships frequently are shaped by the diversity among people rather than by their similarities.

CQ Suppose someone asked you to define the typical American. Could you do it without reference to racial and ethnic categories? ◆ Why, or why not?

Sociological Analysis of Racial and Ethnic Inequality

Despite the rhetoric of equality, American society remains stratified along racial and ethnic lines. To explain this inequality, sociologists draw upon three perspectives—functionalism, conflict theory, and symbolic interaction.

The Functionalist Perspective

Functionalist theorists assume that persistent societal characteristics have positive consequences (or functions) that help to sustain the society in its current form. In making this assumption, they do not argue that inequality is morally good; rather, they state that certain consequences follow from it. Thus, the main function of ethnic and racial inequality is to ensure that unpleasant but important work gets done.

Every society has undesirable jobs—those with low pay, poor working conditions, and little prestige. Yet these jobs must be performed by someone; the question is "by whom?" Functionalist theorists believe that these jobs are assigned to racial and ethnic minorities because these groups lack the power to compete for more desirable positions. Many historical examples are consistent with this belief. For example, Irish and Italian immigrants were originally shunted into menial jobs, and Jewish immigrants ended up working in sweatshops. Today, Mexican immigrants toil as field hands, maids, and gardeners, while recent Asian immigrants work in sweatshops just as Jewish immigrants did before them. Although this form of inequality does not enrich the minority group, it does benefit the broader society (see Merton 1968). Trash gets picked up, crops are harvested, and clothes are manufactured—all of these activities help create wealth and resources for society.

Functionalist theorists further argue that because racial and ethnic minorities typically possess few job skills, have little education, and are not sophisticated in the ways of American culture, low-skilled, low-paying, menial jobs are the best that they can realistically hope to find. As their skills improve, however, they (or their children) will secure better jobs and will rise in the social structure. Newer immigrants then will take their place at the bottom of the social structure, and the cycle will repeat itself. The rise of white ethnic groups seems to support this view, but the history of Native, African, and Hispanic Americans suggests that there is more at work than functionalist theorists imagine.

The Conflict Perspective

Conflict theorists believe that conflict is a basic societal process that underlies virtually all social interaction. According to their thinking, ethnic and racial inequality results from the endless competition among groups for power, wealth, status, and other valuable social resources. The group that wins this competition installs itself as the dominant group, whereas the losers become the subordinate groups (Banton 1983; Collins 1998). Victory, however, may be short lived. If subordinate groups somehow acquire more power, they will demand higher-paying jobs, better working conditions, and more prestige. In the long run, therefore, ethnic and racial inequality almost always results in conflict.

These conflicts are not always confined to clashes between the dominant and minority group. Very often, different racial or ethnic groups clash with one another. As an illustration, consider the case of Korean immigrants who have established grocery stores in the African American neighborhoods of New York, Chicago, Los Angeles, and other cities (Lee 2003). African Americans complain that Korean shopkeepers overcharge them, offer substandard service, and treat them with contempt. In their own defense, Korean grocers say that they are simply earning a living by following the American tradition of free enterprise and that without their stores, African Americans would not have convenient places to shop (Lee 1988; Purdum 1990). This hostility erupted into open violence when Korean stores were attacked by angry crowds during the so-called Rodney King riot mentioned at the beginning of this chapter.

In interpreting the hostility among racial and ethnic minorities, conflict theorists relate the outcomes of the hostility to the position of the dominant group. Conflict theorists therefore argue that hostility between African and Korean Americans actually benefits the dominant group at the expense of the minority groups. As long as

These migrant farmworkers are harvesting cauliflower in California. Functionalists argue that such labor creates wealth and resources for society and that the immigrant farmworkers shown here are doing jobs that many native-born citizens of the United States are unwilling to perform.

CQ What would conflict theorists say about such labor?

racial and ethnic minorities argue among themselves, they cannot focus their energy on combating the dominant group, nor can they look toward broad, societal solutions to the problems of inequity (Bonacich 1972; Reich 1977).

Supporters of the functionalist and the conflict perspectives agree that ethnic and racial groups are subordinate to the majority and occupy the less desirable positions in society. Their perspectives differ, however, in how they explain subordination. Functionalists suggest that even though some jobs are not very desirable, they are important, and that the entire society benefits from having them performed by racial and ethnic minorities. Functional theorists argue further that this situation is fair because racial and ethnic workers are being paid the going rate for their labor. In contrast, conflict theorists emphasize how the dominant group benefits from having racial and ethnic groups perform the "dirty work" of society and that the dominant group keeps the wage rate as low as possible.

The Symbolic Interactionist Perspective

Symbolic interactionists point out that in order for an ethnic or a racial group to exist, its members must develop a "consciousness of kind," or feelings of being like one another and different from outsiders (Hewitt and Hewitt 1986). This consciousness of kind results from the interaction between racial and ethnic groups and the rest of society. To illustrate, for most of American history, Native Americans were treated as a homogeneous group. The government and most people refused to recognize the vast differences between Shawnee and Iroquois, or Navaho and Cheyenne. Instead, all Native Americans were regarded as the same, or simply as "Indians." In effect, Native Americans were forced into a single group, and after three centuries of such treatment, they have adopted a consciousness of kind. Although they recognize and encourage tribal differences, they also regard themselves as Native Americans or American Indians.

A similar process took place among many racial and ethnic groups in the United States. Because of slavery, African Americans lost most of their native culture and consider themselves to be members of a single racial group. Although we commonly think of Italians as an ethnic group, the original immigrants regarded themselves

Comparison of Three Theoretical Perspectives on Race and Ethnicity

PERSPECTIVE[a]	VIEW OF RACIAL AND ETHNIC INEQUALITY	KEY CONCEPTS AND PROCESSES
Functionalism	Sees inequality as beneficial to society because it ensures that unpleasant work gets done	Functions (positive consequences) Job allocation a matter of matching skills to existing opportunities
Conflict Theory	Sees inequality as a process of exploitation and dominance	Competition Conflict for scarce resources
Symbolic Interaction	Sees race and ethnicity as created and sustained through social interaction and shared meanings	Consciousness of kind Identity

TABLE 7.2

[a]The functionalist and conflict perspectives were introduced in Chapters 1 and 2, and symbolic interaction was discussed in Chapter 3.

as Sicilians, Genoans, Venetians, and so on. However, after decades of being treated as a homogeneous group, the original attachments to specific places in Italy were supplanted by a consciousness of kind as Italians. Today, the category of Hispanic includes groups such as Mexicans, Cubans, Puerto Ricans, and Dominicans. If these groups are continually lumped together as one, they might conceivably lose their individual identities and develop a consciousness of kind as one group: Hispanic.

 **Pausing to Think**   **About Sociological Analysis of Racial and Ethnic Inequality**

Functionalists see ethnic stratification as providing some general benefits for society such as ensuring that the unpleasant but important jobs get filled. Conflict theorists focus on how powerful groups in society maintain their favorable position by exploiting minority groups. Symbolic interactionists point out that the interaction between a racial or an ethnic group and the rest of society actually creates the group through the development of a consciousness of kind among the members (see Table 7.2).

CQ What do you think? ◆ Is racial and ethnic diversity good for a society? ◆ What would a conflict theorist say? ◆ A functionalist? ◆ A symbolic interactionist?

Racial and Ethnic Relations in the Twenty-First Century

In a classic study of American race relations in the late 1930s and the 1940s, social scientist Gunnar Myrdal applied the **principle of cumulation** to ethnic relations (Clayton 1996; Myrdal 1944). This principle refers to a vicious circle in which (1) discrimination by the majority keeps the minority in an inferior status, and (2) the minority's inferior status then is cited as "proof" that the minority does not deserve

Principle of cumulation ▲ The process in which discrimination by the majority keeps the minority in an inferior status and that inferior status is then cited as "proof" that the minority does not deserve better treatment.

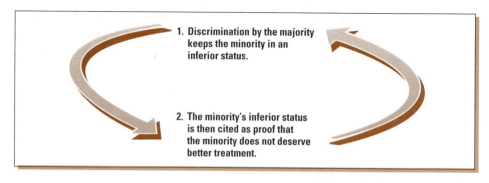

FIGURE 7.3 Principle of Cumulation

This figure shows the circle of prejudice and discrimination. Ethnocentrism among majority group members often gives rise to feelings of prejudice and acts of discrimination toward members of a minority group. Accumulated prejudice and discrimination puts the minority group in a disadvantaged position in society. The disadvantaged position of group members is taken as evidence of their inferiority, and this perception, in turn, produces another round of prejudice and discrimination toward the minority.

STUDY TIP

Meet in a group of three or four. Before you begin to talk, each person should write a downward spiral example of the principle of cumulation on a piece of paper. Then discuss the principle, with each person giving his or her example. Choose one example to work on and, as a group, brainstorm ways in which that downward spiral could become an upward spiral.

better treatment. Even though Myrdal was referring to African Americans, the logic of his argument applies to almost any racial or ethnic group (see Figure 7.3). For example, Mexican Americans suffer discrimination when they try to obtain suburban housing. As a result, they are funneled into the run-down, segregated neighborhoods of the barrio. The Anglo majority observes the depressed housing conditions of Mexican Americans and concludes that even if they had better housing, they would only let it deteriorate.

As Myrdal saw it, the principle of cumulation also could work in reverse. That is, a reduction in discrimination would enable a racial or an ethnic minority to gain better jobs, better housing, and better education, and thus would lead to a decrease in discrimination by the majority. Rather than a vicious circle spiraling downward, this upward spiral eventually would result in equality between the groups. In most societies, unfortunately, the upward spiral has been rare.

Myrdal's principle of cumulation is a powerful tool for analyzing race and ethnic relations, and we use it to acquire insights about the future. What will American racial and ethnic inequality be like in this century? The answer to the question will vary depending on which groups you are asking about. In some cases, an upward spiral may be underway. Japanese, Chinese, and Korean Americans have maintained strong family structures and have excelled at academics—factors that bode well for continued success. Cuban Americans have achieved considerable economic and political success in Florida, and Mexican Americans have shown remarkable family solidarity in the face of poverty. The situation is not as promising for Native Americans. Scattered in relatively small populations in several states, they do not share a common economic interest, nor can they muster sufficient political power to elect many representatives to Congress.

In the future, the African American population may face the most persistent problems. With a white electorate concerned mainly with its own problems, the situation of inner-city African Americans has faded into the background. Yet without structural changes aimed at ending poverty in the inner city, many African Americans will be locked into a cycle in which poverty generates more poverty, and so on without end. The result could be an African American population split into two groups: those who have steady incomes and a middle-class or higher lifestyle, and those who are chronically poor. These matters are complicated by the recent influx into U.S. cities of African refugees from such countries as Somalia who have fled repression at home and hope to build a life in the United States. We can only hope that a solution to this problem will be found soon and that social justice for African Americans once again becomes an important political issue (see Chapter 6; Bonilla-Silva 2000; Feagin 2000; Hacker 1995; Thernstrom and Thernstrom 1998; Wilson 1987).

CQ In reporting on the urban racial violence of the 1960s, former Illinois governor Otto Kerner, Jr., said, "Our nation is moving toward two societies, one black, one white—separate and unequal." Do you think that this prophecy has come true? ◆ Why, or why not?

CONCEPT WEB Race and Ethnic Inequality

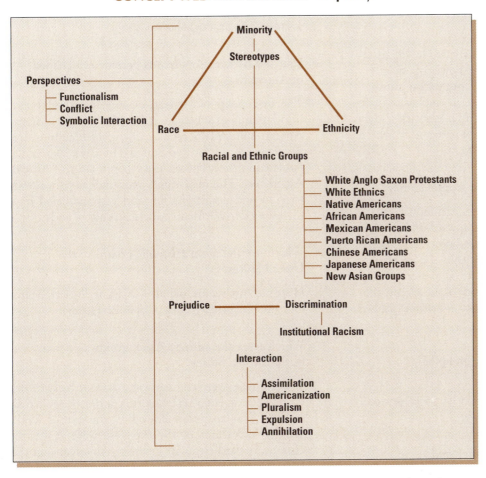

Add the following to this concept web: 1) Cuban Americans, 2) Melting Pot, 3) Korean Americans, 4) Somali refugees, and 5) Principle of Cumulation.

Looking Ahead

Race-ethnicity and social class are major forces dividing societies into groups of people with unequal amounts of wealth, power, and other resources. The third major force that produces vast inequity is gender, the subject of the next chapter.

WHAT YOU SHOULD KNOW ●■▲

1. **How has the Great Social Transformation affected racial and ethnic identity and inequality?**

   Ethnic and racial ties are among the most basic communal relationships that bind people together. Within individual societies, racial and ethnic groups are often unequal in social standing. In industrial, predominantly associational societies, the competition for wealth and political power results in the domination of some groups by other groups.

2. **How are racial and ethnic categories socially constructed?**

   Race and ethnicity are categories created by the interplay of social forces, including the power of one group to impose a racial or an ethnic category on another. Although individuals may choose to emphasize or to deemphasize their racial and ethnic identities, they seldom have any choice about the category to which they are assigned.

3. **What is the foundation of ethnic group identity?**

   By sharing a unique culture and a common identity, ethnic group members are drawn toward one another and feel a strong sense of "oneness," unity, and shared fate. The practice of marriage within the group is a major means by which ethnicity is preserved and passed on to subsequent generations. Race and ethnicity often overlap, and this overlap sometimes causes confusion.

4. **When may a racial or an ethnic group be considered as a minority group?**

   Minority status is based on the relative social power a group has and not simply on its size.

5. **What is the link between prejudice and discrimination?**

   Prejudice refers to the attitudes underlying racism, whereas discrimination refers to actual behavior. Prejudice is encouraged by distorted stereotypes; institutional racism is a form of discrimination that may persist even without prejudice.

6. **Does assimilation lead to a social "melting pot"?**

   A "melting pot" results when both the majority and the minority change and form a new, blended grouping that combines some features of both groups.

7. **Who were the earliest settlers in the United States, and what was their fate?**

   Before the Europeans arrived, the country was occupied by Native Americans divided into hundreds of distinct tribes. By the middle of the nineteenth century, diseases that had been brought to the continent by Europeans, along with dislocation, warfare, genocide, and impoverishment, had greatly reduced the Native American population. Government policy toward Native Americans went through a series of stages: separation, relocation-extermination, forced assimilation, and tribal restoration.

8. **How did African Americans become established in America?**

   The first group of African Americans was brought into Virginia as slaves in 1619. Much of the original African culture was replaced by a slave culture that developed in the United States. The Civil War ended American slavery but not the subordination of African Americans. The civil rights movement of the 1960s tried to end discrimination and was paralleled by a revitalization of African American culture and pride.

9. **Which are the main Hispanic groups in the United States?**

   Hispanic Americans include Mexicans, Puerto Ricans, Cubans, and other groups of Spanish heritage.

10. **Which were the earliest Asian groups to arrive in the United States?**

    The Chinese were the earliest Asian arrivals to the United States, entering California during the gold rush of 1849. The Japanese followed. By the start of World War II, two-thirds of the Japanese were American citizens; nevertheless, all Japanese Americans on the West Coast were rounded up and sent to incarceration centers throughout the West.

11. **How do the functionalist, conflict, and symbolic interaction perspectives explain ethnic inequality?**

    Functionalist theory argues that racial and ethnic inequality helps society adapt to its environment by ensuring that certain important but unpleasant jobs will be accomplished. These jobs are allocated by the majority population to the ethnic and racial minorities because those groups lack the qualifications for more desirable positions.

Conflict theory argues that ethnic and racial inequality results from the competition among groups for power, wealth, status, and other scarce desirables. The group that wins the competition installs itself as the dominant group, while the losers become the subordinate group.

Symbolic interactionists point out that ethnic and racial groups are creations of the dominant society. Groups develop a consciousness of kind, feeling that they are like one another and different from other groups.

12. What does the principle of cumulation contribute to our understanding of the future of racial and ethnic relations?

Over the long run, the majority keeps the minority in an inferior status and then uses that inferior status as "proof" that the minority does not deserve better treatment. The principle can work in reverse—a reduction of inequality enables a minority to gain higher status, which then serves to reduce the amount of inequality between the majority and the minority.

TEST YOUR KNOWLEDGE ●■▲

Key Terms Matching

Match each of these key terms with the best definition or example from the numbered items that follow. Write the letter preceding the key term in the blank before the definition that you choose.

a. Americanization

b. annihilation

c. assimilation

d. barrios

e. discrimination

f. ethnic group

g. ethnic identity

h. ethnic revival

i. ethnicity

j. expulsion

k. institutional racism

l. melting pot

m. minority

n. pluralism

o. prejudice

p. principle of cumulation

q. race

r. racism

s. stereotype

t. symbolic ethnicity

u. WASP

_____ 1. People who share basic cultural features such as language, place of origin, dress, food, and values.

_____ 2. The forceful exclusion of a racial or an ethnic group from a society.

_____ 3. A group that has less power than the dominant group.

_____ 4. The process in which discrimination by the majority keeps the minority in an inferior status, and that inferior status is then cited as "proof" that the minority does not deserve better treatment.

_____ 5. The process within American society in which minority group members change their behavior and in doing so, become more like the majority group.

_____ 6. A situation in which racial and ethnic groups clamor for political autonomy and sometimes demand independence.

_____ 7. An attitude that predisposes an individual to prejudge entire categories of people unfairly.

_____ 8. The unfair and harmful treatment of people based on their group membership.

_____ 9. A group of people who have been singled out on the basis of real or alleged physical characteristics.

_____ 10. The blending of the culture and structure of one racial or ethnic group with the culture and structure of another.

_____ 11. Rigid and inaccurate images that summarize a belief.

_____ 12. A situation in which racist practices become part of the social practices and institutions of a society.

_____ 13. An attempt to preserve and participate in disappearing ethnic roles and culture.

_____ 14. The internalization of ethnic roles as part of a person's self-concept.

_____ 15. White, Anglo-Saxon, Protestant members of American society.

_____ 16. The process by which one ethnic or racial group exterminates another group.

_____ 17. The belief that race determines human ability and that, as a result, certain races deserve to be treated as inferior, whereas other races deserve to be treated as superior.

_____ 18. A situation in which separate racial and ethnic groups maintain their distinctiveness even though they may have approximately equal social standing.

_____ 19. Common cultural characteristics that people share, such as the same language, place of origin, dress, food, and values.

_____ 20. A situation in which the culture and social structure of both the minority and the majority change in such a way that a new, blended grouping emerges that combines some features of both groups.

_____ 21. Ethnic residential neighborhoods primarily made up of Mexican Americans.

Multiple Choice

Circle the letter of your choice.

1. Which of the following contributes to the inability to define race in terms of biological characteristics?
   a. Humans vary along a biological continuum with different societies dividing the continuum differently.
   b. Most schemes of categorizing races are inaccurate.
   c. Humans have migrated for thousands of years, resulting in a mixing of races.
   d. All of the above make it impossible to define race in terms of biological characteristics.

2. With the Great Social Transformation,
   a. racial and ethnic group ties become more important as the building blocks of industrial society.
   b. race and ethnicity become badges that distinguish one group from another as people compete for wealth and political power.
   c. race and ethnicity, along with a strong central government, remain important in social ties.
   d. race is no longer socially important, but ethnicity is important.

3. Which of the following is true about race?
   a. It is a social construction in the sense that biological traits may be endowed with social meaning.
   b. It is a clearly distinguishable set of physical traits, so that all people may be classified as either Caucasoid, Negroid, or Mongoloid.
   c. It determines our mental and physical abilities.
   d. It is a social construction based on cultural characteristics.

4. Who led a campaign against the lynching of blacks in the United States?
   a. Rosa Parks
   b. Martin Luther King, Jr.
   c. Ida B. Wells-Barnett
   d. Harriet Beecher Stowe

5. Which statement is true of stereotypes?
   a. Most people do not have enough contact with members of minority groups to be able to see that the stereotype is inaccurate.
   b. Stereotypes reduce the guilt of those who use them.
   c. Stereotypes separate the group that uses them from the group to which they are being applied.
   d. All of the above are true of stereotypes.

6. Which is an example of institutional racism?
   a. housing segregation
   b. believing that affirmative action provides minorities with an unfair advantage
   c. not hiring someone because of his or her race
   d. stereotyping people on the basis of their ethnicity

7. Irish Americans celebrate St. Patrick's Day with parades, parties, and green beer. This practice is an example of
   a. pluralism.
   b. symbolic ethnicity.
   c. ethnic revival.
   d. Anglo conformity.

8. In the 1970s, the Khmer Rouge of Cambodia killed 2 million fellow Cambodians for supposedly representing capitalist culture. This action was an example of
   a. expulsion.
   b. political reprisal.
   c. annihilation.
   d. ethnic cleansing.

9. On the basis of self-identification, the largest ancestry group in the United States is
   a. Mexican.
   b. English.
   c. African.
   d. German.

10. Which did NOT contribute to the success of Chinese immigrants in the United States?
    a. They had a strong work ethic similar to that in the United States.
    b. They created many self-help organizations.
    c. They placed a high value on education.
    d. They quickly became Americanized.

Identifying Sociological Perspectives on Race and Ethnicity

For each of the following statements, identify the sociological perspective associated with the statement by writing F for functionalist, C for conflict, or SI for symbolic interactionist, in the appropriate blank.

_____ 1. In order for an ethnic or a racial group to exist, its members must develop a "consciousness of kind" that itself results from the interaction between the racial or ethnic group and the rest of society.

_____ 2. Fighting among different racial and ethnic groups benefits the dominant group by diverting the hostilities away from the dominant group.

_____ 3. Racial and ethnic minority groups obtain menial, low-paying jobs because they have few job skills and are not sophisticated in the ways of American culture. However, as their skills improve, they will secure better jobs.

_____ 4. Ethnic and racial inequality results from the endless competition among groups for power, status, and other valuable resources.

_____ 5. Jobs with low pay and poor working conditions are assigned to racial and ethnic minorities because they lack the resources and power to compete for more desirable positions.

_____ 6. The tendency for an ethnic or a racial group to develop a consciousness of kind contributes to the formation of a single homogeneous group replacing the original more diverse identities.

True-False

Indicate your response to each of the following statements by circling T for true or F for false.

T F 1. An ethnic group is one that has been singled out on the basis of physical characteristics.

T F 2. A group can be considered both a race and an ethnic group.

T F 3. A minority group is always smaller in number than the majority group.

T F 4. With more than 1 million students taking the SAT each year, even a small bias will translate into a substantial amount of institutional racism.

T F 5. Native Americans suffered separation, expulsion, and extermination.

T F 6. During World War II, 120,000 Japanese Americans (most of whom were American citizens) were imprisoned, and in the process, they lost their homes, belongings, and businesses.

T F 7. Mexicans are the largest group of Hispanics in the United States.

T F 8. Cuban Americans have the highest average income of all Hispanic ethnic groups in the United States.

T F 9. On average, Japanese Americans have higher education and income levels than white Americans.

T F 10. Poverty and employment differ little by race and ethnicity in American society.

T F 11. Conflict theory argues that ethnic and racial inequality results from the competition among groups for power, wealth, status, and scarce desirables.

T F 12. Symbolic interaction theory argues that racial and ethnic inequality helps society adapt to its environment.

T F 13. Puerto Ricans are a minority group and Mexican Americans are not a minority group.

T F 14. Because of slavery, African Americans have come to consider themselves as members of a single racial group.

T F 15. The diplomatic accord of 1908 known as the "Gentlemen's Agreement" ended Japanese immigration to the United States.

NOTE: The answers to these exercises are at the end of the book.

For additional practice tests and other resources please visit the companion web site at http://www.prenhall.com/curry.

Essay

1. What two civil rights events occurred during the 1950s and what were their effects?

2. Identify and discuss the groups of Asian ancestry. What mechanisms have they used to be successful?

3. Describe the contributions of Ida B. Wells-Barnett.

4. Compare and contrast how functional theory, conflict theory, and symbolic interaction theory explain racial and ethnic inequality.

5. Describe Myrdal's principle of cumulation as it applies to race and ethnic relations.

8

Inequalities of Gender

In September 1991, two thousand naval aviators gathered at the Hilton Hotel in Las Vegas to attend the annual convention of the Tailhook Association—an organization dedicated to promoting naval aviation. The convention featured symposiums, panel discussions, and displays, but as with many other conventions, the Tailhook also served as a social function. It provided an opportunity for naval aviators to gather informally and attend parties ("hospitality suites") sponsored by aviation squadrons. Over the years, the convention gained a reputation as a giant party at which navy fliers drank and caroused freely.

The convention of 1991 was destined to become notorious for an episode of sexual harassment, but a foretaste of that event took place at a morning symposium. The symposium featured a panel of high-ranking admirals, and at one point, a female lieutenant asked the panel when women would be allowed to fly in combat. Her question brought a chorus of boos and jeers from the audience of mostly male fliers. Although one admiral said that someday women would fly combat, no high-ranking officer stepped in to defend the lieutenant or to admonish the audience for its behavior.

That evening a series of hospitality suites were opened, and male aviators lined the hallway, drinking, joking, and shouting. They were also pawing, fondling, and groping any woman who ran their gantlet. In all, 26 women were assaulted that night, and about half of them were naval officers. The incident became public knowledge, and in response to public pressure, the Navy later convened an investigation that ended in mildly rebuking the admiral in charge for his lack of judgment. Another Navy investigation was then undertaken, but it too failed to do anything other than to bemoan the fact that many of the participants at the Tailhook convention did not behave as officers and gentlemen. In the end, no male officer at the convention was ever found guilty of sexual assault or misconduct (Ebbert and Hall 1993).

Tailhook was not an isolated incident of sexual harassment in the military. For example, ever since the Air Force Academy began admitting women in 1976, the campus has been plagued by incidents of sexual harassment, sexual assault, and rape. In a federal court affidavit, a woman cadet testified, "Sexual harassment and improprieties were common and retaliation for reporting them was severe and persistent" (Aguilera and Migoya 2003). In the first six months of 2003 more than 60 current and former women cadets presented allegations of rape, abuse, and mishandling of their cases. Despite efforts by the Academy's administration to solve the problem over the years, little has been accomplished. Some argue that the sexual assault problem is rooted in the Academy's core culture that highly prizes excessive machismo, degradation of women, and loyalty to fellow male cadets over loyalty to the Academy as a whole.

Sexual misconduct is common throughout U.S. society. The federal government recently discovered that 42 percent of female federal employees have personally experienced some form of harassment such as being touched, pinched, subjected to unwanted or lewd comments, and assaulted. The same pattern is found in private industry too. For example, women at the Mitsubishi plant in Tennessee have been pressured to exchange sex for job security and have had their work sabotaged by disgruntled male employees (*New York Times,* September 10, 2000). Recent sociological research offers a hopeful note, however, suggesting that the establishment of open hiring practices decreases gender-based discrimination, especially among managers—people who have the authority to end gender discrimination (Reskin and McBrier 2000).

Although **sexual harassment** is a major social issue, it is also a reflection of a deeper, broader issue: gender inequality (Welsh 1999, 2000). Throughout the world, women are treated as second-class citizens. They have less political influence than men, have lower social status, earn less money, and are not fully protected by the law. In short, almost every society in the world may be described as a **patriarchy**: a social arrangement in which men dominate women. This arrangement, moreover, is supported by **sexism**: an ideology that maintains that women are inherently inferior to men and therefore do not deserve as much power, prestige, and wealth as men.

Chapter Preview

In this chapter we focus on several important topics fundamental to gender inequality. We begin with a discussion of gender inequality and the Great Social Transformation. Next, we discuss gender-role socialization, followed by a discussion of patriarchy and everyday life. After that, we consider gender inequality at work. We then examine feminism. Finally, we look at the sociological analysis of gender inequality, and we conclude with a discussion of gender inequality in the future.

The Great Social Transformation and Gender Inequality

Because we have been socialized into a male-dominated society, some people assume that men are naturally superior to women. This assumption is false, of course, and it did not always exist in its present form. Although patriarchy has been common, in traditional societies there is much greater equality between men and women than in industrial societies. In many small-scale hunting and gathering societies, for instance, men and women play complementary roles, and their lives revolve around many shared activities. No one has a great deal of wealth or power, and men and women often view their relationships in terms of integration and balance (Maybury-Lewis 1992). In horticultural and agricultural societies, however, the balance of power shifts to men, and men begin to dominate women in the economy and other institutions of society. The transition to industrialism changes the relationship between the genders even more. As we noted in Chapter 6, in industrial societies that developed in northern Europe and in England, a stratification system quickly developed that placed the proletariat at the bottom and the bourgeoisie at the top. The proletariat, including women, did the labor, whereas the bourgeoisie became the owners, managers, intellectuals, and professionals. Even among the upper classes, women lost status, and husbands legally controlled the wealth of their wives and dominated the family (cf. Blau 1984). Different traits came to be prized for men and for women. Working outside the home, men were encouraged to be independent and to value objectivity; working inside the home, women were encouraged to be dependent and to value subjectivity (Toffler 1980). Early industrialization thus created sharp differences in the social worlds inhabited by men and women (Friedan 1993).

Gender-Role Socialization

Men and women clearly vary in many biological characteristics: average height, weight, amount of body fat, amount of body hair, and genitals. Starting at an early age, moreover, men and women behave differently. Female infants respond more strongly

Sexual harassment ▲ Unwanted attention or pressure of a sexual nature from another person of greater social or physical power.

Patriarchy ▲ A social arrangement in which men dominate women.

Sexism ▲ An ideology that maintains that women are inherently inferior to men and therefore do not deserve as much power, prestige, and wealth as men.

to faces than to moving objects, whereas male infants respond more strongly to objects. As children mature, a few other differences also emerge. Compared with boys, girls are more sensitive to sound, odor, and touch; they have greater finger dexterity and are more likely to sing in tune. Men are more sensitive to light than women, more adept at manipulating objects in space, and better at visualizing spatial relations in their minds. However, as measured by standardized tests, the genders do not differ in overall intelligence (Peterson 1995; Richardson 1981).

It must be emphasized that these differences are statistical averages and do not characterize every individual in the population. Many women have greater spatial ability than some men, and many men can carry a tune better than some women. Many women are stronger and faster than the average man, and many men have more body fat than the average woman. Thus, you might vary considerably from the averages that describe your gender.

Sociologists agree that men and women differ in some biological characteristics, but they do not conclude that the differences are always socially important. If genetics totally determined social characteristics, then any man would be like all other men, and any woman would be like all other women. Obviously, this is not the case. Every society, therefore, goes beyond biology to establish the more complex social concept of **gender**: the cultural and attitudinal qualities that are associated with being male or female. Those qualities that characterize females are called feminine, and those that characterize males are called masculine. Thus, acting through our society, we actively construct gender roles. A **gender role** is the behavior that society expects for males or for females.

It is not surprising that gender roles differ from one society to the next and change over time. Consider attitudes toward gender among many Native American peoples before the European conquest of North America. Many Native American cultures contained a role, unlike any other male and female roles that we know, called the *berdache*: an individual who took the part of the opposite gender or had that role allocated to them in childhood (Trexler 2002). Among the Mohave, for instance, a male berdache might simulate menstruation by cutting his upper thighs and might mimic the delivery of a stillborn baby by taking drugs that caused the pains of childbirth. A female berdache would take on the masculine role by undergoing a ceremony after which she was permitted to engage in hunting, farming, making magic, and being responsible, as a man, for child rearing. Although berdaches could participate in most of the group's activities, they were not permitted to become formal leaders or warriors. These restrictions suggest that the Mohave imposed some limits on interchanging gender roles (W. L. Williams 1986).

Another example that shows the flexibility of gender involves three tribes living in New Guinea before World War II (Mead 1935). Although the tribes lived fairly close together, they were isolated from one another by mountains and heavy jungle. Thus isolated, each tribe evolved different gender roles. The members of one tribe, the Arapesh, were gentle, passive, and emotionally warm. Among them, both men and women were nurturant and deeply involved in child rearing. In contrast, the Mundugumor were headhunters, and both the men and the women were aggressive and violent. Because neither gender was strongly involved in child rearing, Mundugumor children were often ignored. The third tribe, the Tchambuli, maintained gender roles and identities that were roughly the opposite of traditional American stereotypes. The women were aggressive, domineering, and largely uninvolved in child rearing, whereas, in contrast, the men wore jewelry, were chatty and artistic, and were involved with children. Mead apparently studied the Tchambuli at an unusual period in their history, and the gender roles she described might have been atypical (Gewertz 1981). Nonetheless, those roles existed for a time, and they remind us not to assume that our way of constructing gender is the only way.

Broadly speaking, examples of the three New Guinea tribes and the berdache role among the Mohave Indians show that although the biological endowments of sex are universal, the social meaning attached to those endowments varies from society to

In many hunting and gathering societies, men and women play complementary roles, and no one is particularly powerful. This photograph shows !Kung San women looking for edible roots as they tend their children.

Gender ▲ The cultural and attitudinal qualities associated with being male or female.

Gender role ▲ The behavior society expects for a male or a female.

society. For that reason, gender is a social role, and like other social roles, it is learned through the processes of socialization.

Socialization and Gender

Gender socialization begins virtually at the moment of birth when the physician announces to the parents, "It's a girl (or boy)!" From that moment on, the course of the infant's socialization is set, and girls will follow one path, whereas boys will follow another. Even in newborn infants, gender makes a difference. For instance, newborn boys are handled more than girls, but girls are cuddled much more than boys. On seeing an infant girl smile, people often remark on how cute and pretty the baby is; but on seeing an infant boy smile, the same people will say that the infant is strong and handsome. This distinction is made because infants are often described in terms that anticipate the gender role they will play as adults. Boys, it is traditionally assumed, need to be tough, strong, and assertive to succeed in life, whereas girls need to be family-centered, caring, and physically attractive. These assumptions are changing, to be sure, but they still persist in American culture and may still be seen in the way people interact with infants and children (Young-Eisendrath 1995).

As a consequence of early experiences, by the tenth month of life, children are already identifying themselves as boys or girls, and not too long after that, their gender identity will be firmly fixed (Kohlberg 1966; Richardson 1981). Two-year-old children, for example, will say that boys like to fight and should do chores such as mowing the lawn, whereas girls should do housework. After a few more years, the basic behaviors, attitudes, and social identity associated with each sex are incorporated into the self, and the child is performing a gender role fully (Bleier 1984; Fausto-Sterling 1985; Rossi 1984). By adolescence, gender identity is a basic element in the strategies that people use to cope with life's issues (Renk and Creasey 2003).

Because people treat boys in one way and girls in another, the ability to identify gender is important. To aid in this task, American culture is replete with **gender markers**: symbols and signs that identify a person's gender. For example, in the hospital nursery where newborns are on display, their gender might be indicated by the color of the ribbon attached to the crib or by the color of the dressing gown. Naming infants is another way parents gender-mark their child. Most parents use gender-distinct names for their infants (Lieberson, Dumais, and Bauman 2000). As we mature, gender markers become more prominent, and much of our gender socialization involves learning which markers are appropriate for men and which are appropriate for women. Thus, girls are taught to wear dresses and to behave "properly." When girls grow older, they learn to put on makeup and wear high-heeled shoes. Boys are taught to wear pants and to behave "roughly." When boys grow older, they learn how to shave and how to knot a tie. Although these behaviors are part of everyday life in American society, they also act as gender markers that help us easily to distinguish men from women.

Agents of Gender Socialization

Agents of gender socialization are those who teach gender roles and identities. Parents are the first to serve this function. Virtually from the moment of birth, the parents of newborn infants begin socializing their offspring to become men or women. Following the traditional norms of gender socialization, girls receive toys that encourage them to be passive, sedentary, and receptive, whereas boys receive toys that encourage them to manipulate their environments. For example, parents might give their daughter a coloring book and their son a set of building blocks. The boy's gift encourages him to build things, and the girl's gift encourages her to sit quietly with a book and crayons.

Living Space The living space provided for children has implications for gender socialization. A girl's room will be decorated with floral designs and ruffled bedspreads,

Gender markers ▲ Symbols and signs that identify a person's gender.

Agents of gender socialization ▲ Those who teach gender roles and identities.

Play is an important aspect of socialization.

CQ *What gender roles are these children learning through their play?*

and may be filled with dolls and homemaking toys such as a tea set and a dollhouse. A boy's room will contain sports posters, toy guns, and toy soldiers or action figures such as GI Joe figures (not "dolls"). The only items normally found in the rooms of both boys and girls are musical instruments and books (Reingold and Cook 1975).

Play   This is an important aspect of socialization, and certain toys encourage children to play different roles (Thorne 1993). Through playing cops and robbers with toy guns, boys learn the rudiments of shooting, fighting, and aggressive behavior. Through playing house with dolls, girls learn to work out family relationships, shop and put away groceries, wash dishes, change diapers, and perform other domestic tasks. Many parents will not give their sons dolls because that would imply permission to take on feminine roles. Instead, they give their boys GI Joe action figures (a soldier doll, but no one calls it that). Nor will these parents give their girls boxing gloves, because doing so would encourage them to participate in traditional male pursuits.

Dress   Clothes illustrate another aspect of gender socialization. A quick trip through the children's clothing section of a local department store clearly indicates gender expectations. Boys' clothes are often blue or dark-colored so as not to show dirt. Girls' clothes are in pastel shades that are difficult to clean if soiled. Dresses make it difficult for a girl infant to crawl because the skirt catches under her knees—thus discouraging physical activity.

School   School also reinforces gender roles and gender identity (Evans and Davies 2000). Traditional children's literature depicts boys as active and girls as passive. In stories, girls are usually supporting or minor figures, whereas boys are the central characters. Boys are usually shown in a wide range of occupations, whereas girls are shown in traditional feminine occupations and in domestic roles. Even computer software intended for educational purposes (most of which is fairly new) contains traditional gender images drawn from previous eras (Semrau and Boyer 1990).

Advertising has a strong impact on gender socialization.

What messages do billboard ads like this one for Ralph Lauren send to both men and women?

STUDY TIP

On a sheet of paper, make three columns: "Male," "Female," "Either." In a group of 4–5 students, brainstorm personal qualities (i.e., "gentle," "commanding," "supportive"). As each is called out, decide as a group whether to write it in the "Male" or "Female" column; if you cannot agree, write it under "Either." When you have created substantial lists, discuss how agents of gender socialization have contributed to these particular assignments.

Interaction in the classroom further reinforces gender roles. Teachers call on boys more often than on girls, devote more of their time to boys, and force boys to work through problems while telling girls the answer. When speaking in class, girls are interrupted more often than boys, and boys dominate classroom discussions (Sadker and Sadker 1985). Devoting more teaching attention to boys robs girls of the opportunity to work out solutions for themselves and reinforces the gender stereotype of the "helpless" girl. Conversely, girls are rewarded more highly than boys for nonacademic achievements such as good handwriting, neatness, and getting along with other students. For girls, grades become a reward for being "nice and neat," a result that helps to explain the paradoxical fact that girls typically receive higher classroom grades than boys but make lower scores on standardized tests (Frazier and Sadker 1973; Sadker 1995; Davies 2003).

Recently, educators have become more sensitive to gender issues and are trying to remove gender biases from teaching materials and other school activities. These efforts are especially important in science, mathematics, and other fields that have not encouraged women and that contain few role models for aspiring girls. For instance, popular culture still presents female scientists and mathematicians either as unusually self-sacrificing and dedicated or as daringly adventurous and eccentric—images that are hardly encouraging to young women (LaFollette 1990).

Advertising   Advertising has a particularly strong impact on gender socialization. Men are usually portrayed as powerful, with many interests and diverse occupations. In contrast, women are portrayed as dates, as mothers, or occasionally as businesspeople—but in all cases as being very concerned about their appearance. In most of the pictures that accompany an advertisement, the woman's eyes focus on a man, and the man's eyes focus on important people or gaze directly at the camera. A woman's hands are often used to communicate femininity by touching objects lightly or to express sexuality by caressing a man's face or chest (Goffman 1979; Winship 1983).

A recent trend in advertising depicts men and women in cross-stereotyped roles—for instance, men are shown with children, and women are shown with briefcases. These advertisements draw their power from the surprise of portraying men and women in nontraditional ways. However, women are still more likely than men to be seen in domestic settings, and men's voices are used to narrate over 90 percent of all commercials (Bretl and Cantor 1988). Moreover, advertisements directed at gender-specific audiences are likely to contain powerful gender stereotyping. Men are often the majority audience for televised sporting events, and the advertising on these shows is frequently very stereotypic. For instance, the Super Bowl game that marks the end of the professional football season usually contains commercials that present men in tough, "macho" situations, with attractive women in supportive roles (Craig 1992; Dynes and Humez 1995). Television programming in general is gender oriented. Daytime soap operas have strong romantic interests and are designed with women in mind, whereas evening police dramas are more strongly geared toward men.

Age and Gender-Role Socialization

The United States is one of the most youth-oriented, youth-dominated societies in the world, and many of our ideas about gender roles are heavily laden with assumptions about age. For instance, in all the many debates and discussions of gender-role socialization, it is seldom pointed out that the definitions of masculinity and femininity are based on the characteristics of young men and women (Friedan 1993).

According to American cultural values, young people embody the ideals of beauty, handsomeness, and physical robustness. The aged, in contrast, are stereotyped as being incompetent, frail, and helpless. Although both genders are subjected to the "tyranny of youth," this pattern affects women more than men. In large part, the tyranny strikes women harder because they must, in a patriarchal society, depend heavily on their appearance to achieve success.

The one-sided impact of age on gender may be seen in many areas of everyday life. One area is the media and the visual presentation of women. Chic clothing is designed with the young woman in mind, and print advertisements feature youthful models, many of whom are not old enough to drink, vote, or in some cases, even drive. Films and television also emphasize youthful women, and relatively few roles are written with the middle-aged actress in mind. And those dramas that do feature a middle-aged woman often cast a younger actress in the role.

As people age, their bodies inevitably change, but those changes do not strike men and women equally. Men who put on weight as they grow older are described as mature and stout, whereas women are described as old and overweight. An older man with gray hair is said to be distinguished, whereas an older woman with gray hair is simply said to be old—and therefore less worthy. For this reason, many older women dye their hair, a practice that is less common among men.

Although the youth of society are glamorized, they also face the most pressure to conform to the dominant gender roles. For older people, the pressures are diminished—for instance, men who retire early may also give up the "macho" competitive orientation toward achievement they had in their youth, and they may seek to become more involved in community affairs and the lives of their children and grandchildren. Women in midlife may choose to become more assertive, taking on powerful roles that they avoided during their childbearing years. No longer having to prove that they are "real women" or "real men," the elderly may discover that age has given them freedom from the rigid gender roles that society insisted they play in their youth.

●■▲ Pausing to Think   About Gender Socialization

Although men and women differ in many important biological characteristics, every society goes beyond biology to establish fundamental gender roles associated with being male or female. Because gender roles are socially constructed, they differ from one society to another, and they differ within a given society at different points in time. People are socialized to gender roles by many influences, including the actions of parents, peers, teachers, and the mass media. When combined with age roles, gender roles establish major behavioral expectations for people that shape their lives in important ways.

CQ Have you ever felt constrained by your gender role? ◆ Do you feel that society puts too much pressure on young people to be "real men" or "real women"? ◆ Why can't we just be ourselves?

Patriarchy and Everyday Life

Because gender socialization is so pervasive, we hardly think about it. Nevertheless, gender is expressed in all realms of life, ranging from how likely you are to be elected president to your routine thoughts and activities. In this section, we will discuss how gender affects everyday life and how patriarchy, or male dominance, is ingrained in the way society is organized.

Language and Patriarchy

Language is a subtle yet powerful mechanism that assaults women's self-esteem and helps to perpetuate male dominance (Richardson 1988). Many of the slang words that denote women, such as "bimbo," "chick," or "skirt," are extremely pejorative. The implication of these terms is that women are merely sex objects and that they lack the skills or intelligence needed for success in business or other spheres. Forms of address also subtly imply an unequal gender relationship. Whereas Mrs. or Miss indicates whether a woman is married or single, Mr. gives no indication of a man's marital status. For this reason, many people now prefer the neutral term Ms.

In many situations, a man is addressed by his last name preceded by Mr., Dr., or another title, whereas a woman is addressed by her first name only. Although seemingly harmless, this practice infantilizes women: it implies that they should not be taken as seriously as are men (Jetter, Orieck, and Taylor 1995).

To illustrate, a survey of television sports coverage in Los Angeles found that tennis announcers and commentators called women players by their first name 53 percent of the time as opposed to only 8 percent of the time for men. In addition, when a male tennis player lost a point, the commentators usually said that the loss was due to the opponent's strength; but when a female player lost, the commentators said that the loss was due to nervousness, lack of aggressiveness, failure of confidence, or lack of stamina. In other words, men lost because they were overpowered by a superior opponent, whereas women lost because they lacked the character necessary to achieve victory (reported in *Sports Illustrated*, December 3, 1990:35).

Gender also affects the words we use. A woman who swears is perceived as vulgar, but a man using the same words is perceived as rugged and earthy. If a man says no, people assume he means it. But when a woman says no, people assume that she really means maybe or yes. This phenomenon often lies behind so-called date rapes: the woman rejects the man's sexual advances, but he perceives her rejection as really an acceptance or a "come-on" (Sanday 1992).

The traditional way in which names change when people marry further reflects patriarchy. When a woman marries, she traditionally replaces her last name with that of her husband and becomes Mrs. ———. Although her husband could just as well assume her name, that practice is rare in the United States. Aware that the custom of taking the husband's name reflects patriarchy, many women now are adopting a hyphenated last name that combines the woman's surname with that of the husband. However, even this practice does not entirely end patriarchy in names, because most men continue to use their surname alone. Moreover, most often the woman will place her surname before the hyphen and the man's name after it. Not until this ordering is somehow changed so that it does not indicate which name belongs to the woman and which to the man, and not until men adopt the hyphenated name themselves, will this form of patriarchy end.

Social Interaction and Patriarchy

Gender dominance is also expressed in how men and women interact with one another (Ridgeway and Smith-Lovin 1999). Much of the expression is physical. For example, when a couple are walking side by side, the man often dominates the woman by placing his arm on her shoulder and pushing or pulling her in one direction or another. Although this type of physical dominance is very obvious, other types are more subtle. When a man and a woman are seated next to each other on an airplane, the man usually takes over the armrest and puts his elbow on it, leaving the woman with no place for her arm. Rather than sitting upright, the man may slouch down and spread out in his chair, crowding the woman into a smaller space.

We can also see male dominance in the interactions that take place while men and women are talking. We normally assume that only one person should talk at a time and that each person should contribute about equally to the discussion. Most conversations, however, do not fit this ideal. In conversations that include both genders, men make nearly all of the interruptions. They also set the topic of discussion and ignore the attempts of women to change it. Women ask two to three times as many questions as men, but when women are talking, men seldom ask any questions at all. In sum, men do not take the input of women very seriously (Richardson 1988).

Another example of how men trivialize the role of women comes from a clever study of shopping behavior. When selling new cars, the study found, dealers usually make final offers to women that are about 12 percent higher than the offers they make to men who have shopped for the identical car (American Bar Association 1990).

Evidently, car dealers believe that women are more gullible than men, probably because automobiles are regarded as a male area of interest.

Male dominance also is built into our norms of politeness. Consider: when a couple are planning to dine out and drive to a restaurant, the man drives and takes care of the car, perhaps giving it to the valet at the restaurant door. As the man and the woman walk up to the door, the man opens it for the woman; they enter, and he addresses the maître d'. The man seats the woman at the table, and if they want a bottle of wine, the man orders it. When the bottle arrives, he tastes it and pronounces it satisfactory. The man places the dinner order for the woman. When the meal is finished, the waiter usually offers the check to the man, or perhaps, playing it safe, places the check in the middle of the table and allows the couple to decide who will pick it up. But almost always, and regardless of who actually pays, the man takes care of the check. Upon leaving, the man retrieves their coats and holds hers while she puts it on. Finally, outside the restaurant, the man gives the valet the stub for the car, and when it arrives, the man opens and closes the door for the woman, walks around to the driver's side of the car, tips the valet, and drives off. Although all these behaviors seem very natural and hardly worth comment, they nevertheless assume that men are responsible for women, or conversely, that women cannot cope with even simple tasks (see Table 8.1).

● ■ ▲ **Pausing to Think**   About Patriarchy and Everyday Life

Male dominance remains a predominant feature of many societies (see the Diversity box). Patriarchy is evident in language, in how people refer to or address one another, and in norms of politeness. Patriarchy is so ingrained in our society that most people do not think about it until it has a serious impact on their lives.

CQ In addition to the examples presented in this section, what other examples of patriarchy in everyday life come to mind? ◆ Is patriarchy evident in your neighborhood, your work, your social life?

Gender Inequality and Work

In American society today, work is one of the most important activities we undertake. Our jobs and careers provide us with self-esteem, satisfaction, and, of course, with income (Chapter 9 examines other aspects of work). For these reasons, many sociologists believe that the fundamental source of gender inequality is found in the workplace. Because work is such an important aspect of our lives, we will spend some time discussing it with regard to women.

Working Women

Contrary to the traditional image we have of women as homemakers, women have always worked outside the family. Which women work, however, changed dramatically in the twentieth century. It used to be that women with lower social standing worked, whereas middle- and upper-class women remained in the home. Today, however, women of all social classes participate in the labor force. Thus, an upper-class woman such as the late Jacqueline Kennedy Onassis worked as a book editor even though she was independently wealthy; and Hillary Rodham Clinton worked as an attorney while her husband was governor of Arkansas. Because it is now customary and often necessary for women of all backgrounds to work, the number of working women has increased significantly. In 1950—a time when the ideal of the traditional housewife was prevalent—30 percent of adult women worked full-time. Today, 60 percent work, and by 2006, more than 62 percent will work (U.S. Bureau of the Census 2000). Contrary to what many people might believe, having children does not prevent women

Stereotypic Notions of Gender

FEMININE	MASCULINE
Submissive	Dominant
Dependent	Independent
Emotional	Rational
Receptive	Assertive
Intuitive	Analytical
Timid	Brave
Content	Ambitious
Passive	Active
Cooperative	Competitive
Sensitive	Insensitive
Sex object	Sexually aggressive

TABLE 8.1 • *This table shows the traits traditionally used to describe men and women that contribute to continuing gender stereotypes. Supposedly women are submissive, whereas men are dominant; women are dependent, whereas men are independent; women are emotional, whereas men are rational; women are timid, whereas men are brave; and so on. Even though many women and men share similar profiles in these traits, such cases are usually dismissed as exceptions to the rule. Society has been slow to recognize that men and women are not all one or the other on these traits.*

CQ *Do you think that these stereotypes will continue to exist at the end of the twenty-first century?*

Diversity ●■▲ Equal Rights for Women Is Still a Revolutionary Idea in Many Societies

There are many places in the world where women face especially difficult social conditions and have not begun to share equal rights with men (MacFarquhar 1994; Scupin 1992). In India, for example, newlywed women are sometimes murdered by their husbands because their families did not provide enough dowry money. The murders are passed off as accidents or suicide, leaving the husband free to marry again. There were 110 known cases of such dowry deaths in Delhi in 1989; fewer than 5 percent of the husbands were convicted of any crime. Of course, dowry murders are illegal, but the police often do not have sufficient evidence to press charges.

Baby girls are less desired than baby boys in many countries of Asia and thus are more frequently aborted. Sometimes advanced testing procedures, such as amniocentesis and sonograms, are used to determine the sex of the unborn baby to allow for early abortion. In South Korea, for instance, the use of such procedures has caused male births to exceed female births by nearly three times the worldwide average, and in some provinces of China, there are not enough women of marriageable age for all of the bachelors, who may outnumber their potential spouses ten to one.

In some states in Brazil, a double standard is deeply entrenched and works against women. For example, married men may indiscriminately sleep with other women to prove their masculinity, but married women who have other sexual partners risk being beaten or killed by their husbands. Many such killings go unreported because the police, being men, agree with the double standard, and the courts, further dominated by men, usually will not convict a man on such charges.

More than 80 million African women still undergo an ancient rite called female circumcision or mutilation. This rite involves cutting away parts of the genitalia. Such operations are usually performed by people without medical training, and they frequently cause infection and extensive loss of blood. The operation supposedly deadens the young girls' sexual drive and ensures that they will not voluntarily engage in sex before marriage. Today, many African groups are trying to eliminate this practice. It is worth noting also that in Israel, Jewish religious law prohibits granting a wife a divorce without her husband's consent. At least 10,000 Israeli women, known as the Agunot (the anchored), have husbands who are unwilling to give that permission.

Finally, in many countries, females receive less education than males. Because a lack of education is usually associated with a diminished role in society, societies that discriminate in this way are practicing institutionalized sexism (Bergman and McKnight 1993). The map shows the varying national ratios of females to males in school.

The Global Ratio of Female to Male Secondary School Enrollment

As indicated by this map of the varying national ratios of females to males in school, female enrollment is equal to or superior to that of males in only a few nations. A country's failure to educate young girls is typically due to several factors. Improving female literacy rates is an important way to improve the status of women in society, and it also has significant implications for controlling population growth and reducing infant mortality.

SOURCE: Data from Edward F. Bergman, *Human Geography* (Upper Saddle River, NJ: Prentice Hall, 1995).

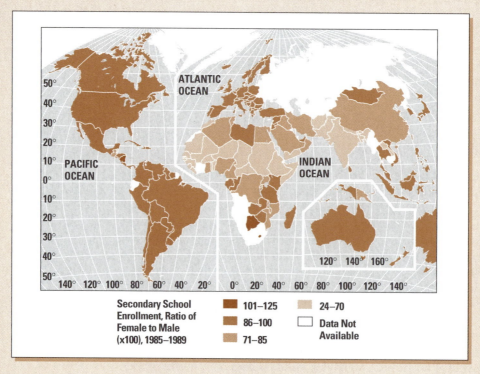

Secondary School Enrollment, Ratio of Female to Male (x100), 1985–1989

■ 101–125
■ 86–100
■ 71–85
□ 24–70
□ Data Not Available

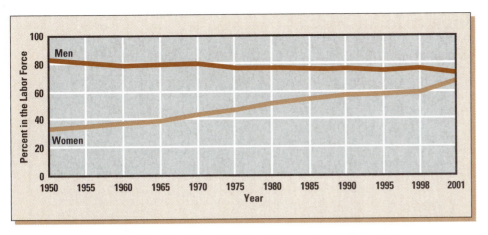

FIGURE 8.1 Participation in the U.S. Labor Force, According to Sex

This figure shows that the majority of both men and women are in the labor force. The overall small decline for men since 1950 reflects the aging of the U.S. population; that is, over the last 50 years, a progressively larger percentage of men have moved from the usual ages of work to the retirement years. The increase in employment for women, even in the face of an aging population, reflects the increasing tendency for women to be employed outside the home even when they are mothers with young children. Opportunity has meshed with necessity in the increasing employment of women.

from working outside the home: Two-thirds of all mothers with children under age 6 still manage to work full-time (U.S. Bureau of the Census 2000). Figure 8.1 shows the increasing participation of women in the U.S. labor force as compared with men.

Work Segregation

Although women have long participated in the workforce, they remain concentrated in a narrow range of jobs (see the Society Today box). For instance, about half of all working women are found in only two broad occupational categories: clerical (such as typist or secretary) and service (such as waitress or nurse). Women constitute an even larger percentage of specific occupational categories. They make up more than 98 percent of secretaries; 75 percent of teachers; 90 percent of professional nurses, bookkeepers, bank tellers, and housekeepers; and 80 percent of waiters, librarians, cashiers, and telephone operators (Roberts 1995; U.S. Bureau of the Census 2000).

Even within occupations that are overwhelmingly female, men dominate the better positions (Whisenant et al. 2002). Women typically wait on tables at inexpensive restaurants, whereas men work in fancy restaurants where the tips are much higher; women remain as word processors, whereas men quickly become administrative assistants; and women nurses care for patients, whereas male nurses become supervisors. In the teaching profession, the higher the level, the more men dominate it (see Chapter 12). Women constitute 98 percent of all kindergarten teachers, 57 percent of all secondary school teachers, 42 percent of all college professors, and 12 percent of all college and university presidents (but predominantly at the smaller, less prestigious institutions) (American Council of Education 1984; U.S. Bureau of the Census 1994). In brief, women have increasingly entered the labor force only to suffer from a double inequity: they are funneled into occupational niches that are neither highly paid nor highly regarded, and even within those niches, they occupy the lower positions.

Despite working as many hours as men, women continue to be responsible for the household and the children. Sociologist Arlie Hochschild referred to this dual responsibility as the **second shift**, meaning that when the woman comes home from her job, she immediately begins working at her second job: cooking dinner, cleaning house, taking care of the children, and doing other household tasks (Dubeck 2002). On average in the United States, working women are responsible for 70 percent of the housework, whereas their husbands and children are responsible for 15 percent each

Second shift ▲ Housework such as cooking, cleaning, and child care that women who work outside the home take on when they arrive home.

Society Today ● ■ ▲

Occupations with the Greatest and Smallest Participation of Women

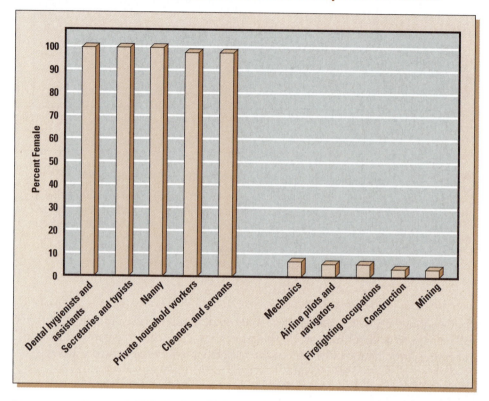

Some occupations are highly feminized: that is, they have a high concentration of women. Some occupations are the opposite; they have a very low concentration of women. You may have noticed this the last time you visited the dentist, or took your car into a garage for repairs, or looked into the cockpit of the airplane you were flying on.

SOURCE: U.S. Bureau of the Census, 2002.

(Hochschild 1997; Perkins and DeMeis 1996). And even when men help, housework remains the woman's responsibility. Before picking up a broom or a dust cloth, most men ask their wives, "What needs to be cleaned?"—a question that implies that the wife is in charge and that the husband is a temporary helper working out of the goodness of his heart. Even among people who have servants, the wife (not the husband) stays home and manages the household (Hochschild 1997).

Although women spend many hours at household tasks, their labor is not counted as productive work. Consequently, statistics on industrial output, productivity, and gross national product do not reflect the labor that women put into running their homes and rearing their children. Moreover, in many nations, women work at home producing woven baskets, boxes, and other products that do not require much technology. Although these products are tangible goods and sell for money, many governments do not count them as part of the nation's productive output. Because of these practices, productivity estimates are far from accurate. If all of the work performed by women was counted, statistics on world productivity would increase by about one-third (United Nations 1991).

Income Inequality

The gender gap can be expressed in terms of money: a woman in the United States earns around 74 cents for every dollar a man earns. The precise amount of the gap

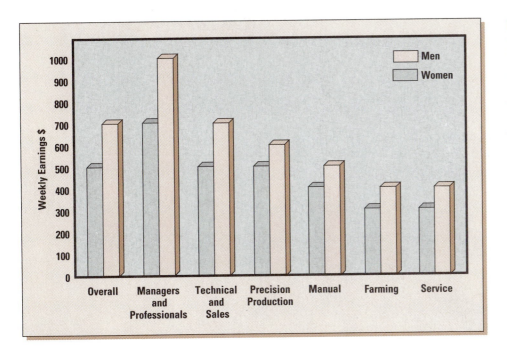

FIGURE 8.2 Weekly Earnings of Men and Women in Major Occupations

Overall, men earn $200 per week more than women. However, a person's occupation makes a difference. Note that men who are managers and professionals make $300 per week more than comparable women.

SOURCE: U.S. Bureau of the Census, 2002.

varies from occupation to occupation, but in none of the thousands of occupations tabulated by the federal census does the average woman earn as much as the average man (U.S. Bureau of the Census 2000). Overall, 73 percent of working women in the United States earn less than $25,000 per year (U.S. Bureau of the Census 2000). In fact, your gender will probably affect your earnings more than your race, ethnicity, age, or educational attainment will (see Figure 8.2). This gender gap in income is true in other countries as well (Van Der Lippe and Van Dijk 2002).

Causes of Gender Inequality in the Workplace   Gender inequality in the workplace has been attributed to several possible causes. These are as follows:

1. *Sexism*   American culture has historically endorsed the sexist belief that women are best suited for jobs that emphasize service, nurturing, or housekeeping, whereas men are best suited for jobs that involve high-level decision making, authority, and production (Reskin and Padavic 1994). Moreover, many people falsely believe that men have the responsibility for supporting the family, whereas women work only for supplemental income. These beliefs are often coupled with the assertion that employed women cannot be relied on because once they become pregnant, they will leave their jobs. Together, these sexist beliefs undercut gender equity in the workplace.

2. *Lack of Qualifications*   Men typically have more education and job experience than women. For instance, 26 percent of men 25 years or older have completed at least four years of college as contrasted to 22 percent of women (U.S. Bureau of the Census 2000). Men also have more job experience because women must take time out for pregnancy and child care. A lack of qualifications for promotion may mean that women are unable to advance beyond entry-level or low-paid positions.

3. *The Glass Ceiling*   Even in the absence of deliberate discrimination, women encounter a **glass ceiling**: subtle and unconscious discrimination that prevents them from reaching higher and better-paying positions for which they are qualified. For instance, women (and members of ethnic minorities) are startlingly absent from the top levels of management. Women and minorities make up 30 percent of the middle managers in the United States but less than 1 percent of the chief executives or the managers who report to the chief executive. In 1990 only 19 of the 4,012 highest-paid officers and directors of top companies were women (Fierman 1990). Federal and

Glass ceiling ▲ Subtle and often unconscious discrimination within organizations that prevents women from reaching higher and better paying positions for which they are qualified.

Atlanta, Georgia: Upper-middle class dual-income family setting. The mother, who is a pediatrician, talks on the telephone while she attends to her daughter. The combination of motherhood with a demanding professional job means long hours and much juggling of work and family commitments.

123 **STUDY TIP**

Select an area of employment that you perceive as displaying elements of gender inequality. Analyze how sexism, lack of qualifications, the glass ceiling, and networking contribute to the gender inequality in this particular area.

state governments have a better record in promoting women, but even so, women account for only approximately one-third of high-level state and local government jobs (Reskin and Padavic 1994).

Why does a glass ceiling exist? One reason is that many corporate executives were socialized to believe that a woman's proper place is in the home and that women do not take their jobs very seriously. Moreover, when thrown into competition with women, some men unconsciously may feel threatened and may try to reduce the threat by excluding women from competing altogether. Changing these decades-old prejudices would require a great deal of long-term resocialization in some cases; in other cases, resocialization might not be effective or practical. Perhaps many old-style executives will have to retire before more egalitarian management practices can be established.

4. Networking   The informal but important practice of networking also contributes to gender inequality in the workplace (Chapter 5). Much of American business and government is conducted outside the office at recreational sites, such as golf clubs, where women are discouraged from participating or even are barred outright. The executive lunch attended by the "old boys" is another network that excludes women and leaves them with no comparable alternative (there is no "old girls'" network). Recently, women have begun to form networks and organizations of their own with the goal of providing information, mutual support, and education about job openings, business opportunities, and important people.

●■▲ Pausing to Think   About Gender Inequality and Work

The majority of women work outside the home, including women with young children. Working women are more heavily concentrated in certain occupations than are men. Differences between men and women in pay, career, and work-related matters are often attributed to sexism, lack of qualifications, the glass ceiling, and male-oriented networking. In recent years, women have begun to form networks of their own whose aim is to provide information, mutual support, and education about job and business opportunities.

CQ What career plans do you have? ◆ Is your career path open equally to men and women? ◆ If not, why not?

Feminism

As we stated at the outset of the chapter, sexism is an ideology that maintains that women are inherently inferior to men and therefore do not deserve as much power, prestige, and wealth as men. **Feminism** is a counterideology that has arisen to challenge sexism and patriarchy and that seeks independence and equality for women (French 1990; Whittier 1995). Betty Friedan is generally credited as being an important catalyst for much of contemporary feminist thought. In her book *The Feminine Mystique* she drew attention to the fact that as long as women achieved their identity in society primarily in terms of their sexual relation to men, they would remain subordinate to them (Friedan 1963). She believed women should break free of the many cultural restraints that bound them to a rigid and narrow social identity. Feminism is often misunderstood as being opposed to the traditional family, but it is more properly understood as seeking independence and equality for women. The following are some of the issues that feminists have championed. These issues have generated much controversy, and debates about them have helped raise people's consciousness of the extent of sexism in society (see the What Do You Think? box).

Gender Equality and the Law

Feminist ideology supports "equal rights under the law." This is called **gender equality**. In the past, the law as it applied to women was frequently a hindrance to them and prevented them from fully participating in society. For example, after the Great Depression struck in the late 1920s and early 1930s, the 1932 Federal Economy Act stipulated that if layoffs were necessary, married women were to be let go first. Federal wage codes, moreover, gave women less pay than men for the same jobs, and women were often fired and their jobs given to men. Gender equality under the law was officially recognized when President John Kennedy signed the Equal Pay Act of 1963 and President Lyndon Johnson signed the 1964 Civil Rights Act, thereby prohibiting many of the discriminatory practices adopted during the Great Depression.

Feminists continued to argue for greater legal protection, and from the mid-1970s through the early 1980s, they advocated passage of an equal rights amendment to the Constitution of the United States. The amendment read, "Equality of rights under the law shall not be denied or abridged by the United States or any State on account of sex." Even though the majority of people in the United States favored

STUDY TIP

Construct a "word web" to illustrate the issues that feminism has addressed. Include descriptions and examples of each.

Feminism ▲ A counterideology that has arisen to challenge sexism and that seeks independence and equality for women.

Gender equality ▲ Equality between men and women under the law.

What Do You Think? ●■▲ Women, Men, and Politics   ?

Question: "Are most men better suited emotionally for politics than most women?"

Over the past decade, approximately one-third of the American public have agreed that men are emotionally better suited for politics than women. Interestingly, almost the same percentage of women hold this opinion as men.

CQ Identify the key terms in the question. What do you think those terms meant to the respondent and to the interviewer?

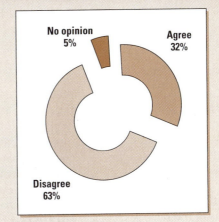

No opinion 5%
Agree 32%
Disagree 63%

SOURCE: General Social Survey 1999.

the amendment, it failed when just 35 states had approved it by the 1982 deadline (passage of a constitutional amendment requires approval of 38 states). Opponents of the amendment claimed that it would ruin American life and destroy the family, and they attacked feminists who supported it as "enemies of every decent society" (Spretnak 1982).

Comparable Worth

Because women (and other minority groups) are most often relegated to narrow, poorly paying, low-prestige positions, it might not do much good to achieve equal pay for equal work. Male and female clerks might earn the same wages, but clerks do not earn very much in the first place. Recognizing this fact, many feminists have rejected the idea of equal pay for equal work and now endorse the concept of **comparable worth**: equal pay for comparable jobs. According to this concept, every job in an organization should be rated as to its value for the organization, and people performing a job with a similar value should be paid a similar wage. Advocates believe that comparable worth would produce greater equity, especially among women whose work traditionally has been devalued. Opponents counter that jobs cannot be evaluated in the way that comparable worth requires, and that in any event, comparable worth would do more harm than good because it would disrupt the way the value of work is now determined (Killingsworth 2002).

Abortion

Feminist ideology tries to counter the prevailing cultural beliefs about women being "naturally" inclined toward motherhood and willing to spend most of their adult lives as care providers. These beliefs often keep women economically dependent on men and limit women's participation in the labor force. The notion that all women want to raise a family is, of course, a false generalization. Feminist ideology sees limitations on abortion as part of a system of beliefs and practices in which men dictate the types of family and gender roles women should perform and ultimately gain control over a woman's life and body.

Feminists generally advocate few restrictions on abortion because they believe that a woman must have the freedom to choose what happens to her body and her life. In seeking greater independence for women, feminists also favor government support for child care, pregnancy leaves from work, and more education about birth control and family planning (Chafetz and Dworkin 1987; Gelb and Hart 1999).

Resistance to Compulsory Heterosexism

Sexual orientation refers to an individual's preference for a particular form of sexual expression. **Heterosexuality** is the desire for a partner of the opposite sex; **homosexuality** is a preference for a person of the same sex; and **bisexuality** is a desire for a person of either sex. Homosexual men are called gays, and homosexual women are called lesbians. Although different types of sexual expression exist and are tolerated to some extent in most societies, all patriarchal societies endorse heterosexuality. In contrast to societies that are relatively open to homosexuality, U.S. society strongly condemns it. This preference is so strong that heterosexuality is virtually compulsory, that is, forced on individuals whether they prefer it or not. For example, in 1986 the Supreme Court ruled that states may criminalize homosexual acts even when they involve only consenting adults in a private home (*Bowers v. Hardwick*). Some feminists—called radical feminists—see compulsory heterosexuality as a form of political coercion that keeps women locked into the biological role of childbearers. They believe that women will not be truly free until they are free to choose whatever form of sexual expression best suits them (Lorber 1995; Stein 1997).

Inclusive Feminism

It is becoming increasingly clear to feminists that inequality in one area of life is related to inequality in other areas. As a result, an approach to inequality called "race,

Comparable worth ▲ Equal pay for comparable jobs.

Heterosexuality ▲ The desire for sexual partners of the other sex.

Homosexuality ▲ The desire for sexual partners of the same sex.

Bisexuality ▲ The desire for sexual partners of either sex.

If you search for the word "feminist" on the Web, you will see that there are over 120,000 sites to chose from. We suggest that you begin with the Feminist Majority Foundation. This site contains fascinating materials relating to current gender issues. For instance, it contains information about Global Feminism, Feminist News and Events, Women and Girls in Sports, and

Feminist Arts, Literature, and Entertainment. After you have explored the Feminist Majority Foundation site, answer the following questions:

What are the central issues for feminists?

All in all, which topics were of most interest to you?

class, and gender" has recently emerged. (The term "race" is short for the longer phrase "race and ethnicity"; and "class" is short for "social class and socioeconomic stratification"). This new perspective focuses on what the causes of inequality are, how the causes are related to one another, and how they affect the individual and society (Anderson and Collins 1997).

Thus, the inequality that women experience because of their gender may be reinforced by their social class and racial characteristics. To illustrate, consider an impoverished Mexican American woman, or Chicana. She belongs to a subordinate gender group, is in the lower social class, and is a member of an ethnic minority. Does any one of her statuses—ethnicity, class, or gender—affect her life more than any other? According to **inclusive feminism**, the answer is no—all forms of inequality are related, and therefore all must be opposed.

Given the controversial nature of feminism, many young women declare that they are not feminists. Yet even nonfeminist women have benefited from feminist ideology. For instance, in 1971, only 43 women were enrolled in the College of Law during the autumn quarter at Ohio State University—just 7 percent of the total class. In 1991, the number was 290—46 percent of the law college's student body. Similar large gains were made in the colleges of business, pharmacy, and veterinary medicine. Nationally, women have gone from 17 percent to 29 percent of chemists, 14 to 44 percent of economists, 3 to 27 percent of industrial engineers, and 24 to 59 percent of public officials (Roberts 1995). Without pressure from feminists, it is doubtful that the proportion of women in these once traditionally male professions would have increased so dramatically over just two decades.

Because feminism strives to end male domination, many men are troubled by it for the obvious reason that they do not want to lose their privileged position. The opposition of some men (and women) to feminism, however, does not mean that all men oppose all aspects of the feminist agenda. For instance, many men believe that masculine roles and identities should be made more flexible and that the separation of men's work from women's is inherently unjust (Kimmel 2000; Kimmel and Messner 1997). Although feminists typically are women, men can be pro-feminist in their ideology, which means that they also want to counter sexism (for additional information on feminism and men's studies, see the Sociology Online box).

●■▲ Pausing to Think   About Feminism

At the heart of feminism is the idea that as long as women achieve their social position and identity primarily in terms of their sexual relation to men, they will remain subordinated to men. Among the issues important to feminists are equality between men and women under the law, the concept of comparable worth, reproductive freedom, resistance to compulsory heterosexism, and an inclusive feminism. Many men support the goals and agenda of feminism, but some men are troubled by feminism because it threatens their privileged position in society.

 What do you think—has feminism provided a valuable counter to sexism in society? ◆ Why, or why not—what are your reasons?

Inclusive feminism ▲ The view that sexism is related to all forms of oppression and that feminist ideology therefore must resist all forms.

Sociological Analysis of Gender Inequality

How can gender inequality be explained? Why does patriarchy exist? Sociologists have answered these questions in terms of three major perspectives: functionalism, conflict theory, and symbolic interaction.

The Functionalist Perspective

From a functionalist perspective, gender inequality has a positive function for the society as a whole. What function could such inequality have? Broadly considered, gender inequality is a mechanism for dividing labor and allocating rewards among the members of a society. It channels women into domestic spheres and nurturing occupations, and it channels men into the paid labor force, commerce, and government.

According to functionalist theorists, it is efficient for society when one spouse remains at home and performs domestic duties while the other spouse works outside the home. This division of labor is accomplished conveniently (at least for some people) by dividing work according to gender. Thus, women are given expressive tasks: smoothing interpersonal problems among family members, defusing hostilities, and creating solidarity. The mother comforts children when they are hurt, gives a birthday party for the father, or does the Christmas shopping. In contrast, men assume instrumental tasks: solving problems, providing resources, and dealing with affairs external to the family unit. The father provides income for the family, deals with financial matters, and makes the major household decisions. Expressive roles require women to be passive, nurturant, and emotional, whereas instrumental roles require men to be aggressive, rational, and competent (Cancian and Oliker 1999). In this way, tasks match behavior and feelings. If men were extremely sensitive to the feelings of others, for example, they might be reluctant to compete for fear of hurting the loser. And if women were insensitive, they could not nurture children (Parsons, Bales, and Shils 1953).

As a consequence of dividing labor and roles along gender lines, women become dependent on men for protection and resources. Masculine activities become more highly valued than feminine activities, and gender inequality becomes deeply ingrained in the society. Both men and women come to take gender inequality for granted and to view it as part of the natural order.

Although functionalist theory highlights the importance of considering the social system as a whole, it does have flaws. First, functionalist theory may be interpreted as an apology for the status quo. Just because women can bear children does not mean that they must be responsible for domestic duties, child care, and expressive roles. Both males and females are capable of being excellent parents (or terrible parents), and both can be expressive or instrumental. Second, an American woman born today can expect to live almost 80 years and to bear (on average) fewer than two children. These statistical facts mean that she will live almost half her life after her children have reached maturity. Under such circumstances, a division of labor that keeps the woman tied to the household and the man to nonfamilial work roles makes less sense than it did in the past. Third, and perhaps most important, is it truly efficient to assign tasks on the basis of gender? Some men are surely more nurturant than some women, and many women are exceptionally well qualified for leadership in business and industry. Would it not be more efficient if the most talented and most highly motivated persons were assigned to these jobs regardless of gender?

The Conflict Perspective

From the conflict perspective, gender inequality is a form of social stratification. The stratification of men and women, however, differs from the type that characterizes racial, ethnic, and class differences. Whereas members of minorities are located disproportionately in the lower strata, women are found throughout the class hierarchy. This fact does not mean, however, that men and women have equal status. Typically, an

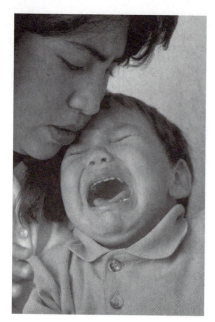

Women are often considered experts at expressive tasks, such as comforting children when they are hurt or unhappy. However, sociologists argue that such skills are learned and are not part of the "natural order of things".

upper-class woman will have more power, prestige, and wealth than any lower-class person, but the same upper-class woman will have less status than an upper-class man. Like functionalists, conflict theorists maintain that the capacity of women to bear children contributes to gender inequality. They claim that men have valued women mainly because women bear children, and without children the society could not survive.

According to conflict theory, the power of men to shape society to their ends means that women will inevitably be a subordinate group (Tilly 1999). Although sexism works against women, conflict theory suggests that women continue to accept it because they have been socialized into a culture that defines women as subordinate. Women have therefore come to believe in sexism and to accept a secondary place in society. In effect, women accept and even support an ideology that works against them—an example of false consciousness (Chapter 6).

There are limits, however, to false consciousness. Although we discuss the women's movement in the last chapter of the book, we should note that women have long opposed patriarchy and have actively campaigned for universal suffrage and an end to sexism. When seen from the standpoint of conflict theory, the women's movement represents an attempt to eliminate the oppression that keeps women in an inferior social position.

The Symbolic Interactionist Perspective

We have already presented much of the symbolic interactionist perspective on gender inequality in the discussion of gender-role socialization earlier in this chapter. To review, however, the symbolic interactionist approach emphasizes the role of meaning and the self in gender socialization. According to this perspective, children must first learn the meaning of "girl" and "boy" and then place themselves in the appropriate category. Young children under 7, for example, often think that appearance is the only distinction between the genders—boys wear pants and have short hair, whereas girls wear dresses and have long hair. As children mature and interact with others, these naive images give way to more accurate conceptions, and they can soon properly define themselves as "girls" or "boys." These definitions are incorporated into the self and become the basis for choosing relationships and activities that reinforce gender identity (Conn and Kanner 1947; Joffee 1971; Theberge 2000).

As adults, men and women take gender distinctions for granted and seldom consider them as social constructions of behavior. They see women as "naturally" inclined toward motherhood and domestic activity, and men as "naturally" inclined toward outdoor activity and work. Many popular books, films, songs, and other agents of socialization reinforce these distinctions, and it becomes difficult for individuals to break free of these cultural expectations. As parents, they socialize their children with the same or similar expectations for gender differences they learned themselves, thus reproducing gender inequality.

● ■ ▲ **Pausing to Think**   **About the Sociological Analysis of Gender Inequality**

Functionalist theorists say that gender inequality benefits society because women are channeled into domestic spheres and nurturing occupations, and men are channeled into the paid labor force of industry, commerce, and government. Conflict theorists say that gender inequality benefits men because it relegates women to lower positions in the system of social stratification. Symbolic interactionists explain gender inequality as the end product of social learning that tends to reproduce itself across generations. (See Table 8.2 for a comparison of the three perspectives.)

CQ   Which theoretical perspective—the functionalist, conflict, or symbolic interactionist—best describes how you think about gender inequality? ◆ Why? Explain your reasons.

TABLE 8.2
[a]The functionalist and conflict perspectives were introduced in Chapters 1 and 2, and symbolic interaction was discussed in Chapter 3.

Comparison of Three Theoretical Perspectives on Gender Inequality

PERSPECTIVE[a]	VIEW OF GENDER INEQUALITY	KEY CONCEPTS AND PROCESSES
Functionalism	Sees gender inequality as an orderly mechanism for dividing labor and allocating rewards	Expressive tasks Instrumental tasks
Conflict Theory	Sees gender inequality as a form of social stratification in which men dominate women	Subordination False consciousness
Symbolic Interaction	Sees gender inequality as transmitted from generation to generation through gender-role socialization	Gender stereotypes Self-definitions

Gender Inequality in the Twenty-First Century

Gender is a social construct based on the biological differences between males and females. The biological differences will not disappear in the future, and therefore gender will not totally disappear either. Society, however, may place less emphasis on insubstantial gender differences and more on people's actual characteristics.

In the last few decades, women of all social classes have entered the labor market in large numbers, gender roles have become more open, and gender identities have grown more flexible. These developments are partially the result of the women's

Lieutenant Kara Hultgreen, one of the first female combat pilots in the U.S. Navy. She was assigned to an aircraft carrier as a pilot of an F-14A fighter bomber.

movement, which we discuss in Chapter 16, and partially the result of new social conditions.

In the past, sexual intercourse was necessarily linked to pregnancy; however, in many parts of the world today, modern contraceptive practices have all but severed that link. At the same time, technology has reduced the importance of physical strength in carrying out many tasks, and most women are strong enough to perform most jobs as well as men can. Perhaps more important, the two-income family is rapidly becoming the norm. Among college students, for instance, both men and women usually expect to marry, have families, and have careers (Astin 1990). As the importance of a woman's income increases, so should her power.

Men also are beginning to recognize that a gender role that requires them to be aggressive, dominant, strong, unemotional, and economically successful might be self-destructive (Kulis and Marsiglia 2000). For example, men are three times more likely than women to commit suicide, six times more likely to be alcoholic, and several times more likely to have a heart attack. These problems often are made worse (or possibly are caused) by the stress associated with fulfilling the male role and living up to the requirement of a masculine identity. In the future, more young men might decide to pay less attention to fulfilling the traditional masculine role. If they do, the sharp distinction between masculine and feminine roles may blur.

A major influence on the future of gender roles will be the aging of the baby boom generation. As the baby boomers retire, they will be replaced by the smaller

CONCEPT WEB Inequalities of Gender

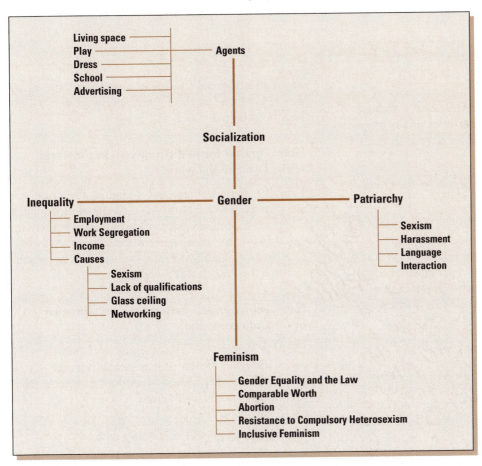

Here is a concept web for gender inequality. Where would you place the topic of "gender roles?"

generation that followed them. As a result, an even larger number of women will be drawn into the workforce. Women may break out of the narrow range of jobs that they now occupy, and the distinction between "women's work" and "men's work" may disappear (Blau and Ehrenberg 2000). For example, men have always been warriors, but in the future, women will surely have an expanded military role. Currently they account for 11 percent of the U.S. armed forces. In 1948, Congress barred women from combat roles, but that bar is now being relaxed. Captain Linda Bray was the first American woman to lead troops in combat when her unit engaged in a skirmish during the invasion of Panama. Of the 35,000 women who participated in Operation Desert Storm during the 1990–91 Persian Gulf War, five died because of hostile action, and thousands came under missile attack while working as truck drivers, intelligence gatherers, helicopter pilots, and medical attendants (Feinman 2000; Hackworth 1991; Hewlett 1991; Jolidon 1990). Even more recently, women flew combat aircraft in Iraq, and thousands served on the ground and at sea.

Looking Ahead

This chapter completes Part Two, Social Inequality. In the next section of the text, we examine issues and theories concerning social institutions. We start the discussion with the economy, an important institution in every society.

WHAT YOU SHOULD KNOW ●■▲

1. *How is gender socially constructed?*

Gender roles arise out of the experiences of a society. As a result, the content of gender roles differs from one society to another, and the roles change through time within a given society.

2. *How has gender equality been affected by the Great Social Transformation?*

In the change from hunting and gathering societies to horticultural and agrarian societies, men begin increasingly to dominate women in the economy and other institutions of society. With the Industrial Revolution, a complex social stratification system develops that places the proletariat, including women, at the bottom and the bourgeoisie at the top.

3. *How are people socialized to their gender role?*

Gender socialization begins at birth as parents set the path for their children to follow—girls going in one direction, boys in another. Gender roles taught to children by their parents are reinforced by several agents of socialization.

4. *How is patriarchy evident in daily life?*

Patriarchy is expressed in all realms of life—in language; in the tendency for women on marrying to adopt the husband's surname rather than the other way around; and in the content and style of social interactions between men and women.

5. *How is gender inequality reflected in the world of employment and work?*

Inequities between men and women in the workforce are seen as a fundamental source of gender inequality. Today most women work outside the home but remain segregated in a narrow range of occupations. Although they are working, most women continue to be responsible for the household and children.

6. *How does inequality between men and women in work affect income?*

On the average, a woman earns approximately 74 cents for every dollar a man earns. Gender has a greater effect on earnings than does race, ethnicity, age, or educational attainment.

7. *What explains gender inequality at work?*

Gender inequality in the workplace is usually attributed to a combination of several factors: sexism, differential qualifications between men and women, the glass ceiling, and male networking.

8. What are the goals of feminism?

Feminism seeks to be independent from male oppression and to achieve economic, social, and political equality between men and women. Among the many issues important to feminists are equality between men and women under the law, equal pay for work of comparable worth, fewer restrictions on abortion, resistance to compulsory heterosexism, and an inclusive feminism.

9. Do societies endorse a particular sexual orientation?

Although different types of sexual expression exist and are tolerated to some extent in most societies, all patriarchal societies endorse heterosexuality. In the United States this preference is so strong that heterosexuality is virtually compulsory. Many feminists see compulsory heterosexuality as a form of state coercion.

10. How do the basic sociological perspectives view gender inequality?

Functionalist theorists say that gender inequality benefits society because women are channeled into domestic spheres and nurturing occupations, whereas men are channeled into the paid labor force of industry, commerce, and government. Conflict theorists say that gender inequality benefits men because it relegates women to lower positions in the system of social stratification. Symbolic interactionists explain gender inequality as the end product of social learning that tends to reproduce itself across generations.

11. What is the future of gender inequality?

In the future, women will increasingly pursue careers that were once dominated by men. The two-income family appears to be the norm, and modern contraceptives provide the means for family planning. The aging of the population means that more young women will be drawn into the workforce. Men are beginning to recognize that the masculine gender role might be self-destructive, and in the future men may be more willing to accept women as their equal partners in life.

TEST YOUR KNOWLEDGE ●■▲

Key Terms Matching

Match each of these key terms with the best definition or example from the numbered items that follow. Write the letter preceding the key term in the blank before the definition that you choose.

a. agents of gender socialization

b. bisexuality

c. comparable worth

d. feminism

e. gender

f. gender equality

g. gender markers

h. gender role

i. glass ceiling

j. heterosexuality

k. homosexuality

l. inclusive feminism

m. patriarchy

n. second shift

o. sexism

p. sexual harassment

_____ 1. The cultural and attitudinal qualities associated with being male or female.

_____ 2. Symbols and signs that identify a person's gender.

_____ 3. The view that sexism is related to all forms of oppression and that feminist idology therefore must resist all forms.

_____ 4. Subtle and often unconscious discrimination within organizations that prevents women from reaching higher and better-paying positions for which they are qualified.

_____ 5. Housework such as cooking, cleaning, and child care that women who work outside the home take on when they arrive home.

_____ 6. The desire for sexual partners of either sex.

_____ 7. Unwanted attention or pressure of a sexual nature from another person of greater social or physical power.

_____ 8. The desire for a sexual partner of the same sex.

_____ 9. Equality between men and women under the law.

_____ 10. Equal pay for comparable jobs.

_____ 11. The desire for a sexual partner of the other sex.

_____ 12. The behavior that society expects from males and females.

_____ 13. An ideology that maintains that women are inherently inferior to men and therefore do not deserve as much power, prestige, and wealth as men.

_____ 14. A counterideology that has arisen to challenge sexism and that seeks independence and equality for women.

_____ 15. A social arrangement in which men dominate women.

_____ 16. The individuals, groups, organizations, and institutions that provide substantial amounts of socialization during the life course.

Multiple Choice

Circle the letter of your choice.

1. Although sexual harassment is a major social issue, it is a reflection of the deeper broader issue of
   a. lack of discipline in the military.
   b. unreported crime in the United States.
   c. genetics determining social characteristics.
   d. gender inequality.

2. In which of the following society/societies does the balance of power between women and men shift to men?
   a. industrial
   b. hunting and gathering
   c. horticultural and agrarian
   d. postindustrial

3. The role in Native American culture in which men simulate menstruation and childbirth is called
   a. gender marker.
   b. matriarchy.
   c. berdache.
   d. inclusive feminism.

4. Margaret Mead concluded from her study of the New Guinea tribes that
   a. gender roles are flexible.
   b. "boys will be boys and girls will be girls."
   c. gender roles are extremely rigid.
   d. biology is more important than socialization.

5. Dressing infant girls in pink and infant boys in blue to identify their sex is an example of
   a. berdache.
   b. gender role.
   c. gender identity.
   d. gender marker.

6. In which of the following ways do parents socialize their children into gender roles?
   a. They encourage girls to sit quietly and display proper manners.
   b. They give to boys those toys that encourage them to manipulate their environment.
   c. They decorate girls' rooms with homemaking toys such as dollhouses and tea sets.
   d. All of the above.

7. Which of the following are agents of gender socialization?
   a. parents
   b. schools
   c. mass media
   d. all of the above

8. Definitions of femininity and masculinity are based on
   a. mature women and men.
   b. middle-aged women and men.
   c. young women and men.
   d. young women and middle-aged men.

9. Which of the following is true about gender?
   a. Gender roles are socially constructed.
   b. Gender roles are similar from society to society.
   c. Gender roles are constant within a society through time.
   d. All of the above.

10. Gender socialization begins
    a. about the time children enter first grade.
    b. virtually at the moment of birth (or earlier sometimes) when the physician announces to the parents that the child is a girl or a boy.
    c. once the child learns to speak.
    d. when girls and boys begin to date.

11. Sarah realizes that the key to promotion in her corporation is making contacts with her superiors, but the men in her company socialize at the racquetball court, on the golf course, and in the locker room. Sarah is being excluded from
    a. the second shift.
    b. the old boys' network.
    c. the glass ceiling.
    d. inclusive feminism.

12. Gender inequality in the workplace has been attributed to all of the following except
    a. sexism.
    b. lack of effort on the job.
    c. lack of qualifications.
    d. networking.

13. When a woman marries, she traditionally replaces her last name with that of her husband. This practice reflects
    a. a matriarchal society.
    b. the breakup of the traditional family.
    c. patriarchy in society.
    d. the establishment of an "old girls' network."

14. Professor Morgan's research focuses on feminist issues and also on inequalities of race and social class. Professor Morgan is practicing
    a. inclusive feminism.
    b. radical feminism.
    c. comparable worth.
    d. berdache.

15. Which of the following statements is a criticism of the functionalist theory of gender inequality?

   a. It fails to recognize the inefficiency of assigning tasks on the basis of gender alone.
   b. It converts the biological fact that women can bear children into the perspective that they must be best-suited to household work.
   c. It fails to recognize that, on average, women live about 40 years after their children are grown and thus it does not make sense to keep them tied to the household.
   d. All of the above are criticisms of the functionalist theory of gender inequality.

Identifying Sociological Perspectives on Gender

For each of the following statements, identify the sociological perspective associated with the statement by writing F for functionalist, C for conflict, or SI for symbolic interactionist, in the appropriate blank.

_____ 1. As a consequence of dividing labor and roles along gender lines, women become dependent on men for protection and resources.

_____ 2. Parents socialize their children with the same or similar expectations for gender differences that they learned themselves, thus reproducing gender inequality.

_____ 3. Gender inequality is a form of social stratification.

_____ 4. Tasks match behavior and feelings: women are channeled into expressive roles such as domestic spheres and nuturing occupations, whereas men are channeled into instrumental roles in the paid labor force, commerce, and government.

_____ 5. The power of men to shape society to their ends means that women will inevitably be a subordinate group.

_____ 6. Gender inequality is a mechanism for dividing labor and rewards among members of a society.

True-False

Indicate your response to each of the following statements by circling T for true or F for false.

T   F   1. In small-scale hunting and gathering societies, men and women play complementary roles, and no one has a great deal of wealth or power.

T   F   2. The structure of gender roles is universal, that is, the same in all cultures.

T   F   3. Girls are more highly rewarded than boys for getting along with others and writing neatness.

T   F   4. Advertisements aimed at gender-specific audiences are free of gender stereotypes.

T   F   5. Pejorative slang words such as "bimbo," "chick," or "skirt" show that language itself can be an assault on the self-esteem of women.

T   F   6. In none of the thousands of occupations tabulated by the federal census does the average woman earn as much as the average man.

T   F   (7.) Working outside the family is a relatively recent development for women.

T   F   8. Over half of all working women have clerical or service jobs.

T   F   9. Symbolic interactionism focuses on the role of meaning and the self in gender socialization.

T   F   10. A major influence on the future of gender roles will be the aging of the baby boom generation.

T   F   11. Feminism is often misunderstood as being opposed to the traditional family.

T   F   (12.) Comparable worth means that men and women should receive the same pay for the same job.

T   F   13. Feminist ideology supports "equal rights under the law."

T   F   14. Functionalism sees gender as a form of stratification in which men dominate women.

T   F   15. The living space provided for children has little in the way of implications for gender socialization.

NOTE: The answers to these exercises are at the end of the book.

For additional practice tests and other resources please visit the companion web site at http://www.prenhall.com/curry.

Essay

1. What are gender markers and how are they formed?
2. What is the "second shift" and why does it characterize the lives of so many women?
3. What factors account for gender inequality in the workplace?
4. What is "inclusive feminism" and what do men and women think about it?
5. Compare and contrast the views on gender inequality of functionalism, conflict theory, and symbolic interaction theory.

9

The Economy

Chapter Outline

Perhaps more than any single person, Steven Jobs brought the average person into the computer age. Like the classic hero of a rags-to-riches story, Jobs was an orphan. Unlike the classic hero, however, he was adopted by middle-class parents and reared in the Silicon Valley of California—now the home of the American computer industry. As a youth, Jobs immersed himself in the counterculture of the 1960s. He meditated, experimented with drugs, and traveled to India seeking spiritual enlightenment.

He later teamed up with Steven Wozniak. Together they developed the Apple computer and subsequently founded the Apple Company. The company succeeded beyond anyone's dreams, but after a time Jobs' weakness at managing people began to show. To better run the company, Jobs hired John Sculley away from Pepsi-Cola. An intense power struggle between the two men followed, and Sculley won: he forced Jobs out of Apple. Jobs quickly rebounded and formed a new computer company that foundered (Butcher 1988; Sculley 1987). He then invested in a software company and his investment made him a billionaire (Markoff 1995).

What happened next seems like fiction. Sculley failed at Apple, and the board of directors recalled Jobs, hoping he could miraculously save the company he founded. After a series of missteps, he brought out the iMAC line of desktop computers and turned Apple into a dynamic, profitable enterprise. Although Apple had always fiercely competed with IBM, in 2003 Apple entered a joint venture with its long-standing rival. The agreement allowed Apple to use a new, powerful IBM chip in its computers. But despite the chip, an Apple computer still is regarded as a unique platform, one that many people like for its graphics and user friendliness.

All societies must have an **economy**: an institution that determines what will be produced, how production will be accomplished, and who will receive what is produced (Samuelson and Nordhaus 1998). In other words, the economy is a cultural universal. In the particular case of the United States, American culture greatly values people who take large risks to achieve success in the marketplace. These people are called **entrepreneurs**, and Steven Jobs is an example of an extraordinarily successful one.

Chapter Preview

In this chapter we examine the economy. We first describe how the economy changed as a result of the Great Social Transformation, and then we compare two contrasting economic systems in contemporary life: capitalism and socialism. We next raise some important issues about the American economy, and we follow that discussion with the sociological analysis of the economic order. Finally, we offer some thoughts about changes in the economy in the future.

The Great Social Transformation and the Economy

Through much of human history, work was a communal activity, and the family or kin group was the chief economic unit of society. For example, in hunting and gathering societies, men hunted together, whereas women gathered and prepared meals. In traditional, agrarian

This photograph shows a robotic arm holding an optical video disc, a medium for storing recorded television images and sound. Many industries now depend on robotics—a new industry that has sprung up to supply computerized machines that can do work cheaper, faster, and with fewer errors than humans.

societies, the family was the primary productive unit of the society because farming involved every family member. Wives and husbands worked together and were helped by their children and other relatives (see Chapter 11).

As we saw in Part One of this book, the nature of work began to change dramatically in the nineteenth century. Industrial output increasingly relied on machines, and machinery required a particular kind of social organization. Factories replaced the family as the primary unit of production, and bureaucratic rules replaced traditional authority. Rather than obeying elders or family members, for instance, workers obeyed impersonal orders that came down from the central administration of the company. And rather than depending on one another for subsistence, workers depended on the paymaster. In short, work was transformed from a communal activity to an associational one and has remained so ever since.

Currently, the vast majority of people in the United States are employed by bureaucratic organizations. From the largest corporation to the smallest business, formal rules and regulations cover almost every aspect of work. Authority flows down from the chief executive officer, to the vice president, to the unit manager, to the office director, and at last, to the worker. At every step of the way, professional managers supervise the work process, and their underlying goal is to increase efficiency, improve productivity, and earn more profits for the company (Caplow 1991). In industrial societies, then, the economy is organized to facilitate large-scale productivity, big business, and mass consumerism. As Figure 9.1 shows, industrialization is spreading throughout the world.

Economy ▲ The social institution that determines what will be produced, how production will be accomplished, and who will receive what is produced.

Entrepreneurs ▲ People who take great risks to achieve success in the marketplace.

Capitalism ▲ An economic system in which the means of production are privately owned and market forces determine production and distribution.

Socialism ▲ An economic system in which the means of production are collectively owned and the state directs production and distribution.

Economy and Society

At the present time, two economic systems are particularly important. The first, **capitalism**, is an economic system in which the means of production are privately owned and market forces determine production and distribution. The other system, **socialism**, is an economic system in which the means of production are collectively owned and the state directs production and distribution. We begin the discussion with capitalism.

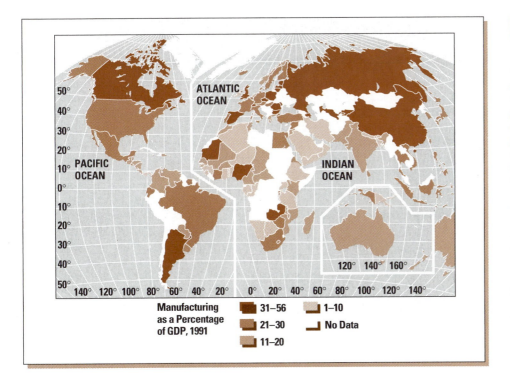

FIGURE 9.1 The Global Distribution of Industry

This map indicates the countries in which industry contributes the highest share of gross domestic product (GDP). GDP is the total value of all the goods and services produced within a country. Manufactured goods generally have a higher value than raw materials or agricultural products, and many nations seek to increase their levels of manufacturing through industrialization. The United States is an interesting example, because even though the share of the U.S. labor force in manufacturing is falling, manufacturing has steadily contributed between 20 and 23 percent of the GDP since World War II.

SOURCE: Edward F. Bergman, *Human Geography: Cultures, Connections, and Landscapes* (Upper Saddle River, NJ: Prentice Hall, Inc., 1995). Data from UNCTAD.

Capitalism

> Every individual endeavors to employ his capital so that its produce may be of the greatest value. He generally neither intends to promote the public interest nor knows how much he is promoting it. He intends only his own security, only his own gain, and he is thus led by an *invisible hand* to promote an end which was no part of his intentions.
>
> —Adam Smith, *The Wealth of Nations*
> (1776 [italics added])

More than 200 years ago, the Scottish philosopher Adam Smith developed a set of economic principles that later became the intellectual foundation for capitalism. His metaphor of the "invisible hand" is still used to represent the free play of economic forces that shape the marketplace and the broader economy.

Industrial capitalism, as we know it, rests on the assumptions that a free market exists, that private individuals may own property, and that people are free to pursue profits for themselves. If you were socialized in a capitalist society, you probably take these assumptions for granted. Without them, however, the economic order in which you live would not exist (see the Diversity box).

1. *Free-Market Competition* According to Adam Smith, impersonal economic forces will guarantee the greatest good for the greatest number of people within a society—provided that the marketplace is free from artificial obstacles. This is called **free-market competition**. In practice, this means that the government must pursue a strict policy of laissez-faire, or not interfering with the free play of economic forces. With the economy thus freed from government interference, the laws of supply and demand ensure that incompetent firms will fail and competent firms will prosper. The result is a marketplace in which high-quality goods and services are available at the lowest possible prices—clearly a benefit to the consumer and to the broader society.

Free-market competition ▲ The buying and selling of goods and services unencumbered by government rules, regulations, and planning.

An issue of growing concern is the role of foreign investment in the United States. On economic grounds, many observers fear that foreign investment in the United States eventually will give outsiders control of the American economy. These outsiders then will convert the United States into a giant marketplace and production center that generates profits for foreign companies. Although these changes may create new jobs and other benefits for people in the United States, the major share of the profits will be carried off to foreign shores.

Other observers take a different view. They point out that foreign investment is not a recent occurrence. For example, even though popular culture portrays the cowboy as an American development, European investors financed many of the largest cattle ranches, railroads, and meat-packing companies of the Old West. At least in this instance, foreign investment contributed to the development of the U.S. economy. Some observers also point out that foreign investors are not conspiring to take over the country. Instead, they are reacting favorably to the strength of the U.S. economy and the stability of the American government. The United States, in other words, is a good place in which to invest. Finally, observers state that most people have very inaccurate notions of how much foreign investment actually has taken place. Overall, total foreign investment in the United States amounts to only 3 percent of the country's total domestic worth. Moreover, and also contrary to popular belief, the largest foreign investors are not the Japanese but the British. In 2000, British investment in the United States was some $108 billion, whereas Japanese investment was $25 billion (U.S. Bureau of the Census 2002). These investments, observers suggest, create jobs and provide capital for expansion. The Honda Company of Japan has invested billions of dollars to develop a manufacturing site in Ohio and has created 10,000 jobs for local workers. In the United States as a whole, foreign investment has created 3.7 million jobs with a total payroll of $112 billion. Just as foreign capital once helped to develop the beef industry on the frontier, today foreign investments create jobs and businesses that otherwise would not exist (Gibney 1998; Powell 1993).

CQ What about you? Do you feel uneasy about foreign ownership of famous American companies? ◆ Would you accept a job with a foreign-owned company? ◆ Why, or why not?

For the economy to remain free, according to capitalist thinking, the government must not compete with private businesses. Thus, rather than build their own aircraft, the military must rely on private companies such as Boeing. The military must also rely on companies like Apple or IBM for computers, and on thousands of small businesses for food items and office supplies.

Although Smith believed in allowing the invisible hand to guide private economic activity, he recognized that economic forces will fail when it comes to providing many public goods and services. There is no economic incentive for private firms to offer welfare, for instance, nor would most people want private firms to supply mercenary soldiers for national defense. In a similar vein, would you want to pay the police for services rendered—paying one fee if they came to your home in response to a burglar alarm, for example, and another fee if they came for a domestic dispute? Most people today would agree that some services should be financed by the government for the good of the society.

2. **Private Ownership**   Although ownership is a common word, it also has a technical meaning. Technically, ownership refers to a bundle of rights associated with the use and disposal of an object or an idea. Thus, if you own this textbook, you have the right to sell it, keep it, destroy it, or otherwise dispose of it. You might someday own a business, factory, or other means of production; as the owner, you will have the right to sell it, expand it, or, should you choose, to do nothing with it. If you as an individual have that right, you enjoy the **private ownership of property**.

Property has value that comes from a combination of scarcity and demand. Commodities that exist in limitless and easily accessible quantities have little or no value; therefore, no one bothers to claim them as property. Air, for instance, is a free good. If air quality continues to deteriorate, however, breathable air could become so scarce that people would gladly pay for it. In a small way, this situation has happened already in smog-filled downtown Tokyo. There, outdoor workers take breaks to breathe from bottles of oxygen, and they gladly pay a fee for this product.

Private ownership of property ▲
The rule of property ownership that vests in the individual the right to own property unencumbered by government rules, regulations, and planning.

In a capitalist society, private individuals own the means of production. Their ownership may be direct, as when an individual owns a business, or it may be indirect, as when many millions of people own stock in a large company. Stock shares are certificates of ownership, and, therefore, anyone who owns a stock share qualifies as a capitalist. A child who has been given a share of common stock in the local utility company by a relative technically qualifies as a capitalist, even if she or he does not realize it.

3. *Pursuit of Profit*   Adam Smith argued that the **pursuit of profit** eventually produces the greatest good for the greatest number of people. Or, as he phrased it, "by pursuing [their] own interests [people] frequently promote that of the society more effectually than when [they] really intend to promote it" (Smith 1952 [originally 1776]). According to capitalists, the pursuit of profit has positive results: the successful entrepreneur earns money, the consumer saves money, and the society becomes more efficient and vigorous.

Although people socialized to believe in American cultural values usually take capitalism for granted, the system is not universally admired. According to some critics, the major problem with capitalism is the negative social consequences it produces (Ashley and Orenstein 1995). For one thing, they contend, the free market is "heartless": changes in supply and demand wipe out industries overnight, devastate entire communities, and destroy families through unemployment and the stress caused by job loss. In addition, capitalist economies rise and fall in cycles. When a recession strikes, millions of people are thrown out of work as firms exercise their right to lay off workers. Even in times of prosperity, the free market ignores the poor because there is little profit to be made from serving them. In 1992, for instance, South Central Los Angeles had only a handful of supermarkets for more than half a million people, mainly because the people in the area were too poor to be "good" consumers (*New York Times*, May 6, 1992:A13). Finally, critics contend, capitalism seems to be more efficient than it actually is. For example, because there are no market incentives to do otherwise, capitalists seeking profits recklessly destroy ecosystems and pollute the environment (Chapter 14). Through overfishing, to illustrate, the once rich waters of Canada and the United States are now almost barren, and commercial fishing is barred. In effect, the quest for profits in the short term destroyed the prospects for profits in the long term (Parfit 1995).

Socialism

Capitalists accept the fact that some people will acquire a greater share of society's wealth than other people. In contrast, socialists believe that everyone should share equally in the goods and services produced by society (Pryor 1985). Rather than relying on the invisible hand to provide the greatest good for the greatest number, socialists argue that the government should decide which goods are produced, how they are distributed, and at what prices they are sold.

The clearest dividing line between socialism and capitalism concerns ownership of the means of production. Under socialism, the government plays a direct role in the economy by acquiring ownership of society's strategic businesses and industries. In many socialist countries, for example, the government owns and operates the railroads, the airlines, television stations, banks, and other services. In addition, the government might own companies that produce chemicals, steel, oil, and other key products. Thus, even though some of the economy remains in private hands, the government is the dominant economic power in the society.

Socialists further believe that the government should own the means of production in the name of the people, whereas capitalists believe individuals should own the means of production in their own name. To put it another way, the issue is private ownership versus public ownership. Capitalists argue that private ownership increases

Pursuit of profit ▲ The system of trade in which those selling goods or services are permitted to charge an amount greater than their costs in producing or buying the good or service.

efficiency and thereby benefits everyone. Socialists argue that private ownership increases inequality and thereby harms most people.

Socialist societies produce more equity than capitalist societies in the sense that more people have access to essential services and that the gap between wealth and poverty is smaller. However, socialist societies suffer from a problem identified by Max Weber: excessive bureaucratization, or red tape. To control the economy, the government must establish a vast network of bureaucratic agencies, each with its own rules, forms, procedures, and long lines of clients. Getting anything done, even for something as routine as acquiring a driver's license, can become such a painful ordeal that many people become frustrated over government inefficiencies.

An example of a socialist economy is Cuba, an island nation just 90 miles from Florida. Cuban socialism began in 1959, when Fidel Castro led a successful revolution. He established a government and seized virtually all private businesses and agricultural lands, nationalized the banks, and drove out foreign corporations. The government also actively managed the economy and undertook many reforms to improve the welfare of the average person. In response to the seizure of property that belonged to American corporations and citizens, the United States imposed a trade embargo on Cuba, limited travel to the island, and established a foreign policy designed to isolate Cuba and to topple Castro from power (Golden 1995).

In spite of U.S. opposition, the Cuban government has succeeded in many of its socialist objectives. Whereas it once employed relatively few workers, by 1970 the government had come to employ 98 percent of the labor force. In addition, wealth was redistributed. The wealthiest Cubans once received about 25 percent of the county's income, but under Castro, that figure fell to about 10 percent (Brundenius 1990).

Evaluating the success or failure of socialism in Cuba, however, depends on your point of comparison. For instance, during the cold war, Cuba received billions of dollars in financial aid from the Soviet Union and found ready customers for its agricultural products within the Soviet bloc. During those boom times, peasants were better off in socialist Cuba than they were in many of the developing nations in Latin America—Cuba was not plagued, as those countries were, by high unemployment, poor health care, illiteracy, and malnutrition. Since the end of the cold war, however, the Cuban economy has faltered. Cuba no longer receives financial aid from the Soviet Union (which no longer exists), and many consumer items that people in the United States take for granted, such as refrigerators, toasters, and television sets, are expensive and scarce (Halebsky and Kirk 1990; McGeary 1998). For these reasons, many young Cubans are becoming disenchanted with their socialist society, and the Cuban government has clamped down on public protests. Fidel Castro's government has begun to allow some individuals to start their own small businesses. Although Cuba's economy has been recovering for the past few years at a rate of 4 percent a year, it remains to be seen whether socialist Cuba can develop a strong economy without massive foreign aid, especially given the U.S. trade embargo (Centre for Development Research 2002).

Mixed Economies: Convergence

Although capitalism and socialism are far apart in theory, in fact the two systems may be converging toward some middle ground or **mixed economy**. There are several reasons for this convergence. First, all industrial societies are affected by similar social forces. Whether an industrial society is capitalist or socialist, it is influenced by new technology, the division of labor, major population shifts, urbanization, and bureaucratization (see Gordon, Edwards, and Reich 1982). And as we discussed previously, given such forces, relationships necessarily become more impersonal, formal, and rational. Regardless of economic ideology, therefore, industrialization creates similar problems that call for similar solutions. For example, as China moves away

Mixed economy ▲ An economy that mixes features of both capitalist and socialist systems, including both public and private ownership of property and limits on free-market competition.

from comprehensive socialism toward a capitalistic economy, it must find ways to motivate workers with monetary incentives, to regulate the economy through persuasion rather than force, and to acquire market outlets for their industrial and agricultural output. Thus China is now the United States' single largest trading partner. Moreover, workers must learn to cope with unemployment because the government no longer guarantees them lifelong job tenure, and families must accept the responsibility for training their children to enter specific careers (Brus and Laski 1989).

Even though the United States is, arguably, the most capitalist society in the world, it began to converge toward a more socialist economy during the Great Depression of the 1930s. The revised version of capitalism that emerged then included a strong measure of **social insurance**: the idea that the government is responsible for guaranteeing a minimum standard of living for everyone. Under this new ideology, social programs were implemented to help the impoverished and to create jobs for the unemployed. For example, the federal government established the Works Progress Administration, an agency that hired people to work on roads, dams, buildings, and other public projects. During the same period, the federal government established Social Security to provide retirement benefits, and laws were passed to regulate employment conditions and job security. After World War II, social programs expanded, and the government even promised to provide everyone with a minimum standard of living (Quadagno 1987). The ability of government to continue to fund such programs has become a major economic and political issue for the twenty-first century (DuBoff 2002).

Sometimes, government intervention is justified on the grounds that a free economy does not work for certain purposes. Under capitalism, to illustrate, pharmaceutical companies have no monetary incentive to develop medicines for rare diseases—the market is simply too small. Congress has therefore granted drug companies certain tax exemptions and a seven-year monopoly on any medicines that treat rare illnesses (Hilts 1992).

In sum, even though socialism and capitalism have different ideological foundations, each system includes some parts of the other. A capitalist country such as the United States provides some social welfare, and socialist countries such as China and Cuba permit some free enterprise (Miller 1991). This blending of elements seems to provide a workable solution for most societies (for information on how to track economic indicators, see the Sociology Online box). Nevertheless, the transition to socialism to capitalism has proved difficult for many societies (Freeland 2000).

STUDY TIP

Construct a visual organizer to illustrate and compare the elements of capitalism and socialism, using different colors for each economic system. Then construct another organizer showing the elements of the mixed economy, using the "capitalism" color for capitalist elements and the "socialism" color for the socialist elements.

Social insurance ▲ The idea that the government is responsible for guaranteeing a minimum standard of living for everyone.

Capitalism is characterized by free-market competition, private ownership of property, and the pursuit of profit unencumbered by government rules, regulations, and planning. Socialism is based on the belief that everyone should share equally in the goods and services produced by the society, that government should own society's strategic businesses and industries in the name of the people, and that the state should play a central role in economic planning. Currently, many countries have economies that mix capitalist and socialist principles.

CQ What did Adam Smith mean by the "invisible hand" of the marketplace? ◆ Do you have faith in the invisible hand? ◆ Why or why not?

The Corporation and Society

In Chapter 5 we discussed the origins of the modern corporation and the way it developed during the Industrial Revolution. In this section we will examine several aspects of the corporation and society, especially in the United States.

The Corporation and the Concentration of Power

On the surface, a corporation appears to be a highly democratic organization, because shareholders vote for directors who oversee the operations of the company. In principle, the shareholders control the company by electing a board and by approving company practices at annual stockholder meetings. The reality of the situation, however, is different (Glasberg and Schwartz 1983). Few small stockholders bother to attend annual meetings, and major shareholders—many of whom are officers of the company—routinely approve of the policies offered by top management. The board also routinely approves new board members, most of whom are selected by top management. Because board members are selected by top management, most of them look on management very favorably, and typically they support whatever the management decides.

The same directors often sit on the boards of more than one company, and most top managers know each other personally. In effect, they form a cozy arrangement of "crony capitalism," an arrangement that is formally called an **interlocking directorate**. More than 80 percent of the United States' 1,000 largest corporations share a director with another large corporation (Davis 2003). The directors of the General Motors Corporation, to illustrate, sit on the boards of many other companies, and as a consequence, General Motors has direct and indirect links to some 700 other corporations (Mintz and Schwartz 1981a, 1981b). Thus, corporate America is not a purely rational, impersonal economic system. Instead, it is governed by a dense network of directors, CEOs, analysts, politicians, and lawyers. Not surprisingly, they share opinions and values, have much the same motivation and goals, and tend to drive the economy along a path that benefits their interests (Davis 2003).

These interlocking directorates wield immense power (Keister 2003). Consider this statistic: the 100 largest American corporations own approximately half of all manufacturing assets in the United States. Or consider this statistic: the ten largest American industrial corporations have combined sales of some $1.3 trillion—a sum greater than the value of all the goods and services produced by many large nations, including Canada, Brazil, India, Russia, and Mexico. These ten companies are Wal-Mart, General Motors, Exxon, Ford Motor, General Electric, Citigroup, Chevron

Interlocking directorate ▲
Members of the boards of directors of corporations sitting on the boards of directors of other corporations, thereby linking the corporations together.

Society Today ● ■ ▲

Ten Largest Businesses in the USA

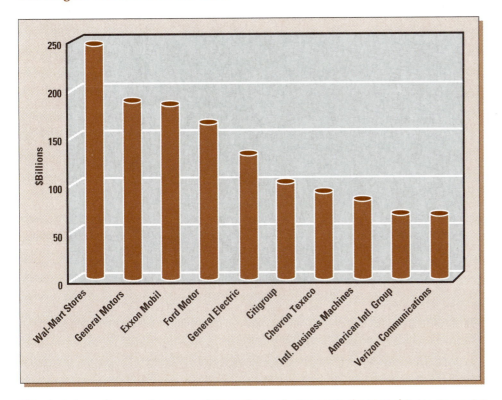

This chart shows the annual revenue of the ten largest businesses in the United States. As a point of comparison, if Wal-Mart was an independent country, it would have the 18th largest economy in the world. Although Wal-Mart deals in retail sales, note how many companies are in manufacturing and production.

 This chart suggest the overwhelming importance of what product?

Texaco, International Business Machines (IBM), American Intel. Group, and Verizon Communications (Fortune 500, 2003; see the Society Today box).

Even though many corporations are already extremely large, some of them are growing even larger, mainly by acquiring other companies. For example, Time and Warner used to be separate companies but merged to form Time-Warner. That media conglomerate recently merged with America Online to form a company with more than $40 billion in annual revenue. Possibly the largest merger in American history took place between Mobile and Exxon. The venture involved $80 billion. Ironically, those companies used to be joined together as part of John D. Rockefeller's original oil empire that was broken up in 1911. Corporate mergers such as these have given rise to **conglomerates**: giant corporations composed of other corporations that produce a variety of products and conduct business in several markets.

A major reason for forming conglomerates is the company's desire to stabilize profits. If one market is depressed, a conglomerate can make money in other markets, thus smoothing out variations in overall profitability. For instance, by acquiring other companies, Philip Morris protects itself against an unfavorable business climate for tobacco products in the United States.

Conglomerate ▲ Giant corporation composed of other corporations that produce a variety of products and that conduct businesses in several markets.

Until recently it was common for American workers to retire at age 65. This is no longer the case. Presently, 68% of workers between 50 and 70 years of age plan to never retire or to work during their retirement (Wild 2003). By 2015, one in five American workers will be 55 years of age or older. Money is a major reason for continuing employment during retirement years. With the economic downturn of the last few years many people have not been able to save enough to cover their projected costs. Also, many have seen their retirement savings greatly diminished in the poor economy. Many of the baby boom generation (born 1946–1965) delayed having children as they pursued their careers, so they are now faced with the problem of paying for the costs of college for their children at a time when they should be saving for retirement. Furthermore, the federal government has increased the age at which workers can collect their full federal Social Security benefits. Social Security was never meant to be a full retirement subsidy. So, in today's economy, workers with no other retirement plan must either continue working or return to work in order to survive.

People plan to work into the retirement years for other reasons too. Older people are healthier and more intellectually active than before. Many see work as a way of not only of obtaining money, but also as way to continue to use their experience and talents, relieve boredom and learn new things, be helpful and contribute to society, stay physically active, and meet new people and socialize with acquaintances and friends (AARP 2003).

It is given that Americans are living longer today than in the past. This is called the "graying" of society as the nation's average age increases (see Chapter 15). And, given that many workers plan to work full- or part-time in their retirement years, America businesses are faced with a growing and unprecedented number of experienced and eager potential older employees. Some businesses are already structuring their work environments to be older-worker friendly. Company characteristics rated as older-worker friendly by the American Association of Retired Persons (AARP) include how aggressively companies seek out older workers, extent of encouragement of older workers to partake of company training programs, provision of health benefits, provision of pension or employee investment opportunities such as profit sharing, and possibilities of flextime and telecommuting. Companies that rate high on these criteria include Baptist Health South Florida, Adecco Employment Services, Children's Health System, The Aerospace Corporation, Principal Financial Group, Deere & Company, Roche, and The Ohio State University Medical Center.

It is unclear what this trend will mean for younger workers. The answer depends on the country's rate of economic growth over the next 20 years.

CQ What is the best way you can prepare for entering a workforce in which the young and old might be competing for jobs?

Another reason for forming conglomerates is to gain access to the technology, skills, and experience of the acquired company. Largely to learn Japanese production techniques, for example, General Motors entered into a joint venture with Toyota to produce cars in California. Conglomerates are also formed to prevent "unfriendly takeovers" by financiers intent on seizing corporate assets for short-term profits. Such takeover attempts were especially common during the 1980s, but they can occur any time that a corporation's assets are worth more than what it would cost to gain control of the company (Nocera 1995). Of course, there may be other reasons for forming conglomerates: companies might buy other companies to gain quick profits. For instance, the ABC and CBS television networks became attractive targets for takeovers when it appeared that Congress was likely to pass legislation to deregulate the communications industry. Such deregulation would allow giant media corporations to increase their profits by increasing the number of radio and television stations they could own (see the Social Change box).

Multinationals

Multinationals ▲ Companies that conduct business in several countries but have their central headquarters in one country.

Business corporations with vast, worldwide holdings are not new. For instance, we mentioned in Chapter 5 how the East India Company helped to create the British colonial empire. What is new, however, is the extent to which corporations are now doing business worldwide. These international companies are called **multinationals**— companies that conduct business in several countries but have their central headquarters in one country. For example, the Caterpillar Tractor Corporation is based in Peoria, Illinois, but operates plants in Scotland, Australia, and Brazil. Honda is headquartered in Japan but has extensive manufacturing plants and marketing operations in the United States. An ironic example of multinational operations concerns baseball, the so-called "great American pastime." Manufacturers of baseballs now ship leather, thread, and yarn from the United States to Haiti. There, low-paid female workers turn the materials into baseballs. The balls are then shipped back to the United States and to other countries such as Cuba, Mexico, and Japan (Barnet 1980).

Multinationals present problems in both power and control. They are difficult to control because they conduct their business in many different countries that have many different laws. Some people even contend that multinationals are rogues—free to operate outside the law. In 1984, for example, a malfunctioning valve at the Union Carbide plant in Bhopal, India, released toxic chemicals that killed more than 4,000 people and permanently maimed thousands more. For seven years the Indian courts ordered the president of the company to come to India and answer to criminal charges. He steadfastly refused, claiming that the Indian courts had no jurisdiction over his behavior. In a final effort, an Indian magistrate ordered the company's Indian assets to be seized, but to no avail (*New York Times*, May 1, 1991:C7). At this writing, the case is still ongoing.

As you might suspect, multinational corporations have vast assets. The largest multinationals control economies as large as those of some countries. Because of their size, these companies exert a strong influence on the economy and politics of the countries in which they operate. Shell, for instance, has extensive petroleum fields in Nigeria, and Shell's decisions to expand or contract petroleum exports exert a powerful influence on the Nigerian economy.

To a certain extent, multinationals benefit their host nations. Multinationals create jobs, generate income, and pay local taxes. They also infuse the culture with new technology and train local workforces. On a broader scale, they establish a general climate conducive to economic growth. At the same time, however, they increase the inequality among nations and make poor nations ever more heavily dependent on wealthy nations (Bergesen 1983; Narula and Dunning 1999). As profit-seeking firms, multinationals extract a country's wealth and send it back to the company's headquarters. Most often these headquarters are located in countries that are already wealthy. For example, most multinationals have their headquarters in the United States and they conduct much of their business through a network of global cities. Capital and resources are moved to whatever global markets seem most profitable (see Figure 9.2; Miller 1995; Sassen 1996). Multinationals, moreover, are often involved in corruption and sometimes tamper with local politics. American firms have paid millions of illegal dollars to government officials in Bolivia, Turkey, Pakistan, and Colombia, and they have been linked to political coups in Chile, Iran, and Guatemala (Barlow 1996).

More than 4,000 people died when toxic chemicals were released from a Union Carbide plant in Bhopal, India, in 1984.

CQ *Should a multinational company with headquarters in one country be held accountable for damages or violation of laws in another country?* ◆ *Why, or why not?*

STUDY TIP

Form a group of three to four students. Before meeting, each student should find and summarize a recent article about a corporation. In a group, discuss the summaries and how this information illustrates the nature and power of the modern corporation as described in the text.

● ■ ▲ **Pausing to Think** About the Corporation and Society

Large corporations employ many workers, control a large amount of society's wealth, and wield considerable social power. The power of many corporations is further increased when they create interlocking directorates, form conglomerates with other corporations, or establish international bases.

 Are we as consumers well served or ill served by the fact that multinationals are becoming increasingly important in the world economy? ◆ What would you expect Adam Smith to say about the development of multinationals?

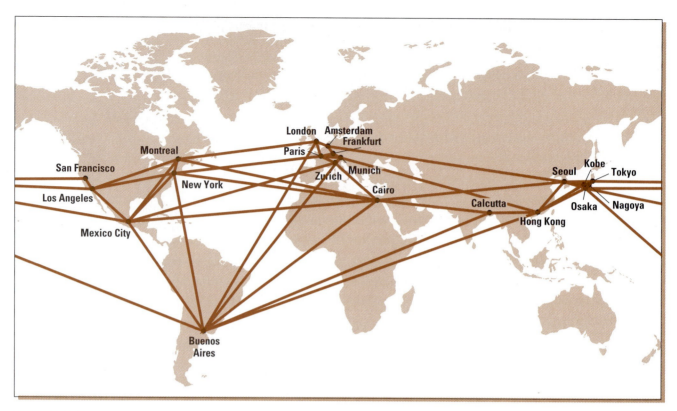

FIGURE 9.2 The Global City in the Global Economy

At the center of the international economic order are the global cities that coordinate and integrate the world system's financial transactions. These global cities are linked in a transnational urban financial system that, on a daily basis, interacts in major financial matters and exchanges. Multinational corporations use this system to move capital and resources to whatever global markets are most profitable (Sassen 1994).

Unemployment and Job Loss Anxiety

Unemployment, or not having a job when you want one, is a feature of industrial societies. It does not exist in traditional societies because the concept of "having a job" does not exist. In traditional societies, people fill roles, and if the role obligations cannot be satisfied, they do something else—but they are not defined as unemployed. For instance, hunters seek game, but if game is absent, the hunters are not considered to be unemployed.

In an industrial society, however, the notion of employment and unemployment takes on great significance. Work is necessary to earn money, but if work is not available, how do you earn a livelihood? Because there is no good answer to this question, unemployment creates many problems for the society and for the unemployed. At the societal level, high unemployment means that human resources are being wasted. The unemployed could be producing goods and services, but they have no opportunity to do so. Unemployment also has an impact on existing societal resources. People without jobs pay little or no taxes and require more government support. They might require job counseling, for example, or welfare subsidies to pay their food and medical bills. At the extreme, desperate people sometimes resort to crime, thereby hurting innocent victims and requiring society to spend even more to apprehend, prosecute, and incarcerate them as criminals.

Because high unemployment strains a society, it typically is a major political issue as well as being a central concern for the individual. In this section, we first discuss the

An unemployed man seeks employment by holding a sign at an intersection during the morning commute. According to the sign, he worked for 36 years in insurance. Insurance companies have taken to exporting many jobs once held by white collar workers to countries where the labor is cheaper. This exporting is called outsourcing and companies do it to increase their profits. Many workers find themselves displaced as a result.

social implications of high unemployment and then turn to a personal problem created by it: anxiety over job loss.

Society and Unemployment

Although it would appear to be a straightforward calculation, the technical aspects of measuring unemployment are fairly complex. To track unemployment, the federal government takes a monthly survey and essentially defines the **unemployed** as people who are without jobs but who are seeking work. Excluded from the survey are children, retired people, and others who are not actively engaged in seeking work. Also excluded are people who have tried to find work but have failed so often that they have stopped trying and have dropped out of the labor force altogether. Like all surveys, the unemployment survey undercounts the homeless, migrants, and people without permanent addresses. These are the very people who are most likely to be without jobs, yet they are the ones most likely to be excluded from the official tallies. In short, the official unemployment rate probably underestimates the true rate by some unknown amount.

Despite its problems, the unemployment rate is one of the most closely watched indicators of economic performance. Even seemingly minor variations in it cause a great deal of concern, because a small but consistent change will produce a large change over the course of a few months. To illustrate, if the current rate is 5 percent, then an increase of half of 1 percentage point every month will increase the rate to about 8 percent in six months—a substantial increase affecting millions of people.

Although political leaders continually try to take measures to lower the unemployment rate, no society can possibly achieve a rate of zero percent unemployment. At any given time, some people will be out of work for various reasons: some may be temporarily sick, and others may be changing jobs, be moving residences, or have personal reasons for not working. The seasons also have an effect. During the harvest, many farmers have jobs that disappear after the season is over. They then must seek other jobs and may experience a period of unemployment. During the early summer, moreover, high school and college graduates enter the labor market, and they are officially unemployed until they find work. For this reason, the unemployment rate typically rises in June.

Unemployed ▲ People who are without jobs but are seeking work.

If zero unemployment is not attainable, what then would be an acceptable level? This question is difficult to answer because so much depends on personal opinion. However, a few statistics might help guide us. First, consider the Great Depression of the 1930s, a period during which unemployment reached a historic high. When the Depression was at its worst, the unemployment rate reached 25 percent. Stated another way, only three out of every four persons wanting work could find a job. This historically high rate produced an army of unemployed. Factories and fields were abandoned, and thousands of people lost their homes. Many of the unemployed took to the road and migrated across the country in search of better opportunities; others "rode the rails" and became "hobos"; and still others scratched for any income possible and relied on charity when scratching was not sufficient. Clearly, the Great Depression indicates that an unemployment rate in the neighborhood of 25 percent produces catastrophic results for society and for the individual.

It is interesting that the lowest unemployment rate occurred not too long after the highest rate. During World War II, the rate fell to under 2 percent, for the obvious reasons that men and women were being called into military service and jobs were plentiful because of wartime production. Since that time, the unemployment rate has never been as low, although from World War II to the 1970s, it remained below 5 percent, and sometimes it fell to 3 percent. During the early 1980s, the rate increased dramatically and reached double digits. Since that time, the unemployment rate has stayed in the range of about 4 to 7 percent. What, then, do the statistics suggest about what is high and what is low unemployment? A rate of 25 percent is clearly high, whereas a rate of less than 2 percent is clearly low. In general, an unemployment rate of around 5 percent or lower is now regarded as acceptable in the United States (see Cohen 1993; U.S. Bureau of the Census 2000).

Although 5 percent might seem to be a fairly low number, it has serious implications for some ethnic groups. In Chapter 7 we called your attention to a persistent problem in American society: the high unemployment rate among segments of the African American population. The black rate is always about twice the white rate, meaning that whenever the white rate is 5 percent, a figure considered acceptable, the African American rate is 10 percent, a figure considered unacceptable. Or to put it another way, when whites are doing about as well as can be expected, many African Americans are doing poorly, and some are experiencing a catastrophe. For example, by 1997 the unemployment rate among disadvantaged young African Americans stood at 37 percent—a rate higher than the highest national rate during the Great Depression. Even in the economic boom of 2000, the unemployment rate of black Americans was 7 percent, as compared with a white rate of 3.9 percent. Economic booms do not bring prosperity to all, and less-skilled workers are more apt to be left behind (Cherry and Rogers 2000).

The impact of unemployment goes well beyond mere numbers, of course. It strikes at people, and people make decisions that affect themselves and their society (Broman, Hamilton, and Hoffman 1990). Without jobs, people may take advantage of whatever opportunity comes their way, and in many cases, the only opportunities are in crime and deviance. Other people might despair and drift along on welfare benefits and the charity of friends and relatives. Ask yourself what you would do if you were not in school and could not find a job. Would you live with your parents or relatives and have them support you? Or would you hang out with other unemployed people about your age and try to survive by whatever means were available?

Such questions are difficult to answer because society stigmatizes the unemployed (Short 1996; Broman, Hamilton, and Hoffman 1990). Especially in a capitalist society, work is a measure of social worth, and the impact of unemployment can therefore be devastating. Being without a job strips away people's sense of identity (see Chapter 3) and separates them from a social world that had been an important anchor in their lives. Cut off from work, they are cast adrift without knowing what to do—a situation Durkheim described as anomic. Some unemployed people suffer feelings of shame and worthlessness, and others fall into severe depression (Riegle 1982). The family and friends of the unemployed also suffer because they vicariously share in the plight. And of course, those people who are directly dependent on the unemployed suffer economically. Although jobless people may have unemployment benefits, such benefits are usually limited to less than a year and do not make up for the income that is lost by not working. Work, even low-paid work, provides a sense of self-worth that the unemployed do not have (Lamont 2000).

Because the economy of most industrial societies shifts and changes over time, there is always the possibility of unemployment. As a result, even people who have jobs suffer from the threat of job loss, a possibility that keeps them in a state of constant anxiety.

Job Loss Anxiety

Unless you are a worker living in a hypothetically perfect world where the unemployment rate is zero, the possibility of losing your job hangs over your head continually. The economy might shift, for example, and sales might plummet; or your company might be bought by another company and then "downsized"; that is, workers might be fired. Nowadays, even companies with robust sales fire workers to be more cost-efficient and productive (Uchitelle 1996). For instance, several years ago, AT&T, a large communications company that was not losing money, announced that it would fire some 30,000 workers. The reason was to become more competitive in the future, when the company anticipated splitting into three smaller companies (Sloan 1996). Ironically, downsizing may be quite profitable to the chief executive officer. The fewer the workers, the more profitable the corporation and the higher the bonuses and incentive pay for the CEO. Evidently, even an employee of a successful company must face the question, Am I next?

In the uncertain atmosphere created by unemployment, many workers now suffer from **job loss anxiety**—that is, anxiety caused by the insecurity of their jobs. Over the course of a year, about 10 percent of the workforce worries about losing their jobs in the near future, and 50 percent wish they had more job security (GSS 2000; gallup.org 2003, accessed September 1, 2003) Recently, one worker in three reported being laid off during the past three years (*New York Times*, September 1, 2003:A8). Education, however, appears to make a difference: the more education workers have the less job loss anxiety they experience (see Figure 9.3, NORC 1998).

Anxiety about job loss has many negative consequences for both the individual and society. It reduces people's confidence in their future, affects the amount of money they are willing to spend, reduces their faith in society, and contributes to voter dissatisfaction (see the What Do You Think? box.) In the United States, both political parties try to capitalize on people's anxieties about work, and when unemployment rises and job loss anxiety increases, each party blames the other (Lewin 1994; Chapter 10).

In some respects, job loss anxiety and unemployment are fundamental to industrial capitalism. The capitalist system relies on the marketplace to decide who is hired and who is fired. Although consumers benefit from the many goods and services cheaply and abundantly provided through capitalism, those same people are also workers, and in that role, they pay a price: the psychological distress of unemployment and nagging anxiety about job loss. Of course, unemployment also occurs under socialism, but socialist societies typically provide generous unemployment benefits, and the government often prevents private companies from engaging in massive layoffs (Tagliabue 1996). In Japan—which has a unique system combining capitalism and socialism—large companies work closely with the government and try to provide loyal workers with lifetime employment.

Job loss anxiety ▲ Anxiety suffered by workers that is caused by the perceived insecurity of their jobs.

FIGURE 9.3 Job Loss Anxiety

Most workers feel fairly secure in their present jobs. However, education makes a substantial difference. Workers with less than a high school education, as the chart shows, are more likely to feel the pressures of job loss anxiety than workers with a graduate degree.

Should they loss their jobs, only a minority of workers think that it will be easy to find another comparable job. With the exception of workers with a bachelors degree, education does not have too much of an effect. For instance, workers with a graduate degree are about as optimistic as workers with less than a high school education.

CQ *Can you suggest some reasons why education makes workers feel secure in their present jobs but does not increase their optimism about finding a comparable job?*

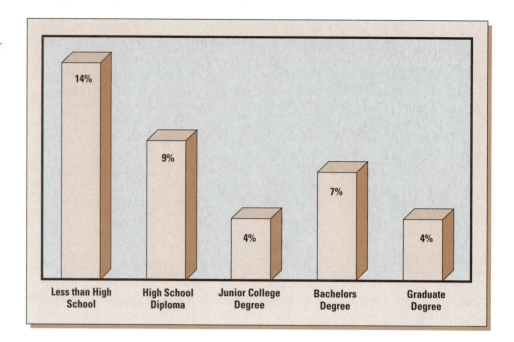

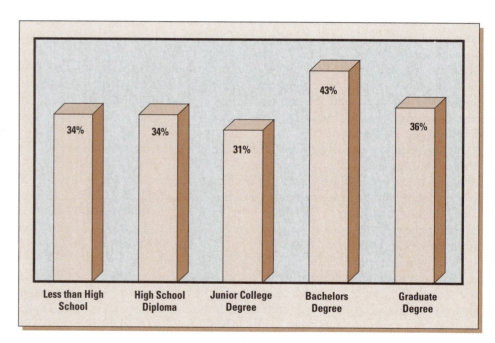

● ■ ▲ **Pausing to Think**   About Unemployment and Job Loss Anxiety

The unemployment rate is watched closely because it indicates the health of the economy and of the broader society. Currently, a rate of 5 percent is considered acceptable, although among some racial-ethnic minorities, the unemployment rate is about twice that figure. Many people suffer from job loss anxiety, and the unemployed may lose confidence in their future and in society, curtail spending, and become dissatisfied with their political leaders.

CQ Are you personally concerned about unemployment and job loss? ◆ How can you best protect yourself from these unpleasant features of the economy? ◆ How important is a good education?

The trust or confidence that people have in societal institutions greatly contributes to the vitality, efficiency, and effectiveness of the society. Such trust is one type of "social capital"; the trustworthiness you attribute to your friends, groups, community, and society is another type (see Putnam 2000). Confidence in business is especially important in a capitalist system. For instance, when confidence is high, people are more likely to invest in the stock market, to buy cars and homes, and to take out loans to pay the cost of going to school. But when confidence is low, people tend to be frugal and to avoid risk, thus pushing the economy down and thereby making a weak economy even weaker.

In the case of the United States, about one-fourth of the people have a great deal of confidence in American business.

Men and women are about the same, but race makes a difference: 30 percent of white Americans have a great deal of confidence in business as compared with 15 percent of African Americans (NORC 1998).

CQ *Can you develop a theoretical assertion to explain why African Americans and whites differ in the amount of confidence they have in American financial institutions?

*To answer this critical question, review the box "What Is Critical Thinking?" in Chapter 1, and pay special attention to the discussion of assertions.

Sociological Analysis of the Economic Order

The three major perspectives in sociology—functionalism, conflict theory, and symbolic interactionism—focus on different aspects of the economic order. In the following pages, we will show how these perspectives help us better to understand the economic aspects of social life. (See Table 9.1 for a comparison of these perspectives.)

The Functionalist Perspective

Functionalist theorists are highly interested in how a society maintains its stability over time. With regard to economic systems, these theorists say that societal stability is achieved by fulfilling the following requirements or functions.

TABLE 9.1

[a]The functionalist and conflict perspectives were introduced in Chapters 1 and 2, and symbolic interaction was discussed in Chapter 3.

Comparison of Three Theoretical Perspectives on the Economic Order

PERSPECTIVE[a]	VIEW OF THE ECONOMY	KEY CONCEPTS AND PROCESSES
Functionalism	Sees the economy as helping society adapt to the environment by efficient production of goods and services	Function Innovation
Conflict Theory	Sees the economy as inherently unstable, producing class conflict and inequality	Worker alienation
Symbolic Interaction	Sees individuals as creating and sustaining the economy through the process of acquiring knowledge and ways of thinking about work and careers	Informal and formal agents of socialization

Andrew Carnegie (1835–1919) was a powerful figure in the history of the steel industry. When he retired in 1901, his net worth exceeded $300 million, and he began donating millions of dollars to charity, mostly to build libraries. Bill Gates is chairman of Microsoft Corporation. A contemporary multibillionarie and one of the nation's wealthiest individuals, Gates is revolutionizing the computer industry and is also donating billions to charity.

CQ *Would you expect to find people with the economic accomplishments of Andrew Carnegie or Bill Gates in a socialist economy?* ◆ *Why or why not?*

Distribution of Goods and Services   Functionalists believe that capitalism, with its emphasis on free markets and profit, is well designed to encourage the production and distribution of goods and services. If a market for a new service or product exists, some entrepreneur is likely to discover it and then to try to profit by it. To illustrate, the Federal Express Company (now FedEx) was the idea of a college student who recognized the need for overnight delivery of packages. The student found backers for his idea, and a new and highly efficient package delivery service came into being. Socialist economies, with their centralized bureaucratic structures, do not respond as quickly because they do not provide the high rewards that encourage people to take risks and develop new businesses.

Production of Wealth and Power   Functionalists argue that a close connection between the economy and political institutions allows for greater efficiency in directing and managing the resources of society. For example, in capitalist societies, economic success allows individuals to accumulate wealth, which they then convert into power (Rosenberg and Birdzell 1986). Power then allows these individuals to influence the government and to seek out new areas of investment. The "robber barons" of the nineteenth century illustrate how economic and political power go together. Capitalists such as John D. Rockefeller, Andrew Carnegie, and Andrew Mellon amassed huge personal fortunes. These fortunes then became the basis for far-reaching political influence, which allowed them to extend their financial empires even further. Eventually, their power was curtailed through antitrust legislation, but by that time, they had succeeded in establishing successful companies and transforming entire industries. In a more recent example, Bill Gates, the cofounder of the Microsoft Corporation at age 20, has done much the same thing, transforming the computer software industry, becoming a billionaire, and then encountering antitrust problems (Elmer-Dewitt 1995; Franklin 2003; Greenfeld 2000; Silverstein 1998).

In socialist societies, the relationship between wealth and power is quite different. Socialist economies produce wealth, but they also redistribute it. Compared with capitalist societies, in socialist societies, a smaller share of the wealth generated by industrialists returns to the entrepreneurs who created it. Consequently, the government usually has to step in and subsidize private investment. For instance, when the Communist Party ruled the former Soviet Union, the state was supposed to create new industry, but important state bureaucrats and politicians benefited the most from the existing economic order. This system proved to be dysfunctional because state bureaucrats lived well even when the economy sagged and productivity declined.

Innovation According to the functionalist perspective, capitalist societies adapt well to changes in their environment because they innovate continually (Samuelson and Nordhaus 1998). The reason is that businesses must continually compete for customers by offering new services and products. Although socialist economies also innovate, they are highly selective in applying their resources. Consumers might be asked to pay more for some products to protect inefficient industries. For example, although Japan has a highly innovative and productive economy in automobiles, steel, and electronics, it lags behind in food, beer, soaps, detergents, and similar consumer goods. In large part, this lag is due to governmental policies that protect inefficient local producers while encouraging innovation in export industries (Nasar 1993; Sterngold 1995).

The Conflict Perspective

In contrast to functionalists, who emphasize stability, conflict theorists emphasize the inherent instability of the economic order. Some conflict theorists even argue that capitalism is self-contradictory and therefore is doomed to failure in the long run.

As we already know, Karl Marx (1844) laid the foundations for the conflict perspective. He and later conflict theorists believed that the free market produces class conflict and worker alienation. Because we have already discussed these aspects of Marx's belief in Chapters 1 and 6, we will concentrate here on how capitalism produces inequity.

When considering the economic order as a whole, conflict theorists often point to the vast inequities produced by capitalism (Granovetter and Tilly 1988; Pampel 2000). For example, the richest 5 percent of American families receive 20 percent of all the income earned by all the families in the United States (U.S. Bureau of the Census 2002). Almost all of the increased wealth generated by the economy goes to the top 20 percent of American families (Rothchild 1995). A student in the top quarter of American families has 19 times the chance of earning a B.A. degree by the age of 24 than a student in the bottom quarter (Gitlin 1995). As these statistics indicate, even though capitalism produces great benefits, it does not distribute them very equally.

The vast inequality produced by capitalism is not perceived as a problem by most people in the United States, however, because capitalism is supported by an ideology that justifies "winners and losers." Accordingly, those people who compete successfully are considered to have earned the right to whatever wealth they manage to accumulate. Thus, the rich can legitimately grow richer while the poor remain impoverished. Finally, conflict theorists point out that the inequities generated by capitalism are self-perpetuating. The children of the rich—who have done little to earn their own wealth—are nevertheless rich because their parents are rich. These same children can thus attend elite schools and interact with others like themselves. They can use their contacts, credentials, and wealth to claim the best-paying, most prestigious jobs in society and thereby distance themselves further from those who do not come from a privileged background. The rich and their children do not suffer from job loss anxiety, and they stand to benefit the most from high corporate profits. The net effect is that inequality becomes a central feature of the social structure that supports capitalism in the first place (see Chapters 6 and 12; Eitzen and Zinn 2000).

During Take Your Daughter to Work Day, a young girl learns what bond trading is all about.

123 STUDY TIP

Analyze the functionalist, conflict, and symbolic interactionist perspectives on the economy. Describe your view of which aspects of each seem to make sense and which do not. Based on your analysis, decide which approach you feel is most accurate.

Career socialization ▲ The process of acquiring knowledge and ways of thinking about work and careers.

Occupational inheritance ▲ Children entering the same occupation as a parent.

The Symbolic Interactionist Perspective

Whereas functionalist and conflict theorists study the operations and consequences of the economic order, symbolic interactionists examine the interactions between the individual, the group, and the economy. In doing so, many symbolic interactionists stress the impact of **career socialization**: the process of acquiring knowledge and ways of thinking about work and careers (Hughes 1958; Shibutani 1986).

Work and career socialization takes place throughout the life cycle, and much of it is conducted by the agents of socialization: individuals and other sources that are especially influential in the learning process. As discussed in Chapter 3, there are two general types of agents: formal and informal.

Informal Agents of Socialization Usually, parents are the earliest and most influential informal agents of socialization. With regard to economic behavior, they influence their children's orientation toward work and set them on certain career paths. Despite the popular image of "rebellious children," children often enter the same occupation as their parents. This process is called **occupational inheritance**. In some cases, occupational inheritance begins when parents bring their children into the family business, first to do odd jobs and later to manage it. In other cases, occupational inheritance involves socialization for a specific profession. To illustrate, the children of a physician have the opportunity to see their parent at work, become familiar with medical jargon, observe the inner workings of a hospital, and meet their parent's medical colleagues. And in the case of physicians, their high incomes make it possible for their children to attend good colleges and universities and to afford medical school. Although occupational inheritance does not mean that all children follow in their parents' footsteps, a large number do. Peers are another important agent of informal socialization. They can be role models, act as a sounding board for ideas about career choices, and serve as a source of information. Peers also can help the novice enter a given field.

The mass media are another important agent of career socialization. Television, films, newspapers, and books provide a steady stream of work-related role models. Although the mass media seldom depict work realistically, they can reinforce cultural values about work and dramatize the rewards attached to certain occupations. For instance, the increasing number of mothers who work full-time has prompted television programs to include working mothers in their casts of characters, thus implicitly reinforcing the idea that women with children can and should work (Cantor and Cantor 1986).

Formal Agents of Socialization While the family, peers, and media provide informal socialization, occupational socialization also takes place formally—that is, through the schools and through work training programs. To illustrate, colleges and universities employ counselors who help students identify possible career tracks and assess their potential for different types of careers. College career counselors like to talk with a student long before graduation, often as early as the junior year. In this way, the student is given adequate time to learn how to search for a job. For example, many students do not know how to prepare an adequate résumé or how to research the companies they would like to work for. Career counselors can also help a student join an appropriate network through informational interviewing, volunteer work, and internships.

Employers themselves are perhaps the most important source of formal career socialization. A large company may require new managers to pass courses in the company's accounting procedures; police departments require rookies to attend a training academy; and the military requires recruits to undergo basic training (see Hodson and Sullivan 1990). In each case, the required training is so specialized that the organization cannot rely on the broader society to provide it. In contrast, other training is so general that new workers arrive on the job almost completely socialized. Secretaries, nurses, engineers, and computer programmers, for example, receive much of their training before starting their careers.

● ■ ▲ **Pausing to Think** About Sociological Analysis of the Economic Order

Functionalist theory argues that the economy distributes goods and services and produces wealth, power, and innovation. Conflict theory emphasizes the inequalities produced by the economic order. Symbolic interaction theory focuses on how the various informal and formal agents of socialization prepare people to enter the world of work.

CQ What are the influences on your choice of career? ◆ Do you plan on visiting a career counselor at your college before you graduate? ◆ Why or why not?

The Economy in the Twenty-First Century

Today the United States has the single largest economy of any nation; still, the American economic order is undergoing fundamental changes. What are these changes, and what will the economy of the United States be like in the future?

One prediction is fairly clear: if the United States is not already a postindustrial society, it soon will be (see Chapter 2; see the Society Today box). A process of **deindustrialization** is taking place, and service jobs now outnumber manufacturing jobs (Alderson 1999). Soon, service-producing activities will account for two-thirds of all employment in the United States. More specifically, employment in health services will increase substantially, and computer and data processing services will lead the way (U.S. Bureau of the Census 2002).

Approximately 5 million of the new jobs created in the postindustrial economy will be in executive, managerial, administrative, or professional occupations. Such jobs are typically well paid, require a college or advanced degree, and provide high worker satisfaction (see Figure 9.4; Simpson and Simpson 1995). However, the

Society Today ● ■ ▲

Disaster and the Internet

The terrorist attack on the World Trade Center on September 11, 2001 resulted not only in terrible loss of life and massive physical destruction but it also resulted in a widespread disruption of vital economic and government communication systems. On that terrible Tuesday of the attack, many global companies had great difficulty in locating their staff and in communicating with their worldwide facilities and offices. This event underlined the importance for companies to have both backup communication systems and plans for disaster recovery.

Several lessons were learned from that attack. First, that it is vital to have redundancy in communication systems. These systems should take full advantage of such things as instant Internet messaging services. Second, that corporate web sites should be used as information clearinghouses for employees and customers. Messages can be posted as to where people are located, what needs they have, and what are expected courses of action. Third, it is important for all staff to have cellphones that may be used during periods when the wireless networks are not overloaded. Fourth, having a text-messaging service that can supplement regular cellphone use. Fifth, having a data backup system located at a remote and secure site.

Finally, it is very important to have a detailed disaster communications system plan that is reviewed and updated regularly. That plan itself should be designed so that the chance is low of it being sabotaged (ebusinessform.com accessed November 11, 2003).

CQ What do you think? How important is it for a company to invest resources in a complex backup communication system?

Deindustrialization ▲ A process of economic change in which an economy is losing jobs in the industrial sector and adding jobs in the service sector.

FIGURE 9.4

In general, workers are fairly well satisfied with their jobs and working conditions. However, as this chart shows, there are a few differences among professionals/executives, white-collar workers, and blue-collar workers.

SOURCE: (Gallop Poll, September, 2003); gallop.com; accessed December, 2003.

CQ *What do you think are the reasons for the differences in job satisfaction?*

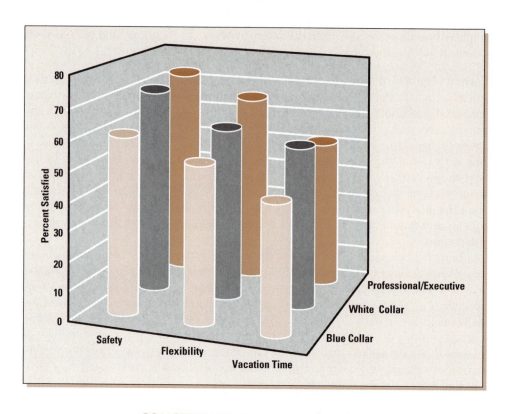

CONCEPT WEB Economy and Society

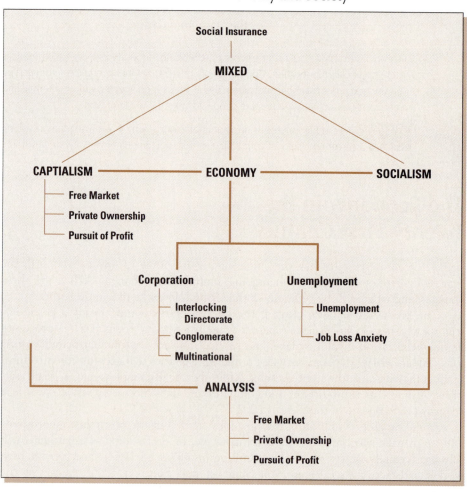

Above is a concept web for Economy and Society. You will note the web includes the characteristics of Capitalism but does not include the characteristics of Socialism. Add the characteristics of Socialism to this web.

majority of the new jobs (about 11 million) will be in the low-paying sector of the service economy: clerical, retail sales, food preparation, cleaning services, and so forth. These jobs generally require less education and do not provide as high worker satisfaction. Moreover, as these lower-tier jobs become more prevalent in a community, the tax base erodes, and it becomes more difficult for taxpayers to fund public schools and other important government services. Thus, as upper-tier "good" jobs become more scarce, there is likely to be increased tension in communities as well as in families. If such a "two-tiered" workforce develops, it may also increase social tensions along racial and ethnic lines, as access to the good jobs becomes ever more competitive (Chapter 7).

A second major trend concerns the role of women in the economic order (Caplow 1991; Chapter 8). Women are now moving into many occupations that were once male dominated, and in the next century, women will be represented in virtually all occupations. Women will also succeed in breaking through several more layers of the glass ceiling and will increase their representation among upper-level corporate managers and highly paid professionals. It will be more common to see women as airline pilots, managers of large corporations, surgeons, and college presidents. With more and more women working outside the home, family size will continue to shrink, and the length of time men and women spend raising children will decrease. Perhaps more people will tend to define themselves in terms of their work or leisure activities, and fewer people will define themselves in terms of parenthood. For that reason, American society will probably become even less child centered than it is today.

Looking Ahead

Although the economy is a fundamental institution, all societies must also have some means of providing political order. Consequently, the next chapter examines the institution of government, the processes of politics, and the general issue of power in society.

WHAT YOU SHOULD KNOW ●■▲

1. **How has the economy changed with the Great Social Transformation?**

In traditional societies, the family or kin group is the chief economic unit of society, and work involves almost every family member. In industrial societies, output relies on machines, factories are the primary unit of production, and businesses become bureaucracies.

2. **What are the basic characteristics of a capitalist economy?**

Industrial capitalism rests on the assumptions that a free market exists, that private individuals may own property, and that people are free to pursue profits for themselves. Adam Smith developed the basic theoretical principles of capitalism and employed the metaphor of the "invisible hand" to represent the free play of economic forces that shape both the marketplace and the broader capitalist economy.

3. **How does socialism differ from capitalism as an economic system?**

Capitalists rely on the free market and assume that some people will acquire a greater share of society's wealth than other people. Socialists believe that everyone should share equally in the goods and services produced by society, and they rely on the government to run the economy.

4. Why is there a tendency today for a convergence toward a mixed economy?

Capitalism and socialism may be converging toward some middle ground. Both capitalist and socialist societies are influenced by new technology, the division of labor, major population shifts, urbanization, and bureaucratization. Given such influences, social relationships necessarily become more impersonal, formal, and rational.

5. What is the nature of the corporation as an economic actor?

The corporation is controlled by a board elected to office by shareholders, but top management holds most of the power because major shareholders routinely approve the policies offered by top management. The board also routinely approves new board members, most of whom are selected by top management.

6. How is the power of the modern corporation manifested?

The sheer size of some corporations makes them powerful, and some corporations are made even more powerful through interlocking directorates. The power of conglomerates lies in their penetration of diverse markets, their control of wealth, and their access to technology. Many giant corporations have worldwide holdings and markets.

7. Why is unemployment a problem both for society and for individuals?

Unemployed people pay little or no taxes, and some require government support. Job loss anxiety is a problem for many people, and unemployed people often lose faith in themselves and in their society, and so they suffer from depression.

8. How do functionalists view the economy?

Functionalists argue that the economy creates and distributes goods and services, encourages innovation, and produces wealth.

9. How do conflict theorists see the economy?

Conflict theorists emphasize the inequities produced by the free-market system. They point out that in the United States most of the wealth is owned by a small number of people, and these people and their offspring benefit the most from the system.

10. How do symbolic interactionists see the economy?

Symbolic interaction theorists emphasize how the various informal and formal agents of socialization contribute to preparing people for entering the world of work. Increasingly, employers are major agents of formal socialization.

11. What can be said of work and the economy in the twenty-first century?

The United States is moving from an industrial to a postindustrial society. Manufacturing jobs are being replaced by low-paying service positions, and women are moving into occupations that were once male dominated. In the future, work may take on even greater importance, and society may become less child centered.

TEST YOUR KNOWLEDGE ●■▲

Key Terms Matching

Match each of these key terms with the best definition or example from the numbered items that follow. Write the letter preceding the key term in the blank before the definition that you choose.

a. capitalism

b. career socialization

c. conglomerates

d. deindustrialization

e. entrepreneurs

_____ **1.** An economic system in which the means of production are privately owned and market forces determine production and distribution.

_____ **2.** Companies that conduct business in several countries but have their central headquarters in one country.

_____ **3.** A process of economic change in which an economy is losing jobs in the industrial sector and adding jobs in the service sector.

_____ **4.** The system of trade in which those selling goods or services are permitted to charge an amount greater than their costs in producing or buying the good or service.

f. free-market competition

g. interlocking directorate

h. job loss anxiety

i. mixed economy

j. multinationals

k. occupational inheritance

l. private ownership of property

m. pursuit of profit

n. social insurance

o. socialism

p. unemployed

_____ 5. People who are without jobs but are seeking work.

_____ 6. Anxiety suffered by workers that is caused by the perceived insecurity of their jobs.

_____ 7. An economic system in which the means of production are collectively owned and the state directs production and distribution of services.

_____ 8. The idea that government is responsible for guaranteeing a minimum standard of living for everyone.

_____ 9. The process of acquiring knowledge and ways of thinking about work and careers.

_____ 10. People who take great risks to achieve success in the marketplace.

_____ 11. The rule of property ownership that vests in the individual the right to own property unencumbered by government rules, regulations, and planning.

_____ 12. Members of the boards of directors of corporations sitting on the boards of directors of other corporations, thereby linking the corporations together.

_____ 13. Giant corporations composed of other corporations that produce a variety of products and conduct business in several markets.

_____ 14. An economy that mixes features of both capitalists and socialist systems, including both public and private ownership of property and limits on free-market competition.

_____ 15. The buying and selling of good and services unencumbered by government rules, regulations, and planning.

_____ 16. Children entering the same occupation as a parent.

Multiple Choice

Circle the letter of your choice.

1. The term for the social institution that determines what will be produced, how production will be accomplished, and who will receive what is produced is
   a. division of labor.
   b. exchange field.
   c. economy.
   d. none of the above.

2. Which of the following did NOT occur as the result of industrialization?
   a. The family became the main economic unit.
   b. Bureaucratic rules replaced traditional authority.
   c. Factories replaced the family as the primary unit of production.
   d. Work became more impersonal.

3. What is the chief economic unit in communal societies?
   a. husband/wife couple
   b. small business
   c. central bureaucratic committee
   d. family or kinship

4. In industrial societies, the economy is organized to facilitate
   a. large-scale producers.
   b. big-business.
   c. mass consumers.
   d. all of the above.

5. Which if the following is a characteristic of a socialist government?
   a. It decides which goods are produced, and how they are distributed.
   b. It owns and operates strategic businesses and industries.
   c. It is responsible for guaranteeing a minimum standard of living for everyone.
   d. All of the above.

6. When the United States adopted the welfare program, it became what type of economy?
   a. capitalist
   b. socialist
   c. mixed
   d. communist

7. Socialism and capitalism have been
   a. growing more unlike each other.
   b. converging toward some middle ground.
   c. incorporating elements of communism.
   d. bypassed by the postindustrial economy.

8. Which of the following is true of conglomerates?
   a. They help stabilize profits.
   b. They facilitate access to the technology, skills, and experience of the acquired company.
   c. They prevent "unfriendly" takeovers.
   d. All of the above.

9. General Motors has direct and indirect links with 700 other corporations because members of its board of directors sit on the other corporations' boards. Therefore, General Motors
   a. is a conglomerate.
   b. is a multinational.
   c. has an interlocking directorate.
   d. is all of the above.

10. Honda is headquartered in Japan, but it has many plants in the United States. Thus, Honda
    a. is a conglomerate.
    b. has an interlocking directorate.
    c. is an entrepreneur.
    d. is a multinational.

11. Which of the following is NOT true of capitalism, according to functionalism?
    a. It encourages innovation.
    b. It encourages entrepreneurialism.
    c. It allows people to convert wealth into power.
    d. It is self-contradictory and will destroy itself.

12. Ted's father was an engineer. When Ted was young, his father would take him to work and teach him about engineering. Ted subsequently became an engineer. What is the term for this process?
    a. entrepreneurship
    b. occupational inheritance
    c. social insurance
    d. none of the above

Identifying Sociological Perspectives on the Economy

For each of the following statements, identify the sociological perspective associated with the statement by writing F for functionalist, C for conflict, SI for symbolic interactionist, in the appropriate blank.

_____ 1. The mass media is an important agent of career socialization by providing a steady stream of work-related models that reinforce cultural values about work.

_____ 2. Schools and work-training programs are important formal agents of career socialization.

_____ 3. Capitalism produces great inequalities among people, with the richest 10 percent of American families controlling more wealth than the remaining 90 percent.

_____ 4. Capitalism, with its emphasis on free markets and profit, is well designed to encourage the production and distribution of goods and services.

_____ 5. Capitalist societies adapt well to change in their environment because they innovate continually.

_____ 6. A close connection between the economy and the political institutions allows for greater efficiency in directing and managing the resources of society.

_____ 7. Most people in the United States do not have a problem with the inequalities created by capitalism because they have an ideology that supports and justifies winners and losers.

_____ 8. Career socialization takes place throughout the life cycle.

True-False

Indicate your response to each of the following statements by circling T for true, or F for false.

T   F   1. Adam Smith's idea behind free-market competition is that it will produce the highest quality goods at the best prices.

T   F   2. The economic policy "laissez-faire" means not interfering with the free play of economic forces.

T   F   3. With more women working outside the home, family size will increase.

T   F   4. Income inequality is greater in socialist systems than in capitalist systems.

T   F   5. Capitalism seems to be more efficient than it actually is, often seeking profits in the short term and thus destroying prospects for profit in the long term.

T   F   6. Socialists believe that all people should get what they work for.

T   F   7. To a certain extent, multinational corporations benefit their host country by creating jobs, generating income, and training local workforces.

T   F   8. Zero unemployment is attainable.

T   F   9. Employers themselves are perhaps the most important source of formal career socialization.

T　F　**10.** In the future, service jobs will be divided into two tiers, one offering well-paying jobs with high satisfaction and the other offering low-paying jobs with little satisfaction.

T　F　**11.** Symbolic interaction theorists emphasize how the various informal and formal agents of socialization contribute to preparing people for entering the world of work.

T　F　**12.** Job loss anxiety reduces people's confidence in their future.

T　F　**13.** Companies that conduct business in several countries are called "multiphased" organizations.

T　F　**14.** Conglomerates tend to focus on the mass production of one good or service.

T　F　**15.** Socialist and capitalist economies are not likely to converge.

NOTE: The answers to these exercises are at the end of the book.

For additional practice tests and other resources please visit the companion web site at http://www.prenhall.com/curry.

Essay

1. What are the formal and informal agents of career socialization?

2. Discuss in detail each of the three assumptions upon which industrial capitalism rests.

3. What evidence is there for the concentration of power among corporations?

4. Why isn't zero unemployment possible?

5. How has economic activity changed as societies go from a hunting and gathering society to an industrialized society?

10 The Political Order

Chapter Outline

Soviet communism began with a massive uprising against Czar Nicholas II. The Bolsheviks seized power on November 7, 1917, and soon communism became a major political rival to Western-style democracy. Following World War II, the United States embarked on a policy of preventing communism from spreading into formerly noncommunist nations, and the cold war began in earnest. For almost the next 50 years, American policy was shaped by the threat of the Soviet Union, China, Cuba, North Korea, North Vietnam, and other communist nations.

To combat communism, the United States entered into military alliances such as the North Atlantic Treaty Organization (NATO), which was originally intended to oppose Soviet expansion in Europe. The United States also entered into wars, bearing the brunt of the fighting during the Korean War to push back the invasion of communist North Korea. During this period, the so-called witch hunts took place—efforts to drive communists and communist sympathizers out of government, private industry, and public service. Many screenwriters and other creative artists were blacklisted for their leftist leanings, and many teachers and professors lost their jobs. Although the furor of the witch hunts slowly diminished, it remained true that an avowed communist would have great difficulty finding employment or entering public service. In 1965 the United States entered the Vietnam War in a major way. As in the Korean War, the goal in Vietnam was to help the pro-Western South fight the communist North. Throughout the cold war, the American military maintained a vast arsenal of nuclear submarines, intercontinental missiles, and long-distance bombers in constant readiness to launch an attack on the Soviet Union (Caplow 1991). The Soviet Union's military was no less impressive, and it countered every American move with a weapon or strategy of its own (Sivard 1986, 1993).

When the Soviet Union collapsed in 1991, almost without warning, the United States suddenly found itself without a monolithic enemy. To a large extent, many of the strategic political questions facing the United States today stem from this sudden change (Beisel 1994; Dandeker 1994). Now, without the threat of the Soviet military, how should the United States use its military power to suppress terrorists? Should the United States seek international support for military operations or go it alone? How much power should the government have to suppress terrorism at home? Questions such as these are inherently **political** because they involve the distribution of power across the institutions, organizations, and individuals of a society. Viewed this way, every society has a particular arrangement of power that is most evident in its form of government, its economy, and its social class structure (see Chapters 6 and 9).

Chapter Preview

We begin with a discussion of the Great Social Transformation and the political order. Next, we introduce some important concepts used to study power and authority in society, and then we broaden the topic to examine the role of states and nations in the contemporary world. We continue the discussion with a description of contemporary political processes in the United States. Next, we compare how the three sociological perspectives might be used to analyze the political institutions of a society, and we close with some thoughts on the political order of the future.

The Great Social Transformation and the Political Order

Throughout most of human history, the political order was relatively simple. In hunting and gathering societies, for instance, tribal members were organized into kinship networks, and elders had the right to settle disputes and to impose punishments. Virtually everyone participated in politics because political processes were informal and were conducted among small groups of coequals (Maybury-Lewis 1999).

With the development of horticultural and agrarian societies, the political order changed. Aristocracies developed through control of land, and government policies were written into codes that established rights. Because these societies were relatively large and complex, consensus was more difficult to achieve, and governmental decisions were enforced by the military or the police. Thus, kings had standing armies, and feudal lords kept armed guards close at hand.

Industrialization brought about new changes in the organization of the political order. The landed aristocracy began to lose power to the industrialists, and in England and northern Europe, a new political order developed around a large middle class composed of professionals, private entrepreneurs, and white-collar workers. In these societies, liberal democracy emerged, which was characterized by competing political parties, voting by the common people, a free press, and a relatively unrestrained capitalistic economy. In other societies, however, dictatorship and other forms of totalitarian control became the rule (Lipset 1995).

Power and the Political Order

The political order ultimately rests on a base of **power**: the ability to achieve ends despite resistance (Weber 1947). Power is, in other words, the key to understanding political processes because in every society it is a valuable resource. Those who have it—the powerful—can control those who are relatively powerless. For this reason, the military openly rules in places like Burma and Iraq, and indirectly rules in places such as Peru and Cambodia. The United States is actually an anomaly in that the American military has enormous power at its disposal, yet it plays a relatively minor and indirect role in shaping public policy within the U.S.

Although power remains a central feature of society, not all power is the same. Max Weber distinguished between using power legitimately and using it illegitimately. A legitimate use of power occurs when society approves of the way in which the power is applied. Thus, the state may imprison people for violating laws; the chief executive officer of a corporation may hire and fire workers; or a schoolteacher may flunk a student. In each case, the person wielding power has the legitimate right to use that power. Weber called this type of power **authority**. In contrast to the legitimate use of power is the illegitimate use of power. For example, a chief executive officer who sexually harasses a worker, or a teacher who flunks a student out of spite, is wielding power, but not in a way that society deems appropriate or legitimate. Weber called this type of power **coercion**.

Weber went on to devise a scheme for categorizing legitimate power—authority—into three types: traditional authority, legal-rational authority, and charismatic authority (Gerth and Mills 1958; Weber 1947). This scheme helps clarify the role that power plays in society, and for that reason, sociologists refer to it frequently.

Traditional Authority

Authority that is legitimated by the historical beliefs and practices of the society is called **traditional authority**. Because it is rooted in tradition, such authority often has

---

Political ▲ Involving the distribution of power across the institutions, organizations, and individuals of a society.

Power ▲ The ability to achieve one's ends despite resistance.

Authority ▲ The socially legitimated use of power.

Coercion ▲ The process of compelling others to do something against their will.

Traditional authority ▲ Authority that is legitimated by the historical beliefs and practices of society.

a sacred or near-sacred quality. Monarchs, emperors, and various kinds of nobility owe their authority to the traditions and customs that bestow power on them. Although followers might disagree with what a traditional ruler does, they rarely question the ruler's right to do it. Traditional authority is a characteristic of the political systems of communal societies (Chapter 2).

Because the traditional ruler's authority is rooted in cherished customs, a radical change in the society's culture must occur before people are willing to accept an alternative form of rule. For instance, it took the devastating defeat of Japan in World War II to change Japanese cultural beliefs about their emperor. According to Japanese tradition, the emperor was divine, and therefore the Japanese people obeyed him without question. After the defeat of Japan, however, the emperor renounced his divinity. As Japan rebuilt, the old traditions surrounding the emperor gradually faded until today he is regarded as a symbol of the nation but not as its divine ruler.

The emperor and empress of Japan. The Japanese emperor traditionally was considered to be divine. Following the Japanese defeat in World War II, however, the emperor renounced his divinity. Today the emperor is considered a symbol of the nation but not its divine ruler.

Legal-Rational Authority

In contrast to traditional authority, **legal-rational authority** derives its legitimacy from the rules and laws that define the rights, duties, and obligations of rulers and followers. In most cases, these rules and laws are laid down in constitutions, charters, articles of incorporation, handbooks, and other written documents. Legal-rational authority commonly characterizes the political leadership of associational societies.

Legal-rational authority resides in the position rather than in the personal qualities of an individual. Thus, minor officials of the Internal Revenue Service, whose function is to collect the federal income tax, can exercise the authority of their position to impose fines and penalties on wayward taxpayers. The taxpayer in question could be a police officer who, acting within the boundaries of his or her position, has the authority to write tickets, arrest suspects, and even shoot people. Once outside these boundaries, however, the IRS official and the police officer have no more and no less authority than the average citizen. A very well-known incident of an official overstepping the boundaries of office was the so-called Watergate scandal of the 1970s. After a lengthy congressional investigation, mounting evidence strongly suggested that President Richard Nixon had obstructed a criminal investigation into the activities of his aides. His actions constituted an illegal use of presidential power, and he eventually had to resign from office.

Charismatic Authority

The third type of authority is perhaps the best known, because the word charisma has become a part of everyday language. Contrary to its everyday meaning, however, Weber defined **charismatic authority** as the power that is legitimated by an individual's exceptional personal attributes, such as a magnetic personality, an extraordinary driving energy, or a powerful aura of wisdom and grace. Through the sheer force of these characteristics, a charismatic individual can inspire devotion and command obedience (Shamir 1994). Charisma is much more than a matter of a charming personality or pearly white teeth, however. In Weber's view, the charismatic person is convinced of some sort of divine election to perform a great task that is usually outside the existing political order, and is able to convince others to share this perception. Truly charismatic people in Weber's sense are rare, but a list might include Joan of Arc, Abraham Lincoln, Martin Luther King, Jr., Mother Teresa, and others who have been able to achieve great feats and inspire multitudes of followers. Because it is so closely tied to an individual's personal attributes, charismatic authority cannot easily be transferred from one person to another. Thus, when a charismatic leader passes from the scene, his or her work may pass as well, since succeeding leaders are unable to attract and organize followers to the same extent as did the charismatic leader.

Charismatic leaders rise above other people in their vision of what society should be or should become. They therefore often spearhead revolutionary movements and

Legal-rational authority ▲ Authority that derives its legitimacy from the rules and laws that define the rights, duties, and obligations of rulers and followers.

Charismatic authority ▲ Power that is legitimated by an individual's exceptional personal attributes, such as a magnetic personality, an extraordinary driving energy, or a powerful aura of wisdom and grace.

Dictator of the Soviet Union from 1924–1953, Joseph Stalin was a charismatic but bloody leader. He exemplifies how charismatic qualities may be combined with evil intent.

rebellions. Chairman Mao Zedong, for instance, inspired millions of Chinese peasants to overthrow the old political order of China and to embrace communism; Mohandas Gandhi led India's drive to gain independence from British rule; and Jesus laid the foundation for Christianity, which soon replaced the many religious cults of ancient Rome. Likewise, Muhammad established Islam, which has become one of the most dynamic religious and political forces in the world today (Chapter 13).

Although charisma is an exceptional quality, it is not necessarily reserved for admirable people. Joseph Stalin, who was dictator of the Soviet Union from 1924 to 1953, has gone down as one of history's most evil figures. He executed, imprisoned, and deliberately starved to death millions of people to accomplish his goals. Yet in face-to-face interactions, Stalin had a riveting personality and remarkable charm. Even experienced diplomats who knew of his bloody record fell under the spell of his charisma (Pipes 1991).

In identifying these three types of authority, Weber knew that they do not exist in pure form. In fact, all three may be present in a society. The United States is an example of this occurrence. The United States was founded on the principles contained in the Constitution, a legal-rational document. Although the Constitution is the foundation of American government, over the course of two centuries, a traditional basis of power has also emerged. For example, nowhere does the Constitution describe the Democratic or the Republican party, yet a two-party system exists and has been legitimated by tradition. Charismatic leaders have also appeared on the scene from time to time. Presidents such as Dwight D. Eisenhower, John F. Kennedy, and Ronald Reagan seemingly commanded large followings by the sheer magnetism of their personalities. These presidents were extremely powerful because they could exercise a combination of legal-rational, traditional, and charismatic authority to further their political agendas.

If the categories of traditional, legal-rational, and charismatic authority are hypothetical, why are they important? The answer is that they provide us with guidelines for identifying the types of power that exist, and furthermore, they indicate how raw power becomes legitimate authority. Stated another way, each category of authority is an **ideal type**: an abstract description, constructed from a number of cases, that reveals the essential features of a concept (Weber 1922).

● ■ ▲ **Pausing to Think**   About Power and the Political Order

Society's political order ultimately rests on power: the politically powerful can control those who are relatively powerless. Power that is legitimated by society is called authority. Max Weber identified three types of authority: traditional, legal-rational, and charismatic. Traditional authority is rooted in society's cherished customs and beliefs; legal-rational authority is rooted in the rules and laws of a society; and charismatic authority is rooted in the personal magnetism of an individual.

 How can a charismatic political leader further his or her political agenda in a way that leaders whose authority is based on the traditional or the legal-rational cannot?

Ideal type ▲ An abstract description, constructed from a number of cases, that reveals the essential features of a concept.

State ▲ The highest political authority within a given territory.

Government ▲ The set of people who are currently engaged in directing the state.

The State and the Exercise of Power

Although the terms *state* and *government* are often used interchangeably in everyday speech, sociologists draw a distinction between them. Technically, the **state** is the highest political authority within a given territory, whereas the **government** is the set of people who currently are engaged in directing the state. Governments come and go, but the state can remain for centuries.

All governments exercise power, but they do not exercise it in the same way or for the same purpose. Governments vary considerably, for instance, in their responsiveness to the people. Sociologists use this variation to categorize states into the following types: authoritarian, totalitarian, and democratic.

Types of States

The Authoritarian State   The **authoritarian state** has three major characteristics. First, the people are excluded from the processes of government; second, little or no opposition to the government is permitted; and third, the government has little interest in the daily lives of the people—provided that the people do not threaten the government or its policies.

At one time in history, the most common type of authoritarian government was a **monarchy**: a system in which political power is passed from person to person on the basis of hereditary claims. This form of rule has existed for thousands of years and continues to exist in some parts of the world. For example, Saudi Arabia and Kuwait are ruled by royal families that claim a hereditary right to power. These families seem to be secure, in part because oil revenues finance generous welfare systems for the people. However, questions remain about the future of these systems. Some Saudi women, for instance, oppose many aspects of the government because they perceive it as being male dominated. At the same time, religious fundamentalists oppose attempts by these governments to modernize. Increasingly, fundamentalist terrorists have targeted Saudi Arabia for attacks. There also remains the nagging question of what will happen when the oil runs out—as it someday must—and the welfare system cannot be so lavishly funded (Bahgat 1998; Faqir 1997; Ijomah 2000; Moghadam 1992).

Another form of authoritarian government is more common: the junta, or rule by a small group of military officers. Juntas frequently hold power in underdeveloped nations. To illustrate, about half of the African nations that have gained independence since the 1960s are now ruled by juntas. These nations, as well as many other Third World countries, are so unstable that the military seems to be the only organization that can guarantee civil order.

The Totalitarian State   In contrast to an authoritarian state, a **totalitarian state** is one in which the government (1) has unlimited power; (2) tolerates no opposition; and (3) exercises close control over its citizens. Some totalitarian regimes are autocracies (rule by a small group), but most are dictatorships (rule by one person). Many dictators have become infamous, among them Joseph Stalin, Adolph Hitler, Saddam Hussein, and "Papa Doc" Duvalier of Haiti.

Whereas authoritarian governments have existed for a long time, totalitarian governments are a relatively new development. Totalitarianism emerged most fully during the twentieth century, in large part because new technology made it possible. For example, a dictator can keep close track of anyone stirring up opposition by using hidden microphones, secret television cameras, telephone taps, and other technological devices. In addition, sophisticated transportation and communication enable the dictator to respond quickly to perceived threats.

Not only do totalitarian regimes suppress political freedoms, but they also exact an immense cost in human suffering. During the late 1970s, the Chinese government punished nearly 1 million college students for supporting Mao Zedong. The government expelled the students from school, paraded them along public streets, and forced them to work in menial jobs (Broaded 1991). In the early 1930s, when dictator Joseph Stalin's communist regime reorganized Soviet agriculture into a system of state-operated collective farms, the resulting chaos caused 7 million Ukrainians to die of starvation. This event eventually figured in the Ukrainian bid for independence from Russia in 1991.

In general, totalitarian regimes have not hesitated to imprison millions of suspected dissenters and to execute them by the hundreds of thousands. Under

King Abdullah II, ruler of Jordan. As a constitutional monarch, his position is secured by both legal-rational authority and traditional authority. A monarchy built into a constitution is a relatively new and somewhat rare form of government.

Authoritarian state ▲ A state that has the following characteristics: (1) the people are excluded from the processes of government; (2) little or no opposition to the government is permitted; and (3) the government has little interest in the daily lives of the people unless they threaten the state's leadership.

Monarchy ▲ A system in which political power is passed from person to person on the basis of hereditary claims.

Totalitarian state ▲ A state that has unlimited power, tolerates no opposition, and exercises close control over its citizens.

totalitarianism, only one official political party exists, such as the Communist Party in North Korea. The party is the political arm of the state, determining everything from who holds public office to what type of music may be played on the radio. Because the party controls access to education, jobs, housing, and other benefits, party membership is highly valued, and only a select few may join. Those who attain membership become an elite class, with power and privileges far greater than those of ordinary citizens.

The Democratic State Totalitarian and authoritarian states are at one end of a continuum, whereas democratic states are at the other end. A **democratic state** allows the people to have an input into government decisions and permits the people to elect and dismiss leaders. Carried to its extreme, a democracy would permit every citizen to participate in every decision made by the government. Because that process is clearly impractical, the representative democracy has evolved. In this form, the democratic state institutionalizes procedures for electing and removing leaders from public office. Typically, candidates from different political parties run for office, and the winners become the representatives of the people (Dahl 2000).

Many totalitarian and authoritarian governments claim to be democracies, and they may even hold elections. In these elections, however, a true choice does not exist because only one party is allowed to run candidates. Under these circumstances, voting might seem to be a meaningless ritual, but voting is important because it adds an aura of legitimacy to the government and state.

Nations and States

We previously defined the state as the highest political authority within a given territory and distinguished between it and the government. It is also important to distinguish between state and nation. A **nation** may be defined as a group that lives within a given territory and that shares a common history, culture, and identity (Gellner 1998). As an example, consider the Iroquois nation. At one time in history, the Iroquois of the Northeast were organized into a league of Six Nations—the Mohawk, Oneida, Onondaga, Cayuga, Tuscarora, and Seneca—all of whom to a greater or lesser extent spoke the Iroquoian language and viewed themselves as members of one nation, especially when dealing with outsiders such as the British (Chapter 7; Maybury-Lewis 1999).

The concepts of nation and state are not mutually exclusive. They may be combined to produce the **nation-state**: the supreme political authority within a territory that incorporates and represents a nation. For instance, Japan is a homogeneous country with a common culture; hence, it is a nation-state. In contrast, the French-speaking population of Quebec constitutes a nation, but it is not the supreme political authority in that territory, because Quebec is a part of Canada (Bourque and Duchastel 2000; Gagnon 1996; Juteau 1994; Mendelshon 2002).

Because of historical circumstances, many countries have political borders that do not correspond with the geographic location of the nations in the region. This arrangement is especially evident in the parts of Africa that were formerly colonized by Great Britain, France, Germany, and Belgium. The colonies later gained independence but retained the territorial boundaries first laid down by their colonial rulers. In some instances, a single nation or tribe in an area was divided among two or more states, whereas in other cases, distinct and sometimes antagonistic nations were thrown together within a single state. Great turmoil and violence has often been the result.

A case in point is Burundi. Once part of German East Africa, Burundi contains several nations, including the Hutus and the Tutsis, within its boundaries (Longman 1999). After Germany's defeat in World War I, Burundi became a Belgian trust, and it received independence in 1962. A series of coups, countercoups, and rebellions followed. Members of the Hutu nation in exile invaded Burundi, and when their

Democratic state ▲ A state that allows the people to have an input into government decisions and permits the people to elect and dismiss leaders.

Nation ▲ A group that lives within a given territory and shares a common history, culture, and identity.

Nation-state ▲ The supreme political authority within a territory that incorporates and represents a nation.

Rwanda: Sculls mark the site of Tutsi massacre. The government keeps the site as a reminder of the horrific slaughter.

invasion failed, some 200,000 Hutus were massacred by the victorious Tutsis. Had the borders of Burundi been drawn to avoid combining two antagonistic nations, perhaps this bloodshed could have been avoided (Drumbl 1999; Niazi 2002; Smith 1995).

It sometimes happens that nations exist but without a state of their own, as illustrated by the history of the Middle East. The Romans conquered Israel in 70 A.D. and destroyed Jerusalem, thus beginning the Jewish diaspora (dispersion). For almost 2,000 years, Jews were scattered throughout the world, eventually settling in countries in Europe, Africa, Asia, and South America (Wirth 1928). Although Jews maintained a culture and an identity, they had no state. Not until 1948 and the founding of Israel did Jews once again have a state that corresponded to their nation.

War and Terrorism

The period 1900 to 2000 has been called the "Century of War." In addition to the hundreds of armed conflicts that took place during that time, two world wars were fought. They are called world wars because so many nations joined sides to form two major blocs: allied and axis. In addition, many nations that did not formally join either bloc were forced to take sides when one bloc or the other threatened or invaded them. In the first of these world wars, approximately 1.8 million soldiers on all sides were killed, along with 1 million civilians. As large as those figures might seem, the toll for the second world war was even larger: 17 million soldiers and 35 million civilians died (Kornblum and Julian 1995:531).

From a sociological perspective, war is a social institution. In other words, every society has a social structure—a collection of firmly entrenched values and norms—that regulates war (Frankel 2003). For instance, the government formally authorizes war on behalf of the nation, passes laws mobilizing the nation to fight the war, and usually agrees to follow the rules of war outlined in the Geneva Convention. **War**, therefore, may be defined as an institutionalized and violent conflict between nations, tribes, and other social entities.

Explanations for War   Because so many wars have been fought throughout human history, many theorists believe that aggression, hostility, and conflict are built into the genetic structure of human beings (for example, Wilson 1993). However, sociologists disagree. Whereas your genes *might* conceivably explain why you get into a fight with

War ▲ An institutionalized and violent conflict between nations, tribes, and other social entities.

another student, your genes cannot explain why your government declares war on another nation. Clearly, the fact that war is an institution requires a social explanation. Several such explanations have been proposed, and in this section we review the most prominent ones.

Carl von Clausewitz and Total War Possibly the best known theory of war was proposed by Carl von Clausewitz, a nineteenth-century Prussian officer and writer (1976 translation). He wrote volumes, but two main points stand out. First, Clausewitz argued that in trying to achieve international goals, nations often clash with each other. To resolve these conflicts, they first attempt diplomatic negotiations. But if that fails, they may go to war. War thus becomes an instrument of foreign policy, or diplomacy pursued by violent means.

Clausewitz's second major point concerns war and society. To him, war was total. He believed that in a time of war, every resource of the society should be redirected towards victory. Civilian factories should be converted to producing war goods, personnel should be conscripted as soldiers, and persons not in the military should be put to work at war-related jobs. In effect, total war pitted the entire military, economic, and social might of one nation against the entire might of another nation.

In the twentieth century, the concept of total war sometimes has been interpreted to mean that little or no distinction should be drawn between civilian and military targets. Accordingly, in World War II both sides carpet bombed cities, causing hundreds of thousands of civilian deaths. The United States also wiped out two entire cities with atomic bombs. Although the morality of these actions is still being debated, the fact remains that more civilians died than soldiers—a statistic that conforms to Clausewitz's notions of total war.

Marxian Theory of War Not surprisingly, Karl Marx linked war to capitalism. He said that as a capitalist economy grows ever larger, it increasingly needs more raw materials, labor, and monetary capital to sustain itself. Soon, domestic resources grow scarce and capitalists seek additional resources from abroad. In some cases, the quest leads capitalists to establish plantations, farms, mines, and assembly plants on foreign soil. The production and profits from these operations then go back to the capitalist nation, leaving little for the host nation. Another strategy, particularly popular during the nineteenth century, was colonization. Strong capitalist countries used the threat of war, or actual war, to establish dominion over weak nations, and to extract resources from them. Were he alive today, Marx would undoubtedly say that the real but unstated goal of the American-led invasion of Iraq was not to reduce the threat from weapons of mass destruction, but to gain control over the flow of Iraqi oil.

Because war reflects capitalism, Marx further pointed out, it indirectly reflects the interests of the bourgeoisie. That occurs because the bourgeoisie control the society, the government supports the bourgeoisie, and so the government goes to war to serve bourgeois interests. Inasmuch as the proletariat have no power, they are forced to fight in a war that benefits the ruling class, but not them.

Institutional Theory While institutional theory recognizes the importance of economic considerations, it emphasizes the relationship among the various institutions of society. This view gained prominence after World War II. At that time, the United States began to disarm, but abruptly reversed course when the Cold War broke out. In the process of rearming, military and industrial leaders formed an informal coalition that became known as the "military-industrial complex."

Institutional theorists argue that the military-industrial complex has so much power that it dominates American society. In effect, the complex bypasses the legislative and the executive branch of the government. That happens because elected officials have neither the expertise nor the desire to evaluate military and industrial decisions. In addition, politicians are easily swayed by industrial lobbyists and special-interest groups.

Currently, many theorists claim the military-industrial complex does not have as much power as it once did. They argue that in practice, the president, high-ranking bureaucrats, and elected officials largely determine whether the nation goes to war, and if so, how the war is conducted. In addition, these theorists say that public opinion exerts a powerful force that the military-industrial complex cannot control. Presidents George Bush and George W. Bush both received substantial boosts in public esteem from the wars with Iraq, thus strengthening their leadership and indirectly reinforcing their hold on the military-industrial complex.

A broader application of the institutional approach takes into account institutions that span separate countries. Consider the United Nations. Although many critics dismiss it as irrelevant, most political leaders do not. They recognize that support from the United Nations and other international bodies helps to build coalitions. For instance, the war to drive Iraq out of Kuwait was conducted under the banner of the United Nations and generated relatively little public controversy. The second Iraq war, however, failed to receive an endorsement from the United Nations. As a consequence, the war did not have clear-cut, international legitimacy—a lack that ultimately made it difficult to obtain support for rebuilding Iraq after the war.

Terrorism

Although terrorism has been used for centuries, September 11 suddenly brought it to the forefront of public concern and led to numerous changes in American society. Possibly the most visible changes can be observed at any U.S. airport. Not too long ago, passengers simply walked aboard their airplane, but not now. Today, airports bristle with armed guards of the newly created Transportation Security Administration, all luggage must pass through scanning machines, and passengers must submit to body searches. At an airport, it is even illegal to joke about security.

Terrorism and war are different, yet related. In contrast to war, **terrorism** may be defined as the noninstitutionalized use of threat, intimidation, and violence to bring about a political objective. Because terrorism is not institutionalized, terrorists freely use any tactic or weapon that suits their purpose. They might attack malls, theaters, and public places with suicide bombing; randomly shoot into a crowded airport; or kill a specific individual. Less common but greatly feared are mass attacks with poisonous gas and biological agents.

Terrorist attacks are not intended to destroy military targets, but to spread fear, discontent, and panic among the enemy population. To achieve that goal, terrorists target two groups, one randomly and the other selectivity. The random group consists of the relatively small number people who happen to be at the "wrong place at the wrong time." Random targeting means that everyone knows that anyone might be a victim at any place and at any time. This knowledge creates uncertainty and fear that spread throughout the entire population. After September 11, for example, virtually everyone in the United States felt threatened—even though they knew that the probability of being personally attacked was minuscule.

The second target consists of selected individuals. These might be high government officials, celebrities, or people with specialized skills and knowledge. Even if the attacks on these people fail, the threat of attack diminishes their ability to function effectively. For example, on September 11 no one knew if President Bush had been targeted; consequently he was closely guarded and kept out of public view. Thus, at a time of great crisis, the president could not immediately step forward to exert public leadership.

The theory of terrorism postulates that as fear spreads throughout a society, people will increasingly lose faith in their government. At some point, they will demand that government agree to terrorists' demands in exchange for an end to the violence. Whether terrorism can actually succeed in this way remains unclear. The fear it creates might lead to a change in a specific policy, but by itself, terrorism cannot bring down the entire government of a major nation.

STUDY TIP

Create a chart that lays out the different sociological explanations for war. Use a different color for each of the three theories.

Terrorism ▲ The noninstitutionalized use of threat, intimidation, and violence to bring about a political objective.

The twentieth century has been characterized by increasing political fragmentation, as shown in the breakup of the former Soviet Union and Yugoslavia and in revolutions in countries such as Guatemala, Cambodia, and Nigeria. Human rights violations and extreme violence, including genocide, massacres, and mass torture, have often accompanied political upheavals. How is it that people who normally are pleasant, thoughtful, generous, and kind to their friends and family can act so viciously toward people they consider enemies? Sociologist William Gamson (1995) has said that such extreme actions do not so much reflect hatred as they do the politics of exclusion.

The politics of exclusion involves identification of the people whom we define as "we" and the people whom we define as "they" (Lamont and Molna'r 2002). This is an important distinction, because the people defined as "we" are those to whom we owe moral obligations. The people defined as "they" are the people to whom we owe no moral obligations. Although it may be convenient to divide the world into two camps—the "we" and the "they"—social life is not that simple. In fact, fine gradations exist between the "we" and the "they."

The politics of exclusion is made possible by certain techniques. For instance, consider the following:

- Demonizing. "They"—the other group—are defined as evil and "we" as good, so that it is natural for the good to attempt to stamp out the evil.
- Shifting-the-Blame. "They asked for it" or "They started it" or "They deserve what they get" are the types of statements supporting extreme violence against racial-ethnic minorities, immigrants, and other such groups. Shifting-

the-blame absolves individuals of blame even before they engage in violent behavior.
- Routinizing-the-Violence. When killing and destruction become defined as "normal," there are fewer inhibitions against violence directed toward others. People typically become numb to their own hostile actions during wartime, and it is often not until much later that they experience guilt.
- Dehumanizing. Treating the other group members as less than human means that violence against them is not really violence against people; rather, it is violence against a subhuman species with no claim to moral protection.

Although people may be excluded from normal social life by the politics of exclusion, the process is reversible. For example, during World War II, Japan and the United States viewed each other as members of opposing camps. In both countries, members of the other group were demonized and dehumanized; each country shifted the blame for the war to the other, and violence against the other side was routinized. Horrible savagery occurred during the war, and neither side felt any moral obligation to people living in the other country. Since the end of the war, however, much of the "we/they" dichotomy in American-Japanese relationships has crumbled. One of the effects of the globalization of trade and the mass media has been that a greater familiarity has developed between the peoples of the United States and Japan. It is unlikely that the two nations could treat each other again with the violence with which they behaved toward each other in the early 1940s.

States and Human Rights

Human rights—those broadly defined rights to which all people are entitled by virtue of their humanity—play an important role in preserving individual freedoms. A Universal Declaration of Human Rights was signed by many governments in 1948, three years after the end of World War II. The declaration states that "Everyone shall live free and equal in dignity and rights." Unfortunately, many governments, including several of those that signed the Universal Declaration, often find excuses to ignore human rights in their dealings with their own people (see the Diversity box for a discussion of the politics of exclusion).

For instance, in 1960 in Lisbon, Portugal, two students raised their glasses in public in a toast to freedom. A short time later, they were arrested and sentenced to seven years of imprisonment. At that time, Portugal was under a repressive dictatorship, and its government punished all such displays. Peter Benenson, a 40-year-old British lawyer, became enraged when he read the newspaper account of the students' arrest and imprisonment. He developed a plan to bring public pressure on governments that unjustly imprison or harass people for their political views. With a few other volunteers, he launched a campaign called "Appeal for Amnesty, 1961" to draw attention to the fate of political prisoners around the world (Stanton, Fenn, and Amnesty International 1991). Since that time, the organization he founded, Amnesty International (AI), has developed into a worldwide voluntary organization with more than 4,200 local groups. Each local group works on behalf of political prisoners in its own

Human rights ▲ Those broadly defined rights to which all people are entitled by virtue of their humanity.

Iraq: Women waiting for food at a welfare station. A United Nations investigation concluded that government rations during Saddam Hussein's autocratic reign accounted for only a third of an average family's nutritional needs. Iraq could be a wealthy nation with enough resources to feed its population if a political order responsive to civilian needs can be established.

country and tries to draw attention to people whose human rights have been violated. The group researches and documents each case and then begins a letter-writing campaign to bring the case to the attention of local, national, and even international audiences. The success of Amnesty International has encouraged the formation of other human rights organizations (see the Sociology Online box).

With the end of the cold war and the collapse of most communist governments, along with the disappearance of some dictatorships, there may be fewer traditional political prisoners. Nonetheless, at the beginning of this decade, Amnesty International reported that there were thousands of people whose political rights had been grossly violated by the state, with thousands more cases unreported. Abuse of human rights has been widespread in the political fragmentation of Yugoslavia and other states. Some researchers believe that reports of human rights violations will increase in the future, because of the instability of governments in many countries and the increased recognition of violence against women that is condoned by their own governments (Chapter 8; Bonner 1995).

The issue raised by Amnesty International and other such human rights organizations is that states and governments routinely violate the rights of their own citizens

Sociology Online

If one types in the term "political" into a good Web browser, one can find more that 37 million hits—more than we could check out in a reasonable amount of time. So, it is necessary to focus on a more narrow topic. We suggest you begin with the Human Rights Watch destination. When you get to the home page of the Human Rights Watch organization, go to the destination titled About Human Rights Watch. From there scroll down to the Divisions listing. There you will find a series of reports on human rights, children's rights, and women's rights violations in Africa (sub-Saharan Africa), Americas (Latin America and the Caribbean), Europe and Central Asia, and the

Middle East (Middle East and North Africa). Choose any two of these areas to investigate.

As you read the reports listed in each of the two areas you selected, note the social characteristics of the people being victimized. Then answer the following questions:

Who seems to be victimized by the state?

Why are these people being selected for punishment, torture, or other forms of human rights violations?

Who will come to the aid of the victims?

and that there is no effective international organization that can prevent such violations (Fein 2000). When governments choose to involve themselves in human rights campaigns, their own ideological beliefs create biases. For instance, during the cold war, the United States was willing to support human rights claims against socialist or communist countries such as Cuba, but it was reluctant to press for human rights in countries that generally supported U.S. policy, such as El Salvador and Guatemala (Halebsky and Kirk 1990; Schirmer 1999). The United States has also been criticized for violating human rights. Prisoners suspected of being members of the terrorist groups al-Qaida and Taliban were routinely tied, blindfolded, denied food and water for long periods, and roughly treated. Many were sent to a special prison at the American naval base in Guantanamo, Cuba, where they were held without being charged or allowed to seek legal aid. Moreover, they were denied status as prisoners of war, and thus none of the traditional and legal protections of the Geneva Convention applied to them. Thus, we are left with the conclusion that even among democratic governments, the first line of defense of human rights is often left to voluntary organizations with little power.

● ■ ▲ **Pausing to Think**   About the State and the Exercise of Power

The authoritarian state excludes the common people from the process of government, permits no political opposition to the ruling group, and has little interest in the daily lives of the people. The totalitarian state resembles the authoritarian state but closely controls the daily lives of its citizens. The democratic state allows the common people to have direct input into governmental decisions and to elect and dismiss political leaders. States may incorporate nations, and this arrangement may lead to political instability and human rights violations. It may also lead to terrorism as different nations seek to obtain their goals.

CQ   To what extent do you feel that the international community has the right to sanction other states that violate the human rights of their citizens? ◆ What should such sanctions consist of?

Political Processes in the United States

Political processes operate at two levels: the formal and the informal. At the formal level, the Constitution lays down the legal-rational basis for the government of the United States. This source of authority is supplemented by several thousand federal laws that specify the rights and obligations of citizens of the United States. Existing alongside the formal system is the informal system, which consists of social processes that are not specified in documents or laws but that are nevertheless important. A great deal of politics gets done through them. In this section, we will examine several informal political processes.

Political Parties

Because of the complexity and the size of most associational societies, individuals are forced to form organizations to further their political goals. Political organizations meant to legitimately influence the government are called **political parties** (see Chapter 16 for a discussion of social movements). Large political parties, such as the Democratic and Republican parties, are sizable bureaucratic organizations. They stand for certain causes and ideologies, they articulate opinions, and they propose solutions to problems. Political parties achieve their goals mainly by raising money for political campaigns and running candidates for political office.

The two main parties in the United States are, of course, the Democratic and the Republican. Third parties, or those not affiliated with the Democratic and/or

Political party ▲ A political organization meant to legitimately influence the government.

Republican party, may be influential, but they seldom win elections. However, the role of a third party may be undergoing change, and in the future, third parties may wield a great deal of power. We return to this possibility later in the chapter.

In the United States, the two-party system seems to work because both parties act as umbrella organizations for a host of specific interests. The Democratic Party is the traditional home to labor unions, ethnic minorities, and liberal causes, whereas the Republican Party is the home to management, the upper classes, and conservative causes. Although the members of each of these groups might not agree among themselves, they willingly set aside their differences during an election and support their party's candidate. For example, some ethnic minorities have long-standing grievances against labor unions with regard to discrimination, yet both minorities and labor will usually support the Democratic candidate in an election (see the What Do You Think? box).

An important goal of a political party is to *influence government policy* (Campbell 2002). In addition to winning office, a party exerts influence by controlling

What Do You Think? ●■▲ Liberal or Conservative? ❓

For most of American history, there have been two major political parties. Today, the Democratic Party attracts liberals, or people who support the so-called left, whereas the Republican Party attracts conservatives, or people who support the so-called right. If asked, most people in the United States can place themselves somewhere along the political continuum "very conservative to very liberal." Recently, the largest percentage of people considered themselves to be moderates or conservatives. Liberals were a distinct minority (Gallup poll, May 2003). These differences in party loyalty and voting patterns mean that liberals and conservatives take different positions on many important issues, as the following table illustrates.

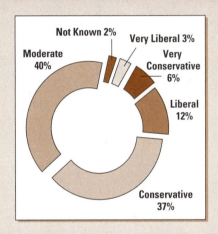

Not Known 2%
Very Liberal 3%
Moderate 40%
Very Conservative 6%
Liberal 12%
Conservative 37%

CQ *What is your definition of a liberal and of a conservative? ◆ Where do you place yourself on this ideological continuum? ◆ What are your reasons? ◆ Do you think liberalism is staging a comeback?

*To answer these critical questions, review the box "What Is Critical Thinking?" in Chapter 1, paying special attention to the discussion of key terms.
SOURCE: Victor Kamber and Bradley O'Leary, *Are You a Conservative or a Liberal?: A Fun and Easy Test to Tell Where You Stand on the Political Spectrum* (Austin, TX: Boru Press, 1996).

FIVE IMPORTANT ISSUES	LIBERAL POSITION	CONSERVATIVE POSITION
Human Nature	People are basically good	People are likely to do bad things
Government	Government should play an active role to improve human nature	Government should play a limited role with an emphasis on defending society from threats
Crime	Eliminate causes of crime, such as poverty, and rehabilitate criminals	Punish criminals severely and keep them in prison for lengthy terms
Business	Businesses must be highly regulated because they seek profit, even if it means ignoring or contributing to social problems	Business should not be regulated because the free enterprise system will solve social problems, and in any event, the government is incompetent
Women and minorities	Government must provide laws, safeguards, and goals to achieve equality	Government mandates are not effective, nor are they fair to everyone

appointments. For example, every new president attempts to appoint judges who are sympathetic to the president's goals. The most notorious case was the 1937 attempt of President Franklin Roosevelt to "pack the Supreme Court." He proposed reorganizing the Supreme Court in a way that would give him the power to appoint six new justices who, presumably, would support his programs and legislation. The attempt ultimately failed, and it seems unlikely that a president will try that again—at least not in the near future. All presidents, however, routinely nominate candidates for federal judgeships. Their nominees must be approved by the Senate, and when the opposing party controls the Senate, the appointments may be held up for years.

Political parties are also important as a *basis for forming coalitions*. This situation is especially true in other countries. To illustrate, in Great Britain, party discipline is strict, and elected representatives almost always vote along party lines. In the United States, however, the situation is different, and political parties are the basis for a loose form of coalition building. Under this system, a party can muster most of its members to vote along party lines most of the time. Depending on the issue, however, some members will cross over and vote with the other party. For example, Clarence Thomas, a Republican nominee for the Supreme Court, was at the center of a heated controversy over charges of sexual harassment made against him. In the end, he was confirmed when 11 of 57 Democratic senators broke ranks with their party and voted for him. A partial exception to this loose form of party discipline occurred after the Republicans won control of the House of Representatives in 1994. A group of newly elected Republican representatives followed the leadership of Newt Gingrich, the Republican Speaker of the House, on almost every bill.

The party in power determines who becomes chair of a committee. By tradition, the leaders of the Senate and the House of Representatives assign committee memberships and give the chairs to those members of their party who have the greatest seniority (length of continuous service). Because legislation must be considered first by a committee, these chairs determine which legislation will come before the full Congress. In effect, the chair can squelch a bill by not letting it out of committee.

Political parties are also the *focal points for conflict* between different segments of society. The Republican Party represents predominantly the white middle and upper classes, whereas the Democratic Party represents the working and lower classes, including most racial and ethnic minority groups. The impact of these constituencies is reflected in the **party platform**: the official statement of the ideology, goals, and plans that each party will implement if its candidates are elected to office. The Republican platform typically stresses individual initiative, free enterprise, less government, technological development, and a strong national defense. The Democratic platform, in contrast, typically emphasizes social programs, the expansion of government, less defense spending, and affirmative action to eliminate barriers to equal opportunity. These platforms differ, but in any given election, candidates from both parties tend to move toward the center on most issues because the majority of American voters are grouped in the middle of the political spectrum and will not support extreme positions on any issue.

Special-Interest Groups

The influencing of legislation has become a big business in the United States at all levels of government. However obscure a bill might be to the general public, it never goes completely unnoticed, because all legislation affects someone. Consequently, the halls of Congress are filled with people who earn handsome fees for influencing congressional votes on certain bills. These people, called **lobbyists**, are employed by large corporations, unions, environmental groups, and organizations of all types. Lobbyists are valuable because they have special insights into the workings of government and enjoy informal contacts with "people in the right places." There are approximately 38 lobbyists for every member of Congress, a figure that suggests the intensity of lobbying efforts.

Party platform ▲ The official statement of the ideology, goals, and plans that a party will implement if its candidates are elected to office.

Lobbyist ▲ A person employed by a large corporation, a union, or other organizations that aim to influence congressional votes on certain bills.

Lobbyists do not work for themselves. Rather, they usually toil on behalf of an **interest group**: an organization formed for the express purpose of swaying political decisions. For example, the American Medical Association is one of the most active interest groups in the nation, and it lobbies intensively for legislation that it deems important. Similarly but far less powerfully, the American Sociological Association attempts to influence legislation, especially bills that affect funding for research. In fact, virtually any interest group that can afford to do so will attempt to influence legislation through lobbying efforts.

Many interest groups draw support from diverse segments of society, and groups may form coalitions that seem improbable on the surface. For instance, the National Abortion Rights Action League focuses on the single issue of a woman's right to an abortion (the pro-choice position). This group draws support from men and women, from whites and nonwhites, and from all social classes. Although these segments of society often oppose one another on other issues, they cooperate when it comes to abortion.

Special-interest groups frequently establish organizations to raise money. These groups are called **political action committees**, or **PACs**. Even though PACs date back to the early 1930s, not until 1971 did federal law permit labor unions, corporations, and other special-interest groups to form PACs of their own. Since that time, PACs have proliferated and now number in the thousands.

PACs have a huge influence on American politics (Fritsch 1996; Steagall and Jennings 1996). The reason is simple: PACs contribute money to candidates, and the more that PACs contribute, the more influence they have. For any national election, PACs will contribute millions of dollars to various candidates, and naturally enough, they expect something in return. Thus, the American Medical Association and other sponsors of PACs can expect those members of Congress who accept their donations to vote for legislation supported by them.

The role played by parties, lobbyists, interest groups, and PACs clearly illustrates the importance of informal political processes even in a political system that is rooted in legal-rational authority. Because these informal political entities represent thousands of different constituencies, they often end up working for different objectives or at cross-purposes. Many sociologists believe that this state of affairs protects democracy because it prevents any one group from acquiring a monopoly on power. Other sociologists, however, warn that because the system is controlled by influential but informal groups, the ordinary citizen cannot do much to influence politics and is therefore becoming disenchanted. Later in the chapter, we will examine how this disenchantment might play out in this century.

Voting

Democracy offers people an opportunity to elect government officials, but many people do not take advantage of that opportunity. In only 5 of the past 18 presidential elections (1932–2000) has more than 60 percent of the voting-age population cast a ballot. In off-year elections for congressional representatives, voter participation is even lower: the 1998 off-year election attracted only a little over 36 percent of those eligible to vote (Infoplease.com 2000). In contrast to these relatively low rates of voting, in Belgium, the rate is 95 percent; in Austria, 92 percent; in Sweden, 91 percent; and in Italy, 90 percent (Piven and Cloward 1989). Why do so few American citizens vote? One set of factors is race, class, and gender. According to federal criteria, almost one person in ten is very poor, and the poor are not very active politically. Poverty is correlated with education, and only about 28 percent of people with eight years or less of formal education voted in the 1996 presidential election. In that same election, however, about 49 percent of high school graduates voted, as did some 73 percent of college graduates (U.S. Bureau of the Census 2000).

On the whole, African Americans are less likely to vote than white Americans, but mainly for reasons of social class. Middle- and upper-class African Americans vote at approximately the same rate as middle- and upper-class whites. In the past, fewer

Interest group ▲ An organization formed for the express purpose of swaying political decisions.

Political Action Committee (PAC) ▲ A political organization established by a special interest group to raise money to support political candidates.

Society Today ● ■ ▲

Soft Money Contributions

Soft money is a contribution made to a national political party for "party building" rather than for support of a particular candidate. In practice, soft money is highly controversial for two reasons: (1) Only a thin and easily crossed line separates "party building" from the "support of a candidate," and (2) there are generous limitations on the size of a soft money contribution.

The chart below shows the soft money donations of the five largest industries.

FIVE LARGEST INDUSTRY DONORS

Industry	$ Millions
Health	$29
Labor	$36
Misc Business	$52
Communications/Electronics	$71
Finance/Insurance/Real Estate	$92
Total Contribution	$209

Reprinted from *http://www.commoncause.org/laundromat/ industry.cfm* by permission of Common Cause, 2003.

Soft money contributions are not equally split between the Democratic and Republican parties. The health industry, for example, contributes more to Republicans while labor unions contribute overwhelmingly to Democrats.

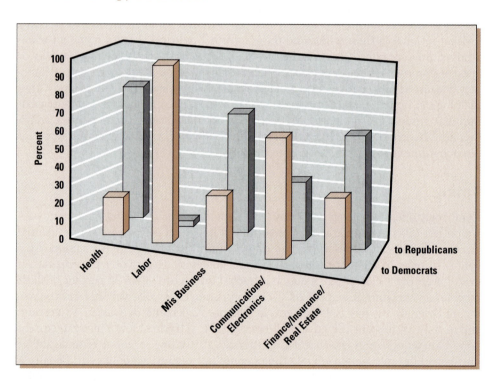

CQ In preparation for the 2004 presidential election, the Republican party raised much more money than the Democratic party. To what extent do you think that such donations reflect popular opinion versus special interests?

than one-third of Hispanic Americans voted (U.S. Bureau of the Census 1994). Evidently, Hispanics tend to distrust the political system. No party represents the full range of their views, nor do they see much hope of improving their lives through political participation.

With regard to gender, women are somewhat more likely to vote than men, and because women live longer, they have an opportunity to vote in more elections than men. Women tend to favor causes such as world peace, child welfare, health care, environmental concerns, and equal pay for comparable work. Because they are the victims of sexual harassment and gender discrimination, women are naturally concerned about those issues as well (Cook, Thomas, and Wilcox 1994).

In the past, voter registration difficulties and requirements have discouraged many potential voters from registering. Now it is possible in many communities for people to register to vote in schools, at places where driver's licenses are issued, and in libraries. This convenience should have the long-term effect of increasing voter participation in elections.

●■▲ Pausing to Think   About Political Processes in the United States

> Political parties attempt to influence government policy, act as a basis for the formation of coalitions, and serve as the focal points for conflicts between various segments of society. Parties also offer platforms and attempt to achieve their major goals by raising money and running candidates for office. Lobbyists, special-interest groups, and PACs try to sway political decisions at all levels of government. Voter turnout in the United States is low compared with that of many other nations, and it varies by race, class, and gender.

CQ How do you view voting in a democracy—as an obligation or a right? ◆ Did you vote in the last election? ◆ Why, or why not?

Power-Elite and Pluralist Models

In a democratic society, the people are supposed to be the ultimate source of authority; yet even a casual observer will note that only a few people actually govern the state. Sociologists know this fact too, and they have analyzed the situation at some length. Is power controlled by a select minority, they ask, or is it spread throughout the society? To answer these questions, sociologists offer two contrasting models: the power-elite model and the pluralist model.

The Power-Elite Model

More than 50 years ago, sociologist C. Wright Mills argued that a small group of people controls the United States (Mills 1956; Mills and Mills 2000; see also Domhoff 1998; Form 1995; Wehr 1994). These people are wealthy, are well placed socially, know each other personally, and frequently marry among themselves. They share a similar worldview and work in concert to achieve a political agenda that suits their interests. Mills called this group the **power elite** (see Figure 10.1).

Mills argued that the power elite dominates American society by exerting control over three major institutional areas: the economy, the government, and the military. Its members are the presidents and board chairmen of major corporations; they hold powerful positions in government; and they are the high-ranking generals and admirals of the military. The elite further consolidate their dominance by circulating from one institution to another. An example of such circulation can be found in the career of Dwight D. Eisenhower. He began as a junior army officer and eventually became the Supreme Commander of Allied Forces in Europe during World War II. He retired from the military, was president of Columbia University for a brief period, and then

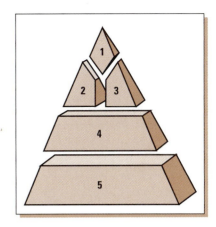

FIGURE 10.1 The Power-Elite Model

The pyramid figure depicts C. Wright Mills' model of the power elite. According to Mills, the power elite consists of the people in the "higher circles," specifically (1) the corporate rich, (2) the executive branch, and (3) military leaders. Less important in controlling the country are (4) leaders of interest groups, the legislative branch of government, and local opinion leaders. Without much power, the (5) unorganized mass of people seldom get to make the important decisions that control their destiny.

SOURCE: Adapted from p. 407 in *Conflict and Order: Understanding Society*, 7th ed. by D. Stanley Eitzen and Maxine Baca Zinn. Copyright © 1995. Reprinted by permission of Allyn & Bacon, Inc.

Power elite ▲ People who are wealthy and well placed socially, who know one another personally, who frequently marry among themselves, who share a similar worldview, and who work in concert to achieve a political agenda that suits their interests.

commanded the North Atlantic Treaty Organization (NATO) when it was first formed. He was then nominated for president by the Republican Party and won an overwhelming victory in 1952. Eisenhower served as president for eight years, and on retirement he became the elder statesman of American politics. He died in 1969, one of America's most beloved heroes. During his lifetime, he had circulated from the army to academia, to an international military organization, and finally to the presidency.

The power-elite model implies that democracy means very little because elites always have the power to achieve their goals. President Eisenhower recognized this problem. In his farewell presidential address, he warned the nation about the dangers of the "military-industrial complex"—a coalition among industrial, military, and political leaders. This coalition of elites dominates both military policy and matters that affect military policy, such as foreign policy. Deals involving billions of tax dollars are struck behind closed doors by people who are not accountable to any public constituency. Evidently Eisenhower's concern was at least partially justified: since he first issued his warning, the military-industrial complex has relentlessly and successfully pursued a policy of expansion. Even today, with the threat of Soviet aggression gone, military spending continues on a vast scale.

In sum, the power-elite model is based on the premise that society is controlled by a small group of people (Hertz 1990; *Mother Jones* 1996). By and large, members of this group circulate among the major institutions of society, know one another personally, and informally but effectively determine the course of government. If the power-elite theorists are correct, then notions of democracy are mostly clichés, and the average person has little real voice in government. But is the power-elite perspective correct? Many sociologists have reservations, and some offer the so-called pluralist model as an alternative.

The Pluralist Model

Whereas the power-elite model argues that power is monopolized by a small elite, the *pluralist model* maintains that power is diffused throughout society (Dahl 1982). Theorists who work in the pluralist tradition point out that a complex nation such as the United States has multiple (or plural) centers of power, such as business associations, unions, schools, churches, civic associations, and special-interest groups. The United States also is an exceptionally heterogeneous nation, and many power centers are thus based on race, ethnicity, and gender. Because power is distributed across many centers, a group can only rarely achieve everything it wishes. Instead, each group must rely on compromise and accommodation, and it must be satisfied with obtaining only part of what it wants.

Theorists following the pluralist model recognize that some people or groups have considerably more power than others, but these theorists also believe that even the most powerful figures in American society are obligated to various constituencies. The politician is obligated to the groups that back him or her; the president of a multibillion-dollar corporation must consult with the company's board of directors; the board, in turn, must be sensitive to the demands of regulatory agencies, banks, public opinion, and millions of stockholders.

Even though a given power center may be relatively weak, according to the pluralist model, it still might be capable of blocking the actions of other groups. As a result, power centers based on race, ethnicity, or gender can make themselves heard, even though they represent relatively small numbers of individuals. African Americans are a statistical minority, but the African American vote often was the difference between winning and losing a close presidential election.

Power centers that are able to block the actions of other groups are known as **veto groups**. At the national level in the United States there are currently several such groups. They include multinational corporations and small and midsize professional and business organizations represented by such bodies as the National Chamber of Commerce and the National Association of Manufacturers. These groups often come into conflict with one another, as in the recent battles over the health dangers of smoking. In this instance, the tobacco lobbies have fought with the insurance companies and with the medical interests over pending legislation and regulation.

In contrast to the power-elite model, the pluralist model is consistent with notions of democracy. Because power is dispersed in a pluralistic system, people who are wealthy and well positioned cannot always have their way. Even individuals with relatively little power can influence outcomes by creating voting blocs, veto groups, and coalitions.

Although pluralism strengthens democracy, the diffusion of power can impede problem solving. Too much pluralism translates into poor leadership, a lack of coordination, and a lack of focus. Certain problems—the war on drugs, the fight to eradicate AIDS, and the preservation of the environment, for example—are extremely large and complex. Some analysts argue that the solutions to such problems will emerge only when concentrated social power is applied to them (Thurow 1980).

Since the 1960s, many studies of power and local decision making have been conducted (for example, Dahl 1961; Domhoff 1983, 1998; Lyon 1999). Some of these studies report the existence of a power elite; others find that power is dispersed throughout the community. In general, pluralism prevails in large, economically diverse communities, whereas a power elite tends to dominate smaller, less diversified communities. In addition, communities with business-oriented governments often are dominated by a power elite.

●■▲ Pausing to Think About Power-Elite and Pluralist Models

The power-elite model argues that a small group of people control the United States; they are wealthy and well placed socially, they know one another personally, and they frequently are linked through marriage. According to the power-elite model, the average person has relatively little say in government. The pluralist model argues that power is diffused throughout society, but it recognizes that certain groups have more power than others. Some of these groups are strong enough to exert veto power over certain actions of the government. Although pluralism strengthens democracy, too much pluralism may translate into political gridlock.

CQ Jean-Jacques Rousseau (1712–1778), a French writer and philosopher, wrote, "In the strict sense of the term, a true democracy has never existed, and never will exist." In applying this statement to the power-elite and the pluralist models, do you agree with him? ◆ Why, or why not?

Society Today ●■▲

Members of Congress

	1981	1995	2001
Black	17	41	39
Asian, Pacific Islander	6	6	NA
Hispanic	6	17	19
Female	21	55	62

NA: not available

SOURCE: U.S. Bureau of the Census, *Statistical Abstract of the United States*, 2002.

Veto group ▲ A group whose power lies primarily in the ability to block actions of other groups.

Sociological Analysis of the Political Order

The three major perspectives in sociology—functionalist, conflict, and symbolic interactionist—are often used to analyze the political order. Because each perspective emphasizes a different aspect of power, taking all three into account enables us to arrive at a broad understanding of the political order. The perspectives are as follows.

The Functionalist Perspective

From the functionalist perspective, the state has achieved a dominant position because it provides society with cohesion and order. The state does so by fulfilling certain functions:

1. *Maintain Order*   A major function of the state is to guarantee order. In extreme instances, the state may resort to force, but the continuous use of force is seldom necessary because every society has mechanisms for regulating conflict. Traditional societies can rely on custom, but industrial societies are so complex that custom cannot always produce the desired result. Accordingly, the state assumes the responsibility for codifying the most important norms into rules and laws, and then enforcing them. Enforcement may be direct, as through the police, or indirect, as through informal sanctions such as ridicule or public disgrace.

Afghanistan, a largely transitional Eastern society, is an example of a country that has failed to maintain order. Once rather peaceful, Afghanistan has been crisscrossed by warring factions ever since civil war broke out some two decades ago. Because Afghan society is organized around tribal units, clans, and interpersonal relationships, these political conflicts have thus become a part of the communal structure of the society itself. Consequently, Afghanistan promises to remain a shifting battleground of warring factions for a long time (Dupree 2002; *New York Times*, February 5, 1996:1, 4).

2. *Interact with Other States*   In the modern world, states must interact with other states to survive. Thus, states sign military treaties with friendly governments, join economic alliances with other states, engage in diplomacy, and sometimes engage in war. None of these tasks could be accomplished without a centralized authority—the state—to act on behalf of the people.

3. *Direct the System*   Societies are complex economic, social, and political systems, and the state is responsible for directing the society. The United States government tries to maintain full employment and prosperity. If the incumbent administration fails at this task, the incumbents may be voted out of office in the next election, as was President Carter in 1980 and President Bush in 1992. Citizens also expect the government to regulate important institutions such as banks and insurance companies, to repair existing roads and build new ones, and to maintain a military defense. None of these and other tasks could be accomplished efficiently without a central authority.

The functionalist perspective emphasizes the role of the state in promoting order and achieving consensus, but obviously the state does not always succeed. In this regard, the conflict perspective acts as a corrective by emphasizing the inequality of power.

The Conflict Perspective

In the nineteenth century, Karl Marx proposed a theory of the state that was to have a profound impact during the twentieth century, when numerous states were founded on Marxist principles. Contemporary conflict theorists still draw on and expand Marx's broad perspective (Gallup 1996). Rather than focusing only on class conflict, however, they recognize that conflicts exist among many groups in modern society. For instance, racial or ethnic groups compete with the dominant group for resources; women compete with men; liberals compete with conservatives; conservationists compete with big business; labor competes with management. The outcomes of these struggles often depend on a group's wealth, its ability to raise large sums of money, and its power to influence government policy. Typically, it is the weak, powerless, or unorganized who lose in these struggles, because they lack the resources even to enter the fray.

Conflict theorists argue further that democracy does not prevent power from being centralized in the hands of a dominant few, nor does democracy ensure that the group with power will relinquish it at the request of the majority. Voting, freedom of speech, and other tools of democracy do not always perform their intended function, especially in poor societies with long traditions of political upheaval and inequality. Even in modern industrial states, women fail to achieve political parity with men. Moreover, if everyone in a society accepts the ideology of the dominant group, that ideology is the norm and goes unchallenged. For instance, if we all accept the ruling class' notion that welfare is bad and that vast inequality is good, then it is unlikely that a socialist government will ever come to power (Bourdieu 1986a; Kidd 1995; Wissinger 2000).

Conflict theory and functionalism are macro-level perspectives that address the role of power in society. As such, they say relatively little about the individual person. The symbolic interactionist perspective, in contrast, focuses on the individual.

The Symbolic Interactionist Perspective

Political parties are more than just formal organizations; they are also ideas in people's minds and part of their social identities (Stets and Burke 2000). These ideas and identities are acquired through the processes of **political socialization**: the formal and informal learning that creates a political self for each individual. Like socialization in general, political socialization focuses specifically on how political attitudes, beliefs, and identities are transmitted from one generation to the next. If people are socialized to think of themselves (for example) as good Democrats or Republicans, their

Political socialization ▲ The formal and informal learning that creates a political self for each individual.

political identities become part of their self-concepts, and their behavior helps create a broad base of support for party action. Also, like socialization in general, political socialization is accomplished by several agents of socialization (Sapiro 1994; Zelditch 2000; see Chapter 3). The first and perhaps the most important of these agents is the family, because that is where children acquire their initial attitudes toward political parties, their respect for authority, and their views on the current political system. Increasingly, however, socialization is accomplished by the mass media, especially television. For example, those who read daily newspapers and watch network television news every day are among the most highly socialized people in regard to political events. People who follow the news are more likely to get involved in politics and to have a favorable view of the political process than those who do not follow the news (Hargrove and Stempel 1995).

Symbolic interactionists further point out that the television image is easy to manipulate and that if voters depend solely on television for their political information, they will be getting very superficial information. This concern actually goes back to the first televised presidential debate between Richard Nixon and John F. Kennedy. Evidently, Kennedy fully prepared for the event and came across as dynamic and bright, whereas Nixon appeared gaunt and gruff. More recently, during the first presidential debate of the 2000 campaign, the Democratic candidate, Al Gore, was criticized for sighing and rolling his eyes when the Republican candidate, George W. Bush, made certain comments. Whether Gore's behavior significantly affected the final outcome of the election is difficult to know, however.

Whereas television once responded to political events, it may now be changing politics to suit its own demands (Alteide and Snow 1991). For example, television is most powerful when the images it shows are dramatic, unambiguous, and centered around well-known themes. For this reason, politicians running for office typically prefer brief advertisements that rely on emotional impact and that center on simple themes. An early example of this tactic again involved John F. Kennedy. Many of his television commercials opened with a brief shot of PT boats splashing through the water—an image that reminded the viewer of his experiences in the South Pacific during World War II. Complicated themes are not well suited to short commercials, so they tend to get suppressed during a campaign.

●■▲ Pausing to Think   About the Sociological Analysis of the Political Order

According to the functionalist perspective, the state provides society with cohesion and social order. To do so, the state maintains order, interacts with other states, and directs the overall social system. According to the conflict perspective, there is a continuing struggle within society for control of the governing institutions of the state, and the group with the most power usually wins. According to the symbolic interactionist perspective, the political system exists as ideas and identities in people's minds, which are acquired through political socialization.

CQ What political socialization have you received? ◆ Has your family been a significant influence (pro or con) on your political views? ◆ Has television been an influence?

The Political Order in the Twenty-First Century

As we mentioned earlier in this chapter, American voters seem to be losing faith in the people who operate the political system. This loss of faith stands in sharp contrast to the situation that existed in the past. A hundred years ago, people in the

Society Today ● ■ ▲

Confidence in Government

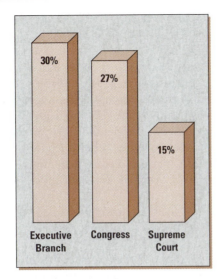

Approximately one-third of American adults say they have "hardly any confidence" in the executive branch of the federal government and in Congress; about half that number express the same feelings about the Supreme Court. Whether these figures are high or low, or good or bad, has been debated for a number of years (GSS 1999).

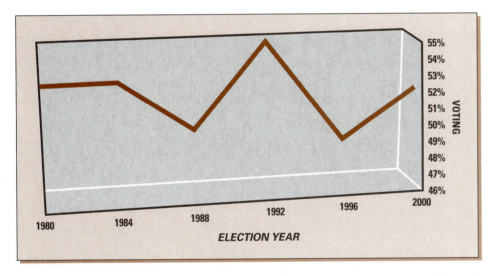

For the past several presidential elections, about 50 percent of all eligible voters actually voted. Compared with many countries, this is a low voter turnout (U.S. Bureau of the Census, 2002).

CQ How much confidence do you have in the executive branch, Congress, and the Supreme Court? Why? ◆ Can you think of a hypothesis that links confidence in the government to voter turnout?

United States were passionately involved in their politics. They enthusiastically joined political parties, for example, because they believed in the importance of being involved in the political process. Most people who could vote did vote, and they worked hard to see that their candidates received the most votes. People were personally acquainted with the local officials they elected, and almost every adult was connected, in some way, to the political system (Lynd and Lynd 1929).

Today, politicians are as far removed from the public as movie stars are, and most people view politics as an intimidating and uninviting process. They become involved only when their private lives or personal interests are threatened (Bellah et al. 1996). For example, fewer than 5 percent of the people are members of a political club, and one-third of American people say that they have hardly any confidence in Congress or the executive branch (NORC 1998).

Although sociologists do not know why people are disenchanted with politics, one reason might be the widespread belief that the individual no longer has any real voice in government; that is, the growth of large government bureaucracies and the increased influence of special-interest groups leave average citizens with the sense that their input will make little difference (Caplow 2000). For example, the vast majority of adults in the United States believe that the government is run by a few big interests looking out for themselves. Once beliefs such as this one take hold, they destroy incentives for the average person to participate in the political process (Barlett and Steele 1992; Caplow 1991; *New York Times*/CBS Poll, reported in the *New York Times*, August 12, 1995:8Y).

Another reason might be the contemporary media's continual revelations about the private lives of politicians. Perhaps revealing too many details about a politician's human weaknesses causes a general loss of respect for politicians. With constant reminders of the sins and scandals committed by politicians, citizens become highly suspicious and generally unwilling to support political leaders. In the 1960s, the press

CONCEPT WEB The Political Order

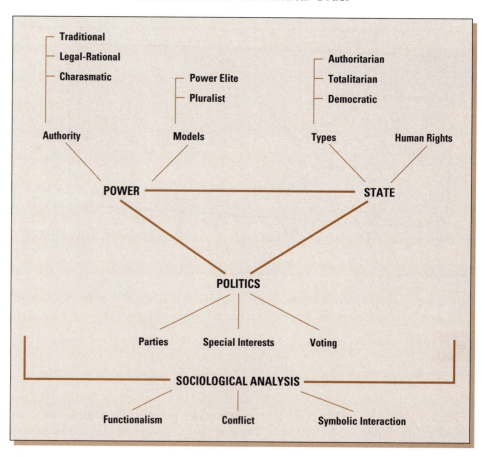

This is a concept web for the Political Order. Not included is the topic of War and Terrorism. How would you include the topic in the web? Try this—write a short essay about how the concepts of state, power, and politics go together.

avoided any mention of the sexual affairs of President Kennedy, and Kennedy enjoyed great popularity; in contrast, during the 1990s, the press eagerly reported on any fact or rumor about President Clinton's extramarital conduct.

It is possible that the citizenry will develop a renewed interest in the political system through the vehicle of protest and counterprotest. Since the events of 9/11, the nation has mobilized to protect itself from terrorist attacks. Consequently, people have been forced to rely on the government because it is the only agent of society capable of waging war. And as the war goes on some people will support it while others will oppose it—but in either case involvement in the political system will increase.

Looking Ahead

The next chapter examines changes affecting the family. The family is the basic social unit of society and is therefore of fundamental importance.

WHAT YOU SHOULD KNOW ●■▲

1. How did the political order change with the Great Social Transformation?

Hunting and gathering societies give elders the right to settle disputes and to impose punishments. Horticultural and agrarian societies have aristocracies that control the land and governments that establish codes and rights. Industrial societies tend to be democratic, but some industrializing societies are totalitarian.

2. What is the key to understanding the political process?

The political order ultimately rests on power. Weber said that authority is legitimate power and that coercion is illegitimate power.

3. What are the three major types of authority?

According to Weber, the three types of authority are traditional, legal-rational, and charismatic.

4. What are the general types of states?

There are three types of states: authoritarian, totalitarian, and democratic. The authoritarian state excludes the common people from the process of government and permits no political opposition to the ruling group, but it has little interest in the daily lives of the people. The totalitarian state resembles the authoritarian state, but it also exercises close control over the daily lives of its citizens. The democratic state allows the common people to have direct input into government decisions and to elect and dismiss political leaders.

5. Are states and nations the same?

No. States are defined by political authority, whereas nations are defined by history, culture, and identity. The concepts of nation and state may be combined to produce the nation-state—the supreme political authority within a territory that represents a single nation.

6. What is the difference between war and terrorism?

War is an institutionalized and violent conflict between nations, tribes, and other social entities. Terrorism is the noninstitutionalized use of threat, intimidation, and violence to bring about a political objective.

7. What are the fundamental political processes in the United States?

The United States has a two-party system, and each party attempts to exert control over the government. Lobbyists, special-interest groups, and political action committees attempt to influence the course of government for the benefit of specific interests or specific individuals.

8. Who actually runs things in the United States?

Some theorists say that a power elite dominates American society through its control of the economy, the government, and the military. Other theorists say that although there may be a number of powerful people who form an elite, a large number of special interests contend with one another to attain their goals. At the local community level, the power-elite model tends to be applicable, whereas at the large community level, the pluralist model tends to be applicable.

9. What insights into politics and the state are offered by the basic sociological perspectives?

The functionalist perspective argues that the state provides society with cohesion and social order, interacts with other states, and directs the social system. The conflict perspective argues that different groups struggle for control of the state and that the powerless usually lose the struggle. The symbolic interactionist perspective emphasizes the role of political socialization as the mechanism through which people learn the political norms and values of their society.

10. What does the future hold for the political order?

Politicians have progressively lost respect among American voters. One result of this political alienation is that people view politics as an intimidating and uninviting process. Since the events of 9/11, people have been forced to rely on government for protection, and have increased their involvement in politics. This involvement is likely to continue.

TEST YOUR KNOWLEDGE ●■▲

Key Terms Matching

Match each of these key terms with the best definition or example from the numbered items that follow. Write the letter preceding the key term in the blank before the definition that you choose.

a. authoritarian state

b. authority

c. charismatic authority

d. coercion

e. democratic state

f. government

g. human rights

h. ideal type

i. interest group

j. legal-rational authority

k. lobbyist

l. monarchy

m. nation

n. nation-state

o. party platform

p. political

q. political action committee (PAC)

r. political party

s. political socialization

t. power

u. power elite

v. state

w. totalitarian state

x. traditional authority

y. veto group

_____ 1. Power that is legitimated by an individual's exceptional personal attributes, such as a magnetic personality, an extraordinary driving energy, or a powerful aura of wisdom and grace.

_____ 2. An organization formed for the express purpose of swaying political decisions.

_____ 3. The official statement of the ideology, goals, and plans that a party will implement if its candidates are elected to office.

_____ 4. A state that allows the people to have input into government decisions and permits the people to elect and dismiss leaders.

_____ 5. The formal and informal learning that creates a political self for each individual.

_____ 6. Authority that derives its legitimacy from the rules and laws that define the rights, duties, and obligations of rulers and followers.

_____ 7. The ability to achieve one's ends despite resistance.

_____ 8. A state where the people are excluded from the processes of government, little or no opposition to the government is permitted, and the government has little interest in the lives of the people unless they threaten the state's leadership.

_____ 9. Authority that is legitimated by the historical beliefs and practices of the society.

_____ 10. The process of compelling others to do something against their will.

_____ 11. The supreme political authority within a territory that incorporates and represents a nation.

_____ 12. A group whose power lies primarily in its ability to block actions of other groups.

_____ 13. An abstract description, constructed from a number of cases, that reveals the essential features of a concept.

_____ 14. People who are wealthy and well placed socially, who know one another, who marry among themselves, who have a similar worldview, and who work in concert to achieve a political agenda that suits their interests.

_____ 15. A political organization meant legitimately to influence the government.

_____ 16. A system in which political power is passed from person to person on the basis of hereditary claims.

_____ 17. Involving the distribution of power across the institutions, organizations, and individuals of a society.

_____ 18. A state that has unlimited power, tolerates no opposition, and exercises close control over its citizens.

_____ 19. The socially legitimated use of power.

_____ 20. The highest political authority within a given territory.

_____ 21. Those broadly defined rights to which all people are entitled by virtue of their humanity.

_____ 22. A political organization established by a special interest group to raise money to support political candidates.

_____ 23. A group that lives within a given territory and shares a common history, culture, and identity.

_____ 24. A person who is employed by a large corporation, a union, or other organization and who aims to influence congressional votes on certain bills.

_____ 25. The set of people who are currently engaged in directing the state.

Multiple Choice

Circle the letter of your choice.

1. Democracy, in general, came with the emergence of which type of society?
   a. hunting and gathering
   b. agricultural
   c. horticultural
   d. industrial

2. The political order ultimately rests on which base?
   a. consent of the governed
   b. power
   c. the economy
   d. quality of leadership

3. Which type of power did Max Weber define as illegitimate?
   a. traditional
   b. charismatic
   c. legal-rational
   d. coercive

4. The president of the United States has particular powers that are specifically and formally defined and that do not accompany the president once he or she leaves office. Which type of power does the president have?
   a. traditional
   b. charismatic
   c. legal-rational
   d. coercive

5. Which of the following is NOT a characteristic of charismatic authority?
   a. It is an illegitimate power.
   b. It is based on an individual's personal characteristics.
   c. Individuals with this power often lead revolutions.
   d. It cannot easily be transferred from one person to another.

6. Which of the following is a system in which political power is passed from person to person on the basis of hereditary claims?
   a. power elite
   b. monarchy
   c. charismatic
   d. kinship

7. Which of the following is a characteristic of an authoritarian state?
   a. The government is not very interested in people's daily lives.
   b. People are excluded from the process of government.
   c. The government does not tolerate much opposition.
   d. All of the above.

8. Japan is a homogeneous country with a common culture, and its territory incorporates and represents this culture. Which term best describes Japan?
   a. state
   b. nation-state
   c. nation
   d. none of the above

9. At one time, the Iroquois of the Northeastern United States lived in a specific territory and shared a common history, culture, and identity. They were a
   a. state.
   b. nation.
   c. government.
   d. political order.

10. Which of these processes is involved in defining a group as "they" during times of political upheaval?
    a. treating members of the groups as less than human
    b. blaming the other group for starting the conflict
    c. labeling the other group as evil
    d. all of the above

11. Which of the following best describes third parties in the United States?
    a. They have a good record in terms of winning elections.
    b. Their candidates seldom win elections.
    c. They usually do well in state elections but not in national elections.
    d. They have done well in times of social turmoil but not in times of social stability.

12. Which of the following is NOT true of political parties?
    a. They are an important basis for forming coalitions.
    b. They sometimes conflict over issues.
    c. They employ lobbyists to influence government policies.
    d. They attempt legitimately to influence government policy.

13. Which of these models stresses that the United States is controlled by leaders of the military, the government, and business?
    a. pluralist
    b. conflict
    c. power-elite
    d. functionalist

14. In the interest of public health, the American Medical Association works to block the actions of tobacco companies. In this context, the AMA is called
    a. a veto group.
    b. a PAC.
    c. a power elite.
    d. an interest group.

15. "Everyone shall live free and equal in dignity and rights" is declared by
    a. the Constitution of the United States.
    b. a Universal Declaration of Human Rights.
    c. the Equal Rights Amendment.
    d. the Family Rights and Privacy Act of 1964 as Amended.

Identifying Sociological Perspectives on the Political Order

For each of the following statements, identify the sociological perspective associated with the statement by writing F for functionalist, C for conflict, or SI for symbolic interactionist, in the appropriate blank.

_____ 1. Democracy does not prevent power from concentrating in the hands of a dominant few.

_____ 2. Groups with the ability to raise large sums of money tend to have more influence over government policy than groups that cannot raise much money.

_____ 3. Political parties are more than just formal organizations; they are also ideas in people's minds and part of their social identities.

_____ 4. Increasingly, political socialization is accomplished by the mass media, especially television.

_____ 5. A central authority is needed to accomplish efficiently the tasks required in overseeing the many institutions in a society with its complex economic and social systems.

_____ 6. The state is needed to maintain order and to interact with other states in the modern world.

True-False

Indicate your response to each of the following statements by circling T for true or F for false.

T F 1. When a person wielding power has a legitimate right to do so, that power is called authority.

T F 2. Most communal societies are ruled by legal-rational authority.

T F 3. A society cannot contain legal-rational, traditional, and charismatic authority at the same time.

T F 4. The junta is a form of authoritarian government.

T F 5. Totalitarian governments are more oppressive than authoritarian governments.

T F 6. There are more members of Congress than there are lobbyists.

T F 7. Men are much more likely to vote than women.

T F 8. According to the power-elite model, democracy in the United States works as it was intended to work.

T F 9. Too much pluralism in a society leads to poor leadership, a lack of coordination, and a lack of focus.

T F 10. The pluralist model maintains that power is diffused throughout society.

T F 11. Terrorism is the noninstitutionalized use of threat, intimidation, and violence to bring about a political objective.

T F 12. Terrorist attacks are more about creating fear than destroying military targets.

T F 13. Marx explained war as something built into the genetic structure of human beings.

T F 14. Politicians have progressively lost respect among American voters.

T F 15. According to the functionalist perspective, there is a continuing struggle within society for control of the government institutions of the state.

NOTE: The answers to these exercises are at the end of the book.

For additional practice tests and other resources please visit the companion web site at http://www.prenhall.com/curry.

Essay

1. Describe C. Wright Mills' power-elite model.

2. What are the four techniques used in the politics of exclusion as "we" become identified as separate from "they"?

3. Discuss Weber's categories of authority. Give an example of each.

4. Compare war with terrorism. Was the World Trade Center disaster a result of an act of war or an act of terrorism? Explain.

5. Why are there third-party movements in American politics?

11

Marriage and the Family

Albert and Lisa have been married for three-and-a-half years. Albert is a machinist; Lisa stays home and takes care of the household. They have one child and are expecting another in six months.

The couple met at a friend's birthday party. Albert was half drunk, and he spotted Lisa sitting on the floor by herself. Immediately attracted, he approached and asked her, "Is this seat taken?" (Blumstein and Schwartz 1983:334). Lisa was put off by his drinking, so she left the party—but Albert would not be deterred. He called her and sent her flowers until she finally agreed to go out with him. Soon they started dating regularly. It was a month before they kissed. Lisa says, "He didn't try anything. He was just really good to me. That made me feel really good. We were both ourselves. . . . I probably fell in love with him before he realized that he was in love with me. And I told him, 'I am not trying to pressure you or anything, but I happen to be in love with you and I'm going to marry you some day, whenever you're ready, and you just let me know whenever the time comes'" (334–336).

Lisa and Albert were married in a big church wedding. They moved into a small, plain house in a pleasant neighborhood with tidy lawns and front yards brightened with flowers in the summer. When the couple married, they agreed that the home was Lisa's responsibility, and Lisa feels guilty when forced to ask Albert for help around the house. "The house and kids are my full-time job," she says. "It's what we wanted" (338). They are both satisfied with their sex life and agree that sex is a special, intimate relationship. Albert says, "There's no indecision on that, because we are both married to each other and we are each other's sexual partner for life" (343).

Lisa and Albert embrace traditional family values so strongly that they appear to be a corny stereotype of the perfect couple. What are the values that have brought Lisa and Albert so much happiness?

Perhaps most obvious is the value placed on love. American culture prescribes that love is a prerequisite for marriage, in part because love provides the emotional motivation to develop intense social relationships and in part because it helps to sustain the couple when difficulties arise. Another value is lifelong commitment; marriage is forever. This assumption is ingrained so deeply in American culture that the idea of marrying for one year, five years, or some other specific number of years seems bizarre—although it is a logical possibility. Because marriage is supposed to be a lifelong relationship, separation or divorce is defined as a personal failure. Marital fidelity is another important part of the commitment, and spouses are supposed to have sexual relations only with each other. To do otherwise is to jeopardize the trust on which the marriage is built. Finally, the sanctity of the family is important; the family is supposed to be a sanctuary from the pressures of life, a "haven in a heartless world" (Lasch 1977). Thus, the privacy of a household is inviolate, and family matters are primarily the business of the family itself. Only in unusual circumstances are friends and relatives to become involved, and only in extreme circumstances is the state to intrude.

As the example of Lisa and Albert illustrates, the traditional American family consists of a mother, a father, and children living together under a single roof, supported by the man's wages and nurtured by the woman's care. This image of the family is portrayed so persistently in American culture that people often feel that any other arrangement is exotic or perverse. Nevertheless, the traditional American family is atypical among the societies of the world, and it is even atypical in the United States. Only about 20 percent of American families now consist of a full-time housewife, a working husband, and one or more children.

Because different societies support different family forms, an adequate explanation of the family must take this diversity into account. What do the various family forms have in common that can serve as a basis for defining the family? Sociologists have identified the following common factors:

1. To be members of a family, individuals must be related to each other by blood or by marriage.

2. Family members reside permanently together, usually under a single roof. In some types of families, members may live in communes, or children might live apart from their parents for a period to attend school or undergo other training. Much less commonly, the husband might live in one dwelling, whereas the wife lives in another.

3. Some family members are entitled to have sexual relations with other family members, and some members are expected to bear children. These family members usually are expected to support and socialize their offspring.

4. Considered as a whole, the family constitutes an economic unit: members share income, own assets jointly, and have the right to use family property.

In brief, a **family** is a group of individuals who are related in some way, usually live together, engage in sex, have responsibility for rearing children, and function as an economic unit (see Eshleman 1984).

Chapter Preview

For many years, a great transformation has been taking place both in the structure of the family as a social institution and in the nature of relationships among family members. To understand this change, we will examine several important questions in this chapter. What types of families are there, and how has the family been transformed? What are kinship systems, and how do they weave together the people in a society? Why do people get married, and why do they get divorced? How does the family as an institution differ in majority and minority populations? What issues face families today? We end the chapter with a discussion of how the three major sociological perspectives view the family and what the future holds for marriage and the family.

The Great Social Transformation and Marriage and the Family

A major change in family structure accompanied the change from communal society to associational society. New employment opportunities fostered social mobility and a redefinition of the family home as a private retreat. As people began to move to urban areas, family size decreased. Prior to industrialization, rural households performed a wide variety of functions and activities, and often served as an abode for a wide assortment of people, including servants, apprentices, orphaned children, elders without relatives, and live-in boarders. In urban industrial societies, however, bureaucracies provide many of the services formerly provided by families: schools watch the children during the day; insurance policies and welfare organizations provide help in times of need; and the police provide protection in times of danger. Individuals thus are more free to establish intimate emotional relationships with a single person, because they do not need the services formerly provided by other family members (Hareven 1994).

Changing family functions and values have also affected child rearing. In preindustrial society, parenting roles were intermixed with social and economic roles.

Family ▲ A group of individuals who are related in some way, usually living together, engaging in sex, having responsibility for rearing children, and functioning as an economic unit.

Children were considered economic assets and were regarded as members of the workforce. Adolescence was virtually unknown as a distinct stage of development, and family members were more integrated into common economic activities that blurred gender and age categories. As a result of industrialization, the family ceased to be a work unit, and, in most cases, it limited its economic activities to consumption and child care.

Types of Families

All societies must perpetuate their populations and must confront the biological fact that human children require a long period of socialization, support, and protection before reaching independence. The universal solution to this problem is the creation of a social unit that has responsibility for rearing the young. Although all societies recognize the family as a basic social institution, different societies give preference to different family forms.

In industrialized societies, the most common type is the **nuclear family**: a unit composed of a husband, a wife, and their children. Most people belong to two nuclear families. One is the **family of orientation**, the nuclear family into which they were born. The other is the **family of procreation**, which consists of their spouse and their children.

For most purposes, a nuclear family acts as an independent decision-making unit. For example, the parents are entrusted with rearing the children and with deciding where to live and what to buy. If the nuclear family cannot be self-supporting, help may come from other individuals or from government welfare agencies, but this help is meant to be temporary (see the discussion of poverty in Chapter 6).

A variation on the nuclear family is the **blended** or **reconstituted family**, in which spouses and their children from former marriages live together as a single

Nuclear family ▲ A social unit composed of a husband, a wife, and their children.

Family of orientation ▲ The nuclear family into which a person is born.

Family of procreation ▲ A person, a spouse, and their children.

Blended or reconstituted family ▲ A form of family in which spouses and their children from former marriages live together as a single nuclear family.

Prior to industrialization, households performed a wide variety of functions and activities. They also served as home to an assortment of different people. This 1876 American lithograph (left) depicts a very busy household from the Revolutionary War period. In contemporary households, most of the economic activity takes place outside the home. The family in the photograph on the right is together now, but soon it will disperse, and each family member will spend most of the day in a bureaucratic setting away from home.

nuclear family. Although the blended family might seem new, it is actually an old form. In past times, when the death rate was high, widows and widowers with children were common; when they remarried, they created a blended family. Nowadays blended families usually result from the remarriage of divorced parents. Divorce also has given rise to the **binuclear family**, in which each divorced parent establishes a separate household and the children spend time in both households. In effect, the children are reared in two separate nuclear family environments. With the growth of binuclear families in American society, more and more children find themselves in the role of a stepchild.

The **extended family** is composed of two or more generations of kin who function as an independent social and economic unit. Extended families are the basic social unit in traditional societies. An extended family might include the spouses, the spouses' children, the spouses' parents, and possibly, the brothers and sisters of the spouses. The extended family is large enough to permit a complex division of labor. Whereas in a nuclear family, the husband and wife must assume total responsibility for providing income and socializing children, in an extended family, those responsibilities may be allocated to different individuals. For instance, the grandparents may nurture the children, whereas the biological parents are responsible for securing the family's income.

Marriage and Kinship

We have talked about some of the variations in family form in the United States. However, systems of marriage and kinship vary considerably across the world, as illustrated by an extreme form of the traditional family practiced by the Nayar of the Malabar region of India. Nayar girls marry before they reach adolescence, and the Nayar wife, once married, probably will never see her husband again. When the married girl matures, she lives in her own hut near her brothers and takes lovers from the Nambudiri, a rich and powerful tribe that resides nearby. She has children by Nambudiri men; yet the biological fathers have nothing to do with their offspring. Child rearing falls to the mother, whereas her brothers assume responsibility for family support.

This arrangement provides substantial advantages to both groups. The Nambudiri have remained wealthy by passing inheritance only to the eldest son of the eldest son, a custom that prevents family holdings from becoming fragmented among several children. Moreover, only the eldest son can marry, and he must marry a Nambudiri woman, thus keeping wealth within the Nambudiri tribe. The younger sons, who are not permitted to marry, take Nayar women as lovers.

The Nayar find this arrangement beneficial because the resulting children are kept under the control of the mother and her brothers without interference from outsiders. The "losers" are the Nambudiri girls who remain single. They live in strict seclusion and may venture outside the house only if they are covered from head to foot, with their faces hidden by an umbrella.

As the example of the Nayar and the Nambudiri suggests, different types of families and kinship systems may be found throughout the world. Despite the differences, however, the fact remains that all societies have some system for creating marital units and kinship networks.

Kinship Patterns

Virtually every individual is embedded in a system of **kinship**: a network of people who are related by marriage, blood, or social practice (such as adoption). Kinship is important because it enables the society to perpetuate itself over time. It does so in at least two ways.

First, all societies must socialize children and transmit property, wealth, and power from one generation to the next. Kinship plays an important role in these

Binuclear family ▲ A family form in which each member of a divorced couple establishes a separate household between which their children divide their time.

Extended family ▲ A family composed of two or more generations of kin that functions as an independent social and economic unit.

Kinship ▲ A network of people who are related by marriage, blood, or social practice (such as adoption).

processes. In the United States, for instance, inheritance usually passes through the kin network, first to the surviving spouse and then, if there is no surviving spouse or when the spouse dies, to the children. Power also follows kinship, as when the eldest son assumes responsibility for making family decisions or when the owner of a family business proclaims that his son or daughter will become the next chief executive officer. Thus, kinship provides continuity between generations and perpetuates culture, organizations, and institutions over time.

A second way in which kinship enables a society to perpetuate itself over time is through the creation of complex social bonds. A marriage that unites members of different families creates **affinal relationships**: social bonds based on marriage. Because many people are involved in any given kinship network, affinal relationships may unite hundreds (or even thousands) of people who otherwise would have no bonds among themselves. Although affinal kinship produces highly unified groups, different affinal groups sometimes clash as they compete for power and wealth. These clashes may have far-reaching consequences if one group assumes power and systematically vanquishes members of the opposing group (Goldschmidt 1990). Nevertheless, kinship is a mechanism for placing individuals into a broader social network that helps to order social relationships.

In the United States, kin typically include an individual's family of procreation and of orientation, along with grandparents, aunts, uncles, and cousins. All other relatives are considered distant kin and for most purposes are treated as nonkin. In this regard, the American system is somewhat unusual, as many societies restrict kinship to either the mother's or the father's relatives (see the Social Change box, From Clan to Couple).

Affinal relationship ▲ Social bonds based on marriage.

Social Change ●■▲ From Clan to Couple

We often praise the modern nuclear family as an ideal family form. But we may be unaware that a common Native American family structure, the matricentric clan, survived for thousands of years before the coming of the white settlers. For instance, among the preindustrial Creek Indians of Florida, power was vested in the women of the clan. The women were assisted by their brothers, who helped maintain clan loyalty and discipline by supporting their sisters and mothers (Spoeher 1947).

A woman's brother, whom we would call the "uncle on the mother's side," oversaw his sister's children. If the children became ill, the uncle would tend to their health, and when they were older, he would help select their spouses. The uncle was also the primary authority figure in political matters. As a consequence of this arrangement, the biological father played a limited role. Relieved from the autocratic role of disciplinarian, the father had less stressful relations with his children and welcomed the participation of the uncle. In the event of divorce or the father's death, the uncle would assume complete responsibility for the care of the children.

The Creek matrilineal system, however, was undermined through contact and conflict with whites. The extended-kin organization gradually shifted to a system based on marriage and the nuclear family (Goldschmidt 1990). The biological father assumed more responsibility for education and discipline, and the uncle lost his former position of authority. Personal property came to be inherited by the father's children, rather than by his sister's children. As females and uncles lost status, the very nature of the extended-kin arrangement changed.

Under the new arrangement, an economically successful Creek had little reason to remain socially close to less successful clan members. Intermarriage further encouraged a breakdown of clan relationships. Creeks with white spouses adopted white customs and learned English and business skills that moved them further from their Creek roots. Allegiance to the clan was further undermined by the boarding schools that were introduced to educate Creek children. With the children physically separated from their families and under the domination of missionary teachers, the ties between the individual and the clan sometimes dissolved completely.

To the Creeks, the domination of the uncle and the reduced role of the biological father had always seemed a natural and sound arrangement. They reasoned that the brother (who became the uncle) had grown up with his sister and therefore knew her better than the husband, who had come upon the scene later in her life. The uncle, moreover, was a member of the same clan as his sister and hence would always have the clan's welfare in mind.

CQ What did the Creek Indian family lose as it was forced to change from a clan-based family structure to one based on couples? ◆ What did it gain?

Tokyo, Japan. A bride and groom pose for a formal wedding picture in front of Meiji-jingu Shrine, Tokyo's most splendid Shinto shrine. Romantic love is becoming more important in Japan, once a very traditional nation.

Traditional societies often are organized by elaborate family networks, but in industrial societies, members of the nuclear family are the center of each person's most important kin relationships. The ultimate responsibility for children, jobs, housing, finance, and a host of other matters resides with the nuclear family rather than with the extended kin. To be sure, the extended kin might gather to celebrate weddings, holidays, and other events, but on a day-to-day basis, these kinfolk usually go their separate ways.

Marriage

When two individuals become involved in a socially approved relationship that involves intimate, mutual long-term obligations, and when they have fulfilled the customary or legal requirements, their relationship is termed **marriage**. Every society has rituals and laws that define a valid marriage. The rituals might be sparse, requiring only standing before a justice of the peace, or extraordinarily elaborate, as in weddings of kings and queens that involve thousands of people. In either case, once the couple is married, the two parties are expected to have sexual relations with each other—although societies vary as to how strictly they demand that sex take place only within marriage.

In most societies, people marry for pragmatic reasons such as wealth or power. In a minority of societies, however (including the United States), people are expected to marry for love. This expectation occasionally might be breached in practice, but most people in the United States are opposed to marrying for purely pragmatic reasons. Rather, they assume that sometime during maturity all people will fall in love, marry, have children, and then live out their lives in a home of their own. In the United States, this cultural assumption is overwhelmingly powerful: 60 percent of the population is currently married, and about 20 percent have been married.

Why do so many people marry? How do the matching and the sorting of prospective spouses take place? What guides this process? The answer is romantic love (sometimes simply called "love"). Although romantic love is seldom defined very clearly, people presumably recognize love by symptoms such as an almost obsessive yearning to be with that special person, by sexual desire for that person, and by excitement and joy when in that person's company.

Romantic Love

American teenagers, particularly young women, are often pictured as being overly susceptible to the influences of romantic love. Popular radio stations aimed at the youth market play songs that emphasize love and romance, and the videos on MTV show couple after couple falling in love. Research has shown, however, that teenagers share a belief that love is important but not all-important in male-female relationships (Simon, Eder, and Evans 1992).

Romantic love is an emotional identification between two individuals that is so intense that they are convinced they cannot be happy without each other (Fisher 1996). Although romantic love might seem to be a modern phenomenon, the conventions of romantic love in Western culture date back to the Middle Ages. Knights pledged their services to a noblewoman, who would lavish praise on them in return. This early form of romantic love was an idealized display that was never intended to culminate in sexual relations or marriage (Beigel 1951).

During the nineteenth century, romantic love was recognized but was not an important consideration in marriage. The dowry, family standing, and political ties were the basis for marriage, especially among the upper classes. To be sure, the spouses might develop affection for each other over time, but loving (or even liking) was not an overriding consideration in making a match.

Marriage ▲ A state that occurs when two individuals are involved in a socially approved relationship that involves intimate, mutual long-term obligations, and they have fulfilled the customary ceremonial or legal requirements.

Romantic love ▲ An emotional identification between two individuals that is so intense that they are convinced that they cannot be happy without each other.

Today, romantic love as a basis for marriage seems to be more highly valued in societies that have weak extended family ties and less valued in traditional societies in which kinship networks reinforce the relationship between marriage partners (Simmons, von Kolke, and Shimizu 1997). Why should this be so? The answer is to be found in the rise of industrialization and the growth of the nuclear family (Cherlin 1981; Goode 1982; Kammeyer 1987).

In industrial societies, romantic love provides an incentive to marry and to form families. In contrast, where the culture prescribes that people marry for economic and political reasons, romantic love is viewed as a disruption to an orderly society. The Chinese, for example, traditionally have married for economic reasons, but under the current influence of foreign popular culture, some Chinese youths now are marrying for love (WuDunn 1991).

Another reason that romantic love is more highly valued in industrial societies is that romantic love provides a source of support in times of stress. In a nuclear family system, social support is particularly important for young couples, who are expected to solve their family problems with minimal help from relatives. In extended-family systems, love is not as important because couples can draw on their kin for help.

Finally, when spouses are in love, they become committed primarily to each other rather than to their families of orientation. Thus, romantic love helps to transfer commitment from the existing kin to the newly created family of procreation. This transfer must be accomplished if the new couple is to become an independent social unit.

Like many social phenomena, romantic love appears to be an expression of "human nature," but it is actually a social process that facilitates marriage in some societies. The typical American, who expects to fall in love, might spend years waiting for the "right person" to begin courtship. On the other hand, an individual socialized into a society that does not recognize romantic love would not expect to "fall in love" and so could accept a marriage to a virtual stranger arranged by his or her parents (Dion and Dion 1996).

Courtship

Courtship is the relationship between people who are preparing for marriage to each other. In the United States, the media portray courtship as a heightened period of love that can strike without warning and without logic. This aspect of love is celebrated continually in stories that involve "two star-crossed lovers" who meet, fall in love, and suffer whatever consequences the author has in store for them. A moment of critical thinking, however, raises doubts about the randomness of Cupid's arrow. People overwhelmingly choose spouses of their own race, ethnicity, religion, and social class—a phenomenon called **endogamy**. When they marry outside their own group, they are engaging in **exogamy**. Some social forces must be causing people to marry individuals like themselves. What are the factors that render romantic love nonrandom? The factors are propinquity, ethnicity and race, and values.

Propinquity Propinquity, or physical closeness, constrains romantic love for the simple reason that people cannot fall in love unless they meet, and they are unlikely to meet if they are far apart. The tendency to choose prospective spouses from neighbors, coworkers, and classmates produces endogamy because people who live close to one another tend to have similar social backgrounds. Consider that schools have roughly homogeneous student populations drawn from mostly homogeneous local neighborhoods. In these circumstances, students are likely to meet others of the same race and similar social class at school. Having met, they are likely to fall in love and marry, thus perpetuating endogamy (Whitbeck and Hoyt 1994).

Ethnicity and Race In general, people tend to marry within their own racial and ethnic group. Less than 1 percent of whites are married to blacks; even among racial groups that have married out the most, such as Japanese Americans, the majority

Endogamy refers to marriage within one's racial or ethnic group. Exogamy refers to marriage outside one's racial or ethnic group.

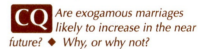 *Are exogamous marriages likely to increase in the near future?* ◆ *Why, or why not?*

 **STUDY TIP**

In a small group, consider the randomness of romantic love. Do you think it is random, or do you think it is affective by specific factors such as propinquity, ethnicity and race, or values? Has the effect of such factors changed in the last generation? As you discuss, stay open to new perspectives and ideas.

Courtship ▲ The relationship between a male and a female who are preparing for marriage to each other.

Endogamy ▲ Marriage in which the couple are members of the same race, ethnicity, religion, or social class.

Exogamy ▲ Marriage in which the couple are from different races, ethnic groups, religions, or social classes.

Propinquity ▲ Physical closeness.

marry within the group (Jiobu 1988). When endogamy is considered along ethnic rather than racial lines, however, intermarriage is more common. For instance, 60 percent of Irish Americans and 75 percent of Italian Americans currently marry someone from another white ethnic group. Religion is an important ethnic factor that contributes to endogamy. Even though marriages across religious lines are more common now than in the past, people still tend to marry someone of the same or a similar religion. Indeed, many religions discourage interreligious marriages by requiring that both partners be of the same faith.

Values   Marital endogamy is reinforced by the values of American culture. For example, television advertisements invariably depict racially endogamous couples. Several popular television quiz shows have contestants select their dream dates, but only from a field of candidates of the same race. At the interpersonal level, friends and family further reinforce the values of endogamy. This support is so strong that in some instances, a young person marrying outside the group risks being ostracized by friends and family. Even so, the rate of exogamy has been on the rise in contemporary American society.

Dimensions of Marriage and the Family

The Nayar and the Nambudiri, discussed earlier, illustrate how different marriage and kinship systems can work effectively. The same groups also illustrate another point: the basic biological unit of the family is the mother and her children (recall that Nayar women rear the children). Given this fact, all societies must determine how to fit the man into the family unit. It is not surprising that different societies have resolved this issue in different but effective ways.

Limited Marriage Patterns   Marriage can involve only a limited number of combinations of spouses. Most familiar to Westerners is **monogamy**, a marriage consisting of one male spouse and one female spouse (Kanazawa and Still 1999). In recent years, gay rights groups have been pressuring state legislators to define marriage as consisting of a bond between two spouses of different or the same sex. In contrast, a marriage consisting of multiple spouses is called **polygamy**. This form falls into three types: (1) *polygyny*, a marriage of one husband and two or more wives; (2) *polyandry*, a marriage of one wife and two or more husbands; and (3) *group marriage*, a marriage of several wives and several husbands, each of whom is married to all of the other spouses.

Polygamy is permitted widely throughout the world but is now illegal in the United States. In the past, however, the most notable American polygamists were the Mormons of the nineteenth century. At that time, Mormons believed that plural marriage (as they called it) was decreed by God, and furthermore, that it eliminated the evils of prostitution and the tendency for men to divorce their wives in favor of younger women. The Mormon Church officially abandoned plural marriage in 1890 (Elisha 2002). Even so, it is estimated that perhaps ten thousand to thirty thousand Mormons still practice plural marriage, especially in isolated rural areas where bigamy laws are not strictly enforced.

In most societies, the motivation for having multiple wives is based less on sex than on economics and politics. For example, Ibn Saud, the founder of the ruling Saud family of Saudi Arabia, had a total of 35 wives, chosen from the independent tribes that once dotted the Arabian Desert. In accordance with Muslim tradition, however, he never had more than four wives at one time. He married them to cement the political affiliations that were part of his successful campaign to unite Arabia under one rule and to form the modern country of Saudi Arabia.

Although about three-fourths of all societies favor a form of marriage other than monogamy, most men in the world have only one wife (Murdock 1949). A major reason is that many societies in which polygamy is practiced are small, and most of the world's population lives in monogamous societies. Another reason is that even where

Monogamy ▲ A marriage consisting of one male spouse and one female spouse.

Polygamy ▲ A marriage consisting of multiple spouses.

The man in this photo is pictured with his nine wives. This is an example of a polygynous marriage in Utah, a state founded by the Mormons, who once practiced polygamy.

polygyny is accepted, it can be practiced only by wealthy men who can afford to support more than one wife and the many children that multiple marriages produce.

In contrast to polygyny, group marriage and polyandry are rare and occur only in atypical social circumstances. One example is the Toda of India. They practiced female infanticide, and as a result, they suffered from a chronic shortage of marriageable women. To alleviate this problem, they adopted polyandry. Thus, when a Toda woman married, she became the wife of a man and of all of his brothers. The brothers shared the wife and were collectively responsible for supporting her.

Descent   Every society has norms regarding **descent**, the system by which kinship is traced over generations. In effect, descent tells people who their relatives are and specifies their rights and obligations with respect to one another. Logically, descent could pass through either the mother's side of the family, the father's side, or both. Because men dominate most pastoral and agrarian societies, in those societies, kinship and inheritance pass through the man's side of the family. This system is called patrilineal descent. The opposite situation occurs in matrilineal descent, in which kinship and inheritance pass through the mother's side of the family. In *bilineal* descent, lineage and inheritance pass through both sides of the family. Unlike most other societies, the United States and many other Western, industrialized societies support bilineal descent.

Residence   Societies develop norms about where married couples should reside. In traditional societies, marriage unites kinship networks, and the couple is expected to live with or near the kinfolk. In some of these societies, the newly married couple lives with the kinfolk of the wife's mother—a *matrilocal arrangement*—whereas in other societies, the couple lives with the kinfolk of the husband's father—a *patrilocal arrangement*. Marriage in industrial societies, however, is less a unification of kin networks than a joining of individuals. Consequently, newlyweds typically reside in their own, independent households apart from their relatives—a *neolocal arrangement*.

A new form of neolocal residence has emerged in recent years. As women have entered the labor force in large numbers, some families have had to adopt a new commuting pattern because the wife's employment is in a different community from her husband's. In this situation, each spouse maintains a separate residence in the city of

Descent ▲ The system by which kinship is traced over generations.

Society Today ● ■ ▲

Is Premarital Sex Morally Wrong?

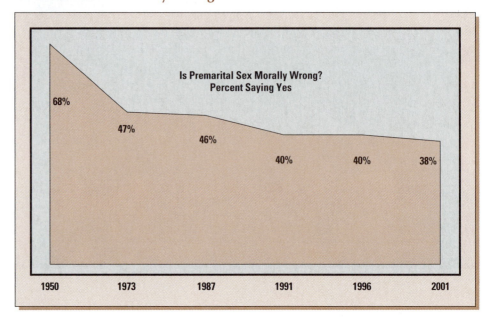

Is Premarital Sex Morally Wrong?
Percent Saying Yes

68% 47% 46% 40% 40% 38%

1950   1973   1987   1991   1996   2001

Premarital sex is now much more acceptable than in the past. Nevertheless, note that about four out of ten adults *say* that it is morally wrong (gallop.com; accessed October 10, 2003).

CQ Do think that what people say about the morality of premarital sex prevents them from engaging in it? ◆ If so, to what extent? ◆ What is your reasoning?

employment, and the spouses reunite regularly on weekends and vacations. As a result, the couple regularly spend time in both residences (Anderson and Spruill 1993). Such a commuting couple is said to be a bilocal household.

Power   A family system in which a man (usually the husband or the eldest male) has the most power is a patriarchy. Historically, patriarchy has been the predominant family system in the world (see Chapter 8). Although a society theoretically could vest most of the family power in women—in a system known as a *matriarchy*—no known society ever has been truly matriarchal. Family systems in which women hold some power are fairly common, however; these are called *matricentric* families. The Nayar, mentioned earlier, are an example (the Nayar also are matrilocal). In the United States, African American families are more likely to be matricentric than are white families, and about one-half of all black children are reared in a matricentric setting.

● ■ ▲ Pausing to Think   About Marriage and Kinship

In communal societies, most of a person's life takes place within the family, whereas in associational societies, family life is separated from a person's job, recreation, and other activities. Marriage and kinship determine who is responsible for supporting and rearing children and enable the society to perpetuate itself. Societies have developed different systems of marriage and kinship. The reliance on romantic love is one of the less common methods of family formation, but it is well suited to the nuclear family in industrial society.

CQ Why does American society emphasize romantic love but practice endogamy?

Alternative Family Forms in the United States

Although the family has been one of the most stable institutions in American history, the traditional family cannot satisfy all of the demands placed on it by the millions of people living in a society that is passing from the industrial to the postindustrial stage. Whereas in 1980, one American household in three consisted of a married couple with children under 18 (a "traditional family"), that description now applies to only one American household in four. This decline, however, does not mean that marriage is no longer associated with the family. The overwhelming majority (77 percent) of families in the United States still include a married couple (U.S. Bureau of the Census 2002). Moreover, as Figure 11.1 shows, of those children living with married-couple parents, the overwhelming majority live with their mother and father.

In the past, people could opt to marry or to remain single. It was assumed, however, that single people were destined to a life of loneliness and that married people were fulfilling the natural course of human events. Today several marital options exist, and society is more tolerant of alternative living arrangements. What are some of these alternatives?

Serial Monogamy

American culture and law permit a person to have more than one spouse, but not at the same time—a pattern called **serial monogamy**. An individual thus can marry, divorce, remarry, redivorce, and so on without limit (Pinsof 2002). Apparently the record for serial monogamy is held by a woman who had 61 husbands (Wallechinsky and Wallace 1975). Because divorce is so common, serial monogamy is now almost the statistical norm: 46 percent of all marriages in a given year involve a groom or a bride (or both) who were married previously (U.S. Bureau of the Census 1997).

Serial monogamy is popular because marriage is popular. Many people like being married but cannot establish a lifetime commitment to one particular person. The pattern of marriage, divorce, and remarriage enables people to participate continually in the institution of marriage, but with different partners. The result is that the typical American man will marry more women over his lifetime than the typical man living in a polygamous society (Bernard 1982).

The Single-Parent Family

In 2000, there were 17 million single-parent families in the United States (U.S. Bureau of the Census 2002). Although many people believe that the single-parent family is a product of loose morality and premarital pregnancies, that belief is incorrect. The majority of single-parent households result from the divorce or separation of spouses.

Becoming a single parent adversely affects women more than men—women on average experience a 27 percent decrease in their standard of living, whereas men experience a 10 percent increase (Peterson 1996; Weitzman 1987). Approximately one-third of all families with children now live below the federal poverty line, and one-fifth of those impoverished families consist of a single mother and her children (U.S. Bureau of the Census 1994). As these figures suggest, poverty strikes disproportionately at women (and their children); that is, poverty is becoming feminized.

One reason for the feminization of poverty is that women earn less than men. Thus, the loss of the man's income causes a proportionately greater loss for the woman than the loss of the woman's income causes for the man. Another reason is that women do not accumulate much economic security. They have little in the way of retirement funds, insurance benefits, savings, and other assets. When children are involved, the courts grant custody to the woman in more than 90 percent of the cases, but about half of all husbands refuse to make child-care payments. Despite the law,

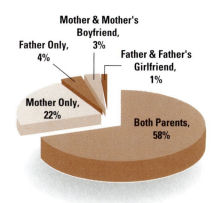

FIGURE 11.1 Living Arrangements of Children

Most children in the United States live with both parents while a smaller but substantial number live with their mothers.

SOURCE: U.S. Department of Commerce. 2003. "Two Married Parents the Norm," *Commerce News,* July 12.

Serial monogamy ▲ A cultural pattern that permits a person to have more than one spouse, but not at the same time.

avoiding payment is relatively easy. For instance, it is all but impossible to collect when the delinquent man lives out of state, and even when he lives in-state, it is difficult: he must be served with a judgment, taken to court, and ordered to pay by a judge. If he still does not pay, the services of a marshal must be obtained to serve a payment order. Faced with this tangle of legal bureaucracy, many women lack the resources to prosecute their ex-husbands, and therefore they drop the matter (Associated Press 1995a).

For children, growing up in a single-parent family may be more difficult than growing up in a two-parent family. As yet it is not clear the extent to which children from single-parent family settings are socially or emotionally disadvantaged as compared with children from two-parent homes (Cherlin 1999).

Gay and Lesbian Families

After years of "hiding in the closet," gays and lesbians are proclaiming their sexual preferences and openly establishing gay and lesbian families. At Stanford University, for instance, gay and lesbian student couples have the same housing, health care, and campus privileges as married students (Dodge 1991). With few exceptions, however, most religious bodies will not perform a marriage ceremony for a gay or lesbian couple, and the legal standing of any such marriages is ambivalent in many states (Tully 1994). There may be unresolved issues—for instance, if one spouse in a homosexual marriage dies, does the survivor automatically inherit all of the deceased person's property, as is usually the case in a heterosexual marriage?

Some progress toward resolving these and other legal issues has been made recently. Several cities, including Seattle and San Francisco, have passed laws that permit a gay or lesbian couple to declare publicly and legally that they are "domestic partners." Although these partnerships are not equivalent to marriage in the traditional sense, they give same-sex couples many of the same rights as any married couple.

There are marked gender differences in relationships between homosexual partners. Lesbian female partners tend to be faithful, but gay male partners often have sexual relationships outside the family setting: some 90 percent of gays living in a family relationship have sexual contacts with other men. Gay and lesbian couples cannot

Gay male couple eats dinner with their two adopted Hispanic children in dining room. Sociologists would have little trouble defining such an arrangement as a family because it fulfills all the functions of a traditional family. American society, however, has yet to fully accept such arrangements.

procreate biologically, of course, but one member of a lesbian pair may bear a child through artificial insemination (Haimes and Weiner 2000). Sometimes a woman with children enters into a lesbian alliance, thus creating a lesbian family with children. (The same process occasionally occurs among gay men.) Child custody may become a hotly contested issue in these situations, but in a marked departure from past practices, courts sometimes grant custody to the homosexual parent. Research shows that children with lesbian and gay parents develop psychologically, intellectually, behaviorally, and emotionally in a positive direction (Fitzgerald 1999).

Cohabitation

When partners share a household and engage in intimate social and sexual relations without being formally married, they are engaged in **cohabitation**. Overall, about 2 million American couples are cohabiting; the practice is particularly popular among the young. Almost half of all cohabiting couples expect eventually to marry their partner. If they fulfill this expectation, cohabitation becomes a conventional marriage (Blumstein and Schwartz 1983). The law now recognizes that a cohabiting partner might have a claim on the other partner's assets, and in some cases, monetary support (sometimes called "palimony") has been granted when a couple separates.

Before the 1960s, cohabitation—"living in sin"—was widely viewed as deviant, and the open cohabitation that did take place occurred mostly among the less affluent. Cohabiting couples often had difficulty in finding a place to live, and they were an embarrassment to their families. In most places, cohabitation was illegal, but there was little need to enforce the law, because social sanctions prevented most people from trying it. Cohabitation now is more widely accepted and for many couples a step in the courtship process leading to marriage (Techman 2003). However, critics contend that cohabitation loosens family ties and places emphasis on personal values at the expense of family values (Hunt and Hunt 1987). Couples who cohabit before marriage are more likely to experience marriage dissolution than those who do not cohabit, so it appears that cohabitation does not provide a successful introduction to the married state (Smock 2000).

Independent Living

One of the fastest-growing segments of the American population consists of people who live by themselves. Their number has more than doubled, from 11 million in 1970 to nearly 26 million today (U.S. Bureau of the Census 2002). Although this number is growing, we should not assume that independent living is forced on people or that those who live alone are in some way odd. In fact, the majority are 25 to 54 years old and college educated. They have dated recently, are in good health, and are working for pay (Glick 1994).

The increase in singlehood has several causes. One is the trend among young people to postpone marriage. During the 1970s, the typical woman was 21 years old when she married for the first time, and the typical man was 23 years old. Currently these figures are 26 for men and 24 for women (U.S. Bureau of the Census 2002). As a result, people are living alone longer. Another reason for the increase in independent living is the increase in longevity. When a spouse dies after decades of marriage, the survivor may not have anyone to live with or may prefer to live alone. Because the elderly are a substantial segment of those who live independently, the ever-growing number of elders means that the number of people living independently will increase in the future (McGarry and Schoen 2000). Divorce is another reason for the increase in adults who are living alone. Although many divorced persons eventually remarry, there is a time between marriages during which the divorced person without children will establish a single-person household. Finally, our culture has become more accepting of single adulthood as a normal state of living. Earlier in this century,

Cohabitation ▲ A situation in which partners share a household and engage in intimate social and sexual relations without being formally married.

Society Today ● ■ ▲

Living Alone

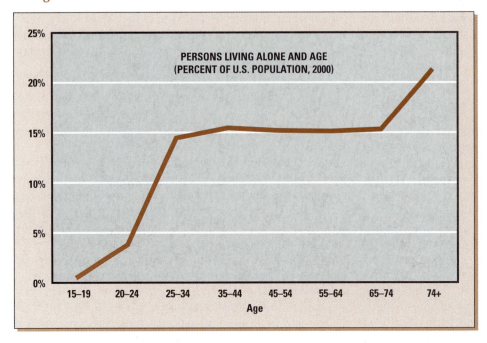

At younger ages, relatively few people live by themselves. However, beginning at about the mid-twenties, people begin to live alone. The percentage remains fairly constant until age 65 or so, and then increases to a little over 20 percent (U.S. Bureau of the Census, 2002).

 Most college students do not live alone, and very few have ever lived alone. After you graduate, would you prefer to live alone? ◆ Why or why not?

123 **STUDY TIP**

Make a chart naming and describing the alternative family forms in the United States. Include information about why each alternative has developed.

the single adult was looked on as someone who simply did not fit in with the normal life cycle.

More women than men live alone—women account for about 40 percent of all single people (U.S. Bureau of the Census 2002). One reason for this statistic is women's longevity. There are more widows than widowers, and (as mentioned before) female elders often live alone. Moreover, divorced women are less likely to remarry, in part because they typically have custody of children and have low incomes, and in part because they choose to live independently (see the Society Today box, Living Alone).

● ■ ▲ Pausing to Think   About Alternative Family Forms in the United States

The number of people in traditional families is declining, whereas the number of people living in alternative family forms is increasing. These changes are occurring because of divorce, toleration of alternative arrangements, a willingness to leave a bad marriage, and the tendency for the young today to postpone marriage. Nevertheless, the overwhelming majority of families still include a married couple.

 Is there a typical American family? ◆ Do alternative family forms fulfill the same functions as the traditional family? ◆ Why, or why not?

Racial and Ethnic Variations in Family Forms

As we saw in Chapter 7, race and ethnicity are powerful forces that shape American social institutions. It is not surprising, therefore, that the family forms found in various racial and ethnic groups differ from the prevalent form found among white Anglo-Saxon Protestants (WASPs). These differences are illustrated by African Americans and Mexican Americans, the two largest racial-ethnic minorities in the United States.

The African American Family

As we discussed in Chapter 7, many African Americans live in poverty. Because of the resulting economic uncertainty, they may find it difficult to form families that are similar to the traditional American family. Whereas some 75 percent of whites with children live in two-parent families, 40 percent of African Americans live in such family groups (U.S. Bureau of the Census 2002). Statistics such as that illustrate how the African American family differs from the traditional white family, but how are the differences explained? What are the consequences?

One answer to these questions was suggested during the upheavals of the civil rights movement in the 1960s. Daniel Moynihan, a social scientist who later became a U.S. senator, argued that the African American family was a product of slavery and therefore was matricentric in form. Furthermore, this type of family was dysfunctional in modern American society because it produced a continual stream of deviance, poverty, and welfare dependency (Moynihan 1965). Moynihan predicted that over time the problems would grow worse: new generations of African Americans would mature, form matricentric families of their own, and repeat the cycle of poverty. Moynihan was immediately embroiled in controversy. Critics charged that he was "blaming the victim"—that is, faulting African Americans for problems that really originated in the racism of the broader society (Healey 1997).

After more than 40 years, the controversy has subsided, and several conclusions may be drawn. First, Moynihan's idea that slavery produced the matricentric family has not been verified by historical evidence. In the period immediately following the end of slavery, African American families typically were composed of husband and wife (Gutman 1976); the matricentric black family was a later development. Second, most sociologists now believe that matricentric families are not inherently pathological, as Moynihan suggested; therefore, matriarchy is not at the center of the problems faced by African Americans. African American men historically have been denied access to well-paying jobs, and without steady incomes, they cannot fill the conventional roles of husband and father. African American women have helped to fill these voids by assuming family dominance. In doing so, they provide a family stability that otherwise would not exist. Had whites faced the same barriers, this argument implies, a white matricentric family would also have developed. Finally, sociologists and other social scientists know that different family forms come into existence in different circumstances. Consequently, the matricentric family is a problem only to people who have been socialized to believe that patriarchy is the only proper family form.

Currently the African American population is divided into "haves" and "have-nots." About one-third of African Americans have reached middle-class standing, and their family structure resembles that found in the broader society. In this regard, they are more fully assimilated into American society than other blacks. In contrast, a segment of the African American population is chronically poor and separated from middle-class black society and from the larger American society as well (see Chapter 6; Wilson 1987). Isolated in neighborhoods filled with crime, deviance, and drugs, these African Americans have few resources or role models to help them achieve upward mobility. To cope with this environment, they have developed an alternative family structure; and in doing so, they have done remarkably well by drawing on the extended family and by forming mutual support systems. For example, an African American family living in the inner city might consist of a mother who works while the grandmother watches the youngest child, and of an older sister who attends school. Such resourcefulness has enabled many African Americans to rear children and to cope with daily life despite the disadvantages they encounter at almost every turn (Healey 1997; Kamo 2000).

The Mexican American Family

Like African Americans, Mexican Americans (Chicanos) are targets of discrimination and typically live in segregated neighborhoods. Chicanos are not far from their country of origin, and the steady stream of new immigrants helps to perpetuate Mexican American culture. For these reasons, the Chicano family may experience a relatively slow pace of change; nevertheless, change is inevitable. It can be described in terms of three major characteristics that originated during the Spanish colonial period in Mexico and the United States (Moore and Cuellar 1970; Moore and Pachon 1985).

First, Mexican Americans are highly familistic, and Chicanos value the family so highly that it has priority over the individual. They maintain extended families that include aunts, uncles, cousins, grandparents, and compadres—persons outside the family who are chosen to be godparents of the family's children. Compadres are usually close friends and are treated as members of the extended family. The practice of compadrazgo (godparentage) knits families together, providing security and mutual aid to individual family members, and it lasts a lifetime.

Patriarchy is a second traditional characteristic of the Chicano family. Mexican American women are subordinate to men and serve as devoted daughters, wives, and mothers. Thus, women are responsible for managing the household and for socializing children. Mexican American women exert behind-the-scenes influence in performing these roles, but their husbands retain the final word in most matters. Perhaps for that reason the language used to describe Mexican American families refers to them by the masculine term *Chicano* rather than the feminine term *Chicana*.

Mexican American patriarchy is linked closely to the Hispanic concept of **machismo**, a value system embracing highly masculine behaviors and including a double standard (Hardin 2002). Whereas wives are expected to be faithful and daughters are expected to be chaste, husbands and older sons are expected to display their machismo by engaging in sexual activity outside the family. Of course, a double standard cannot be put into practice if all women are chaste and faithful. Chicano culture therefore divides womanhood into two types: (1) "good women," whose virtues are unquestioned and whose loyalties and sexuality are channeled into the marital role; and (2) "bad women," who are available for sex and who do not qualify as marriage partners.

The third characteristic of the Mexican American family is authoritarian child rearing. In keeping with the emphasis on machismo, Chicano fathers typically are strict with their children, especially with older boys and girls. Although the mother may administer the punishment, the father is the final disciplinary authority.

The Chicano family tends to be child centered. Children are expected to show respect to their elders, and parents try hard to protect children from bad influences. In addition, men are particularly protective of their sisters and mothers. Divorce is uncommon and is not favored by the Catholic Church.

In this family setting, Chicano children develop a sense of ethnic belonging and identity by age 5 or 6. They feel that they are part of "the people" (La Raza), and they sense that Chicano culture helps them to cope with an Anglo-dominated society (Healey 1997). Language is an important aspect of this coping process; for many Mexican Americans, Spanish is the language of choice even though they may speak

Machismo ▲ A value system embracing highly masculine behaviors and including a "double standard."

English well. Spanish not only facilitates communication with older Chicanos and recent immigrants but also provides the speaker with a private world safe from Anglo penetration.

Currently, some characteristics of the Chicano family are changing in response to changes in American society. Patriarchy is on the decline. Many Mexican American women are now entering the professions and are attaining identities of their own in the process. These women expect to participate in decision making, and they are constructing new roles for themselves. This tendency is especially true among younger, better-paid Chicanas living in urban areas (Grebler et al. 1970; Simpson and Yinger 1985). In addition, the Chicano extended family is losing its central place in Mexican American life, largely because mutual aid is less vital than it used to be. As Chicanos assimilate, they become less dependent on their kin and more able to seek aid from the government when necessary.

●■▲ **Pausing to Think**   **About Racial and Ethnic Variations in Family Forms**

The African American family is often matricentric and represents a response to racism. Mexican American families tend to be patriarchal and have retained the more traditional family arrangements of Mexico.

 If the incomes of African American and Mexican American families were to increase dramatically, would the pace of assimilation also increase? ◆ Why or why not?

Issues in Marriage and the Family

Like all other institutions, the family is always changing. Some changes have gone largely unnoticed by the public, but others have been defined as major social issues.

Marital Dissolution

In a traditional marriage ceremony, the couple vows to stay married "until death do us part." This vow, however, is fairly likely to be broken: half of all American marriages now end in divorce in an average of seven years, or stated another way, the typical marriage lasts seven years or less. The actual rate of marital dissolution is probably higher than statistics indicate because divorce is only one of several types of dissolution. Technically, **divorce** is the dissolution of the legal ties that bind a married couple, but socially it constitutes the recognition that the marriage is over. A *legal separation* is an arrangement whereby spouses agree to take up separate residences. This type of separation is recognized by law and usually precedes a divorce. In contrast, an *informal separation* is not recognized by law but is very common. Perhaps one couple in six has informally separated for at least 48 hours because of disagreements (Kitson 1985). **Desertion** is the social dissolution of marriage that occurs when one spouse leaves the other or simply walks away from the marriage for a prolonged period. Desertion is sometimes called the "poor person's divorce" because it achieves marital dissolution while avoiding the costs and red tape associated with a legal divorce.

Divorce does not occur with equal frequency in all segments of American society. Teenagers are especially prone to separation or divorce because often they have short courtships and may not know each other very well. In addition, teenagers often are financially insecure, inexperienced in worldly matters, and immature in their social relationships. Although romantic love is supposed to conquer all, reality can intrude rudely in a marriage.

Divorce ▲ The dissolution of the legal ties that bind a married couple; socially it constitutes the recognition that the marriage is over.

Desertion ▲ The social dissolution of marriage that occurs when one spouse leaves the other or simply walks away from the marriage for a prolonged period.

Society Today ● ■ ▲

Divorce and Marriage Rate

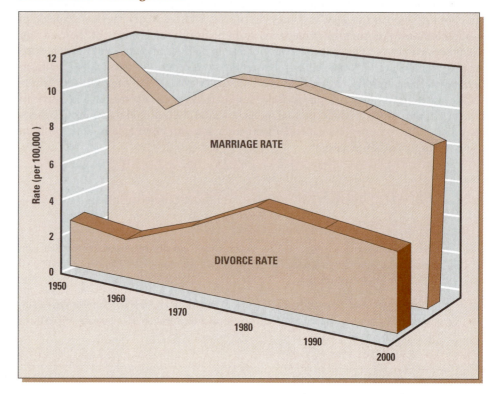

Contrary to popular belief, the divorce rate has actually been decreasing over the last 20 years, and so has the marriage rate. Currently, approximately two marriages take place for every divorce (U.S. Bureau of the Census 2002).

African Americans have higher rates of marital dissolution than whites, apparently in response to the poor economic conditions in which many African Americans live. At the other extreme, divorce rates among Asian Americans are very low, largely because divorce stigmatizes the extended family. As Asian Americans assimilate, their divorce rates should begin to approximate those found among other segments of society.

Whether marital dissolution takes the form of divorce, desertion, or separation, it is one of the most stressful events that an individual can experience (Masterson 1984). Men are more likely to be fired from their jobs after a divorce, and the death rate for divorced men and women is higher than that for married people (Emery et al. 1984; Weiss 1975). Moreover, the typical divorce involves one child, and almost invariably that child suffers from emotional and economic distress (Bartfeld 2000; Seltzer 1994) (see the Society Today box, Divorce and Marriage Rate).

Explaining Marital Dissolution

Virtually everyone enters a marriage believing that it will last forever. Why does this belief go unfulfilled so often? Why do marriages fail routinely? Several intertwined factors are at work.

Society   As discussed earlier in this chapter, the family and society are closely related. In an extended family system, marriage represents the union of kinship lines, political alliances, and economic interests. Divorce is discouraged or prohibited because it would necessitate the dissolution of many valuable, complex relationships. In a nuclear family system, however, divorce requires that only two people disentangle their relationship, and it affects the extended kin only indirectly. Hence there are fewer restraints on marital dissolution.

In addition, the nuclear family is vulnerable to many stresses. It is an independent unit that has relatively few outside resources on which to draw in times of crisis. The loss of a job, for example, can mean economic ruin for the family. A serious illness can mean that no one is available to care for the children. The death of a child may leave a lingering guilt that erodes the emotional bonds between the parents.

To a great extent, the vulnerability of the nuclear family is also affected by social class. An upper- or upper-middle-class family is connected to institutions that can cushion the shocks that a working- or lower-class family must absorb directly. For example, generous severance pay for managers provides a monetary cushion in times of unemployment; health insurance covers expensive medical treatment; and banks are more willing to lend money to people with a history of affluence than to poor people.

Falling Out of Love   In contrast to societies in which love plays only a minor role, in industrial societies, people are expected to marry for love. Romantic love is passionate and unpredictable, however, and people may fall out of love. Without love, a couple may conclude that there is no longer any reason to be married. This situation may be compounded when a couple fails to recognize that married life involves changing diapers, cleaning bathrooms, mowing lawns, stretching paychecks, and other unromantic tasks. As romantic passion gives way to this reality, the couple may conclude that their marriage is foundering and thus may decide to part. This outcome is particularly likely when married people remain open to relationships with others and live in a community in which there is a large supply of people who are potential alternative spouses (South and Lloyd 1995).

Women's Changing Roles   The changing status of women also has contributed to the acceptance of marital dissolution and has reduced the social pressures to marry. The typical married woman now works outside the home and finds increasing social support for combining a career with motherhood and marriage. Financial security was a major reason for staying married in the past, but this reason has become less important. This loosening of economic dependency has had consequences for men as well: A divorced man whose former wife has a job can more easily escape the need to make child-care payments while leaving the woman with the burden of rearing the children. Even so, the gender gap in pay means that women suffer a greater economic loss through divorce, a fact that many men refuse to admit (see Chapter 8).

In sum, sociologists emphasize the social factors involved in marital dissolution. Many of these factors reside in society. It follows from this emphasis that we should not consider every dissolved marriage to be a failure, nor should we always blame the individuals involved.

Domestic Violence

According to our cultural ideals, the family should be a place of love, happiness, and tranquillity. Too often, however, these ideals are shattered by domestic violence. Such violence comes in many forms—physical, psychological, emotional, sexual, and verbal—but always involves the abuse of one family member by another. Abuse of wives and children is the form most commonly studied, but domestic violence also involves wives abusing their husbands, and children abusing their parents.

Spouse Abuse   It is estimated that one-fifth of adult women have been abused by the husband or partners (gallup.com, accessed October 10, 2003). The most common type of physical abuse is battery, either with fists or with weapons. Between 2,000 and 4,000 women are beaten to death each year by their husbands. In fact, battery is the most significant cause of injury to women, even more prevalent than auto accidents, rape, or mugging (Gelles 1979; Skolnick and Skolnick 1998).

There are significant class differences in spouse abuse. Lower- and working-class men often punch their wives in the face, thus leaving highly visible traces of their violence. In contrast, middle- and upper-class men attack the woman's torso and other portions of the body that are not visible to casual observers. When domestic violence occurs, lower-class families are more likely than middle- and upper-class families to call the police (Kammeyer 1987). Because of these differences in reporting and in the visibility of injuries, the typical wife abuser is commonly and incorrectly stereotyped as a working-class or lower-class man. In fact, however, abuse occurs throughout American society (Palermo 1994).

Why do abused wives stay with their husbands (Nabi and Horner 2001)? What prevents them from fighting back? Fear of retribution to their relatives or children is a typical reason; many abusive husbands threaten to seek revenge on other loved ones if the wife leaves. Abused wives, moreover, often have no place to go and no one to care for them (Strube and Barbour 1983). Of equal importance, many abused wives have been reduced to a state of psychological dependence that renders them incapable of leaving. They believe that a failed marriage is an admission of their personal failings and that eventually they will be able to change their husbands for the better. Finally, a battered woman may stay because of her personal history. Women who were abused by their parents tend not to flee an abusive marriage because they have been socialized into playing the part of the victim. Unable to flee, the abused wife becomes even more vulnerable to further abuse.

As the prevalence of wife abuse is coming to be more widely known, steps are being taken to alleviate the problem. More than seven hundred shelters for battered women exist across the country (Berk, Newton, and Fenstermaker 1986; Gondolf 1997). The legal system now provides more protection to battered wives than before, and welfare agencies recognize spouse abuse as a major problem. Other organizations also are becoming aware of the problem. Physicians report suspected cases of wife beating more often than in the past, and police take the crime more seriously.

Not all abuse takes places among spouses. A distressing amount takes place among dating couples. A study of college students found that almost all dating couples had experienced arguments involving crying, sulking, swearing, insults, spiteful acts,

Spousal abuse is a problem in many societies. This photograph shows a mother and her children at a shelter for victims of domestic violence in Tel Aviv, Israel.

CQ *Many people still consider spousal abuse a private matter rather than a social problem. What would a conflict theorist say about this issue?*

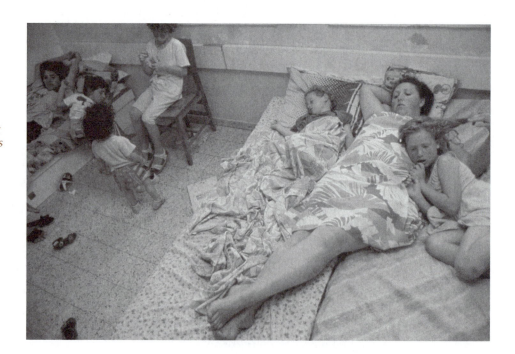

and threats to hit or throw an object at a partner (Lane and Gwartney-Gibbs 1985). Another study of college students found that 40 percent of the respondents surveyed knew of an incident in which threats, pushing, and slapping took place among dating couples. Although women are more often the victims, they are as likely as men to initiate the violence (Makepeace 1981, 1986).

Spouse abuse is found throughout the world. For example, researchers have argued that in parts of India, violence against women reflects their devalued status (Gupta 1993). Throughout her early and teenage years, the young Indian woman's life is controlled in all essential ways by the family's males, and there is much pressure on the young woman to marry rather than to make independent decisions about her future. Marriage is viewed more as a property transfer than a celebration of romance. After marriage, a woman's life is one of drudgery and child rearing with little or no emotional fulfillment. Thus the violence she endures is not physical abuse but psychological abuse in which her dreams, individuality, and identity are sacrificed in servitude to her husband.

In addition to the more subtle forms that abuse can take, as in the example from Indian society, overt physical violence may reflect the level of violence within a culture. For example, in Nigerian villages, researchers have found a pattern of serious spousal battering in which husbands and wives alike are seriously injured. The researchers attribute this pattern to the overall Nigerian culture, which freely accepts physical aggression as a way of settling interpersonal disputes (Kalu 1993).

Spousal abuse may also reflect the tensions and stresses that accompany social change within a society. For example, in Papua New Guinea, incidents of spouse abuse have been increasing. This increase has coincided with the more numerous contacts that Papuans have been making with industrialized societies. As a result of these contacts, traditional Papuan culture is losing its importance, and the levels of uncertainty, stress, and violence are rising (Morley 1994).

●■▲ Pausing to Think   About Issues in Marriage and the Family

Many factors contribute to family problems, including economic pressures, the end of love between husband and wife, and the changing roles of women. Domestic violence can take the form of physical, psychological, emotional, sexual, or verbal abuse. (See the Sociology Online box for additional examples of family issues.)

CQ In your judgment, is violence in the family a cause for alarm in society? ◆ To what extent should society become involved in attempting to limit domestic violence?

Sociology Online   WWW

Family well-being has been a major focus of government policy and action for many years; not just in the United States but worldwide as well. To examine the scope of these activities, we suggest that you begin with the United States Agency for International Development (USAID) web site. USAID's Population and Reproductive Health program has been one of its most successful ventures and has encompassed family planning, health, and nutrition programs for countries in the developing world. Locate information on these programs and answer the following questions:

What is the stated mission of USAID?

What are the programs that USAID sees as essential for Africa, Asia and the Near East, Europe and Eurasia, and Latin America and the Caribbean?

CQ What do you think? ◆ Should the U.S. government be involved in distributing information about family planning? ◆ What benefits do U.S. citizens gain from such international efforts?

STUDY TIP

Describe the functions of the family as described in the functionalist view of marriage and the family. Explain each function by using a family—your own or an another—as an example.

Sociological Analysis of Marriage and the Family

As a fundamental institution of society, the family arises from the biology of procreation. Humans, however, are social beings; they have created intricate institutions that require sociological explanation. We now discuss the three major sociological perspectives on the family.

The Functionalist Perspective

Every society has some type of family structure. This fact suggests that the family satisfies functions that are common to all societies. Some of these functions are as follows:

Socialization   Unlike the young of other species, which require little or no parental care, the human infant must be supported for many years. To satisfy this requirement, all societies have established a particular group—the family—and have made it responsible for primary child care and socialization. Although industrial societies assign many of these functions to the school, the church, and other organizations, the child's first major socialization experiences take place within the family and often shape the remainder of his or her life.

Replacement of Members and Regulation of Sexual Behavior   Societies require procreation to survive, and all societies therefore have norms and mores to regulate sexual behavior. Thus, family and kin encourage or require individuals to choose their mates from a pool of other people with certain characteristics. The resulting endogamy provides an orderly—but not necessarily a just—means of perpetuating the society's population.

Economic Functions   By custom and law, family assets are passed from parent to offspring, and wealth is kept within the family line. This process can result in a substantial accumulation of riches. Of the wealthiest individuals in the United States, approximately half attained their wealth exclusively through inheritance.

The family is also embedded in the economic process of production and consumption. The economies of many nonindustrial societies are organized around small family farms and family-owned businesses, whereas the economies of industrial societies typically are organized around partnerships and corporations. In both types of societies, however, the family is an important unit of consumption. Food and shelter usually are purchased for the family rather than for the individual, and radios, television sets, cars, and other major items are owned in the names of the adult family members. The custom of giving gifts for Christmas, birthdays, anniversaries, and graduations is another form of family-related consumer behavior.

Support and Comfort   For most people, families are a major source of support and comfort. When a family member is too ill to work, other members may help financially; or a young couple might ask their parents for money for a down payment on their first home. In times of stress, the family is the social institution most responsible for providing comfort. When people lose their jobs, contract a serious disease, or end a relationship with an intimate, the family becomes a refuge in which they can find shelter and heal their emotional wounds.

Social Placement   Although inheritance is most commonly considered in terms of money, children also inherit their parents' social class and place in society. Societal stability thus is maintained, but often at the expense of the less wealthy. Children also belong to the same ethnic group as their parents, and they usually accept their parents' religion, political preferences, and social values. These family background characteristics are among the most important determinants of an individual's social status, especially before she or he reaches maturity.

Functionalist theorists often hail the traditional family as being ideally suited to carry out the tasks necessary for the survival of the society and the well-being of the individual (Dennis 1993). Other theorists, however, suggest that just because these functions are being satisfied does not mean that the traditional family is superior to all other family forms. Conflict theorists, in particular, emphasize the role of power within the traditional family and suggest that the family is one source of inequality.

The Conflict Perspective

Conflict theorists emphasize the power relationships that exist within the family, the family's role in perpetuating social inequality based on ascribed characteristics, and the dominance of men over women (that is, patriarchy). An early but still influential analysis of family power was developed by Friedrich Engels (1902). He said that the monogamous family developed in early agrarian and horticultural societies that were productive enough to create surpluses of wealth. Because men controlled this wealth, they became leaders, financiers, and power brokers, whereas women were restricted to providing services to men as sex objects, childbearers, nurturers, and domestic workers. Eventually the family developed into an institution that was the model for the patriarchy that characterizes all of industrial society.

Although Engels knew that the family can take many forms, he believed that monogamy was best suited for controlling wealth. The essential characteristic of a monogamous marriage, he said, is the wife's fidelity. If she has sexual relations exclusively with her husband, the offspring must be legitimate and thus eligible to inherit property. If inheritance is restricted to legitimate offspring, wealth can pass between generations and accumulate within the family.

In contrast to Engels, many contemporary conflict theorists place more emphasis on the sexual aspects of marriage. They suggest that men's size, strength, and aggressiveness first enabled them to dominate women as sexual prizes. Female sexuality became a man's property, and the right to this property became the defining characteristic of a marriage. Accordingly, in most legal jurisdictions, a marriage is not binding until the couple has had sexual intercourse; the concept of marital rape was not recognized by the law until recently, and the wife's infidelity was sure grounds for divorce (see Collins 1975). In short, conflict theorists maintain that marriage is a societally enforced arrangement that still grants the husband more power than the wife. The state, through various policies and social programs, manages to maintain men's dominance even while it attempts to overcome some race and class inequality (Curran and Abrams 2000).

Critics of conflict theory point out that although the norms of family life require women to do most of the child care and domestic chores and typically give them less sexual freedom than men (the double standard), women nonetheless find marriage and family life attractive. Love and cooperation can exist even in unbalanced power relations, they say, and conflict theorists overestimate people's desire for absolute equality.

The Symbolic Interactionist Perspective

According to symbolic interactionists, the family exists not as some ideal type, but as people who make decisions daily as they interact with one another. No two families are exactly alike, and people are active participants in the evolution of the family and ultimately create the mosaic of family life. Moreover, the family is a source of major roles and identities, such as mother, father, son, daughter, wife, and husband. These roles and identities become part of the individual's self-conceptions and help to define his or her commitments and relationships with others.

When people interact, they first define the situation by identifying what is expected of themselves and others. The resulting interaction requires both role taking and role making (McCall and Simmons 1978). Thus, the traditional marriage consists of taking the standard roles of husband and wife and making them into more personalized roles that are better suited for particular individuals. To illustrate, in the traditional family role, the husband is expected to be the chief breadwinner, but in some families, the wife may earn more than the husband earns. To facilitate the wife's work, the husband might adjust his role by contributing greater support services for his wife and their children. He might leave work early to pick up the kids from school and stop at the supermarket for the items he will cook for dinner.

During the process of modifying standard roles and identities, new conceptions of reality emerge as each partner learns to take the role of the other. Over time, the couple that shares activities successfully will develop a common memory and a joint biography: "I" and "you" become "we" (Berger and Kellner 1975). Other couples never develop a unified view of their married life. Rather, each partner continues to engage in experiences not shared by the other. These different experiences might complement one another in some cases, but in other cases, the experiences are based on social realities that are not interrelated (Bernard 1972). In extreme cases, the experiences may be so different that each spouse has a separate conception of the marriage.

Lesbians and gays who form alternative families must go through this same process of turning an "I" and a "you" into a "we." They also have to find compatible role arrangements, without the help of the standard husband-and-wife roles of heterosexual marriages (Blumstein and Schwartz 1983; Rothberg and Weinstein 1996). In addition, they must fight against social norms that suggest they cannot have a "real family" because they are not heterosexuals. From the perspective of symbolic interaction, however, embracing a lesbian or gay identity does not require a renunciation of family, but it does require a new symbolic groundwork. The concept of the alternative family as the "family we choose" becomes their vision of self-determination. This chosen family might incorporate friends, lovers, and children in any combination. What counts are the bonds of affection among the family members (Weston 1995).

TABLE 11.1

[a]The functionalist and conflict perspectives were introduced in Chapters 1 and 2, and symbolic interaction was discussed in Chapter 3.

Comparison of Three Theoretical Perspectives on Marriage and the Family

PERSPECTIVE[a]	VIEW OF MARRIAGE AND THE FAMILY	KEY CONCEPTS AND PROCESSES
Functionalism	Sees marriage and the family as performing tasks necessary for the survival of society and the well-being of individuals	Socialization of children and other functions
Conflict Theory	Sees marriage as dominance of men over women and the family as perpetuating social inequality	Patriarchy The double standard
Symbolic Interaction	Sees the family as defined by the social interactions of its members	Role taking Role making

Conflict theorists suggest that the family maintains social class inequality and that it empowers men over women, and adults over children. Functionalist theorists emphasize how the family socializes the young, regulates sexual behavior, and provides emotional support in times of stress. Symbolic interactionists emphasize how family may be analyzed in terms of role expectations, interactions, emotions, behavior, and cognitions (see Table 11.1).

CQ Is the family the most important institution in society? ◆ What would a functionalist say? ◆ A conflict theorist? ◆ A symbolic interactionist? ◆ What do you think? ◆ What are your reasons?

Marriage and the Family in the Twenty-First Century

Currently, there is much controversy over the state and the future of the family. This controversy exists, in large part, because the American family has changed more in the last 40 years than in the previous 250 (Blumstein and Schwartz 1983; Benokraitis 2000). Two opposing trends seem to be in conflict at the moment (Hunter 1991; see the Society Today box, Types of Families).

Society Today ●■▲

Types of Families

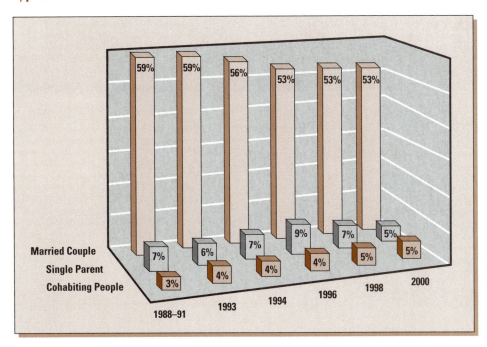

The percentage of married couple families in the United States has decreased somewhat since 1988–1991. At the same time, cohabitation has slightly increased and the single-parent family has slightly decreased. The married couple family remains the most common type of family, by far (U.S. Bureau of the Census, 2002).

Society Today ●■▲

No Gay Men as Boy Scout Leaders: Discrimination or Family Values?

The United States Supreme Court ruled in June 2000 that the Boy Scouts of America (BSA) had the legal right of free association and therefore could exclude gay males as members. The ruling set off a debate in many communities over the appropriateness of the action. Those supporting the decision saw it as an affirmation of traditional family values. The BSA has long been a symbol of the "American way of life," and that way of life emphasizes heterosexuality as the norm (Gross 2000; Chapter 8). Those opposed to the decision see it as a form of discrimination against gay men and view it as being as objectionable as excluding blacks or Jews. From this view, denial of membership is a violation of civil rights. They point out that other youth groups, such as the Girl Scouts and the Boys and Girls Clubs of America, have no such policies; most foreign scouting organizations also have no homophobic policies (Cohen 2000).

Churches, schools, charities, and other organizations that have long supported the BSA have begun to reassess their commitment to the organization because of this policy of exclusion. Although membership in the BSA has increased from the addition of new members, some parents have removed their children from the organization because they do not want their children to be part of an organization that discriminates against persons because of their sexual orientation. They hope that the BSA will reverse its decision and open its membership to all boys and men. Meanwhile, the boys in the BSA, who are mostly interested in camping and outdoor activities, are caught in the middle of a moral battleground over family values.

CQ What about you? ◆ Do you see the debate over this policy of exclusion of gays in the BSA as a healthy dialogue or as a serious rift in the organization?

The television series Will and Grace depicts the interactions of Will, a gay man, and Grace, a heterosexual woman. A comedy series, the show explores the dynamics of courtship and traditional and alternative family forms through the interactions of Will, Grace, and their friends. The show won three Emmy Awards in 2000.

On one side of the debate, according to James Davidson Hunter (1991), many people value an idealized form of the traditional family. In their view, the family is, and should be, a male-dominated unit that serves as a retreat from the harsh realities of life. People who support this view—called traditionalists by Hunter—support government policies designed to prevent alternative family forms from gaining strength and try to persuade the public that alternative family forms are deviant. The traditionalists believe that women are responsible for domestic chores and that men are responsible for providing income for the family. Traditionalists opposed the Equal Rights Amendment discussed in Chapter 8, believing that it would undermine male domination of the family. Because traditionalists feel that childbearing is the activity that gives womanhood meaning, they oppose abortion on demand and any other activity that reduces the role of women as mothers.

On the other side of the debate are those who see the idealized traditional family as one of many alternatives. Such people—called progressives by Hunter—generally favor a more equal sharing of household tasks and believe that men should be more involved in domestic chores and child rearing. Progressives also seek an inclusive view of the family that includes the childless couple, the homosexual family, the single parent, the cohabitor, and the serial monogamist. The essential requirement for these units is that the people involved should love and care for each other. Thus, progressives favor policies that would strengthen alternative family forms and would support laws that protect the economic interests of domestic partners, should their marriage end.

According to Hunter, the future of the American family depends on which side wins this cultural debate. If the traditionalists win, the alternative family forms will be seen as less desirable approximations of the "true family," and the health of the family as an institution will be judged by the extent to which the traditional family form is dominant. If the progressives win, the traditional family will become just one of many alternatives.

What Do You Think? ●■▲ How Do You See Morality and Marriage? **?**

Many issues of traditional morality surround marriage today. Recently a poll was conducted of 13- through 17-year-olds (Gallup, 2003). It found that 66 percent of the teens found divorce to be "morally acceptable." Fifty-seven percent said that sex between an unmarried man and women was morally acceptable. Forty-two percent said that having a baby outside of marriage was morally acceptable, and only 10 percent thought it moral for a man to have more than one wife at a time. Few teens found it moral for married men and women to have an affair—5 percent.

Where do you stand on these issues?

	MORALLY ACCEPTABLE	MORALLY UNACCEPTABLE
Divorce	_____	_____
Sex between an unmarried man and woman	_____	_____
Having a baby outside of marriage	_____	_____
Polygamy—a man having more than one wife at one time	_____	_____
Married men and women having an affair	_____	_____

CQ What are the implications for society if most members check the "morally acceptable" answers? ◆ What are the implications if most members check the "morally unacceptable" answers?

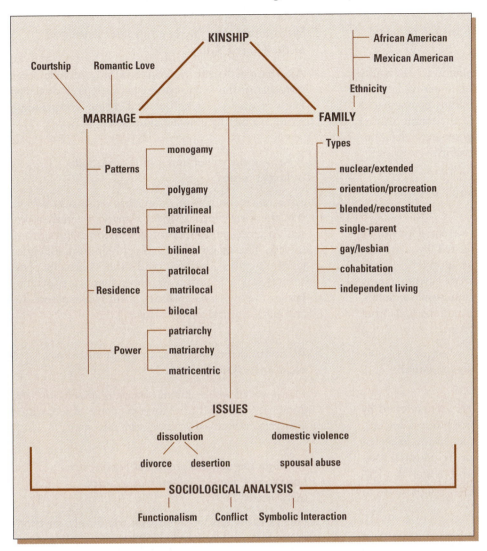

This is a concept web for Marriage and the Family. Not included is the concept of serial monogamy. How would you include it in the web?

Looking Ahead

Even though the family bears much of the responsibility for socializing children, it is no longer the primary source of formal education. Society has become so complex that separate institutions have arisen for that purpose. The next chapter explores the various social facets of education.

WHAT YOU SHOULD KNOW ●■▲

1. **How has the family changed with the Great Social Transformation?**

   In industrial societies, the most common type of family is the nuclear family, whereas in communal and transitional societies, the extended family is common. As societies changed, the structure of the family shifted from an emphasis on the multipurpose extended family to an emphasis on the nuclear family.

2. **What is kinship, and how has its role in society changed?**

   Every individual is embedded in a system of kinship—a network of people who are related by marriage, blood, or social practice (such as adoption). Traditional societies often are organized by elaborate family and kin networks, whereas in industrial societies, the kin may be replaced by organizations and other institutions.

3. **What forms of marriage and family are found in the world's societies?**

   Western, industrialized societies are characterized by monogamy and are likely to practice bilineal descent. In traditional societies, married couples are expected to live near or with kinfolk, whereas in industrial societies, newlyweds reside in their own households independent of their kin. Patriarchy is the arrangement in which men have the most power.

4. **What factors during the Great Social Transformation promoted the development of the nuclear family?**

   The nuclear family gained importance as a result of three main factors: the migration of people from rural areas to cities in search of employment; social mobility that weakened kinship bonds; and a decline of the functions performed by the extended family.

5. **Why do people marry and form families?**

   In most societies, people marry for wealth, security, or power. In some societies, people are expected to marry for love. According to American culture, romantic love is a prerequisite for marital happiness, but in many societies, marriage rests on material grounds, and both spouses are content with such arrangements.

6. **What alternative family forms have developed in the United States?**

   Alternatives to the traditional family include serial monogamy, the single-parent family, gay and lesbian families, and cohabitation. In addition, independent living is a rapidly growing alternative.

7. **What are the racial and ethnic variations in family forms?**

   After much controversy, most sociologists now believe that the matricentric African American family represents a successful adaptation to American culture and society. This adaptation involves help from extended family members, sharing, and other mutual support activities. The Mexican American family is characterized by the high value placed on family life, patriarchy, and authoritarian child rearing.

8. **What are the major issues in the family as a social institution?**

   Major social issues include marital dissolution and domestic violence in the form of spouse abuse, which is largely committed against women by men.

9. **What do the major sociological perspectives have to say about the family as a social institution?**

   Functionalist theory states that the family functions to socialize children; replace members; regulate sexual behavior; produce and consume goods; transfer wealth; provide support and comfort; and pass on ethnic identity, social class, religion, political preferences, and social values. Conflict theory emphasizes the power relationships that exist within the family, the family's role in perpetuating social inequality, and the dominance of men over women. Symbolic interaction theory emphasizes how people interact and define their situation with regard to family life.

10. **What does the twenty-first century hold for the family as an institution?**

   Currently, a cultural debate is under way as to whether the idealized traditional family is to be considered the dominant family form or simply one of many possible arrangements. How we view the family of the future depends on the outcome of that debate.

Key Terms Matching

Match each of these key terms with the best definition or example from the numbered items that follow. Write the letter preceding the key term in the blank before the definition that you choose.

a. affinal relationships

b. binuclear family

c. blended or reconstituted family

d. cohabitation

e. courtship

f. descent

g. desertion

h. divorce

i. endogamy

j. exogamy

k. extended family

l. family

m. family of orientation

n. family of procreation

o. kinship

p. machismo

q. marriage

r. monogamy

s. nuclear family

t. polygamy

u. romantic love

v. serial monogamy

_____ 1. A situation in which partners share a household and engage in intimate social and sexual relations without being formally married.

_____ 2. A marriage consisting of one male spouse and one female spouse.

_____ 3. A network of people who are related by marriage, blood, or social practice (such as adoption).

_____ 4. The dissolution of the legal ties that bind a married couple; socially it constitutes the recognition that the marriage is over.

_____ 5. A social unit composed of a husband, a wife, and their children.

_____ 6. A family form in which each member of a divorced couple establishes a separate household between which their children divide their time.

_____ 7. A marriage consisting of multiple spouses.

_____ 8. The nuclear family into which a person is born.

_____ 9. A person, a spouse, and their children.

_____ 10. Social bonds based on marriage.

_____ 11. Marriage in which the couple are members of the same race, ethnicity, religion, or social class.

_____ 12. An emotional identification between two individuals that is so intense that they are convinced that they cannot be happy without each other.

_____ 13. The social dissolution of marriage that occurs when one spouse leaves the other or simply walks away from the marriage for a prolonged period.

_____ 14. The relationship between a male and a female who are preparing for marriage to each other.

_____ 15. Marriage in which the couple are from different races, ethnic groups, religions, or social classes.

_____ 16. A state that occurs when two individuals are involved in a socially approved relationship that involves intimate, mutual long-term obligations, and they have fulfilled the customary ceremonial or legal requirements.

_____ 17. A group of individuals who are related in some way, usually living together, engaging in sex, having responsibility for rearing children, and functioning as an economic unit.

_____ 18. A cultural pattern that permits a person to have more than one spouse, but not at the same time.

_____ 19. A form of family in which spouses and their children from former marriages live together as a single nuclear family.

_____ 20. A family composed of two or more generations of kin that functions as an independent social and economic unit.

_____ 21. A value system embracing highly masculine behaviors and including a "double standard."

_____ 22. The system by which kinship is traced over generations.

Multiple Choice

Circle the letter of your choice.

1. What changes in the family occurred as a result of the Great Social Transformation?
   a. Its economic activity became limited to consumption.
   b. Its size decreased.
   c. Adolescence became a distinctive stage.
   d. All of the above.

2. Mary and her sons and Ted and his daughters formed a family. Which term best describes their family?
   a. extended family
   b. blended family
   c. family of orientation
   d. bilocal family

3. Which of these types of society is often organized by elaborate family networks?
   a. familial
   b. extended
   c. traditional
   d. modern

4. Individuals tend to choose prospective spouses from neighbors, coworkers, and classmates because of
   a. propinquity.
   b. affinal relationships.
   c. endogamy.
   d. exogamy.

5. When Michael, who is Jewish, and Amy, who is Catholic, became engaged, Michael's parents were not happy that Michael was marrying outside the Jewish faith. Michael's parents, therefore, believe in
   a. serial monogamy.
   b. endogamy.
   c. exogamy.
   d. romantic love.

6. When a Toda woman (from India) marries a Toda man, she becomes the wife of all his brothers as well. This system is called
   a. serial monogamy.
   b. polyandry.
   c. group marriage.
   d. polygamy.

7. Shannon and Chris got married and moved into an apartment down the street from Shannon's parents. This pattern of residence is called
   a. matrilocal.
   b. neolocal.
   c. patrilocal.
   d. bilocal.

8. Actress Elizabeth Taylor has been married and divorced eight times. Which of the following terms describes her practice?
   a. serial monogamy
   b. polygamy
   c. polyandry
   d. cohabitation

9. The second most common type of family after the traditional family is the
   a. divorced couple.
   b. single parent.
   c. binuclear.
   d. gay.

10. Which of the following is true of homosexual partners?
    a. Lesbian couples tend to be faithful.
    b. Gay male partners often have sexual relations outside the family setting.
    c. Courts sometimes grant custody of children to a lesbian in a stable relationship.
    d. All of the above.

11. When a married couple has separate residences but unites on weekends and vacations, the couple is
    a. in a trial marriage.
    b. in a bilocal pattern of residence.
    c. not legally married.
    d. in a limited cohabitation arrangement.

12. Being highly family centered, being patriarchal, and having authoritarian child-rearing practices is characteristic of
    a. Mexican American families.
    b. African American families.
    c. single-parent families.
    d. gay and lesbian families.

13. Which of the following is NOT an explanation for marital dissolution?
    a. Women's roles are changing.
    b. Divorces are fairly easy to get.
    c. People fall out of love.
    d. People fail to have a long courtship before marriage.

14. Which of the following groups has the lowest divorce rate in America?
    a. whites
    b. African Americans
    c. Hispanic Americans
    d. Asian Americans

15. Equal sharing of household tasks and an inclusive view of family that includes the childless couple and the homosexual family are characteristic of which of these views?

    a. traditionalist
    b. progressive
    c. polygamist
    d. monogamist

Identifying Sociological Perspectives on Marriage and the Family

For each of the following statements, identify the sociological perspective associated with the statement by writing F for functionalist, C for conflict, or SI for symbolic interactionist, in the appropriate blank.

_____ **1.** The family perpetuates social inequality on the basis of ascribed characteristics and the dominance of men over women.

_____ **2.** The family exists not as some ideal type, but as people who make decisions daily as they deal with one another.

_____ **3.** All societies have norms and mores to regulate sexual behavior so that societies will procreate in an orderly way.

_____ **4.** Families are a major source of support and comfort.

_____ **5.** The traditional family is ideally suited to carry out the tasks necessary for the survival of the society and the well-being of the individual.

_____ **6.** Marriage is a socially enforced arrangement that still grants to the husband more power than to the wife.

True-False

Indicate your response to each of the following statements by circling T for true or F for false.

T F **1.** Traditional societies have small nuclear families as each person's most important kin relationship.

T F **2.** Research shows that children with lesbian and gay parents develop psychologically and emotionally in a positive direction.

T F **3.** Romantic love is more highly valued as a reason for marriage in societies with weak extended family ties.

T F **4.** Desertion is sometimes called the "poor person's divorce."

T F **5.** Independent living has decreased in the United States since 1970.

T F **6.** Each year in the United States, more women are battered by their husbands than are injured in car accidents.

T F **7.** Low- and working-class wife abusers tend to hit their wives in more visible places than do middle- and upper-class wife abusers.

T F **8.** The changing status of women has increased the social pressure to marry.

T F **9.** Couples who cohabit before marriage are more likely to experience marriage dissolution than those who do not cohabit.

T F **10.** If the traditionalists win the culture debate, then the health of the family as an institution will be judged by the extent to which the traditional family form is dominant.

T F **11.** Symbolic interaction theory emphasizes the power relationships within the family.

T F **12.** Most sociologists now believe that matricentric African American family represents a poor adaptation to American culture and society.

T F **13.** In most societies, people marry for wealth, security, or power.

T F **14.** According to Engels, monogamy was best suited for controlling wealth.

T F **15.** The Chicano family tends to be child centered.

NOTE: The answers to these exercises are at the end of the book.

For additional practice tests and other resources please visit the companion web site at http://www.prenhall.com/curry.

Essay

1. What are several explanations for marital dissolution?

2. What are four alternatives to the traditional nuclear family?

3. How did industrialization change family structures and functions?

4. In general, what are the differences between Mexican American families and African American families?

5. How does the blended or reconstituted family differ from the binuclear family?

12 Education

Chapter Outline

Eugene Lang was the son of poor immigrant parents. He graduated from East Harlem's Public School 121, one of the lowest-ranked elementary schools in New York City. At age 14, while waiting on tables in a restaurant in East Harlem, he met a customer who turned out to be a trustee of Swarthmore College. With his help, Lang won a full scholarship to Swarthmore and graduated at age 19.

Fifty years after attending Public School 121, Lang was asked to return to the school and give the commencement address. After meeting the students, he quickly realized that his planned remarks would be irrelevant to the inner-city youths who sat fidgeting before him. So he set aside his prepared notes and instead began speaking from his heart about Martin Luther King, Jr. and his "I Have a Dream" speech. Almost offhandedly he said that he would personally finance the college education of every member of the sixth-grade class, if they would just stay in school.

The school's principal predicted that even with Lang's generous offer, only one or two of the 62 students would go on to college. Somewhere along the way, most of them inevitably would fall victim to poverty, welfare dependency, low expectations, teenage parenthood, crime, and drug abuse. Yet contrary to the principal's prediction, 90% of the class graduated from high school or its equivalent, and 60% enrolled in a community college or a four-year college. Lang subsequently was deluged with questions from people who wanted to adopt elementary school classes of their own. In response to the demand, Lang organized the "I Have a Dream" Foundation.

The foundation caught the imagination of lay people and educators alike. As support poured in, the foundation expanded its activities. In addition to sponsoring entire grades from elementary schools, the foundation began sponsoring entire age groups from public housing projects. These programs now support the children, or "Dreamers" as they are called, for 12 to 16 years. Once graduated from high school, Dreamers are provided additional support for college or vocational school. Currently "I Have a Dream" projects in 20 states support some 6,000 children.

The "I Have a Dream" program has been influential beyond its own activities. It has inspired similar programs throughout the country. For example, in 1998 Congress adopted the "I have a Dream" model for an educational program called GEAR UP. Administered by the Department of Education, GEAR UP supports schools and state agencies in their efforts to help low-income students prepare for college (ihid.com; accessed October 10, 2003).

Lang has donated more than $25 million to education, but he believes that the money itself is not the most significant factor in changing the lives of disadvantaged children. The major problem, he says, is the lack of social support to motivate young children and guide them through school. Once that is in place, the Dreamers themselves will carry forward to success (Kelly 1990; Nieves 1991).

What sociological lesson lies buried in Lang's experiences with Public School 121? Perhaps the most significant point is this: dropping out of school and being swallowed by a hostile environment has little do with innate ability but much to do with the economic and social resources available to students. Many lower-class children find that higher education is out of reach because so many barriers lie in their path and they lack the social support systems to ease their way.

Chapter Preview

To better understand education as a social institution, this chapter examines several important questions: What fundamentally is education, and how is it connected with formal schooling? How was education transformed as societies industrialized? What are the basic characteristics of the American educational system, and how is it similar to or different from education in societies such as Japan? What basic problems and issues face education today? What do the major social theories tell us about education? And how is education likely to change in the future?

The Great Social Transformation and Education

Education is the transferral of the knowledge, values, and beliefs of a society from one generation to the next. In communal societies, education is largely informal and is passed on through highly personalized social relations between parents and children. Among the social transformations accompanying industrialization have been the rise of professional educators and an increase in the number of years of mandatory schooling. Industrial societies have such complex cultures that informal socialization is inadequate; a more systematic method of transmitting knowledge is necessary. Consequently, industrial societies rely on **formal education**—the transmission of knowledge, skills, and attitudes from one generation to the next through systematic training. This training usually takes place in organizations that specialize in providing instruction conducted by professional teachers and supervised by professional administrators—that is, in **schools**.

In industrial societies, formal education has come to play an unquestioned role in preparing individuals for participation in the mainstream of economic life. The benefits of education are not just for the workplace, however. In contemporary society, education nourishes social innovation through research and support of creative activities in areas such as health care, consumer issues, politics, and family life. Consequently, education affects virtually everyone in society.

Education ▲ The transferral of the knowledge, values, and beliefs of a society from one generation to the next.

Formal education ▲ The transmission of knowledge, skills, and attitudes from one generation to the next through systematic training.

Schools ▲ Places of formal educational instruction.

Mother interacts with her three children as they engage in arts and crafts during home school. While some people find home schooling appropriate and beneficial for their children, most others find public or private schools more attractive. The American system of education seems able to accommodate a wide variety of choices and solutions to the problem of education of children.

Cross-Cultural Comparisons: The United States and Japan

Since 1945, when World War II ended, Japan has become one of the world's preeminent industrial powers, giving the United States (and many other countries) fierce competition in economic areas. When asked why the Japanese work so hard and so efficiently, people typically cite better education as the most important reason (Stevenson 1989). Is this answer correct? Have the Japanese developed an educational system that produces a superior, more knowledgeable, better motivated, and more loyal workforce? Answering this question and related ones requires some understanding of the educational systems of both countries. Let us consider the United States first.

Education in the United States

People in the United States have an abiding faith in the value of education. They see education as necessary for participating in democracy, for righting injustices, and for attaining personal happiness (Brint 1998; Davis and Smith 1987). Belief in education transcends the social divisions of race, class, and gender: whites and nonwhites, women and men, the poor and the wealthy all believe that education is vital for the survival of a free people and for the individual's social and economic advancement. This belief has led the United States to spend more than $600 billion a year on education and to develop the most comprehensive educational system in the world. Nearly all American citizens receive both a primary and a secondary education (U.S. Bureau of the Census 2000). Every person, it is assumed, has the right to at least a high school education funded by public revenues. Moreover, those who qualify have the additional right to a higher education, which is heavily subsidized by government at both the state and the federal levels.

Of course, the high cultural value now placed on education does not exempt the educational system from controversy and criticism. Many observers feel that the American educational system is failing. They point out that although more than 80 percent of the population is now graduating from high school, more than 11 percent of the population is **functionally illiterate**—unable to read and write well enough to carry out the routine activities of everyday life (Reich 1992). The functionally illiterate cannot read a newspaper with any real understanding, follow directions on a medicine bottle, or write a personal letter. Dropouts are another persistent problem: in 1997 alone, nearly 3.7 million high school students dropped out of school (U.S. Bureau of the Census 2000; see the Society Today box). In short, American society values learning but tolerates an educational system that is far from perfect. The educational system of the United States has several characteristics that, in combination, make it unique among nations; this system produces both outstanding results and, paradoxically, a high rate of failure. Its characteristics may be summarized as follows.

Decentralized Control   The United States is a republic composed of states; each state has the broad responsibility for educating its citizens. Within each state, this responsibility is delegated to local communities and school districts that act through elected boards to decide matters of curriculum, administration, and teaching. The United States contains approximately 16,000 independent school districts that are free—within state-imposed limits—to pursue their own school calendars, curricula, and teaching methods.

Although the United States has a decentralized educational system, the federal government plays a major role in education. To be sure, federal spending for education has decreased in response to tight budget restraints, but the government continues to spend more than $75 billion per year on education (U.S. Bureau of the Census 2000). Much of this money goes to various funding programs that exert a strong though indirect influence on local schools.

Functionally illiterate ▲ Lacking the ability to read and write well enough to carry out the routine activities of everyday life.

Society Today ● ■ ▲

College Graduation Rates

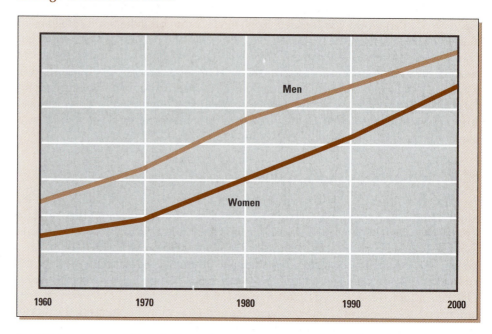

For the past 40 years, the percentage of women and men with a college degree has steadily been increasing. Note that the statistics are for persons 25 or older and do not include currently enrolled students (U.S. Bureau of the Census 2002).

CQ Why do you think proportionately more men have college degrees than women?

Decentralized control also means that local community leaders make the crucial decisions about the allocation of resources to specific schools. The net result of this decision-making pattern is that in many communities schools within the same school district get allocated fewer resources than others (Condron and Roscigno 2003). Children in the poorly funded schools perform at a lower level than students in well-funded schools. All too often, the poorly funded schools are the ones that serve the poor and minority children.

Mass Education   The United States was the first industrial nation to adopt the notion of **mass education**—the idea that everyone is entitled to a certain amount of publicly provided education and is obligated to obtain it. Thus, by 1850, excluding the children of slaves and Native Americans, approximately half of all school-age children were enrolled in school (Baker 1999). By 1900, all states required children to attend school, usually until age 16; that is, **mandatory education** had become the norm.

The principles of mass education and mandatory education trace their roots to two sources. The first is the belief that education and democracy go hand in hand. Thomas Jefferson supported the principle of mass schooling because he believed that education would enable citizens to understand the important events and issues of the day. Although in Jefferson's time, political participation was limited to affluent white adult males, the notion of mass education gradually expanded to include women and members of minorities.

The second source of mandatory mass education is industrialization. By the 1900s, organized labor and other groups concerned with child welfare were demanding that

Mass education ▲ The idea that everyone is entitled to a certain amount of publicly provided education and is obligated to obtain it.

Mandatory education ▲ Education to a certain age specified by law.

children attend school rather than being sent to work. Their demand was motivated in part by a sincere desire to protect children from being exploited, and in part by the fear that children were taking jobs that otherwise would have been held by adults. The factory system was yet another industrial force behind the drive for mass education; factories depended on workers who were punctual, regular in attendance, submissive to authority, and orderly. Thus, the schools taught reading, mathematics, science, history, and the behaviors required of successful factory workers.

Consistent with the requirements of the factory system, the so-called Lancaster schools emerged in the nineteenth century. The schools, which were named after their founder, Joseph Lancaster, often were located near urban industrial areas. Lancaster schools were conducted like educational factories. One teacher, with the assistance of several dozen student monitors, oversaw the mass teaching of 400 to 500 elementary schoolchildren. Seats were arranged in neat, efficient rows; students were required to sit quietly, to raise their hands if they needed to speak, and to keep their eyes on their own desks. These requirements were enforced with strict discipline. Much of what passed for education was merely rote memorization (Parelius and Parelius 1978).

The United States is one of the few nations that extend the principle of mass education to higher education. Under the Land Grant College Act of 1862 (the Morrill Act), the federal government granted each state 30,000 acres of land, or its equivalent, for each state senator and representative. The states then sold their land to finance the establishment of "land grant" universities. These schools originally emphasized agriculture and mechanics, but over time they broadened their offerings to include liberal arts, sciences, humanities, and professional courses (Collier 2002). Carrying the principle of mass higher education even further, many states have developed elaborate systems of junior colleges that make the first two years of higher education available at the local community level. Junior colleges are a uniquely American contribution to the structure of higher education, and they have been extremely popular. Some 800 two-year institutions were founded between 1900 and 1965.

As a result of the widespread belief in mass education, the American school system has grown to be the most extensive in the world. Over 90 percent of school-age children and approximately half of all youths (18–21 years) are in some type of school. And even among three- and four-year-olds, half attend preschool. Furthermore, two-thirds of high school graduates now go on to college, and by 2008, 20 million students a year will be enrolling in an institution of higher learning (U.S. Census Bureau 2000, 2002). In comparison, in Western Europe, only 20 percent of 16- and 17-year-old youths attend school, and only about 10 percent of all children go on to college.

Practicality   American culture emphasizes practicality and Yankee know-how—even in education. Thus, American schools teach subjects related to occupational careers (such as bookkeeping) and subjects meant to enhance students' lives directly (such as health and hygiene). Mathematics often is justified on the basis that it is useful for solving real-world problems, whereas reading and writing are said to be vital to job success. Art and music classes, less easily justified on the basis of practicality, are often the first to be eliminated when school districts retrench.

The emphasis on practicality also increasingly pervades higher education. During the 1960s, half of all college-bound high school seniors intended to major in the liberal arts; today fewer than one-quarter intend to do so. Now the fastest growing majors are computer science and professional or business-related disciplines that are highly marketable (Delucchi 2000). Moreover, in a recent poll, half of all freshmen said that they were attending college in order "to be well off financially". This economic orientation toward education typically grows stronger whenever the competition for jobs increases.

Credentialism   Sociologist Randall Collins (1979) suggests that in the United States, academic degrees are viewed as credentials that indicate the holder's

Society Today ● ■ ▲

Average Annual Earnings

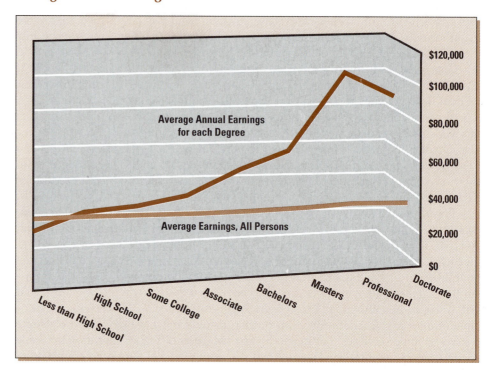

Average Annual Earnings for each Degree

Average Earnings, All Persons

$120,000
$100,000
$80,000
$60,000
$40,000
$20,000
$0

Less than High School · High School · Some College · Associate · Bachelors · Masters · Professional · Doctorate

Education does not guarantee you high earnings nor does a lack of education condemn you to perpetual poverty. In general, though, the more education you have, the more you will earn. As this chart shows, people with professional degrees earn over six times more than what high school dropouts earn, and over three times more than what the average person earns (U.S. Bureau of the Census 2002).

CQ Can you offer a reason why, on average, people with professional degrees earn more than people with doctorates?

qualifications to perform certain jobs and social roles. He calls this **credentialism**. Applying this test, corporations may require clerks to have high school diplomas, and universities may require professors to have doctoral degrees. In neither case does a degree prove that the degree holder has the ability to perform the job, but it acts as a credential that screens out many would-be applicants (Brown 2001). A person lacking the proper credentials simply is not considered. For employed workers, research has shown that those with more years of schooling and more educational and training certificates earn more than what would be predicted on the basis of their job skills alone (Hunter and Leiper 1993).

Credentialism results in **educational inflation**—the situation in which the credentials required to obtain a job increase while the skills necessary to perform the job remain the same. Although many modern jobs are admittedly complicated, the overwhelming increase in the demand for credentials comes from educational inflation rather than from increases in job complexity (Collins 1979). To be a waiter or a factory worker, for example, once required only an eighth-grade education, but today the same job may require a high school diploma. In the past, the standard requirement for becoming a nurse was a diploma from a hospital school of nursing; today a bachelor's degree in nursing from a four-year college or university program is becoming the necessary credential. As a result of educational inflation, a high proportion of the

Credentialism ▲ The view that academic degrees indicate the holders' qualifications to perform certain jobs or roles.

Educational inflation ▲ The situation in which the credentials required to obtain a job increase while the skills necessary to perform the job remain the same.

Society Today ● ■ ▲

Foreign-Born Students

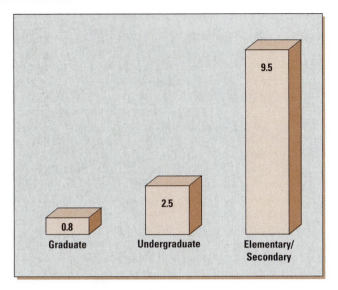

9.5

2.5

0.8

Graduate   Undergraduate   Elementary/
                              Secondary

Although people who grow up in the United States tend to take the American educational system for granted, people in many other countries highly prize American education—especially from an American college or university. That is a major reason for the presence of foreign-born students on campuses in the United States.

American labor force may be overeducated for the jobs they now hold (Shockey 1989).

Although educational inflation seems wasteful, overeducation has many benefits in other respects. At a minimum, education prepares people for occupational changes that are impossible to predict. The more education that people have, the greater their flexibility about future career choices. Perhaps of more importance, education is not solely about job qualifications; ideally, it engages the intellect and broadens the horizons. It helps people to achieve a more meaningful life and to participate wisely in democracy. For these reasons, a person can never be overeducated.

Education in Japan

Both Japan and the United States have become modern, industrial, associational societies; yet they have developed different systems of education (Arai 2003). Whereas education in the United States reflects the cultural values of practicality, mass education, decentralized control, and credentialism, the Japanese educational system rests on the traditional values of conformity, selectivity, and standardized planning. Education in Japan may be likened to a pyramid: a broad base of elementary schools supports a smaller number of academic high schools, which in turn support a tiny number of elite universities (Brint 1998; Shields 1989). Because of intense competition, only a small fraction of the children who enter preschool will graduate from an elite university.

Unlike people in the United States, who believe that different individuals have different abilities, the Japanese believe that all students have much the same innate ability and that differences in academic performance must be due to differences in effort (Stevenson 1989). Therefore, the key to superior performance is hard work, which begins at an early age. Before most Japanese children even enroll in school,

What Do You Think? ●■▲ Has the Time Come for Year-Round Schooling?

?

Summer vacation is a holdover from the last century, when children were needed to work on the family farm during the summer. As the United States industrialized, the need for child farm labor declined, but the nine-month school year remained. The result is that schoolchildren in the United States spend an average of 180 days per year in school, a relatively small number of days by world standards. In Japan, children spend 243 days a year in school; in Israel, 216; in Germany, 210; in the Netherlands and Thailand, 200 (reported in *USA Today*, August 28, 1991:7A).

As it stands, the nine-month school year is inefficient. Although many school systems are overcrowded, school facilities remain underutilized or empty during the summer. On the other hand, year-round schooling would involve substantial increases in budgets to pay for additional salaries, supplies, and support services. Such a change would cost California and New York more than $120 million annually. Would taxpayers support such expenditures when they are already reluctant to pass current school levies? Possibly the answer is no. In the past, when overcrowding was more severe than it is today, many school systems adopted a year-round schedule, but they reverted to the nine-month school year when overcrowding decreased.

From a teaching perspective, summer vacation is wasteful, because students rapidly forget what they learned during the school year and become slack in their study habits. Teachers therefore must devote much of September to reviewing the previous year's material. Students from disadvantaged families are especially affected because during the summer vacation, they have fewer educational resources in the home (such as books) and fewer opportunities to visit libraries and museums or to benefit from the learning that is associated with travel.

Some educators predict that the disadvantages of the extended summer vacation are so great that by the next century, the majority of students will be attending school all year

(Mydans 1991). Already some 1.3 million students in 23 states attend year-round schools. Although this figure represents only 2.5 percent of all students in kindergarten through grade 12, it is double the number of students who attended year-round schools in 1989.

In the future, technology will undoubtedly play an important role in year-round schooling (Gehl and Douglas 2000). Already, more teachers are putting syllabuses, lecture notes, tests, and other materials on the Internet (Hafner 1995). As schools become equipped with this advanced technology, more students will be able to learn at home during the summer by using a personal computer. Teachers could even videotape their lectures and show them over cable television, and they could conduct examinations by means of dial-in modems.

The greatest impediment to year-round schools, however, may be the resistance that occurs when a long-cherished tradition is threatened by a new arrangement. Summer vacation has become so deeply ingrained in American culture that the life tempo of children, parents, and teachers revolves around it. The family vacation traditionally is taken during the summer months, when children are out of school. Teachers typically are paid for nine months of service, but many say that the three most valuable fringe benefits of teaching are "June, July, and August"—a period when they are free to work on advanced degrees, to find summer work, or to pursue personal interests. Despite the economic and social advantages of year-round schooling, only a bare majority of the public (51 percent) favors that system (Gallup Poll 1991).

CQ What implications does year-round attendance have for financing education? ◆ Thinking back on your own experience, would year-round attendance have improved your academic skills?

Public Schools with Access to the Internet

	1995	1998	1999	2000
With Internet Access	50%	89%	95%	98%

SOURCE: U.S. Bureau of the Census, 2002.

Schools have enthusiastically adopted computer technology. To illustrate this point, the table shows that in five years the percentage of public schools with Internet access nearly doubled. Now almost all schools are online.

their parents—usually their mothers—have taught them numbers, the alphabet, and some art skills. By age 4, more than 90 percent of Japanese children are attending preschool to receive a head start on their education. The typical Japanese student spends six to seven hours a day in school, five full days a week and a half day on Saturday. The summer break lasts 40 days, but during this break, students have specific assignments to be completed each day of the week (see the What Do You Think? box).

At age 14, all Japanese students take a screening examination that determines who will go to an academic high school and who will go to a vocational high school. Because so much is determined by these examinations, Japanese students are driven to study

with extreme intensity. The life of a Japanese student is a life of study. At 10 P.M., the subways of Tokyo are crammed with older students returning from the juku—private schools that meet after regular school hours. The juku trains students for the infamous "hell week" of college entrance examinations that are given in February and March.

A recent development concerns Japanese children who live outside of Japan. There are considerable number of them because Japanese businesses routinely send their employees to work in other countries. While living abroad may be educational, when it comes to college examinations these children cannot effectively compete with native-schooled Japanese. At high school age, therefore, many of these expatriate children move back to Japan to attend special schools. There they receive extra instruction aimed at passing the college examinations. Graduates of these schools have been very successful, so much so that many parents in Japan now send their children to live abroad just so they can qualify to return and attend the special schools (Kobe Institute Symposium 2001).

As in the United States, Japanese universities vary in prestige. Unlike the system in the United States, however, graduation from an elite university is virtually the only gateway to a job with a top Japanese corporation or a high-level government position (Rosenbaum and Kariya 1989). And unlike the United States, students at elite universities are all but guaranteed a good position in business or industry. One feature of the Japanese university strikes outsiders, especially those from the United States, as peculiar in the extreme. It is assumed that anyone who passes the entrance examination to an elite university is qualified to graduate. Hence, Japanese college students hardly ever study, and they routinely miss classes. Instead of studying, they spend most of their time at parties and banquets and just hanging out. These informal activities forge social ties among students from different regions and backgrounds, and these ties will follow the students throughout their careers.

What happens to Japanese high school students who fail the college entrance examinations? In effect, they become students from an academic high school with no college to attend. Most such students study for an additional year or two at a private school that specializes in teaching them to pass their college examinations. During that time, their parents often are so embarrassed that they will not mention their children's names in public.

On the whole, the Japanese educational system receives high marks, especially the primary and secondary schools. These high marks, however, extract high costs

STUDY TIP

Outline or word web the elements of the U.S. and Japanese school systems, using colors—for example, one color for United States and one color for Japan, or different colors for each of the aspects of education (structure, values, etc.). In your visual, include your own evaluation of the pros and cons of each system.

American high school students generally do not compare well academically with Japanese high school students. Students in the United States spend less time on homework and have longer summer breaks. Moreover, many schools suffer from overcrowding or inadequate facilities. This photograph shows students meeting in a hallway in an overcrowded high school.

(Kariya 2000). First, the system demands that parents invest a great deal of energy and money into educating their children. Women especially are expected to sacrifice their own identity for that of their children. Second, because Japanese schools demand so much commitment, little time is left for activities that American students take for granted, such as dating, sports, and part-time work. Third, the screening examinations make no allowance for individual differences. Learning-disabled students, the handicapped, and students whose pace of development is not synchronized with the official curriculum are often left behind. Fourth, those who are left behind are deemed failures and bring shame and embarrassment on themselves and their families.

●■▲ Pausing to Think   About Cross-Cultural Comparisons

Education is one of the major institutions through which formal knowledge, skills, and attitudes are passed from one generation to the next. The educational systems of the United States and Japan differ greatly. In Japan, the educational system forms a pyramid, and relatively few Japanese ever achieve the rewards that are associated with reaching the top of the pyramid—attendance at a leading university. In contrast, the American school system emphasizes mass education, with the hope that most people will attain a college degree.

CQ Japanese students and their parents pay a high social price for educational success in high school. Would you have wanted your high school to stress extremely rigorous academic training? ◆ Why, or why not?

Education and Minority Issues

People in the United States typically believe that education is the key to individual advancement and the solution to problems of social inequality (Jencks et al. 1979). As a result of this attitude, issues of fairness and justice are very important in education. If some students are given an unfair advantage through attending better schools, these advantages will increase their chances of obtaining a better job and ultimately, a more secure grip on the American dream of material success. For these reasons, the schools are often an arena of controversy and violent conflict over scarce resources. Many of these conflicts involve issues related to racial and ethnic minorities, women, and class privilege (Brint 1998; Moss and Tilly 2001; Roscigno and Ainsworth-Darnell 2000; see Chapters 6, 7, and 8).

The Coleman Report and Unequal Education

In 1966, sociologist James Coleman published a massive study of some four thousand American public schools. The study showed that the great majority of students attended racially segregated schools, that predominantly white schools had more educational resources than predominantly black schools, and that African American students did not perform as well as white Americans. These facts were not surprising; far more surprising were the findings regarding the role of educational resources.

Common sense suggests that schools with ample resources will provide better education than schools with meager resources (Arum 2000). Facilities such as air-conditioned classrooms, computers, laboratories, and libraries should result in superior learning. Despite what common sense suggests, however, Coleman found that students from schools with ample resources did not perform substantially better than students from schools with meager resources, once other factors were taken into account. What was responsible for superior performance? The answer was family background. African Americans did not perform well because many came from families of lower socioeconomic status. Whites, on the other hand, came mostly from middle- and upper-class families and were raised in relatively affluent environments that stressed the importance of education.

Since the Coleman report was published, additional evidence has shown the importance of teacher-student interactions. In keeping with Coleman's findings, British research shows that schools with the most expensive equipment and facilities do not necessarily provide the best education. This research, however, emphasizes quality of teaching rather than the element of social status emphasized by Coleman. It found that students from disadvantaged backgrounds benefited greatly from teachers who cared about them, who were well organized, and who could maintain discipline (Rutter 1979). Coleman later reached similar conclusions when he compared students in private schools with those in public schools (Coleman, Hoffer, and Kilgore 1982).

On the whole, it appears that at least two factors contribute to students' performance: social status and high-quality teacher-student interaction. Unfortunately, many minority children come from disadvantaged backgrounds and attend schools that lack a scholastic culture in which high-quality teaching can take place (Danziger and Waldfoggel 2000; Hedges and Nowell 1999).

Mandatory Busing to End Segregation

Historically, American schools have been segregated, largely by race. Native Americans, for instance, attended separate schools located on reservations. In Northern and Western urban areas of the United States, children attended neighborhood schools that were segregated by ethnicity and social class. In the South, one educational system existed for African Americans and another for whites. In 1954, the Supreme Court ordered an end to racial segregation of the public schools—an order that has yet to be implemented fully.

Thus far, the only practical way to achieve school integration has been by busing students to schools outside their local neighborhoods. Opposition to busing sometimes has been intense and sometimes has produced **white flight**, an upsurge in white families' moving to suburban neighborhoods to avoid mandatory busing (Jonas 1998). White flight has had two consequences for the schools. First, in many school districts, it has caused increases in segregation. When whites flee, the proportion of African Americans (and members of other minority groups) becomes higher in city neighborhoods. The out-migration of affluent whites also caused the tax base of the city to

Schools have occasionally been a focal point of racial-ethnic conflicts, as shown in this photograph of an antibusing protest in Boston. There have been protests against busing for almost half a century, and the controversy promises to extend well into the twenty-first century.

White flight ▲ An upsurge in white families moving to suburban neighborhoods to avoid mandatory busing.

shrink just as the costs associated with busing increased. As a result, many schools were forced to shift funds from classroom instruction to busing. Not all whites fled the central city solely because of school integration, of course. Many left for better housing, more job opportunities, and to get away from high-crime areas. For whatever reasons, though, affluent whites departed, leaving behind urban school districts with many financial problems. The people who inherited these problems were African Americans, Hispanics, and others too poor to move (Kantor and Brenzel 1994).

Nowadays, public opinion strongly favors the principle of school integration. This is particularly true for today's younger adults (Andolina and Mayer 2003). Almost nine out of ten white respondents believe that students of all races should go to the same schools, and six out of ten would not object to sending their children to a school where more than half of the students are African American. Endorsement of a principle, however, is different from favoring a specific practice: two out of every three white adults oppose mandatory busing (NORC 1998). In addition, some African Americans argue today that all the money put into busing would be better spent if it were invested in improving existing schools in existing black neighborhoods (Fuerst and Petty 1992).

How much of the opposition to busing is due to racism, and how much is due to other concerns? This question has no clear answer. Some people undoubtedly object to busing on racist grounds, but others object because it destroys the concept of the neighborhood school and violates a sense of community identity. These people maintain that children are best served when they spend most of the day surrounded by neighborhood peers. Other people object to using the schools and schoolchildren as political tools. They contend that the battles over integration should be fought by adults and that children should remain protected from such ugliness.

What has busing produced? Has school integration been achieved? The answer is clearly no: one-third of African American children now attend schools that are predominantly black, and more than 90 percent of white children attend schools that are predominantly white. Has mandatory busing improved the education of urban schoolchildren? The answer is unclear. Academic performance seems to be approximately the same whether children are bused or not (Coleman and Hoffer 1987; St. John 1975). Has mandatory busing increased harmony in society? Again the answer is unclear. In some cases, busing has been met with protests, strikes by students, and violence. As a rule, however, people opposed to busing have confined their opposition to bureaucratic and legal channels rather than taking to the streets. In short, even though busing to achieve integration has been practiced for more than 50 years, the anticipated results have not been achieved. Busing remains mired in social and legal controversies.

Many communities have developed **magnet schools** as a way of integrating their students. Magnet schools offer specialized programs or intensive studies in certain subjects such as science, math, physical education, foreign language, and culture or theater. These schools attract students from all areas of the community, thereby mixing racial and ethnic groups (Goldring and Hausman 1999). The schools are usually located in minority neighborhoods in the hope of attracting children from the entire city, regardless of race, ethnicity, or social class (Archbald 1996; Gamoran 1992; Henig 1989). Through the development of magnet schools, a public school system may retain its students within the system; however, magnet school programs require massive busing of students, which raises educational costs. In addition, once parents have the choice of where to send their children, the parents of white and wealthier parents may elect to avoid sending their children to schools with high percentages of poor or minority children. If this pattern would spread, it would contribute to a resegregation of local schools (Saporito 2003).

The Language of Instruction

Although the United States has no official language, English customarily is used and taught in schools. Until recently this custom was not a political issue, but the rapid

Magnet schools ▲ Schools that offer specialized programs or intensive studies in certain subject areas to draw students from all residential areas of the community.

increase in non-English-speaking immigrants has brought the issue of an "official language" to a head. The vast majority of people in the United States favor curtailing immigration and the issue has spilled over into education (NORC 1998). Should classes be taught in English, or should some accommodation be made for pupils whose native tongue is not English (Fong 2000; Williams 1992)?

This question has no easy answer. If immigrant children are placed in special classes while they learn English, they are likely to fall behind in their regular studies. They also will fall behind, however, if they are placed in regular classes taught in English, because they do not understand the language very well. A possible solution to this dilemma is to teach some subjects in the immigrants' native language, and at the same time to supplement their regular education with special instruction in English.

Although this solution is appealing, it presents some problems. First, multi-language instruction creates an economic burden on school systems that are already struggling to meet their budgets. For example, the Los Angeles school system enrolls children who speak some 80 different languages, and it obviously cannot afford to have multilanguage classes in all of them (Schrag 1994). Second, some critics believe that multilanguage instruction leads immigrants to think they can prosper even if they remain isolated in their own ethnic world. In reality, these critics believe the quickest path to success is to join the mainstream—and to speak correct, unaccented English. Finally, critics argue that multilanguage instruction will fragment American culture into distinct regional and ethnic cultures, thereby weakening national cohesion.

The rapid increase in non-English-speaking immigrants in some communities has strengthened the need for adult education in English as a Second Language (ESL). This photograph shows a white male teacher asking questions of an ESL class of Hispanic women with their children.

Testing and Educational Inequality

Although the United States has no system of comprehensive standardized tests administered by the federal government, some 46 million students from kindergarten through high school take more than 150 million standardized tests each year (Lemann 1995b). In the United States, perhaps the closest approximations to nationwide standardized tests for college-bound students are the Scholastic Aptitude Test (SAT) and the American Achievement Test (ACT). Almost 2 million high school students take these tests each year as part of the process of applying to colleges and universities.

As you might know from having taken it, the SAT measures both quantitative and qualitative skills. The outcomes for the various sections of the test are summed into a total score, and it is this total that draws the most attention. These totals vary substantially by racial-ethnic background and gender (Wright, Palmer, and Miller 1996). For example, Asian Americans typically have the highest total scores, followed by white Americans, Native Americans, Mexican Americans, Puerto Rican Americans, and African Americans. The ACT produces a similar ranking of groups (reported in *USA Today*, August 27, 1991:1; *Chronicle of Higher Education Almanac*, September 5, 1990:13).

What accounts for these differences in SAT scores? Possible explanations range from genetics—an explanation that sociologists reject almost uniformly—to cultural forces (see Chapter 3). One fact, however, is clear: no standardized test is completely free of cultural and social class bias. To perform well, individuals must somehow learn to answer the test questions in the culturally acceptable way. The following is a typical question on a typical standardized test:

Painter is to painting as _____ is to sonnet.

a. *driver*

b. *poet*

c. *priest*

d. *carpenter*

The correct answer is "poet" because a poet creates a sonnet just as a painter creates a painting. Although this question might seem to be free of biases, in fact it assumes that the student is familiar with the terms being used, especially sonnet. This

A student taking a standardized test. Critics charge that such tests reflect a white, male, middle-class bias and therefore penalize women and students from different cultural and class backgrounds.

CQ *Should colleges rely on standardized tests when they make decisions about admitting students?*

Cultural literacy ▲ The extent to which a person possesses the basic information needed to thrive in the modern world.

assumption also suggests a class bias: children reared in middle- and upper-class homes are more likely to have come across poetry and to recognize sonnet than children from lower-class homes. The question also assumes that the student is familiar with the form of a logical syllogism (A is to B as C is to D), is adept at taking multiple-choice tests, and is familiar with art. Finally, the question may be interpreted in two ways: painting could be a verb, meaning that the painter is engaged in creating a picture, or a noun—that is, a type of picture. The student therefore must know enough about English to realize that painting has these two meanings.

What type of student is most likely to answer this and similar questions correctly? Clearly, it is the student who has been socialized from birth into white middle- or upper-class culture. Such a student speaks English, has received a good education up to the point of the time of the test, is highly motivated, has been raised in a household that stresses education, and has been well socialized into the culture of the dominant white group. Because standardized tests are constructed by testing companies dominated by middle-class white males, such tests almost invariably contain subtle but real biases that penalize women and students from different cultural and class backgrounds (Lemann 1995a, 1995b).

The Debate over Cultural Literacy

E. D. Hirsch, Jr., a noted conservative educator, popularized the term **cultural literacy**: the extent to which a person possesses "the basic information needed to thrive in the modern world" (Hirsch 1987:xiii). Hirsch lists some five thousand items of information that a culturally literate person in the United States should know, such as the names John Adams and Susan B. Anthony, the location of the Caribbean Sea, and the meanings of *semper fidelis* and *e pluribus unum*. Although a culturally literate individual would not necessarily know a great deal about these items, he or she would know enough to feel comfortable when encountering them.

Hirsch suggests that cultural literacy is important because it enhances communication and mutual understanding. Without a common culture and a knowledge of that culture, national unity would erode and perhaps even vanish (see Hirsch 1987; Kerewsky 1989). Hirsch and other proponents of the cultural literacy movement believe that the schools have a special responsibility for ensuring that all students are well versed in the core culture of the society. Unfortunately, they contend, today's schools permit students to pursue idiosyncratic collections of easy courses; as a result, the cultural core of American society is being lost (Christenbury 1989). To rectify this situation, Hirsch says, students should be required to know certain facts and should demonstrate their knowledge by passing difficult tests. Until a student has done so, he or she should not be permitted to graduate. (For other conservative views on education, see the Sociology Online box.)

Sociology Online   **WWW**

Education is a very important social institution. It is no surprise, therefore, that there are many web sites for educational matters. One popular search engine recently identified 4.3 million web sites for elementary education, 5.6 million for secondary education, and 7.6 million for higher education. Clearly, there are several sites to choose from. We suggest you begin with the National Association of Scholars (NAS). The stated purpose of this organization is to advance the "restoration of intellectual substance, individual merit, and academic freedom in the university." These are lofty goals, but what exactly do they mean? Find an answer to this question by clicking on the book titles or underlined topics provided by the NAS. We suggest that you begin with the one marked Information. When you have finished your exploration, answer the following questions:

Is the NAS opposed to multiculturalism?

What issues or controversies in education are the NAS identified with?

Although critics of the cultural literacy movement agree that the educational system is not perfect, they argue that cultural literacy is not the solution. They believe that the cultural literacy approach encourages superficial learning, with an emphasis on memorizing lists of facts rather than acquiring true understanding.

Cultural literacy has also drawn fire from **multiculturalists**—individuals who believe that culture should be viewed from the perspective of different groups (Kivisto and Rundblad 2000). Multiculturalists point out that most of the items that have been suggested as part of the core culture of the United States are drawn from Western European traditions and reflect the thinking of "DWEMs"—dead white European males. The viewpoints of ethnic and racial minorities, women, and individuals from the lower social classes are overwhelmingly ignored (Olneck 1993). To illustrate, schoolchildren are taught that Christopher Columbus discovered the Americas in 1492 and thus began the development of the New World. In contrast, multiculturalists point out that the Americas already were inhabited by native peoples, many with highly complex civilizations. What the Europeans regarded as a major discovery was, from the viewpoint of Native Americans, the beginning of wars, forced relocations, disenfranchisement, and broken promises (see Chapter 7).

The multicultural viewpoint is especially important because ethnic populations in the United States are growing rapidly and thus gaining influence. In the Southwest, for instance, Mexican Americans are being elected to school boards and to committees that review and recommend school textbooks. One result of their participation is an increased sensitivity to the multicultural viewpoint. One textbook was rejected because it illustrated a passage about Mexican Americans with a single photograph—that of an illegal immigrant being arrested by the border patrol (Celis 1991). This focus on illegal immigration ignores the fact that the majority of Mexican Americans were born in the United States, are American citizens by birth, and live perfectly legal lives.

Tracking and Educational Inequality

Most high schools in the United States **track** students: that is, they assign them to different programs on the basis of their ability or interests. (Sometimes these decisions are based on standardized tests that contain cultural assumptions, as discussed before.) Schools usually provide three tracks: vocational, general, and college preparatory. The college preparatory track is for students who have the greatest academic ability and who intend to pursue higher education. The other tracks are for students who presumably are less capable academically and who plan to enter the labor force immediately on graduation. In some countries, students on different tracks attend different schools, but students in the United States typically attend the same school regardless of their track.

Tracking seemingly permits students to take courses appropriate to their abilities, interests, and goals in life. Proponents of tracking claim that it contributes to an efficient use of resources because it matches individuals who have a given set of qualifications with an appropriate societal position or job. For example, proponents claim that it makes little sense for students who are not planning to attend college to be in a college preparatory curriculum. They are better served if they are in a curriculum that provides them with the skills they need to earn a living directly after high school. Also, if students who are unable to do the work are placed in a college preparatory course, teachers may react by lowering standards for everybody. As a result, the most capable may become bored and lose their motivation to work.

There are significant variations among schools both in the processes that assign students to instructional tracks and in the effects of tracking on students' academic achievement (Hallinan 1992, 1994; Kubitschek and Hallinan 1996). Ideally, individuals should be sorted without regard to race, ethnicity, gender, or social class. Therefore, schools emphasize criteria such as objective grades, standardized tests, and impartial written evaluations. In reality, however, the poor, women, and members of minority groups encounter obstacles that prevent them from gaining the full benefits

Multiculturalism ▲ The belief that culture should be viewed from the perspective of different groups.

Tracking ▲ Assigning students to different educational programs on the basis of their abilities or interests.

of the educational system through tracking (Ansalone 2003; Lucas and Berends 2002). As we will see later in this chapter, this is one reason why conflict theorists believe that tracking favors students from wealthier backgrounds.

Gender Bias

As stated previously, people in the United States typically believe that education is the key to individual advancement. This belief, however, is often applied to men in one way and to women in another. Until the mid-1970s, in fact, women generally were expected to advance through their husbands' achievements. Accordingly, the school system prepared women for domestic roles and childbearing. In high school, girls were required to take classes in home economics, where they would learn to cook and sew; they were not allowed to take "boys' classes" such as auto mechanics and woodworking. Girls who did not aspire to college were tracked into typing, bookkeeping, and other courses that taught them skills for relatively low-paying jobs with few prospects for advancement. Women were expected to quit their jobs when the right man came along and to become homemakers and mothers. These stereotypical expectations prevailed on the college campus as well: most college women, it was assumed, were attending school to find a suitable spouse. Few women majored in math, chemistry, and engineering—disciplines that are highly quantitative.

What accounts for the scarcity of women in quantitative fields (Tang 2003)? In early grades, girls show about the same mathematical aptitude as boys, but by high school, they score lower than boys on standardized tests. Evidently, mathematical and other quantitative subjects have been labeled "masculine" (Damarin 2000). As a result, girls are not eager to excel in these areas, because such an achievement would make them appear unusual and perhaps unattractive to their peers. Another factor is unconscious bias on the part of teachers and guidance counselors. Despite increased sensitivity to minority and women's issues, counselors still steer women away from college preparatory courses in mathematics and the sciences (Renzetti and Curran 1998). Finally, many fields contain so few women that they supply no role models for younger women.

Gender inequality in education is highly visible on college campuses (Fisher 2001). Even though women make up more than half of all college students, they account for only about one-third of the faculty. The lack of women in fields such as

Doonesbury   BY GARRY TRUDEAU

Gender bias frequently occurs when teachers call on boys in the classroom and ignore the girls. As this cartoon shows, such practices convey the idea that girls are less important than boys.

physics, mathematics, computer sciences, and biology is particularly acute. In many schools, these departments have no women at all. (There is a similar lack of African American faculty members in these areas [*Chronicle of Higher Education* 1993; U.S. Department of Education 1990].)

Although gender bias in education remains a problem, it may be declining. Compared with the situation that existed for women in the United States in 1950, today's women have many more opportunities. Many schools consciously attempt to promote nonsexist attitudes and to use textbooks, films, and videos that reflect an egalitarian outlook. Gender discrimination is illegal; and according to federal law (Title IX), schools that receive federal funds must provide equal opportunity for both genders (Sigelman and Wahlbeck 1999). The existence of these and other laws makes it possible to challenge sexism in the courts. In one case, the Detroit school board was prevented from instituting all-male academies for African American students. Even though the academies were designed explicitly to address the problems faced by African American boys, the American Civil Liberties Union and the National Organization for Women argued successfully that such programs discriminated on the basis of sex and denied female students equal opportunity to participate.

In many respects, the educational system can address only partially many of the issues facing the broader society. Women who rely on their identities as mothers and spouses to sustain them throughout life are especially vulnerable. They can be economically devastated by divorce, widowhood, or abandonment, especially if they lack the education necessary for a well-paying job. Much of the poverty among single mothers stems from their failure to receive adequate job skills through formal education (Chapter 8). This issue, along with those of race and class inequality, goes far beyond the confines of education and requires a broad-based societal solution.

Freedom of Choice

Closely connected with the whole issue of competition and school financing is the controversy over whether tax money should be used only for public schools or whether such funds could be used to pay for tuition at private or church schools. In response to the growth of an educational bureaucracy that seems out of control to many people, there is an increasing call for greater parental choice in the selection of schools for their children (Boyd 1993). A freedom of choice approach would transfer tax funds from schools to families in the form of a voucher that families could use to send their child to any school for which the child qualifies, including private schools. This approach would mean that money would flow out of the public school system to private schools. If parents were given free choice in selecting schools for their children, school funding would probably be further hurt (Powers and Cookson, Jr. 1999).

Proponents of the movement argue that children have the right to attend a particular school regardless of where it is located, and at public expense. They suggest that the government issue vouchers that could be used to pay tuition and other expenses at any approved school. Thus, parents could send their children either to a public magnet school located across the city or to a private school located just a few blocks away. Paradoxically, people like freedom of choice, and they like the public schools.

If enacted, freedom of choice would alter the fundamental structure of American education. It would do away with the principles of the neighborhood school and of community control, which have guided the development of the American educational system for decades. Equally (if not more) controversial is the possibility that parents would use government vouchers to send their children to religious schools. In effect, critics argue, freedom of choice would amount to government subsidy of religious education and would violate the long-standing separation of church and state. Although the public supports freedom of choice, only about one American in three supports the use of government vouchers to pay for private or parochial schooling (Gallup Poll 1991). However, these attitudes may change, particularly if the public schools are perceived as failing to provide quality education.

STUDY TIP

Name and summarize the minority issues in the U.S. educational system. List and define the terms related to those issues.

Today, inequality in education is a major issue for minority groups in the United States. Connected to the issue of inequality are several other issues: (1) mandatory busing of students in many communities in response to court decisions aiming to desegregate the schools; (2) language of instruction; (3) standardized testing; (4) cultural literacy; (5) tracking; (6) gender bias; and (7) freedom of choice.

CQ In the following three controversies, what are the underlying pros and cons for each side of the debate? ◆ Which side are you on in each of the controversies? ◆ Why?

- Busing to achieve racial integration
- Language of instruction
- Cultural literacy

Sociological Analysis of Education

The three broad modes of sociological analysis—functionalism, conflict theory, and symbolic interactionism—provide different perspectives on education. Functionalism emphasizes the societal benefits provided by a standard education that provides everyone with a common language, useful academic skills, and similar core values and norms. Conflict theory emphasizes the role of education in perpetuating social inequality. Symbolic interaction theory emphasizes the dynamics of classroom interaction in forming an academic identity.

The Functionalist Perspective

From the functionalist perspective, the institution of education helps to maintain an orderly and efficient society. It does so in several specific ways.

Socialization   In technologically simple societies, the family and the peer group teach the young almost everything they must know to carry out their adult responsibilities. As societies grow more complex, however, the required knowledge becomes so vast that a system of formal education emerges to help prepare children for their adult roles. Family and peer group remain important agents of socialization, but the responsibility for formal learning passes into the hands of professional teachers under the governance of school boards and departments of education.

Elementary schools concentrate on teaching basic academic subjects such as mathematics, history, and English. The scope and the depth of the subject matter expand in secondary school, and increase again in college. Schools also teach the dominant cultural values and norms of the society, but without much awareness that such teaching is taking place. These lessons are called the **hidden curriculum**, because they do not appear as part of the formal lesson plans and learning objectives (Wren 1999). For example, teachers teach obedience to authority and order when they praise children for sitting quietly, for lining up promptly, and for showing respect to adults. Competitiveness is taught through sports and through academic games such as classroom spelling bees, in which students are challenged to spell difficult words. The student who makes the fewest mistakes wins a prize. As children mature, the hidden curriculum emphasizes punctuality, lining up, avoiding conflicts with peers, and acting interested and attentive even when one is bored (Ballentine 2001; Illich 1983).

Integration into Society   Heterogeneous societies confront the problem of integrating various ethnic, racial, religious, and language groups into a national culture. With more than 200 racial and ethnic groups, the United States is one of the most heterogeneous societies in the world, and the school system is used to help assimilate newcomers and minorities. Because immigrants are concentrated in large cities, urban

Hidden curriculum ▲ Lessons taught in school that do not appear as part of the formal lesson plans and learning objectives.

These fifth-grade children in a multi-ethnic classroom are learning about books. Functionalists generally believe that society would run more smoothly if all children were assimilated to the same set of core values. Conflict theorists point out that so-called core values usually represent the interests of the dominant group in society.

school systems have shouldered most of the responsibility for assimilating newcomers (Jackson and Cooper 1989). To illustrate, the Los Angeles school system has students from more than 28 ethnic groups (*USA Today*, May 13, 1985:1). In New York City, one out of four children under the age of 10 has non-English-speaking parents; it was expected that by the year 2000, one out of three children in the New York public school system would belong to a minority group (*Time*, July 8, 1991:15). In more than half of the 20 largest school districts in the United States, the majority of students are members of racial or ethnic minorities (Boyer 1983). If the pace of immigration continues, the public schools will be called on increasingly to help socialize and assimilate recent arrivals and their children.

Functionalists generally believe in assimilation as the most efficient means of handling large numbers of immigrants (Chapter 7). Because they value assimilation so highly, functionalists tend to prefer English as the main or only language of instruction, and they emphasize standardized testing and cultural literacy. Of course, this treatment means that children whose parents do not speak English must struggle to learn English in the classroom while at the same time learning the subject matter. They must also learn the cultural history of the dominant society, while deemphasizing the history of their own ethnic group. Although functionalists realize that these practices work against the interests of some racial and ethnic minority group members, functionalists are more concerned with the smooth operation of society, which they feel is enhanced by common societal norms, values, and a universal language.

Social Placement Based on Ability   According to functionalists, the school system helps to sort young people into various social statuses or positions. Schools do this by evaluating students and pointing them toward certain broad types of careers (tracking). Functionalists believe that as a result of these processes of evaluation and tracking, "the best and the brightest" students go to the most selective colleges and eventually enter the most demanding occupations. Ideally, the placement of individuals into appropriate societal positions will produce an efficient and stable society based on merit (see Chapter 6; Chapter 7; Parrillo 1996).

The Conflict Perspective

Conflict theorists emphasize how the educational system perpetuates social inequality. Probably few people would disagree with the principle that academic rewards should be

In this photograph, a student has been forced to wear a "dunce cap" and sit in a corner with his back to the class. This punishment was meted out to students who violated rules or who did not perform well. The cap labeled the student as a dumb person or "dunce."

CQ *Can you think of any contemporary educational practices that serve the same function as the dunce cap?*

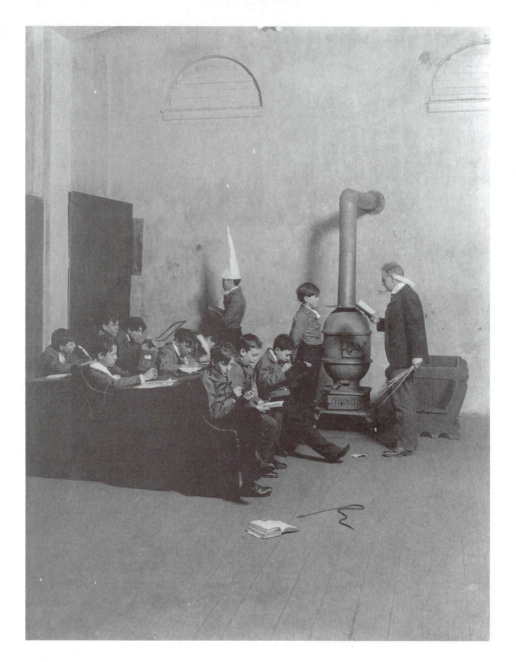

based on academic merit, but most people do not realize that academic merit is defined and measured in terms of middle- and upper-class expectations. Working- and lower-class students, having been socialized in a different environment, must adapt to a different set of norms, many of which put them at a disadvantage (Bowles 1977). According to conflict theorists, the hidden curriculum works against working-class students because it instructs them not to challenge authority. Thus the hidden curriculum benefits managers, owners, political officials, and other powerful people (Connell et al. 1982). In general, the higher the parents' class standing, the higher their children's educational achievements; upper-class students are six times more likely to graduate from college than are lower-class students (see Sewell 1971; Sewell and Hauser 1980).

Approximately one-fourth of private schools in the United States are preparatory schools that charge high tuition and principally serve upper-class families. The students at these schools ("preppies") enjoy the benefits of small classes, rigorous teaching, and the intangible but valuable advantage of being immersed in a school culture that assumes that everyone will attend a high-prestige college or university (see Coleman and Hoffer 1987; Coleman et al. 1982).

According to conflict theorists, the prestige hierarchy of colleges and universities also contributes to the reproduction of inequality. Elite colleges and universities largely enroll students from elite preparatory schools and from high schools located in affluent suburbs. In turn, graduation from an elite college or university greatly enhances an individual's chances for prestigious employment or admission to a good graduate or professional school. Once out of school, the graduate benefits from the social ties established while in school. Overall, students with a degree from an elite college or university have lifetime earnings 85 percent higher than those of students with degrees from the typical undergraduate school (Coleman and Rainwater 1978).

In general, conflict theorists see the issues of language of instruction, standardized testing, and cultural literacy as issues of power, whereby the more powerful are forcing the less powerful members of society to adapt to their customs. Although these practices often appear to be applied fairly, inevitably they favor students whose native language is English and who come from an upper-class background.

According to conflict theorists, tracking is yet another social mechanism that actually undermines individual achievement and reinforces social inequality (Gamoran 1992; Gamoran and Mare 1989; Knipprath 2000). This process occurs in several ways:

1. A definite social class bias is associated with tracking. A study of one high school revealed that 80 percent of the sophomores from high socioeconomic backgrounds were on the college track as contrasted to 52 percent of the sophomores from low socioeconomic backgrounds. Yet the two groups made similar scores on standardized achievement tests. Of course, students from privileged backgrounds are also more likely to be white Anglo-Saxon Protestants, and generally they are overrepresented on college preparatory tracks (Coleman and Hoffer 1987; Vanfossen, Jones, and Spade 1987).

2. Tracking affects an individual's earnings. Vocational graduates earn much less over their lifetimes than do students who go on to complete college. In view of this probability, should not all students be encouraged or required to go on to college?

3. Learning is unequal. Students on the college preparatory track learn more and score higher on standardized tests than students on the other tracks (Goodland 1984).

In short, conflict theorists argue that what transpires inside the classroom often contributes to social inequality throughout society. It creates another form of capital—cultural capital—that is used to secure and justify upper-class privilege (Chapter 6).

The Symbolic Interactionist Perspective

Symbolic interactionist theory emphasizes the school as a social setting that influences the playing of social roles and the development of the self. The self-definitions formed in schools may have consequences for life both inside and outside the classroom. For example, a teacher may define some students as intelligent and others as slow learners. These definitions may be based on small differences in performance—differences that may have been the result of some students' slower rates of maturation or of test bias. Nevertheless, because the teacher is an authority within an authoritative organization, these definitions or labels may be internalized by the students, who then will conform to the expectations implied by the labels. Children who are labeled "good learners" approach their schoolwork with confidence and usually succeed, thereby reinforcing their positive self-definitions. In contrast, children who are labeled "poor learners" approach learning reluctantly and thereby fail. Their failure then reinforces their original negative self-definition. These labels follow them from grade to grade, their performance is noted on their official records, and the gap between the two groups of students becomes ever wider. The labeling process thus creates a **self-fulfilling prophecy**, whereby the teacher's (or some other authority's) expectations and assumptions cause behavior that fulfills those expectations and assumptions (Alexander, Entwisle, and Thompson 1987; Bidwell and Friedkin 1988;

Self-fulfilling prophecy ▲ Process whereby an authority figure's expectations and assumptions cause behavior that fulfills those expectations and assumptions.

Students whom teachers label as "good learners" tend to perform better than those labeled "poor learners." This process is known as the self-fulfilling prophecy.

STUDY TIP

In a pair or group of three, talk about self-fulfilling prophecy as it relates to education. Think ahead of time about a self-fulfilling prophecy that has been part of how you perceive yourself as a learner—or choose one from a person or situation that you know of. Discuss how you can turn around a damaging self-image that comes from a self-fulfilling prophecy.

TABLE 12.1

[a]The functionalist and conflict perspectives were introduced in Chapters 1 and 2, and symbolic interaction was discussed in Chapter 3.

Brophy 1983; Crano and Mellon 1978; Dusek 1985; Sewell and Hauser 1980; Wilkinson and Marrett 1985).

Labeling may affect behavior outside the classroom as well. For instance, the supposedly slow learners may choose careers that are less demanding intellectually and may not strive to improve their academic skills. Thus, they self-select themselves out of important jobs and leadership positions that might have been theirs were it not for the label.

In contrast to functionalists and conflict theorists, symbolic interactionists stress that interaction—what actually goes on in the classroom—is important to study (see Table 12.1). For example, the interaction between students and teachers is often affected by ascribed characteristics. To illustrate, lower-class children—many of whom are members of racial and ethnic minorities—sometimes display aggressive behaviors that are a normal part of their peer group interactions, but middle-class teachers interpret these behaviors as hostility and conclude that these children cannot be taught in a normal classroom. Yet many of these students are as intelligent and have as much academic potential as the typical middle-class student. Gender also affects classroom

Comparison of the Three Theoretical Perspectives on Education		
PERSPECTIVE[a]	**VIEW OF EDUCATION**	**KEY CONCEPTS AND PROCESSES**
Functionalism	Sees education as essential for an orderly and efficient society	Socialization and other functions Official and hidden curriculum
Conflict Theory	Sees educational system as perpetuating social inequality	Prestige hierarchy of schools Cultural capital
Symbolic Interaction	Sees education as interaction in the social setting of the school	Labeling Self-fulfilling prophecy

interactions. Teachers often reward girls for silence, neatness, and conformity while tolerating rebellious behavior in boys. When this treatment happens, boys dominate classroom discussions and receive an inappropriate amount of the teacher's attention (Delamont 1983; Frazier and Sadker 1973; Richardson 1981; Walker and Barton 1983).

Because symbolic interactionists view human behavior as highly situational and as dependent on the actual interaction that occurs, they are mostly interested in studying how interaction takes place within a given school and how it affects students' self-concepts. For instance, tracking has implications for the development of self-concepts. Students on the vocational track often are unnecessarily stigmatized, because the student culture of many high schools defines vocational students as intellectually inferior to and less refined than students on the college track. Students are aware of this stigma, and assignment to a vocational track may damage self-esteem and stunt the development of many skills not directly related to academic ability. Teachers who are aware of this bias could counter by affirming the value of vocational training, by pointing out that employees in skilled trades earn good wages, and by emphasizing the value of a successful manufacturing plant to a community. Similarly, symbolic interactionists would approach their analysis of the issues of language of instruction and cultural literacy through the interaction processes at work in the classroom. Cultural diversity implies that we recognize the contribution of many different ethnic and racial groups, and this recognition could be done in such a way as to praise the contributions made by people of color, women, and other groups.

● ■ ▲ **Pausing to Think**   About the Sociological Analysis of Education

According to functionalists, formal education is important because it transmits formal knowledge, common social values, and norms that maintain an efficient society. In contrast, conflict theorists emphasize how formal education serves to legitimate and perpetuate social inequality. Symbolic interactionists focus on how teacher-student interactions affect a person's self-concept, self-esteem, and identity.

CQ   Were you assigned to a "track" in your high school? ◆ If so, how did you feel about that treatment? ◆ Compare how functionalists, conflict theorists, and symbolic interactionists view tracking. Which perspective do you agree with the most?

Education in the Twenty-First Century

As we have discussed throughout this chapter, education and society are closely related; in general, education reflects the dominant structure and concerns of the society. This characteristic means that what you do as a student will be affected by the changes that occur in your society. Conversely, your ability to prosper through education rests heavily on the match between the type of education you acquire and the nature of your social environment.

How can you as a college student get a good education now—one that will prepare you for the emerging postindustrial society of the United States? This is an especially important question when you consider the rising cost of college (see the Society Today box, Costs of Higher Education). Sociologists Jerald Hage and Charles Powers (1992) have examined this question, and, although their complete answer is rather involved, part of it can be summarized here.

In postindustrial society, they argue, the ability to solve problems is crucially important. The value of a computer programmer/analyst, for example, lies in the person's ability to find solutions to problems involving complex computer systems rather than in her or his ability to follow instructions, fill out forms, or engage in routine interactions with other employees. So, while in college, you want to learn how to solve problems and to enjoy the challenge of working through difficult situations until solutions are found.

123 STUDY TIP

From reading the chapter, synthesize what you consider to be the "Ten Most Dominant Elements of Public Education in the United States." For each, name significant consequences and note whether you consider those consequences to be pros or cons. Finally, name the element that you believe needs to be rethought in the twenty-first century and state why.

Society Today ● ■ ▲

Costs of Higher Education

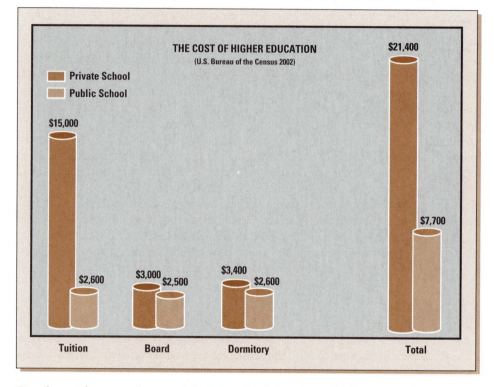

THE COST OF HIGHER EDUCATION
(U.S. Bureau of the Census 2002)

- Private School
- Public School

$21,400

$15,000

$7,700

$2,600 $3,000 $2,500 $3,400 $2,600

Tuition   Board   Dormitory   Total

Over the past few years, the cost of obtaining a bachelors degree has been rising faster than the cost of living. This graph shows that at a private college or university, you can expect to pay over $21,000 per year for tuition, food, and dormitory space. By comparison, public schools are inexpensive, prompting many people to say that a good public college or university is a "bargain".

CQ If you are reading this book, then you must be in school; and if you are in school, then you must think that the cost of a higher education is worth it. What makes higher education worth the cost? ◆ In your opinion, what can be done to make higher education more affordable?

Hage and Powers believe that the economic core of an industrial society is the production of material goods, whereas the economic core of a postindustrial society is creativity. The industrial worker is treated mainly as a standardized factor of production, but the postindustrial worker will be regarded as a valuable source of ideas. So, during your time in college, you should develop your creativity, both inside and outside the classroom.

Whereas industrial societies emphasize standardization and homogenization, the postindustrial society will move beyond mere standardization. Individuality will be prized. For example, computers will be assigned the task of giving standardized instruction, whereas teachers will focus on the problems of a particular student as an individual. Businesses will look at their customers less in terms of categories and more in terms of unique combinations of social backgrounds, personal interests, and sociological identities. As a college student, you can work on combining individuality with the high standards people have come to expect through standardization. One way of doing this is to become a critical thinker and to develop individuality in your academic work.

For certain, the increasing diversity of society will require all of us in this century to get along with many different types of people. One way to develop your interpersonal skills is to form friendships with as many different types of people as you can.

There is little doubt that the workplace of the future will involve high technology. These elementary schoolchildren are now learning to solve problems on the computer—a skill that they will surely need in the next century.

CONCEPT WEB Education

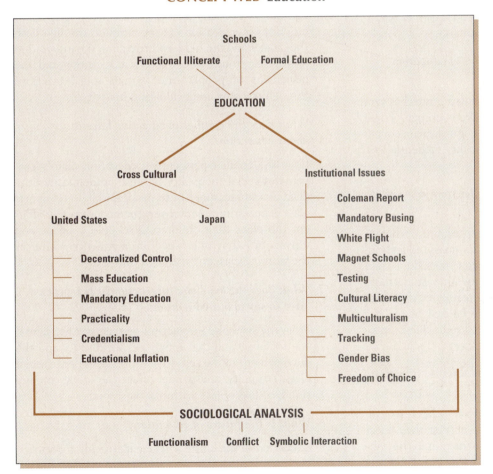

This is a concept web for Education. The portion of the web dealing with education in Japan has not been developed. Add features of the Japanese educational system to the web. Would it be reasonable to move *functional illiterate* to the Institutional Issues section? Why or why not?

If you interact with others who are different from you, then you will become socially skilled, but of more importance, you will learn to appreciate diversity.

In short, the postindustrial society of the next century will demand a talent for problem solving, creativity, individuality, and an ability to work with others from diverse backgrounds. Regardless of your major, these appear to be universal skills that will be well suited to the society that lies ahead.

Looking Ahead

Education is a key institution in contemporary society. In the next chapter, we discuss religion, an institution that throughout human history has been important in giving meaning to people's lives.

WHAT YOU SHOULD KNOW ●■▲

1. How has education changed with the Great Social Transformation?

In communal societies, education takes place in personal settings, and the teacher is often a parent, relative, or other member of the communal group. With industrialization, education becomes formal, and the responsibility for educating children is given to teachers, counselors, and other professionals.

2. What are the basic characteristics of education in the United States?

The educational system of the United States has several basic characteristics that make it unique. These characteristics are decentralized control, mass education, mandatory education, practicality, credentialism, and educational inflation.

3. How does education in Japan differ from education in the United States?

The Japanese system forms a steep pyramid, whereas the American system emphasizes mass education. Japanese children spend more time in school than students in the United States, and they study more intensely. Academic failure is a matter of shame to Japanese families, whereas in the United States, accomplishment or failure is believed to be due to individual ability.

4. What are the principal educational issues affecting minorities?

Today, several issues face the public school system: (1) busing of students to schools outside their local neighborhoods; (2) language of instruction in the public schools; (3) standardized testing that mostly reflects middle- and upper-middle-class culture; (4) cultural literacy; (5) tracking; (6) gender inequality in educational opportunities and instruction; and (7) freedom of choice, or programs that propose to give students vouchers that can be used to attend any school of their choice, including schools with religious affiliations.

5. What does the functionalist perspective have to say about education?

From the functionalist perspective, education helps to maintain an orderly and efficient society. The major functions of education are socialization through both the official and the hidden curriculum, the integration of various groups into mainstream society, and the placement of people into various social positions through tracking and evaluating students.

6. What does the conflict perspective have to say about education?

From the conflict perspective, education mainly perpetuates social inequality because academic merit is defined and measured in terms of middle- and upper-class expectations. Moreover, the economically affluent can place their children in schools, colleges, and universities that offer superior instruction, whereas the working class and the poor cannot.

7. What does the symbolic interactionist perspective have to say about education?

From the symbolic interaction perspective, the school is a social setting that influences social roles and the development of the self. In addition, a student's social class, ethnicity, and gender affect the social interaction that takes place within a classroom.

8. What is the future of education?

Education in the future will face many calls for reform. Nevertheless, a good way to prepare yourself for the postindustrial society is to educate yourself to be flexible socially, to be good at solving problems, and to be creative. In addition, you should develop the ability to work with people from diverse backgrounds.

TEST YOUR KNOWLEDGE ●■▲

Key Terms Matching

Match each of these key terms with the best definition or example from the numbered items that follow. Write the letter preceding the key term in the blank before the definition that you choose.

- **a.** credentialism
- **b.** cultural literacy
- **c.** education
- **d.** educational inflation
- **e.** formal education
- **f.** functionally illiterate
- **g.** hidden curriculum
- **h.** magnet schools
- **i.** mandatory education
- **j.** mass education
- **k.** multiculturalism/multiculturalists
- **l.** schools
- **m.** self-fulfilling prophecy
- **n.** tracking
- **o.** white flight

_____ **1.** Lessons taught in school that do not appear as part of the formal lesson plans and learning objectives.

_____ **2.** The extent to which a person possesses the basic information needed to thrive in the modern world.

_____ **3.** Places of formal educational instruction.

_____ **4.** The situation in which the credentials required to obtain a job increase while the skills necessary to perform the job remain the same.

_____ **5.** The belief that culture should be viewed from the perspective of different groups; those who hold that belief.

_____ **6.** Assigning students to different educational program on the basis of their abilities or interests.

_____ **7.** The transferal of the knowledge, values, and beliefs of a society from one generation to the next.

_____ **8.** Lacking the ability to read and write well enough to carry out the routine activities of everyday life.

_____ **9.** Education to a certain age specified by law.

_____ **10.** The transmission of knowledge, skills, and attitudes from one generation to the next through systematic training.

_____ **11.** An upsurge in white families moving to suburban neighborhoods to avoid mandatory busing.

_____ **12.** The idea that everyone is entitled to a certain amount of publicly provided education and is obligated to obtain it.

_____ **13.** Process whereby an authority figure's expectations and assumptions cause behavior that fulfills those expectations and assumptions.

_____ **14.** Schools that offer specialized programs or intensive studies in certain subject areas to draw students from all residential areas of the community.

_____ **15.** The view that academic degrees indicate the holders' qualifications to perform certain jobs or roles.

Multiple Choice

Circle the letter of your choice.

1. In communal societies, education
- **a.** takes place in complex bureaucratic organizations.
- **b.** is formal and systematic.
- **c.** is largely informal and is passed on through highly personalized social relations.
- **d.** is largely formal and is passed on through professional administrators.

2. The principle of mass education in the United States goes back to Thomas Jefferson's belief that education and which of the following go hand in hand?
- **a.** religion
- **b.** democracy
- **c.** farming
- **d.** industrialization

3. Which of the following is NOT true of education in the United States?
- **a.** It is criticized because many young people are functionally illiterate.
- **b.** Control of education is highly centralized.
- **c.** The United States was the first industrialized nation to implement mass education.
- **d.** It is based on the value of practicality.

4. Universities funded by the Morrill Act that originally emphasized agriculture and mechanics but that over time became large, comprehensive research universities are called

   a. liberal arts universities.
   b. magnet schools.
   c. Ivy League schools.
   d. land grant universities.

5. Roland has the skills necessary to performs the duties of a manager, but the company will not hire him because he does not have a college degree. This condition is called

   a. educational inflation.
   b. mass education.
   c. credentialism.
   d. cultural illiteracy.

6. Jacalyn's father was hired at the local factory without a high school diploma. However, now the company requires a high school diploma for that same job. This condition is called

   a. educational inflation.
   b. credentialism.
   c. practicality.
   d. mass education.

7. Which of the following findings was NOT included in the Coleman report?

   a. African American children perform more poorly than white children.
   b. American children attend racially segregated schools.
   c. Predominantly white schools have more educational resources than predominantly black schools.
   d. Students in schools with more educational resources perform much better than those from schools with fewer educational resources.

8. Which of the following was the result of white flight?

   a. increased racial and ethnic segregation
   b. decreased city tax base
   c. increased financial problems in central city schools
   d. all of the above

9. Schools that offer specialized subjects like science, math, and arts and that hope to attract students to their schools because of the specialized subjects are called

   a. neighborhood schools.
   b. hidden curriculum schools.
   c. magnet schools.
   d. tracking schools.

10. In the United States, school integration

    a. is strongly supported by most people.
    b. has been achieved by mandatory busing.
    c. is evident in that over 90 percent of white children attend integrated schools.
    d. has created equal funding of schools.

11. In Uma's high school, students are placed in one of three groups: vocational, general, or college preparatory. This process is called

    a. labeling.
    b. tracking.
    c. magnet schooling.
    d. tailoring education.

12. When Brian's mother was in high school, she was required to take typing and home economics even though she preferred woodworking. Brian's mother was subjected to

    a. labeling.
    b. tracking.
    c. gender bias.
    d. prejudice.

13. A latent function of education in the United States is that children learn to be on time, to line up properly, and to be patriotic. This situation is referred to as

    a. the hidden curriculum.
    b. cultural literacy.
    c. cultural capital.
    d. assimilation.

14. One consequence of the freedom to choose schools will be that

    a. money would flow out of the public school system to private schools.
    b. most people will desert public schools.
    c. property taxes would be increased to pay for increased busing.
    d. religious schools will become entirely publicly financed.

15. Mark was labeled as a slow learner by one of his teachers. As a result, he developed a negative self-image and started performing poorly in school. This outcome is called

    a. cultural illiteracy.
    b. self-fulfilling prophecy.
    c. functional illiteracy.
    d. gender bias.

Identifying Sociological Perspectives on Education

For each of the following statements, identify the sociological perspective associated with the statement by writing F for functionalist, C for conflict, or SI for symbolic interactionist, in the appropriate blank.

_____ 1. Assimilation is the most efficient means for society to handle a large number of immigrants; therefore, there should be school instruction in one language only.

_____ 2. It is important to focus on the social interaction between teachers and students to understand what is actually happening in the classroom.

_____ 3. Evaluation and tracking help direct the best and the brightest students to the most selective colleges, therefore helping them enter the most demanding occupations.

_____ 4. The hidden curriculum works against working-class students because it instructs them not to challenge authority.

_____ 5. The educational system is well designed to teach students what they need to know to fill their adult roles.

_____ 6. Such issues as the language of instruction, standardized testing, and cultural literacy are issues of power in which the more powerful force the less powerful to adapt to their customs.

True-False

Indicate your response to each of the following statements by circling T for true or F for false.

T F 1. In industrial societies, education is highly formal and takes place mainly in schools.

T F 2. The United States and Japan have extremely similar educational systems, in that both are highly industrial societies.

T F 3. The federal government plays a very small role in the United States educational system.

T F 4. The factory system held back the development of mass education in America.

T F 5. College life for Japanese students is much easier than college life for American students, because the Japanese assume that anyone who passes the entrance exams is qualified to graduate.

T F 6. In the United States, belief in education transcends the social divisions of race, class, and gender.

T F 7. Most standardized educational tests, including the ACT and SAT, are free of cultural and class bias.

T F 8. Two out of every three white adults oppose mandatory busing.

T F 9. Regardless of what your major is, problem solving, creativity, individuality, and the ability to work with others from diverse backgrounds will be universal skills necessary in postindustrial society.

T F 10. The economic core of an industrial economy is the production of material goods, whereas the economic core of a postindustrial society is creativity.

T F 11. The Morrill Act of 1862 created the conditions for the founding of the land grant universities.

T F 12. Many communities have created *compass* schools as a way of integrating their school system.

T F 13. Conflict theorists think that tracking students favors students from wealthier backgrounds.

T F 14. Among the findings of the Coleman report was that predominantly white schools had more resources than predominantly black schools.

T F 15. Labels attached to children by teachers or others, such as a being "good learner," tend to create a *self-fulfilling prophecy*.

NOTE: The answers to these exercises are at the end of the book.

For additional practice tests and other resources please visit the companion web site at http://www.prenhall.com/curry.

Essay

1. What are some compelling arguments for year-round schooling? What is the greatest impediment to the idea?

2. Contrast how functionalism, conflict theory, and symbolic interaction see education.

3. Contrast the characteristics of education in Japan with the U.S. system.

4. Why do high schools track students and what are the problems with tracking students?

5. What evidence is there for the presence of gender bias in the U.S. system of education?

13

Religion

Today, the term *puritan* refers to a person who has an extremely strict sense of religious morality and who regards games, levity, and lose behavior as sinful. The term derives from the original Puritans, who in 1692 lived in Salem, Massachusetts. In that year, two young girls in Salem town began displaying hysterical behaviors. Unable to diagnose much less cure these afflictions, town elders began to suspect that the girls had been possessed by the Devil. After being question by the elders at some length, the girls named three older women as witches.

The three women were imprisoned and one confessed to being a witch. Greatly alarmed, the elders established a special court to root out all the witches in Salem. As the witch hunt mounted in fury, several more women and a few men were arrested, interrogated, and convicted. In June, one man was hanged; in July and in August ten people were executed; in September an accused man was pressed to death (suffocated by placing large stones on his chest) for refusing to participate in his trial; and later that month eight more people were executed. With the last executions, the witch trial seems to have run its course. The governor of Massachusetts stepped in, dissolved the special court, and freed the remaining prisoners. The legislature of the colony subsequently annulled the trials altogether and indemnified the families of the executed people.

Historians have long studied the Salem Witch Trial, and so have sociologists (Starkey 1949). For example, a sociological study by Kai Erikson (1966) remains influential to this day. He argues that the trial served to reinforce Puritan culture. It did so by vividly reminding the Puritans of (1) the Devil's power to lead ordinary people into ungodliness; and (2) the dreaded consequences of succumbing to the Devil's temptations. On a broader scale, the Salem Witch Trial has been used as a metaphor for scapegoating. To illustrate, the play and several film versions of *The Crucible* are based on the Salem Witch Trial. They have been interpreted as a protest against the witch hunt for communists in the 1950s; and today they are often used as a metaphor to denounce the scapegoating of Muslim Americans for the events associated with 9/11.

Witches and witchcraft survive in America today. Increasingly, people have been turning to Wicca as a spiritual home. Wicca is a modern form of an ancient pagan naturalistic religion. Wiccans are guided by the principle, "If it harm none, do what you will." Witchcraft has been closely associated with Wicca, but Wiccans are not Satanists. Traditional churches today do not accept Wicca as a comparable way of approaching the deity.

Although Wicca is controversial in traditional religious circles, we emphasize that sociologists do not judge religious practices as right or wrong, logical or illogical, good or bad. Instead, sociologists point out that beliefs about the sacred, or **religion,** are a cultural universal. As scientists, sociologists ask questions such as these: What are the consequences of religion for society? How is religion related to other social institutions? How are churches organized? How do people develop a religious identity? In the pages that follow, we will delve into these questions, because the answers can help us better understand our social world and ourselves.

Chapter Preview

We begin this chapter by examining the effects of the Great Social Transformation on religion. Next, we describe the elements of religion, and then we discuss the major religions of the world. Following that discussion, we present the sociological analysis of religion. Lastly, we examine the forces that are changing religion and then look at religion in the twenty-first century.

The Great Social Transformation and Religion

The roots of religion lie in an ancient communal past, a time when the institution of religion was supreme in the social organization of society. In many communal societies, religion permeated all aspects of society and was woven into daily life. The aboriginal Hopi of Arizona, for instance, performed elaborate rituals concerning the essentials of life, such as securing rain, growing crops, preventing sickness, and raising children. The ceremonies lasted from a few days to two weeks or more, and they occurred at least once a month (Maybury-Lewis 1992).

In contrast to communal society, in contemporary industrial society, the institution of religion has become separated from many social and economic activities. Most of us go to work, earn money, attend school, and buy groceries in places that are devoid of religious ceremony. Increasingly, religion has become a matter of private expression, with silent prayers substituting for communal rituals. Community involvement in religion occurs on a particular day of the week and on certain special occasions during the year, but it does not interfere with the demands of an industrial economy.

The classical sociologist Max Weber recognized the fundamental importance of religion, particularly in regard to the emergence of capitalism in Western Europe. In his book *The Protestant Ethic and the Spirit of Capitalism*, he argued that there was a close connection between the virtues espoused in the Protestant Reformation—hard work,

Religion ▲ A system of beliefs, rituals, and ceremonies that focuses on sacred matters, promotes community among its followers, and provides for a personal spiritual experience for its members.

Traditional Hopi dancers. The Hopi performed elaborate rituals concerning the essentials of life, such as growing crops and preventing disease. They are shown here wearing traditional garb with "butterfly" headdress near the Grand Canyon in Arizona.

honesty, and prosperity as a sign of God's favor toward the individual—and the values of a capitalist economic system—initiative, thrift, and competition (Weber 1958). Although scholars disagree today on which caused which—whether the Protestant Reformation caused the rise of capitalism or whether the rise of capitalism created the right conditions for the emergence of the Protestant Reformation—there is agreement that both political change and religious change were closely connected in the transformation of European society from traditional to associational (Inglehart 1997).

The Elements of Religion

Regardless of what people believe about sacred matters, all religions have certain elements in common. The presence of these common elements makes different religions similar and enables sociologists to recognize, categorize, and analyze the relationships between religious systems and society. Viewed broadly, these common elements or characteristics of religion are as follows:

Characteristics of Religion

1. Beliefs   Émile Durkheim was one of the first sociologists to study religion scientifically. He pointed out that in the course of our lives, we all encounter religious mysteries that defy common sense, logic, and science (Durkheim 1912/1947). Our inability to explain these mysteries does not prevent us from believing in them. Christians believe, for instance, that Jesus's mother, Mary, was a virgin. Although science and common experience indicate that a virgin birth is impossible, Christians continue to believe in the notion of the virgin birth. The validity of this particular belief is a matter of faith; but the social consequences of the belief are a matter of sociology. Similarly, you undoubtedly do not approve of witch hunts, but you can better understand the puritan worldview, and hence their motivation, by taking into account their belief in witchcraft. In sum, beliefs explain the logically unexplainable within the believer's level of knowledge about the world, and as we discuss next, they separate the sacred from the profane.

2. The Sacred and the Profane   According to Durkheim (1912), all religions distinguish between the sacred and the profane. The **sacred** are those things that have supernatural significance and qualities, whereas the **profane** are those things that are regarded as part of ordinary life. Anything can be endowed with sacredness, but common examples taken from Christianity are the crucifix, the rosary, and holy burial ground. Explicitly profane behaviors (again, from the Christian viewpoint) are greed, selfishness, and adultery. In many places, moreover, a church is regarded as a sacred place where people can seek refuge from civil authorities (see the Sociology Online box on page 381).

3. Rituals and Ceremonies   All religions have some form of routinized behaviors that express and reinforce the faith; that is, all religions have **rituals**. Prayers, chants, and incantations are common rituals, as are stylized body movements and sayings. Thus, Catholics traditionally kneel before the crucifix and recite the rosary (a form of stylized prayer), whereas Buddhist monks chant and light incense sticks. To the participants, these rituals are an important part of their worship, but to a sociologist, they are important for a much different reason. Durkheim argued that rituals are social mechanisms through which the sacred and the profane are brought together temporarily. The ceremonial lighting of candles on a menorah commemorates the Jewish Festival of Lights (Hanukkah) and links Jews both to their common group experiences and to their God; the daily prayer cycle of Muslims and Catholics permits believers to approach the divine with praise, worship, and supplication. In short, rituals permit worshipers—who might be contaminated by the profane—to approach their deity

Sacred ▲ Those things that have supernatural significance and qualities.

Profane ▲ Those things that are regarded as part of ordinary life.

Ritual ▲ Commonly routinized behaviors that express and reinforce religious faith.

The lighting of a menorah is an ancient ritual associated with Hanukkah, an important Jewish holiday. By participating in the rituals of their religion, people of the same faith are linked to a common group experience.

temporarily and safely. To sociologists, such rituals help bind people together into a society. Rituals celebrate the possibility of social solidarity in spite of all the moral conflicts and profane aspects of everyday life. For a few brief moments, everyone is united in spite of their many other differences (Glazier 1996; Pickering 1984).

4. Moral Communities Religions are organized around communities of people who share the same beliefs and values. The religious community is important for several reasons. It provides continuity from one generation to the next, thereby ensuring the survival of the religion. The religious community looks after mundane business matters, such as paying rent on church buildings and purchasing materials for worship. Equally important, it provides social support for its members. In times of distress, members offer aid; in times of joy, they offer congratulations; and in times of threat, they come together for self-protection.

5. Personal Experience Religion is obviously a powerful force in human affairs, in part because it is intertwined with an individual's personal experience. The so-called born-again Christians are possibly the best-known group in the United States that requires personal involvement. According to their beliefs, the participant must have a highly intense, emotional, and personal religious experience in which he or she is "born again" as a Christian. In contrast to the dramatic experiences required of born-again Christians, Zen Buddhists, Sikhs, and Quakers believe that quiet meditation will transport the participant to a peaceful level of altered consciousness. The personal experience obtained through religion can give meaning to people's lives, sometimes resolving personal problems or resolving guilt. For instance, a few years ago, a woman who was being questioned about the deaths of her two children finally confessed to killing them—after the police investigator, whom she had come to trust, knelt with her in prayer and asked God for guidance (*New York Times*, August 4, 1995:A7; Stark 1987).

Although all religions contain these common elements, the emphasis may differ. Some religions are very rich in ceremony, whereas others are fairly sparse. In a traditional Hindu marriage, for example, the ceremony goes on for hours and hours, whereas a contemporary Protestant ceremony may be completed in less than half an hour. Some belief systems are extremely complicated, whereas others are extremely simple. To illustrate, the belief system of Catholicism is so elaborate that the church has developed special courts to adjudicate religious disputes. In contrast, the ancient Romans believed that religion was primarily a family matter. Each Roman household had its own gods, and the Romans were quite tolerant of the religious beliefs of the various societies they conquered. They made no attempt to develop a complex, comprehensive religious order, but instead practiced pantheism—the tolerant acceptance of the worship of all gods (Maybury-Lewis 1992). Thus, even though religion is a cultural universal, cross-cultural differences also exist and therefore must be taken into account when trying to explain religion sociologically.

Types of Religion

All religions exist within the broader society and must come to some accommodation with other societal institutions. Some religions are well accepted, whereas others are not (Troeltsch 1931). On the basis of this variation in acceptance, religions may be classified into different types of organizations.

Church and Denomination   In casual speech, the terms church and denomination often are used interchangeably, but each term has a specific, sociological meaning. A formal religious organization that is well established and well integrated into society is a **church**. A church has certain characteristics: it is organized bureaucratically, has a large membership, follows well-established rituals, and is accepted widely by the population (see Troeltsch 1931; Wallis 1975; Weber 1958). These characteristics give churches stability and solidify their relationship with the broader society. Churches claim authority over the profane as well as over the sacred; in doing so, they assert the right to judge and supervise the morality and ethics of everyday life.

Some churches find so much favor that they become the state's official religion. When that event occurs, everyone in the nation is automatically a member of the religion by virtue of birth. Such a religion is called an **ecclesia**. For example, some Latin American nations formally recognize Roman Catholicism as the official religion, or ecclesia, of the state. Other ecclesiae include Lutheranism in Norway, Sweden, Denmark, and Iceland; Islam in Pakistan; and Buddhism in Burma. Even though Protestantism is the dominant American religion, the United States does not recognize an ecclesia. In fact, the opposite is true—people in the United States strongly oppose having an ecclesia, and the Constitution prohibits the mixing of church and state. Article I of the Bill of Rights says, "Congress shall make no law respecting an establishment of religion, or prohibiting the free exercise thereof. . . ."

In pluralistic societies such as the United States, religions usually take the specific form of a **denomination**: a religion that maintains friendly relations with the government and with other religions but that does not claim to be the nation's only legitimate faith. Over 1,500 religious denominations exist in the United States (Melton 1998). Major American denominations include (among others) Baptists, Catholics, Lutherans, Episcopalians, Reform Jews, Methodists, Presbyterians, and Unitarians. Although members of a particular denomination might believe that their faith is the only true faith, they also recognize the right of other people to hold different views. Nevertheless, historically, Protestant denominations have maintained and continue

STUDY TIP

Write a short essay detailing the elements of religion—beliefs, the sacred and profane, rituals and ceremonies, moral communities, and personal experience—as they appear in one particular world religion.

Church ▲ A formal religious organization that is well established and well integrated into its society.

Ecclesia ▲ A church that is a state's official religion.

Denomination ▲ A religion that maintains friendly relations with the government and with other religions but that does not claim to be the nation's only legitimate faith.

A boy studying the Qur'an in Lahore, Pakistan.

to maintain a desire for a competitive religious market—one that is free of government regulation. Success in the free marketplace of religion is judged by the number of "converts" gained from other denominations. Many times, though, denominations that have reached a peaceful yet mildly competitive accommodation in an associational society may in traditional or transitional societies actively compete against one another for converts. For example, Catholics and Pentecostals, who get along well in American society, work very hard against each other to gain converts in the Caribbean and Latin American countries (Fortuny-Loret, de Mola, and Cabayet 1994; Novaes 1994). Among the most aggressive denominations in America's religious marketplace today are Baptists, Methodists, Jehovah's Witnesses, and Mormons.

Sect   Another form of religious organization is the sect. In contrast to a church, which accepts the broader society, a **sect** actively rejects the social environment in which it exists (Johnson 1963). Many, if not most, sects come into existence by breaking away from a larger religious organization. Members of the sect are deeply committed to their beliefs, and they view themselves as guardians of a true doctrine. In some cases, they have used armed violence to gain their ends (see Bellah et al. 1985).

In contrast to church services, which are ritualized, routinized, and sometimes passive, sect services are emotional, spontaneous, and active. During the service, sect members often rise from their seats to shout encouragement and to express their fervor. They may dance about, sing, and rejoice in their personal experience of the divine presence.

Sects are loosely organized and are relatively nonbureaucratic compared with churches. The absence of much formal organization coupled with nonprofessional leadership renders sects vulnerable to economic misfortune and mismanagement. Sects seldom last long, although a few exceptions are now well known: Baptists, Presbyterians, Seventh Day Adventists, Quakers, and Jehovah's Witnesses all began as sects and grew into major denominations and churches (Crotty 1996).

Cult   Sometimes religious groups develop around a particular charismatic leader and have little or nothing in common with conventional religious traditions. These groups are called **cults**. Usually, cult members disavow the broader society because they view it as degenerate, and they further believe that each person must establish better relations with the spiritual. To accomplish these ends, cults sometimes require members to live together in group quarters or to move into communes.

People join cults for many reasons. Because some recruits are isolated and lonely, they seek the companionship that membership brings. Other recruits are attracted by the cult's philosophy, and still others join as a result of persuasion and social pressure (Knox 1999). Possibly the most common reason for joining, however, is the leader's charisma. For this reason, cults are often closely associated with a particular person (Lofland and Richardson 1984). For example, Sun Myung Moon believed he was Christ returned to earth. On the basis of this belief, he formed the Unification Church in Korea and, in 1959, he brought it to the United States, where his followers became known as "Moonies." The cult leader David Koresh also believed that he was divinely inspired, and he established a commune near Waco, Texas. His commune ended tragically. Surrounded by federal authorities after a gun battle, the compound burst into flames when agents attacked it with a tank outfitted to blow tear gas through the building walls. Koresh's followers apparently set fire to their own commune at his orders, and more than 80 people died, including many children. The fiery end to Koresh's cult has become a defining moment for some militia groups, which interpret the federal response as excessive and unnecessary.

Cults are generally smaller than sects, are less structured, and lack ties to established churches and denominations. Most cults die out rather quickly, but a few have longer lives. When a cult becomes established, it typically accommodates itself to the broader society, and hostility toward it diminishes.

Sect ▲ A loosely organized, non-bureaucratic religious organization with nonprofessional leadership that actively rejects the social environment in which it exists.

Cult ▲ A religious organization that has little or nothing to do with conventional religious traditions and believes that society is degenerate and that the members of the organization must withdraw together from normal life and live apart in group quarters or a commune.

All religions have elements in common: they are systems of belief that distinguish between the sacred and the profane; they have rituals and ceremonies; they are organized around a core community; and they provide people with powerful emotional experiences. Religions may be grouped into churches, denominations, sects, and cults.

CQ Do you know of any cults in your state? ◆ What are their major characteristics? ◆ Do you consider cults a danger or a blessing to society?

Varieties of Religion

Thousands of religions exist today, and thousands more existed in the past. Although many of these religions vanished without a trace, other have continued to thrive over the centuries. The largest of these—the so-called world religions—have some 3.1 billion adherents, a number equal to more than half the world's population. It is particularly important to know about these major religions, because people, cultures, and societies once isolated from one another are now in regular contact (Beyer 1994). One result has been an escalation of conflict. For instance, religious differences among Croatian Catholics, Serbian Eastern Orthodox Christians, and Bosnian Muslims were at the center of the conflict in Bosnia-Herzegovina; and religious differences among Jews, Christians, and Muslims have frequently led to hostility and tragedy in the Middle East. We now turn to a description of world religions, but in keeping with the sociological viewpoint, our description emphasizes social organization (see the World Today box, Major Religions of the World on page 383).

123 STUDY TIP

Develop a chart to summarize the different types of religions. For each, include the defining elements, goals, relation to society, and examples.

Christianity

Christianity is the world's largest single religion, with 1.96 billion believers divided among three major branches. The largest branch is the Roman Catholic, followed by the Protestant, and then by the Orthodox Christian (also known as Eastern Orthodox). Although large pockets of Christians are found throughout the world, most Christians live in Europe, North America, and South America.

Christianity began as a tiny cult whose members believed that Jesus of Nazareth was the long-promised Messiah of the Jews. Jesus was arrested, tried for treason, and executed by crucifixion. His followers claim that he rose from the dead and ascended to heaven in fulfillment of religious prophecy.

In the tenth century, Christianity split into two bodies: the Roman Catholic Church and the Orthodox Church, which is based in what is now Istanbul. Largely isolated from Western influences, the Orthodox Church was bypassed by many of the events that shaped Western culture, such as the Renaissance and the rise of capitalism (Blasi 1989). A second major division in Christianity occurred during the sixteenth century, when Martin Luther (1483–1546) and other reformers broke away from the Roman Catholic Church and formed independent churches of their own. To this day, Protestantism is characterized by splinter groups that form around different beliefs, rituals, and other religious matters.

Islam

Muslims (or Moslems) are followers of the Islamic religion. They believe that the *Qur'an* (Koran) is the word of Allah (God) as set down by the prophet Muhammad over a span of 20 years. Muslims maintain that there is no god but Allah and that Muhammad is His messenger; they pray daily, give alms, fast during religious periods of the year, and hope to make a pilgrimage to the holy city of Mecca at least once in

Muslims believe that prayers must be offered daily, and when they pray, they face toward Mecca, the birthplace of the prophet Muhammad. These Muslims are praying in front of a large mosque in India. Islam is the second-largest world religion, and it is growing rapidly.

World Today ● ■ ▲

Muslims Throughout the World

LOCATION	MILLIONS
Asia	812.0
Africa	315.0
Europe	31.4
North America	4.3
Latin America	1.6
Oceania	.2

SOURCE: U.S. Bureau of the Census, *Statistical Abstract of the United States*, 2000.

their lifetime. Although Muslims are affected strongly by local influences, their veneration of the holy writings imposes a common body of tradition and beliefs across the many different cultural settings in which Islam has flourished.

Although Westerners often regard Islam as an Arabic religion, in fact most Muslims do not live in the Arabic countries or in the area of the world usually thought of as the Middle East (Houben 2003). For example, some 812 million Muslims live in Asia, and 4.3 million live in North America (see the World Today box). With a total membership of more than 1 billion people, Islam is now the second-largest religion in the world, and it continues to grow. By the turn of the twenty-first century, Islam had grown to account for one-fifth to one-quarter of the world's population.

The social organization of Islam is quite unlike that of Christianity. For example, in contrast to the bureaucratic and centralized leadership of the Catholic Church, Islam does not have a centralized authority structure. Rather, local clerics act as leaders, and some acquire widespread political influence. Strict Islamic countries, such as Saudi Arabia and Iran, look to the Qur'an for guidance in all matters and make no distinction between religious and civil life. For example, crimes are punished according to the Qur'an, and the penalties can be harsh by Western standards.

There are several splits within Islam, but the deepest is between Sunni (orthodox) and Shiite Muslims. This division arose centuries ago. Following the death of Muhammad, a controversy arose over the issue of who should succeed him. Some Muslims supported Abu Bakr, a friend of Muhammad and the first convert to Islam. Others supported Ali, Muhammad's son-in-law and cousin. Supporters of Abu Bakr became known as Sunni; Ali's supporters became known as Shiite. Over the centuries, political and theological issues have continued to differentiate Sunni from Shiite, and the two groups remain distinct divisions within Islam.

Islam is the fastest growing religion in the United States. In addition to Muslim migrants from the Middle East, African Americans are the largest convert group. About 90% of African American Sunni Muslim converts are located in large cities. Urban mosques have become core institutions in inner-city neighborhoods of many large communities (Kahera 2002).

Judaism

Numerically, Judaism is the smallest of the world religions. It accounts for less than 1 percent of the world's population. The Jewish population of the United States (6 million) is larger than the Jewish population of Israel (4 million). France, Russia, and the Ukraine also have substantial Jewish populations (approximately half a million) (American Jewish Yearbook 2002; census.gov [accessed October 20, 2003]).

A distinctive feature of Jewish faith concerns the covenant (agreement) under which Jews became God's "chosen people." Also central to Judaism is the *Torah*, the name given to the first five books of the Bible (Kolatch 1994). According to Jewish beliefs, God revealed the Torah (including the Ten Commandments) to Moses on Mount Sinai more than three thousand years ago. Jewish holy writings also include the remainder of what is generally known as the Old Testament, and the *Talmud* (commentaries on the Jewish law by Torah scholars; see Kolatch 1994).

As with Islam and Christianity, major divisions exist within Judaism. Orthodox Jews dress distinctively, segregate men from women at religious services, and adhere strictly to regulations regarding food (everything that is eaten must be kosher according to dietary law). In contrast, Reform (liberal) Jews are less strict in their practice and observance of Jewish customs. Conservative Jews represent a middle ground between the Orthodox and the Reform branches.

Jews first migrated to the United States during the seventeenth century, but the largest numbers came from Europe during the last decades of the nineteenth century. Some of these early immigrants established small businesses; others entered the professions. The greatest bulk of Jewish immigrants, however, scratched out a living as sweatshop workers and laborers. Prejudice and discrimination against Jews, known as anti-Semitism, grew, and employers, social clubs, and colleges routinely barred Jews or admitted only a small number under a quota system. In Europe, anti-Semitism reached its height during the late 1930s. The most thorough and wide-ranging genocide in history culminated during World War II when the Nazis systematically killed 6 million Jews (Chapter 7).

Although Christianity, Islam, and Judaism appear to be vastly different, they share some beliefs in common. Each worships one god, a practice known as **monotheism**. In addition, each uses the portion of the Bible known to Christians as the Old Testament. For that reason, the three groups are all called the *People of the Book*. (See the Sociology Online box.)

Monotheism ▲ Belief in and worship of one god.

Sociology Online

www

For your study of religion, we suggest that you begin with a search for the Christian Bible. You will find many sites. See if you are able to search various versions of the Bible for passages. A passage of the Old Testament that is important to Christians, Jews, and Muslims involves the Ten Commandments. Many people also consider the Ten Commandments an important part of the cultural heritage of the United States. Do you know of those commandments? If so, how many can you list by heart?

You can check the accuracy of your list by typing in the passage "Deuteronomy 5." Next, select a version of the Bible, such as the NKJV (New King James Version), and then choose Lookup. How many of the Commandments were you able to list correctly?

 CQ What do you think the social functions of the Ten Commandments might have been in biblical times?

Buddhist worshipers in Kamakura, Japan, praying before a 50-foot bronze statue of Buddha that was cast in 1252. Buddha's disciples spread his teachings throughout Asia, and from Asia, Buddhism spread to the West.

Eastern Religions

Three major belief systems are generally considered to be Eastern religions because they originated in that area of the world. Of course, today many thousands of people who believe in these religions live throughout the world. The major Eastern religions are Hinduism, Buddhism, and Confucianism.

Hinduism   With 793 million adherents, Hinduism is the largest of the Eastern religions (U.S. Bureau of the Census 2000). Dating back to prehistoric times, it is one of the oldest religions in the world. Hinduism took a firm hold on the Indian subcontinent, and today almost half of all Hindus live in India (McDonald 2003). Hinduism is such an integral part of the Indian social structure that the two cannot be separated (see Chapter 6).

Unlike Christianity and Islam, Hinduism does not rest on the teachings or revelations of a single person. Instead, the central belief of Hinduism is the dharma: the idea that a special moral force exists throughout the universe. This force makes demands on the individual and imbues day-to-day life with a sacred quality. The dharma also upholds the traditional caste system of India. In addition, Hinduism includes a belief in karma: the development of the spirit as expressed in reincarnation. After death, a person's spirit is reborn in another body, and the quality of the new life is determined by the quality of the previous life. The only escape from this cycle of death and birth is spiritual perfection: an individual attaining such perfection reaches the state of nirvana and no longer undergoes reincarnation. Hindus believe in a universal moral order, a belief that suggests monotheism. Yet they also accept multiple deities, a conception that suggests **polytheism**, the belief in many gods. To complicate matters further, an individual Hindu is free to be a monotheist, a polytheist, or even an atheist.

Like all other religions, Hinduism has ceremonies and rituals. Some rituals are personal, such as the prescribed cleansing that must be performed after a high-caste Hindu comes in contact with a member of a low caste. Other rituals are public, such as the Kumbh Mela. This ritual occurs every 12 years, when Hindus travel to the Ganges River to bathe in its sacred water. The last Kumbh Mela attracted 10 million believers. Hindus also regularly bring offerings to their temples in the belief that deities dwell there (Johnson 1989).

Buddhism   Buddhism has more than 325 million followers and is the second-largest Eastern religion after Hinduism. Buddhism originated with a single individual, Siddhartha Gautama, who was born the son of a king in about 563 B.C. in what is now southern Nepal. Because a sage had warned the king that his son would threaten him and would become a universal monarch, the king confined Gautama to home. Gautama later escaped, however, and wandered about Asia in search of peace. Eventually he came upon the Tree of Enlightenment. After living under the tree for many years and practicing meditation, Gautama became *Buddha*, the enlightened one.

Buddha's disciples were monks and lay people who spread his teachings throughout Asia. They established monasteries, provided religious instruction, and conducted religious services that consisted of a sermon, scripture readings, meditation, and confession. Today various forms of Buddhism are found in southern Asia, Sri Lanka, the Himalayas, Tibet, Mongolia, China, Korea, and Japan. Asian immigrants brought Buddhism to the United States and, during the 1960s, it became popular among many college students and other youths. Currently there are 67 Buddhist temples in the United States (as well as 1,700 miscellaneous Eastern churches [U.S. Bureau of the Census 1997]).

Many Buddhists do not worship a deity but try to live a good life inspired by the example and teaching of Gautama. They believe that life on earth is full of suffering but that life is transitory. Like Hindus, Buddhists maintain that the goal of existence is to reach nirvana and that an individual's life on earth reflects the spiritual

Polytheism ▲ Belief in and worship of more than one god.

achievements of an earlier existence. Only by attaining enlightenment can a person break the cycle of reincarnation and find peace. Also like Hindus, Buddhists believe that everyday life has significance. The manner in which routine activities are performed causes spiritual improvement or spiritual decline. Thus, Buddhists are anxious to engage in the so-called "right practices": to have the right views and intentions, to employ the right speech and actions, to make the right effort, to have the right concentration, and to experience the right ecstasy. In some forms of Buddhism, a supernatural element has been added to Buddha's role so as to emphasize the importance of his ethical teachings.

Confucianism The third major Eastern religion, with 5 million followers, is Confucianism. Like many other religions, Confucianism originated with a single person: K'ung Fu-tzu, or Confucius, as he is better known in the West. Born in northern China around 551 B.C., Confucius devoted his early teachings to solving the practical problems of daily living. The bulk of his wisdom is summarized in the Analects: a collection of precepts that deal with the proper management of society. Underlying the specific advice of the Analects is a particular vision of human existence. Central to this vision is jen: a human-hearted sympathy that binds all people together. Jen is expressed most frequently in the five basic relationships of human life: sovereign and subject, parent and child, older brother and younger brother, husband and wife, and friend and friend. Of these five, Confucius emphasized the parent-child relationship. He also recognized that even though jen is powerful, it cannot always overcome the misunderstandings and disagreements that may exist in human relationships. To make relationships flow more smoothly, Confucius also emphasized Li: proper etiquette and ritual.

Confucianism became an integral part of the Chinese culture, in part because many of Confucius' students were important government officials. The religion went into an eclipse between the third and seventh centuries A.D. but later regained prominence and maintained its hold on Chinese society until contemporary times. In the twentieth century, Chinese revolutionaries believed that Confucianism promoted stagnation, imperial leadership, and a lack of concern for the people. In the Chinese revolution of 1911, students burned Confucius in effigy and called for an end to the state that was based on his teachings (Johnson 1989). The current Chinese government relegates Confucianism to a low position and has attempted to replace Confucian aspects of Chinese culture with the political ideology of communism. Nevertheless, Confucianism still remains an important part of Chinese culture (So and Chiu 1996).

In contrast to religions that emphasize a supernatural being, Buddhism and Confucianism are **ethicalist** belief systems. Their followers aspire to attain spiritual excellence by practicing rituals and by following the ethical principles set forth in their religion. In this sense, the emphasis is on living a "good" life rather than on worshiping a deity.

World Today ● ■ ▲

Major Religions of the World
(US Bureau of the Census 2000)

This chart shows religious affiliation across the globe. Note that Christians and Muslims combined make up over half of the earth's population.

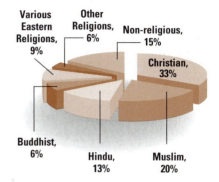

Various Eastern Religions, 9%
Other Religions, 6%
Non-religious, 15%
Christian, 33%
Buddhist, 6%
Hindu, 13%
Muslim, 20%

STUDY TIP

Create a word web that names and describes the varieties of world religions. Show how the religions relate to one another through connector lines. Note similarities by putting characteristics (i.e., monotheism) in separate circles or boxes and using lines to connect appropriate religions to the boxes (you may want to use a different color for the lines leading to each characteristic).

● ■ ▲ Pausing to Think   About the Varieties of Religion

The largest single religion is Christianity, which is divided into Roman Catholic, Protestant, and Orthodox. Islam is the second-largest world religion and contains several branches, the sharpest division being between Sunni and Shiite. Although more Jews live in North America than in Israel, the state of Israel is widely viewed as the official Jewish state. Hinduism, Buddhism, and Confucianism are the major Eastern religions. Figure 13.1 illustrates the worldwide distribution of the major religions.

CQ The English playwright Robert Burton (1577–1640) said, "One religion is as true as another." What do you think he meant by this? ◆ What would be a sociological response to his statement?

Ethicalist ▲ A belief system that emphasizes living a "good" life rather than worshiping a deity.

FIGURE 13.1 The Global Distribution of World Religions

The preponderance of the inhabitants in each of the colored areas on the map share the religious tradition indicated. In certain eastern Asian nations, many people have plural religious affiliations and are shown here as Buddhist. Israel is the only state where Jews are in the majority; however, significant Jewish populations exist elsewhere as indicated. The map reveals an interesting fact about South America. Although many believe that almost everyone in South America is Roman Catholic, Protestantism has made rapid gains since the 1950s. If the present rates of conversion hold, many nations in South America will have Protestant majorities in this century. Animism, a belief in the existence of spirits or spiritual forces, has many adherents among native peoples of Africa, the Amazon basin, Borneo, New Guinea, and Australia.

SOURCE: From *Human Geography: Cultures, Connections, and Landscapes,* by Edward Bergman, © 1995. Reprinted by permission of Prentice Hall, Inc., Upper Saddle River, NJ.

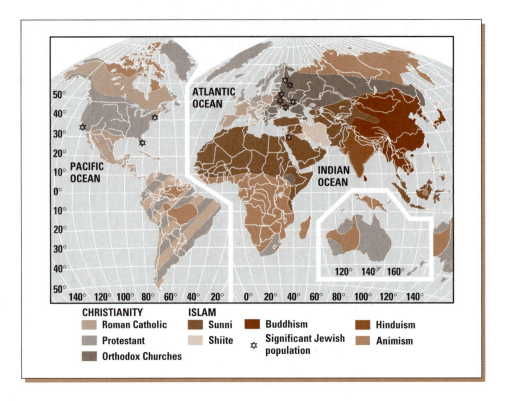

Sociological Analysis of Religion

Sociologists agree that religion is one of society's basic institutions, but sometimes they disagree as to which approach should be used to analyze it. Although no single approach is ideally suited for all purposes, the three major perspectives of sociology—the functionalist, conflict, and symbolic interactionist—have proved useful.

The Functionalist Perspective

In a classic work, *The Elementary Forms of the Religious Life* (1912), Émile Durkheim laid the foundations for the functionalist approach to religion. Unlike some of his contemporaries who regarded religion as an outmoded relic of times past, Durkheim argued that religion played an important role in society. All religions, he said, have social rather than supernatural origin; hence, all religions can be explained sociologically.

Durkheim also said that all social institutions—including religion—contribute to the harmony and stability of society. Having common rituals, he noted, drew people together by forcing them to engage in the same activities at the same time. For example, the practice of observing the Sabbath and engaging in periodic prayers gives people something in common and reaffirms the customary norms and values of the broader society. Moreover, religion provides a standard belief system and a common morality, both of which help to unite individuals with one another and with the broader society. Finally, religion provides a set of symbols, such as the Christian cross or the Jewish Star of David. These symbols represent the religion to outsiders and remind insiders of their common faith and unity.

Following on Durkheim's lead, functionalist theorists have identified several other functions of religion:

1. **Cohesion** In keeping with Durkheim's position, most sociologists agree that religion contributes to societal cohesion, and it does so in several ways. For example, by

participating in religious activities, people are drawn into a group, thus reducing any sense of isolation that they might suffer and also increasing the social solidarity of the group (Lawson 1999). Religion also provides a moral code and a plan for living a worthy life. Insofar as adherents follow this morality and this plan, group cohesion is increased. Finally, religion provides social and emotional support in times of conflict, stress, and hardship (Meyer and Lobao 2003). When a loved one dies, for example, religious beliefs and ritual provide solace to the bereaved. Most people find it comforting to believe that the deceased has passed on to a higher existence, and funeral services provide a time and a place for sharing memories of the recently departed.

2. Social Control Many of life's most critical junctures concern birth, marriage, death, and other important events. Virtually all religions claim authority over how such events are to be interpreted and ritualized. Thus, without the proper rituals, a youth may not enter adulthood; and a funeral conducted without the proper religious ceremony could jeopardize the status of the deceased in the afterworld. Because these events are so commonplace, religion inevitably controls many important points in a person's life cycle.

Religion also imposes social control in another way. When norms are based on religion, normative violations are offenses not only against civility but also against the sacred. However, unlike the penalties imposed by civil courts, which punish people while they live, religious punishments can extend into the afterlife and can last for all eternity. The specter of eternal damnation in Christianity or perpetual reincarnation into lower and lower animal forms in Hinduism can exert influence over the behavior of the living. Thus, priests, ayatollahs, shamans, and other religious authorities are leaders of a spiritual community, and their judgments embody religious authority based in a moral code.

For religious controls to be most effective, the religious group must dominate the community. To illustrate, in places where the majority of young people do not attend church, religion will not prevent juvenile delinquency, even for those teenagers who are religious. In contrast, if everyone in the community is deeply religious, then religion may have a strong impact on curbing delinquency (Curry and Jiobu 1995; Stark 1987).

3. Provision of Purpose In the normal course of life, people encounter many anxieties about the future, about social relationships, and about economic security. Religion helps to reduce such anxieties by providing answers to broad questions about the meaning of life, existence, and the hereafter. Religion further helps people to comprehend and accept why bad things happen to good people, as well as (perhaps even more unsettling) why good things happen to bad people (see Ebaugh, Richman, and Chafetz 1984).

The functionalist perspective emphasizes how religion increases the cohesion of society and controls the behavior of the individual. The conflict perspective, as we now discuss, emphasizes the role that religion plays in justifying the status quo and inequality.

The Conflict Perspective

Karl Marx believed that the ruling class used religion as a weapon to achieve its own ends. For instance, consider Christianity. It was (and still is) the predominant religion of Europe. Among its many teachings is the promise that no matter how miserable life is on earth, people will reap their rewards in the afterlife if they follow Christ. This promise has the weight of sacred authority, and Marx said that it encourages people to be obedient, docile, and complacent—characteristics that make them better workers and thus more valuable to the ruling class.

Not only does religion legitimate inequality; according to Marx, the existence of religion also illustrates the fact that humans can create social institutions, can come

Gather in a group of three. Before you meet, each person should select and summarize one of the sociological approaches to religion—functionalist, conflict, and symbolic interactionist. Then meet together and take turns presenting each of your approaches (be sure to include examples in your descriptions to help one another understand). Then talk about each approach and whether you agree or disagree with its position. If you can, come to a conclusion about which approach seems to make the most sense to you as a group.

to be dominated by their creation, and can eventually believe that the domination is legitimate. This is false consciousness in the profoundest sense of the concept. Why does it come about? The answer, according to Marx, is that religion deflects the attention of the lower classes away from the upper classes, who are the true source of oppression. Because Christianity holds that a person's conduct on earth leads to rewards or punishments in the afterlife, it encourages people to accept their situation passively. In this way, the otherworldly orientation of Christianity acts as a narcotic that dulls the pain created by inequity and concentrates the beliefs of the lower classes on the better life awaiting them in the hereafter.

Marx opposed not only Christianity but also its relationship with capitalism. In general, he portrayed religion as a conservative force that perpetuates oppression and supports inequity. However, as you might suspect, many scholars disagree with his assessment. They say that religion can actually promote change and reduce inequity. For example, some Christian leaders and theologians promote a doctrine called *liberation theology*. Priests and clergy who advocate liberation theology blend Christian principles with political activism; they work among the poor and try to counter oppression by the ruling classes. In Latin America, liberation clergy have been active since the 1960s, and several, including the archbishop of San Salvador—Oscar Arnulfo Romero—have been killed in the process. Although Pope John Paul II has condemned the movement for mixing left-wing politics with traditional church doctrine, the liberation theology movement continues to find adherents (Neuhouser 1989).

The Symbolic Interactionist Perspective

From the symbolic interactionist perspective, religion is important because it affects individuals and their social relationships. Perhaps the most significant impact of religion on the individual concerns the development of social identity. By virtue of being a member of a religion, the individual can more fully answer the question "Who am I?"

A strong religious identity is important because it serves as a reference point that affects many aspects of daily life. For some people, in fact, religion is their primary means of identifying with others. For instance, Evangelical or Pentecostal Christians may try to live their lives according to the ethical and moral precepts of their church and may interact almost exclusively with others who share their beliefs. Similarly, Orthodox Jews may prefer to live in a community governed by Jewish ritual and law, and devout Confucians may spend most of their free time contemplating the moral life (Heilman 1999, 2000).

Many other people, in contrast, keep religion confined to a specific area of their lives. Christians who attend church only on Christmas are affiliated loosely with their religion, although personal religious beliefs might be important to their self-concepts (Hewitt 1989). To cite another example of how religious identity may be compartmentalized, many Japanese follow both a Buddhist tradition with regard to honoring the dead and a Christian or Shinto tradition with regard to marriage. The Japanese also are inclined to change religions without a great deal of mental anguish. Because Buddhism and Shintoism are ethical religions, conversion to a religion with a deity is not a matter of deep concern. The important consideration is to live an ethical and a moral life.

A radical or dramatic change of faiths, such as converting from Christianity to Islam or to Judaism, may involve a fundamental shift in identity (Hewitt and Hewitt 1986). Not only must the convert's entire belief system change, but his or her position in society may change as well. A Christian in the United States who converts to Judaism also becomes, among many other things, a member of a minority group. Similarly, an Israeli Jew who converts to Islam joins a group that is a minority in Israel.

Whereas some people convert, others may actively reject their earlier religious identity. Such people—called apostates—have a recognizable social profile. They tend to be young, highly educated single males who are mobile and politically independent. As apostates grow older, however, they often return to religion and become more religious than before they became apostates (Greeley 1989; Hadaway and Roof 1988).

Religious identity, as well as the beliefs and values associated with religion, are the products of socialization. As we explained in Chapter 3, a great deal of socialization takes place informally, as when the family prays before a meal or attends services on the Sabbath. Though informal, these experiences are nevertheless the origins of deep-seated ideas about the afterlife and about proper conduct. When children grow older, childhood images linger and are both a source of comfort and a source of fears that reinforce the moral authority of the religion (Richardson 1981, 1997).

The school is also an agent of religious socialization. Despite the avowed separation of church and state, public schools in the United States are oriented toward Christianity, especially Protestantism. For instance, virtually all public schools take vacations at Easter and Christmas, two important Christian holidays, but most public schools do not close for Passover or Yom Kippur. To celebrate these occasions, Jewish students attending public school must ask to be excused and then must make up on their own time the schoolwork they missed. In other communities with large Jewish populations, however, teachers may not give tests or introduce new material on major Jewish holidays. And in upstate New York, a group of Hasidim (a Jewish sect) have attempted to create their own school district.

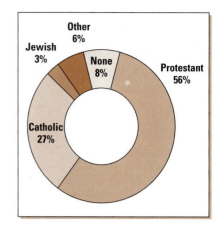

Religious Preferences in the United States

(U.S. Bureau of the Census 2002)

When asked about their religious preferences, about half of all adults say they are Protestant; about one-fourth say Catholic; and 8 percent have no preference at all.

CQ *American values embrace the notion of religious tolerance. Yet we know that many religious groups have been—and still are—discriminated against. Examples of this are Catholics, Mormons, Hindus, and more recently Muslims.*

Are most American people just hypocrites? ◆ Or can you offer a sociological reason that helps to explain the contradiction between the value of religious tolerance and antireligious discrimination?

● ■ ▲ **Pausing to Think**   About the Sociological Analysis of Religion

Functionalists believe that religion helps to unify society and provides people with a sense of where they stand in relation to the infinite. Conflict theorists argue that religion mainly supports the ruling class. Symbolic interactionists examine the role of religion in shaping social identity and locating the individual in society.

CQ Karl Marx made one of the most famous statements in sociology: "Religion is the sign of the oppressed creature. . . . It is the opiate of the people." What do you think Marx meant by this? ◆ Do you agree with him? ◆ Why, or why not?

Social Change and Religion

Whereas the pace of social change once was rather slow, today change takes place rapidly, dramatically, and often unpredictably. The institution of religion is changing, too—in part because society is changing, in part because there are internal dynamics in religion, and in part because changes in religion trigger changes in society, which then feed back to cause further changes in religion (see the Social Change box). Sociologists have identified several broad changes now at work in the United States.

Religion and Women

The social position of women in American society has been changing over the last 50 years or so. Today many women are entering or attempting to enter the ministry. In some instances, their efforts have not been entirely successful. For example, Catholic women have been arguing for an expanded role within the church. As a result, in many smaller communities where parishes lack full-time priests, women have been appointed as parish administrators. The Catholic Church nevertheless continues to prohibit women from becoming priests (Dillon 1999). Although Pope John Paul II asserted in 1995 that women and men were equal in the sight of God and the church, he further asserted that each gender has characteristics that make them suited for separate roles in the church and in life. The tension generated over this issue has

Social Change ●■▲ Religious Revival in Russia

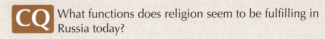

The people of Russia have experienced a great amount of social, political, and economic change in the last decade or so. They have seen the collapse of the Soviet Union, the fall of communism, the rise of democracy, and the emergence of a new market economy. They have also experienced a religious revival.

The fall of communism created a great void in Russian society. The communist government had attempted to substitute the ideology of communism and the functions of government for the role of the church. Just how successful these attempts were can be debated, but for the most part, church life was driven underground. Today the situation is obviously different, and Russians appear to be returning to the church in ever-increasing numbers. A recent survey found that many of

these returnees are young people who are seeking new meaning or purpose in their lives amid the wrenching turmoil that their nation is now undergoing (Greeley 1994).

Although the religious revival in Russia may appear to be a unique event, we should not overlook the fact that in many other countries, people have responded to change in a similar fashion. Any time that society suddenly and radically changes, people seek stability and a new meaning in life. In this quest, they often return to their traditional religion because it is a secure foundation for a new equilibrium.

CQ What functions does religion seem to be fulfilling in Russia today?

---

already produced splinter groups of Catholic women who, without official church approval, hold their own services in which women fulfill all the religious roles.

Some branches of Judaism and Protestantism have been opened to women. Today women rabbis and ministers routinely conduct services and are responsible for the organization and administration of their synagogue or church. Such changes have not gone unchallenged, and some members of these religions continue to oppose an expanded role for women (Lockhart 2000). Nevertheless, it seems likely that as time goes on, women will assume increasingly important positions in religious organizations.

Secularization

To some extent, religion and science compete to explain the same phenomena. For example, people used to believe that plague was caused by the wrath of God, that the bodies of the mentally ill were inhabited by the devil, and that there were witches with supernatural powers. As science developed, however, it increasingly replaced religion as a source of explanation. The germ theory of disease could explain plague, mood-altering drugs and psychotherapy could help or cure mental illness, and the idea of witches with supernatural powers became obsolete. In short, as science explains more and more, religion explains less and less (Johnstone 1996; Lechner 1991; Yamane 1997). This process is called **secularization**: the declining influence of religion combined with an increasing influence of science (Smith 2003).

Religious groups that stress the moral aspects of their beliefs often blame secularization for increases in crime, teenage pregnancy, drug abuse, and other social maladies. As these religious groups see it, only a reaffirmation of traditional religion and an expansion of religious influences will solve such problems.

In principle, continuing secularization might eventually be expected to diminish the influence of religion, and perhaps even cause religion to vanish altogether. Although this outcome is perhaps possible, most sociologists do not believe that it will occur, because secularization is not an all-powerful force (Stark 1987). Instead, it proceeds at an uneven pace and does not systematically replace the beliefs and values of other institutions. More properly understood, secularization is a process that transforms religion without destroying it. As Figure 13.2 shows, even in the highly secularized culture of the United States, most people hold traditional religious beliefs (Greeley and Holt 1999).

Secularization ▲ The declining influence of religion in life combined with an increasing influence of science.

In some cases, secularization may even be reversed by a return to fundamentalist religious beliefs. For example, during the 1960s and 1970s, the Shah of Iran secularized much of Iran's economy and military, and he curtailed the influence of the clergy. He also drove the Ayatollah Khomeini—his major religious opponent—into exile. After

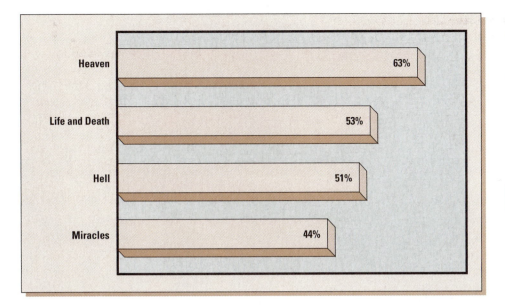

FIGURE 13.2 Religious Beliefs in the United States

This chart shows the percentage of adults in the United States who say they definitely believe in heaven, life after death, hell, and miracles. In addition, another 20 percent (not shown on the chart) say that they probably believe in heaven, life after death, hell, and miracles.

SOURCE: GSS, 1999.

CQ *After examining these data, would you say that religiosity in the United States is very high, high, moderate, low, or very low?*

15 years, however, Shiite Muslims managed to return Khomeini to power. Khomeini then led a religious revival and obliterated virtually all of the efforts the Shah had made to secularize Iran (Hadden 1995).

Civil Religion

According to sociologist Robert Bellah, traditional religion is being supplanted by **civil religion**: quasi-religious beliefs that link people to society and country. "Civil" refers to the nonreligious aspects of life (what Durkheim called the profane), whereas "religion" refers to a system of beliefs or faith (the sacred). Strictly speaking, combining the two words into a single term is a nonlogical union of opposites, but as Bellah intended, the term has come to mean the combination of the profane and the sacred.

Civil religion is not a direct substitute for traditional religion. In fact, the societies with the highest development of civil religion also have the most highly developed traditional religions, and in some places, civil society merges with civil religion. Thus, in some places, crimes against the state are also crimes against God, and crimes against God are crimes against the state (Bellah 1967, 1975; Bellah and Hammond 1980). For example, many states, among them Ohio, Virginia, and West Virginia, restrict or prohibit the sale of alcohol on Sunday. These "blue laws" are an attempt by the government to reserve Sunday for sacred activities. Similarly, American society has reserved December 25 to celebrate the birth of Christ. We all recognize, of course, that Christmas has many economic implications, and the secular aspects of gift-giving have thus merged with religion.

Although we most often associate religion with the worship of a deity, many other aspects of our lives have religious overtones. The notion of patriotism, to illustrate, has much in common with civil religion because we are socialized to believe in the goodness and sacredness of our country. Consequently, we respond to our country with awe, love, and obedience, and we express these feelings by participating in rituals and worshiping symbols of the nation (Rowbottom 2002). In the United States, holidays such as the Fourth of July and Thanksgiving, and sports events and other public gatherings provide the setting for many such rituals. At these events, stirring speeches are made and the national anthem is played. Sometimes the audience rises and sings the "Star-Spangled Banner" or recites the Pledge of Allegiance, a vow that openly links the nation to religion with the phrase "one nation under God." In addition, we often regard the American flag as a cherished symbol of our country, and many people favor

Civil religion ▲ Quasi-religious beliefs that link people to society and country.

Patriotism can be seen as a civil religion, and people who change their citizenship are often treated like converts to a new religion. This photograph captures some of the emotion felt by thousands of Hispanic residents as they become American citizens. The Pledge of Allegiance and the flag are important symbols of the United States, and they are used in the naturalization ceremony.

Society Today ● ■ ▲

The Religion Factor in the Election of 2000

Religion played an important role in the presidential election of 2000. Al Gore, the nominee of the Democratic Party, selected Joe Lieberman, a Senator from Connecticut, as his running mate for vice president. Lieberman was the first Jew to run for the vice presidency, breaking a long-existing absence of Jews at "the top of the ticket." Gore and Lieberman won the popular vote by a small margin but lost the election to George Bush, Jr. and Richard Cheney in the Electoral College vote. Exit polls showed the strong effects of religion on white voters.

RELIGIOUS AFFILIATION	PERCENT VOTING FOR GORE	PERCENT VOTING FOR BUSH
Protestant	34	63
Catholic	45	52
Jewish	80	17

SOURCE: Exit poll results provided by <CNN.com/Election/2000>.

a constitutional amendment that would make desecration of the flag a federal offense. These and other civil rituals and symbols invoke emotions that are similar or identical to the emotions felt at religious services. Thus, civil religion in an associational society reinforces core values and strengthens communal bonds (Beckford 1989).

The Revival of Religion in the United States

Religious commitment in the United States remains; over 90 percent of the American adult population say that they attend regular religious services (NORC 1998). Nevertheless, the increasing secularization of American society, coupled with the growth of civil religion, has altered the nature of religious commitment in the United States (see Figure 13.3). Traditional mainstream religions have been losing ground to churches and sects that stress renewed commitment to doctrine, personal experience, and religious morality. This movement, which is called "religious fundamentalism," places a high emphasis on basic religious value. Although mainly a Protestant movement because Protestantism is the predominant religion of the country, fundamentalism also has taken root among Catholics, Jews, and Muslims (see the Society Today box, The Religion Factor in the Election of 2000).

Protestant fundamentalists typically believe that the Bible is literally true; that moral standards have sunk to alarming depths; and that people can attain salvation only by accepting Christ as their savior. An important part of fundamentalism is the belief that each individual must establish a personal relationship with Christ through an emotional and enlightening experience; that is, they must be "born again." For this reason, Christian fundamentalists sometimes display the sign "John 3.3," a reference to the biblical passage that tells of salvation through spiritual rebirth.

More than most other religious groups, Protestant fundamentalists focus on sin. They view society as threatened by sexual lewdness, drunkenness, gambling, homosexuality, lapses in faith, and other behaviors that they loathe. Fundamentalists also tend to have a conservative political agenda. They oppose what they consider to be pornography and other forms of lewd behavior. They oppose abortion on demand, and they want to teach the theory of creationism—a religious account of human origins—alongside the theory of evolution (see the box What Do You Think?—Creationism

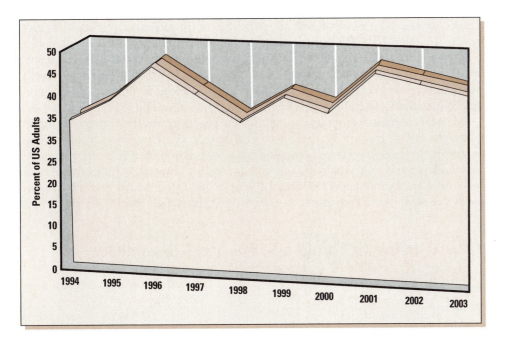

FIGURE 13.3 Religious Affiliation in the United States

The term "religiosity" refers to the strength of religious feelings. One indication of religiosity is whether people regularly attend religious services. The chart shows the percentage of U.S. adults who seldom or never attend church or synagogue.

 What do these data suggest?
◆ *Is religiosity increasing, decreasing, or staying about the same?*

What Do You Think? ●■▲ Creationism versus Evolution ❓

Because of the religious revival in the United States and the growing influence of conservative Christians, Darwin's theory of evolution has increasingly come under attack. Essentially, the theory of evolution holds that (1) the earth is very old; (2) plant and animal life has evolved over millions of years; (3) evolution has proceeded from simple life forms to more complex forms; (4) life forms best adapted to the environment have been the ones to survive and evolve; and (5) today's humans have evolved, as have other life forms, over millions of years from simpler life forms.

The theory of evolution stands in direct contradiction to the account of human life known as creationism. According to creationism, (1) the earth is comparatively young; (2) each species and creature was specially hand-crafted by God; (3) people were created directly by God, so that today's humans are not different in important ways from the first people; and (4) human limitations arise from people's sinfulness and not from maladaptations to the environment.

Creationists argue that evolution has become the dominant paradigm of biological science to the exclusion of creationism. They further contend that evolutionists, by virtue of their positions of power within the educational system, have kept creationists from teaching their theory as an alternative to the theory of evolution. Creationists further feel that they have been persecuted for their beliefs, and they contend that evolutionists have driven many creationist teachers from their teaching positions (Eve and Harrold 1994; Scott 1997).

The current arguments between evolution and creationism echo the Scopes trial held in Dayton, Tennessee, in 1925. At that time, Tennessee had a law that forbade the teaching of any theory that denied the biblical account of creation. John Scopes, a local high school teacher, violated that law by teaching evolution. To test the law, Scopes agreed to stand trial. The widespread interest in the trial attracted two of the greatest lawyers of the day—William Jennings Bryan for the prosecution and Clarence Darrow for the defense. After a long and difficult trial, Scopes was found guilty and fined $100. Scopes' conviction was later reversed on appeal. The outcry over the case discouraged many states from passing similar laws. However, the law remained on the books in Tennessee until 1967.

To date, the courts have held that creationism is religion and not science, and that to require its teaching in the public schools would violate the separation of church and state. As religious fundamentalism spreads in the United States, the issue of teaching creationism in the public schools will continue to be debated (Segerstale 1996; Holden 2002; Moore 2003).

CQ *How do you define and distinguish between "science" and "religion"?

---

*To answer these critical questions, review the box What Is Critical Thinking? in Chapter 1, paying special attention to the discussion of key terms.

versus Evolution). Fundamentalists are distrustful of the federal government, in part because they fear that it limits their ability to control the communities they live in.

Today, about 33 percent of the U.S. population think of themselves as fundamentalists; some 40 percent claim to have had an experience in which they "felt as though they were very close to a powerful, spiritual force that seemed to lift them out of themselves"; and 38 percent claim to have been born again (Gallup Poll 1983; NORC 1994).

Many fundamentalist groups promote their beliefs aggressively by preaching in public places and going door-to-door to distribute documents. In addition, fundamentalists can be trained to perform their religious roles by attending one of the 450 Bible colleges and more than 18,000 fundamentalist Christian schools throughout the United States. Fundamentalists can also read about their beliefs and activities in one of the more than 275 periodicals designed to spread their word (Cox 1995).

● ■ ▲ **Pausing to Think**   About Social Change and Religion

The Catholic Church does not accept women as priests, but women are gaining increasing acceptance as rabbis and ministers. Although American society is highly secularized, religiosity may nevertheless be increasing. Civil religion is proving popular. A religious revival seems to be under way in the United States, and Protestant fundamentalism may be spreading.

CQ What social changes involving religion have the greatest impact on your life? ◆ For instance, have you been caught up in the religious revival, or have you gotten involved in the controversy over greater involvement of women in the leadership of the church?

Religion in the Twenty-First Century

Despite our increasing reliance on science and technology, the basic human questions of life's meaning and our fate remain unanswered. Religion offers some answers to these timeless questions and therefore remains a powerful force in contemporary society. For that reason, the commitment to religion will probably not change very much in the future; what will change is the social organization within which religious expression takes place.

Already visible are two new forms of religious organization. Both are associated with an important trend in the United States—declining church attendance. Even though people claim strong religious beliefs, many find it difficult to get themselves out to religious services (Caplow 1991). As a result, religious groups have had to become more aggressive in bringing their message to the people. One strategy has been to rely on the new communications technology and to develop the so-called electronic church. Another way has been to centralize many activities within the church thus and to develop the so-called mega-church.

The Electronic Church

As society increasingly comes to rely on sophisticated and far-reaching communication networks, we can expect religion to change as well. One aspect of this change is already highly visible and will probably become even more important in this century: the so-called **electronic church**. This term refers to the broadcasting of religious services through the mass media, notably television. Programming on a typical Sunday morning is almost exclusively devoted to church services, while special channels and cable television regularly televise services. The electronic church has been popular. Some 25 percent of adults in the United States regularly tune in religious services on television or radio (NORC 1998). Overall, the electronic church is now a $2 billion

Electronic church ▲ Church or ministry that broadcasts its religious services through the mass media, notably television.

enterprise, and some 1,400 radio stations and 220 television stations are devoted exclusively to religious programming. Several of these stations broadcast 24 hours a day to an audience numbering some 13 million people. Of this number, about half contribute money to television ministries. Electronic preachers, or **televangelists**, stress fundamentalism, and like all other fundamentalists, they call for a return to what they perceive as traditional values. Ironically, they criticize modernity while using modern technological devices to spread their message (Bendroth 1996; Hughey 1990).

The development of the electronic church was made possible by changes in federal policy. Local television stations are required by the Federal Communications Commission (FCC) to broadcast public interest messages. In the past, stations have met this requirement by giving away free time for religious programs during Sunday mornings or very late at night. Originally, mainstream religious groups developed these programs, but in the 1960s, a new type of religious broadcaster emerged because of changes in federal regulations. The FCC ruled that stations could sell additional broadcast time to religious organizations and credit the time to their public interest obligations (Hadden 1987). This expanded commercial time was purchased by the new breed of televangelist preachers, who aggressively used sophisticated technology and showmanship to build large electronic ministries. Soon, Pat Robertson, Robert Schuller, and other electronic preachers became household names.

In addition to spreading fundamentalism, televangelists usually solicit donations to support their ministries (Hadden 1987). They also use their air time to market religious products, such as self-help books they have written, videotapes of their sermons, and travel packages. Although virtually all religious bodies draw on their congregations for financial support, the sheer amounts of contributions that come through television are unprecedented.

What is not well understood at this time is whether the neighborhood church will be able to compete with the electronic church. As more and more people watch services on television, it may become extremely difficult to maintain or construct many new churches. Television may also promote passivity, and church members who rely on television might not be as committed to community service as they have been in the past.

Televangelists ▲ Fundamentalist ministers who espouse traditional religious values and regularly use television to spread their message.

Interior view of Dr. Robert H. Schuller's Crystal Cathedral in Garden Grove, California. The Crystal Cathedral qualifies as a mega-church because it attracts thousands of worshipers and, moreover, provides a wide range of activities and services that extend beyond religion per se.

The Mega-Church

Another way to attract more people to religion is to increase the facilities, services, and activities associated with a church. The so-called **mega-church**—one that draws more than 2,000 worshipers each week—typically offers its members many more reasons to come to church than to hear a sermon or visit with a priest. In fact, the idea of the church as a place of worship is replaced by the idea of the church as a life center or a hub around which people organize their daily routines and social commitments. From this viewpoint, church members are first and foremost consumers with many diverse needs. The mega-church strives to meet these needs by incorporating nontraditional services and facilities into a total religious package.

Take, for example, Dallas's First Baptist Church (Grossman 1991a, 1991b). It was one of the original mega-churches. It featured programs aimed at meeting the spiritual, emotional, recreation, and entertainment needs of its members. To that end, the church had a secondary school, a nursery, a child care center, television studio, bowling alley, racquet ball court, exercise facility (including a Jacuzzi), library, atrium, and theater.

The success of the First Baptist mega-church prompted other churches to follow suit. As a result, the First Baptist church remains important but no longer dominates the religious in Dallas. Whereas 8,000 people used to attend weekly services,

Mega-church ▲ A large religious congregation in which the church becomes a life center around which people organize their activities and provides its members with many nontraditional services and facilities.

CONCEPT WEB Religion

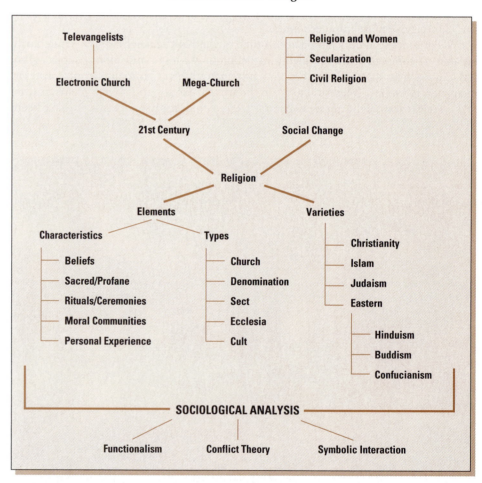

This is a concept web for Religion. Try this. Enter the concept *religious revival* into the web.

attendance is now down to 5,000 people, a figure surpassed by several churches in the area. To revitalize the program, the First Baptist church recently embarked on a fund-raising drive aimed at amassing $48 million to expand its programming and physical plant. The plan includes many new features: a Christian bookstore-coffee bar modeled after Barnes and Noble, a sports styled snack bar, a large banquet hall for dinner-theater, and a commercial kitchen to cater downtown events off of church property. The building also will have a prayer room with a view overlooking the city from eight stories high (DallasNews.com; accessed October 12, 2003)

All churches must attend to mundane matters such as finance and maintenance. Thus, bingo games, ice cream socials, festivals, and picnics are part of a church's routine activities. The mega-church, however, is distinguished by sheer size coupled with an aggressive outreach into all aspects of people's lives. In effect, the mega-church uses business tactics to incorporate a wide range of secular activities into a sacred setting.

Looking Ahead

The next chapter concerns medicine and health care, a rapidly changing institution that is vital for our personal and social well-being. Major topics of that chapter include health and society, sociological issues in medicine and health care, and medicine and health care in the future.

WHAT YOU SHOULD KNOW ●■▲

1. **How in general does religion differ between communal and associational societies?**

In many communal societies, religion permeates all aspects of society and is woven throughout people's daily lives. In industrial associational societies, religion is separated from other social and economic activities and has become a matter of private expression.

2. **What are the general characteristics of religion?**

All religions are systems of belief that perform the following functions: they distinguish between the sacred and the profane, provide people with powerful emotional experiences, have rituals and ceremonies permitting worshipers to approach the deity and to celebrate social solidarity, and contain a community of people who provide social support for members.

3. **How do churches differ from denominations?**

Churches are formal religious organizations that are well established, are well integrated into their society, and claim moral authority over all aspects of life. Denominations maintain friendly relations with the government and with other denominations but do not claim to be the exclusive religious faith of the country.

4. **How do religious sects and cults fit into their society?**

Sects are loosely organized and reject the social environment in which they exist. Their members are deeply committed to their beliefs. Most cults develop around a charismatic leader, and cult members disavow the broader society. In comparison with sects, cults are generally smaller, less structured, and lack ties to other established religious bodies.

5. **Which religious bodies are known as the "People of the Book"?**

Christians, Muslims, and Jews are known as the "People of the Book."

6. **Which are the principal religious bodies of Eastern societies?**

Hinduism, Buddhism, and Confucianism are the principal religious bodies of Eastern societies.

7. What insights into religion are provided by the functionalist theoretical perspective?

According to the functionalist perspective, religion helps to organize society, gives people a sense of where they stand in relation to the infinite, provides people with a sense of purpose, and is a source of social cohesion and social control.

8. What contributions are made by conflict theory to understanding religion as a social institution?

Conflict theorists argue that religion benefits the ruling class by legitimizing social inequality and by perpetuating the status quo. Marx referred to religion as "the opiate of the people" because he thought that religion blinded people to the reality of their oppressed condition.

9. How does symbolic interaction theory view religion?

From the symbolic interactionist perspective, religion is important because it affects individuals and their social relationships. By virtue of being a member of a religion, the individual can more fully answer the question "Who am I?" For some people, religion is their primary means of identifying with others.

10. How has social change affected religion?

Many religions are rethinking the role of women, and some religions accept women as ministers or rabbis. Both secularization and civil religion are growing in importance, yet at the same time, a worldwide religious revival seems to be under way. In the United States, this revival is most evident in the spread of Protestant fundamentalism.

11. What does the future hold for religion?

Religion offers some answers to timeless questions and therefore remains a powerful force in contemporary society. The commitment to religion will probably not change very much in the future; however, the way in which religions are organized may change a great deal. New forms of religious organization—the electronic church and the mega-church—are already in place.

TEST YOUR KNOWLEDGE ●■▲

Key Terms Matching

Match each of these key terms with the best definition or example from the numbered items that follow. Write the letter preceding the key term in the blank before the definition that you choose.

  a. church
  b. civil religion
  c. cult
  d. denomination
  e. ecclesia
  f. electronic church
  g. ethicalist
  h. monotheism
  i. polytheism
  j. profane
  k. religion
  l. ritual
  m. sacred
  n. sect
  o. secularization
  p. televangelist

_____ **1.** A religion that maintains friendly relations with the government and with other religions but that does not claim to be the only legitimate faith.

_____ **2.** A formal religious organization that is well established and well integrated into its society.

_____ **3.** Belief in and worship of one god.

_____ **4.** Fundamentalist ministers who espouse traditional religious values and regularly use television to spread their message.

_____ **5.** Belief in and worship of more than one god.

_____ **6.** Those things that have supernatural significance and qualities.

_____ **7.** A religious organization that believes that society is degenerate and that the members of the organization must withdraw together and live apart in group quarters or a commune.

_____ **8.** Commonly routinized behaviors that express and reinforce religious faith.

_____ **9.** A belief system that emphasizes living a "good" life rather than worshiping a deity.

_____ 10. A loosely organized, nonbureaucratic religious organization with nonprofessional leadership that actively rejects the social environment in which it exists.

_____ 11. A system of beliefs, rituals, and ceremonies that focuses on sacred matters, promotes community among its followers, and provides for a personal spiritual experience for its members.

_____ 12. Quasi-religious beliefs that link people to society and country.

_____ 13. The declining influence of religion in life combined with an increasing influence of science.

_____ 14. Those things that are regarded as part of ordinary life.

_____ 15. Church that is a state's official religion.

_____ 16. Church or ministry that broadcasts its religious services through the mass media, notably television.

Multiple Choice

Circle the letter of your choice.

1. Unlike communal society, religion in contemporary industrial society has become
   a. closely integrated in all parts of work and school.
   b. less bureaucratic.
   c. separated from many social and economic activities.
   d. more magical.

2. Which of the following is characteristic of religion?
   a. holding rituals and ceremonies
   b. making the distinction between the sacred and the profane
   c. having beliefs
   d. all of the above

3. From the Christian point of view, the crucifix and the rosary are which type of objects?
   a. sacred
   b. associational
   c. profane
   d. bureaucratic

4. What sociologist argued that there was a close connection between the virtue of Protestantism and the value of capitalism?
   a. Émile Durkheim
   b. Max Weber
   c. Robert Bellah
   d. Auguste Comte

5. The Roman Catholic Church has found so much support in many Latin American countries that it has become the state's official religion in those countries. In such countries, the Roman Catholic Church is
   a. a sect.
   b. a denomination.
   c. an ecclesia.
   d. a cult.

6. According to the text, which of the following is NOT a reason that people join cults?
   a. They are attracted to the cult's philosophy.
   b. They are lonely and isolated.
   c. They identify with the elaborate rituals of the cult.
   d. They are attracted to the leader's charisma.

7. With less than 1 percent of the world's population as followers, which of the following is the smallest of the world religions?
   a. Islam
   b. Judaism
   c. Hinduism
   d. Christianity

8. Which of the following religions believes in a covenant between the people and God that is expressed in the Torah and the Talmud?
   a. Buddhism
   b. Judaism
   c. Hinduism
   d. Confucianism

9. Which of the following religions believes that the manner in which routine activities are performed creates spiritual improvement or decline?
   a. Buddhism
   b. Christianity
   c. Islam
   d. Judaism

10. Which of the following religious groups are called "People of the Book"?
    a. Confucians, Buddhists, and Jews
    b. Hindus, Muslims, and Christians
    c. Muslims, Christians, and Jews
    d. Muslims, Buddhists, and Jews

11. Which of the following religions proposes that after death, a person's spirit is reborn into another body and that the quality of the new life is determined by the quality of the old life?
    a. Judaism
    b. Hinduism
    c. Islam
    d. Confucianism

12. Which of the following religions emphasizes jen, or human-hearted sympathy, that binds all people together?
    a. Confucianism
    b. Hinduism
    c. Buddhism
    d. Islam

13. In the United States, science has been growing more influential in explaining disease, climatic changes, and mental health, while the influence of religion has been declining. Which of the following terms do sociologists use to describe this process?
    a. ritualism
    b. secularization
    c. modernization
    d. scientific transformation

14. Which of the following groups typically believes that the Bible is literally true, that moral standards have sunk to alarming depths, and that people can attain salvation only by accepting Christ as their savior?
    a. Protestant fundamentalists
    b. Liberal Protestants
    c. Roman Catholics
    d. Reform Jews

15. The mega-church strives to attain the idea that
    a. the church should be a life center or a hub around which people organize their daily routines and social commitments.
    b. it is important to have one large ecclesia.
    c. the church should reach out through the Internet to reach as many people as possible.
    d. all religions can be a part of one church.

Identifying Sociological Perspectives on Religion

For each of the following statements, identify the sociological perspective associated with the statement by writing F for Functionalist, C for Conflict, SI for Symbolic Interactionist, in the appropriate blank.

_____ 1. Perhaps the most significant impact of religion on the individual concerns the development of social identity.

_____ 2. Religion is important because it affects individuals and their social relationships.

_____ 3. Both religious identity and the beliefs and values associated with religion are the products of socialization.

_____ 4. Religion contributes to social cohesion, controls many important points in a person's life cycle, and helps reduce anxiety by providing answers to broad questions about the meaning of life.

_____ 5. Religion, as well as other social institutions, contributes to the harmony and stability of society.

_____ 6. Religion is a conservative force that perpetuates oppression and supports inequality.

True-False

Indicate your response to each of the following statements by circling T for true or F for false.

T F 1. In communal societies, religion permeates all aspects of life.

T F 2. Confucianism is the world's largest religion.

T F 3. Christianity began as a tiny cult whose members believed that Jesus was the long-promised Messiah of the Jews.

T F 4. Followers of Islam believe that the Qur'an is the word of Allah as set down by the prophet Muhammad.

T F 5. The central belief of Hinduism is the idea that a special moral force exists throughout the universe that makes demands on the individual and gives everyday life a sacred quality.

T F 6. Durkheim said that religion was a narcotic that dulled the pain of inequality.

T F 7. To some extent, religion and science compete to explain the same phenomena.

T F 8. It seems likely that as time goes on, women will be less likely to hold important positions in religious organizations.

T F 9. Liberation theology is a blend of Christian principles with political activism.

T F 10. More than most other religious groups, Protestant fundamentalists focus on sin.

T F 11. Dallas' First Baptist Church is an example of a mini-church.

T F **12.** Within a society, civil religion is a direct substitute for traditional religion.

T F **13.** The theory of evolution stands in direct contradiction to the account of human life known as creationism.

T F **14.** Karl Marx believed that the middle class used religion in their struggle against the ruling class.

T F **15.** The roots of religion lie in an ancient communal past.

NOTE: The answers to these exercises are at the end of the book.

For additional practice tests and other resources please visit the companion web site at http://www.prenhall.com/curry.

Essay

1. What are five characteristics of religion? Give examples of each.

2. How did Buddhism originate? What are the central beliefs in Buddhism and where is it practiced today?

3. Max Weber recognized the connection between the Protestant Reformation and capitalism. What was the connection?

4. Describe the different types of religious organizations.

5. What are the characteristics of a mega-church today?

14

Medicine and Health Care

Chapter Outline

Throughout the course of history, humans have been at war with the microbe world. A host of viruses, bacteria, or multicelled creatures have found human tissues to be a sustaining source of food and reproduction (McNeill 1976). Some of these microbes cause acute disease in humans. Some kill quickly, some slowly, and some convert the host body into the disease carrier without making the host noticeably ill. Many microbe attacks take the form of an **epidemic**. An epidemic is a widespread outbreak of a contagious disease. If the outbreak occurs over a very large area or is worldwide it is called a **pandemic**.

Major epidemics and pandemics have had serious impacts on society. Examples of these outbreaks include the fourteenth century's Black Death, the cholera epidemics of the nineteenth century, the influenza epidemic of 1910–1918, the AIDS pandemic of the last 30 years, and the SARS outbreak of 2003. Not only did these plagues kill large numbers of people, but they also disrupted the functioning of key social institutions.

With the growth of science and technology humans have been able to develop tools to fight many contagious diseases. However, in spite of medical and public health advances, new diseases continue to appear and old ones return in more resistant forms (Weiss 2002). Since 1970, 30 new diseases have been recognized including AIDS, Ebola, and hepatitis C. In addition, there has been the reemergence of more than 20 old diseases that had been well controlled. These include yellow fever, malaria, and cholera.

At the beginning of the twenty-first century AIDS is the worst and most widespread pandemic. It was first detected in the United States in gay men in 1981. By 1983, an AIDS epidemic was recorded among heterosexuals in Central Africa. By 1985, every region of the world reported AIDS cases. In 1987, the first antiretroviral AIDS drug, AZT, was approved for use in the United States. In 1984, AIDS became the leading cause of death in the United States for people between the ages of 25 and 44. By 1995, it had become clear that AIDS was transmitted through intravenous drug use as well as sexual contact. In 1998, the first large-scale trial of an AIDS vaccine was undertaken in North America and Europe. By the start of the twenty-first century, AIDS had killed worldwide more than 20 million men, women, and children (Klesius 2002). In 2003 alone more than 5 million people were infected with AIDS and 3 million people died of the disease. Another 40 million were living with HIV (World Health Organization 2003).

With the globalization of disease, a global response has developed to fight AIDS and other killer epidemics. The global fight against disease has been led by the World Health Organization and other international organizations. However, national governments have not devoted the resources needed to assure victory in the microbe war. Some countries are too poor to do much. Other countries have different priorities. The fight against disease is both medical and political.

Because sickness places strains on the social system and on individuals, every society has the institution of medicine. To be sure, there are cultural differences in the organization of the institution, but all societies must somehow deal socially with the problems of disease, injury, and sickness. Consequently, the study of medicine as a social institution is an important area of sociology.

Recognizing the social aspects of medicine, sociologists define disease and health in special ways. To sociologists, a **disease** is a pathology that disrupts the usual functions of the body, and **health** is the capacity to satisfy role requirements (Parsons 1953, 1975). From these definitions, it follows that people are sick to the extent that they cannot meet their role obligations because of disease. To illustrate this point, suppose that you have a severe cold but you continue to study as you normally do. However, rather than interacting with your friends, you spend the remainder of your time in bed. A sociologist observing you would say that because you could not continue to interact with your friends in the usual manner, you were sick with regard to your friendship role; but because you did not change your study habits, you were healthy with regard to your academic role. The ability to fulfill role obligations, in short, is the defining characteristic of sickness and health. Even though this approach to defining sickness and health might seem odd, it is valuable because it recognizes both that sickness occurs in a social environment and that it has social consequences.

Chapter Preview

In this chapter, we begin by briefly discussing how the Great Social Transformation has affected medicine and health care. Next, we focus on health and society: we explore the historical development and the social organization of medicine today. We then move on to study issues in health care. A section on the sociological analysis of medicine and health care follows, and we conclude with a look at medicine and health care in the future.

The Great Social Transformation and Medicine and Health Care

In contrast to the way in which most people in the United States view disease, in preindustrial, communal societies, disease is a matter that involves the entire community. When an individual becomes seriously sick, everyone joins in an effort to make the patient well again. To illustrate this process, consider the Iroquois before they had contact with European settlers. In those times, an Iroquois who fell sick was treated by a shaman—a healer thought to have special powers—and by the adults of the tribe. Working together, each adult would put on a stylized mask that portrayed a particular disease; then they would all ceremoniously dance around the sick person to chase away the spirits causing the sickness (Keesing 1958). Today, such behavior might strike some people as strange, but is it really? Consider a roughly similar approach to healing that is still followed in some communities of the United States. When a person becomes sick and goes to a hospital, the patient's family and friends gather in the waiting room. There, they pray continuously until relieved by someone who takes their place. These prayers go on for as long as the patient is in the hospital or until the patient passes away (Taylor 1995). Hence, both the Iroquois of the past and the people in some contemporary communities make a communal response on behalf of the sick person. In both cases, they can do so because they know one another personally, share a common history, and anticipate a common future.

In contrast to a communal response, industrialized, associational societies take a far different approach to sickness. Sickness becomes a matter of science, and science works the same way on all people whether we know them personally or not. Rather than calling on the community to pray or to drive out evil spirits, sick people call on healers trained in scientific medicine, and they place their faith in drugs, surgery, and sophisticated technology. Because sickness is fought off with science, the interaction

Epidemic ▲ A widespread outbreak of a contagious disease.

Pandemic ▲ An outbreak of contagious disease over a very large area or worldwide.

Disease ▲ A pathology that disrupts the usual functions of the body.

Health ▲ The capacity to satisfy role requirements.

between patients and healers becomes impersonal, focused, and rational. For example, the doctor who performs surgery on you might spend no more than 20 minutes talking to you, and most of that short time will be devoted to discussing medical problems. In all likelihood, moreover, you did not know the surgeon before you became sick, and after you recover, you will probably never see the surgeon again. Finally, your surgery probably will take place in a hospital, an organization that is governed by impersonal rules and bureaucrats. In short, industrial societies rely on science and technology to combat disease and on associational relationships to control the human interaction that takes place in medical settings.

Health and Society

As we said at the beginning of this chapter, all societies have the social institution of medicine, but the development and organization of that institution varies considerably throughout the world. In this section, we focus on the organization of medicine and health care in the United States.

The Historical Development of Medicine in the United States

Before the development of scientific medicine, many physicians believed that good health resulted from a proper balance of fluids within the body. These fluids were called humors. On the basis of this belief, a physician might treat a patient by cutting a vessel in the arm and allowing the blood to flow out until the proper balance of humors was restored. If the patient recovered, the physician concluded that the humors had been brought into balance; if the patient died, the physician concluded that the patient had not bled enough. A notable victim of this practice was George Washington. In 1799, he contracted what is now believed to have been a severe cold, but his physicians bled him so much that he died. In retrospect, Washington would have been much better off if his physicians had followed the Iroquois practice described earlier and danced around him in masks.

In Washington's time and until the latter part of the nineteenth century, physicians could do little actually to cure a disease or to alleviate suffering. Consequently, medicine suffered from low esteem, and physicians did not receive much respect. As Benjamin Franklin commented cynically, "God does the healing and physicians reap the fee."

Medical practices remained crude by contemporary standards until well into the nineteenth century. In 1845, only three states issued medical licenses, and the entire curriculum of the typical medical school could be learned in four months. Physicians rarely consulted among themselves because they wanted to keep their treatments as trade secrets. Nor did they earn much money. For many of them, treating patients was a part-time job (Starr 1982).

The situation began to change in the middle of the nineteenth century. The newly introduced theory of germs laid the foundation for understanding communicable diseases; the development of anesthetics made it possible to perform extensive surgery; and improved sanitation reduced the gangrene, blood poisoning, and other infections that had killed most of the people who managed to survive the surgeon's knife. Physicians started to wash their hands, and midwives used clean dressings. Nursing became an accepted profession, and patients received better care.

All of the changes in medicine were taking place within a changing society. Increased urbanization and the growth of industrial capitalism forced people to rely less on their personal knowledge and more on the specialized knowledge of other people. This reliance extended to physicians, who were now applying science to cure disease. With their growing success, physicians gained greater influence and won greater respect from the public.

FIGURE 14.1 Mortality

For several years now, heart disease and cancer have been the leading causes of death in the United States. To a significant extent, these diseases can be slowed or prevented by diet and exercise, and by avoiding environmental hazards. For youths, however, the leading causes of death are not disease, but accident, homicide, and suicide. We know comparatively little about reducing these types of death rates.

SOURCE: Center for Health Statistics, 2000.

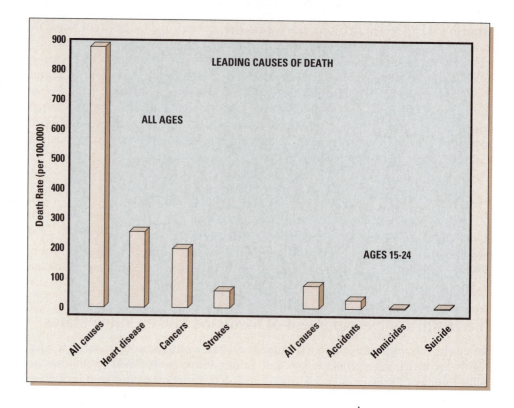

The American Medical Association (AMA), which was founded in the middle of the nineteenth century, had an important influence on the acceptance of the medical profession. Spurred on by the AMA, legislatures outlawed "quack" healing practices and granted the AMA control over training new physicians. By the twentieth century, the AMA had gained a near-monopoly on the practice of American medicine and had begun to recognize various specialties. The AMA now recognizes 27 specialties, of which internal medicine is the largest (Stevens 1998). As one of the most powerful organizations in the United States, the AMA actively participates in setting national health goals, approving medical legislation, and certifying physicians.

Today, medicine is an established institution in the United States, and the vast majority of people have confidence in it (NORC 1998). We typically regard medicine as good; we respect healers, especially medical doctors; and we believe that medical science will eventually provide cures for health problems that now seem hopeless. Most people remain optimistic that science will eventually find the cause and then the cure for AIDS and other diseases that are among the leading causes of death in the United States (see Figure 14.1 and the Sociology Online box).

Sociology Online

www

We suggest you begin your exploration of health care with a very important topic, the global epidemic of HIV/AIDS, by selecting United Nations Joint Programme on HIV/AIDS. Choose the World AIDS Campaign homepage, and then answer the following questions:

What percentage of HIV infections worldwide occur through sex between men and women?

What percentage occur through sex between men?

Why does UNAIDS believe that engaging men as partners in fighting HIV/AIDS is the surest way to change the course of the epidemic?

Also check out the site for the World Health Organization and the site for the National Centers for Disease Control.

The Social Organization of Medicine

One way to examine the social organization of an institution is to focus on the key positions within it. In this section, we describe the key positions in medicine, beginning with medical doctors.

Physicians Undoubtedly, the most powerful position in medicine belongs to the physician. Although physicians constitute just 10 percent of all American health care workers, they have considerably more than 10 percent of the power. For example, consider how much legal authority that physicians possess. According to the law in most jurisdictions, physicians have broad rights to diagnose a disease, prescribe drugs, and perform surgery. And in many jurisdictions, only a physician can legally pronounce a person dead, certify that someone is mentally incompetent, or give testimony in court as an expert in medical matters. Frequently, the presence of physicians is considered so important that they can obtain special license plates that allow them to park in places that the ordinary citizen cannot; and their prestige is so high that they are treated with deference, respect, and courtesy wherever they go (Starr 1982; Wessel 1986).

In capitalist societies, medicine generates huge amounts of money, and, despite recent declines, physicians are among the most highly paid workers in the nation. The typical physician earns $194,000 after expenses, a sum more than five times the earnings of the average worker. Specialists earn even more—obstetricians and gynecologists average $214,000 per year, and orthopedic surgeons $268,000 per year. Family practitioners, on the other hand, average "only" $142,000 per year (U.S. Bureau of the Census 2002).

With the advances in medical knowledge and technology, physicians have increasingly specialized in practices such as cardiovascular diseases, pediatrics, and neurology, whereas the number of traditional "family doctors" has declined. Currently, fewer than 9 percent of all physicians are in general and family practice (U.S. Bureau of the Census 1997). As a result, smaller communities have difficulty attracting physicians, because specialty practices are profitable only in large population centers. Specialization has also led to increased costs, a problem we discuss later.

Nurses At one time, nursing was held in low esteem, and no "proper" woman would dream of entering the profession. In the nineteenth century, however, Florence Nightingale changed the image of nursing in Great Britain, as described in the Profiles box. Her influence spread to the United States, and the first U.S. nursing school was established in 1873 at New York's Bellevue Hospital. Since that time, nurses have played an important part in establishing contemporary medicine. In 1901, for example, a group of nurses in Boston originated the idea of prenatal care, and nurse Margaret Sanger led the fight to give people access to contraception (Anticaglia 1975). She invented the term *birth control* and helped to found the Planned Parenthood Federation of America.

Although nurses used to train mainly at three-year schools affiliated with hospitals, that pattern is changing. An increasing number now attend four-year universities, major in nursing, and receive bachelor's degrees on graduation. Most nurses then enter the workforce, but a few attend graduate school with an eye toward pursuing research careers or obtaining higher-level positions in medicine. Because graduate training in nursing is a very recent development, very few of the 2.6 million employed registered nurses in the United States hold master's degrees, and fewer than 1 percent have doctorates (Miller 1992). However, with the continued development of nursing as a profession, it is estimated that in the next few years, there will be a need for another 299,999 nurses with master's and doctoral degrees (Schwirian 1998).

Even though nurses are trained professionally, they can work only under the supervision of physicians, most of whom are men (Jecker and Self 1991). Ironically, the nurse gets to know the patient very thoroughly, but the physician remains in control of the patient's treatment. This situation sometimes results in discomfort or harm to

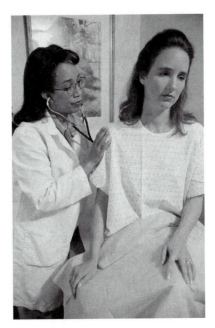

The most powerful position in medicine is still that of the physician. This photograph shows a female doctor listening through a stethoscope while examining a patient.

Although most people have heard of Florence Nightingale, the average person knows little, if anything, about her. Some people actually believe that she is a character from a novel, but in fact, Nightingale was a real person. She is famous for revolutionizing health care and for pioneering the profession of nursing. Born in 1820 to an upper-class British family, she died in 1910.

In many ways, Nightingale's achievements are especially remarkable because she lived at a time when upper-class women neither worked outside the home nor went to college. She had to study medicine on her own and had to fight for hospital apprenticeships in Germany and France. In 1853, at the age of 33, she became supervisor of nurses at a London hospital that catered to middle- and upper-class women. She was not paid for her work.

Nightingale's opportunity for national service came the following year, when Britain joined Turkey and France to fight against Russia in the Crimean War. The fighting went well for the allies but not for wounded British soldiers. They were sent to military hospitals, where many died. For example, at the hospital in Scutari, Turkey, half of the soldiers died shortly after arrival. Such a mortality rate was high even for Victorian times, and it was caused largely by the appalling conditions at the hospital. Supplies were scarce, and hot food was lacking. The water was bad. Beds were infested with fleas; rooms were invaded by rats. Sheets were washed in cold water and then were reused without being cleaned thoroughly. Drains were clogged, and the sewer trenches running under the building gave off an overpowering stench.

When newspaper reports about the hospital conditions reached Britain, an outraged public demanded action, and Florence Nightingale stepped forth. The *London Times* financed her efforts, and soon she organized a corps of 38 nurses for service in the war. The high command of the British army opposed Nightingale, but she was a formidable political foe. Because of her upper-class background she knew people in high places, and soon she and her nurses were on their way to Turkey.

At the Scutari hospital, Nightingale set up a hot-water laundry and installed an extra kitchen to provide hot food. She cleaned the floors and walls, installed better ventilation, improved the water supply, and rerouted the sewers. At night she made endless rounds among the wounded soldiers, tending to their needs by lamplight. Some six months after her arrival, the mortality rate at the hospital had fallen from approximately 50 percent to just 2 percent. Nightingale was a national hero: the *Times* wrote glowing accounts of her work, and the famous poet Henry Wadsworth Longfellow immortalized her in poetry. In sum, Nightingale revolutionized health care, not by making breakthroughs in medical science but by providing an environment in which healing could take place.

The British army, however, had mixed reactions. It adopted her sanitation reforms and agreed to gather more accurate health statistics, but it rejected her proposals to grant more authority to the medical staff. Rather than diluting power by giving it to surgeons and nurses, the army decided to keep it in the hands of military officers (Smith 1982).

Nightingale's work with the army was joined by Harriet Martineau (see the Profiles box, Chapter 1). Between the two of them they were able to muster much social pressure on the army, and that helped improve the help care for wounded soldiers (McDonald 2001).

Nightingale later founded the Nightingale Training School for Nurses, an important development for health care in general. Nurses today are regarded as professionals, but in Victorian times, they had a reputation for drunkenness and sexual promiscuity. Some actually were prostitutes. For this reason, Nightingale had been a severe taskmaster in Turkey and demanded that her nurses conduct themselves professionally and with circumspection. Their accomplishments and conduct, and later the school, helped to establish the modern profession of nursing.

CQ What lasting contributions did Florence Nightingale make to the practice of modern medicine? ◆ What did she teach us about the importance of nurses in maintaining health?

the patient. For instance, when physicians prescribe drugs in dosages that are incorrect, the nurses may recognize the problem but be unable to correct it.

Currently, more than 95 percent of registered nurses in the United States are women. And as in most feminized occupations, nurses are compensated less well than members of comparable male professions (Riska and Wegar 1993; Chapter 8). Because nursing does not pay especially well and because nurses are frequently resentful at their professional subordination to physicians, unions have been successful in organizing the profession.

Health Care Organizations

Physicians, nurses, dentists, and other medical practitioners work with patients in a variety of organization settings. We now examine several key medical organizations that are a part of the American health care system.

Hospitals Although at one time hospitals had a grim reputation as "places where you go to die," the contemporary hospital is a place where you are treated for serious diseases or injuries. Because we normally associate hospitals with medicine, it is easy to forget that hospitals are also bureaucracies (see Chapter 5). As anyone who has ever been hospitalized knows, every hospital is staffed by bureaucrats, has a huge number of rules and regulations, and generates a vast amount of paperwork. As a bureaucracy, however, hospitals are interesting because they do not follow the usual principles of hierarchy. Rather than having a single, clear line of authority, most hospitals have two lines: (1) physicians, who retain authority over medical matters; and (2) hospital administrators, who have authority over business matters. These two lines of authority are often in uneasy balance. Physicians, who have a great deal of prestige, are the hospital's main source of patients. Consequently, administrators give medical matters a wide berth and try to meet the demands of physicians whenever possible. Nevertheless, the physicians' authority is not unlimited. The hospital provides much of the equipment, facilities, and support staff that the physicians require. For instance, the hospital finances costly equipment such as CAT scanners, maintains sterile operating rooms, and provides nursing care. Without these supports, physicians could not adequately treat their patients. Physicians realize, moreover, that without access to a hospital, they would have no place to send their patients and could not maintain a full practice (Califano 1994).

Currently, the ever-increasing cost of medical care has forced hospitals to change their old ways of doing things. Although we discuss these changes in greater detail later, we here note the formation of *multihospital* systems. These are a combination of two or more hospitals that are owned or managed by a single corporation (Fennel and Alex 1993). By taking advantage of pooled resources, these corporations hope to cut costs and improve services. Hospitals have also tried to cut costs by hiring physicians directly. Under this arrangement, the physician becomes a hospital employee whose salary is directly controlled by the administration. If this practice becomes widespread, it would strengthen the authority of administrators and weaken the authority of physicians. Perhaps it would even end the system of having two lines of authority within the hospital. Whatever specific changes occur, however, within a decade or two, the hospital system we now know will probably have become a relic of the past.

Health Maintenance Organizations and Managed Care The **health maintenance organization (HMO)** is an insurance plan combined with a physical facility for delivering care. Members of an HMO pay a set monthly fee in much the same way they would pay an insurance premium. In return, the HMO provides comprehensive health coverage. If a patient's problem cannot be resolved by the HMO physician, the patient may be referred to a specialist who has agreed to provide services at a rate set by the HMO. As proposed originally by President Richard Nixon in 1971, HMOs were designed to bring some logic and planning into the nation's health care system and to serve as more efficient health care providers. The original plan anticipated that most of the U.S. population would eventually be enrolled in an HMO of some type, but this is not yet the case (Starr 1982). A related health care delivery system is the PPO, or Preferred Provider Organization. As compared with the HMO, the PPO gives the patient a greater range of options in selecting personal physicians.

Another way to provide health services is through *managed care:* a program that integrates the delivery and financing of health care services into a single plan. Some managed care programs are offered through HMOs. Typically, managed care programs offer a package of health care benefits provided through physicians who are part of the program. Patients are usually required to see a primary care physician for most of their

The National Naval Medical Center in Bethesda, Maryland. This federal facility has an excellent reputation and provides care to navy personnel, to members of Congress, and to the president of the United States. The United States has some of the best medical care facilities in the world, but access to such facilities is not universal.

Health maintenance organization (HMO) ▲ An insurance plan combined with a physical facility for delivering health care.

needs and are not allowed to visit specialists without the consent of their primary care physician. Managed care is bringing a major change to the career of many physicians. Rather than maintaining an independent practice, many physicians are becoming employees of corporate managed care plans and organizations (Hoff, Whitcomb, and Nelson 2002). Indeed, the AMA has even considered forming a physicians' union. Managed care is a controversial approach to delivering health services (Schied 2003). Although such programs appear to lower medical costs, both to the patient and to society, many people fear that the emphasis on cost control results in inferior health care and prevents patients from seeing a physician of their own choice (American Nurses Association 1998).

●■▲ Pausing to Think   About Health and Society

In the past, physicians could do very little to cure disease, and their prestige and income were low. As scientific medicine developed, however, medicine became a major institution. Nursing also became a respected profession and was recognized as an important part of the healing process. Today, medicine involves large bureaucracies, among the most important of which are hospitals, health maintenance organizations, and managed care programs.

 What is the difference between an HMO and a hospital? ◆ Do they serve different purposes?

Society Today ●■▲

American Lifestyles and Health

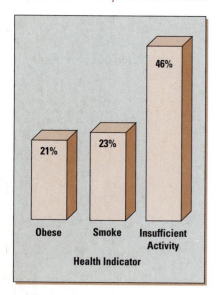

This chart shows that one-fifth of the people in the United States are not just overweight, they are obese. A similar fraction smokes and almost half do not get enough physical activity.

SOURCE: Statistical Abstract, 2002.

 What implications do these data have for improving the level of health in the United States and for decreasing health costs?

Sociological Issues in Medicine and Health Care

The inefficient, patchwork social organization that constitutes the American institution of medicine; the high cost of many medical treatments; and the amazing developments in medical technology raise several issues that will eventually affect everyone. We now discuss some of these issues.

Inequality in Health and Health Care

As we know from previous chapters, the three major dimensions of inequality are class, race, and gender (see Chapters 6–8). It is not surprising, therefore, to find that these dimensions are associated also with inequality in medicine.

Social Class   In all societies, the upper classes enjoy the highest levels of health. These people are knowledgeable about the symptoms of disease, and, of equal importance, they have the necessary resources to obtain professional help of the highest caliber. In addition, they live and work in generally healthy environments and have the time and money to exercise, enjoy recreation, eat properly, and otherwise take care of their health. Obesity, smoking, and a lack of regular exercise characterize poor and uneducated people more than wealthy, highly educated people (U.S. Bureau of the Census 1997; see Society Today, American Lifestyles and Health). Although the difference between the lifestyles of the wealthy and of the poor might not affect their health immediately, over the course of many years, it invariably takes a toll on the poor (Cockerham 1988; Ross and Wu 1995).

In contrast to the upper classes, less affluent people live in generally unhealthy environments and cannot afford to visit posh country clubs and tennis courts as a way to get fit. Such people also live in areas with limited access to medical facilities, and those facilities that are available are overcrowded and understaffed. In many states, for example, county hospitals provide health care for the poor, and these hospitals also absorb the costs of public health services. When funds for public services are severely cut, these hospitals become financially strained and therefore shut down many of their basic services to the poor (Humphries and Van Doorslaer 2000; Meyer 1995; Murphy 2000; Veenstra 2000).

Race and Ethnicity There are substantial health differences between African Americans and white Americans. Consider these statistics: compared with whites, African Americans have a higher incidence of chronic diseases that prevent them from working; an African American woman is more than four times more likely than a white woman to die during childbirth; an African American baby is twice as likely to die as a white baby; and an African American male is seven times more likely to die of homicide than a white male (U.S. Bureau of the Census 2000). As these statistics indicate, racial and ethnic minorities who lack power and wealth suffer poorer health than that of the dominant majority.

One reason for the disparity is the overlap between socioeconomic status and race and ethnicity. Many African Americans, Hispanics, and people in the lower classes have relatively little control over their lives and therefore believe that they have little control over their health. In effect, they become fatalistic and careless about their diet, exercise, and other preventive measures (Ross and Wu 1995). Racial and ethnic discrimination also plays a role. For instance, residential segregation forces many members of minority groups into crowded urban areas with unhealthy environments, few physicians, and inadequate health facilities (Falcone and Broyles 1994).

To some extent, racial and ethnic minorities typically receive poor health care because so few physicians are members of minority groups. For example, only some 3 percent of all physicians in the United States are African American or Hispanic. These statistics have hardly changed over the past ten years or so and probably will not change substantially for the foreseeable future (U.S. Bureau of the Census 1994).

Gender Whether you are a man or a woman has a substantial impact on your health, for several reasons (Cook 1995; Baunach 2003; see Table 14.1 on page 415). Like members of some racial and ethnic minority groups, women suffer from the problems faced by people who lack power and wealth. In addition, medicine is a male-dominated institution, which has traditionally viewed women's diseases as less important than men's diseases (Scully and Bart 2003). For instance, menstrual cramps, morning sickness, difficulties with lactation, and other female ailments receive low research priority. Even breast cancer, which will attack about one woman in eight during her lifetime, has not been given the same research priority as ailments that primarily afflict men. In addition, less is known about women's medicine. All too often, male patients are used as the primary subjects for research and clinical drug testing. Thus, the widely known research finding that shows that taking an aspirin a day significantly reduces the risk of heart attacks comes from a study based on 22,000 men but no women (Laurence and Weinhouse 1994).

A large number of women work in the health care field, as nurses, technicians, and administrators—but not as physicians. In effect, women are overrepresented in positions of lesser power and underrepresented in the most powerful positions. Currently, about one physician in five is a woman. Although this statistic is a substantial increase over a time when virtually no woman could gain admittance to medical school, the statistic also shows that a gender gap remains (Zimmerman 2000). Currently, however, the gap is declining, since women now constitute 40 percent of new medical students. If this trend continues, the number of female physicians will increase dramatically in this century (Laurence and Weinhouse 1994; U.S. Bureau of the Census 1994).

In sum, health care is very unevenly distributed across American society. Those segments of the population that are powerful and wealthy are healthier than those segments that are powerless and poor. The inequities in health thus parallel the inequities we discussed in Part Two of this book.

 STUDY TIP

Describe the three major dimensions of inequality as they relate to health and health care. For each, give two reasons why the inequality persists and name two specific examples of how that inequality manifests itself.

The Cost of Health Care

Although inequity in health care is a major problem, it is by no means the only problem besetting the American health care system. The United States now spends almost $1 trillion per year on health and related matters, and during this century, the annual figure could reach $2 trillion (U.S. Bureau of the Census 2000). Medical costs, in other words, are devouring an ever-growing share of the nation's resources, thereby leaving less for other uses. What accounts for the spiraling costs of health care? Several factors are involved, as follows:

1. *Physician Fees* In the United States, physicians typically earn their living from the fees that they charge their patients. This practice, common among many professions, is called "fee for service." Today, the net incomes of physicians account for 20 percent of all health care expenditures in the United States (U.S. Bureau of the Census 2000).

Fees have grown because physicians now conduct extensive diagnoses and treatments. In part, this trend has been spurred by technology-intensive medicine. Physicians now routinely rely on sophisticated tests and diagnostic machines that are expensive to operate and to maintain. The trend has also been spurred by the practice of "defensive medicine." Many physicians rely heavily on tests to evaluate a patient's problem, and sometimes they order tests of only marginal usefulness. By doing so, these physicians hope to compile a folder of evidence that shows that they have not been negligent in treating a particular patient and hence that they are not liable should they be sued (Rodwin 1995).

Although the practice of defensive medicine often results in needless expense, legal action is a very real possibility. Most physicians are sued several times during their careers and, accordingly, they pay large amounts for liability insurance. General practitioners will pay some $8,000 annually, whereas obstetricians—who get sued more frequently—will pay approximately $35,000 annually (U.S. Bureau of the Census 2000). Most of these insurance costs eventually get passed along to whomever is paying the physician's fees.

2. *Hospitals* Hospitals charge high fees, in part because hospitals are large, complex bureaucracies with high costs (Woolhanler and Himmelstein 1997). For example, it costs a typical hospital about $1,000 per day to support the average patient (U.S. Bureau of the Census 2000). Included in these costs are the wages and salaries of support personnel, the cost of equipment, unpaid bills of indigent patients, maintenance of the physical plant, and administrative overhead. If a hospital has more revenues than costs, the resulting profit goes either to shareholders (in the case of a for-profit hospital) or to the sponsoring organization (in the case of a nonprofit hospital).

Expenses incurred by the hospital cannot fully explain why hospital charges have consistently grown faster than the rate of inflation. Another part of the explanation is the desire of hospitals to earn profits and their ability to raise prices. They can do so, within limits, because patients are not free to shop for the best hospital at the lowest price. Any given community has only a few hospitals from which to choose; and in any event, patients almost always enter a hospital selected by their physician. For these reasons, the costs associated with hospitals account for about one-third of all medical spending in the United States (DiMaggio and Anhuer 1990).

3. *Technology* Changes in medical science also contribute to the higher cost of medical care. As medicine has become more dependent on sophisticated devices and procedures, the price of treatment has gone up. To treat heart disease, for instance, a physician can call on an extensive array of technologies and specialized skills: a tiny balloon inserted in the arteries can open the passageways for blood circulation; a small motor can regulate the heartbeat; or an entirely new heart can replace the old one. These and other advances require elaborate equipment and highly trained personnel,

Society Today ● ■ ▲

The Ever-Rising Costs of Medical Care in the United States

(U.S. Bureau of Labor Statistics 2002)

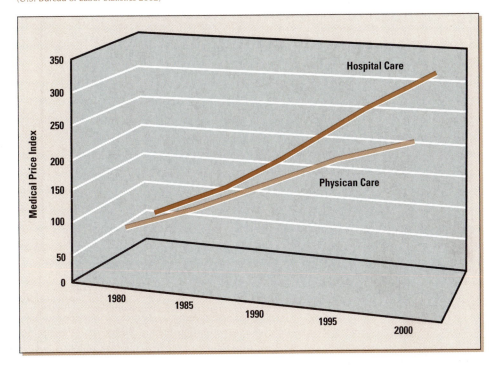

The chart shows that the medical price index has continually increased over the past 20 years, precipitating a crisis in health care. Despite attempts to cut costs by reducing physician fees, shortening hospital stays, delaying surgery, and reducing health insurance benefits, the cost of medical care continues to rise—and there seems to be no end in sight.

CQ Why do you think medical costs keep going up even though attempts are continually being made to hold them down?

all of which contribute to medical costs (see the Society Today box, The Ever-Rising Costs of Medical Care in the United States).

The problem of increasing health costs has recently led to calls for health care reform (Williams 1999). Most of these calls have focused on changing health insurance plans. Consequently, health insurance has also become a major issue in medicine.

Health Insurance

Because health care costs so much, especially when it involves heart disease, cancer, and other major problems, most people turn to some form of health insurance. Currently, about seven out of ten people in the United States have private health insurance, usually purchased through their employer or their labor union as part of a benefits package (U.S. Bureau of the Census 2002). Although many businesses used to pay the health insurance premiums for their workers, today most employers pay only part of the premium. The employee pays the rest (Jimenez 1997).

Whether government or private, however, very few health insurance plans pay for all medical expenses. Most plans require the patient to pay costs up to a fixed amount (the deductible) or to pay a part of any costs (a copayment). Insurance plans also contain exclusions and limits on how much they will pay in total. As a result, even

Society Today ● ■ ▲

Health Insurance: Who Is Not Covered?

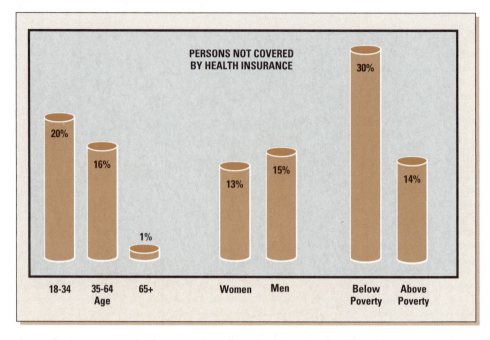

PERSONS NOT COVERED BY HEALTH INSURANCE

18-34	35-64	65+		Women	Men		Below Poverty	Above Poverty
20%	16%	1%		13%	15%		30%	14%

Age

Currently, insurance is the biggest political issue concerning health. Both President Clinton and President Bush favored expanding health insurance coverage, but in different ways. Despite these efforts, significant numbers of people still do not have health insurance. Not surprisingly, one's position in American society makes a difference (U.S. Bureau of the Census, 2002).

people with insurance are only partially protected. For example, patients who have major surgery frequently receive bills for $100,000 or more. If the patient's insurance pays 80 percent, the patient must pay the remaining 20 percent, or $20,000—a sizable sum that is beyond many people's reach.

Today, three categories of people tend to be uninsured (see Society Today, Health Insurance: Who Is Not Covered?). The first category consists of racial-ethnic minorities. Approximately a fifth of African Americans and a third of Hispanic Americans have no health insurance of any kind, as compared with 15 percent of white Americans. The second group consists of young people, aged 18 to 34. People in this age category either change jobs frequently or go in and out of the workforce while attending school. As a result, they tend not to work for businesses that provide long-term health insurance. Finally, the poor tend not to be insured.

Attempts to control costs have inspired some innovative insurance programs. The state of Oregon is experimenting with an insurance plan that gives the highest priority to measures that improve health, such as prenatal care, family planning, immunization, and proper diet. Although these measures are not very dramatic, they do affect a large number of people at a relatively low cost. In contrast, procedures such as organ transplants are dramatic but relatively inefficient because they affect only one person at great cost.

Both major political parties in the United States have endorsed some type of health care reform, and both have set their sights on reducing the growing costs of Medicare. The **Medicare** program was established in 1965 by President Lyndon Johnson as a way to provide health insurance for the elderly (see the What Do You Think? box). It services people 65 or older and the disabled. The program is financed through a tax that is levied on people who are working and on their employers.

Medicare ▲ A federal health insurance program for the elderly, financed by taxes on working people and on their employers and by a monthly fee for those enrolled in the program.

The term subjective health refers to how you rate your own health. This figure shows that the older people become, the less likely they are to rate themselves as being in excellent health.

CQ *Can you think of any social assertions that would explain why subjective health declines with age? ◆

Also, can you think of any sociological reasons that would explain why less than half of those respondents aged 18 to 25 rate themselves as being in excellent health?

*To answer these critical questions, review the What Is Critical Thinking? box in Chapter 1, paying special attention to the discussion of assertions.

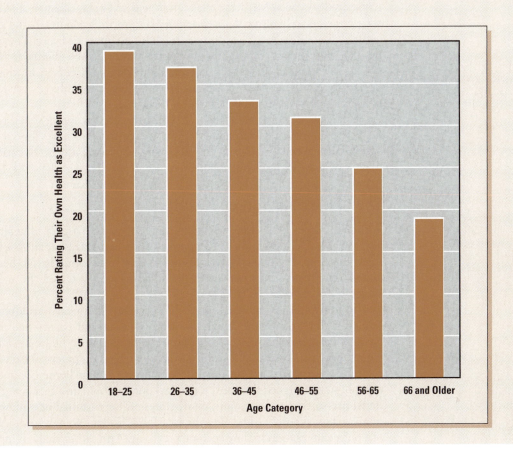

In addition, people enrolled in Medicare pay a monthly fee. Currently, almost 40 million people are enrolled, and the program spends more than $220 billion annually; by 2005, it will spend $356 billion (Lee 1992; U.S. Bureau of the Census 2002).

The problems of Medicare are mostly linked to financing. The current funding is insufficient, and the program will, it seems, go bankrupt sometime in this century. To prevent that event from happening, drastic changes will have to be made. The details of these changes are highly technical, but the overall issue of how to expand coverage, especially for prescription drugs, remains an unsolved and highly controversial issue. In the future, some form of managed health care will play a larger role. More people will have to join HMOs or health plans organized by groups of physicians and investors. Patients will have fewer choices in whom they see and in what services they receive. Physicians will earn less, and hospitals will have to cut costs. Many will simply go out of business, leaving patients with even fewer choices. Whatever the details of the outcomes, though, the institution of medicine will be far different from the one we know now.

Medicaid was enacted jointly with Medicare. As a smaller federal health insurance program administered at the state level, **Medicaid** is targeted to the poor and disabled (Hill, Zimmerman, and Fox 2002). In 2000, nearly 41 million aged, blind, disabled, or poor persons with families received Medicaid benefits. The cost of these benefits to the federal government was in excess of $142 billion—some $72 billion more than was spent in 1975 (U.S. Bureau of the Census 2000). In 1995, Congress attempted to pass legislation that would cap the amount of money that the federal government disburses to the states—thus forcing states to find more economical ways to provide health care to those who can least afford it. Although these proposed changes are controversial, there is little doubt that some form of cost containment will be implemented. As with Medicare, the future will see major changes being made in how the poor receive health care. Even more so than with Medicare, the poor will almost certainly be compelled to use some form of highly managed care. They will have fewer options than they do now, and many of them may not be eligible for Medicaid benefits at all. Despite Medicaid, however, about one poor person in four has no health insurance at all (Summer 1994). As a result, these people have very limited access to physicians, hospitals, and other health facilities.

Ironically, even though the cost of health care is a major social issue, the role of medicine continues to expand, thereby increasing the cost. This process has been going on since the nineteenth century, but now it is rapidly accelerating (Hacker and Skocpol 1997; Schroeder 2000).

The Medicalization of Society

Although most of the issues in medicine involve some aspect of health care, there is also a growing concern about the power of medicine as a social institution. Increasingly, medicine has taken over areas of life that were formerly handled by the family, courts, churches, and other institutions. This trend is called the **medicalization of society** (Conrad 1992; Clarke et al. 2003).

To illustrate how medicalization has proceeded, consider childbirth. For most of human history, people regarded childbirth as a natural occurrence rather than as a medical problem. In times past, babies were delivered in the home, aided by a family member or perhaps by a midwife (a woman with much practical experience in delivering babies but without much formal training). As medicine became more influential, physicians argued that only a medical doctor could ensure a healthy delivery, and under pressure from physicians, many states either curtailed or outlawed the practice of midwifery (Laurence and Weinhouse 1997). Today, women routinely seek the care of a physician as soon as they become pregnant. And rather than giving birth at home, most women go to hospitals, where the baby is delivered by a team of specialists under the direction of a medical doctor. Thus, what was once regarded as a natural occurrence has now become defined as a medical problem.

Medicalization has taken place in other realms of social life as well. For instance, people who drank too much were once thought to lack the willpower necessary to quit. Today, people with the same problem are regarded as sick. If they are suffering from a disease, then it follows that they should be treated by medical doctors. Similarly, people suffering from an addiction to gambling or sex, or from a variety of other behavioral disorders, are now being defined as sick, and their disorder is therefore defined as a medical problem.

The recognition of mental problems as medical problems has further opened the way to medicalizing large areas of human behavior. Emotions, feelings, drives, needs, and other psychosocial and psychobiological aspects of human behavior have been brought into the domain of medicine (Nash 2000). Violent mood swings, depression, and self-destructive behavior are recognized as sicknesses, and people suffering from these problems seek the help of physicians. Because one out of every four people in the United States suffers from some form of mental disorder every year, the medicalization

Medicaid ▲ A federal health insurance program administered at the state level targeted to the poor and the disabled.

Medicalization of society ▲ The expansion and taking over of areas of life by medicine that were formerly part of another social institution.

of mental illness brings a substantial part of life under the control of the medical establishment.

Physical attractiveness is also being medicalized. Wearing braces on the teeth, a practice that is fairly common among children, is now becoming popular among adults. The shape of one's nose, ears, chin, and other body parts is routinely altered for the sake of appearance. Surgeons, moreover, can repair deformities caused by accidents and birth defects. These tragedies were once regarded as a matter of fate, but now they can be medically treated. Eventually, even height might become medicalized (Table 14.1).

Although American society is well along the path to medicalization, some critics contend that the consequences are not uniformly good. The medicalization of child-birth undoubtedly has saved lives, for instance, but it has also led to an enormous increase in Cesarean sections (a surgical procedure to remove the baby from the mother's womb). As medicalization continues, moreover, it gives more authority to medicine and takes it away from religion, law, education, and other institutions concerned with social control. Many people find this trend deeply troubling. In their view, it undermines the notions of morality, self-control, and social responsibility. Without these, they say, society has no way to control individual behavior.

●■▲ Pausing to Think   About Sociological Issues in Medicine and Health Care

A major issue facing American society is the unequal distribution of health care. Poor people, racial-ethnic minorities, and women tend to receive inferior care. Costs are another issue. As costs have escalated, people have increasingly turned to health insurance and to publicly supported health plans such as Medicare and Medicaid. Society is also becoming more medicalized, and critics worry that medicine is eroding the traditional basis of moral authority and individual responsibility.

CQ Why are only some people in the United States covered by health insurance? ◆ Why don't all citizens receive a minimum amount of coverage?

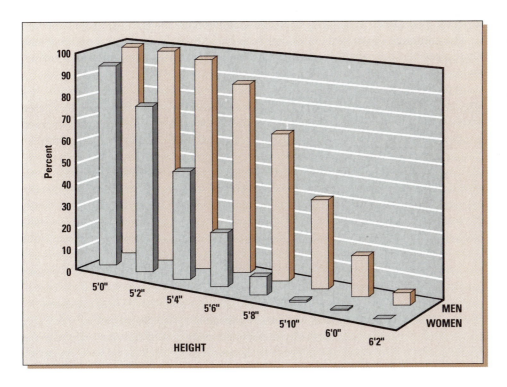

TABLE 14.1 Height of the American Population
(National Center for Health Statistics 2002)

The chart shows the percentage of women (front row) and men (back row) who are taller than a given height. For example, more than 90 percent of women and more than 98 percent of men are taller than 5'0"; and almost 20 percent of women and almost 90 percent of men are taller than 5'6".

In the absence of other data, height might be used to crudely measure the overall health of a population. All else equal, favorable environmental factors—such as good diet, sanitation, and medical care—will increase the average height of a group of people.

CQ *Should height be considered a medical condition?*

Sociological Analysis of Medicine and Health Care

As mentioned several times before, sociology has three major perspectives: functionalist, conflict, and symbolic interactionist. Each perspective highlights a different aspect of society and of the individual, thus providing different but equally valuable insights into social behavior (see Table 14.2).

The Functionalist Perspective

Healthy citizens are the greatest asset any country can have.

—Sir Winston Churchill, prime minister of Great Britain, 1943

When Winston Churchill made this remark, Britain was fighting World War II and was straining to sustain the war effort. Millions of men and women were needed to serve in the military, to maintain agricultural production, and to work in factories. Without a healthy workforce, Churchill feared, the war effort would fail.

From the functionalist viewpoint, Churchill's analysis illustrates a basic function of medicine: to keep people healthy so that they can serve the society. Clearly, a society will collapse if it does not have enough people capable of producing goods and providing services. Although this possibility might seem far-fetched with regard to the United States, it has happened repeatedly throughout history. For example, highly developed civilizations existed in North, Central, and South America before the arrival of Christopher Columbus. Europeans, however, brought with them diseases that decimated the Native American population—8 million Native Americans died in the Caribbean alone (Josephy 1994; Palmer 1992). And with the loss of those populations, many of those societies vanished as well.

Another function of medicine, of course, is to treat and cure sickness. Different societies, as we previously discussed, approach this problem with different theories about the cause of sickness and with different ideas about what constitutes an appropriate cure. Nevertheless, because all societies recognize that sick people cannot perform their roles as well as healthy people, all societies have the institution of medicine.

The contemporary treatment of disease is based heavily on science, and medical research goes on continuously. As a result, medicine serves the function of spurring

TABLE 14.2

[a]The functionalist and conflict perspectives were introduced in Chapters 1 and 2, and symbolic interaction was discussed in Chapter 3.

Comparison of Three Theoretical Perspectives on Medicine and Health Care

PERSPECTIVE[a]	VIEW OF MEDICINE AND HEALTH CARE	KEY CONCEPTS AND PROCESSES
Functionalism	Sees medicine and health care as performing essential functions for society	Sick role Malingering
Conflict Theory	Sees medicine and health care as big business in capitalist societies	Inequalities of care
Symbolic Interaction	Sees medicine and health care as interaction among patients, physicians, and nurses in a social context	Socialization Social networks of support

scientific research. Better treatments are always welcomed, but even more pressing is the search for cures for diseases that are now incurable. Gene therapy, for example, holds some promise, but more research will have to be done before it becomes an acceptable treatment procedure (Anderson 1995). Although research careers in medicine are seldom as financially rewarding as the practice of medicine, in the long run, research is essential.

Medicine also serves another important function: it encourages people to follow the norms, values, and behaviors of conventional society. That is, medicine acts as an agent of social control. It does so by certifying that certain people are qualified to perform certain tasks; that is, medicine acts as a gatekeeper. To illustrate, a physician may be asked to certify that an enlistee is healthy enough to join the armed services, that a student can participate in athletics, or that a new employee is qualified to perform a certain job. It is interesting that medicine can now act as a gatekeeper to death. With the development of life-sustaining technology, premature babies can be saved, and the lives of patients in comas can be prolonged for a considerable period, perhaps years. Very often, in these cases, a physician determines whether a patient lives a while longer or dies immediately. Going a step further, over half of the American people believe that under appropriate conditions, physicians should have the right to assist patients in committing suicide (Cohen, Fihn, and Boyko 1994).

Finally, as we have already discussed, in capitalist societies, medicine and health care are big businesses that generate huge sums of money. This function of medicine—the production of wealth and prestige—makes entering the medical profession extremely attractive, provided that you are willing to make the necessary sacrifices and that you have the necessary resources.

The Sick Role Functionalist theorists emphasize that society must somehow exert social control over sickness. Addressing this issue, sociologist Talcott Parsons (1953, 1975; Turner and Samson 1995) suggested that every society must confront the problem of **malingering**: pretending to be sick to achieve some personal or social goal. Although a little malingering might seem harmless, widespread malingering places severe strains on the social system. What would happen, for example, if a group of students in your sociology class pretended to be sick and were excused from turning in their term papers on time? You probably would regard those students as "cheaters" who were unfairly taking advantage of the system. You might even take action against

Malingering ▲ Pretending to be sick to achieve some personal or social gain.

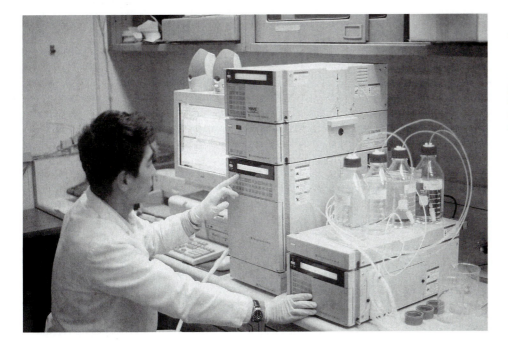

This photograph shows a geneticist analyzing variability of human genes in DNA samples. Medical research into genetics is very promising. It may lead to early detection of a patient's potential medical problems and suggest preventative measures that can be taken before symptoms of a disease appear.

them because they were undermining the validity of the grades and the value of the course. You would feel this way because you have learned that with regard to sickness, certain expectations are appropriate, and other expectations are inappropriate. Talcott Parsons summarized these expectations as the **sick role** and organized them under the following four major headings:

1. *Sick people are not responsible for their condition.* Parsons recognized that being sick is unpleasant and that under ordinary circumstances, no one would voluntarily become sick. In addition, getting sick is not a matter of moral choice; instead, it is a matter of physiological processes, and people are stricken by sickness through no fault of their own. Hence, if you become sick, you are not to be blamed or punished for your condition.

2. *Sick people may withdraw from normal activities.* According to Parsons, sick people may withdraw from normal activities without incurring penalties or sanctions. Business organizations, for example, permit workers to take time off for illness ("sick days"); schools excuse students for sickness; and in general, sick people are excused from their normal duties. As a general rule, the sicker you are, the more exemptions you receive. If you have a mild cold, your boss will expect you to show up for work, but not if you have pneumonia. And in some cases, a sick person may actually be prohibited from working. Jet pilots, for example, may not fly if they have a cold.

3. *Sickness is undesirable, and sick people should want to be well.* According to this norm, sick people should regard their condition as undesirable and thus should want to recover as quickly as possible. This expectation guards against using sickness as a way to gain special favors or treatment. That is, it prevents malingering. A sick person who fails to meet this expectation will be stigmatized as a deviant.

4. *The sick should seek treatment.* Finally, Parsons said, the norms of the sick role demand that sick people obtain qualified help. Home remedies might suffice for a minor problem, but a serious disease requires professional help. In fact, over half of all adults in the United States see a physician every year (NORC 1998). Merely seeking help, however, is not enough. The sick role also requires that the patient cooperate with qualified healers or risk being shunned, ridiculed, or otherwise sanctioned.

As developed originally by Parsons, the concept of the sick role gained immediate and widespread currency; yet it is not without shortcomings. One shortcoming concerns the norm of responsibility. According to the norms that Parsons identified, sick people are not to be blamed for their condition. Yet we know that many diseases carry a stigma and that people are, in fact, blamed for their condition. To illustrate, a person with a sexually transmitted disease might be stigmatized as being sexually promiscuous, and a child with a physical deformity might be ridiculed by thoughtless playmates. Therefore, Parsons's concept of the sick role applies most appropriately to diseases that do not carry a moral stigma. Another problem with the sick role is the expectation that the patient will try to recover. In many instances, this expectation is unrealistic: people sometimes suffer from an incurable condition that lingers for years and eventually causes death. Instead of trying to recover—which might be impossible— these people adapt their lifestyles to the demands of their sickness. Finally, conflict theorists and symbolic interactionists believe that the concept of the sick role exempts the role of the physician from analysis and also fails to account for the dynamic quality of the interaction between patients and physicians (Friedson 1970; Levine 1987).

Although these criticisms show that the concept of the sick role should not be accepted uncritically, it remains a useful concept. It links our behavior as individuals suffering from sickness to the society in which we live. Without this link, functional theorists believe, our behavior when sick would be disorderly, unpredictable, and therefore dysfunctional to society as a whole.

STUDY TIP

Gather in a group of three or four and brainstorm a number of illnesses. Then, consider each in terms of the four aspects of the sick role. Does the sick role apply to a person with each of these illnesses? Why or why not? In each case, how does the behavior of the sick person affect others?

Sick role ▲ A social role developed by society for the sick, who, if they play the role correctly, are released from life's normal obligations for the duration of the illness.

The Conflict Perspective

Medical care and cure has become big business.

—Emily Mumford, *Medical Sociology*, 1983

In this brief statement, Emily Mumford remarks on the capitalistic nature of American medicine. To many conflict theorists, this feature lies at the core of what is wrong with medicine and health care in the United States. They point out that even with the most expensive and technologically advanced health care system in the world, the United States compares unfavorably with the less expensive and less elaborate health care systems of other industrial countries. In one survey of 18 industrialized nations, for instance, the United States ranked the highest in total spending, yet it was the lowest in the proportion of the population protected by public health insurance (Sivard 1993).

Conflict theorists also stress the inequality of medicine and health care with regard to racial and ethnic minorities, women, and other groups that lack power (Bates 2000; Farmer 1999). As we have already discussed in the section on health and inequality, racial and ethnic minorities suffer from poorer health than do whites; diseases that primarily or exclusively afflict women tend to be downplayed in importance; and the poor are less healthy than the rich. Sociologists are also finding that people with alternative sexual preferences suffer from poor health (see the Diversity box).

Conflict theorists point out that the institution of medicine does not function as smoothly as functionalist theorists believe. In fact, conflict theorists say, major interest groups are always fighting among themselves. Physicians, hospitals, insurance companies, drug companies, and government regulatory bodies all have huge stakes in medicine, and they continually compete with one another for power. To illustrate, physicians have such massive influence that they have maintained their legal monopoly on the prescription of drugs and have prevented nurses and other healers

Diversity ●■▲ Stress and the Mental Health of Gay Men

In the past, researchers have found that members of minority groups have experienced psychological distress because of their stigmatized minority group status. Given that gay men are a minority, do they experience psychological distress from their status as do members of other minorities? Ilan Meyer (1995) set out to answer this question in a study of 741 AIDS-free gay men in New York City.

To measure psychological distress, Meyer employed a variety of mental health measures, including demoralization or feelings of dread, anxiety, sadness, helplessness, poor self-esteem, perceived health problems, and confused thinking; guilt, which includes both rational and irrational feelings of guilt; suicide, which measures both intent and attempted suicide; and traumatic stress response, which measures AIDS-related preoccupation, avoidance, nightmares, panic attacks, and problems in daily functioning.

The findings show that gay men who had high levels of stress because of their gay status were two to three times as likely to suffer from high levels of psychological distress. How does stress from their gay status work to produce high levels of psychological distress? One way is through internalized homophobia. This term refers to the internalization of society's negative definition of homosexuality, thereby creating a negative self-image that could not be entirely shaken by publicly coming out as gay. The more the gay men had internalized homophobia, the more psychological distress they manifested. Another way is through the negative effects of stigma and labeling, which refer to the expectations the gay men had about being rejected or discriminated against in their relationships with others because of their homosexuality. The more they expected to be rejected or discriminated against, the more psychological distress they manifested. The third way is through discrimination, which refers to the extent to which they had personally experienced antigay violence or discrimination. The more antigay violence or discrimination they had experienced, the more distress they manifested.

This study showed that gays, because of their status as a minority group within society, are vulnerable to psychological distress and mental health problems. What can be done to lessen the psychological distress experienced by these men? Meyer suggests that the distress can be lessened through proactive coping—through such measures as obtaining social support from other gays that affirms and validates gay culture and values, and by devaluing the stigmatizing values of the dominant culture. In other words, gay men can improve their mental health by forming a communal-type social system that buffers them from the hostile elements of mainstream society.

from expanding their professional spheres. Physicians have also blocked efforts to provide government-sponsored insurance programs for all citizens, in spite of the fact that millions of Americans want greater health care coverage (NORC 1994). Nonetheless, the power of physicians is being challenged. Insurance companies and government agencies now actively pressure the health care system to rely more on nurse practitioners, midwives, and other less costly alternatives to physicians. In addition, the practice of hiring physicians as employees of HMOs, hospitals, and other care-giving organizations reduces their autonomy and reduces their power as well. Physicians claim that these restrictions on their authority will affect the care received by their patients and that ultimately patients will suffer from the power struggles in medicine.

The Symbolic Interactionist Perspective

Whereas the functional and conflict perspectives mainly apply to the macro-level of analysis, the symbolic interactionist perspective focuses on the individual and on social interaction. With regard to medicine and health care, symbolic interactionists have closely studied socialization, the interaction between physicians and patients, and social support for sick people (Mattingly and Garro 2000).

Socialization of Physicians and Nurses Because physicians deal with life-and-death matters, they must undergo intensive training before being allowed to practice independently. They begin their educations as undergraduates who major in "pre-med," a curriculum requiring many courses in the biological and physical sciences. As you undoubtedly know, excellent grades and high scores on entrance examinations are minimum requirements for acceptance into a medical school.

Medical school usually follows the attainment of a bachelor's degree and usually takes four years to complete. Typically, it is an intense, stressful introduction to the knowledge, values, and attitudes associated with the medical profession. Although many medical students begin their training with lofty ideals about serving society, these ideals soon give way to more practical concerns about surviving medical school itself. Students quickly learn to be dispassionate and unemotional about sickness and to look upon medicine as primarily a technical and scientific process. Because there is so much medical knowledge to absorb and so little time to absorb it, medical students become adept at anticipating what the faculty think is important rather than mastering everything. By the time they leave medical school, most students have come to view themselves as doctors and have taken on the physician's detached view of healing as a rather impersonal process. Such a view may be functional, given the typical stresses involved in handling many patients during an eight-hour day (Becker et al. 1961; Ben-Sira 1990).

Nurses typically major in nursing during their four years of undergraduate education. As they learn the nursing role, they are socialized to think of themselves as professionals who value patient care and rational knowledge. Nurses tend to maintain a high level of altruism and dedication to people throughout their training.

After nurses graduate, they sometimes find that their values of compassion and caring are not the dominant values of the medical bureaucracy in which they work. They also find that many physicians insist on controlling every aspect of patient care, leaving the nurse little room for independent decision making. Although nurses must deal with the suffering of their patients on an hourly basis, they lack the legal authority to treat their patients—something only a physician may do. For this reason, nurses often experience a great deal of stress and quickly "burn out" (Schwirian 1998; Twaddle and Hessler 1987).

Physician-Patient Interaction Typically, the interaction between physician and patient appears to be very one-sided: the physician is the authority who gives orders, and the patient obeys. However, social reality is much more complicated than that picture. Not all patients respond to illness in the same way. For example, there are important ethnic-racial differences in how people respond to pain. Physicians have noted that Asian Americans often respond to pain quietly and stoically, whereas

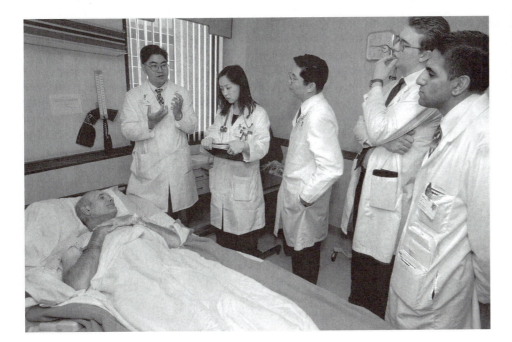

The attending physician discusses a patient's condition with medical students in a hospital room. The patient is listening passively as is his part in the sick role.

Italian Americans are more likely to express their discomfort forcefully and to demand relief loudly (Alonzo 1984; Zborowski 1969). Similarly, athletes often sustain broken bones and torn muscles that would incapacitate the average person, yet they continue to play, and they treat such injuries as a normal occurrence. In fact, athletes often hide symptoms of injury from physicians (Curry 1993). As these examples suggest, patient-doctor interaction is fraught with opportunities for misunderstandings, even though it appears to be straightforward.

Nurses play an important role in facilitating communication between physician and patient. In a hospital, the physician sees the patient for a few minutes a day, whereas the nurse sees the patient throughout the day. As a result, the patient gets to know the nurse, and conversely, the nurse gets to know the patient. To take advantage of this situation, in some hospitals, the traditional one-to-one relationship between the physician and the patient has given way to a team approach that includes the patient, doctor, nurse, and other medical practitioners.

Social Support and Recovery from Disease   Symbolic interactionists have become increasingly interested in the patient's subjective experience of illness on a day-to-day basis, and in the impact that illness has on the lives of the patients and their caregivers (Lawton 2003). Symbolic interactionists are especially interested in the social context within which healing takes place. Often, the social context can affect the speed and course of recovery. Generally, patients who belong to networks of friends, family, and coworkers do better than patients who are isolated. The social networks provide emotional and material support and help the sick person to maintain hope. In addition, a network provides information about treatments, physicians, and hospitals. Isolated patients, in contrast, receive little or no help from other people, lack information, and may not have the emotional strength to face the disease alone (Bloom et al. 1991; Koomen et al. 1990).

● ■ ▲ **Pausing to Think**   **About the Sociological Analysis of Medicine and Health Care**

According to the functionalist view, medicine and health have a number of functions: to keep people healthy so that they can contribute to society; to cure sickness; to engage in medical research; to act as agents of social control; and to produce wealth and prestige.

Healthy People 2010

The U.S. Public Health Service now sponsors a program called "Healthy People 2010." The program has identified several priority areas. Improvements in these priority areas should improve the health of the American population by the year 2010. Here are five examples that concern prevention:

PRIORITIES

Improved physical fitness

Better nutrition

Less use of tobacco, alcohol, and other drugs

Improved mental health

Responsible sexual behavior

SOURCE: U.S. Department of Health and Human Services, 2000. www.health.gov/healthypeople.

---

123 STUDY TIP

Construct a time line of the history of medical care, from communal societies through the Great Social Transformation, into modern day. Use key terms and include the most significant elements of each stage of the development of medical care.

Preventive medicine ▲ Medical treatments and information that aim at the prevention of disease and the maintenance of health.

Functionalists also note that society has developed the sick role. People who are physically ill and fulfill the social expectations of the sick role are released from the normal obligations of life until they return to health. Conflict theorists argue that American medicine is big business that results in high costs and that it downplays the problems of women, racial-ethnic minorities, and the less affluent. Conflict theorists also argue that physicians, hospitals, insurance companies, drug companies, and government regulatory bodies are constantly in conflict. Symbolic interactionists emphasize the socialization of health care professionals, patient-physician interaction, and the social support systems for recovering patients.

CQ Most Americans, apparently, are not bothered by the poor health found among the lower social classes and among racial-ethnic minorities. How would a conflict theorist explain this indifference? ◆ A functionalist? ◆ A symbolic interactionist?

Medicine and Health Care in the Twenty-First Century

Historically, the primary goal of medicine has been to cure disease, and that remains an important goal today. In the future, however, another medical goal will take on greater importance. Rather than emphasizing cure, medicine in the future will emphasize the maintenance of health and the prevention of disease (Jamner and Stokols 2000). This trend, referred to as **preventive medicine**, should grow stronger in the future, for three reasons. First, it makes sense to emphasize prevention because small changes in lifestyle can have large effects on the health of a population. The effects of smoking, alcohol, poor diet, and lack of exercise now cause half of the mortality from the ten leading causes of death. Yet changes in just two of these factors—smoking and diet—have been responsible for more than half of the decline in the death rate from heart disease. Such changes doubtless have had a greater impact on reducing death from heart disease than has open heart surgery (Califano 1986; Caplow 2000). Similarly, HIV infection and other sexually transmitted diseases can be prevented through the use of a variety of "safe sex" practices, and, in the case of HIV, through a better understanding of how the disease is acquired through blood transfusions. Because a cure for AIDS is not yet available and drugs to fight the disease are very expensive, prevention is the only real defense.

Second, changes in the age structure of the population will encourage health maintenance and prevention in the future. By the first quarter of this century, 60 million people in the United States will be over 65 years old (see Chapter 15). Because the need for medical care increases with age, the United States soon will have to spend enormous sums for Medicaid, Medicare, veterans' hospitals, and other medical programs. As we discussed earlier, sheer economic necessity will force the government to stress health maintenance and prevention as a way to combat health costs (see Society Today, Healthy People 2010).

The third factor behind the health maintenance trend is a changing view of health itself. Health will soon become a global concept encompassing a society's medical system, social arrangements, political power, and place in the world system (Larkin 1999). The World Health Organization (WHO), an international organization with projects in many countries, already defines health as a state of physical, mental, and social well-being (Raphael et al. 1997; World Health Organization 2000). To achieve health by this definition requires vast changes in many societies: full employment, with wages high enough to buy nutritious foods; greater attention to equal rights for women and to women's health issues; the implementation of universal education; and the avoidance of war and civil strife (Mosley and Cowley 1991; United Nations 1995). Statisticians at the United Nations have devised a "Human

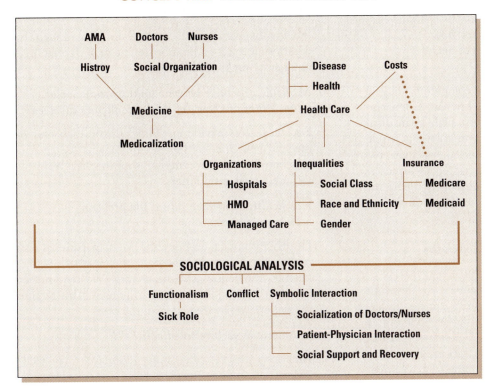

Here is a concept web for medicine and health care. Try this: add *cultural competence* to the web. In the web *costs* and *insurance* are connected by a dotted line. The dotted line indicates a potential direct link between the concepts. Write a paragraph connecting the two concepts thereby changing the dotted line to a solid line. What other potential links between concepts in the web are there?

Development Index" that gives a rough indication of which societies have achieved these conditions.

Health care in this century will place greater emphasis on **cultural competence**. Cultural competence is the ability of the health care system to provide care tailored to the specific cultural needs of patients with diverse values, beliefs, and behaviors (Betancourt, Green, and Carrillo 2002). Cultural competency recognizes that in a diverse society, for health care to be sound, compassionate, and efficacious it must be sensitive and responsive to the diverse cultural context of its many patients. Sociologists, anthropologists, and other social scientists will help inform the health care system of the nature and needs of specific cultural groups. This will result in the growth of applied and clinical sociology (Kallen 2002).

Looking Ahead

This chapter concludes the study of major social institutions. Sometimes, institutions seem too massive for any individual to change. The next chapter deals with population, the environment, and cities. These topics have much to do with the quality of life we will experience in the twenty-first century. As we shall see, high rates of population growth and massive movement of people to cities have profound implications for the environment. To counteract this impression, the final chapter discusses collective social action, a topic that suggests how individuals can work together to change the society in which they live.

Cultural competence ▲ The ability of the health care system to provide care tailored to the specific cultural needs of patients with diverse values, beliefs, and behaviors.

WHAT YOU SHOULD KNOW ●■▲

1. **How has the institution of medicine and health care changed with the Great Social Transformation?**

In communal societies, the entire community may be involved in the healing process, whereas in associational societies, specialized healers, such as medical doctors and registered nurses, are primarily responsible for curing the sick. In industrialized, associational societies, moreover, sickness is regarded as a matter of science, interactions between healers and patients tend to be impersonal, and treatment is offered in bureaucratic organizations.

2. **How did scientific medicine develop in the United States?**

In the middle of the nineteenth century, the development of germ theory laid the foundation for understanding communicable diseases; the development of anesthetics made extensive surgery possible; and improved sanitation reduced the infections that often killed patients. These changes combined with changes in the medical profession to produce the scientific medicine that we know today.

3. **Who occupies the key positions in the medicine and health care institution?**

Physicians are the most powerful group in medicine and health care because they have broad rights to diagnose and treat illness. Nurses are in close contact with patients but are subordinate to physicians. Because this arrangement often causes frustration and anxiety on the part of nurses, many of them leave the profession at an early age.

4. **Which are the leading health care organizations?**

Hospitals are the central organizations in the delivery of health care. Hospitals provide physicians with much of the equipment, facilities, and support staff that they require to conduct their practice, whereas physicians provide hospitals with paying patients. The increasing cost of medical care has led to the creation of the multihospital system, health maintenance organizations, and managed care.

5. **How is social inequality manifest in the delivery of health care?**

The upper classes enjoy the highest levels of health, have the most knowledge about good health practices, and have the resources to obtain the best in medical attention. Racial and ethnic minorities lag behind the dominant majority in health. Women's health issues are usually given less attention than those of men. In addition, women and minorities are underrepresented among the ranks of physicians.

6. **Medical costs have become an important social issue. What are some of the basic factors involved?**

Several factors have contributed to the high cost of medical care. Among these are physicians' fees, hospital charges, and the complex, sophisticated technology used in treating illness.

7. **Has health insurance solved the problem of increased costs?**

Health insurance was devised to help patients pay high medical costs, but the poor, the racial-ethnic minorities, the young, and the unemployed tend not to be insured. In addition, most insurance plans require the patient to pay some part of the costs.

8. **Is American society "medicalized"?**

American society is becoming more and more medicalized. Medicalization gives more authority to medicine and takes it away from other institutions. Critics say that medicalization tends to undermine traditional notions of personal morality, self-control, and social responsibility.

9. **What contribution to our understanding of medicine and health care has been made by the functionalist perspective?**

Functionalists argue that the institution of medicine and health care fulfills several important social functions, including keeping people healthy, treating the ill and curing sickness, engaging in scientific research on disease, acting as an agent of social control, and producing wealth and prestige for physicians. Functionalists also inform us that society has developed a specialized role—the sick role. People who are physically ill and fulfill the social expectations of the sick role are released from the normal obligations of life until they return to health.

10. **What contributions to our understanding of medicine and health care have been made by the conflict perspective?**

Conflict theorists point out that medicine has become big business. This trend has led to high costs and to the unequal distribution of health care, especially for the poor, for racial and ethnic minorities, and for women. Conflict theorists also say that physicians, hospitals, insurance companies, drug companies, and government regulatory bodies are in constant conflict as they attempt to advance their own special interests.

11. *The symbolic interactionist perspective has also contributed to our understanding of medicine and health care. What are some of its main insights?*

Symbolic interactionists tend to focus on the individual and social interaction. They have studied the socialization process of health care professionals, patient-physician interaction, and the social support systems of recovering patients.

12. *What does the future hold for medicine and health care?*

The future will see a greater emphasis on the maintenance of health and the prevention of disease. As the U.S. population ages, preventive medicine will become increasingly important. To achieve health as defined by the World Health Organization, many societies will have to make vast improvements in their social arrangements and standard of living.

TEST YOUR KNOWLEDGE ●■▲

Key Terms Matching

Match each of these key terms with the best definition or example from the numbered items that follow. Write the letter preceding the key term in the blank before the definition that you choose.

a. disease
b. health
c. health maintenance organization (HMO)
d. malingering
e. Medicaid
f. medicalization of society
g. Medicare
h. preventive medicine
i. sick role

_____ **1.** The capacity to satisfy role requirements.

_____ **2.** The expansion and taking over of areas of life by medicine that were formerly part of another social institution.

_____ **3.** An insurance plan combined with a physical facility for delivering health care.

_____ **4.** A social role developed by society for the sick, who, if they play the role correctly, are released from life's normal obligations for the duration of the illness.

_____ **5.** A federal health insurance program administered at the state level targeted to the poor and the disabled.

_____ **6.** Medical treatments and information that aim at the prevention of disease and the maintenance of health.

_____ **7.** A federal health insurance program for the elderly financed by taxes on working people and on their employers and by a monthly fee for those enrolled in the program.

_____ **8.** A pathology that disrupts the usual function of the body.

_____ **9.** Pretending to be sick to achieve some personal or social goal.

Multiple Choice

Circle the letter of your choice.

1. Compared with communal societies, health care in associational societies is
  a. more scientific.
  b. less personal.
  c. more rational.
  d. all of the above.

2. Which of the following is NOT true of nurses?
  a. They often burn out because of job stress.
  b. They can make independent decisions about a patient's treatment.
  c. They are increasingly attending four-year universities.
  d. In hospitals, they generally spend more time with patients than the doctors do.

3. Which of the following is true of the relationship between doctors and hospital administrators?
  a. They often have an uneasy relationship.
  b. Administrators defer to physicians on medical matters.
  c. Physicians rely on administrators to provide them with equipment.
  d. All of the above.

4. What is the term for a combination of two or more hospitals that are owned or managed by a single corporation?

   a. multiplex
   b. multihospital system
   c. hospice
   d. joint care facility

5. What is the reason that members of the upper classes are usually healthier than members of the lower classes?

   a. The upper classes live and work in generally healthy environments.
   b. The wealthy tend to smoke less and exercise more.
   c. Members of the upper classes are usually educated about diseases and can recognize symptoms.
   d. All of the above.

6. Compared with whites,

   a. African Americans have a higher incidence of chronic diseases that prevents them from working.
   b. African American women are four times more likely to die during childbirth.
   c. African American babies are twice as likely to die.
   d. all of the above.

7. Why does being male or female have a substantial impact on your health?

   a. Medicine is male dominated.
   b. Medicine has viewed women's diseases as less important than men's diseases.
   c. Male patients are used as the primary subject for research and clinical drug tests.
   d. All of the above.

8. Medical costs

   a. are devouring an increasing share of the nation's resources.
   b. could reach $2 trillion.
   c. in part reflect the impact of increased technology in medicine.
   d. all of the above.

9. As compared with the HMO, the PPO (Preferred Provider Organization) gives

   a. the patient a greater range of options in selecting personal physicians.
   b. lower rates across all services, thus keeping costs down.
   c. nurses more authority when caring for patients.
   d. those who are sick the ability to malinger.

10. Which of the following is NOT a factor in the increasing costs of health care?

   a. Most people are now covered by health insurance.
   b. Physician fees are high, accounting for 20 percent of all health care expenditures.
   c. Hospitals are large, complex bureaucracies with high costs.
   d. Medicine is dependent on sophisticated and expensive devices and procedures.

11. At one time, alcoholics were considered immoral people. Now, they are defined as having a disease of addiction. This change is an example of

   a. sick role.
   b. malingering.
   c. medicalization of society.
   d. stigmatization of the sick.

12. Critics argue that the medicalization of society

   a. gives courts more control over individual behavior.
   b. undermines morality, self-control, and social responsibility.
   c. results in fewer people being treated for serious illness.
   d. undermines advances in women's health.

13. Which of the following is NOT an aspect of the sick role?

   a. Sick people are not responsible for their condition.
   b. Sick people should want to get well.
   c. Sickness is an undesirable condition.
   d. Sick people should still try to fulfill their role obligations.

14. Preventive medicine makes sense because

   a. small changes in lifestyle can have large effects on the health of a population.
   b. society is getting younger, and young people care more about their health.
   c. it shifts costs from Medicaid to Medicare.
   d. it helps the medicalization of society.

15. When studying medicine and health care, symbolic interactionists look at

   a. the socialization of physicians and nurses.
   b. physician-patient interaction.
   c. social support and recovery from disease.
   d. all of the above.

Identifying Sociological Perspectives on Medicine and Health Care

For each of the following statements, identify the sociological perspective associated with the statement by writing F for functionalist, C for conflict, or SI for symbolic interactionist, in the appropriate blank.

_____ 1. Social networks provide patients with emotional and material support and information about treatments, physicians, and hospitals.

_____ 2. The purpose of medicine is to keep people healthy so that they can serve society.

_____ 3. Medical school provides an intense and stressful introduction to the knowledge, values, and attitudes associated with the medical profession.

_____ 4. Medicine acts as an agent of social control by deciding which people can administer it.

_____ 5. Medicine encourages scientific research and thereby results in better treatments.

_____ 6. Physicians have such great influence that they have a legal monopoly on the prescription of drugs and have prevented nurses from expanding their professional spheres.

True-False

Indicate your response to each of the following statements by circling T for true or F for false.

T F 1. Because sickness places a strain on the social system and on individuals, every society has the institution of medicine.

T F 2. The formation of the American Medical Association reduced gangrene, blood poisoning, and other infections that killed most surgical patients.

T F 3. Physicians occupy the most powerful position in medicine.

T F 4. Those segments of the population that are powerful and wealthy are healthier than those segments that are powerless and poor.

T F 5. Most hospitals have two lines of authority: doctors and nurses.

T F 6. The overlap between race and class is one reason that African Americans have poorer health, on average, than whites.

T F 7. Critics of the concept of the sick role state that, in reality, people are sometimes stigmatized for their illnesses.

T F 8. There is not much variation in patient-doctor interaction from one racial or ethnic group to the next.

T F 9. Focus on preventive medicine will probably decline in postindustrial society.

T F 10. The World Health Organization defines health as a state of physical, mental, and social well-being.

T F 11. Florence Nightingale and Harriet Martineau worked to improve the health care conditions of wounded British soldiers.

T F 12. Cultural competence in health care means the ability of the health care system to provide care tailored to the specific cultural needs of patients with diverse values, beliefs, and behaviors.

T F 13. A basic function of medicine is to keep people healthy so that they can serve society.

T F 14. Conflict theory sees medicine and health care as performing functions for society.

T F 15. Hospitals charge high fees in part because they are large, complex bureaucracies with high costs.

NOTE: The answers to these exercises are at the end of the book.

For additional practice tests and other resources please visit the companion web site at http://www.prenhall.com/curry.

Essay

1. How do communal and associational societies differ in their approach to the treatment of illness and death?
2. Give examples of how social class, race and ethnicity, and gender all impact the quality of health care one receives.
3. What three factors have contributed to the rise in health care costs?
4. While nursing is gaining prestige, what are remaining issues for nurses in health care?
5. Why are physicians increasingly becoming employees rather than being independent professionals?

15

Population, Ecology, and Urbanization

A tiny speck in the South Pacific, Easter Island is one of the most isolated bits of inhabited land in the world. Today, the island is known mainly for the gigantic stone statues that dot its landscape. The Polynesians referred to these statues as moi. They have been a mystery every since Captain Cook came upon the island in 1772.

The people who created the moi came to the island around A.D. 400. At the time of their arrival, the island was heavily forested with palm trees and had abundant marine and bird life. The early settlers enriched the island with domesticated animals, edible plants, and fruit trees. Living in a rich environment, the population grew rapidly and had reached a height of nearly 20,000 people by 1680.

The islanders believed that they could win favor from their gods by constructing moi. Soon, the different clans on the island were competing to build the largest and most splendid statue. The competition grew fierce, and the islanders increasingly had to tax the limited resources of their island. To haul the statues around, the islanders made rope from native shrubs until there were no more shrubs. They cut the trees to use for fuel and to make logs over which they rolled the moi, until all the trees were gone. Without timber, they could not build canoes; and when the old canoes disintegrated, they could no longer fish in the open sea, nor could they leave the island. Deforestation also dried and eroded the soil, causing water to run off the barren land into the sea. Since the land could no longer produce, food became scarce. Soon, the clans began to fight among themselves over food. Their warfare was merciless and savage. Food was so scarce that even the winners had little to eat, and so they ate the dead.

When European explorers visited the island, they found only a windswept, barren land inhabited by some 2,000 people living in caves. The explorers also found the great moi scattered about, but by this time, the statues had been broken and disfigured by warring clans and so became the remnants of a time when the island was forested, beautiful, and bountiful (Bahn and Flenley 1992).

The history of Easter Island illustrates the importance of a society's population in determining what happens to it. When food was abundant, the island could support many people, and so it soon experienced a **population explosion**: a rapid, unchecked growth in the number of people inhabiting an area. As the population expanded, however, the food supply quickly began to run out, triggering a **population implosion**: a rapid, unchecked decline in the number of people inhabiting an area. Although concepts such as these necessarily involve numerical analysis, the lesson of Easter Island further illustrates that numbers ultimately get back to real, living people, and that what happens to some people—even in distant places and a long time ago—has implications for our lives today.

Chapter Preview

In this chapter, we will cover three closely related topics: population, ecology, and urbanization. We begin with the key concepts used in studying the growth and decline of populations—fertility, mortality, and migration. We then explore the issue of whether continual population growth threatens to exhaust the world's resources. Easter Island and the ideas of Robert Malthus play an important part in that discussion. After that, we present an

Three giant moi statues, each weighing 16 tons, face out to the sea on Easter Island. The moi were created by the early settlers of the island, probably Polynesians who came by canoe around A.D. 400. Believing that the moi would look after them, these people overpopulated their island and depleted its resources.

ecological framework for studying the connections between a population and its environment. The last major topic is urbanization and the urban way of life. This topic explores such issues as the quality of life in large urban centers and the very rapid growth of cities. We conclude with a discussion of some trends concerning population growth, environment, and urbanization in the future.

The Great Social Transformation and Population, Ecology, and Urbanization

Although overpopulation is currently a major problem, for most of human history, the earth was big enough and abundant enough to accommodate everyone with relatively little strain. When the first humans began moving onto the open savannas of Africa, the entire human population of the world probably amounted to no more than a few hundred thousand people and was growing very slowly. By about 1000 B.C., the population had expanded to 5 million, but growth was still relatively slow. However, as we saw in Chapters 1 and 2, the shift from agriculture to industrialization was accompanied by many changes. One of the most significant was the increasingly fast rate of population growth. In 1650—generally considered to mark the onset of the industrial era—the world's population was perhaps 500 million. But as industrialization proceeded, growth rapidly increased. By 1800, the world's population had almost doubled from its 1650 level, and by 1900, it had reached 1.7 billion people. Today, the population of the world is some 6.3 billion. Put another way, starting in 1650, it took about 150 years for the population to double, but in this century, it took less than 90 years for it to triple (see Figure 15.1). Present rates of growth cannot continue indefinitely, for at some point the number of deaths will begin to exceed the number of births, and the population will stabilize or, possibly, decrease. The question, therefore, is what will the world be like when these changes occur and the population is held in check? We will address this issue later in this chapter.

Demographic Analysis

Because population is such an important aspect of social life, a separate area of sociology is devoted to it. This area, **demography**, is the scientific study of the size, growth, and composition of the human population (Hauser and Duncan 1959; Stockwell 1976). Although the study of demography involves mathematics and statistics, the goal of most demographers is to understand how social forces affect the population and how the population affects society. For instance, if a society is experiencing rapid growth, we can generally expect the birth rate to be high and the number of young people in the population to be large. Society then will need to direct its resources toward schools, teachers, and child care. But if a society is experiencing slow growth, or no growth, then the number of older persons will be large, and society will have to devote more resources to health problems, retirement funds, and elder care. The sheer size of the population, moreover, may be an important social force in its own right (Organski and Organski 1961:246). For example, a large population provides soldiers for the military, workers for farms and industry, scientists for research, and people to fill the many other roles that must be filled if society is to run smoothly (see Figure 15.2).

In some respects, changes in the population are easy to understand, because only three factors affect it. These factors are fertility, mortality, and migration. Each of these, in turn, is measured by a rate. Some of these rates are tedious to calculate even with a computer and, in any case, are difficult to understand. In the next section, therefore, we will confine ourselves to discussing just the basic rates. (See Figure 15.3 for a description of a basic demographic tool, the population pyramid.)

Population explosion ▲ A rapid, unchecked growth in the number of people inhabiting an area.

Population implosion ▲ A rapid, unchecked decline in the number of people inhabiting an area.

Demography ▲ The scientific study of the size, growth, and composition of the human population.

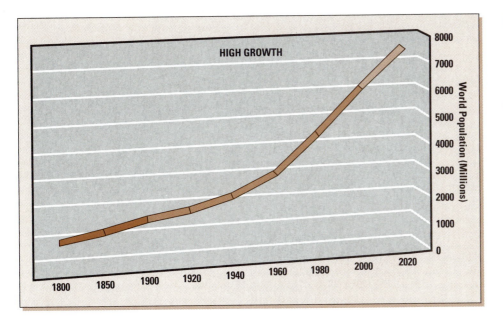

FIGURE 15.1 Growth of the Earth's Population

The world's population increased dramatically during the twentieth century, and projections indicate that the growth will continue well into the twenty-first century.

The annual growth rate of the world's population peaked in 1980 and began to decline. Even so, that does not mean that the world's population will also decline. Instead, it will continue to grow, but at a slower pace than in the past.

Even with a declining growth rate, every year millions of people are added to the earth's population. In 2000, some 70 million people were added annually, and by 2040 approximately 40 million people will be added annually.

CQ *What implication do these data have for the future of the "population problem?"* ◆ *Do they suggest that the problem will be solved by the middle of the twenty-first century, and that we no longer need to worry about it?*

SOURCE: InfoTrac 8th edition by Weeks. Copyright © 2002. Reprinted with permission of Wadsworth, a division of Thomson Learning: www.thomsonrights.com. Fax 1-800-730-2215.

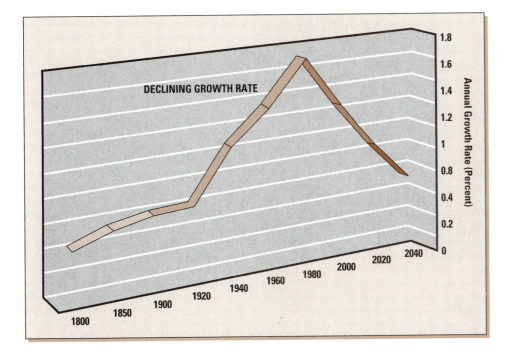

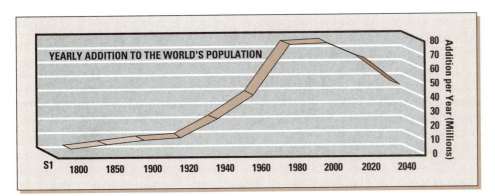

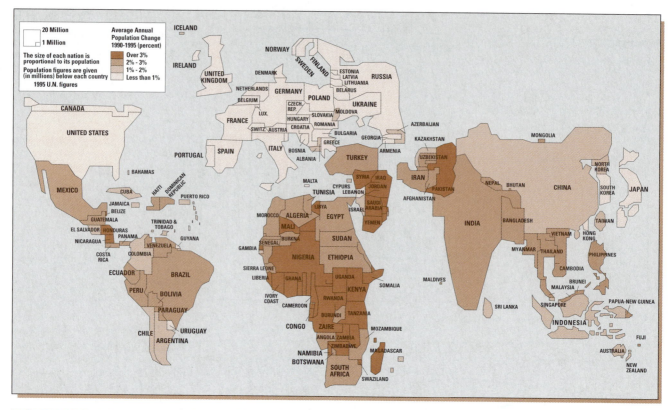

FIGURE 15.2 A Cartogram of the World Population

In Figure 15.2, the size of the population of each country determines its relative size on the map. Maps such as this one that convert statistical data to graphic form are termed cartograms. Figure 15.2 also uses color coding to convey information about the rate of annual population increase. In looking at the map, you can see quickly not only which countries contain large populations but also which ones are growing rapidly. For instance, India, whose population is over 900 million and growing rapidly, dwarfs the United States and Russia, whose populations and growth rates are lower.

SOURCES: Data from the World Resource Institute, *World Resources 1994–1995* (New York: Oxford University Press, 1994), pp. 268–269; Edward F. Bergman, *Human Geography: Cultures, Connections, and Landscapes,* © 1995. Reprinted by permission of Prentice-Hall, Inc., Upper Saddle River, NJ.

Fertility

You probably have a general understanding of this term already, but demographers use it in a technical sense. Strictly speaking, **fertility** is the number of births that occur over a specific period, usually one year. This topic is probably studied more than any other in demography because it has the greatest long-term impact on the growth or decline of a population. And because only women can bear children, fertility is usually discussed mainly in relation to women.

The period in a woman's life when she is capable of having children is between the onset of menstruation and the onset of menopause—or roughly thirty years. During this period, a woman could conceivably bear approximately thirty children, but that number would be extremely rare. If you believe the *Guinness Book of Records,* however, in the eighteenth century, a Russian woman was pregnant 27 times and had 69 children.

With regard to social groups, the Hutterites are one of the most fertile on record. They are a religious sect that migrated to the United States from Switzerland in the late nineteenth century. During the 1930s, each Hutterite woman bore an average of 12 children, a level far above that which is found today even in the high-fertility

Fertility ▲ The number of births that occur over a specific period, usually one year.

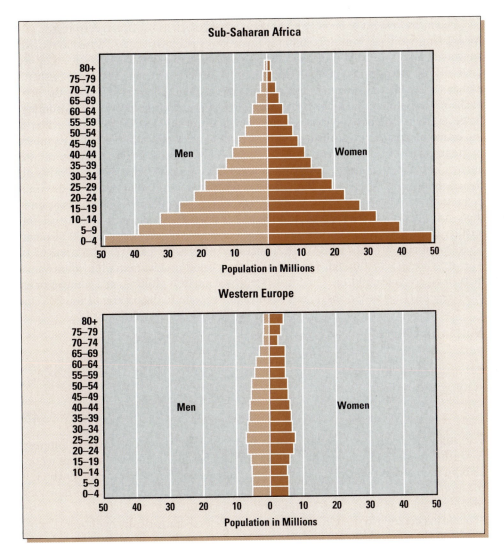

Sub-Saharan Africa

Men | Women

80+
75–79
70–74
65–69
60–64
55–59
50–54
45–49
40–44
35–39
30–34
25–29
20–24
15–19
10–14
5–9
0–4

50 40 30 20 10 0 10 20 30 40 50

Population in Millions

Western Europe

Men | Women

80+
75–79
70–74
65–69
60–64
55–59
50–54
45–49
40–44
35–39
30–34
25–29
20–24
15–19
10–14
5–9
0–4

50 40 30 20 10 0 10 20 30 40 50

Population in Millions

FIGURE 15.3 **The Population Pyramid**

Demographers often provide a graphic display of a society's population through a figure called a population pyramid. The pyramid shows the number of men and women for each five-year age group in the population. These two illustrations show the population pyramids for two world regions—Africa south of the Sahara Desert, and Western Europe. In comparing the two pyramids, we learn the following: (1) there are many more people in sub-Saharan Africa than there are in Western Europe, because the total area represented by sub-Saharan Africa is much larger; (2) the population of sub-Saharan Africa is much younger than is Western Europe's population, because proportionately more people in the African population as compared with Western Europe's population are concentrated in the base of the pyramid, which represents the younger age groups; and (3) the sub-Saharan African population has a greater potential for future growth than does Western Europe, because so many more Africans than Europeans are presently in the younger age groups and have yet to go through their own childbearing years.

CQ *How is Western Europe's low fertility level reflected in its population pyramid?*

SOURCE: *Population Bulletin* vol. 49, no. 4 (1994). Reprinted by permission of the Population Reference Bureau.

regions of the world. In large part, the Hutterites' fertility was due to their strict religious beliefs, sound health practices, and early marriages (Weeks 1998).

American culture once placed a high value on large families, but those values have changed. American women now marry at an older age than they used to, and many of them work full-time after having children. The difficulty and cost of supporting a large family has also acted as a brake on American fertility. Consequently, the average birthrate for women in the United States works out to slightly less than two children per woman during a lifetime. This rate is below *replacement level*: the number of children required to replace the population as people die. Were it not for the steady stream of immigrants who arrive here each year, the American population would eventually grow smaller.

Men and women who wish deliberately to control their fertility must rely on sexual abstinence or contraception. The most effective method of contraception is oral contraceptives, commonly called "the pill," but it is not foolproof. Approximately 2 percent of couples using it experience a pregnancy. Another way to control fertility is through abortion. Even though it is illegal in many places, and has become a political issue, abortion is the single most used method of birth control worldwide (Oaks 2003). For instance, in Kenya, strict antiabortion laws make family planning available only to married women. Unwed pregnant women have few options and may choose to terminate their pregnancy with an illegal and often unsafe abortion. As a result, abortion is responsible for one-third of the maternal deaths in Kenya (Lorch 1995; Sibanda 1999).

The measurement of fertility is based on records such as baptismal certificates, entries in family Bibles, or most commonly nowadays, birth certificates. Whereas records are generally well kept in wealthy industrial nations, in less wealthy societies they are often inaccurate or not kept at all. In those places, authorities are reluctant to spend money for a seemingly meaningless task; and even when money is available, the people keeping the records may be poorly educated and not highly motivated. Assuming, however, that the necessary records are available, the simplest measure of fertility is the **crude birthrate**: the annual number of births in a population per 1,000 members of the population. For instance, in 2000, the crude birthrate for the United States was about 15; that is, there were 15 births for every 1,000 people in the country. Although the crude birthrate is easy to compute, it is not very precise. It is based on the total population, which includes men, babies, and elders—people who cannot bear children. For that reason, demographers often prefer a more sensitive measure: the general fertility ratio. This is the annual number of births in a population per 1,000 women aged 15 through 44 years. In 2000, the **general fertility ratio** for U.S. women was 67.6. The age category 15 through 44 represents the period in a woman's life when she is most likely to have children. Obviously, some women bear children at a younger or an older age, but the exceptions do not occur often enough to distort the measure.

Mortality

> Declining mortality, not rising fertility, is the root cause of current world population growth. It is not that people breed like rabbits; rather, they no longer die like flies.
>
> (Weeks 1986:142)

The study of death or mortality strikes many people as a rather morbid interest. Nevertheless, death is important to demographers because it affects the size of a population. In analyzing this topic, demographers distinguish between **mortality**, which is the number of deaths that occur during a year, and **life expectancy**, which is how long people probably will live.

Life expectancy in the United States has increased dramatically over time. For instance, at the turn of the century, the average person probably lived 49 years, whereas today the figure is 76 years. This figure varies, however, according to race and sex. Women live longer than men, and whites live longer than African Americans. Thus, a white male now has a life expectancy of 74 years, a white female 79 years, a black male 68 years, and a black female 76 years. Although some of these differences might have genetic origins, most are due to differences in lifestyle, wealth, education, and access to health care. We discuss these factors in Chapters 6, 7, and 14.

There are many conflicting and exaggerated claims to longevity, but there are well-documented cases of a Japanese man who lived to be 119 years old and a French woman who lived to be 120 years old. Because at least a few people have reached those ages, the **life span**—the theoretical maximum length of life—could be that long (Weeks 1998). In other words, even though life expectancy is increasing, there is plenty of room for it to increase even more.

The most critical portion of life is the first year. During this period, infants are highly susceptible to infectious diseases, poor diet, and lack of care. Although diseases have biological causes, social factors are responsible for spreading diseases. As we discuss in Chapter 14, relatively simple practices, such as washing your hands and covering your mouth when you sneeze, have greatly reduced the spread of communicable diseases and the incidence of infections.

After the first year of life, mortality declines and stays low for a considerable duration. For the young and middle aged in contemporary societies, the major cause of death is not sickness, but accidents, warfare, or catastrophe. To illustrate, in the United States, car crashes and other accidents are the leading causes of death from the ages of 1 to 39 (U.S. Bureau of the Census 2000). Mortality begins to increase after

Crude birthrate ▲ The annual number of births in a population per 1,000 members of the population.

General fertility ratio ▲ The annual number of births in a population per 1,000 women aged 15 through 44 years.

Mortality ▲ The number of deaths that occur during a year.

Life expectancy ▲ How long people probably will live.

Life span ▲ The theoretical maximum length of life.

middle age, and as people near their life expectancy, it increases dramatically. In wealthier societies, death results mainly from heart problems, cancer, stroke, and infections of the respiratory system. In less wealthy societies, the main causes are infectious diseases and the consequences of malnutrition.

As with fertility, the measurement of mortality is based on records that are often inaccurate or not kept at all. But if the correct information is available, the **crude death rate** is easily calculated. It is the annual number of deaths per 1,000 members of the population. In 2003, for instance, the United States rate was 9 deaths per 1,000, whereas in Mexico it was 5 per 1,000. The reason is that the United States has an aging population, but Mexico does not: roughly 13 percent of the U.S. population is 65 or older, whereas only 5 percent of the Mexican population is in that age range. As with the crude fertility rate, demographers would prefer a more refined measure of mortality, but often the crude rate is the only one available.

When demographers compare the number of people being added to the population through birth with the number of people leaving the population through death, a very powerful index of population change is obtained. It is called **natural increase**: the number of births in a given time period minus the number of deaths in the population for the same time period. When births exceed deaths, there is natural increase. When the number of deaths exceeds the number of births, there is **natural decrease**. For example, in the United States in 2000, there were 5 million births and 3 million deaths. Thus, the United States was experiencing natural increase.

Migration

Of the three factors that can change the size of a population, migration is undoubtedly the most controversial at the present time. Technically, **migration** is the movement of people from one area of residence to another; **immigration** is the movement of people into a place; and **emigration** is the movement of people out of a place. To illustrate these differences in U.S. terms, migration consists of emigrants who leave their homeland and immigrate to the United States.

Because migration of all types is increasing, there are now Turkish migrants in Scandinavia and Germany; Pakistani and Indian migrants in Great Britain; Indian migrants in Uganda, South Africa, and other African countries; Arab migrants in France; Chinese migrants in Vietnam, Thailand, Japan, and other Asian nations; and Filipino migrants in Kuwait. Thus, countries are becoming increasingly diverse, and this trend will probably continue well into this century.

People migrate for two broad reasons. The first reason, called *push factors*, are the reasons for leaving a place. Although there may be any number of personal reasons for leaving, the underlying reasons are mostly political and economic. For instance, during the nineteenth century, the failure of the potato crop in Ireland "pushed" thousands of Irish to the United States. *Pull factors*, on the other hand, are the forces that attract migrants to a place, such as a congenial government or good weather conditions. Push and pull factors work together. People being pushed from one place will, if they have a choice, go to places that have many pull factors.

Historically, the United States has received immigrants in large numbers. Between 1901 and 2000, for example, more than 67 million people came to the United States, by far the largest number of people to be accepted into any country in that time period (U.S. Bureau of the Census 1994, 2002). Many of these people immigrated to the United States to seek a better life. Early Chinese immigrants, for instance, called the United States the Gold Mountain because they thought that they would migrate, prosper, and then return to China secure for life (Chapter 7).

Although migration across national boundaries receives the most attention, people can also move from place to place within a country or society. This type of movement is called *internal migration*. In the United States, the pattern of internal migration has mainly consisted of movement from the Atlantic coast to the Pacific coast. This east-to-west flow has been taking place since colonial times, and today about one

Crude death rate ▲ The annual number of deaths per 1,000 members of the population.

Natural increase ▲ The number of births in a population in a given time period minus the number of deaths in the population for the same time period, where births exceed deaths.

Natural decrease ▲ The situation in which the number of deaths in a population exceeds the number of births.

Migration ▲ The movement of people from one area of residence to another.

Immigration ▲ The movement of people into a place.

Emigration ▲ The movement of people out of a place.

American in five lives in the West. Early in the twentieth century, a substantial south-to-north migration also took place as African Americans moved from the agricultural South to find better jobs in the industrializing North. Currently, however, this migration stream is flowing in the opposite direction. Improvements in economic and social conditions in the South are the most common reasons cited for the reversal. Another reason is the popularity of Florida, Arizona, Texas, New Mexico, and other so-called Sun Belt states as retirement havens.

Compared with fertility and mortality, migration is difficult to measure, for three reasons. First, although the federal government monitors the flow of legal immigrants into the United States, no one knows how many illegal immigrants enter the country clandestinely. Second, there is the problem of how to designate people who make temporary, short moves. For example, should college students who move home for the summer but return to the dormitory in the fall be counted as internal migrants? Although the answer is debatable, the federal government classifies such students as "movers" rather than as migrants. Finally, in the United States and many other countries, people have the right to move about freely and are not required to report their residence to a central authority. Consequently, few records about migration exist, making it difficult to gather reliable and current data on internal migration.

If proper data are available, the **net migration rate** may be calculated as the annual difference between the number of people who enter a place and the number who leave, per 1,000 people of that place. For instance, in 2000, the net migration rate was 3; that is, 3 more people (per 1,000 residents) moved to the United States than left the United States. This figure has been roughly the same for the past 30 years. Even though the media often describe migration to the United States as a "clamor at the gates," "a flood of people," or a "swelling horde," the amount of migration will probably remain the same or will slightly decline over the next 50 years (U.S. Bureau of the Census 2000).

Although a net migration rate of 3 hardly constitutes a flood, over a prolonged period the total number of immigrants in the country could increase substantially. Most of the controversy over immigration, however, has focused on short-term effects. Despite the accumulated evidence showing that immigrants usually take jobs that native-born groups do not want, some politicians insist that immigrants threaten the jobs of those in the middle class (Bean and Bell-Rose 2000). The number of illegal immigrants in the United States, as mentioned, is unknown, but the figure might be

Net migration rate ▲ The annual difference between how many people enter a place and how many leave, per 1,000 people of that place.

roughly 5 million. Although 5 million is a large number, it amounts to only 2 percent of the total U.S. population—hardly the "horde" that many politicians would have us imagine. In the light of statistics such as these, many sociologists suspect that anti-immigration rhetoric is simply a disguised appeal to racism—a topic we discuss in Chapter 7 (see also Foner et al. 2000).

The Demographic Transition and the Growth of Population

At the beginning of this chapter, we briefly discussed the great increase in world population since the advent of the industrial era. We now wish to explain in more detail how the growth in population came about. Essentially, it involves the link between the birthrate and the death rate. From studying this rate over time, especially in Europe, demographers have identified a growth pattern they call the **demographic transition**. The demographic transition proceeds through four stages:

Stage 1. *Preindustrial—High Birthrate and High Death Rate.* This stage describes the stable populations found in preindustrial societies. In such societies, medical science was not available, nor could much be done to lessen the impact of famine, floods, droughts, and other factors that directly controlled the food supply. Under these conditions, the death rate was high. The birthrate was also high because more people meant more labor, and more labor meant a higher standard of living for the family. An additional motive for high fertility was security in old age. Children typically supported their parents when they could no longer work. Under conditions of high mortality, however, parents had to have many children in order to ensure that a few survived into adulthood. The overall result of these social forces was that the high death rate offset the high birthrate and that the population neither increased nor decreased dramatically.

Stage 2. *Transitional—High Birthrate and Declining Death Rate.* The second stage of the demographic transition characterizes societies as they move from the communal to the transitional. People continue to value large families, but the material reasons for having children decline. At the same time, advances in technology, medicine, and social conditions cause the death rate to fall. Deaths then no longer offset births, and the population begins rapidly to rise as a sustained natural increase adds large numbers of people to the population.

Stage 3. *Transitional—Declining Birthrate and Low Death Rate.* This is a period of smaller families as societies move from the traditional toward the associational form of organization. The gap between fertility and mortality declines, and by the end of this stage, the population is growing at a very slow rate of natural increase. Mortality approaches a minimum level because of advances in health care, nutrition, steady food surpluses, and prenatal care.

Stage 4. *Industrial—Low Birth and Death Rates.* In the final stage of the demographic transition, both birthrates and mortality rates are low. Although the population might periodically show slight gains or losses, over the long run, it neither grows nor declines. In short, the population has stabilized. This stage is typical of industrial societies.

The demographic transition is not so much a theory as a description of European history. It therefore might not apply to other societies. But if the European experience is repeated, the theory offers a basis for optimism. In 1992, to illustrate, transitional societies were characterized by high birthrates, but their death rates were relatively low, or about the same as those of the industrialized nations. This situation resembles Stage 2 of the demographic transition. Presumably, as greater industrialization takes place, the birthrates of the transitional societies will decline, and they will move into Stage 4 of the demographic transition. At that point, their populations will be stable (Bongaarts and Bulatao 1999; Caldwell 1999; Heuveline 1999; see Figure 15.4).

Demographic transition ▲ The change through time in the dynamics of population growth in a society from high fertility and high mortality to low fertility and low mortality.

This illustration is from an old print, circa 1900. It shows women operating massive mill machinery. The industrial revolution transformed the textile industry. Prior to the coming of the mills, textiles were produced at home. As women and men left the home to work in the factories, urban areas expanded, and family life changed.

● ■ ▲ **Pausing to Think** **About Demographic Analysis**

Demographic change is closely related to social change, and the goal of most demographers is to understand how social forces affect the population and how, in turn, the population affects society. Demographers focus on three basic factors: fertility, mortality, and migration. According to the theory of the demographic transition, as societies move from preindustrial to industrial, changes in mortality and fertility cause them to go through a series of stages that eventually end in a stable population.

CQ Are you concerned about the population explosion? ◆ How do you think that situation will affect your life in the next century?

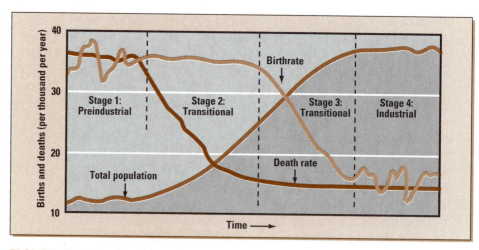

FIGURE 15.4 Demographic Transition Model

High birth and death rates characterize Stage 1 (preindustrial) of the demographic transition model. During Stages 2 and 3 (transitional), death rates drop to lower levels, while birthrates remain high. In Stage 4 (industrial), birthrates have come into balance with death rates. Meanwhile, as this figure shows, the total population has skyrocketed because of the difference between birth and death rates. Experts disagree about whether this model will apply to all countries undergoing industrialization or whether it applies mainly to the demographic history of Northern European countries.

SOURCE: Paul L. Knox and Sallie A. Marston, *Places and Regions in Global Context*, © 1998. Adapted by permission of Prentice-Hall, Inc., Upper Saddle River, NJ.

Population Growth and the Environment

Population affects the quality of our lives, in large part, through affecting our society's **ecosystem**: an interlocking, stable group of plants and animals—including humans—living in their natural habitat. The relationship between population and ecosystem was foretold by Thomas Robert Malthus (1766–1834), a parson, an economist, and an academic. Had he known about the example of Easter Island that was described at the beginning of this chapter, he would not have been surprised. Those events aptly illustrate many of his ideas about population growth and the environment.

The Malthusian Trap

Malthus lived during the Industrial Revolution and was influenced by the poverty, misery, and wretched working conditions he saw all around him. The source of the misery, according to him, was overpopulation. He said that when the population is small, there are enough resources to sustain everyone at a comfortable level. But when the population is large, those same resources must be spread so thinly throughout the society that most people live in poverty and distress.

Malthus further noted that the human population is capable of very rapid growth. To illustrate this growth, consider that each of us has two biological parents, each of our parents has two parents, each of our parents' parents has two parents, and so forth. Mathematically, this sequence of numbers is a geometric progression, much like the string of numbers 2, 4, 8, 16, 32, 64, 128. . . . Malthus further believed that raw land—the major source of food in an agrarian society—can be brought into production only one parcel at a time. This process is relatively slow and laborious. It approximates an arithmetic rate of increase, similar to the numbers 2, 4, 6, 8, 10, 12, 14. . . . Comparing the two strings of numbers, we can see that after seven steps, the geometric progression reaches 128, whereas the arithmetic progression reaches only 14. These contrasting strings of numbers, which can represent the growth of the population and its food supply, led Malthus to an inescapable conclusion: if nothing were done, the population would quickly outgrow its food supply, and everyone would starve.

What could be done to avoid this fate? Malthus believed that the solution to the problem was contained in the laws of nature and society. This solution, however, was not very comforting. He predicted that as the population grew, certain "positive checks" would eventually increase the death rate and reduce population size. These positive checks consisted of famine, war, and plague. He allowed for the possibility of slowing population growth by "preventive checks," practices that included postponement of marriage and abstinence from sex within marriage. He was not very optimistic about the preventive checks, however, and he was especially dubious about sexual restraint.

Malthus suggested that most societies were doomed to alternating periods of prosperity followed by periods of famine, war, and plague. Once the positive checks had reduced the population sufficiently, prosperity would return. But when prosperity returned, the population would grow once more until another cycle of famine, war, and plague again reduced its size. Clearly, Malthus painted a grim picture of the future, and soon he was known as the "Gloomy Parson."

Malthus's ideas provide a good perspective for understanding what happened on Easter Island; fortunately, though, what happened there has not come true for the rest of the world. With advances in industrialization, children have lost their value as extra work hands, and the birthrate has not continued to increase as Malthus feared. Advanced technology has increased food production tremendously, an outcome that Malthus did not consider in his calculations. However, the fact that Malthus's predictions have not yet come true for the world in general does not mean that they will not, or have not, come true for many of the world's societies.

Ecosystem ▲ An interlocking, stable group of plants and animals living in their natural habitat.

The Contemporary Debate over Malthus's Predictions

Malthus lived over a hundred years ago, but his writings nevertheless continue to draw the attention of scholars and policy makers (Petersen 1998). Although sociologists do not agree with everything he wrote, the core of his ideas may be used to analyze the relationship between the environment and population growth. Currently, the controversy over population and resources pits one school of thought, the so-called neo-Malthusian, against another school, the so-called Cornucopian (cf. Schnaiberg 1980).

According to the Cornucopian view, human inventiveness will cope with any scarcities caused by overpopulation. Cornucopians support their position by citing the success of the "Green Revolution." (Das 2002) This term refers to the new plants, improved fertilizers, better soil preparation, and other changes in agriculture that have vastly increased farm productivity. Between 1960 and 1986, for instance, the world's grain harvests doubled even though the amount of land under cultivation actually declined. In India between 1980 and 1990, more good land was taken out of production than was actually used. Such savings bode well for the future, because most of the good lands in the world are already being farmed. On the basis of the experience of the Green Revolution and other technological advances, proponents of the Cornucopian view conclude that the earth can support more than twice the number of people now on the planet.

Although neo-Malthusians recognize the benefits of the Green Revolution, they emphasize two environmental trends. The first trend concerns the consequences of relying on technology as a cure for scarcity. They point out that the Green Revolution makes heavy use of chemical fertilizers and hybrid plants. These chemicals pollute the environment and use water extravagantly; moreover, hybrid plants drive out native vegetation. They further point out that the mechanization of agriculture gives an enormous advantage to large, corporate farms but leaves little for small farmers (Gore 1992; Lewis 1992).

The second trend is equally ominous. Neo-Malthusians say that a Malthusian disaster is not something we have to wait for; in fact, it is already happening. This recognition also increasingly emphasizes the pivotal role of women. Because only women can bear children, nowhere in the world are the costs and risks of childbirth shared equally by men and women. However, in many societies, the sharing is extremely unequal. In sub-Saharan Africa, for example, a woman will typically bear six to eight children during her lifetime, but because life expectancy is about 50 years, she will either be pregnant or breast-feeding an infant for half of her adult life. In addition, the possibility of dying during the birth process is far from negligible. In these societies, the chance that a woman will survive through her reproductive years is about one in six.

This boy is transplanting rice in Bihar, India. Because children provide valuable labor in many developing countries, larger families mean more family workers. A growing population, however, puts added stress on the environment and creates more people to feed, a process that in turn encourages people to have even larger families.

Given the high risks and costs associated with childbearing, it would make sense for these women to reduce their fertility. But just the opposite is now occurring. Lacking power, these women have no choice but to produce children who can contribute to the family's welfare. To illustrate, in some parts of India, young children tend animals, care for younger siblings, fetch water, and collect firewood. Their labor is extremely valuable, and by age 10 to 15, many will work longer hours than most adults.

A growing population, of course, puts stress on the environment. To collect wood, children have to trek farther and farther because the nearest trees are the first to be cut down. As nearby wells dry up and become polluted, wearisome trips to far-off water sources must be made. And as the soil becomes depleted, more hours are required to farm land that yields less and less. To accomplish these increasingly difficult tasks, people need additional workers, and hence they have more children. These additions to the population, in turn, stress the environment even more . . . and the cycle goes on (Dasgupta 1995). Figure 15.5 depicts the size of the population in industrial and nonindustrial traditional and transitional societies. It is in the latter societies where neo-Malthusians find the greatest likelihood of famine, war, and plague.

Human Ecology

The contemporary debate pitting Cornucopians against neo-Malthusians represents one aspect of a broad perspective in sociology. This perspective, called **human ecology**, examines the relationship between society and the environment. It rests on the assumption that groups cooperate and compete with each other for the use of environmental resources. It further assumes that interplay between social and environmental forces determines what happens to the environment and what happens to society. For instance, the controversy over timbering in the old forests of the Pacific Northwest pits private forestry companies against conservation groups. Forestry companies are seeking profits, whereas conservation groups want to keep the forests for their aesthetic and social value.

Over 30 years ago, the ecological approach was applied to the problem of air pollution in metropolitan Los Angeles. Starting from the ecological premise that environment and society affect each other through competition, Otis Dudley Duncan (1959) proposed a model that consisted of four factors: population (P), social organization (O), environment (E), and technology (T). This model is called "POET" for short. Duncan applied the POET model to the problem of Los Angeles smog, as follows:

1. *Population* Migration had caused the Los Angeles population to grow enormously.

2. *Organization* Although Los Angeles had a system of public transportation, for the most part, people traveled around in their private cars.

3. *Environment* Los Angeles is ringed by mountains that trap and concentrate the polluted air, thereby intensifying its effects.

4. *Technology* The relatively inefficient gasoline engine created by-products that combine with sunlight to form toxic chemicals and smog.

Each of these four factors by itself could produce smog, but when all four of them interacted, the smog problem greatly intensified. For example, as the population of Los Angeles increased and people chose to use cars as their primary means of transportation, the demand for public transportation fell, and the demand for cars increased. More cars required more roads, freeways, and parking lots, which made driving more convenient and increased the demand for cars even more. Especially before the development of pollution controls for automobiles, the gasoline engine was highly inefficient and gave off large amounts of pollution. Consequently, as the number of cars increased, the amount of pollutants in the air increased. This polluted air was trapped over

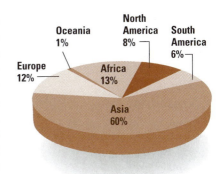

FIGURE 15.5 World Population: Where People Live

The people are not evenly spread across the earth. The majority of people in the world live in Asia, and only 1 percent live in Oceania

SOURCE: U.S. Bureau of the Census 2002.

123 **STUDY TIP**

Outline and describe the four factors of the POET model developed by Otis Dudley Duncan. Following the example in the text (how the POET model was applied to Los Angeles smog), name another environmental issue and analyze it using the POET model.

Human ecology ▲ The study of the relationship between society and the environment.

Trapped by surrounding mountains, smog accumulates in the Los Angeles basin. Although technological strides have reduced smog considerably, the growing population undermines the progress that is made.

Los Angeles because the surrounding mountains prevented it from leaving the area. The result was a hazy, murky atmosphere that caused breathing problems and burning lungs. On certain smoggy days, schoolchildren were kept indoors, and adults were advised not to run or otherwise strain themselves. The smog also laid down a thin layer of pollution on buildings, cars, plants, and anything else that was outdoors.

The response to the smog problem required changes in technology and social organization. The city responded organizationally by enacting laws that restricted business activities during periods of heavy smog, whereas the state responded by setting extremely tight emission standards for new cars sold in California. The development of the catalytic converter offered a technological boost by eliminating some 90 percent of smog-producing pollutants before they escaped into the air. Unfortunately, nothing could be done to alter environmental factors. A few people proposed drilling huge tunnels through the mountains to create fresh air passages, and others proposed using atomic power to blast out canyons for the same purpose. These proposals were never taken seriously.

In all, human ecology offers a viewpoint that is especially well suited to analyzing environmental problems caused by human activity. It points to the importance of both social and technological factors, and of the interplay among them. With environmental problems multiplying worldwide, among scholars there is currently a resurgence of interest in the sociology of the environment and the ecological approach (Gelbspan 2000; for additional materials on threats to the environment such as global warming and acid rain, see the Sociology Online box).

Attitudes about the Environment

The decades of the 1960s and 1970s were important turning points in changing American attitudes toward the environment (Potter 2000). The environmental movement, which is discussed in Chapter 16, galvanized public opinion about the dangers of pollution and the deteriorating quality of life. Currently, most people in the United States are environmentally concerned, at least to some extent. Only one-third of adults in the United States believe that we are overly concerned about the environment; some three-fifths feel that the pollution of the waterways is dangerous; and about three-fourths believe that the government should pass laws to make business protect the environment, even if doing so interferes with businesses' rights to make their own decisions (Kirn 2000; NORC 1994).

Unfortunately, positive attitudes about the environment do not always translate into action. Although most people say that they support efforts to save the environment, most of them are not very willing to make substantial personal sacrifices to do so. If saving the environment means paying higher taxes or higher prices, or suffering a decrease in their standard of living, most Americans express an unwillingness to act (NORC 1994). Perhaps reflecting these ambivalent feelings on the part of voters,

Sociology Online

www

Go online to the web site for the Environmental Protection Agency (EPA). You know you have arrived at the correct location when you see the EPA logo. The EPA site contains a vast amount of information. We suggest you begin by clicking on Browse EPA Topics, then on Air. There are several choices to make here, and all of them deal with environmental issues that impact our world. For instance, you can choose the Global Warming Home Page. Here you can learn about the Climate system, the emission problem, the impacts of global warming,

and what actions are being taken. After you have explored several of these sites, answer the following questions:

What is meant by "Global Warming"?

What are "Greenhouse Gases"?

How serious a threat do these gases pose?

What is being done?

What can you do?

Water May Be Dangerous to Your Health

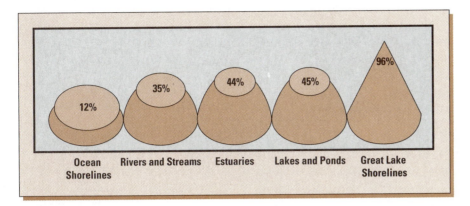

Despite substantial progress, the quality of the environment still remains questionable. This chart indicates that almost all the shorelines of the Great Lakes are polluted, and that almost half of all lakes and ponds also are polluted (EPA 1998, *Report to Congress*).

CQ Conflict theorists would say that pollution is primarily caused by private businesses that put profit ahead of the public good. Do you agree? ◆ Why or why not?

politicians are moving toward deregulating industry and loosening environmental controls (Chapter 9). Ironically, even those people who express great concern for the environment do not always behave in the appropriate manner. In a clever study, a researcher interviewed nearly 500 people in a public place and found that 94 percent of them favored cleaning trash from the streets. Yet when these same people finished the interview, fewer than 2 percent of them bothered to pick up the trash that the researcher had quietly planted in their path. When asked why they had refused to pick up the trash, respondents said it was somebody else's responsibility (Bickman 1972; Forsyth 1995; see the Society Today box).

● ■ ▲ Pausing to Think About Population Growth and the Environment

According to Thomas Robert Malthus, the human population is capable of growing so rapidly that it may outpace the ability of the environment to support it. Cornucopians believe that human ingenuity will overcome any problems caused by overpopulation, whereas neo-Malthusians believe the opposite. Human ecology is a branch of sociology that pays particular attention to the relationships among population, social organization, the environment, and technology. Most people in the United States are environmentally concerned, yet most of them are reluctant to make any personal sacrifices to benefit the environment.

CQ Thinking back to the Easter Island example, could you explain what happened there in terms of the POET model? ◆ Do you see any similarities to what has happened in Los Angeles?

Urbanization

When we think about the great cities of the past, we often think of Athens, Carthage, and Rome, while overlooking the great cities created by Native Americans. For example, by A.D. 1000, the Mississippian people of North America had established a

Monks Mound at Cahokia. For several hundred years, Cahokia was a major Native American city. Today the site has been abandoned, and the people who lived there have long since been absorbed into other Native American groups.

string of communities along the Mississippi, Ohio, Missouri, Tennessee, Arkansas, and Red rivers. This river network formed a complex trade route that linked the Gulf of Mexico to the Great Lakes and the eastern seaboard. At the center of trade stood the city of Cahokia, located along the Mississippi River across from today's St. Louis.

Cahokia was continuously inhabited for 700 years, and at its peak more than 10,000 people lived within it, governed by an elite class of war chiefs, politicians, and religious figures. The most powerful of these leaders was the absolute ruler, or "Great Sun." He and his family lived on the flattened top of a ten-story-tall earthen mound that had a base larger than that of an Egyptian pyramid. From there, the Great Sun extended his rule beyond Cahokia to cover thousands of square miles and to touch the lives of millions of people.

Although Cahokia was a great city, by the sixteenth century, it lay in ruins. Over time, the city was gradually abandoned, and its inhabitants were absorbed into the many different Native American groups living in North America. No one knows precisely why Cahokia collapsed, but researchers speculate that the city might have grown so large that it could no longer sustain itself (Josephy 1994).

Despite its size and importance, Cahokia was not like New York, Beijing, or Tokyo. Although it was huge for its time, now it would be classified as a small urban place, or perhaps as a large rural community. And whereas life in modern cities is driven by scientific technology and associational relationships, life in Cahokia was preindustrial, traditional, and communal—characteristics that described Native American society as a whole.

Although cities such as Cahokia contained only a small proportion of the population, they represent the beginning of a major, worldwide trend that is still going on: **urbanization**, or the increase in the percentage of the population residing in cities. A **city**, in turn, is a large and densely settled concentration of people. In this section, we will first examine the historical development of the city, and then we will examine the nature of urbanization in traditional and industrial societies. We conclude the section with a discussion of the quality of urban life.

The Historical City

As we discussed in Chapter 2, for the largest part of human history, people sustained themselves by hunting and gathering, a mode of subsistence that required everyone's

Urbanization ▲ The increase in the percentage of the population residing in cities.

City ▲ A large, densely settled concentration of people.

participation. But even with everyone contributing, hunting and gathering was not efficient enough for the group to accumulate large surpluses of food. With the rise of horticultural and agrarian societies, however, the situation changed. Now it was possible for some surplus to accumulate, and with the accumulated surplus on hand, a few people could be spared from the daily grind of producing food. Thus freed, these individuals could serve as political and religious leaders, construct permanent shelters, create art, and develop technology. With some surplus, moreover, people began to form permanent settlements, and a few of these settlements grew large and were transformed into something we might call a city (Palen 2002).

The first cities apparently evolved in the valleys of the great river systems—the lower Tigris and Euphrates (3500 B.C.), the Nile (3300 B.C.), the Indus (2500 B.C.), the Huangho (1650 B.C.)—and in Mesoamerica (200 B.C.). Several favorable conditions encouraged urban development in these places. The terrain, climate, and technology enabled farmers to produce enough food to feed themselves, with enough left over to feed people living in the city. In addition, some of these cities were strategically located along the key trade routes of antiquity. One of the more recent of these legendary trade route cities was Tombouctoo ("Timbuctoo" in modern slang). It was situated on the Niger River, where the river bends north into the Sahara Desert. First settled around A.D. 1000, it prospered for centuries as a point of departure for camel caravans trekking across the Sahara. The city withered, however, when alternative sea routes around Africa were discovered in the fifteenth century (Bergman and McKnight 1993; Spielmann and Eder 1994).

With the rise of the Roman Empire, urbanization spread throughout Europe. Many contemporary cities, such as London, Brussels, Utrecht, and Seville, originated as forts, administrative centers, and trading towns of the Roman Empire (Schwab 1992; Sjoberg 1960). By contemporary standards, these early cities were small. For instance, Rome probably never exceeded 350,000 people, a population size surpassed by 48 American cities today (U.S. Bureau of the Census 2002). Despite their small size, however, these early cities forever changed the organization of society in several ways.

Before gunpowder, walled cities were virtually impregnable to direct assault, and people would flee to them as natural points of defense whenever danger threatened. Cities were also centers of government. Secure in the city, rulers could extend their power over the hinterlands and dominate vast expanses of territory. Cities were also the seat of religion, and many important religious ceremonies were held there. A few authors even argue that religion was the main reason that cities came into existence (Mumford 1961:10). Because people were concentrated in one place, they could support many specialized occupations. Artisans could begin to ply their craft there, and scholars could establish libraries and offer classes. Thus, the city became home to early universities, libraries, hospitals, and scientific laboratories.

Until the Industrial Revolution, city life throughout the world was much like life in Cahokia. In the absence of scientific technology, it was impossible to house, feed, and care for very large urban populations. This limitation restricted the number and growth of cities for some eight thousand years. However, by the early stages of the Industrial Revolution, the situation began to change. Because the food supply increased dramatically, farmers were freed to work in the factories that were beginning to turn out industrial and consumer goods. Factory employment, in turn, produced an expansion of secondary activities to supply workers with shelter, food, and clothing. Job opportunities in these secondary occupations attracted more migrants and accelerated the rate of city growth even more. Along with urbanization came a change in society. Large-scale manufacturing required a larger and more rational system of organization and management. This new organizational form was the bureaucracy, which became dominant in both industry and government (see Chapter 5). Because factory work adds jobs to society and because bureaucratic office work adds even more jobs, the number of occupations increased, and the division of labor grew ever more complex. Thus, technology and urbanization created societies that could produce goods in unprecedented quantities and that were socially organized in ways different from what

Aerial view of Mexico City at sunset with traffic and city lights. Mexico City is by far the largest city in Mexico.

CQ *What key term do sociologists use to describe the dominance of such large cities in traditional societies?*

World Today ● ■ ▲

Urbanization by Major World Regions, 2003

PERCENTAGE OF TOTAL POPULATION IN CITIES

World	47
More Developed Countries	75
Less Developed Countries	40
Africa	33
Asia	38
Latin America	68
North America	79
Europe	73
Oceania	69

SOURCE: Population Reference Bureau 2003. 2003 World Population Data Sheet. Washington, DC.

Urban primacy A pattern of urbanization in which one city grows extremely large and dominates the society, whereas the rest of society remains rural.

people had known before. In short, what we now think of as the modern city came into existence.

Cities Today

Today, about 47 percent of the world's population is urban, but this figure obscures the difference between industrial and traditional societies (Population Reference Bureau 2003) (see the World Today box). Traditional societies are about one-third urban, whereas industrial societies are about three-fourths urban. And as we noted when discussing Cahokia, in traditional societies, the quality of urban life is different from that in industrial societies. Consequently, we will discuss urbanization in both kinds of societies.

Urbanization in Traditional Societies   In traditional societies, urbanization takes place very unevenly. Usually one city grows extremely large and dominates the society, whereas the rest of the society remains rural. This pattern is called **urban primacy** (Macionis and Parrillo 2004; Palen 2002). In Thailand, to illustrate, about 80 percent of the population is rural, but the capital city of Bangkok has 7 million people. Bangkok's population is approximately 50 times more than that of the second-largest city in Thailand (Palen 1997; Sassen 1994). Similarly, Mexico City has a population of 28 million, which is about eight times larger than Mexico's second-largest city.

Urban primacy today results from both natural increases and migration (Schwab 1992). Even though urban fertility is lower than that in rural areas, it is still significantly higher than the urban mortality rate. Hence, the primate city grows from an excess of births over deaths. It is urban migration, however, that accounts for most of the growth.

Why are migrants attracted to the primate city, a place where there are more workers than jobs, affordable housing is scarce, and government aid is almost nonexistent? One reason is a broad push factor: however bad the situation in the city might be, it is better than where they came from. There is also a pull factor at work. When a primate city reaches about 20 percent of the nation's total population, almost everyone in the country will have at least one relative there (Schwab 1992:78). These relatives can welcome new arrivals and provide them with temporary shelter, tips on urban living, possible employment opportunities, and general social support. Thus, migrants are simultaneously pushed off the land and pulled into the primate city.

Because housing is scarce, urban migrants form spontaneous settlements: shanty-towns, slums, and other areas that they take over without official permission. These people are sometimes called *squatters*. In Cairo, for instance, squatters live in old graveyards; in Manila, they construct cardboard shacks on top of mounds of refuse in the city dump; and in Mexico City, they live in open fields near the outskirts of the city.

Despite the harsh living conditions, these settlements have some features of communal life. People know each other personally and follow the traditions they bring with them from the countryside. Families form neighborhood communities. Leaders emerge, and an informal government comes into being. Many sociologists believe that the communal elements of the spontaneous settlements give their inhabitants the strength and vitality to cope with their bleak urban environment (Herzer et al. 2000).

Local authorities usually have ambivalent opinions about spontaneous settlements. Some authorities regard them as eyesores and as a breeding ground for crime and political discontent. Because the settlements are viewed as a threat, the police periodically sweep through them, destroying dwelling units and driving people out. However, the squatters usually have no other place to go, and so they quickly return after the police have left. Short of occupying the area with troops, it has proved impossible to keep squatters permanently out of certain areas (Macionis and Parrillo 2004).

More recently, authorities have adopted a more positive attitude toward spontaneous settlements. Rather than trying to abolish them, authorities have tried to use them as the starting point of community development. The Indonesian government, for example, has provided settlements with basic municipal services, while other governments have offered land to help squatters establish permanent homes and a self-sufficient community.

As the discussion of spontaneous settlements implies, urban growth in traditional societies is rapid and chaotic. The huge number of migrants overwhelms the capacity of the city to respond, while the society as a whole cannot create enough wealth to support everyone at a comfortable level. Under these conditions, the primate city drains resources from the rural portion of society for its own benefit. Rural poverty then rises, and more people leave for the primate city. This cycle of migration and poverty will end only when the society as a whole has enough wealth for everyone.

Urbanization in Industrial Societies   The course of urbanization has been different in industrial societies. Compared with growth in traditional societies, urban growth has been slow, and primate cities have not developed (see Figure 15.6 for U.S. urban population statistics). To illustrate, the largest American metropolitan area is New York with a population of about 20 million people, whereas the second-largest metropolitan area is Los Angeles with a population of about 15 million. Although large, New York is not primate; it does not dominate the nation in the way that Mexico City and Bangkok dominate Mexico and Thailand.

During the 1920s, sociologists at the University of Chicago developed an explanation of city growth called the concentric zone model (Burgess 1925; Gold 2002). According to this model, cities grow as a series of rings, or concentric zones. The first zone consists of the central business district, or the "downtown area." The next zone is called the "zone of transition" and mainly contains light manufacturing and wholesaling activities. Also found in this zone are bars, pawnshops, cheap hotels, and some inexpensive residences. This area usually has a reputation for being a "bad neighborhood." The next three rings consist of residential housing. The ring next to the zone of transition is the poorest, whereas the outermost ring is the most affluent. Although patterns of concentric zones did not accurately describe every city in the United States, the model was roughly accurate for many cities during the first half of the twentieth century.

At the time that the concentric zone model was being developed, many thriving businesses were located in the central business district and in the zone of transition.

FIGURE 15.6 Urban Population
of the United States

*The figure shows the percentage of the
American population living in urban
places since 1840. Actually, the percentages are not strictly comparable
because land area of the United States
has changed over time, and because
the definition of "urban" also has
changed over time.*

SOURCE: Population Reference Bureau,
Population Bulletin 2000; U.S. Bureau of the
Census 2002.

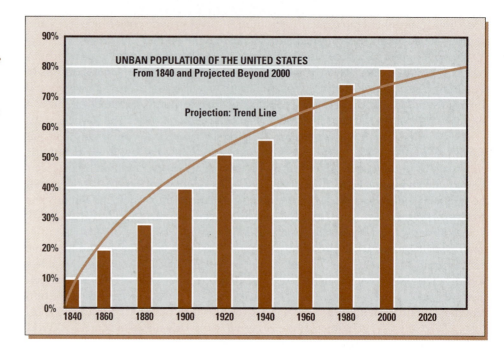

People lived in these areas because they wanted to be near their work. After a time, these people accumulated some wealth and could afford to commute between work and to purchase the more expensive housing in the outer rings. New migrants were eager to move into vacancies thus created, and so a continual flow of people from the inner to the outer rings was established. African Americans were exceptions to this pattern. Because of racial discrimination, they could not move, and a portion of the inner city became permanently African American.

The concentric zone model was proposed during a time before extensive suburbs existed, before privately owned cars were common, before there were freeways, and before industry had moved to the outskirts of the city. As life changed, the model became less accurate and was subsequently modified by other analysts (see Figure 15.7). The so-called sector model added the possibility that some parts of the city grew along irregularly shaped sectors moving outward from the central city. A sector of expensive housing might, for instance, follow a street from the downtown area to the outskirts of the city. Another variation of the model recognized the existence of multiple nuclei, or several areas that adopt specialized uses. For instance, one section of the city might specialize in financial businesses, whereas another might specialize in tourist attractions. Each of these sections, or nuclei, then becomes the center of a small community, with other businesses and residences growing outward from it. For example, in San Francisco, the Embarcadero (a financial center) and Fisherman's Wharf (a tourist center) would be considered nuclei.

Even more recently, cities have begun merging into one single **metropolitan community**: a large city and the surrounding areas that are integrated on a daily basis with the city. These surrounding areas are the well-known "burbs," or **suburbs**: communities with metropolitan areas that are outside the central city. For instance, the Los Angeles metropolitan community consists of the city of Los Angeles and the various communities near the city, such as Santa Monica (a residential community on the beach), Monterey Park (an Asian American community to the east), and the City of Commerce (a community that is almost all industry and almost no residences). Many people who live in these communities work, shop, and do business in Los Angeles. They also read the *Los Angeles Times* and watch Los Angeles television stations. Although these people technically live in separate municipalities, for most practical purposes, they are a part of the Los Angeles metropolitan community.

Although many people live in the suburbs and commute to the downtown areas of the city, many more people live in the suburbs and work there as well. This pattern

Metropolitan community ▲ A large city and the surrounding areas that are integrated on a daily basis with the city.

Suburbs ▲ Communities with metropolitan areas that are outside the central city.

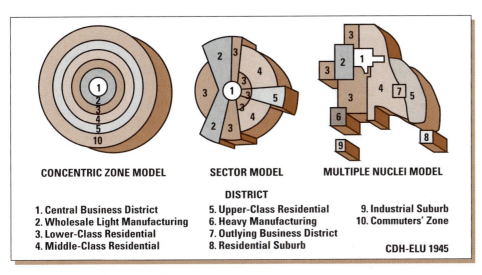

CONCENTRIC ZONE MODEL   **SECTOR MODEL**   **MULTIPLE NUCLEI MODEL**

DISTRICT

1. Central Business District
2. Wholesale Light Manufacturing
3. Lower-Class Residential
4. Middle-Class Residential

5. Upper-Class Residential
6. Heavy Manufacturing
7. Outlying Business District
8. Residential Suburb

9. Industrial Suburb
10. Commuters' Zone

CDH-ELU 1945

FIGURE 15.7 **The Internal Structure of Cities**

As we see in this figure, the concentric zone model portrays the city as being organized around a central core that is the main business district. Moving from the city's center to the periphery, there are a series of different land uses—wholesaling and light manufacturing, lower-class residential, middle-class residential, and the commuter zone. This model is attributed to Robert Park and Ernest Burgess of the University of Chicago. They used it to describe the city of Chicago earlier in this century as it was growing and expanding in industry and population.

Other researchers did not think the concentric zone model could be generalized to all cities, so they proposed models that they thought better described the cities they investigated. These include the sector and multiple-nuclei models. Today researchers recognize that, in fact, most cities combine features of all three models.

 Can you identify characteristics of a nearby city that correspond to one of these three models?

SOURCE: Chauncy P. Harris and Edward L. Ullman, "The Nature of Cities," in *The Annals of the American Academy of Political and Social Science* 244 (1945):7–17.

of living and working in the same area developed because the suburbs have become communities in their own right, complete with their own neighborhoods, governments, schools, libraries, and shopping centers. As a result, approximately twice as many people both live and work in the suburbs as live in the suburbs and work in the downtown area.

The suburbs developed in response to several social forces. The multilane freeways that go around the perimeter of the city (the outer belts) spurred the development of suburban places along the city's rim. Now, rather than going from the suburb to the central city to work, to shop, to see a doctor, or to enjoy the movies, suburbanites can obtain the same services by driving along the outer belt from one suburban community to another. Another factor has been the decentralization of jobs. Faster transportation and communications have encouraged manufacturing plants and distribution centers to relocate from the central city to the outer rings of the city—that is, to the suburbs. Yet another factor has been the aging of the central city. Facilities in many downtown areas are simply worn out or obsolete. Parking is expensive and inconvenient; buildings are dirty and run-down. In contrast, suburban shopping malls and industrial centers typically have bright new facilities and ample parking.

While the suburbs have been increasing in importance, the central business districts of many cities have been declining. Offices stand empty, retailers complain of disappointing sales, and the streets, buildings, sewage lines, and other parts of the physical infrastructure are decaying and sometimes collapsing. For example, in Columbus, Ohio, a pedestrian in the downtown area was almost killed by a falling brick that broke loose just at the moment the pedestrian passed under an old building. Another serious problem has been caused by migration. The outflow of wealthier people to the suburbs has left behind those people who are less well off financially. Very often these people are predominantly African Americans, Hispanics, or members of other minority groups. In effect, the metropolis is increasingly becoming two worlds: one is the world of the inner city inhabited by people with limited means, and the other is the world of the affluent suburb.

As metropolitan communities have grown, those located fairly close to each other have merged to form a *megalopolis*: a giant metropolitan complex that functions, in many ways, as a single urban community. The New York megalopolis, for instance, is centered on the city of New York, but it includes cities in New Jersey and Connecticut and other cities in New York State. Together, this group forms a single, huge urban community. Government officials of New Jersey, for example, often live in Connecticut alongside commuters who make a daily trek into Manhattan. In the future, more and more people will live in these giant urban areas because smaller metropolitan communities are becoming megalopolises, and megalopolises themselves are merging with each other to form *urban regional areas*. There are already signs of such regions: the corridor from Washington, D.C., to New York City is almost an unbroken stretch of urban landscape, as is the stretch between Los Angeles and San Diego.

Finally, a new form of city is emerging as a response to globalization—the *global city*. Cities such as New York, London, and Tokyo are global cities. What makes them "global" is that they contain in them the organizations that run the worldwide economy. On a daily basis, these cities are connected through financial transactions, exchange of services, and modern communications. What happens in one of these cities on any given day has consequences for what happens in the other cities (Sassen 1991; Chapter 9).

Urbanism: The Urban Way of Life

The concept of **urbanism** refers to the patterns of social life found in cities (Flanagan 2002). These patterns are much different, many sociologists have argued, from life in a rural town. There are differences of sheer size, of course, but in addition there may be differences in the quality of social interaction. It is often said, for instance, that city people are cold and always in a rush, whereas rural townsfolk are friendly, soft-spoken, and in tune with nature. These and other possible differences were noted some 100 years ago by the German sociologist Ferdinand Toennies (1855–1936). In *Community and Society* (1887) he developed the concepts of *Gemeinschaft* and *Gesellschaft*. By *Gemeinschaft*, Toennies meant a place where people know each other personally and are deeply concerned about each other. These people follow old traditions and customs; they believe in the family; and they worry about the well-being of their community. Typically, small rural communities have a strong sense of *Gemeinschaft*. In contrast, *Gesellschaft* refers to a place where social relations are based on pragmatic, practical interests. Because people do not know each other personally, they become formal and impersonal. They do not follow tradition very closely, nor are they especially concerned with the well-being of their community. Toennies said that cities are typically *Gesellschaft* in orientation.

As you might guess, Toennies had a negative view of urban life—a view that was shared by Louis Wirth (1939) of the University of Chicago. Roughly a contemporary of Toennies, Wirth had similar ideas, which he applied to American cities. Wirth argued that urban life was distinguished by three characteristics, as follows:

1. *Size* Wirth believed that size was associated with social diversity. According to him, the contemporary city was a mosaic of ethnic communities, specialized land uses, and neighborhoods of different social classes. In this environment, communal bonds are replaced by formal institutions such as the law, the police, government, and private enterprise. Separately and collectively, these institutions maintain order and provide social solidarity across the urban spectrum.

Urban size, furthermore, forces people to interact in terms of roles rather than whole personalities. For example, in a supermarket, the important thing is not who the checkout clerk is, but how efficiently the clerk gets the job done. With an eye

Urbanism ▲ The pattern of social life found in cities.

toward the end rather than the means, urban dwellers emphasize formality, rationality, and goals. Even the exchange of pleasantries such as "How are you?," "Thank you," and "Have a nice day!" are rituals that are aimed at maintaining a social role rather than expressing personal emotions.

2. **Density** Urban existence is highly dense because many people live in a small area. Wirth believed that high density reinforces the effects of large size and alters the nature of social interaction. The sheer number of contacts with strangers means that each interaction must be transitory and brief. The barrage of stimuli from strangers, shop signs, and media forces people to screen out the unimportant ones and to prioritize those that are important enough for attention. For example, when walking down a busy street, urbanites will brush off a panhandler as unimportant but will stop and chat with a coworker, who is important. Urbanites also attend closely to visual symbols because symbols indicate the roles people play. A brown uniform signals a United Parcel Service driver, a hard hat denotes a construction worker, and a blue uniform a police officer. These visual clues keep interaction impersonal but greatly increase the efficiency of urban life.

Density also increases jostling on the sidewalk and congestion on the freeway. Peace, quiet, and privacy are difficult to obtain in the city. As a result, people become anxious, hostile, and sometimes violent. Making the situation even worse, urban life proceeds at a quick tempo: people walk down the street hurriedly, constantly glancing at their watches to see whether they are late. In fact, Wirth wrote that the clock and the traffic signal aptly symbolized the formal, hurried pace of urban life.

3. **Heterogeneity** Because cities are large, Wirth said, they are heterogeneous—home to many different religious, ethnic, racial, and social groups. Wirth maintained that so much diversity makes urbanites more tolerant of different lifestyles and more open to different ethnic groups. An urbanite might work with people of many different racial backgrounds, for example, or have neighbors with alternative sexual preferences. For the typical urbanite, surrounded by diversity, what is different becomes normal, and urbanites might not even be aware of their own tolerance.

In the minds of many early sociologists, as illustrated by Toennies and Wirth, city life was fundamentally different from life in the hinterlands. Rural life was communal, and urban life was associational. And to them, that was the fundamental problem of the city. For instance, these sociologists said that urban crime was caused by the absence of communal social controls, such as the family, church, and neighborhood. Mental illness occurred more in urban areas, they further said, because people could not cope with the cold and impersonal social environment of the city. In general, they concluded, the quality of life was worse in the city than in the countryside.

In contrast to the rather pessimistic views held by many early sociologists, most contemporary sociologists regard the city as a series of communities within a broader whole—a mosaic of business districts, tourist attractions, residential areas, and specialized neighborhoods. For instance, the area around many urban colleges is, essentially, a "student neighborhood." Most of the houses and apartments are rented to students; most of the businesses cater to students; and most of the people walking the streets are students. The area also has a communal culture that supports the social needs of young people who are learning to live independently while attending school. In short, the neighborhood is a community. Although this example concerns students, essentially the same points can be made about neighborhoods composed mainly of certain ethnic groups, of musicians, of surfers, and of others who have a distinctive lifestyle. These vibrant cultures buffer the urbanite from many of the potentially negative effects of city living (Fisher 1984:36; Gans 1982; Gottdiener and Hutchison 2000).

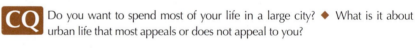

●■▲ Pausing to Think   About Urbanization

The first cities arose in agrarian societies and were located in the valleys of the great river systems. Industrialization encouraged the growth of cities, and today industrial societies are heavily urbanized. In many industrial societies, cities grew progressively outward from their core, and the suburbs now contain the bulk of the urban population. Many social theorists argue that urbanization is extremely unpleasant, but other social theorists argue that communal neighborhoods protect urbanites from the negative effects of city living.

CQ Do you want to spend most of your life in a large city? ◆ What is it about urban life that most appeals or does not appeal to you?

Population, Ecology, and Urbanization in the Twenty-First Century

Thirty years ago, scientists, such as Paul Ehrlich in his influential book *The Population Bomb* (1968), along with other researchers feared that the world was fast approaching a population calamity. They were wrong. Fertility actually decreased, and food production increased. These facts, however, do not mean that their warning was misguided and should be ignored.

Despite lower fertility, the population will continue to grow and put pressure on the environment. There are large numbers of young women in the world, and as they enter the childbearing period of their lives, more people will be added to the population. A large part of this growth will take place in poorer, traditional societies—those that can least afford it. In those places, urban growth will be especially great, and urbanites will suffer even more from overcrowding, pollution, congestion, and above all, poverty. Unless a major breakthrough in technology is achieved very soon and accompanied by a reduction in fertility, the urban future looks grim for many societies in the world today.

Another pessimistic prediction concerns animal and plant life. Technology, population, pollution, and urbanization are continually pushing many species of animals and plants into extinction. The permanent loss of genetic diversity upsets the balance

Logging companies burn the rain forest to facilitate removal of lumber. This photograph shows a fire in the Amazon basin. Between 1991 and 1995, 11 percent of the world's forest area was lost (Brown, Renner, and Flavin 1997). As a result, many plant and animal ecosystems were destroyed. In addition, because the forest helps remove carbon dioxide from air, the quality of the air we breathe has also suffered. In many parts of Asia, smoke clouds from the burning rain forests hang over the countryside and over cities, causing burning eyes, coughing, choking, and severe respiratory ailments.

of complex ecological systems and could be extremely costly in the long run. The cost to the human spirit is perhaps equally important, for as Theodore Caplow said, "When the last wild elephant dies, the world will be less beautiful" (Caplow 1991:28).

Although some aspects of the future appear bleak, the future is not fixed in stone. For instance, the trend toward more efficient land use, which was mentioned earlier, can reduce the pressures on ecological systems. The introduction of small-scale technology, such as the cookstove discussed in the Social Change box, can decrease

Social Change ●■▲ Cookstoves for the Developing World

In many societies, traditional cooking methods are very inefficient. Most of the heat released from burning wood or charcoal is wasted—only 10 to 20 percent actually finds its way to the cooking pot or other cooking utensil. In addition, cooking is a serious health hazard. The fumes and smoke from the traditional cooking stove or open fire cause respiratory diseases that directly or indirectly kill 4 to 5 million children worldwide. Clearly, improvements in the efficiency and safety of traditional cooking methods would help improve health, while also reducing deforestation.

For several decades, international aid organizations have been trying to find simple and economical ways to improve traditional cooking practices. Progress has been slow, however. Many of the initial attempts failed because the "improved" stoves did not meet the needs of the people who were expected to use them or were too expensive.

Recently, however, several women's organizations have formed in developing countries around issues such as community health and protecting the environment. These groups have worked closely with the women who actually prepare the meals, and they have been able to make several key suggestions that have led to a more successful design of the family

cooking stove. In Kenya, for instance, women's groups suggested a new shape for the cookstove that allowed a ceramic insert to be used. The new stove was called the Jiko, which means "stove" in Swahili. The Jiko directs at least twice as much heat to the cooking pot as the ordinary metal stove and uses an average of 1,300 fewer pounds of fuel per year per family. Some women in urban areas have been able to save as much as a fifth of their annual income by using the Jiko stove, and many have invested the money in starting small businesses or in paying school fees for their children. Local manufacturing of the Jiko has developed into a large-scale commercial industry and has brought the price down to a reasonable level.

Almost 1 million households now use the Jiko. Women's groups are continuing to encourage its use in Kenya and neighboring countries. The Jiko cookstove reinforces an important sociological point: as the world's population continues to increase, a vast array of energy-saving projects must be undertaken to reduce waste and pollution. All of us, not just those in the developing countries, will need to reexamine our daily energy use to find ways to economize on fuel and to decrease pollution (Kammen 1995).

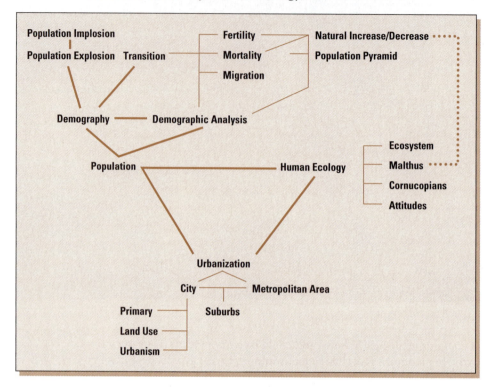

This is a concept web for three important connected topics: population, environment, and urbanization. Try this: Notice that *Malthus* is connected by a dotted line to *natural increase/decrease*. What did Malthus have to say that would justify this connection?

pollution and increase the efficient use of scarce resources. And national governments throughout the world can establish policies that address the problems of population, environment, and urbanization. After all, as one critic of current environmental policy points out, it is much more effective to prevent pollution from occurring rather than to deal with pollution after it is produced (Commoner 2000). As Chapter 16 discusses in greater detail, what we do now can change the future.

Looking Ahead

Population change and institutional change seem too massive for any individual to change. To counteract this impression, the final chapter discusses collective action, a topic that suggests how individuals can work together to change the society in which they live.

WHAT YOU SHOULD KNOW ●■▲

1. What do demographers study?

Fertility, mortality, and migration are the basic processes studied by demographers. Changes in population size are caused by changes in the numbers of births and deaths and by changes in the amount of immigration and emigration.

2. How is the demographic transition related to the Great Social Transformation?

According to the demographic transition, preindustrial societies are characterized by high birthrates and high death rates. As societies change, birthrates remain high, but death rates decline. Mature, industrial societies are characterized by low birthrates and low death rates. Demographers used to think that all societies would pass through the demographic transition.

3. What did Thomas Malthus say?

Thomas Malthus argued that there are enough resources to sustain everyone at a comfortable level when the population is small but not when the population is large. Malthus further argued that the human population can grow so fast that it may outpace the ability of the environment to support it. The Malthusian argument continues today as neo-Malthusians and Cornucopians debate the extent to which the world's population can be supported by our environment.

4. What does the perspective of human ecology contribute to our understanding of the link between population and environment?

Human ecology is a sociological perspective that examines the relationship between society and the environment. It assumes that groups cooperate and compete with one another for the use of environmental resources, and it pays particular attention to the relationship among the population, social organization, environment, and technology.

5. How committed are Americans to improving the environment?

Most people in the United States express concern about the quality of the environment and support efforts to improve it. Nevertheless, most are not willing to pay higher taxes or higher prices or to suffer a decline in their level of living to improve the environment.

6. What factors gave rise to the first cities?

The first cities arose in the fertile valleys of great rivers. The terrain, climate, and technology of these places enabled farmers to produce enough food to feed themselves and still have enough left over to feed people living in the city. In addition, some of these cities were strategically located along the key trade routes of antiquity.

7. How does urbanization in today's traditional societies differ from urbanization in industrial societies?

In many traditional societies, one or two extremely large cities dominate the society. These cities contain the principal administrative and economic activities of the society, and they attract large numbers of migrants from rural areas. In contrast, industrial societies typically have several large cities that grow as industrial centers. The populations of these cities grow progressively outward and eventually form outlying suburbs.

8. What does the city's population size, density, and heterogeneity mean for the lives of urbanites?

Many social theorists argue that the large size, dense settlement, and heterogeneous population of the industrial city combine to create a disjointed, unpleasant lifestyle. Other social theorists argue that cities contain pockets of communalism and neighborhood groups that buffer urbanites from the many negative aspects of city living.

9. What does the future hold for population, the environment, and urbanization?

Despite decreasing world fertility, the world's population will grow, especially in poorer, traditional societies. In addition, technology, population growth, pollution, and urbanization will continue to push many species of animals and plants into extinction. On the other hand, many governments are now trying to reduce population growth and promote efficient land use. The introduction of alternative technologies, moreover, can help to reduce pressures on the environment.

TEST YOUR KNOWLEDGE ●■▲

Key Terms Matching

Match each of these key terms with the best definition or example from the numbered items that follow. Write the letter preceding the key term in the blank before the definition that you choose.

a. city

b. crude birthrate

c. crude death rate

d. demographic transition

e. demography

f. ecosystem

g. emigration

h. fertility

i. general fertility ratio

j. human ecology

k. immigration

l. life expectancy

m. life span

n. metropolitan community

o. migration

p. mortality

q. natural decrease

r. natural increase

s. net migration rate

t. population explosion

u. population implosion

v. suburbs

w. urban primacy

x. urbanism

y. urbanization

_____ 1. The annual number of deaths per 1,000 members of the population.

_____ 2. The situation in which the number of deaths in a population exceeds the number of births.

_____ 3. An interlocking, stable group of plants and animals living in their natural habitat.

_____ 4. The number of deaths that occur during a year.

_____ 5. Communities with metropolitan areas that are outside the central city.

_____ 6. The study of the relationship between society and the environment.

_____ 7. The increase in the percentage of the population residing in cities.

_____ 8. A large city and the surrounding areas that are integrated on a daily basis with the city.

_____ 9. A rapid, unchecked growth in the number of people inhabiting an area.

_____ 10. A large, densely settled concentration of people.

_____ 11. The situation in which the number of births in a population exceeds the number of deaths.

_____ 12. The number of births that occur over a specific period, usually a year.

_____ 13. The movement of people from one area of residence to another.

_____ 14. The annual number of births in a population per 1,000 members of the population.

_____ 15. A description of how the growth of the world population has proceeded through four stages, each stage being a unique relationship between the birthrate and the death rate of the population.

_____ 16. The movement of people into a place.

_____ 17. The movement of people out of a place.

_____ 18. The annual difference between how many people enter a place and how many leave, per 1,000 people of that place.

_____ 19. A rapid, unchecked decline in the number of people inhabiting an area.

_____ 20. The patterns of social life found in cities.

_____ 21. A pattern of urbanization in which one city grows extremely large and dominates the society while the rest of the society remains rural.

_____ 22. The scientific study of the size, growth, and composition of the human population.

_____ 23. The theoretical maximum length of life.

_____ 24. How long people probably will live.

_____ 25. The annual number of births in a population per 1,000 women aged 15 through 44 years.

Multiple Choice

Circle the letter of your choice.

1. The Easter Island example shows how
   a. unrestrained population growth and cultural values that neglect the environment will quickly destroy an ecosystem.
   b. brave, seafaring people can migrate from one place to another and prosper.
   c. a society's population concentrated in the young ages can be stable.
   d. giant statues, called the moi, can bring a divided people together in times of trouble.

2. A large population provides
   a. soldiers for the military.
   b. workers for farms and industry.
   c. people to fill the many roles required in order for the society to run.
   d. all of the above.

3. Moving from Columbus, Ohio, to Phoenix, Arizona, is an example of
   a. natural population increase.
   b. internal migration.
   c. external migration.
   d. natural population decrease.

4. Which of the following describes societies in Stage 1, the preindustrial, of demographic transition?
   a. high birthrate and high death rate
   b. high birthrate and declining death rate
   c. declining birthrate and low death rate
   d. low birthrate and low death rate

5. In Stage 2, the transitional, of the demographic transition, a high birthrate and a declining death rate cause the
   a. population size to be stable.
   b. population size to decrease.
   c. population size to rapidly increase.
   d. population size to slowly increase.

6. Which of the following describes the situation in Stage 4, the industrial, of the demographic transition as many transitional societies move from preindustrial to industrial?
   a. high birthrate and high death rate
   b. high birthrate and declining death rate
   c. low birthrate and low death rate
   d. declining birthrate and low death rate

7. Which of the following did Thomas Malthus argue?
   a. that the Green Revolution would provide sufficient food for the world's population
   b. that nature did not provide sufficient food for the world's population
   c. that population growth eventually would outpace growth in food supply
   d. that Stage 2 of the demographic transition was the ideal stage

8. Which of the following points of view argues that human inventiveness will cope with any scarcities caused by overpopulation?
   a. Malthusian
   b. Cornucopian
   c. Green Revolution
   d. Neo-Malthusian

9. Which of the following is NOT part of Otis Dudley Duncan's POET ecological model?
   a. environment
   b. opportunity
   c. population
   d. technology

10. Positive attitudes about the environment on the part of Americans

   a. have translated into aggressive actions to clean up the environment.
   b. do not always translate into action.
   c. have led to a majority of people picking up trash when they come across it.
   d. have led to a majority feeling that we are overly concerned about the environment.

11. Mexico City is eight times larger than Mexico's second largest city. This condition is an example of

   a. suburbanization.
   b. *Gemeinschaft*.
   c. *Gesellschaft*.
   d. urban primacy.

12. Which of the following is consistent with Burgess's concentric zone model of city growth?

   a. The outermost ring is the most affluent.
   b. The ring next to the zone of transition is the richest area.
   c. The zone of transition contains high-rent luxury apartments.
   d. The innermost ring has a reputation for being a "bad neighborhood."

13. Developments in transportation technology, such as the interstate highway system, helped the development of which of the following models of city growth?

   a. Concentric zone
   b. Sector
   c. Malthusian prediction
   d. *Gemeinschaft*

14. According to Ferdinand Toennies, small farming villages most likely have a strong sense of

   a. *Gesellschaft*.
   b. organic solidarity.
   c. *Gemeinschaft*.
   d. heterogeneity.

15. Which of the following is NOT one of the ways that Louis Wirth distinguished cities from rural areas?

   a. distance from the industrial core to the outer ring
   b. population size
   c. density
   d. heterogeneity

True-False

Indicate your response to each of the following statements by circling T for true or F for false.

T F 1. Overpopulation has been a problem for most of human history.

T F 2. A population's fertility level is at replacement if enough children are born to replace the population as people die.

T F 3. Were it not for the steady stream of immigrants who arrive in the United States each year, the American population would eventually grow smaller.

T F 4. Life expectancy in the United States has changed very little in the past century.

T F 5. For the young and the middle-aged in the United States, the major cause of death is sickness and disease.

T F 6. Migration is currently increasing the diversity in many countries in the world.

T F 7. The current migration pattern within the United States continues to be from the southern states to the northern states.

T F 8. Postindustrial societies will be characterized by low birthrates and low death rates, according to demographic transition theory.

T F 9. Malthus referred to famine, war, and plague as positive checks that would increase the death rate and reduce a population's size.

T F 10. Today about 45 percent of the world's population is urban.

T F 11. In the twenty-first century, despite the world having a lower fertility than in the past, population will continue to grow and put pressure on resources.

T F 12. The first cities arose in the desert.

T F 13. Louis Wirth believed that high density in cities reinforces the effects of large size and alters the nature of social interaction.

T F 14. Currently only a small percentage of Americans are environmentally concerned.

T F 15. Neo-Malthusians recognize the benefits of the Green Revolution.

NOTE: The answers to these exercises are at the end of the book.

For additional practice tests and other resources please visit the companion web site at http://www.prenhall.com/curry.

Essay

1. What three characteristics did Louis Wirth use when describing urban life and what were their effects?

2. Contrast how the patterns of social interaction differ between Tonnies' *Gemeinschaft* (rural life) and *Gesellschaft* (city life).

3. Which model of urbanization—sector, concentric zone, or multiple nuclei model—best fits your home town? Explain.

4. Discuss the "Green Revolution." What is it, how did it start, and what are its prospects?

5. What can you tell about a population from a population pyramid? Illustrate by drawing one.

16 Collective Social Action

Chapter Outline

In 1986, students throughout China began engaging in protest marches. These protests grew in strength, and on May 4, 1989, more than 100,000 students gathered in Tiananmen Square, Beijing. Part of China's emerging prodemocracy social movement, they were demanding more freedom, an end to political corruption, and greater opportunity for political participation. All the major U.S. television networks filmed the students as they engaged in hunger strikes, marches, and other forms of nonviolent protest. To all outward appearances, the students were on the verge of winning a major victory and opening China to democratic reform. At that point, however, the Chinese government hardened its position and sent troops and tanks into Tiananmen Square. Soldiers pushed through the crowds, firing on the students. More than 700 people were killed. Although the live television transmissions had been stopped, videotapes of the shootings were smuggled out of China and were broadcast to a horrified world (Bergman and McKnight 1993).

Faced with the threat of jail and even death, what prompted the students to come out and demand more freedom? Several factors lay behind their decision. In general, the students lived a dreary life. Most of their professors had lost interest in teaching, dormitories were crowded, and parties and dating were frowned upon. The future was not promising, either: a minor position in a state agency was the best job awaiting a college graduate. More importantly, the students knew of the prodemocracy movements sweeping through Eastern Europe and felt that they were being left behind (Kwan 1990; Chapter 9).

What happened in Tiananmen Square illustrates several points about collective behavior and social action, but for the moment, let us concentrate on an aspect that is sometimes overlooked: the role of the individual in promoting social change. By banding together with others, each individual student in Tiananmen Square was able to affect the course of China's history. For one thing, after Tiananmen Square, the United States demanded that the Chinese government pay closer attention to human rights, and Congress threatened to revoke certain trade privileges that China enjoyed. The Tiananmen Square incident also exposed the totalitarian nature of the Chinese government and reduced the prestige of China throughout most of the world. And finally, the image of a single Chinese student standing in front of a column of tanks won the admiration of television viewers around the world.

Tiananmen Square's events still haunt the Chinese. Many of the young people there that day still experience government harassment (Smith 2001). Their phones are tapped. Some are watched and regularly followed by the police, and some are restricted from travel within China and to other countries. Take Fang Zheng as an example. Before the Tiananmen event he was an athlete, a sprinter. On the day of government reprisals for the demonstrations, Fang was run over by a tank as he was helping his girlfriend over the railing to the sidewalk. Both of his legs were amputated. Later, he trained himself to throw the discus and javelin. He won two gold medals in the national disability games, and was selected to participate in the Far East and South Pacific Disability Games. Once the Chinese organizers learned how he had lost his legs, he was told to pack his things and move far away so no foreign reporters could interview him. The police warned his girlfriend that if she stayed with him, she could be in trouble. To this day, the police often question him and his friends, and potential employers are afraid to hire him. He has paid a major price for leading 40 college students to Tiananmen Square that day.

Viewed sociologically, the students in Tiananmen Square were participating in **collective social action**: cooperative attempts to achieve a social goal (see Figure 16.1). Tiananmen Square is, of course, an example of collective social action, but so are less dramatic episodes of human behavior. You have undoubtedly been involved in some type of collective social action yourself. You may have, for instance, joined in a protest march, run onto the field to tear down the goalposts after a football game, or washed cars on a Saturday afternoon to raise money for a special event. Collective social action does not even require you to be in close physical proximity to others. The Internet allows people to come into contact with others who share a common interest or social complaint. For example, in 1995, political protests on one hundred college campuses against the political agenda of newly elected House Republicans were organized and coordinated through the Internet, thereby making it clear that social action was now being pursued in a new form—the e-mail movement (Herszenhorn 1995).

The protest at Tiananmen Square also illustrates the fact that young people sometimes have a special role in initiating collective social action (Lauer 1991). As compared with older people, the young are not as attached to the past or to the status quo. For that reason, the young may be more willing to consider alternatives to the current situation. To be sure, young people have less experience than older people, but they have enthusiasm, which, if properly channeled into collective social action, can become a powerful force for social change.

Chapter Preview

In this chapter, we first examine the impact of the Great Social Transformation on collective social action. Then, we take up the nature of collective behavior and focus on crowds, riots, panics, and rumors. Next, we examine social movements and see how people use movements to reform society or to promote social revolution. In our discussion of specific American social movements, we cover the civil rights movement, the women's movement, and the environmental movement. We then examine the topic of social action and working for change. Finally, we look to the future and suggest that social movements and collective social action will probably increase as we enter this century.

The Great Social Transformation and Collective Social Action

Collective behavior, social movements, and social action play important roles in transforming society from communal to associational. Collective social action is not a new element of human behavior, however. Ancient Rome experienced protests and outbursts, especially during games, religious festivals, and other popular events at which people were gathered together in large numbers (Vanderbroeck 1987). Similarly, during the Middle Ages, spontaneous peasant revolts and riots sometimes occurred during festivals and other gatherings. As these instances demonstrate, communal societies have tensions, and individuals sometimes organize to take collective social action.

Contemporary, associational societies also have tensions that result in collective social action. In this chapter, for instance, we discuss how industrialization has produced dangerous chemicals and tons of toxic waste and how individuals have demonstrated, marched, and in some cases, engaged in violence aimed at cleaning up

Collective social action ▲ Cooperative efforts to achieve a social goal.

the environment. We also discuss how the tensions generated by racial and gender inequalities have spurred collective social action. In short, associational societies embrace many peoples with different values and resources, and the conflicts over these values and resources eventually lead to collective social action.

Collective Behavior

In familiar situations—when we are at work, in class, or at home with our families—we know what is expected of us and of other people. But sometimes we find ourselves in situations that are not well structured, and we have little or no idea about what to expect or how to behave. Faced with such novelty, we are apt to engage in **collective behavior**: that is, to engage in social interactions that are a response to unstructured, ambiguous, or unstable situations. Because there are many situations that are relatively unstructured, the concept of collective behavior covers a broad range of behaviors—being caught up in a crowd, a riot, or a panic, or even simply responding to rumors, stories, or news items that turn out to be false.

Although collective behavior might appear to be irrational and unexplainable, sociologists believe otherwise. In particular, sociologist Neil Smelser (1962) has suggested a theory of structural strain that links existing societal conditions to the emergence of collective behavior. According to this theory, collective behavior will emerge when six social conditions are met:

1. *Structural Conduciveness* This condition refers to the preexisting conditions that make collective behavior likely. For example, rumors might start flying around the headquarters of a large corporation when profits fall and several high-ranking executives are fired.

2. *Structural Strains* Conditions that cause people to feel anxious or strained set the stage for collective behavior. To illustrate, a racial or an ethnic riot is likely to break out if relationships among various ethnic groups are already tense, or a revolution might occur if large segments of the people feel that they are being unjustly deprived and discriminated against.

3. *Generalized Beliefs* Before collective behavior can occur, people must develop a set of beliefs about their situation and about the appropriate action to take to change that situation. For instance, members of a protest crowd might develop the belief that nothing can be done to change the situation except to engage in violence, thus increasing the likelihood of a violent outburst.

4. *Precipitating Factors* An incident that triggers or precipitates the collective behavior must take place. Many so-called race riots have broken out, for example, following an incident involving a minority member and the police.

5. *Mobilization for Action* For collective behavior to occur, people must join together or mobilize to achieve their goal. Mobilization usually occurs as the result of a leader's encouraging people to follow a certain line of action. Thus, in 1995, French union leaders urged their followers to hold a nationwide strike to shut down all public services. To further their goal, they organized massive demonstrations, and a few of those gatherings led to violent confrontations with the police.

6. *Failure of Social Control* Collective behavior is more likely to take place if the agencies of social control are indecisive and fail to act swiftly and firmly. For instance, a football victory celebration may turn into a student riot if the local police cannot control the crowd quickly.

Structural strain theorists argue that these conditions will lead to an episode of collective behavior only if all six conditions are met. If any one condition is not

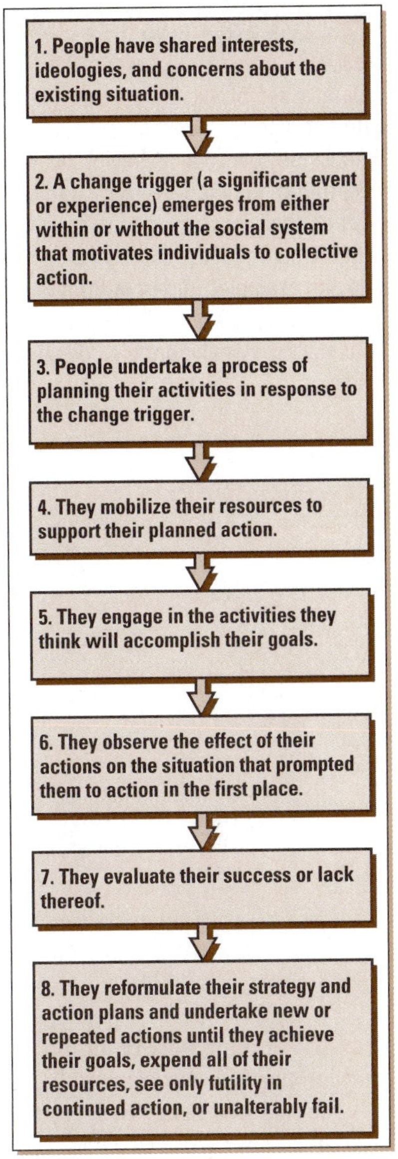

FIGURE 16.1 Steps in Social Action

Whatever the focus of social action and whoever the social actor, social action passes through this series of stages (Schwirian and Mesch 1993).

Collective behavior ▲ Social interactions that are a response to unstructured, ambiguous, or unstable situations.

present, then no collective behavior will take place. Thus, even if the first five conditions are met, a riot will not erupt unless there is a failure of social control.

Many sociologists think that the theory of structural strain is overly complicated, and they point out that the theory is difficult to test scientifically. Nevertheless, they agree that the presence of one or more of the six conditions makes collective behavior more likely than if none of the conditions were present. This is consistent with the common view of the social world, and, for that reason, college presidents become alert when the local football team is about to play an archrival, and police chiefs order their officers to stand by when an incident occurs pitting a racial or ethnic minority against the establishment.

As the discussion of structural strain implies, collective behavior includes a variety of collective actions. It is therefore useful to discuss each type in greater detail (Marx and McAdam 1994; Turner and Killian 1987).

Crowds

The crowd probably catches the attention of the public more than any other type of collective behavior. In the public mind, the crowd is synonymous with the "mob," but sociologists do not equate the two terms. A **crowd** is a temporary grouping of individuals who are physically close enough to engage in social interaction. In contrast, a **mob** is a special type of crowd, one that is wildly out of control and intent on doing violence and harm (Gale 1996; McPhail 1997).

According to these definitions, most people are routinely members of a crowd but are rarely members of a mob. For example, you are in a crowd whenever you walk down a busy hallway talking to other students, or when you weave your way along a busy street, or when you attend a popular public event. In contrast to simply being in crowds, however, most people dislike violence and will leave a crowd if it appears to be turning into a mob. We will have more to say about mobs when we take up the topic of riots.

Even though everyone is frequently a member of a crowd, not all crowds are the same. Sociologists distinguish among the following types:

Crowd ▲ A temporary grouping of individuals who are physically close enough to engage in social interaction.

Mob ▲ A special type of crowd that is wildly out of control and is intent on doing violence and harm.

Casual crowd ▲ A type of crowd that consists of people who are passive and have a low emotional engagement and little social interaction with those nearby.

Conventional crowd ▲ A type of crowd that is a relatively structured grouping in which conventional norms govern social behavior.

Solidaristic crowd ▲ A crowd that provides its members with a sense of unity or social solidarity.

1. *Casual Crowd*   A **casual crowd** consists of people who are passive and have a low emotional engagement and little social interaction with those nearby. People continually move in and out of a casual crowd with little notice. If you have ever been to a fair, for example, and joined a group of people watching a demonstration of a cooking gadget, you were a member of a casual crowd. Because they cause little disruption in normal social life, casual crowds are not usually considered to be a social problem.

2. *Conventional Crowd*   A **conventional crowd** is a relatively structured grouping in which conventional norms govern social behavior. Although members of a conventional crowd follow the well-known norms governing the situation, each person has little interaction with the other people in the group. For instance, the people gathered at a bus stop, waiting in a supermarket line, or lining up to board an airplane form a conventional crowd. As these examples suggest, conventional crowds are concerned with goal-directed behavior and are mechanisms through which many normal activities are accomplished.

3. *Solidaristic Crowd*   A crowd that provides its members with a sense of unity or social solidarity is called a **solidaristic crowd**. Many people feel personally empowered by being a member of a solidaristic crowd (Drury and Reicher 1999). The "Million Man March" on Washington in 1995 was an expression of solidarity for African American men. These men gathered in an attempt to form a consensus that social life in the African American community must be governed by greater peace, love, and tolerance (Marriott 1995; Messner 1997). Other solidaristic crowds include students attending pep rallies before major sports events, people attending religious revival meetings such as the Billy Graham Crusade, and people attending patriotic events such as parades on the Fourth of July.

4. *Expressive Crowd*   When people gather to change their mood, emotions, and behavior, they are members of an **expressive crowd**. If you have been to a rock concert, for example, you were part of an expressive crowd. You may have noticed how crowd members sang, danced, swayed, clapped, and otherwise used the event as an emotional outlet and as an opportunity to express their feelings. In some cases, the crowd itself creates the emotions to be expressed. You might, for instance, attend a rock concert even though you do not especially like the group that is performing. Once there, however, you become caught up in the sound and excitement of the event and become highly expressive. Because expressive crowds occasionally become unruly, officials are greatly concerned whenever a situation arises that might prompt the formation of an expressive crowd.

5. *Acting Crowd*   When crowd members become angry and engage in smashing windows, overturning cars, setting fires, or attacking members of certain groups, the crowd has moved beyond mere expression. It has, instead, become an **acting crowd** and now constitutes a mob (Drury 2002).

Because acting crowds often initiate social change, sociologists have studied them at some length. Herbert Blumer offered a now-classic symbolic interactionist account of how an acting crowd comes into existence (1939). According to him, an acting crowd goes through five stages as it interprets events: (1) people become restless, apprehensive, and susceptible to rumors; (2) something startling occurs, and people become preoccupied with it; (3) people then start milling about and discussing what is going on; (4) people next focus on some aspect of the event or on certain people involved in the event; (5) finally, crowd members come to a general agreement as to the best action to take.

The action that is produced by this five-staged process may be something as childish as a cafeteria food fight or as serious as an overthrow of a government. The point that Blumer made, however, is well taken—as people in crowds interact, they develop an interpretation of events, and this interpretation guides their actions. As we discussed with regard to the student protest in Tiananmen Square, an acting crowd can play a major role in changing the course of a government.

Riots, Panics, and Rumors

When people engage in collective behavior, they sometimes do things they would not do under normal circumstances. This tendency can be seen most clearly in a **riot**: relatively large-scale, violent collective behavior that grows from a shared anger, frustration, and sense of deprivation. Compared with mob violence, a riot involves many more people, takes place across a wider area, and may last for days. Although riots are often set off by a single incident, they typically reflect underlying strains in the social structure.

Riots are nothing new to the American social scene. One of the most infamous riots in American history occurred in New York City during the Civil War. The riot began as a protest against the government's policy of conscripting men into the army, but at some point it turned into a rampage in which the participants burned, looted, and attacked anyone who tried to stop them. This riot was not unique by any means, and almost one hundred years later, urban riots were still commonplace. During the 1960s, riots became a routine summer occurrence in American cities. Although the media called these outbursts "race riots," in fact there was relatively little violence between whites and African Americans. Instead, the outbursts appeared to be caused by long-simmering frustrations about racial inequality and the failure of American society to live up to its promises of equal opportunity.

The photograph shows a woman hugging a man with a U.S. flag in the background at an interfaith vigil after the terrorist attack on September 11, 2001. Expressive crowds are important emotional outlets that help people express strong feelings that need to be released after such a terrible event.

Expressive crowd ▲ A type of crowd people join to change their mood, emotions, and behavior.

Acting crowd ▲ A type of crowd in which the members turn into a mob, becoming angry and aggressive and engaging in violent acts.

Riot ▲ Relatively large-scale, violent collective behavior that grows from a shared anger, frustration, and sense of deprivation.

A demonstrator tries to put a stop to the gas bombs being thrown by Seattle Police while others duck for cover during the World Trade Organization protests in downtown Seattle, November 30, 1999. The protests were planned as nonviolent activities, but some members engaged in smashing windows and starting fires, and the police reacted with force.

CQ *What concept do sociologists use to describe a crowd whose members have become angry and begin smashing windows?*

Another form of collective behavior that may have serious consequences is the **panic**: a collective but irrational reaction to a serious threat. A panic is a highly dramatic event that often draws the attention of the mass media. For example, films portray thousands of people madly fleeing before an oncoming monster or a theater audience wildly dashing for the exits as flames burst out all around them.

Although the dramatic image of a panic is commonplace, sociologists now believe that true panics occur only rarely. Faced with a flood, a hurricane, an invading army, or other impending catastrophe, people seldom become hysterical, irrational, selfish, or antisocial. Very often, the problem is not mass flight, but resistance to leaving. Unless ordered, many residents of a threatened community will choose to ride out the catastrophe at home.

Furthermore, people react to threats in a fairly predictable manner. Rather than blindly fleeing from a burning theater, for example, most people will follow conventional norms about public behavior. They will wait their turn in line and go through the emergency exit in an orderly manner. Tragically, however, the flames and smoke may spread so fast that most people will not reach the exit in time and may perish standing in line.

Riots, panics, and other forms of collective behavior are often fueled by rumors. A **rumor** is a false or an unverified report communicated from one person to another and readily spreads through social ties among people (Lai and Wong 2002). Because rumors travel informally, they are difficult to verify and are easily exaggerated as time goes by (Rosnow and Fine 1976). For example, soon after Elvis Presley died, rumors began to circulate that he was still alive. Similarly, rumors of conspiracy began circulating soon after the assassination of President John Kennedy, and other rumors will undoubtedly arise in the future when a famous and beloved public figure passes away.

Rumors can be thought of as attempts to understand what is happening in an unstable and novel situation. Stated another way, rumors are a type of improvised or made-up news. For that reason, they frequently arise after devastating storms, battles, or other events that cause television and radio stations to go off the air, newspapers to stop publishing, and other channels of communication to fail. Even in the tranquil setting of a bureaucratic office, a rumor might begin when a high-ranking official suddenly steps down or when a merger with another company is about to take place. In

Panic ▲ A collective but irrational reaction to a serious threat.

Rumor ▲ A false or unverified report communicated from one person to another.

such situations, workers will be anxious about how they will be affected by the event. Consequently, if no official announcements are forthcoming, rumors will begin as people struggle to understand the new situation (Murphy 1985).

Rumors sometimes serve as precipitating events for other forms of collective behavior (Subramaniam 1999). Most of the riots that occurred during the 1960s were triggered or precipitated by a rumor. To illustrate, just before the riots in the Watts section of Los Angeles in 1965, a rumor began circulating that the police had stopped a pregnant African American woman and had beaten her. In fact, no such incident had occurred, yet the rumor seems to have precipitated the riot, one of the most devastating in American history. Once an episode of collective behavior begins, moreover, new rumors may emerge that offer an easy but inaccurate explanation for what is taking place. Thus, during a so-called race riot, it may be rumored that the police are shooting all African Americans on sight, or that African American mobs are attacking any white person they encounter.

As we can see, the broad term collective behavior refers to many kinds of social activity. These different kinds of behavior are, however, related to one another. Thus, a crowd gathered to watch a soccer game might become involved in a riot. And what happens during the riot might trigger rumors that circulate back through the crowd and excite it to new action. This example, and others we have offered, leads to the conclusion that collective behaviors are fluid, dynamic, and evolve as they take place. Because episodes are continually changing and because events happen quickly and sometimes without warning, it is difficult systematically to study collective behavior. Nevertheless, sociologists have long been intrigued by the topic of collective behavior and have offered explanations for it. We now turn to various explanations of the crowd.

Social Theory and Crowd Behavior

Sociologists have developed three main theories of crowd behavior. These are designated contagion theory, convergence theory, and emergent norm theory. These theories do not fall neatly into the categories of functionalism, conflict theory, or symbolic interaction, and so will be presented in their historical order.

Contagion Theory Early sociologists believed that people in collective situations lost their individuality and became swept up in the behaviors of others. For example, in 1852, Charles MacKay said that when normal people were in a crowd, they seemingly "went mad," adopted a "herd mentality," and became "disgraceful and violent" (MacKay 1852). Gustave LeBon, an early and influential student of collective behavior, said that people in crowds often felt that they were free to do almost anything they wished. In these situations, LeBon further said, the crowd develops a collective mind of its own, and a contagion sweeps through the crowd, releasing people's destructive tendencies (1895). In the early part of the twentieth century, sociologist Robert Park claimed that the give-and-take communication among crowd members took the form of a circular reaction: false information at one stage was rapidly communicated to others in the crowd, who then embellished the misinformation and communicated it to other crowd members (Park and Burgess 1921).

Although LeBon's ideas continue to shape the popular image of the "mob," sociologists have abandoned his ideas about a collective mind (McPhail 1991; Wethington 2000). His notion of contagion, however, remains intriguing. For example, consider a crowd that is gathering for a rock concert. As the time for the concert gets closer, a few people begin pushing forward to get good seats. On seeing them, other people quickly conclude that all the good seats will soon be taken, so these people also begin pushing forward. As they do so, they stimulate themselves and other people to push even faster and harder. Soon a melee is breaking out as everyone is rushing forward. The people at the front of the crowd can no longer resist the weight of the crowd, and they are now being helplessly pushed forward. A few of them get trapped against a wall, and a few others stumble and are immediately pushed to the ground. Unable to move forward yet unable to prevent the mass of people behind them from pushing forward, those trapped against the wall start to suffocate and soon die, while those on the ground are trampled underfoot.

Although an incident like this might appear to be a violent, irrational act, in fact, it is caused by the mutual stimulation of people seeing other people moving forward and by the desire of everyone to get to the good seats first. In that sense, it is a normal social reaction to an unusual set of circumstances. It might be noted, incidentally, that events such as these have led promoters of rock concerts to sell only assigned seats (Forsyth 1998).

Convergence Theory   Another explanation for crowd behavior, convergence theory, assumes that crowd unity results from the like-mindedness of members and that this like-mindedness exists before people join the crowd. The behavior of the crowd, in other words, is determined by the similarity of its members. For example, a crowd of students might gather to protest the firing of a popular professor. Although many of these students may be strangers to one another, they tend to be about the same age, to share the same norms, and to have similar values. The fact that they have gathered to protest the firing also means that they already agree on the issue that brought them together in the first place. However, once the crowd has formed, it may behave in unconventional ways. To show their displeasure with the college's decision, for instance, protesting students might suddenly decide to start throwing rocks or turning over cars—behaviors that they would never engage in as individuals.

Emergent Norm Theory   Because crowd behavior often appears to be irrational, there is a tendency to regard the crowd as a special kind of social behavior. According to emergent norm theory, however, little is unique about the crowd (Turner 1996). In most situations, our behavior is guided by norms, and so it is when we are members of a crowd. The problem is that in a crowd, we may be agitated, excited, and uncertain about what behavior is appropriate. Under these conditions, we are likely to latch on quickly to the norms that emerge from interacting with other crowd members. For example, if a group of protesting students develops a norm of nonviolence, then students who engage in violent acts will be booed and jeered by other crowd members, and perhaps driven from the scene. On the other hand, if a norm of violence emerges, then those students who throw rocks and attack bystanders will be cheered and otherwise rewarded by the crowd.

In practice, all three theories of crowd behavior could apply to a crowd in a given situation. As an example, consider the actions of a crowd gathered at the base of a tall building. Everyone is looking up at a man who is standing on the ledge of the building and threatening to commit suicide by jumping. In this situation, a crowd will sometimes urge the person to jump and will jeer at police officers who are attempting to prevent the suicide. What explains this seemingly irrational, antisocial behavior? Some deeper understanding of this situation emerges from applying the three theories we have just discussed. First, convergence theory suggests that some people in the crowd are predisposed to act in antisocial ways. Either through chance or choice, these people join the crowd and bring with them their personalities and emotional characteristics that predispose them to bait the person on the ledge. Second, contagion theory implies that the shouts of the people who are urging the person on the ledge to jump, spread the idea of baiting to other people. And third, as the idea of baiting spreads through the crowd, norms of callousness and cruelty emerge that make the baiting seem normal in the context of the situation. Following these norms, other crowd members join the baiting, thus doing something they would not do under ordinary circumstances (Turner and Killian 1987).

 STUDY TIP

Come up with three visual representations—drawings or collages—that represent the three theories of crowd behavior (contagion theory, convergence theory, and emergent norm theory).

Pausing to Think   About Collective Behavior

Collective behavior appears most often when people are faced with novel situations and have few preexisting norms to guide them. The theory of structural strain suggests that the causes of collective behavior are linked to existing social conditions. Several types of collective action exist, including crowds, riots, panics, and rumors. Contagion theory maintains that people in a crowd agitate one another and lose control over their usual behavior. Convergence theory assumes that people who are already predisposed to act in a certain way converge on a common site to form a crowd. Finally, emergent norm theory holds that people in crowds respond to norms that develop while crowd behavior is under way.

CQ Think about a time when you were part of a conventional, solidaristic, or expressive crowd. Did participation in this crowd evoke strong feelings in you? ◆ Did these feelings lead you to engage in new or different behavior?

Social Movements

The study of collective behavior also includes the study of social movements. A **social movement** is an organized but noninstitutionalized effort to change society through collective action. Compared with crowd behavior, a social movement is relatively well organized and may involve literally millions of people. With so many people involved, most participants will be strangers to one another, and at any given time, they will be involved with only a minority of the people in the movement.

Types of Social Movements

Social movements differ from one another primarily in their goals. On the basis of goals, sociologists often recognize the following types:

1. *Reform*   The goal of a **reform movement** is to change society in a limited way. Very often, a reform movement focuses on the passage or repeal of specific laws. For example, the original goal of the temperance movement was to outlaw the manufacture and sale of alcoholic beverages. This goal was accomplished in 1919 when the Eighteenth Amendment to the U.S. Constitution was adopted, an amendment that legalized prohibition. Similarly, the women's suffrage movement aimed to give women the right to vote, a goal that was achieved with the passage of the Nineteenth Amendment. Other examples of reform movements are the Progressive movement, which resulted in the passage of legislation to regulate the meat-packing industry and to provide for the recall of corrupt public officials; the disabled rights movement; the victims' rights movement; the antipornography movement; and the anti–drinking-and-driving movement.

2. *Revolutionary*   Unlike a reform movement, the goal of a **revolutionary movement** is to replace the existing social order with a completely new order. Revolutionary movements usually arise when simply reforming the existing social order seems insufficient. To people reared in the United States, the best-known revolutionary movement occurred in 1776. Many colonists came to believe that the injustices they were suffering at the hands of the British monarchy could be corrected only by the establishment of a new country.

3. *Resistance*   A **resistance movement** is a countermovement. That is, its goal is to stop or reverse changes that are taking place. An example is the movement for the repeal of Prohibition. This movement came into existence after Prohibition went into effect and eventually succeeded when Prohibition ended in 1933. Another example is

Social movement ▲ An organized but noninstitutionalized effort to change society through collective action.

Reform movement ▲ A social movement whose goal is to change society in a limited way.

Revolutionary movement ▲ A social movement whose goal is to replace the existing social order with a completely new order.

Resistance movement ▲ A countermovement whose goal is to stop or reverse changes that are taking place.

In 1954, 35 percent of the nonagricultural labor force was unionized. By 1991, union membership had shrunk to less than half that figure. If the trend of declining union membership continues, by the year 2005, unions will be a negligible factor in the labor force—perhaps as few as 5 percent of private-sector personnel will be union members.

Several factors are responsible for the decline in union membership. First, unions began as resistance movements, and the aggressive unions of the early twentieth century were highly successful in eliminating unsafe and economically exploitive conditions faced by workers. Many nonunion workers now take for granted the improved conditions in the workplace that were won through hard-fought battles waged by unions many decades ago. Justice in the workplace is protected by many federal and state laws, and workers have become complacent about their rights. Union leadership itself has become less willing to challenge corporate owners and often acknowledges the corporation's superior ability to define conditions in the workplace. Also, union leadership has stopped resisting corporate leaders because it feels less powerful.

Second, public support for unions has eroded because of a series of highly publicized disclosures about corrupt union officials. Numerous union leaders have been linked to underworld crime families, and the Teamsters Union was placed in trusteeship by the federal courts because of corrupt officials. Corporations encourage this antiunion sentiment and try to portray union demands as excessive and selfish (Craver 1993).

Third, the traditional union base of blue-collar workers is shrinking. Millions of blue-collar manufacturing jobs have been lost through automation or deindustrialization and the use of low-paid workers outside the United States. In addition, corporations define white-collar workers as part of management, thus creating a wedge between white- and blue-collar workers. Thus, even though many white-collar workers might gain greater job security and better benefits through unionization, they are reluctant to join.

Fourth, unions were slow to include minority and female workers in their membership and have only recently turned their attention to recruiting members from these groups. As a result, many employers have been able to weaken unions by using women or minority-group members as replacement workers during periods of labor conflict.

Although unions have faced difficult times, the movement may be on the upswing again. To illustrate, in 1997 the Teamsters Union with 185,000 members went on strike against United Parcel Service and shut down the package delivery company for two weeks. The Teamsters received financial help from the AFL-CIO, and UPS soon agreed to most of the union's demands. Some observers speculated that the victory—the largest union victory in more than a decade—might be a turning point in the union movement. Former Secretary of Labor Robert Reich said, "This is something of a watershed. But only the future will tell how much a watershed it is" (www.nytimes.com. 1997. "Victory for Labor, But How Far Will It Go?").

CQ Would you join a labor union if you thought that doing so would increase your job security? ◆ Do you think that the labor movement ought to become more of a resistance movement again? ◆ Why, or why not?

---

the labor movement, which began as an attempt to resist the power of management and to establish the right of workers to make certain decisions and to work in a safe environment (see the Social Change box "What Happened to the Labor Movement?"). A more recent illustration is the pro-life movement, which is opposed to abortion. It came into existence to counter the pro-choice movement, which had won a significant legal battle when the Supreme Court affirmed the right of a woman to have an abortion.

4. *Expressive* The goal of an **expressive movement** is to provide gratification through self-expression. One example is the charismatic movement that is currently occurring among both Catholics and Protestants. This movement urges people to open themselves to the direct actions of the Holy Spirit. People who do so often speak in tongues, swoon, and experience other emotional releases. Another example is the New Age movement, whose goal is for individuals to develop a new sense of personal, physical, and spiritual well-being. Similarly, men's groups have formed to allow men the freedom to express whatever thoughts, fears, and anxieties they have about being men. Some of these groups beat drums and chant to free up their inner masculine selves.

The various forms of collective behavior we described earlier can play a part in shaping a social movement. Protesting crowds might call attention to a movement's

Expressive movement ▲ A type of social movement whose goal is to provide gratification through self-expression.

goals, or the outbreak of a riot might cause the government to take certain actions. Even a rumor could influence the outcome by providing an explanation that might be untrue but might nevertheless be believed. For example, the string of demonstrations and so-called urban race riots that occurred throughout the 1960s sensitized the American public to the conditions faced by African Americans and spurred the government to institute reforms ranging from Head Start (a program for preschool children) to laws that prohibited discrimination on the basis of race, color, creed, and gender.

In contrast to many other forms of collective behavior, social movements tend to be large, formal, and enduring. Hence, they are somewhat easier to explain. We now turn to various explanations of social movements.

Social Theory and Social Movements

As with explanations of crowd behavior, explanations of social movements do not fall neatly into the categories of functionalism, conflict theory, and symbolic interaction—the perspectives that we used to analyze social inequality and social institutions earlier in the text. There are three principal explanations of social movements: relative deprivation theory, resource-mobilization theory, and mass society theory (Lyman 1995).

Relative Deprivation The theory of *relative deprivation* assumes that a social movement is likely to develop when people perceive a gap between what they feel their situation *should* be and what their situation *actually* is (Gurney and Tierney 1982; Marx and McAdam 1994; see Figure 16.2). Feelings of relative deprivation often arise when people compare themselves with other people and conclude that those other people have more wealth, power, freedom, and other social goods than they themselves have. Feeling deprived, they might then form or join a social movement as a way to close the gap between what they feel should be and what actually is.

The concept of relative deprivation helps to explain why people may feel wronged even though they may appear to be fairly well off in absolute terms. For example, poor people in the United States are fairly wealthy compared with poor people in China. Nevertheless, poor people in the United States may feel highly deprived because they compare themselves, not with the poor in China, but with the American middle and upper classes.

An intriguing prediction follows from the concept of relative deprivation, namely, that people are more likely to engage in collective social action when their situation is getting better rather than when it is getting worse. The Chinese student protesters we discussed at the beginning of this chapter might serve as an example. As long as the Chinese government was totally repressive and dictatorial, the students were forced to live a dreary life with no hope of having a voice in government or even in the decisions that controlled their careers. As the government slowly began introducing small reforms, however, the students began to see some hope for political freedom. As the process of reform accelerated, the possibility of even more freedom increased until the students began to believe that they could play a role in changing their government. As a result of their newly fueled optimism, they initiated a freedom movement that culminated in the mass protest at Tiananmen Square. As we know, the government responded with overwhelming force and apparently returned to its former ways.

Resource-Mobilization Theory A problem with relative deprivation theory is the fact that in all industrial societies, some people have less than others. In effect, relative deprivation is always present, but collective social action does not always take place. How can this situation be explained (Williams and Benford 2000)?

The *resource-mobilization theory* argues that resources are the key ingredient for a successful social movement (Zald and McCarthy 2002). The resources necessary

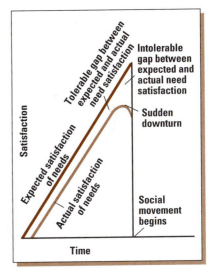

FIGURE 16.2 Relative Deprivation Theory

This figure represents the relationship between rising expectations and social movements. Social movements often occur after a period of social and economic betterment, when a sudden downturn fuels concern that gains will be lost (Davies 1962).

	Leadership Style
Preliminary	*Rabble-rouser* who awakens interest among the people
Popular	*Visionary* who articulates a vision of a better future through collective action
Formal Organizational	*Tactician* who provides action plans and operational leadership
Institutional	*Administrator* who knows how to make a bureaucracy work effectively

FIGURE 16.3 Successful Leadership Style and Stages of a Social Movement

Leaders are important resources for a social movement, and this figure shows the type of leader who is most effective at each stage of a social movement. During the preliminary stage, the rabble-rouser awakens the people to their problem and calls them to action. During the popular stage, people are willing to seek a change in their situation but require a visionary leader to articulate the future toward which they should strive. As the movement becomes formally organized, it needs a good tactician who can bring the diverse elements of the movement together and coordinate and lead the specific actions most likely to achieve the movement's goals. Once the movement becomes institutionalized and accepted as a regular component of society, it needs a good administrator to keep the bureaucracy moving toward the movement's goals.

to launch and maintain a social movement include money, members, leaders, offices and communication facilities, ties with other active groups and influential people, and contacts with the media. In addition, people must agree that the movement is correct, proper, and right; that is, they must define the movement as legitimate (Einwohner et al. 2000; McCarthy and Zald 1973, 1977; Marx and McAdam 1994). Successful movements may even require a number of different leaders at different stages (Figure 16.3).

Clearly, any social movement requires a certain level of resources to sustain it. Office space must be rented, telephones paid for, and postage stamps bought. And today, of course, a nationwide social movement will probably have to spend millions of dollars to advertise its cause on television, hire publicists and advertising agencies, and secure the services of lobbyists, fund-raisers, and other specialized personnel who can establish ties with members of Congress and other key people. The resources available also determine the tactics of social protest. These tactics can range from organizing public meetings to organizing a nationwide strike, and different tactics imply different reactions on the part of the public (see also Society Today: Contributions to Charity).

Like the theory of relative deprivation, resource-mobilization theory suggests that social movements are likely to arise when prosperity is increasing. With economic prosperity, individuals, businesses, charities, and other private organizations have more discretionary income; some of this income may be used to support a social movement. When the economy is deteriorating, however, discretionary income declines, and there is relatively little to support a social movement, no matter how worthy its cause appears to be.

Mass Society Theory According to *mass society theory*, as industrialization advanced, political, religious, and social systems became highly impersonalized, and people became isolated from one another. In effect, the society changed from communal to associational; and with that change came alienation, anomie, and excessive rationalization (Chapters 2 and 5; Kornhauser 1959; Marx and McAdam 1994; Smelser 1998). An example of a social movement arising in mass society is the democracy movement in Czechoslovakia. That nation was formerly a communist state, and the communist government outlawed organized religion, political parties, and independent trade unions—institutions that had traditionally helped to hold Czech society together. From the perspective of mass society theory, the absence of these institutions produced alienation, and out of alienation grew the democracy movement. It was popular because it drew people together, providing them with a common cause and a sense of community. Eventually, the democratic movement led the fight to abolish the communist form of government. As a result, Czech society adopted a free-market economy and democratic government, but Czechoslovakia eventually split into two countries: the Czech Republic and Slovakia.

As with explanations of crowd behavior, each theory can increase our understanding of a social movement. For instance, within a predominantly associational society, one segment of the population might be socially isolated and suffering from relative deprivation, but it might not have the resources to launch a successful social movement. At the same time, another segment of the population might be isolated and have resources but not feel any sense of relative deprivation; hence, it would not attempt a social movement either. These and other possibilities we might outline indicate that each theory provides us with insights as to why and how a social movement emerges, matures, and withers away.

●■▲ **Pausing to Think** **About Social Movements**

The four main types of social movements are reform, revolutionary, resistance, and expressive movements. Relative deprivation theory suggests that social movements will emerge when there is a perceived gap between what people want and what they have.

Resource-mobilization theory suggests that social movements emerge and succeed only when they have the resources to support them. Finally, mass society theory suggests that social movements occur when the broader society becomes impersonalized and people become isolated from one another.

CQ When does a social movement stop being a reform movement and become a revolutionary movement?

Social Movements in the United States

Currently there are several social movements under way in the United States, including the pro-life, the pro-choice, and the disability rights movements (Freeman and Johnson 1999). Although each movement is important, in this section of the chapter, we will focus on three movements that are especially relevant to contemporary life: the civil rights movement, the women's movement, and the environmental movement.

The Civil Rights Movement

One of the most important movements in American history concerns the quest for racial and ethnic equality. This struggle for civil rights began early in American history (Lauer 1991), but we shall pick up the struggle just after the Civil War.

With the end of the Civil War in 1865, the issue of slavery was resolved in the sense that those states that permitted slavery had been defeated militarily. The end of legal slavery, however, did not end the economic and political oppression of African Americans. Many states, especially in the South, passed so-called Jim Crow laws that established a fully segregated way of life. Under this system, African Americans could not attend the same schools as whites, eat in the same restaurants, live in the same neighborhoods, hold political office, or vote. In effect, African Americans were forced into an inferior economic, political, and social position. Throughout the late nineteenth and into the middle of the twentieth century, Jim Crow was reinforced by violence, and African Americans were routinely lynched for "stepping out of line" (Franklin and Moss 1988).

Even though African Americans protested as best they could, as long as the majority of whites believed in Jim Crow, black protests could not substantially change the situation. The National Association for the Advancement of Colored People (NAACP), which was founded in 1910, took the lead in moving social protest into the courts. Over the years, the NAACP won several victories, but the most important was the 1954 Supreme Court decision *Brown* v. *Board of Education* (Wilson 1995). The court ruled that "separate educational facilities [for whites and African Americans] are inherently unequal." In effect, the decision banned racial segregation in the public schools. This decision sparked a wave of social action in support of civil rights. Boycotts of segregated public transportation, sit-ins in restaurants, and marches turned the movement into a full-fledged social movement (Skrenty 2002).

To carry the movement further, another series of protests developed. This part of the movement was led by Martin Luther King, Jr., and his followers in the Southern Christian Leadership Conference (SCLC). The rise of King and other African American ministers in the civil rights movement is explained by a little-recognized fact. During the first decades of the twentieth century, many rural African Americans moved to urban areas to seek employment. Living close together in urban neighborhoods, they turned to the African American church for spiritual guidance and social support. The ministers of these churches were soon taking on key leadership roles, and several of them eventually became the mainstay of the civil rights movement in the South (McAdam et al. 1988).

Dr. King's wing of the civil rights movement favored a nonviolent approach to social change—an approach that made him especially popular among whites. The

A parade in honor of Martin Luther King, Jr., winds its way down Colfax Avenue in Denver on January 17, 2000. Today, the civil rights movement has become an institutionalized part of American society, and Martin Luther King Day is a federal holiday.

television coverage and photographs of police dogs attacking African American protest marchers caused outrage among many white viewers, with the result that many whites joined the movement for racial equality.

Within the civil rights movement itself, a number of more militant groups began to follow such leaders as Bobby Seale of the Black Panthers and Elijah Muhammad and Malcolm X of the Nation of Islam. According to this branch of the movement, African Americans should actively take their destiny into their own hands and should turn away from whites. Thus, the Black Power movement extolled the beauty and dignity of African American culture and rejected the goal of assimilating into white society. It argued rather for the development of economic, cultural, educational, and political institutions created and shaped by African Americans themselves for their own benefit.

Today, the civil rights movement has become an institutionalized part of American society and has served as a model for other social movements both in the United States and abroad (Morris 1999). Although most people in the United States accept the goals of racial and ethnic equality, they disagree about the best means to achieve those goals. In particular, many whites strongly oppose affirmative action (NORC 1998). They say that affirmative action has turned into a quota system that is, in effect, a kind of discrimination against whites. And in any event, these whites say, they had nothing to do with slavery, Jim Crow, and other forms of past inequality. Consequently, they ask, why should they be the ones to suffer from the negative effects of affirmative action? Following this type of reasoning, in 1996, California voters passed a referendum known as Proposition 209 that prohibited all state-run affirmative action programs (*New York Times*, November 7, 1996). The controversy over civil rights will certainly follow American society throughout this century. One issue that has already emerged is the payment of reparations by the federal government to African Americans for slavery (Nuruddin 2002). How this issue will develop and how it will be resolved remains unknown (Healey 1997).

The Women's Movement

The women's movement originated in the 1840s when feminists sought the right to vote and the right to divorce. The early movement was widely viewed as an attack on the sexual morality of the time and on the integrity of the traditional family. Because its goals were considered highly radical at the time, the movement was largely unsuccessful. The status of women was greatly undermined in 1872 when the U.S. Supreme Court ruled that the "innate weaknesses" of women made them unfit for many occupations (*Bradwell v. Illinois* 1872). Some 20 years later the Supreme Court further ruled that women were not even "persons" under the law. This ruling came about, it is interesting to note, when a woman in Virginia applied for a license to practice law. The applicable Virginia statute stated that "any person" with a license to practice law could do so in the state. Her application was rejected, however, on the grounds that the phrase "any person" actually meant "any man," an interpretation upheld by the Supreme Court.

By the early 1900s, the Women's Christian Temperance Union (WCTU) had gained legitimacy and was actively crusading against alcohol abuse and prostitution and for better employment conditions, child labor laws, kindergartens, and moral purity. In many areas of the country, the WCTU's drive against alcohol was heavily supported, and some of that support extended to women's rights. By the 1920s, major changes in gender roles were beginning to take place. The model of the newly liberated woman was the "flapper"—the youthful woman who wore short dresses, danced the Charleston, and smoked and drank in public. Also in 1920, the women's movement won a great victory when women in the United States finally gained the right to vote. Contrary to some predictions, however, women did not vote in a massive bloc. Instead, they split their vote in much the same way that men did, thus dissipating their potential power.

During the Great Depression of the 1930s, the women's movement suffered a series of setbacks. The 1932 Federal Economy Act stipulated that if layoffs were necessary, married women were to be let go first; federal wage codes gave women less pay than men for the same jobs; and many organizations fired women to create openings for men.

During World War II, women entered the labor force in huge numbers, but after the war, they were displaced by returning male veterans. In the boom years of the 1960s, President John Kennedy signed the Equal Pay Act of 1963, and President Lyndon Johnson signed the 1964 Civil Rights Act. This latter act made it illegal for employers of 15 or more workers to discriminate on the basis of race, color, national origin, religion—or sex. There were some exceptions, however—the act permitted hiring actors and actresses on the basis of sex for film roles. Nevertheless, the general expectation that some jobs should be performed by men and others by women was no longer accepted as valid. This provision of the law, it might be noted, applied to both men and women. Thus, men could no longer be denied employment as flight attendants because customers expected to be served by women, just as women could not be denied employment as construction workers because men traditionally performed such work.

During the 1970s, the National Organization for Women (NOW) and other women's rights organizations heavily supported the Equal Rights Amendment to the U.S. Constitution. If passed, this amendment would have constitutionally guaranteed equal treatment of men and women. Even though the majority of voters favored the amendment, it failed when only 35 states approved it (passage of a constitutional amendment requires approval of 38 states).

Today, the women's movement continues to pursue matters of particular interest to women in an international context (Soule et al. 1999; Chishti 2002). As we have mentioned before, women have been intensely involved on both sides of the abortion issue (Jacoby 1998). Other major concerns are the state of women's health (Chapter 14), equal pay and the glass ceiling (Chapter 8), the feminization of poverty (Chapter 6), and the role of women in the family and society (Chapters 11 and 12). Because these are major issues with no easy solutions, the women's movement will be a part of American and global society for most of the next century.

A woman campaigning for the Equal Rights Amendment. Because the amendment failed to secure the support of 38 states, it was never ratified into law.

The Environmental Movement

The environmental movement includes a wide variety of loosely networked groups and organizations (Lutzenhiser 2002; Buttel 2002; McLaughlin and Khawaja 2000;

Theodore Roosevelt, 26th President of the United States, stands with naturalist John Muir on Glacier Point, above Yosemite Valley, California, in 1903. Both men were advocates of nature and outdoor pursuits. Roosevelt liked to hunt and could identify many birdcalls. Muir was a famous mountaineer who climbed many peaks in the High Sierras. Muir, a founder of the Sierra Club, persuaded Roosevelt to make Yosemite a national park. Today, millions of tourists visit Yosemite and enjoy much the same uncluttered scenery Roosevelt and Muir enjoyed over a century ago.

CQ *What do you think?* ◆ *Will Yosemite's scenery still be as beautiful in 2103?* ◆ *Or will population growth in California and other western states doom Yosemite Valley to overcrowding, pollution, and smog?*

Schnaiberg and Gould 1994:150). The diffuse nature of the movement and the resulting lack of overarching goals reflects the diversity of environmental concerns, with different problems affecting different industries and different people. For example, the problem of water pollution in the Great Lakes has little to do with the defoliation of the rain forests in South America; and the problem of preserving wetlands has little to do—at least on the surface—with the problem of air pollution. As a result, environmental conflicts often produce seemingly odd coalitions of groups. During the 1970s, to illustrate, the antinuclear movement was heavily supported by the coal industry. The reason had less to do with the dangers of radioactivity than with the economic gains to be had if coal rather than nuclear fuel were used in power plants.

Because the problems of the environment are so diverse, success in environmental action usually requires groups to form complex coalitions with other groups (Schnaiberg and Gould 2000; Shaffer 2000). The affected groups pool their resources to promote a specific outcome in a specific conflict. After the issue is resolved, however, the coalition quickly dissolves. The fluid nature of these coalitions helps to distinguish the environmental movement from other social movements with long-lasting coalitions.

The roots of the environmental movement are found in American history. As the issues facing the United States changed, so did the nature of the environmental movement. During the *exploitation period*, the ecosystem was viewed either as a vast storehouse of resources ripe for exploitation or as a series of obstacles to be overcome. During the westward expansion, farmers commonly burned the forest to clear it for agriculture. Thus, trees that were hundreds of years old were routinely chopped down, and because there was so much wood available for fuel, the felled trees were burned where they lay. Occasionally these fires got out of control. The fires burned up not only the standing trees but, of more importance, the piles of timber, branches, and cut trees that were on the ground, left over from the logging operations. In one such instance, the community of Peshtigo, Wisconsin, burned to the ground, and before it was over, 1,500 people had perished.

Exhibiting a similar disregard for the environment, the federal government encouraged hunters and settlers to kill the millions of buffalo that were the main food supply for many Native American tribes living on the Great Plains. Not only did this slaughter clear the buffalo from farmlands, but it also destroyed the main food supply of the Plains Indians, thus forcing them to accept life on the reservation. Because there was little scientific knowledge about ecosystems and because natural resources seemed so abundant, few people worried about what was happening.

Beginning with the latter part of the nineteenth century and extending to the end of World War II, the environmental movement entered the conservation period. During this time, the environment became a controversial issue, and two approaches emerged: preservation and conservation. The ultimate goal of the preservationists was to protect the environment from economic exploitation. Accordingly, they argued that certain ecosystems should be set aside and protected from any outside influences that would change them. In effect, they believed that certain natural ecosystems should be preserved, or left in their original state. In contrast, conservationists believed in accommodating economic development whenever possible; thus, they supported programs aimed at soil management, water purification, and ecologically sensitive management of lumbering, fishing, and hunting (Cylke 1993; Schnaiberg and Gould 2000).

By the end of the conservation period, both preservationists and conservationists had made several important gains. The National Park system had been created; federal, state, and local governments had established agencies to protect the environment; educational programs about the environment had been established in many schools; and public awareness of environmental concerns had greatly increased.

After World War II, the so-called ecological period of the environmental movement began, and it has lasted to the present day (see the Profiles box). By 1970, several private organizations in the ecological movement had become politically powerful, and the first Earth Day was held in that year. The main result of Earth Day was to heighten the public's awareness of environmental problems. Currently, environmental organizations have their own separate goals, and they regularly lobby legislatures about environmental matters. In addition, many local environmental organizations have sprung up, and these have had a major influence on issues affecting communities. They

Profiles ●■▲ Rachel Carson

When the book *Silent Spring* appeared in 1962, it caused a public furor. Before *Silent Spring*, hardly anyone had heard the words "pesticide" and "herbicide," but after the book was published, they became a part of our common vocabulary. Written by Rachel Carson (1907–1964), the book warned that the use of chemicals in agriculture was poisoning our health and destroying the environment. In a sense, Rachel Carson's book symbolically marks the beginning of the modern environmental movement in the United States. The history of *Silent Spring* is worth knowing, because it shows how an individual critical thinker can affect the course of society.

Although the book seemed to appear from nowhere, in fact it was the culmination of years of work and experience. Carson actually published her first story when she was only 11 years old. As a teenager, she won a scholarship to the Pennsylvania College for Women, where she wrote for the student newspaper and studied biology. After graduation, she studied zoology at Johns Hopkins University and earned a master's degree. She then joined the U.S. Fish and Wildlife Service, where she enjoyed a highly successful career. While there, she wrote and edited government booklets and subsequently became editor-in-chief.

Carson loved nature, and when she was not working, she enjoyed exploring the Maine coast. During her free time, she wrote lyrically about the sea as a natural environment. Carson believed that we ought to respect all of life, down to the tiniest creatures. She believed that nature was in a delicate ecological balance, and she was appalled when people failed to respect that balance (Gartner 1983:107). Her writings were so successful that eventually she was able to quit her government job and become a full-time author.

During the late 1950s, she began to receive letters from angry and frightened people. They told her that government agencies were spraying the pesticide DDT to control mosquitoes, that farmers were applying chemicals to kill weeds and pests, and that industries were dumping chemical wastes into the water.

In those days, people thought that chemicals would be harmlessly absorbed by the earth. Carson, however, suspected that the chemicals did not disappear. Instead, they were being absorbed by plants; the plants were being eaten by small animals that thus became contaminated; the small animals were being eaten by larger animals that also became contaminated; and so on throughout the food chain. And because humans are also part of nature, we too were absorbing these harmful chemicals from the food we ate.

Carson knew that it would be difficult to change people's opinions and that she was challenging agriculture—a powerful industry with vested interests in continuing the status quo. Consequently, she amassed her evidence carefully, and *Silent Spring* presents the case against pesticides and herbicides almost like a legal brief. She warned Americans that toxic chemicals would destroy the environment unless action was taken immediately. Although Carson focused on the indiscriminate use of chemicals, she implied something deeper: she was attacking the idea that environmental damage was the inevitable price of progress (Brooks 1972).

Predictably, Carson was attacked by the agricultural industry, and, not surprising for the time, she was belittled because she was a woman. In the end, though, she won. Other scientists soon came to her support; the media joined her crusade; and the public became concerned about the environment. The government took action. DDT was banned outright, and standards were established for chemical fertilizers, pesticides, and additives. But of most importance, her belief that we are all part of nature and that we all stand to win or lose together became an accepted part of American culture. No longer was the destruction of the environment an acceptable price to pay for "progress."

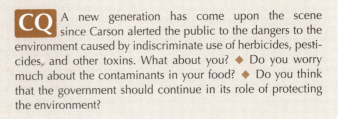

CQ A new generation has come upon the scene since Carson alerted the public to the dangers to the environment caused by indiscriminate use of herbicides, pesticides, and other toxins. What about you? ◆ Do you worry much about the contaminants in your food? ◆ Do you think that the government should continue in its role of protecting the environment?

Toyota Motor Corp President Fujio Cho smiles next to Toyota's all-new "Prius" gasoline-electric hybrid car during an unveiling in Tokyo. The new Prius is equipped with the next-generation Toyota Hybrid System (THS II), developed around the concept of the Hybrid Synergy Drive that represents a sophisticated fusion of ecology and power. This model is available for purchase now in the United States and promises to deliver over 50 miles to the gallon in city traffic.

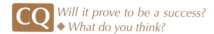 Will it prove to be a success? ◆ What do you think?

have forced polluters to clean up contaminated waste sites, have succeeded in having bans placed on the aerial spraying of pesticides, and have suggested tearing down dams to protect salmon runs.

The environmental movement is now divided into three factions:

1. **Mainstream Ecology** Supporters of *mainstream ecology* mainly work in formal organizations funded by independent financial contributions. These organizations have professional staffs but depend heavily on volunteer workers.

2. **Populist Ecology** The *populist ecology* faction emphasizes individual and corporate responsibility and generally ignores collective political action. With this emphasis, populist ecology resembles an expressive social movement more than it does a reform movement (Marx and McAdam 1994).

3. **Radical Ecology** The *radical ecology* faction, which is the smallest part of the movement, offers an alternative to the rest of the environmental movement. Some radical ecologists follow Gaia, or the view that the earth's living matter—including the air, oceans, and land—are components of a self-regulating organism. Some radical ecologists are **eco-feminists**: They claim that the "oppression of nature" is caused by the same male-dominated institutions that oppress women and minorities.

Deep ecology is a faction that argues that humans require a fundamental change in their consciousness to bring about ecological sustainability. Another branch of radical ecology is social ecology, which argues that the current environmental movement is not capable of solving the world's environmental problems because it is too closely linked with the status quo. A true solution, they believe, will come about only when a new social order has been created.

The environmental movement faces opposition from a number of powerful sources. Particularly influential in the United States are politicians who feel that economic development in the regions they represent has been slowed by environmental concerns (Harper 2000; Lacayo 1995). Many powerful business concerns are also opposed to legislation that forces them to reduce pollution, clean up waste sites, and take the environment into account when expanding facilities (see Chapter 4 and Chapter 15). For instance, Rockwell International has been cited by the state of

Eco-feminists ▲ Feminist social activists who claim that the "oppression of nature" is caused by the same male-dominated institutions that oppress women and minorities.

What Do You Think? ●■▲ Would You Like to Take a Toxic Tour?

?

When we think of taking a vacation, we usually think of going on a luxury cruise to the Caribbean, visiting the museums of Europe, or just hanging out on a beach in Florida with our friends. But how would you like to take a tour to Mexico to see the impoverished shantytowns outside Tijuana, or to Vietnam to visit the sweatshops where shoes and clothes are made for import to the United States, or to San Francisco to explore the world of the garment workers of Chinatown and to dig in the toxic waste dumps of the Mission district? These are just some of the so-called toxic or reality tours now available. The people who take these tours are usually knowledgeable about social problems but lack direct experience. They have read about poverty, exploitation, and other issues, but have not seen poverty face-to-face, or walked through a toxic dump, or talked with sweatshop workers.

CQ *Would you be willing to go on a toxic tour and pay for it? ◆ If so, what would you like to see? ◆ What personal implications do you think a toxic tour would have for you?

*To answer these critical questions, review the "What Is Critical Thinking?" box in Chapter 1, paying special attention to the discussion of personal implications.
SOURCE: *Los Angeles Times*, February 15, 1998:A1, A38.

California and the federal government for repeated violations of environmental laws. One Rockwell plant was responsible for creating 166 hazardous waste dumps, and in 1994, two Rockwell physicists were killed in an explosion. Critics believe that the explosion resulted from sham tests that were really designed to allow the company to dispose of hazardous wastes cheaply (Britt, Knight, and Jacobs 1995; see also the What Do You Think? box). Nonetheless, many people support laws that protect the environment, and younger people are inclined to give the environment priority over the economy (Figure 16.4).

Relations Among Social Movements

Although we have discussed the civil rights movement, the women's movement, and the environmental movement separately, they are related to one another and to other

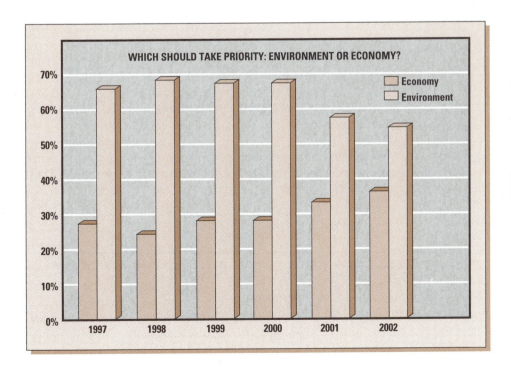

FIGURE 16.4 Concern for the Environment

When asked "Which should take priority, the environment or economic growth?" most people say, "the environment." Nonetheless, in recent years support for the environment has declined (Gallup News Service, April 22, 2002; gallup.com; accessed November 11, 2003).

CQ *Do you think that support for the environment will continue to decline? List the reasons for your answer.*

Society Today ● ■ ▲

Contributions to Charity

Social movements cost money, and donations to charities are an important source of revenue for some organizations.

The greater the household income, the greater the dollar amount contributed to charity. As the chart shows, households with the lowest annual incomes (< $10,000) contributed less than $1,000 annually, while households with the highest incomes contributed almost $5,000 annually.

Although the wealthy contributed more money in absolute dollars, they sacrifice less. That is, the wealthiest households contributed three percent of their annual income to charity while the poorest households contributed seven percent.

SOURCE: U.S. Bureau of the Census 2002.

CQ How do you explain the fact that the poor contributed less in absolute dollars than the wealthy, but at the same time the poor contribute a greater percentage of their household income?

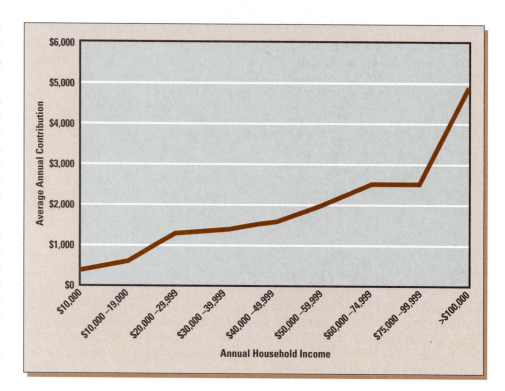

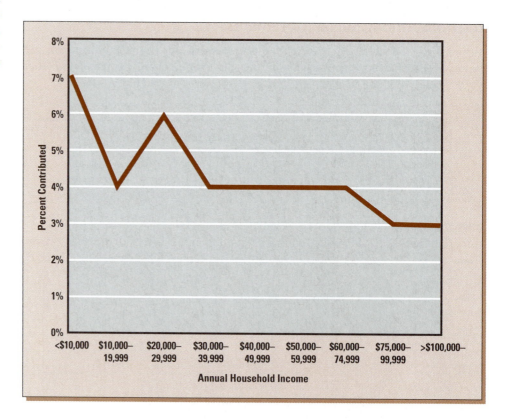

movements we have not discussed (Van Dyke 2003). The civil rights movement, by drawing attention to the inequalities of race and ethnicity, implicitly drew attention to other forms of inequality as well. Thus, movements focusing on gay and lesbian rights have benefited because the public and the government had already been sensitized to the broader issue of inequality. Similarly, as the environmental movement grew, many racial and ethnic minorities came to realize that they are the groups most affected by air pollution, chemical waste, lead poisoning, asbestos, and other environmental hazards. Although two movements sometimes compete for resources, they can sometimes benefit by joining forces to achieve a common goal. In short, the various social movements taking place within a large, associational society often are linked, and often in ways that the founders of the movements did not foresee.

●■▲ Pausing to Think   About Social Movements in the United States

Three social movements have had an especially strong influence on contemporary life in the United States. The civil rights movement originated from the efforts of African Americans to gain equal opportunity and then expanded to include other people of color. Today, civil rights are an accepted part of life in the United States. The women's movement began over a hundred years ago when women collectively sought to gain independence from men and to gain the right to vote. More recently, the movement has actively supported such initiatives as the Equal Rights Amendment to the Constitution and equal pay. The environmental movement is a looser collection of groups and individuals that share a concern for the environment. Because environmental issues are widely diverse, many of these groups form coalitions to achieve specific goals.

 Can you identify any social movements that are counter to the civil rights, women's, and environmental movements?

123 **STUDY TIP**

Make a time line, or an outline organized chronologically, for each of the significant social movements in the United States—the civil rights movement, the women's movement, and the environmental movement. Include in your time lines/outlines an indication of the movements' principal goals.

Collective Social Action and Working for Change

The study of social movements shows us that societies are often changed by individuals who join with other people to engage in collective social action. In this section, we will discuss how efforts to implement change may be targeted at the individual, the organization, or the social institution.

Changing Individuals

One of the most effective ways to shape people's knowledge, values, and attitudes is through instruction—formal schooling, adult programs, classes and workshops, home-study courses, and other educational activities. With regard to formal education, most people in the United States feel strongly that the school system should teach academic subjects while at the same time preparing students to participate in society. The schools, therefore, have been given the responsibility for driver education, sex and health education, the development of vocational skills, and other subjects aimed at helping young people to take their place in the community (see Chapter 12). Because the schools are so crucial in the socialization process, groups wanting to change society often single out the educational system as their primary target. Thus, for instance, the so-called Moral Majority wants the public schools to teach the biblical version of human creation alongside the scientific version; moreover, the Amish distrust public education so much that they have established their own school system.

Cassius Clay was indicted by a Federal Grand Jury for his refusal to be inducted into the armed forces in 1967, during the Vietnam War. When ask why, he said "I'm doing this for my religion. I'm serious, I'm ready to die for my religion." Clay appealed his conviction, which was later reversed by the Supreme Court. Clay changed his name to Muhammad Ali when he took on the Islamic faith. He became famous worldwide for his boxing ability and social conscious. He is a good example of how people can be changed through socialization.

Sometimes individuals are most effectively changed if approached as members of groups (Chapter 5). This method relies on group norms to bring people into conformity. For this reason, group discussions are a better format for changing individual norms than is a lecture (Lauer 1991). And as we have already discussed in Chapter 5, even the most outrageous behavior may seem to be normal when there is a group consensus about it.

Changing Organizations

Because formal organizations are such an important feature of society, they are often the target of change. In attempts to change organizations such as business firms and government agencies, several principles come into play (Lauer 1991). First, *organizations are more effectively changed when the rate of the members' participation in the organization is high.* People trying to change organizations need first to make sure that all members of the organization are involved. People who participate are more likely to support organizational change than those who do not participate. Second, *those people working to bring about change need to be sensitive to the personal needs of the organization's members.* For example, some people put a high value on the personal relationships formed on the job. If these relationships are disrupted by firings, changes in work schedules, or redeployment, the morale of the remaining workers may plummet. Counseling sessions may be required to deal with the strong emotions generated by change.

Third, *the expectations of people working for change are important.* Expectations affect behavior. If the people in the organization are approached positively, they are more likely to cooperate than if they are uninformed or viewed as malcontents who oppose change. For instance, when the Chase Manhattan Corporation was taken over by the Chemical Banking Corporation in 1996, 12,000 people lost their jobs. A "huge insecurity complex" took root among the bank's employees because they were not informed as to what was going to happen to them, and many bad feelings resulted (Kleinfield 1996).

Fourth, *those working for change must know the social structure and operations of the organization being changed.* If a part of a system is to be changed, the whole system is affected. Thus, it is not sufficient to change one part of an organization without considering how that change will reverberate throughout the organization. The effects of an organizational change may linger for years, and people will need to work hard to reestablish effective communications to replace informal arrangements that may have been swept away.

Changing Institutions

We opened this chapter by describing the student protest in Tiananmen Square. In examining that event, we said that people who are in power usually try to stay in power and often use violence to accomplish their goal (see Gamson 1975). Violence is not always necessary, however, and a nonviolent response is not necessarily a weaker course of action. In fact, nonviolence sometimes brings about a profound change in society. Mohandas Gandhi—who led the fight against political, legal, and economic oppression in South Africa and then in India—is perhaps the best-known proponent of nonviolent confrontation and protest. Evidently, his strategy consisted of the following nine elements (Bondurant 1969):

1. Try to resolve conflicts and grievances through negotiation and arbitration without compromising the group's fundamental principles.
2. Prepare the group for direct action, and prepare members to suffer the consequences of their actions.
3. Engage in demonstrations and propaganda.
4. Once again attempt to persuade the opponent to accept the group's demands, and explain that refusal will bring further actions.
5. Initiate strikes, boycotts, and similar types of actions.
6. Begin a program of noncooperation with authorities.
7. Engage in civil disobedience to laws related to objects of change.
8. Take over some of the government's functions (if the government is the opponent).
9. Establish a parallel organization to perform government functions that have been taken over.

These nine elements represent a progression from little overt action to maximum overt action while always remaining nonviolent. At the same time, Gandhi's approach was anything but passive. It advocated strikes, boycotts, civil disobedience, and other forms of collective action as part of the nonviolent strategy.

Individuals who actively work for social action are out to change society. To them, the present situation might be satisfactory in some ways, but the future should be better in more ways. With regard to the future, what outcomes are these individuals likely to create or to encounter? We turn to that question in the final section of this chapter.

Why People Resist Change

Change in individuals, organizations, or social institutions seldom comes easily. To return to the Tiananmen Square incident that began this chapter, why did government leaders resist the students so fiercely? In part, the answer to this question involves legitimacy and self-interest. Many of the entrenched leaders were elderly men who had fought in World War II against the Japanese and had served in the communist revolution that brought their faction to power. In their view, the existing government was the only legitimate government of China, and anyone who wanted to change that was therefore an enemy of the state. With regard to self-interest, these same leaders had an investment in the status quo. They stood to lose a great deal of their power, their material wealth, and perhaps most important, their standing in society. Another question we can ask is, why is it that people often resist change even when it may be in their best

Mohandas Gandhi in 1931. As a sign of respect, he is sometimes referred to as Mahatma, or Great Teacher. Led by the Mahatma, India gained independence in 1947, but five months later, he was dead—assassinated by a religious fanatic.

interest to support or accept the change? One reason is that most people accept their lot in life because they accept the legitimacy of existing institutions that have defined their life for them—it is only when enough people deny legitimacy to existing institutions and institutional arrangements that mass social action is possible (McGeary 2000). Another reason is a rational calculation that leads people to conclude, rightly or wrongly, that they stand to lose something they value if change takes place. In other words, they feel that they have a vested interest in the status quo. A third reason is social inertia. People may be comfortable in their life situation even though they are disadvantaged. Change means that they must confront something new and personally disturbing, and they would rather avoid this if at all possible (Lauer 1991).

Because there is often resistance to change, people wishing to bring about change must expect and understand the nature of this resistance. That is they must listen to the concerns that others have about the proposed change and engage them in calm and rational discussion. Working for change is often difficult and time-consuming. However, without such efforts, social injustices would never be righted.

● ■ ▲ **Pausing to Think**   **About Collective Social Action and Working for Change**

Social action may focus on individuals, organizations, or institutions. When individuals are the focus of change, one of the most effective tools is education and reeducation along prescribed lines. When an organization is the focus, the people within the organization must become involved in the change process. When a social institution is the focus, the tactic of nonviolence has often been used. People resist change for several reasons, varying from self-interest to social inertia.

CQ   At what point do you think a group committed to nonviolent change should rethink its commitment? ◆ Is violence ever justified in working for change?

Collective Social Action in the Twenty-First Century

As we have emphasized throughout this book, change is an ever-present feature of human social life. This has been the case in the past and will be so in the future (see the Sociology Online box). Today, most sociologists concentrate their efforts in the more traditional sphere of the sociologist as social scientist, but a growing number feel that sociology should take a more active role in improving people's lives (Hall 1995). Accordingly, sociologists Gary Marx and Douglas McAdam (1994) suggest the following in this century:

- We will enter a period of heightened collective action. Movements emerge during periods when political systems are receptive to challenge. The fall of communism coupled with the introduction of capitalism and democracy will introduce many opportunities for change in many societies.

- The growing gap between the rich and the poor will stimulate collective action.

- As transportation and communications become easier and swifter, protest and terrorism will become easier and swifter as well.

- The issue of race will continue to divide people, and this trend will produce collective social action aimed at achieving social, political, and economic equality.

- Nationalist ethnic movements will sweep the globe as more ethnic groups act on their own behalf.

 STUDY TIP

In a group of three to five students, discuss Marx and McAdam's predictions for collective and social action in the twenty-first century. Do you agree or disagree with these predictions? What do you think will be the consequences if these predictions come true? What kind of change do you want to see happen in the twenty-first century—and what kind of collective action do you think might help to bring about that change?

Sociology Online

Go online and explore the web sites for the various social movements. A good place to start is with the Social Movements and Culture web site. This site is a project of the students and faculty of the American Studies Program of Washington State University. The site contains information on a variety of social movements, such as AIDS Activism, American Indian, Civil Rights, Environmental, Labor, Transnational/Global, and Women's. Select any three of the social movements listed on the homepage of the web site, read through the material provided, and then answer the following questions:

What is the history of the movement?

What significant events are associated with the movement?

What resources and references does the site provide for additional research on this movement?

Of the three social movements you examined, which seems to you to be mostly likely to bring about lasting change in society?

Not only will the social order change in the future, but sociology itself will undoubtedly change as well. Already, some sociologists argue that we need to place more emphasis on humanist sociology, or on "the study of human freedom and of all the social obstacles that must be overcome in order to insure this freedom" (Scimecca 1995:1). This call is actually an echo of calls made by Harriet Martineau, Max Weber, Émile Durkheim, Karl Marx, and other classical sociologists who initially

CONCEPT WEB Collective Social Action

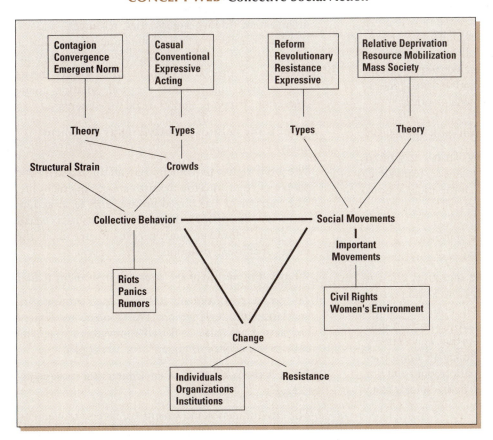

Here is a concept web for Collective Social Action. Try this. Connect "Resistance" to the box with the various social movements. Write a paragraph about the resistance that you see to each of the three social movements in the box. Also, what ongoing social movement would you add to the box? What is its importance for society?

framed the discipline and whose ideas we studied at the beginning of this book. Thus, we have come full circle, and we now confront again the issues raised by the sociological pioneers. How should we respond to a changing world and to the continuing social problems generated by poverty, ignorance, and human greed? Is there a way to avoid the constraints of bureaucracy and yet enjoy the fruits of sound organization? As we weaken the communal ties that bind us together, how do we control the violence and antisocial actions of the few against the many? With the sheer increase of human populations and environmental pressures, can we be optimistic about the future?

WHAT YOU SHOULD KNOW ● ■ ▲

1. What effect has the Great Social Transformation had on collective social action?

Collective social action takes place in communal societies when people respond to accumulated tensions. In associational societies, people with different values and resources may enter into conflicts that produce collective social action.

2. What contribution has structural strain theory made to our understanding of collective behavior?

Structural strain theory links the existing social conditions within a society to the emergence of collective behavior. According to this theory, collective behavior will emerge when all of the following social conditions are met: structural conduciveness, structural strains, generalized beliefs, precipitating factors, mobilization for action, and failure of social control.

3. What forms does collective behavior most often take?

Collective behavior takes many forms. Common forms are casual, conventional, solidaristic, expressive, and acting crowds. Other common forms include riots, panics, and rumors.

4. What are the three main theories of crowd behavior, and what do they tell us?

Contagion theory emphasizes the imitative, circular reactions that may sweep through crowds and prompt people to action that may or may not be rational. Convergence theory argues that crowd unity results from a like-mindedness of members that may actually exist before they come together. Emergent norm theory stresses that even in crowd situations our behavior is guided by norms that may actually arise quickly from the interaction of crowd members.

5. What types of social movements are there?

Social movements differ in terms of their overall goals. Reform movements aim to bring only limited change to existing social institutions. Revolutionary movements strive to change society's whole structure. Resistance movements work to halt social changes that some people feel are destructive of things that they hold dear. Expressive movements aim to bring about change within individual members.

6. What do the main sociological theories of social movements tell us?

Relative deprivation theory suggests that social movements arise because people feel deprived when they compare themselves with others. Resource-mobilization theory argues that resources—money, leaders, members, offices, communication facilities, connections to other active groups—are the key ingredients for a social movement. Mass society theory suggests that impersonalization and isolation create alienation, which promotes social movements.

7. What is the nature of the civil rights movement today?

The civil rights movement has attempted to bring people of color into the mainstream of American life. The movement has mixed protest with legal action, and today most people accept civil rights as a regular part of life. However, many people disagree about the merits of affirmative action.

8. What is the nature of the women's movement today?

The women's movement has combined protest with legislation and legal action. The women's movement has shared with the civil rights movement a general concern for economic equality for all people.

9. What is the nature of the environmental movement today?

The environmental movement is a diverse movement, containing many different groups with different goals, agendas, and strategies. Often, these groups form short-term coalitions during a conflict over a specific issue.

10. *What is involved in changing individuals, organizations, and social institutions?*

For individuals, education is one of the most effective means for bringing about change; for organizations, sensitivity to the concerns of the members is often a key; and for changing a social institution, nonviolent protest has been tried.

11. *Why do people resist change?*

People resist change for several reasons: they accept the existing social institutions; they rationally calculate that they stand to lose more than they will gain from change; and they feel that it is easier to keep things as they are rather than exposing themselves to the unknowns of change.

12. *What does the future hold for collective social action?*

According to some people, the next century will be a time of heightened social action stimulated by global inequality, technology, racial divisions, and ethnic movements. The discipline of sociology may also become more humanistic. Such a change would bring sociology full circle and back to the major concerns of many of its founders.

TEST YOUR KNOWLEDGE ●■▲

Key Terms Matching

Match each of these key terms with the best definition or example from the numbered items that follow. Write the letter preceding the key term in the blank before the definition that you choose.

a. acting crowd

b. casual crowd

c. collective behavior

d. collective social action

e. conventional crowd

f. crowd

g. eco-feminists

h. expressive crowd

i. expressive movement

j. mob

k. panic

l. reform movement

m. resistance movement

n. revolutionary movement

o. riot

p. rumor

q. social movement

r. solidaristic crowd

_____ 1. A type of crowd that consists of people who are passive and have a low emotional engagement and little social interactions with those nearby.

_____ 2. A type of crowd that is a relatively structured grouping in which conventional norms govern social behavior.

_____ 3. A type of crowd that provides its members with a sense of unity or social solidarity.

_____ 4. A type of crowd that people join to change their mood, emotions, and behavior.

_____ 5. A type of crowd in which the members turn into a mob, becoming angry and aggressive and engaging in violent acts.

_____ 6. A type of social movement whose goal is to provide gratification through self-expression.

_____ 7. A false or an unverified report communicated from one person to another.

_____ 8. A temporary grouping of individuals who are physically close enough to engage in social interaction.

_____ 9. A collective but irrational reaction to a serious threat.

_____ 10. Feminist social activists who claim that the "oppression of nature" is caused by the same male-dominated institutions that oppress women and minorities.

_____ 11. An organized but noninstitutionalized effort to change society through collective action.

_____ **12.** Social interactions that are a response to unstructured, ambiguous, or unstable situations.

_____ **13.** Relatively large-scale, violent, collective behavior that grows from a shared anger, frustration, and sense of deprivation.

_____ **14.** A special type of crowd that is wildly out of control and intent on doing violence and harm.

_____ **15.** Cooperative attempts to achieve a social goal.

_____ **16.** A social movement whose goal is to change society in a limited way.

_____ **17.** A social movement whose goal is to replace the existing social order with a completely new order.

_____ **18.** A countermovement whose goal is to stop or reverse changes that are taking place.

Multiple Choice

Circle the letter of your choice.

1. According to Smelser, which of the following is NOT a condition necessary for collective behavior to occur?

  a. structural conduciveness
  b. precipitating factors
  c. failure of social control
  d. ready availability of media resources

2. New Year's celebrations are popular. Which of the following types of crowd gather to celebrate the New Year?

  a. solidaristic
  b. acting
  c. expressive
  d. conventional

3. According to Herbert Blumer's classic symbolic interactionist account of how an acting crowd comes into existence, which of the following is NOT one of the five stages?

  a. People share basic social characteristics even before they join the crowd.
  b. People become restless, apprehensive, and susceptible to rumors.
  c. Something startling occurs and people become preoccupied with it.
  d. People start milling around and discussing the event.

4. Which of the following theories of crowd behavior proposes that the crowd develops a collective mind that releases people's destructive tendencies so that they feel free to do almost anything they wish?

  a. relative deprivation
  b. resource mobilization
  c. contagion
  d. emergent norm

5. Which of the following theories of crowd behavior states that crowd unity forms from members who share similar views and attitudes?

  a. convergence
  b. relative deprivation
  c. emergent norm
  d. resource mobilization

6. Which of the following theories states that social movements occur when people perceive an intolerable gap between what they feel their situation should be and what it actually is?

  a. resource mobilization
  b. relative deprivation
  c. emergent norm
  d. resistance

7. Which of the following theories states that industrialization has led to anomie, alienation, and excessive rationalization that have, in turn, led to social movements?

  a. emergent norm
  b. mass society
  c. resource mobilization
  d. relative deprivation

8. In the 1954 Supreme Court decision in _Brown_ v. _Board of Education_, the court found that

  a. separate educational facilities for whites and African Americans are inherently unequal.
  b. Jim Crow laws were unconstitutional.
  c. California's Proposition 209 was unconstitutional.
  d. the innate weakness of women made them unfit for many occupations.

9. The social period in which the environment was viewed as an obstacle to be overcome was the

  a. conservationist.
  b. preservationist.
  c. exploitative.
  d. ecological.

10. The period of the environmental movement that began after World War II and continues to the present is the
    a. exploitative.
    b. ecological.
    c. preservationist.
    d. conservationist.

11. The present-day social movement that is divided into several factions, making it difficult to define a single overarching goal, is the
    a. environmental.
    b. women's.
    c. civil rights.
    d. expressive resistance.

12. The faction of the environmental movement that emphasizes individual and corporate responsibility and that generally ignores collective political action is
    a. mainstream ecology.
    b. populist ecology.
    c. radical ecology.
    d. feminist ecology.

13. Which of the following is the term for the view that the earth's living matter, including the air, oceans, and land, are components of a self-regulating organism?
    a. Gaia
    b. human ecology
    c. web of life
    d. eco-feminism

14. When it comes to changing organizations, which of the following is true?
    a. Organizations are more effectively changed when the rate of member participation in the organization is high.
    b. People working to bring about change need to be sensitive to the personal needs of the organization's members.
    c. The expectations of the people working for change are important.
    d. All of the above.

15. Which of the following is NOT a reason why people resist change?
    a. They accept the legitimacy of existing institutions.
    b. They have a vested interest in the status quo.
    c. They are experiencing social inertia.
    d. They are concerned that their actions will be seen as unlawful.

True-False

Indicate your response to each of the following statements by circling T for true or F for false.

T F 1. Most people are frequently members of crowds but seldom are members of mobs.

T F 2. Riots, mobs, and acting crowds either are violent or have the potential for violence.

T F 3. Many of the riots in the 1960s were triggered by rumors.

T F 4. Most natural disasters result in large-scale panics.

T F 5. People often engage in collective social action when things are getting worse for them.

T F 6. Contagion theory argues that resources are the key ingredient for a successful social movement.

T F 7. The women's movement originated in the 1940s when feminists entered the labor force in huge numbers.

T F 8. The National Park system was created during the exploitation period of the environmental movement.

T F 9. One element of nonviolent action is to engage in civil disobedience to laws related to the objects of change.

T F 10. In the future, the issue of race will continue to divide people, thus producing collective social action aimed at achieving equality.

T F 11. Relative deprivation theory suggests that social movements arise because people feel deprived when they compare themselves with others.

T F 12. Collective social action does not take place in communal society.

T F 13. Social movements emerge during periods when political systems are receptive to change.

T F 14. Some people resist social change simply because they are satisfied with their life situation.

T F 15. When changing an organization it is good practice to be sensitive to the personal needs of the organization's members.

NOTE: The answers to these exercises are at the end of the book.

For additional practice tests and other resources please visit the companion web site at http://www.prenhall.com/curry.

Essay

1. Why do people resist change?

2. Describe the main factions of the environmental movement.

3. Describe the types of social movements and give an example of each.

4. Discuss the theories of crowd behavior.

5. Describe the various types of crowds.

Study Guide Answers

Chapter 1—What Is Sociology?

Key Term Matching

1. aa. sociology; 2. o. population; 3. z. social structure;
4. a. alienation; 5. j. manifest functions; 6. b. anomie;
7. v. sample; 8. d. dysfunctions; 9. k. mechanical solidarity;
10. n. perspectives; 11. i. life history; 12. s. rationalization;
13. dd. theory; 14. w. scientific method;
15. x. social interaction; 16. f. experimental group;
17. y. social power; 18. t. representative sample;
19. p. qualitative methods; 20. g. functions;
21. q. quantitative methods; 22. c. control group;
23. bb. structured interview; 24. m. participant
observation; 25. h. latent functions; 26. cc. survey;
27. r. random sampling; 28. l. organic solidarity;
29. u. research methods; 30. e. experiment

Multiple Choice

1. d; 2. b; 3. c; 4. c; 5. d; 6. b; 7. a; 8. b; 9. c; 10. a; 11.
c; 12. b; 13. b; 14. d; 15. a; 16. c; 17. c; 18. a; 19. d;
20. b

True False

1. T; 2. F; 3. T; 4. F; 5. T; 6. T; 7. T; 8. T; 9. T;
10. F; 11. T; 12. T; 13. T; 14. T; 15. T

Chapter 2—Culture, Society and Culture Change

Key Term Matching

1. j. folkways; 2. m. hunting and gathering societies;
3. x. society; 4. aa. Great Social Transformation (GST);
5. z. taboos; 6. c. communal society; 7. r. mode
of subsistence; 8. n. ideology; 9. a. agrarian societies;
10. t. muticulturalism; 11. p. invention;
12. f. cultural universals; 13. u. norms;
14. l. human agency; 15. b. associational society;
16. y. symbol; 17. v. pastoral societies;
18. q. language; 19. h. discovery; 20. bb. transitional
societies; 21. s. mores; 22. o. industrial societies;
23. k. horticultural societies; 24. e. cultural relativism;
25. cc. values; 26. d. cultural lag; 27. w. postindustrial
societies; 28. i. ethnocentrism; 29. g. culture

Multiple Choice

1. c; 2. b; 3. d; 4. a; 5. b; 6. c; 7. a; 8. d; 9. b; 10. d;
11. d; 12. b; 13. a; 14. c; 15. a

True-False

1. F; 2. T; 3. T; 4. F; 5. T; 6. T; 7. T; 8. F; 9. F;
10. T; 11. F; 12. T; 13. T; 14. F; 15. T

Chapter 3—Socialization

Key Term Matching

1. c. total Institution; 2. h. looking glass self; 3. a. agents
of socialization; 4. r. superego; 5. o. self; 6. d. id;
7. f. repression; 8. i. moral socialization; 9. c. epigenic principle; 10. p. socialization; 11. m. role model;
12. b. ego; 13. n. secondary socialization; 14. k. resocialization; 15. g. life course; 16. j. primary socialization

Multiple Choice

1. d; 2. b; 3. d; 4. a; 5. d; 6. d; 7. a; 8. b; 9. a; 10. d;
11. d; 12. c; 13. d; 14. a; 15. b

True-False

1. T; 2. T; 3. T; 4. T; 5. F; 6. T; 7. F; 8. F; 9. T;
10. F; 11. T; 12. T; 13. T; 14. T; 15. F

Chapter 4—Deviance

Key Term Matching

1. g. internal social control; 2. d. deviance; 3. k. common
law; 4. j. aging out; 5. n. white collar crime;
6. aa. victimless crime; 7. r. labeling; 8. c. crime;
9. o. civil law; 10. w. deterrence; 11. dd. sociopaths;
12. q. adversarial principle; 13. t. social controls;
14. s. crime against the person; 15. a. hate crimes;
16. z. corporate crime; 17. m. retribution; 18. y. stigma; 19.
h. restitution; 20. v. crimes against property;
21. i. laws; 22. l. external social controls;
23. p. criminal justice system; 24. b. organized crime;
25. f. rehabilitation; 26. bb. religious law;
27. u. incapacitation; 28. e. plea bargaining;
29. cc. index crimes; 30. x. criminal recidivism

Multiple Choice

1. a; 2. d; 3. d; 4. b; 5. c; 6. d; 7. d; 8. d; 9. d;
10. b; 11. c; 12. a; 13. b; 14. a; 15. c

True-False

1. F; 2. F; 3. F; 4. F; 5. F; 6. T; 7. F; 8. F; 9. T;
10. T; 11. F; 12. T; 13. T; 14. T; 15. T

Chapter 5—Interaction, Groups, and Organizations

Key Term Matching

1. e. competition; 2. j. exchange; 3. q. leader; 4. s. norm of reciprocity; 5. f. conflict; 6. y. role; 7. ff. status set;
8. z. role conflict; 9. i. ethnomethodology; 10. o. in-groups;
11. m. groupthink; 12. cc. secondary groups;
13. c. bureaucracy; 14. t. oligarchy; 15. d. coercion;
16. v. out-groups; 17. h. corporation; 18. r. master status;
19. l. group; 20. a. achieved status; 21. w. primary groups;
22. p. instrumental group; 23. ee. status; 24. aa. role strain;
25. b. ascribed status; 26. x. reference group;
27. bb. role stress; 28. u. organization; 29. n. impression management; 30. k. expressive leader; 31. g. cooperation;
32. dd. social interaction

Multiple Choice

1. c; 2. a; 3. d; 4. d; 5. b; 6. b; 7. b; 8. c; 9. b;
10. c; 11. d; 12. b; 13. d; 14. a; 15. b

True-False

1. T; 2. F; 3. T; 4. T; 5. F; 6. F; 7. T; 8. T; 9. F;
10. T; 11. F; 12. F; 13. T; 14. T; 15. T

Chapter 6—Inequalities of Social Class

Key Term Matching

1. f. culture of poverty; 2. a. absolute poverty; 3. g. esteem;
4. c. class consciousness; 5. n. socioeconomic status;
6. i. ideology; 7. k. prestige; 8. b. caste system; 9. q. truly disadvantage; 10. p. structural mobility; 11. l. relative poverty; 12. d. class consistency; 13. o. status consistent;
14. m. social stratification; 15. j. intergenerational mobility; 16. h. false consciousness; 17. e. class system

Multiple Choice

1. d; 2. c; 3. b; 4. a; 5. d; 6. a; 7. a; 8. a; 9. c; 10. c

Identifying Sociological Perspectives

1. C; 2. F; 3. SI; 4. F; 5. SI; 6. C; 7. F; 8. SI

True-False

1. F; 2. F; 3. T; 4. T; 5. T; 6. F; 7. T; 8. T; 9. T;
10. F; 11. F; 12. F; 13. T; 14. T; 15. T

Chapter 7—Inequalities of Race and Ethnicity

Key Term Matching

1. f. ethnic groups; 2. j. expulsion; 3. m. minority;
4. p. principle of cumulation; 5. a. Americanization;
6. h. ethnic revival; 7. o. prejudice; 8. e. discrimination;
9. q. race; 10. c. assimilation; 11. s. stereotype;
12. k. institutional racism; 13. t. symbolic ethnicity;
14. g. ethnic identity; 15. u. WASP; 16. b. annihilation;
17. r. racism; 18. n. pluralism; 19. i. ethnicity;
20. l. melting pot; 21. d. barrios

Multiple Choice

1. d; 2. b; 3. a; 4. c; 5. d; 6. a; 7. b; 8. a; 9. d; 10. d

Identifying Sociological Perspectives

1. SI; 2. C; 3. F; 4. C; 5. F; 6. SI

True-False

1. F; 2. T; 3. F; 4. T; 5. T; 6. T; 7. T; 8. T; 9. T;
10. F; 11. T; 12. F; 13. F; 14. T; 15. T

Chapter 8—Inequalities of Gender

Key Term Matching

1. e. gender; 2. g. gender markers; 3. l. inclusive feminism;
4. i. glass ceiling; 5. n. second shift; 6. b. bisexuality;
7. p. sexual harassment; 8. k. homosexuality; 9. f. gender equality; 10. c. comparable wealth; 11. j. heterosexuality;
12. h. gender role; 13. o. sexism; 14. d. feminism;
15. m. patriarchy; 16. a. agents of gender socialization

Multiple Choice

1. d; 2. c; 3. c; 4. a; 5. d; 6. d; 7. d; 8. c; 9. a;
10. b; 11. b; 12. c; 13. c; 14. a; 15. d

Identifying Sociological Perspectives

1. C; 2. SI; 3. SI; 4. F; 5. C; 6. F

True-False

1. T; 2. F; 3. T; 4. F; 5. T; 6. T; 7. F; 8. T; 9. T;
10. T; 11. T; 12. F; 13. T; 14. F; 15. F

Chapter 9—The Economy

Key Term Matching

1. a. capitalism; 2. j. multinationals; 3. d. deindustrialization;
4. m. pursuit of profit; 5. p. unemployed; 6. h. job loss
anxiety; 7. o. socialism; 8. n. social insurance;
9. b. career socialization; 10. e. entrepreneurs; 11. l. private
ownership of property; 12. g. interlocking directorate;
13. c. conglomerates; 14. i. mixed economy;
15. f. free-market competition; 16. k. occupational
inheritance

Multiple Choice

1. c; 2. a; 3. d; 4. d; 5. d; 6. c; 7. b; 8. d; 9. c;
10. d; 11. d; 12. b

Identifying Sociological Perspectives

1. SI; 2. SI; 3. C; 4. F; 5. F; 6. F; 7. C; 8. SI

True-False

1. T; 2. T; 3. F; 4. F; 5. T; 6. F; 7. T; 8. F;
9. T; 10. T; 11. T; 12. T; 13. F; 14. F; 15. F

Chapter 10—The Political Order

Key Term Matching

1. c. charismatic authority; 2. i. interest group; 3. o. party
platform; 4. e. democratic state; 5. s. political socialization;
6. j. legal-rational authority; 7. t. power; 8. a. authoritarian
state; 9. x. traditional authority; 10. d. coercion;
11. n. nation-state; 12. y. veto group; 13. h. ideal type;
14. u. power elite; 15. r. political power; 16. l. monarchy;
17. p. political; 18. w. totalitarian state; 19. b. authority;
20. v. state; 21. g. human rights; 22. q. political action
committee (PAC); 23. m. nation; 24. k. lobbyist;
25. f. government

Multiple Choice

1. d; 2. b; 3. d; 4. c; 5. a; 6. b; 7. d; 8. b; 9. b;
10. d; 11. b; 12. d; 13. c; 14. d; 15. b

Identifying Sociological Perspectives

1. C; 2. C; 3. SI; 4. SI; 5. F; 6. F

True-False

1. T; 2. F; 3. F; 4. T; 5. F; 6. F; 7. F; 8. F; 9. T;
10. T; 11. T; 12. T; 13. F; 14. T; 15. F

Chapter 11—Marriage and the Family

Key Term Matching

1. d. cohabitation; 2. r. monogamy; 3. o. kinship;
4. h. divorce; 5. s. nuclear family; 6. b. binuclear family;
7. t. polygamy; 8. m. family of orientation; 9. n. family of
procreation; 10. a. affinal relationships; 11. i. endogamy;
12. u. romantic love; 13. g. desertion; 14. e. courtship;
15. j. exogamy; 16. q. marriage; 17. l. family; 18. v. serial
monogamy; 19. c. blended or reconstituted family;
20. k. extended family; 21. p. machismo; 22. f. descent

Multiple Choice

1. d; 2. b; 3. c; 4. a; 5. b; 6. b; 7. b; 8. a; 9. b;
10. d; 11. b; 12. a; 13. d; 14. d; 15. b

Identifying Sociological Perspectives

1. C; 2. SI; 3. F; 4. F; 5. F; 6. C

True-False

1. F; 2. T; 3. T; 4. T; 5. F; 6. T; 7. T; 8. F;
9. T; 10. T; 11. F; 12. F; 13. T; 14. T; 15. T

Chapter 12—Education

Key Term Matching

1. g. hidden curriculum; 2. b. cultural literacy;
3. l. schools; 4. d. educational inflation;
5. k. multiculturalism/multiculturalists; 6. n. tracking;
7. c. education; 8. f. functionally illiterate; 9. i. mandatory
education; 10. e. formal education; 11. o. white flight;
12. j. mass education; 13. m. self-fulfilling prophecy;
14. h. magnet school; 15. a. credentialism

Multiple Choice

1. c; 2. b; 3. b; 4. d; 5. c; 6. a; 7. d; 8. d; 9. c;
10. a; 11. b; 12. c; 13. a; 14. a; 15. b

Identifying Sociological Perspectives

1. F; 2. SI; 3. F; 4. C; 5. F; 6. C

True-False

1. T; 2. F; 3. F; 4. F; 5. T; 6. T; 7. F; 8. T;
9. T; 10. T; 11. T; 12. F; 13. T; 14. T; 15. T

Chapter 13—Religion

Key Term Matching

1. d. denomination; 2. a. church; 3. h. monotheism;
4. p. televangelist; 5. i. polytheism; 6. m. sacred;
7. c. cult; 8. l. ritual; 9. g. ethicalist; 10. n. sect;
11. k. religion; 12. b. civil religion; 13. o. secularization; 14.
j. profane; 15. e. ecclesia; 16. f. electronic church

Multiple Choice

1. c; 2. d; 3. a; 4. b; 5. c; 6. c; 7. b; 8. b; 9. a;
10. c; 11. b; 12. a; 13. b; 14. a; 15. a

Identifying Sociological Perspectives

1. SI; 2. SI; 3. SI; 4. F; 5. F; 6. C

True-False

1. T; 2. F; 3. T; 4. T; 5. T; 6. F; 7. T; 8. F; 9. T;
10. T; 11. F; 12. F; 13. T; 14. F; 15. T

Chapter 14—Medicine and Health Care

Key Term Matching

1. b. health; 2. f. medicalization of society; 3. c. health
maintenance organization (HMO); 4. i. sick role;
5. e. Medicaid; 6. h. preventive medicine; 7. g. Medicare;
8. a. disease; 9. d. malingering

Multiple Choice

1. d; 2. b; 3. d; 4. b; 5. d; 6. d; 7. d; 8. d; 9. a;
10. a; 11. c; 12. b; 13. d; 14. a; 15. d

Identifying Sociological Perspectives

1. SI; 2. F; 3. SI; 4. C; 5. F; 6. C

True-False

1. T; 2. F; 3. T; 4. T; 5. F; 6. T; 7. T; 8. F; 9. F;
10. T; 11. T; 12. T; 13. T; 14. F; 15. T

Chapter 15—Population, Ecology, and Urbanization

Key Term Matching

1. c. crude death rate; 2. q. natural decrease;
3. f. ecosystem; 4. p. mortality; 5. v. suburbs;
6. j. human ecology; 7. y. urbanization; 8. n. metropolitan
community; 9. t. population explosion; 10. a. city;
11. r. natural increase; 12. h. fertility; 13. o. migration;
14. b. crude birth rate; 15. d. demographic transition;
16. k. immigration; 17. g. emigration; 18. s. net migration
rate; 19. u. population implosion; 20. x. urbanism;
21. w. urban primacy; 22. e. demography; 23. m. life span;
24. l. life expectancy; 25. i. general fertility ratio

Multiple Choice

1. a; 2. d; 3. b; 4. a; 5. c; 6. c; 7. c; 8. b; 9. b;
10. b; 11. d; 12. a; 13. b; 14. c; 15. a

True-False

1. F; 2. T; 3. T; 4. F; 5. F; 6. T; 7. F; 8. T; 9. T;
10. T; 11. T; 12. F; 13. T; 14. F; 15. T

Chapter 16—Collective Social Action

Key Term Matching

1. b. casual crowd; 2. e. conventional crowd; 3. r. solidaristic crowd; 4. h. expressive crowd; 5. a. acting crowd;
6. i. expressive movement; 7. p. rumor; 8. f. crowd;
9. k. panic; 10. g. ecofeminists; 11. q. social movement; 12.
c. collective behavior; 13. o. riot; 14. j. mob;
15. d. collective social action; 16. l. reform movement;
17. n. revolutionary movement; 18. m. resistance
movement

Multiple Choice

1. d; 2. a; 3. a; 4. c; 5. a; 6. b; 7. b; 8. a; 9. c;
10. b; 11. a; 12. b; 13. a; 14. d; 15. d

True-False

1. T; 2. T; 3. T; 4. F; 5. F; 6. F; 7. F; 8. F; 9. T;
10. T; 11. T; 12. F; 13. T; 14. T; 15. T

Glossary

Absolute poverty The poverty of people who cannot afford some minimum of food, clothing, shelter, and other necessities regardless of how they compare with other people.

Achieved status A status over which people can exert at least some control.

Acting crowd A type of crowd in which the members turn into a mob, becoming angry and aggressive and engaging in violent acts.

Activity theory A theory of aging that argues that the elderly should participate actively in society.

Adversarial principle A tradition where guilt or innocence is determined by a contest between the prosecution and the defense.

Affinal relationship Social bond based on marriage.

Agents of gender socialization Those who teach gender roles and identities.

Agents of socialization The individuals, groups, organizaions, and institutions that provide substantial amounts of socialization during the life course.

Aging out Refers to fact that the rate of crimes people commit declines sharply after their mid-30s.

Agrarian societies Societies whose technology of food production is such that annual food surpluses are used to support larger populations and permanent settlements.

Alienation A situation in which people are estranged from their social world and feel that life is meaningless.

Americanization The process within American society in which minority group members change their behavior and in doing so become more like the majority group.

Annihilation The process by which one ethnic or racial group exterminates another group.

Anomie A social condition in which social norms are conflicting or entirely absent.

Ascribed status A status assigned to people whether they wish to have it or not.

Assimilation The blending of the culture and structure of one racial or ethnic group with the culture and structure of society.

Associational society A society in which social relationships are often highly impersonal and the main social units are organizations, corporations, and bureaucracies.

Authoritarian state A state that has the following characteristics: (1) the people are excluded from the processes of government; (2) little or no opposition to the government is permitted; and (3) the government has little interest in the daily lives of the people unless they threaten the state's leadership.

Authority The socially legitimated use of power.

Barrios Ethnic residential neighborhoods primarily made up of Mexican Americans.

Binuclear family A family form in which each member of a divorced couple establishes a separate household between which their children divide their time.

Bisexuality The desire for sexual partners of either sex.

Blended or reconstituted family A form of family in which spouses and their children from former marriages live together as a single nuclear family.

Bureaucracy A form of organization based on explicit rules, with a clear, impersonal, and hierarchical authority structure.

Capitalism An economic system in which the means of production are privately owned and market forces determine production and distribution.

Career socialization The process of acquiring knowledge and ways of thinking about work and careers.

Caste system A fixed arrangement of strata from the most to the least privileged, with a person's position determined unalterably at birth.

Casual crowd A type of crowd that consists of people who are passive and have a low emotional engagement and little social interaction with those nearby.

Category A cluster of people who share a social trait such as age, sex, or race.

Charismatic authority Power that is legitimated by an individual's exceptional personal attributes, such as a magnetic personality, an extraordinary driving energy, or a powerful aura of wisdom and grace.

Church A formal religious organization that is well established and well integrated into its society.

City A large, densely settled concentration of people.

Civil law Law that is imposed on society from above by civil authority.

Civil religion Quasi-religious beliefs that link people to society and country.

Class consciousness An awareness by members of a social class that it is being oppressed and that membership in the class dooms everyone to the same fate.

Class consistency The similarity among the characteristics that define class strata.

Class system A system in which social standing is determined by factors over which people can exert some control, such as their educational attainment, their income, and their work experience.

Coercion The process of compelling others to do something against their will.

Cohabitation A situation in which partners share a household and engage in intimate social and sexual relations without being formally married.

Collective behavior Social interactions that are a response to unstructured, ambiguous, or unstable situations.

Collective social action Cooperative attempts to achieve a social goal.

Common law Law that is developed over time by the accumulation of many cases.

Communal society A society characterized by rich personalized relationships and in which the main social units are family, kin, and community.

Comparable worth Equal pay for comparable jobs.

Competition The process through which two or more parties attempt to obtain the same goal.

Conflict A form of interaction in which the parties attempt to physically or socially vanquish each other.

Conformity An adaptation to structural strain within a society in which the conformist accepts both the conventional goals of society and the conventional means to obtain them.

Conglomerate Giant corporation composed of other corporations that produce a variety of products and that conduct businesses in several markets.

Continuity theory A theory of aging that states that successful aging is a matter of maintaining the same level of engagement experienced as an adult.

Control group In an experiment, the group not exposed to the experimental stimulus but used as a comparison with the experimental group.

Conventional crowd A type of crowd that is a relatively structured grouping in which conventional norms govern social behavior.

Cooperation The process in which people work together to achieve shared goals.

Core nations According to world systems theory, nations that are highly industrialized, powerful, and control the world system.

Corporate crime Illegal actions of a corporation or people acting on behalf of a corporation.

Corporation A group that, through the legal process of incorporation, has been given the status of a separate and real social entity.

Courtship The relationship between a male and a female who are preparing for marriage to each other.

Credentialism The view that academic degrees indicate the holders' qualifications to perform certain jobs or roles.

Crime An act that has been declared illegal by some authority.

Crimes against the person Violent crimes or the threat of violence directed against people.

Crimes against property Crimes that involve theft or destruction of property belonging to others.

Criminal justice system The social system of police, courts, and prisons officials that responds to violations of the law.

Criminal recidivism When people convicted of crimes commit subsequent offenses.

Crowd A temporary grouping of individuals who are physically close enough to engage in social interaction.

Crude birthrate The annual number of births in a population per 1,000 members of the population.

Crude death rate The annual number of deaths per 1,000 members of the population.

Cult A religious organization that has little or nothing to do with conventional religious traditions and believes that society is degenerate and that the members of the organization must withdraw together from normal life and live apart in group quarters or a commune.

Cultural lag The tendency for elements of material culture to change more rapidly than elements of nonmaterial culture.

Cultural literacy The extent to which a person possesses the basic information needed to thrive in the modern world.

Cultural relativism The belief that each culture is unique and must be analyzed and judged on its own terms.

Cultural universals Similar cultural solutions in different societies for similar problems of survival.

Culture The mutually shared products, knowledge, and beliefs of a human group or society.

Culture of poverty The set of norms and values that helps the poor to adapt to their situation.

Deindustrialization A process of economic change in which an economy is losing jobs in the industrial sector and adding jobs in the service sector.

Democratic state A state that allows the people to have an input into government decisions and permits the people to elect and dismiss leaders.

Demographic transition Long-term decline in a population's birth- and death rates from high to low.

Demography The scientific study of the size, growth, and composition of the human population.

Denomination A religion that maintains friendly relations with the government and with other religions but that does not claim to be the nation's only legitimate faith.

Descent The system by which kinship is traced over generations.

Desertion The social dissolution of marriage that occurs when one spouse leaves the other or simply walks away from the marriage for a prolonged period.

Deterrence The use of punishment to discourage crime.

Deviance Any violation of a widely held norm.

Diffusion The transmission of a cultural element from one group or society to another.

Discovery Noticing something that has not been noticed before.

Discrimination The unfair and harmful treatment of people based on their group membership.

Disease A pathology that disrupts the usual functions of the body.

Disengagement theory A theory of aging that emphasizes the importance of the elderly gradually disengaging from their roles in society.

Divorce The dissolution of the legal ties that bind a married couple; socially it constitutes the recognition that the marriage is over.

Dysfunctions Actions that have negative consequences for society.

Ecclesia A church that is a state's official religion.

Eco-feminists Feminist social activists who claim that the "oppression of nature" is caused by the same male-dominated institutions that oppress women and minorities.

Economy The social institution that determines what will be produced, how production will be accomplished, and who will receive what is produced.

Ecosystem An interlocking, stable group of plants and animals living in their natural habitat.

Education The transferral of the knowledge, values, and beliefs of a society from one generation to the next.

Educational inflation The situation in which the credentials required to obtain a job increase while the skills necessary to perform the job remain the same.

Ego Freud's term for the part of the psyche that is conscious and in touch with reality.

Electronic church Church or ministry that broadcasts its religious services through the mass media, notably television.

Emigration The movement of people out of a place.

Endogamy Marriage in which the couple are members of the same race, ethnicity, religion, or social class.

Entrepreneurs People who take great risks in order to achieve success in the marketplace.

Epidemic A widespread outbreak of a contagious disease.

Epigenic principle Erik Erikson's formulation that states that humans develop through a biologically predetermined unfolding of personality through eight stages.

Esteem The honor that accrues to the individual filling a position in a social system.

Ethicalist A belief system that emphasizes living a "good" life rather than worshiping a deity.

Ethnic group People who share basic cultural features such as language, place of origin, dress, food, and values.

Ethnic identity The internalization of ethnic roles as part of a person's self-concept.

Ethnic revival A situation in which racial and ethnic groups clamor for political autonomy and sometimes demand independence.

Ethnicity Common cultural characteristics people share, such as the same language, place of origin, dress, food, and values.

Ethnocentrism The belief that one's own culture is superior to all other cultures.

Ethnomethodology The methodology for studying the common understanding of everyday life.

Exchange The process through which people transfer goods, services, and other items with each other.

Exogamy Marriage in which the couple are from different races, ethnic groups, religions, or social classes.

Experiment A method for studying the relation between two or more variables under highly controlled conditions.

Experimental group In an experiment, the group to whom the experimental stimulus is administered.

Expressive crowd A type of crowd people join in order to change their mood, emotions, and behavior.

Expressive leader A group leader whose activities are aimed at promoting group solidarity, cohesion, and morale.

Expressive movement A type of social movement whose goal is to provide gratification through self-expression.

Expulsion The forceful exclusion of a racial or ethnic group from a society.

Extended family A family composed of two or more generations of kin that functions as an independent social and economic unit.

External social controls The societal mechanisms external to the individual that prevent deviance.

False consciousness A class's acceptance of an ideology that is contrary to the best interests of the class.

Family A group of individuals who are related in some way, usually living together, engaging in sex, having responsibility for rearing children, and functioning as an economic unit.

Family of orientation The nuclear family into which a person is born.

Family of procreation A person, a spouse, and their children.

Feminism A counter-ideology that has arisen to challenge sexism and that seeks independence and equality for women.

Fertility The number of births that occur over a specific period, usually one year.

Folkways Norms concerning relatively unimportant matters.

Formal education The transmission of knowledge, skills, and attitudes from one generation to the next through systematic training.

Free-market competition The buying and selling of goods and services unencumbered by government rules, regulations, and planning.

Functionally illiterate Lacking the ability to read and write well enough to carry out the routine activities of everyday life.

Functions Actions that have positive consequences for society.

Gender equality Equality between men and women under the law.

Gender markers Symbols and signs that identify a person's gender.

Gender role The behavior society expects for a male or a female.

Gender The cultural and attitudinal qualities associated with being male or female.

General fertility ratio The annual number of births in a population per 1,000 women aged 15 through 44 years.

Gerontology The study of aging and the elderly.

Glass ceiling Subtle and often unconscious discrimination within organizations that prevents women from reaching higher and better-paying positions for which they are qualified.

Government The set of people who are currently engaged in directing the state.

Great Social Transformation (GST) The profound change in social relationships from communal to associational brought about by industrialization, urbanization, bureaucratization, rationalization, and globalization.

Group A collection of people who take each other's behavior into account as they interact, and who develop a sense of togetherness.

Groupthink Intense social pressure within a group for individuals to conform to group norms and abandon individual and critical thinking.

Hate crime A crime motivated by racial prejudice or other biases against a person or a person's property.

Health maintenance organization (HMO) An insurance plan combined with a physical facility for delivering health care.

Health The capacity to satisfy role requirements.

Heterosexuality The desire for sexual partners of the other sex.

Hidden curriculum Lessons taught in school that do not appear as part of the formal lesson plans and learning objectives.

Homosexuality The desire for sexual partners of the same sex.

Horticultural societies Societies in which the cultivation of domestic plants satisfies most needs for food.

Human agency The activities of individuals or groups aimed at attaining a goal or end.

Human ecology The study of the relationship between society and the environment.

Human rights Those broadly defined rights to which all people are entitled by virtue of their humanity.

Hunting and gathering societies Societies that obtain their sustenance primarily through hunting game animals and gathering nuts, berries, and other wild plants; and that are held together by kinship ties and by a simple division of labor based on age and gender.

Id Freud's term for the basic drives of humans.

Ideal type A composit of characteristics based on many specific examples.

Ideology The pattern of beliefs that legitimizes or justifies a particular societal arrangement.

Immigration The movement of people into a place.

Impression management The conscious manipulation of props, scenery, costumes, and behavior in an attempt to present a particular image to other people.

Incapacitation Refers to keeping the most dangerous criminals locked away.

Inclusive feminism The view that sexism is related to all forms of oppression and that feminist ideology therefore must resist all forms.

Index crimes Eight crimes given special attention in the Uniform Crime Reports published by the Federal Bureau of Investigation.

Industrial societies Societies that rely on technology and mechanization as the main source of sustenance.

In-group Group to which people feel that they belong.

Innovation An adaptation to structural strain within society in which the innovator accepts the goals of society but rejects the socially approved means and thus opts for deviance in order to attain the goals.

Institutional racism A situation in which racist practices become part of the social practices and institutions of society.

Instrumental leader A group leader whose activities are aimed at accomplishing the group's tasks.

Interest group An organization formed for the express purpose of swaying political decisions.

Intergenerational mobility Upward and downward mobility in socioeconomic status measured by the standing of children compared with that of their parents.

Interlocking directorate Members of the boards of directors of corporations sitting on the boards of directors of other corporations, thereby linking the corporations.

Internal social controls Social controls seated within the individual that are learned through socialization.

Invention A new material or nonmaterial product resulting from the combination of known cultural elements in a novel manner.

Job loss anxiety Anxiety suffered by workers that is caused by the perceived insecurity of their jobs.

Kinship A network of people who are related by marriage, blood, or social practice (such as adoption).

Labeling The process by which a definition is attached to an individual.

Language Words that are symbols and rules for conveying complex ideas.

Latent functions Functions that are unintended or unrecognized by others.

Laws A body of rules governing the affairs of a community that are enforced by a political authority, usually the state.

Leader A person who can consistently influence the behavior of group members and the outcomes of the group.

Legal–rational authority Authority that derives its legitimacy from the rules and laws that define the rights, duties, and obligations of rulers and followers.

Life course Consists of the stages into which our life span is divided, such as adolescence or middle age.

Life expectancy How long people probably will live.

Life history A long interview, or series of interviews, in which the researcher attempts to discover the essential features, decisive moments, or turning points in a respondent's life.

Life span The theoretical maximum length of life.

Lobbyist A person employed by a large corporation, a union, or other organizations that aim to influence congressional votes on certain bills.

Looking glass self The process through which people imaginatively assume the reactions of people.

Machismo A value system embracing highly masculine behaviors and including a "double standard."

Magnet schools Schools that offer specialized programs or intensive studies in certain subject areas to draw students from all residential areas of the community.

Malingering Pretending to be sick to achieve some personal or social gain.

Mandatory education Education to a certain age specified by law.

Manifest functions Functions that are intended or recognized by others.

Marriage A state that occurs when two individuals are involved in a socially approved relationship that involves intimate, mutual long-term obligations, and the individuals have fulfilled the customary ceremonial or legal requirements.

Mass education The idea that everyone is entitled to a certain amount of publicly provided education and is obligated to obtain it.

Master status A status, ascribed or achieved, that is so important that a person organizes his or her life and social identity around it.

Mechanical solidarity Social solidarity based on shared values.

Medicaid A federal health insurance program administered at the state level targeted to the poor and the disabled.

Medicalization of society The expansion and taking over of areas of life by medicine that were formerly part of another social institution.

Medicare A federal health insurance program for the elderly financed by taxes on working people and on their employers and by a monthly fee for those enrolled in the program.

Mega-church A large religious congregation in which the church becomes a life center around which people organize their activities and provides its members with many nontraditional services and facilities.

Melting pot A situation in which the culture and social structure of both the minority and the majority change in such a way that a new, blended grouping emerges that combines some features of both groups.

Metropolitan community A large city and the surrounding areas that are integrated on a daily basis with the city.

Migration The movement of people from one area of residence to another.

Minority A group that has less power than the dominant group.

Mixed economy An economy that mixes features of both capitalist and socialist systems, including both public and private ownership of property and limits on free-market competition.

Mob A special type of crowd that is wildly out of control and is intent on doing violence and harm.

Mode of subsistence The manner in which a society obtains the basic materials necessary to sustain itself; the most basic feature of a society.

Monarchy A system in which political power is passed from person to person on the basis of hereditary claims.

Monogamy A marriage consisting of one male spouse and one female spouse.

Monotheism Belief in and worship of one god.

Moral socialization Socialization to the "moral" values of society.

Mores Norms concerning very serious matters.

Mortality The number of deaths that occur during a year.

Multiculturalism The belief that culture should be viewed from the perspective of different groups.

Multinationals Companies that conduct business in several countries but have their central headquarters in one country.

Nation A group that lives within a given territory and shares a common history, culture, and identity.

Nation-state The supreme political authority within a territory that incorporates and represents a nation.

Natural decrease The situation in which the number of deaths in a population exceeds the number of births.

Natural increase The number of births in a population in a given time period minus the number of deaths in the population for the same time period.

Net migration rate The annual difference between how many people enter a place and how many leave, per 1,000 people of that place.

Norm of reciprocity A strong norm that says that if you do something for a person, then that person must do something of approximately equal social value in return.

Norms The specific expectations about how people behave in a given situation.

Nuclear family A social unit composed of a husband, a wife, and their children.

Occupational inheritance Children entering the same occupation as a parent.

Oligarchy A small clique of people who rule an organization for their own benefit.

Organic solidarity Social solidarity based on a functional interdependence among people.

Organization A group that is deliberately constructed, with well-defined roles and positions that differ in prestige and power, and has rules and sanctions for violation of those rules.

Organized crime Crime conducted by businesses supplying illegal goods or services and that routinely use corruption and violence to gain their ends

Out-group Group to which people feel that they do not belong.

Panic A collective but irrational reaction to a serious threat.

Pandemic The outbreak of a disease that occurs over a very large area or is worldwide.

Participant observation Type of observation in which the researcher participates in the activities of the group in order to obtain an in-depth and intimate understanding of it.

Party platform The official statement of the ideology, goals, and plans that a party will implement if its candidates are elected to office.

Pastoral societies Societies that derive most of their sustenance from raising domesticated animals.

Patriarchy A social arrangement in which men dominate women.

Perspectives Our mental pictures of the relative importance of things.

Plea bargaining A commonly used procedure whereby defendants agree to plead guilty to a lesser charge rather than to proceed to a formal trial.

Pluralism A situation in which separate racial and ethnic groups maintain their distinctiveness even though they may have approximately equal standing.

Political Involving the distribution of power across the institutions, organizations, and individuals of a society.

Political Action Committee (PAC) A political organization established by a special interest group to raise money to support political candidates.

Political party A political organization meant to legitimately influence the government.

Political socialization The formal and informal learning that creates a political self for each individual.

Polygamy A marriage consisting of multiple spouses.

Polytheism Belief in and worship of more than one god.

Population In the context of a research project, any group that the researcher is studying, such as all the students in a class, all the inmates in a prison, or all the women in a society.

Population explosion A rapid, unchecked growth in the number of people inhabiting an area.

Population implosion A rapid, unchecked decline in the number of people inhabiting an area.

Postindustrial societies Societies based primarily on the creation and transmitting of specialized knowledge.

Power The ability to achieve one's ends despite resistance.

Power elite People who are wealthy and well-placed socially, who know one another personally, who frequently marry among themselves, who share a similar worldview, and who work in concert to achieve a political agenda that suits their interests.

Prejudice An attitude that predisposes an individual to prejudge entire categories of people unfairly.

Prestige The honor associated with an occupation or other position in a social system.

Preventive medicine Medical treatments and information that aim at the prevention of disease and the maintenance of health.

Primary group Group characterized by intimate, warm, cooperative, and face-to-face relationships.

Primary socialization Early socialization that stresses the basic knowledge and values of the society.

Principle of cumulation The process in which discrimination by the majority keeps the minority in an inferior status and that inferior status is then cited as "proof" that the minority does not deserve better treatment.

Private ownership of property The rule of property ownership that vests in the individual the right to own property unencumbered by government rules, regulations, and planning.

Profane Those things that are regarded as part of ordinary life.

Propinquity The tendency to chose prospective spouses from people who live close to each other.

Pursuit of profit The system of trade in which those selling goods or services are permitted to charge an amount greater than their costs in producing or buying the good or service.

Qualitative methods Research techniques designed to obtain the subjective understanding, interpretation, and meaning of social behavior.

Quantitative methods Research techniques designed to produce numerical estimates of human behavior.

Race A group of people who have been singled out on the basis of real or alleged physical characteristics.

Racism The belief that race determines human ability and that as a result, certain races deserve to be treated as superior.

Random sampling A sampling procedure in which everyone in the population has an equal chance of being selected as a respondent.

Rationalization The replacement of traditional thinking with rational thinking, or thinking that heavily emphasizes deliberate calculation, efficiency, and effectiveness in the accomplishment of explicit goals.

Rebellion An adaptation to structural strain within society in which the rebel rejects the goals and means of society and replaces them with new goals and means.

Reference group Group whose values, norms, and beliefs come to serve as a standard for one's own behavior.

Reform movement A social movement whose goal is to change society in a limited way.

Rehabilitation The use of education and other programs to reform offenders to prevent future offenses.

Relative poverty Poverty determined only by comparison with others.

Religion A system of beliefs, rituals, and ceremonies that focuses on sacred matters, promotes community among its followers, and provides for a personal spiritual experience for its members.

Religious law Law that is believed to stem from divine authority.

Representative sample A sample that in its characteristics mirrors the population from which it comes.

Repression Freud's term for the process of maintaining appropriate thoughts in the conscious mind.

Research methods The techniques, practices, and ethics involved in gaining new knowledge.

Resistance movement A countermovement whose goal is to stop or reverse changes that are taking place.

Resocialization A process that aims at reforming or altering an inmate's personality through manipulation and control of the environment.

Restitution A policy of attempting to restore things, as much as possible, to the way they were before a crime was committed.

Retreatism An adaptation to structural strain within society in which the retreatist rejects both the means and the goals of society but does not replace them with anything that the society regards as worthwhile.

Retribution An act of vengeance by which society inflicts on the offender suffering comparable to that caused by the offense.

Revolutionary movement A social movement whose goal is to replace the existing social order with a completely new order.

Riot Relatively large-scale, violent collective behavior that grows from a shared anger, frustration, and sense of deprivation.

Ritual Commonly routinized behaviors that express and reinforce religious faith.

Ritualism An adaptation to structural strain within society in which the ritualist has no interest in the conventional goals of society, yet goes through the motions by following the prescribed rules and behaviors.

Role conflict The incompatibility of different roles played by a single person.

Role model A person who serves as an especially important reference point for our thoughts and actions.

Role strain The incompatibility of expectations within a single role.

Role stress The anxiety produced by being unable to meet all role requirements at the same time.

Role taking Assuming the role of another person and then judging oneself from the viewpoint of that other person.

Role The expected behavior associated with a status.

Romantic love An emotional identification between two individuals that is so intense that they are convinced that they cannot be happy without each other.

Rumor A false or unverified report communicated from one person to another.

Sacred Those things that have supernatural significance and qualities.

Sample A small number of cases selected to represent the entire population.

Schools Places of formal educational instruction.

Scientific method An objective and judicious approach to empirical evidence. Scientists are objective because they do not allow their personal opinions to enter into their scientific work; and they are judicious because they require a substantial, if not overwhelming, body of objective evidence before arriving at a conclusion.

Second shift Housework such as cooking, cleaning, and child care that women who work outside the home take on when they arrive home.

Secondary group Group characterized by limited participation and impersonal and formal relationships.

Secondary socialization Socialization following primary socialization that emphasizes synthesis, creativity, logic, emotional control, and advanced knowledge.

Sect A loosely organized, nonbureaucratic religious organization with nonprofessional leadership that actively rejects the social environment in which it exists.

Secularization The declining influence of religion in life combined with an increasing influence of science.

Self A perception of being a distinct personality with a unique identity.

Self-fulfilling prophecy Process whereby an authority figure's expectations and assumptions cause behavior that fulfills those expectations and assumptions.

Serial monogamy A cultural pattern that permits a person to have more than one spouse, but not at the same time.

Sexism An ideology that maintains that women are inherently inferior to men and therefore do not deserve as much power, prestige, and wealth as men.

Sexual harassment Unwanted attention or pressure of a sexual nature from another person of greater social or physical power.

Sick role A social role developed by society for the sick, who, if they play the role correctly, are released from life's normal obligations for the duration of the illness.

Social controls Mechanisms that monitor behavior and sanction the violation of norms.

Social evolution theories Theories of social change that assert that societies evolve from the simple to the complex.

Social insurance The idea that government is responsible for guaranteeing a minimum standard of living for everyone.

Social interaction The acts people perform toward one another and the responses they give in return, which may consist of spoken words, subtle gestures, visual images, or even electronically transmitted digits.

Social movement An organized but noninstitutionalized effort to change society through collective action.

Social power The ability to get others to conform to one's wishes even against their own desires.

Social stratification The arrangement of society into a series of layers or strata on the basis of an unequal distribution of societal resources, prestige, or power, such that the stratum at the top has the most resources.

Social structure The relatively permanent components of our social environment.

Socialism An economic system in which the means of production are collectively owned and the state directs production and distribution.

Socialization The process by which people learn the skills, knowledge, norms, and values of their society, and by which they develop their social identity.

Society A grouping that consists of people who share a common culture, obey the same political authority, and occupy a given territory.

Socioeconomic status A person's ranking along several social dimensions, particularly education, occupational prestige, and income.

Sociology The scientific study of social structure and social interaction and of the factors making for change in social structure and social interaction.

Sociopaths People who commit wanton murder or serial killings apparently because they lack any internal social controls.

Solidaristic crowd A crowd that provides its members with a sense of unity or social solidarity.

State The highest political authority within a given territory.

Status A position within society.

Status consistent Having a similar ranking along the various dimensions of socioeconomic status.

Status set The collection of statuses a person occupies at any one time.

Stereotype Rigid and inaccurate images that summarize a belief.

Stigma A social marker that brings shame on a person.

Structural mobility The movement of entire categories of people due to changes in society itself.

Structured interview A procedure in which respondents are asked the same series of questions and the answers are recorded in a standard format.

Suburbs Communities with metropolitan areas that are outside the central city.

Superego Freud's term for the cultural values and norms internalized by an individual.

Survey A systematic procedure for gathering information, usually through the application of standardized interviews or questionnaires.

Symbol A representation that stands for something else.

Symbolic ethnicity An attempt to preserve and participate in disappearing ethnic roles and culture.

Taboos Norms about matters that are so serious as to be almost beyond comprehension.

Televangelists Fundamentalist ministers who espouse traditional religious values and regularly use television to spread their message.

Terrorism The non-institutionalized use of threat, intimidation, and violence to bring about a political objective.

Theory An explanation for the relationship between certain facts.

Total institution A setting in which people are isolated from the rest of society and controlled by an administrative staff.

Totalitarian state A state that has unlimited power, tolerates no opposition, and exercises close control over its citizens.

Tracking Assigning students to different educational programs on the basis of their abilities or interests.

Traditional authority Authority that is legitimated by the historical beliefs and practices of society.

Transitional societies Societies that are partly agrarian and partly industrial and whose population members are largely peasants.

Truly disadvantaged People who live predominantly in the inner city and who are trapped in a cycle of joblessness, deviance, crime, welfare dependency, and unstable family life.

Unemployed People who are without jobs but are seeking work.

Urban primacy A pattern of urbanization in which one city grows extremely large and dominates the society, whereas the rest of society remains rural.

Urbanism The pattern of social life found in cities.

Urbanization The increase in the percentage of the population residing in cities.

Values The preferences people share about what is good or bad, right or wrong, desirable or undesirable.

Veto group A group whose power lies primarily in its ability to block actions of other groups.

Victimless crimes Violations of law in which there are no obvious victims.

War An institutionalized and violent conflict between nations, tribes, and other social entities.

WASP White, Anglo-Saxon, Protestant members of American society.

White-collar crime Crime committed by people of high social status in the course of their occupation.

White flight An upsurge in white families moving to suburban neighborhoods to avoid mandatory busing.

References

ABC (American Broadcasting Corporation). 1995. Poll results were presented on September 29 on the *Good Morning America* show; the poll was conducted on September 28 after the prosecution and defense had presented their final summations.

Aguilera, Elizabeth and David Migoya. 2003. "A Culture of Hostility." *Denver Post*. August 17. www.denverpost.com/cda/article.

Alderson, Arthur S. 1999. "Explaining Deindustrialization: Globalization, Failure, or Success?" *American Sociological Review* 64:701–721.

Alexander, Karl L., Doris R. Entwisle, and Maxine S. Thompson. 1987. "School Performance, Status Relations, and the Structure of Sentiment: Bringing the Teacher Back In." *American Sociological Review* 52 (October):665–682.

Alonzo, Angelo A. 1984. "The Illness Behavior Paradigm: A Conceptual Exploration of a Situational–Adaptation Perspective." *Social Science Medicine* 19:499–510.

Alteide, David L., and Robert P. Snow. 1991. *Media Worlds in the Postjournalism Era*. New York: Aldine de Gruyter.

American Bar Association. 1990. Reported in the *New York Times*, December 13:A12.

American Council of Education. 1984. Reported in John J. Macionis, *Sociology*. 3rd ed. Englewood Cliffs, NJ: Prentice-Hall, 1991.

American Nurses Association. 1998. "Managed Care: Challenges & Opportunities for Nursing." Online. www.ana.org/readroom.

American Sociological Association. 1995. *Careers in Sociology*. Washington, DC: American Sociological Association.

American Sociological Association. 1997. *Code of Ethics*. Washington, DC: American Sociological Association.

Anderson, A. B., and J. S. Frideres. 1981. *Ethnicity in Canada*. Toronto: Butterworths.

Anderson, Elaine A., and Jane W. Spruill. 1993. "The Dual-Career Commuter Family: A Lifestyle on the Move." *Marriage and Family Review* 19:131–147.

Anderson, Margaret L., and Patricia Hill Collins. 2000. *Race, Class, and Gender: An Anthology*. Belmont, CA: Wadsworth.

Anderson, Patrick R. and Donald J. Newman. 1998. *Introduction to Criminal Justice*. 6th ed. Boston: McGraw-Hill.

Anderson, W. French. 1995. "Gene Therapy." *Scientific American* 273 (September): 124–128.

Andolina, Molly W. and Jeremy D. Mayer. 2003. "Demographic Shifts and Racial Attitudes: How Tolerant Are Whites in the Most Diverse Generation?" *The Social Science Journal* 40:19–31.

Aneshensel, Carol S. 1992. "Social Stress: Theory and Research." *Annual Review of Sociology* 18:15–38.

Ansalone, George. 2003. "Poverty, Tracking, and the Social Construction of Failure: International Perspectives on Trackung." *Journal of Children and Poverty* 9:3–20.

Anticaglia, Elizabeth. 1975. *12 American Women*. Chicago: Nelson-Hall.

Applebaum, Richard P. 1978: "Marx's Theory of the Falling Rate of Profit: Towards a Dialectical Analysis of Structural Social Change." *American Sociological Review* 43 (February):64–73.

Arai, Katsuhiro. 2003. "A Comparative Study of Educational Assessment Systems in Japan and the United States." *The Journal of Educational Sociology* 72:37–52.

Archbald, Doug A. 1996. "SES and Demographic Predictors of Magnet School Enrollment." *Journal of Research and Development in Education* 29:152–162.

Archer, Melanie, and Judith R. Blau. 1994. "Class Formation in Nineteenth-Century America: The Case of the Middle Class." *Annual Review of Sociology* 19:17–41.

Arum, Richard. 2000. "Schooling and Communities: Ecological and Institutional Dimensions." *Annual Review of Sociology* 26:395–418.

Asch, Solomon E. 1952. *Social Psychology*. New York: Prentice-Hall.

——. 1955. "Opinions and Social Pressure." *Scientific American* 193(5):31–55.

Ashley, David, and David Michael Orenstein. 1995. *Sociological Theory*. 3rd ed. Boston: Allyn & Bacon.

Associated Press. 1994. Reported in *Columbus Dispatch*, September 17:1A.

——. 1995a. "Deadbeats: A Challenge for Clinton." Reported in *Columbus Dispatch*, February 22:1A, 2A.

——. 1995b. "Internet's Size Depends on What's Being Counted." Reported in *Columbus Dispatch*, February 7:3E.

Astin, Alexander. 1990. "The American Freshman: National Norms for Fall 1990." American Council on Education and the University of California at Los Angeles, excerpted in *Chronicle of Higher Education*, January 30:A30–31.

Babbie, Earl R. 2001. *The Practice of Social Research*. 9th ed. Belmont, CA: Wadsworth.

Bahgat, Gawdat. 1998. "The Gulf Monarchies: Economic and Political Challenges at the End of the Century." *Journal of Social, Political, and Economic Studies* 23:147–175.

Bahn, Paul, and John Flenley. 1992. *Easter Island, Earth Island*. London: Thames and Hudson.

Baker, David P. 1999. "Schooling all the Masses: Reconsidering the Origins of American Schooling in the Postbellum Era." *Sociology of Education* 72:197–215.

Ballantine, Jeanne H. 2001. *The Sociology of Education*. 5th ed. Upper Saddle River, NJ: Prentice-Hall.

Ballard, Robert D. 2000. "Environmental Racism." Pp. 267–274 in Jerome H. Skolnick and Elliott Currie (eds.), *Crisis in American Institutions*. Boston: Allyn and Bacon.

Banfield, Edward C. 1974. *The Unheavenly City Revisited*. Boston: Little, Brown.

Banks, James A. 1979. "The Implications of Multicultural Education for Teacher Education." Pp. 1–30 in F. H. Klassen and D. M. Gollnick (eds.), *Pluralism and the American Teacher: Issues and Case Studies*. Washington, DC: American Association for College Teacher Education.

Banton, Michael. 1983. *Racial and Ethnic Competition*. Cambridge, England: Cambridge University Press.

Barak, Greg. 1991. *Gimme Shelter: A Social History of Homelessness in Contemporary America*. New York: Prager.

Barlett, Donald L., and James B. Steele. 1992. *America: What Went Wrong?* Kansas City: Andrews and McMeel.

Barlow, Hugh D. 1996. *Introduction to Criminology*. Boston: Little, Brown.

Barnet, R. J. 1980. *The Lean Years: Politics in an Age of Scarcity*. New York: Simon & Schuster.

Bartfeld, Judi. 2000. "Child Support and Post Divorce Economic Well-Being of Mothers, Fathers, and Children." *Demography* 37: 203–213.

Bartollas, Clemens, and Simon Dinitz. 1989. *Introduction to Criminology: Order and Disorder*. New York: Harper & Row.

Bates, Eric. 2000. "The Shame of Our Nursing Homes." Pp. 52–62 in Jerome H. Skolnick and Elliott Currie (eds.), *Crisis in American Institutions*. Boston: Allyn and Bacon.

Baunach, Dawn Michelle. 2003. "Gender, Mortality, and Corporeal Inequality." *Sociological Spectrum* 23:331–358.

Bean, Frank D., and Stephannie Bell-Rose (eds.). 2000. *Immigration and Opportunity: Race, Ethnicity, and Employment in the United States*. New York: Russell Sage Foundation.

Beck, E. M., and Steward E. Tolnay, 1990. "The Killing Fields of the Deep South: The market for Cotton and the Lynching of Blacks, 1882–1930." *American Sociological Review* 55:526–539.

Becker, Howard S. 1963. *Outsiders: Studies in the Sociology of Deviance*. New York: Free Press.

Becker, Howard S., et al. 1961. *Boys in White: Student Culture in Medical School*. Chicago: University of Chicago.

Beckford, James A. 1989. *Religion and Advanced Industrial Society*. London: Unwin Hyman.

Beeghley, Leonard. 1999. *The Structure of Social Stratification in the United States*. Boston: Allyn & Bacon.

Beigel, Hugo C. 1951. "Romantic Love." *American Sociological Review* 16:326–334.

Beisel, David R. 1994. "Looking for Enemies." *Journal of Psychohistory* 22(1):1–38.

Bell, Daniel. 1973. *The Coming of Post-Industrial Society*. New York: Basic Books.

Bell, Derrick. 1993. *Faces at the Bottom of the Well*. New York: Basic Books.

Bellah, Robert N. 1967. "Civil Religion in America." *Daedalus* 96:1–21.

———. 1975. *The Broken Covenant*. New York: Seabury.

Bellah, Robert N., and Philip E. Hammond. 1982. *Varieties of Civil Religion*. New York: Harper & Row.

Bellah, Robert N., Richard Madsen, William Sullivan, Ann Swidler, and Steven Tipton. 1985. *Habits of the Heart: Individualism and Commitment in American Life*. Berkeley, CA: University of California Press.

Bellah, Robert N., Richard Madsen, William Sullivan, Ann Swidler, and Steven Tipton. 1995. *The Good Society*. New York: Knopf.

Bellow, Adam. 2003. *In Praise of Nepotism: A Natural History*. New York: Doubleday. Boston, MA: McGraw Hill.

Bell-Fialkoff, Andrew. 1996. *Ethnic Cleansing*. New York: St. Martin's Press.

Bendroth, Margaret Lamberts. 1996. "Fundamentalism and the Media, 1930–1990." Pp. 74–84 in Daniel A. Stout and Judith M. Buddenbaum (eds.), *Religion and the Mass Media: Audiences and Adaptations*. Thousand Oaks, CA: Sage.

Benedict, Jeff. 1997. *Public Heroes, Private Felons: Athletes and Crimes Against Women*. Boston: Northeastern University Press.

Benedict, Ruth R. 1934. *Patterns of Culture*. Boston: Houghton Mifflin.

Benokraitis, Nijole V. 2000. *Feuds About Families: Conservative, Centrist, Liberal, and Feminist Perspectives*. Upper Saddle River, NJ: Prentice-Hall.

Benokraitis, Nijole, and Joe Feagin. 1994. *Modern Sexism: Blatant, Subtle, and Covert Discrimination*. Englewood Cliffs, NJ: Prentice-Hall.

Ben-Sira, Zeev. 1990. "Universal Entitlement for Health Care and Its Implications for the Doctor–Patient Relationship: A New Perspective on Medical Care." *Advances in Medical Sociology* 1:99–128.

Berger, P. L. 1967. *The Sacred Canopy*. Garden City, NY: Doubleday.

Berger, Peter L., and Hansfried Kellner. 1975. "Marriage and the Construction of Reality." In Dennis Brisset and Charles Edgley (eds.), *Life as Theater*. Chicago: Aldine.

Bergesen, Albert, ed. 1983. *Crisis in the World-System*. Beverly Hills, CA: Sage.

Bergman, Edward F. 1995. *Human Geography: Cultures, Connections, and Landscapes*. Upper Saddle River, NJ: Prentice-Hall.

Bergman, Edward F., and Tom L. McKnight. 1993. *Introduction to Geography*. Englewood Cliffs, NJ: Prentice Hall.

Bergman, George, and Melanie Killen. 1999. "Adolescents' and Young Adults' Reasoning About Career Choice and the Role of Parental Influences." *Journal of Research on Adolescence* 9:253–275.

Berk, Richard A., Phyllis J. Newton, and Sara Fenstermaker. 1986. "What a Difference a Day Makes: An Empirical Study of the Impact of Shelters for Battered Women." *Journal of Marriage and the Family* 48:481–490.

Berman, Dennis K. and Alma Latour. 2003. "World Com's Ebbers Enters Plea of Not Guilty in Oklahoma Case." *Wall Street Journal*, September 4:A3.

Bernard, Jessie. 1972. *The Future of Marriage*. New York: Bantam.

———. 1982. *The Future of Marriage*. New Haven, CT: Yale University Press.

Beyer, Peter. 1994. *Religion and Globalization*. Thousand Oaks, CA: Sage.

Bian, YanJie. 2002. "Chinese Social Stratification and Social Mobility." *Annual Review of Sociology* 88:91–116.

Bianchi, Suzanne M. 1999. "Feminization and Juvenilization of Poverty: Trends, Relative Risks, Causes, and Consequences." *Annual Review of Sociology* 25:307–333.

Bickman, L. 1972. "Environmental Attitudes and Actions." *Journal of Social Psychology* 87:323–324.

Biderman, Albert D. and James P. Lynch. 1991. *Understanding Crime Incidence Statistics: Why the UCR Diverges from the NCS*. New York: Springer-Verlag.

Bidwell, Charles, and Noah Friedkin. 1988. "The Sociology of Education." In Neil J. Smelser (ed.), *Handbook of Sociology*. Newbury Park, CA: Sage.

Biel, Steven. 1996. *Down with the Old Canoe: A Cultural History of the Titanic Disaster*. New York: W. W. Norton.

Billings, Andrew C. and Susan Taylor Eastman. 2002. "Selective Representation of Gender, Ethnicity, and Nationality in American Television Coverage of the 2000 Summer Olympics. *International Review of the Sociology of Sport*. 37:351–370.

Blackman, Ann, Cathy Booth, Jon D. Hull, Sylvester Monroe, and Lisa H. Towle. 1994. ". . . And Throw Away the Key." *Newsweek*, February 7:54–59.

Blake, Wayne H., and Carol A. Darling. 1994. "The Dilemma of the African American Male." *Journal of Black Studies* 24:402–415.

Blasi, Anthony J. 1989. "Sociological Implications of the Great Western Schism." *Social Compass* 36:311–325.

Blau, Francine D. 1984. "Women in the Labor Force: An Overview." Pp. 297–315 in *Women: A Feminist Perspective*. 3rd ed. Palo Alto, CA: Mayfield.

Blau, Francine D., and Ronald G. Ehrenberg (eds.). 2000. *Gender and Family Issues*. New York: Russsell Sage Foundation.

Blau, Peter M. 1986. *Exchange and Power in Social Life*. New York: Wiley.

Blau, Peter M., and Otis Dudley Duncan. 1967. *The American Occupational Structure*. New York: John Wiley.

Blau, Peter M., and Marshall W. Meyer. 1987. *Bureaucracy in Modern Society*. 3rd ed. New York: Random House.

Bleier, Ruth. 1984. "Occupational Segregation and Labor Market Discrimination." In Barbara Reskin (ed.), *Sex Segregation in the Workplace*. Washington, DC: National Academic Press.

Blessing, Patrick J. 1980. "Irish." Pp. 524–545 in Stephan Thernstrom (ed.), *Harvard Encyclopedia of American Ethnic Groups*. Cambridge, MA: Belknap Press of Harvard University Press.

Bloom, Joan R., Pat Fobair, David Spiegel, Ricks Cox, Anna Varghese, and Richard Hoppe.

1991. "Social Supports and the Social Well-Being of Cancer Survivors." *Advances in Medical Sociology* 2:95–114.

Blumer, Herbert. 1939. "Collective Behavior." In Robert E. Park, (ed.), *Principles of Sociology*. New York: Barnes and Noble.

———. 1986. *Symbolic Interactionism: Perspective and Method*. Englewood Cliffs, NJ: Prentice Hall.

Blumstein, Philip, and Pepper Schwartz. 1983. *American Couples: Money, Work, and Sex*. New York: William Morrow.

Boelen, W. A. Marianne. 1992. "Street Corner Society: Corneville Revisited." *Journal of Contemporary Ethnography* 21(1):11–51.

Bonacich, Edna. 1972. "A Theory of Ethnic Antagonism: The Split Labor Market." *American Sociological Review* 37:547–559.

Bondurant, Joan. 1969. *Conquest of Violence*. Berkeley, CA: University of California Press.

Bongaarts, John, and Rodolfo A. Bulatao. 1999 "Completing the Demographic Transition." *Population and Development Review* 25:515–529.

Bonilla-Silva, Eduardo. 2000. "Understanding the Present Understanding the Future: Toward a New Civil Rights Movement Agenda." Paper presented at the Annual Meetings of the American Sociological Association. August 12–16. Washington, DC.

Bonner, Fred A. II. 2000. "African Americans Giftedness: Our Nation's Deferred Dream." *Journal of Black Studies* 30:644–663.

Bonner, Raymond. 1995. "Trying to Document Rights Abuses." *New York Times*, July 26:A4.

Bourdieu, Pierre. 1986a. "The Forms of Capital." In J. G. Richardson (ed.), *Handbook of Theory and Research in the Sociology of Education*. New York: Greenwood Press.

———. 1986b. *In Other Words: Essays Toward a Reflexive Sociology*. Stanford, CA: Stanford University Press.

Bourque, Gillis, and Jules Duchastel. 2000. "Erosion of the Nation-State and the Transformation of National Identities." Pp. 183–198 in Janet Abu-Lughod (ed.), *Sociology for the Twenty-First Century*. Chicago: U. of Chicago Press.

Bowles, Samuel. 1977. "Unequal Education and the Reproduction of the Social Division of Labor." In Jerome Karabel and A. H. Halsey (eds.), *Power and Ideology in Education*. New York: Oxford University Press.

Boyd, William Lowe. 1993. "Choice and Market Forces in American Education: A Revolution or a Non-Event?" *Oxford Studies in Comparative Education* 3:105–127.

Boyer, Ernest L. 1983. *High School*. New York: Harper & Row.

Bremmer, Ian, and Ray Taras, (eds.). 1992. *Nations and Politics in the Soviet Successor States*. New York: Cambridge University Press.

———, (eds.). 1996. *New States, New Politics: Building the Post Soviet Nations*. New York: Cambridge University Press.

Bretl, Daniel J., and Joanne Cantor. 1988. "The Portrayal of Men and Women in U.S. Television Commercials: A Recent Content Analysis and Trends over 15 Years." *Sex Roles* 18:595–609.

Brewer, Rose M., Cecilia A. Conrad, and Mary C. King. 2002. "The Complexities and Potential Theorizing of Gender, Caste, Race, and Class." *Feminist Economics* 8:3–18.

Brint, Steven. 1998. *Schools and Societies*. Thousand Oaks, CA: Pine Forge Press.

Britt, Russ, Tony Knight, and Chip Jacobs. 1995. "Raid a Result of Rockwell Corporate Culture?" *Orange County Register*, August 27:B2, B4.

Broaded, C. Montgomery. 1991. "China's Lost Generation: The Status Degradation of an Educational Cohort." *Journal of Contemporary Ethnography* 20(3):352–379.

Broman, Clifford L., V. Lee Hamilton, and William S. Hoffman. 1990. "Unemployment and Its Effects on Families: Evidence From a Plant Closing Study." *American Journal of Clinical Psychology* 18:643–659.

Brooks, Paul. 1972. *The House of Life: Rachel Carson at Work*. Boston: Houghton Mifflin.

Brophy, Jere E. 1983. "Research on the Self-Fulfilling Prophecy and Teacher Expectations." *Journal of Educational Psychology* 75:631–661.

Brown, David K. 2001. "The Social Sources of Educational Credentialism: Status, Culture, Labor Markets, and Organizations." *Sociology of Education*. Extra Issue: 19–34.

Brown, Larry J. 1987. "Hunger in the U.S." *Scientific American* 256:37–41.

Brown, Lee. 1990. "Neighborhood-Oriented Policing." *American Journal of Police* 9:197–207.

Brown, Lester R., Michael Renner, and Christopher Flavin. 1997. *Vital Signs 1997*. New York: W. W. Norton.

Brown, Roger. 1965. *Social Psychology*. New York: Free Press.

Browne, M. Neil, and S. M. Keeley. 1998. *Asking the Right Questions: A Guide to Critical Thinking*. 5th ed. Englewood Cliffs, NJ: Prentice-Hall.

Brundenius, Clares. 1990. "Some Reflections on the Cuban Economic Model." Pp. 143–156 in Sandor Halebsky and John Kirk (eds.), *Transformation and Struggle: Cuba Faces the 1990s*. New York: Praeger.

Brus, Wlodzimierz, and Kazimierz Laski. 1989. *From Marx to the Market: Socialism in Search of an Economic System*. Oxford, England: Clarendon Press.

Bugliosi, Vincent. 1996. *Outrage: The Five Reasons Why O.J. Simpson Got Away with Murder*. New York: Dell Publishing.

Burgess, Ernest. 1925. "The Growth of the City." In Robert Park, Ernest Burgess, and R. D. McKenzie (eds.), *The City*. Chicago: University of Chicago Press.

Bush, Diane Mitsch, and Roberta G. Simmons. 1990. "Socialization Over the Life Course." In Morris Rosenberg and Ralph H. Turner (eds.), *Social Psychology: Sociological Perspective*. New Brunswick, NJ: Transaction.

Butcher, Lee. 1988. *Accidental Millionaire: The Rise and Fall of Steve Jobs at Apple Computer*. New York: Paragon House.

Buttel, Frederick H. 2002. "Has Environmental Sociology Arrived?". *Organization and Environment* 15:42–54.

Cahill, Sandra, and Philip Cahill. 1999. "Scarlet Letters: Purusing the Corporate Citizen." *International Journal of the Sociology of Law* 27:153–165.

Califano, Joseph A. Jr. 1986. *America's Health Care Revolution: Who Lives? Who Dies? Who Pays?* New York: Simon & Schuster.

Califano, Joseph A. 1994. *Radical Surgery: What's Next for America's Health Care*. New York: Time Books.

Caldwell, John. 1999. "The Delayed Western Fertility Decline: an Examination of English-Speaking Countries." *Population and Development Review* 25:479–513.

———. 1994. *Radical Surgery: What's Next for America's Health Care*. New York: Times Books/Random House.

Campbell, Bernard. 1995. *Human Ecology*. 2nd ed. New York: Aldine De Gruyter.

Campbell, E. Q. 1969. "Adolescent Socialization." Pp. 831–860 in D. A. Goslin (ed.), *Handbook of Socialization Theory and Research*. Chicago: Rand McNally.

Campbell, John L. 2002. " Ideas, Politics, and Public Policy." *Annual Review of Sociology*. 28:21–38.

Campbell, Mary E. 2000. "Payback Time: Racial, Ethnic, and Gender Differences in the Effects of Education on Annual Income and Earned Income, 1976–1998." Paper presented at the Annual Meeting of the American Sociological Association. August 12–16. Washington, DC.

Cancian, Francesca M., and Stacey J. Oliker. 1999. *Caring and Gender*. Lanham, MD: Rowman & Littlefield.

Candiotti, Susan. 2000. "Tobacco Chief Says His Company Is Changing." Retrieved online

June 15 from (www.cnn.com/2000/law/06/14/florida.smoke).

Cantor, Muriel G., and Joel M. Cantor. 1986. "Audience Composition and Television Content: The Mass Audience Revisited." Pp. 214–225 in Sandra J. Ball-Rokeach and Muriel G. Cantor (eds.), *Media, Audience, and Social Structure*. Newbury Park, CA: Sage.

———. 1992. *Prime-Time Television: Content and Control*. Newbury Park, CA: Sage.

Caplow, Theodore. 1991. *American Social Trends*. Orlando, FL: Harcourt Brace Jovanovich.

Caplow, Theodore, Louis Hicks, and Ben J. Wattenberg. 2000. *The First Measured Century: An Illustrated Guide to Trends in America, 1900–2000*. Washington, DC: AEI Press.

Caren, Eric, and Steve Goldman (eds.) 1998. *Extra Titanic: The Story of the Disaster in the Newspapers of the Day*. Edison, NJ: Castle Books.

Carson, Rachel. 1962. *Silent Spring*. Boston: Houghton Mifflin.

Celis, William III. 1990. "Responding to Critics, SAT Ponders Change." *New York Times*, October 28:12Y.

———. 1991. "Texas Lawmakers Confront School Financing Issue Anew." *New York Times*, July 19:8A.

Centre for Development Research. 2002. "Whither the Cuban Economy After Recovery? The Reform Process, Upgrading Strategies, and the Question of Transition." *Journal of Latin American Studies* 34:365–395.

Chafetz, J. S., and A. G. Dworkin. 1987. "In the Face of Threat: Organized Anti-feminists in Comparative Perspective." *Gender and Society* 1:33–60.

Charles, Camille Zubrinsky. 2003. "The Dynamics of Racial Residential Segregation." *Annual Review of Sociology* 29:167–207.

Cherlin, Andrew. 1992. *Marriage, Divorce, and Remarriage*. Cambridge, MA: Harvard University Press.

Cherry, Robert, and William M. Rogers III (eds.). 2000. *Prospects for All: The Economic Boom and African Americans*. New York: Russell Sage Foundation.

———. 1999. "Going to Extremes: Family Structure, Children's Well-Being, and Social Science." *Demography* 36:421–428.

Chin, Kolin. 2001. "The Social Organization of Chinese Human Smuggling." Pp. 216–234 in David Kayle and Rey Koslowski (eds.), *Global Human Smuggling: Comparative Perspectives*. Baltimore: Johns Hopkins University Press.

Chishti, Maliha. 2002. "The International Women's Movement and the Politics of Participation for Muslim Women." *The American Journal of Islamic Social Sciences* 19:80–99.

Christenbury, Leila. 1989. "Cultural Literacy: A Terrible Idea Whose Time Has Come." *English Journal* (January):14–17.

Chronicle of Higher Education. 1993. Almanac Issue (August 25):15.

Chudacoff, Howard P. 1999. *The Age of the Bachelor: Creating an American Subculture*. Princeton, NJ: Princeton University Press.

Clark, Don. 1998. "Bug Hunting Emerges as a Hot Campus Sport." Pp. 545–546 in Borgna Brunner (ed.), *The Time Almanac*. Boston, MA: Information Please LLC.

Clarke, Adel E., Janet K. Shim, Laura Mamo, Jennifer Ruth Fosket, and Jennifer R. Fishman. 2003. "Biomedicalization: Technoscientific Transformations of Health, Illness, and U.S. Bipmedicine." *American Sociological Review* 68:161–194.

Clausewitz, Carl vov. 1976. *On War*. Edited and translated by Michael Howard and Peter Paret. Princeton, NJ: Princeton University Press.

Clayton, Obie. 1996. *An American Dilemma Revisited: Race Relations in a Changing World*. New York: Sage Foundation.

Coates, Jennifer. 1999. "Women Behaving Badly: Female Speakers Backstage." *Journal of Sociolinguistics* 3:65–89.

Coakely, Jay J. 1991. *Sport in Society: Issues and Controversies*. St. Louis, MO: C. V. Mosby.

Coakley, Jay J. 1998. *Sport in Society: Issues and Controversies*. Boston, MA: McGraw Hill.

Coakley, Jay J. 1998. *Sport in Society: Issues and Controversies*. St. Louis: Mosby.

Coakley, Jay J., and Peter Donnelly. 1999. *Inside Sports*. New York: Routledge.

Cockerham, William C. 1988. "Medical Sociology." Pp. 575–599 in Neil J. Smelser (ed.), *Handbook of Sociology*. Beverly Hills, CA: Sage.

Cohen, Jonathan S., Stephan D. Fihn, and Edward J. Boyko. 1994. "Attitudes Toward Assisted Suicide and Euthanasia Among Physicians in Washington State." *New England Journal of Medicine* 331:89–94.

Cohen, Randy. 2000. "Demerit Badge." The *New York Times Magazine* July 23, Section 6:19–20.

Cohen, Robin, and Paul Kennedy. 2000. *Global Sociology*. New York: New York University Press.

Cohen, Roger. 1993. "Europeans Consider Shortening Workweek to Relieve Joblessness." *New York Times*, November 22:A1, A6.

Coleman, James S. 1982. *The Asymmetric Society*. Syracuse, NY: Syracuse University Press.

———. 1993. "The Rational Reconstruction of Society." *American Sociological Review* 58:1–15.

Coleman, James S., and Thomas Hoffer. 1987. *Public and Private High Schools: The Impact of Communities*. New York: Basic Books.

Coleman, James, Thomas Hoffer, and Sally Kilgore. 1982. *High School Achievement: Public, Catholic, and Private Schools Compared*. New York: Basic Books.

Coleman, James S., and Lee Rainwater. 1978. *Social Standing in America: New Dimensions of Class*. New York: Basic Books.

Coleman, John R. 1983. "Diary of a Homeless Man." *New York Times*, February 21:26–35.

Collier, James, 2002. "Scripting the Radical Critique of Science: The Morrill Act and the American Land Grant University." *Futures* 34:182–191.

Collins, James W., and Richard J. David. 1990. Reported in Columbus Dispatch, June 5:9A.

Collins, Patricia Hill. 1998. *Fighting Words: Black Women and the Search for Justice*. Minneapolis: University of Minnesota Press.

Collins, Randall. 1975. *Conflict Sociology*. New York: Academic Press.

———. 1979. *The Credential Society*. New York: Academic Press.

———. 1986. *Max Weber: A Skeleton Key*. Newbury Park, CA: Sage.

———. 1994. *Four Sociological Traditions*. New York: Oxford University Press.

Columbus Monthly. 1989. "The Titans" (June 6): 29–37.

———. 1991. "Buying America: Foreign Investment Threat is Overstated." *Columbus Dispatch*, November 13:8A.

Commoner, Barry. 2000. "Why We Have Failed." Pp. 263–266 in Jerome H. Skolnick and Eliott Currie (eds.), *Crisis in American Institutions*. 11th ed. Boston: Allyn and Bacon.

Comte, Auguste. 1896 [orig. 1830–1842]. *Positive Philosophy of Auguste Comte*. Translated by H. Martineau. London: Bell.

Condron, Dennis J. and Vincent J. Roscigno. 2003. "Disparities Within: Unequal Spending and Achievement in an Urban School District." *Sociology of Education*. 76:18–36.

Conn, J. H., and L. Kanner. 1947. "Children's Awareness of Sex Differences." *Journal of Child Psychiatry* 1:3–57.

Connell, R. W., D. J. Ashenden, S. Kessler, and G. W. Dowsett. 1982. *Making the Difference: Schools, Families and Social Division*. Sydney: George Allen & Unwin.

Connor, W. 1972. "Nation-Building or Nation-Destroying?" *World Politics* 24:319–355.

Conrad, Peter. 1992. "Medicalization and Social Control." *Annual Review of Sociology* 18:209–232.

Cook, Elizabeth Adell, Sue Thomas, and Clyde Wilcox, (eds.). 1994. *The Year of the Women: Myths and Realities*. Boulder, CO: Westview Press.

Cook, Rebecca J. 1995. "Gender, Health, and Human Rights." *Health and Human Rights* 1:350–366.

Cookson, Peter W. Jr., and Caroline Hodges Persell. 1985. *Preparing for Power*. New York: Basic Books.

Cooley, Charles Horton. 1902. *Human Nature and the Social Order*. New York: Scribner's.

Corsini, Raymond. J. 1977. "A Medley of Current Personality Theories." Pp. 399–431 in Raymond Corsini (ed.) *Current Personality Theories*. Itasca, IL: F.E. Peacock Publishers.

Coser, Lewis A. 1956. *The Functions of Social Conflict*. Glencoe, IL: Free Press.

Coser, Lewis A., and Bernard Rosenberg. 1964. *Sociological Theory: A Book of Readings*. New York: Macmillan.

Coser, Rose Laub. 1991. In *Defense of Modernity: Role Complexity and Individual Autonomy*. Stanford, CA: Stanford University Press.

Cottingham, Clement. 1982. "Conclusion: The Political Economy of Urban Poverty." Pp. 179–208 in Clement Cottingham (ed.), *Race, Poverty, and the Urban Underclass*. Lexington, MA: Lexington Books.

Covington, Jeanette. 1995. "Racial Classification in Criminology: The Reproduction of Racialized Crime." *Sociological Forum* 4:547–568.

Cowan, James G. 1992. *The Elements of Aborigine Tradition*. Rockport, MA: Element.

Cox, Harvey. 1995. "The Warring Visions of the Religious Right." *Atlantic Monthly* (November):59–69.

Craig, Steve, (ed.). 1992. *Men, Masculinity, and the Media*. Newbury Park, CA: Sage.

Crano, William D., and Phyllis M. Mellon. 1978. "Causal Influence of Teachers' Expectancies on Children's Academic Performance: A Cross-Lagged Panel Analysis." *Journal of Educational Psychology* 70:39–49.

Craver, Charles B. 1993. *Can Unions Survive?: The Rejuvenation of the American Labor Movement*. New York: New York University Press.

Cress, Daniel M., and David A. Snow. 2000. "The Outcomes of Homeless Mobilization: The Influence of Organization, Disruption, Political Mediation, and Framing." *American Journal of Sociology* 105:1063–1164.

Crosby, Faye J., (ed.). 1987. *Spouse, Parent, Worker*. New Haven, CT: Yale University Press.

Crotty, Robert T. 1996. "Redefining the Church and Sect Typology." *Australian and New Zealand Journal of Sociology* 32:38–49.

Cumming, Elaine and William Henry. 1961. *Growing Old: The Process of Disengagement*. New York: Basic Books.

Cumming, Elaine. 1976. "Nobody Ever Died of Old Age: In Praise of Old People." Pp. 19–41 in Cary S. Kart and Barbara B. Menard, eds., *Aging in America: Readings in Social Gerontology* Sherman Oaks, CA: Alfred Publishing.

Curran, Laura, and Laura S. Abrams. 2000. "Making Men Into Dads: Fatherhood, the State, and Welfare Reform." *Gender and Society* 14:662–678.

Currie, Elliott. 1989. "Confronting Crime: Looking Toward the 21st Century." *Justice Quarterly* 6:5–25.

Curry, Timothy Jon. 1993. "A Little Pain Never Hurt Anybody: Athletic Socialization and the Normalization of Sport Injury." *Symbolic Interaction* 16(3):273–290.

———. 2000. "Booze and Bar Fights: A Journey to the Dark Side of College Athletes." Pp. 162–175 in Jim McKay, Michael Messner, and Don Sabo (eds.), *Masculinities, Gender Relations, and Sport*. Thousand Oaks, CA: Sage Publications.

Curry, Timothy J., and Richard M. Emerson. 1971. "Balance Theory: A Theory of Interpersonal Attraction?" *Sociometry* 33:216–238.

Curry, Timothy Jon, and Robert M. Jiobu. 1995. "Do Motives Matter: Modeling Gambling on Sports Among Athletes." *Sociology of Sport Journal* 12:21–35.

Cylke, F. Kurt Jr. 1993. *The Environment*. New York: HarperCollins.

Dahl, Robert. 1961. *Who Governs?* New Haven, CT: Yale University Press.

———. 1982. *Dilemmas of Pluralist Democracy: Autonomy vs. Control*. New Haven, CT: Yale University Press.

———. 2000. *On Democracy*. New Haven, CT: Yale University Press.

Dahrendorf, Ralf. 1959. *Class and Conflict in Industrial Society*. Stanford, CA: Stanford University Press.

———. 1988. "Totalitarianism Revisited." *Partisan Review* 55:541–554.

Damarin, Suzanne K. 2000. "The Mathematically Able as a Marker Category." *Gender and Education* 12:69–85.

Dandeker, Christopher. 1994. "New Times for the Military: Some Sociological Remarks on the Changing Role and Structure of the Armed Forces of the Advanced Societies." *British Journal of Sociology* 45(4):635–654.

Daniels, Roger and Harry H.L. 1994. *Asian Americans: Emerging Minorities*. Englewood Cliffs, NJ: Prentice-Hall.

Danziger, Sheldon, and Jane Waldfogel (eds.). 2000. *Securing the Future: Investing in Children from Birth to College*. New York: Russell Sage Foundation.

Das, Raju J. 2002. "The Green Revolution and Poverty: A Theoretical and Empirical Examination of the Relations Between Technology and Society." *Geoforum* 33:55–72.

Dasgupta, Partha S. 1995. "Population, Poverty, and the Local Environment." *Scientific American* (February):40–45.

Davidson, James West, and Mark Hamilton Lytle. 1982. *After the Fact: The Art of Historical Detection*. New York: Knopf.

Davies, James C. 1962. "Toward a Theory of Revolution." *American Sociological Review* 27(1):5–19.

Davies, Julia. 2003. "Expressions of Gender Analysis of Pupils' Gendered Discourse Styles in Small Group Classroom Discussions." *Discourse and Society* 14:115–132.

Davis, Gerald F. 2003. "American Cronyism: How Executive Networks Inflated the Corporate Bubble. *Contexts* (Summer):34–41.

Davis, J. A., and T. W. Smith. 1987. *General Social Surveys, 1972–1987: Cumulative Codebook*. Chicago: National Opinion Research Center.

Davis, Kingsley. 1953. "Reply to Tumin." *American Sociological Review* 18(August): 394–397.

Davis, Kingsley, and Wilbert E. Moore. 1945. "Some Principles of Stratification." *American Sociological Review* 10(2):242–249.

Delamont, Sarah. 1983. *Interaction in the Classroom*. New York: Routledge, Chapman and Hall.

DeLisi, Matt. 2002. "Not Just a Boys' Club: An Empirical Assessment of Female Career Criminals." *Women and Criminal Justice* 13: 27–45.

Della Fave, L. Richard. 1980. "The Meek Shall Not Inherit the Earth: Self-Evaluation and the Legitimacy of Stratification." *American Sociological Review* 45:955–971.

Delnick, Edward. 1990. "When Faith and Medicine Collide." Washington Post, September 25:WH14.

Delucchi, Michael. 2000. "Staking a Claim: The Decoupling of Liberal Arts Mission Statements from Baccalaurate Degrees Awarded in Higher Education." *Sociological Inquiry* 70:157–171.

Dennis, Norman. 1993. Rising Crime and the Dismembered Family: Choice in Welfare Series No. 18. London: Institute of Economic Affairs.

Denton, Nancy A., and Douglas S. Massey. 1989. "Residential Segregation of Blacks, Hispanics, and Asians by Socioeconomic

Status and Generation." *Social Science Quarterly* 69:797–816.

Denzin, Norman K. 2002. "Much Ado About Goffman. *The American Sociologist* 33:105–117.

Derber, Charles. 2004. *The Wilding of America: Money, Mayhem, and the New American Dream*. New York: Worth Publishers.

Desmond, Edward W. 1989. "Puppies and Consumer Boomers." *Time*, November 13:53.

Deutscher, Irwin. 1973. *What We Say, What We Do: Sentiments and Acts*. Glenview, IL: Scott, Foresman.

Deutschman, Alan. 2000. *Second Coming of Steve Jobs*. New York: Broadway Books.

De Vita, Carol J. 1996. "The United States at Mid-Decade." *Population Bulletin* 50(4):19.

De Witt, Karen. 1991. "U.S. Finds Schools Costing More to Achieve Less." *New York Times*, August 29:A14.

Diamond, Jared. 1991. "Speaking with a Single Tongue." *Discover* (February):78–85.

Didsbury, Howard F. Jr., (ed.). 1989. *The Future: Opportunity Not Destiny*. Bethesda, MD: World Future Society.

di Leo, Rita. 1992. "The Soviet Communist Party, 1981–1991: From Power to Ostracism." *Coexistence* 29(December):321– 334.

Dilla Alfonso, Haroldo. 2000. "The Cuban Experiment: Economic Reform, Social Restructuring, and Politics." *Latin American Perspectives* 27:33–44.

Dillon, Michele. 1999. "The Catholic Church and Possible 'Organizational Selves': The Implications for Organizational Change." *Journal for the Scientific Study of Religion* 38:386–397.

DiMaggio, Paul J., and Helmut Anhuer. 1990. "The Sociology of Non-Profit Organizations and Sectors." *Annual Review of Sociology* 16:137–159.

Dinitz, Simon. 1989. Personal communication.

Dion, Karen, and Kenneth L. Dion. 1996. "Cultural Perspectives on Romantic Love." *Personal Relationships* 3:5–17.

Dirlik, Arif. 2001. "Markets, Culture, Power. The making of a 'Second Cultural Revolution' in China." *Asian Studies Review* 25:1–33.

Dobriner, William M. 1969. *Social Structure and Social Systems*. Pacific Palisades, CA: Goodyear.

Dodge, Susan. 1991. "Vigorous Civil-Rights Drives by Homosexual Students Bring Both Changes and Resentment on Campus." *Chronicle of Higher Education*, April 3:A31.

Domhoff, William G. 1974. *The Bohemian Grove*. New York: Harper & Row.

_____. 1983. *Who Rules America Now: A View from the 80s*. Englewood Cliffs, NJ: Prentice-Hall.

_____. 1990. *The Power Elite and the State: How Policy Is Made in America*. New York: Aldine de Gruyter.

_____. 1998. *Who Rules America: Power and Politics in the Year 2000*. New York: Mayfield.

Douglas, Jack D., et al. 1980. *Introduction to the Sociology of Everyday Life*. Boston: Allyn & Bacon.

Drury, John. 2002. "When Mobs Are Looking for Witches to Burn, Nobody's Safe. Talking About the Reactionary Crowd." *Discourse and Society* 13:41–73.

Drury, John and Steve Reicher. 1999. "The Intergroup Dynamics of Collective Empowerment: Substantiating the Social Identity Model of Crowd Behavior." *Group Processes and Intergroup Relations* 2:381–402.

Drumbl, Mark A. 1999. "Sobriety in a Post-Genocidal Society: Good Neighborliness Among Victims and Agressors in Rawanda?" *Journal of Genocide Research* 1:25–41.

DuBoff, Richard B. 2002. "A Slippery Sloap: Economists and Social Insurance in the United States." Pp. 311–321 in Vincente Navarro (ed.), *The Political Economy of Social Inequalities: Consequences for Health and Quality of Life*. Amityville, NY: Baywood.

Dubeck, Paula. 2002. "Are We There Yet? Reflections on Work and Family as an Emergent Social Issue." *Sociological Focus* 35:317–330.

Duncan, Otis Dudley. 1959. "Human Ecology and Population." In Philip M. Hauser and Otis Dudley Duncan, *The Study of Population*. Chicago: University of Chicago Press.

Dunn, Dana. 1993. "Gender Inequality in Education and Employment in the Scheduled Castes and Tribes of India." *Population Research and Policy Review* 12:53–70.

Dupree, Nancy Hatch. 2002. "Cultural Heritage and National Identity in Afghanistan." *Third World Quarterly* 23:977–989.

Durkheim, Émile. 1947 [orig. 1912]. *The Elementary Forms of Religious Life*. New York: Free Press.

_____. 1966 [orig. 1897]. *Suicide: A Study in Sociology*. Translated by John A. Spaulding and George Simpson. New York: Free Press.

_____. 1966 [orig. 1893]. *The Division of Labor in Society*. New York: Free Press.

Dusek, Jerome B., (ed.). 1985. *Teacher Expectancies*. Hillsdale, NJ: Erlbaum.

Duster, Alfred M., (ed.). 1970. *Crusader for Justice: The Autobiography of Ida B. Wells*. Chicago: University of Chicago Press.

Dynes, Gail, and Jean M. Humez, (eds.). 1995. *Gender, Race, and Class in Media*. Thousand Oaks, CA: Sage.

Ebaugh, Helen R. F., Kathy Richman, and Janet Saltman Chafetz. 1984. "Life Crises among the Religiously Committed: Do Sectarian Differences Matter?" *Journal for the Scientific Study of Religion* 23:19–31.

Ebbert, Jean, and Marie-Beth Hall. 1993. *Cross Currents: Navy Women from WWI to Tailhook*. Washington, DC: Brassey's.

Eckholm, Erik. 1995. "Studies Find Death Penalty Often Tied To Victim's Race." *New York Times*, February 24:A1, A11.

Edgerton, Robert B. 1979. *Alone Together: Social Order on an Urban Beach*. Berkeley, CA: University of California Press.

Ehrlich, Paul R. 1968. *The Population Bomb*. New York: Sierra Club/Ballantine.

Einwohner, Rachael L., Jocelyn A. Hollander, and Toska Olson. 2000. "Engendering Social Movements: Cultural Images and Movement Dynamics." *Gender and Society* 14:679–699.

Eitzen, D. Stanley, and Maxine Bacca Zinn. 2001. *In Conflict and Order*. Boston: Allyn & Bacon.

_____. 2003. *Social Problems*. 9th ed. Boston: Allyn & Bacon.

Eldering, Lotty. 1996. "Multiculturalism and Multicultural Education in an International Perspective." *Anthropology and Education Quarterly* 27:315–330.

Elisha, Omri. 2002. "Sustaining Charisma: Mormon Sectarian Culture and the Struggle for Plural Marriage, 1852–1690. Nova Religio: *The Journal of Alternative and Emergent Religions*. 6:45–63.

Elmer-Dewitt, Philip. 1995. "Mine, All Mine." *Time*, June 5:46–54.

Emanuel, Ezekiel J., David Wendler, Christine Grady. 2000. "What Makes Clinical Research Ethical?" *Journal of the American Medical Association* 283:2701–2711.

Emery, Robert F., et al. 1984. "Divorce, Children, and Social Policy." In Harold W. Stevenson and Alberta E. Seigal (eds.), *Child Development Research and Social Policy*. Chicago: University of Chicago Press.

Emirbayer, Mustafa. 1996. "Useful Durkheim." *Sociological Theory* 2:109–130.

Engels, Friedrich. 1902. *The Origin of the Family, Private Property, and the State*. Chicago: Charles H. Kerr.

Entessar, Nadar. 1988. "Criminal Law and the Legal System in Revolutionary Iran." *Boston College Third World Journal* 8(1):91–102.

Erikson, Eric. 1963 (orig. 1950) *Childhood and Society*. New York: Norton.

Erikson, Kai. 1966. *Wayward Puritans: A Study in the Sociology of Deviance*. New York: Wiley.

_____. 1968. *Identity: Youth and Crisis*. New York: Norton.

Eshleman, J. Ross. 1984. *The Family: An Introduction*. Boston: Allyn & Bacon.

Espiritu, Yen Li. 1996. "Colonial Oppression, Labor Importation and Group Formation: Filipinos in the U.S." *Ethnic and Racial Studies* 19:29–48.

Etzioni, Amitai. 1975. A Comparative Analysis of Complex Organizations. New York: Free Press.

Evans, Lorraine, and Kimberly Davies. 2000. "No Sissy Boys Here: A Content Analysis of the Representation of Masculinity in Elementary School Reading Text Books." *Sex Roles* 42:255–270.

Eve, Raymond A., and Francis B. Harrold. 1994. "Who Are the Creationists? An Examination of a Conservative Christian Social Movement." *Population Review* 38:65–76.

Fairchild, Erika and Harry R. Dammer. 2000. *Comparitive Criminal Justice Systems*. Belmont, CA: Wadsworth.

Falcone, David, and Robert Broyles. 1994. "Access to Long Term Care: Race as a Barrier." *Journal of Health Politics, Policy, and Law* 19:583–595.

Faqir, Fadia. 1997. "Emerging Democracy and Islam in the Arab World." *Third World Quarterly* 18:165–174.

Farmer, Paul. 1999. *Infection and Inequalities: The Modern Plagues*. Berkeley, CA: University of California Press.

Fausto-Sterling, Anne. 1985. *Myths of Gender*. New York: Basic Books.

Feagin, Joe R. 1989. *Racial and Ethnic Relations*. 3rd ed. Englewood Cliffs, NJ: Prentice-Hall.

———. 2000. "Social Justice and Sociology: Agendas for the 21st Century." Presidential Address presented at the Annual Meetings of the American Sociological Association. August 12–16. Washington, DC.

Feagin, Joe R., and Clarice Booker Feagin. 1998. *Race and Ethnic Relations*. Upper Saddle River, NJ: Prentice-Hall.

Featherman, David L., and Robert M. Hauser. 1978. *Opportunity and Change*. New York: Academic Press.

Federal Bureau of Investigation. 1996. Crime in the United States. Washington, DC: U.S. Government Printing Office.

Fein, Helen. 2000. "No Brave New World: Life Integrity Rights and Freedom in the World, 1997 and 1987." Paper presented at annual meeting of the American Sociological Association. Washington, DC.

Feinman, Ilene Rose. 2000. *Citizenship Rights: Feminist Soldiers and Feminist Antimilitarists*. New York: New York University Press.

Felson, Richard B. 1985. "Reflected Appraisal and the Development of the Self." *Social Psychological Quarterly* 48:71–78.

Fennell, Mary L., and Jeffrey A. Alex. 1993. "Perspectives on Organizational Change in the U.S. Medical Care Sector." *Annual Review of Sociology* 19:89–112.

Ferrell, David. 1990. "To Live and Die in LA." *Los Angeles Times Magazine*, August 12:8–14, 33–35.

Ferrarotti, Franco. 2002. "On Genocide, Old and New." *International Journal of Contemporary Sociology* 39:169–174.

Fierman, Jaclyn. 1984. The Urban Experience. San Diego: Harcourt Brace Jovanovich.

———. 1990. "Why Women Still Don't Hit the Top." *Fortune*, July 30:40 ff.

Fisher, Bernice Malka. 2001. *No Angel in the Classroom: Teaching Through Feminist Discourse*. Upper Saddle River, NJ: Prentice-Hall.

Fisher, Helen. 1996. "The Origin of Romantic Love and Family Life." *National Forum* 76:31–34.

Fisher, Seymour and Roger P. Greenberg. 1977. *The Scientific Credibility of Freud's Theories and Therapy*. New York: Basic Books.

Fitzgerald, Bridget. 1999. "Children of Lesbian and Gay Parents: A Review of the Literature." *Marriage and Family Review* 29:57–75.

Fitzpatrick, Joseph P. 1980. "Puerto Ricans." Pp. 858–867 in Stephan Thernstrom (ed.), *Harvard Encyclopedia of American Ethnic Groups*. Cambridge, MA: Belknap Press of Harvard University Press.

Flanagan, William G. 2002. *Urban Sociology: Images and Structure*. Boston: Allyn & Bacon.

Flippen, Annette R. 1999. "Understanding Group Think from a Self-Regulatory Perspective." *Small Groups Research* 30:139–165.

Foner, Nancy, Ruben G. Rumbaut, and Steve Gold (eds.). 2000. *Immigration Research for a New Century*. New York: Russell Sage Foundation.

Fong, Timothy P. 2000. "The First Suburban Chinatown: The Remaking of Monterey Park, California." Pp. 369–380 in Peter Kivisto and Georganne Rundblad (eds.), *Multiculturalism in the United States: Current Issues, Contemporary Voices*. Thousand Oaks, CA: Pine Forge Press.

Form, William. 1995. "Mills at Maryland." *The American Sociologist* (Fall):40–67.

Forsyth, Donelson R. 1994. *Our Social World*. Pacific Grove, CA: Brooks/Cole.

———. 1998. *Group Dynamics*. Pacific Grove, CA: Brooks/Cole.

Fortune. 1994. "Fortune 500 Companies," as compiled by Columbus Dispatch, March 29:F1.

Fortuny-Loret, de Mola, Patricia and Luisa Cabayet. 1994. "Pentecostalism: Its Power of Transformation in Jalisco and Yucatan." *Nueva Antropologia* 13:49–56.

Frankel, Joseph. War (Britannica.com; accessed October 20, 2003).

Franklin, John Hope, and Alfred A. Moss Jr. 1988. *From Slavery to Freedom*. 6th ed. New York: Knopf.

Franklin, M.I. 2003. "We are the Borg: Microsoft and the Struggle for Controlling the Internet." *Amsterdams Sociologisch Tijdschrift* 30:223–253.

Frazier, Nancy, and Myra Sadker. 1973. *Sexism in School and Society*. New York: Harper & Row.

Freeland, Chrystia. 2000. *Sale of the Century: Russia's Wild Ride from Communism to Capitalism*. New York: Crown Business.

Freeman, Derek. 1983. *Margaret Mead and Somoa: The Making and Unmaking of an Anthropological Myth*. Cambridge, MA: Harvard University Press.

Freeman, Jo, and Victoria Johnson. 1999. *Waves of Protest*. Upper Saddle River, NJ: Prentice-Hall.

French, Marilyn. 1990. "Feminism." Pp. 42–48 in Kurt Finsterbusch and George McKenna (eds.), *Taking Sides: Clashing Views on Controversial Social Issues*. Guilford, CT: Dushkin.

Freud, Sigmund. 1961 (orig. 1930). *Civilization and Its Discontents*. Standard edition (vol. 21) London: Hogarth Press.

———. 1957 (orig. 1914). *On the History of the Psycho-analytic Movement*. Standard Edition (vol. 14, pp. 1–67).

Friedan, Betty. 1963. *The Feminine Mystique*. New York: W. W. Norton.

———. 1993. *The Fountain of Age*. New York: Simon & Schuster.

Friedman, Lawrence M. and Robert V. Percival. 1981. *The Roots of Justice*. Chapel Hill, NC: University of North Carolina Press.

Friedman, Thomas L. 1994. "Trade Ties Bind, Indeed." *New York Times*, May 25:C1.

Friedson, Eliot. 1970. *Professional Medicine*. New York: Dodd-Mead.

Frisco, Michelle L. and Kristi Williams. 2003. "Perceived Housework Equity, Marital Happiness, and Divorce in Dual-Earners Households." *Journal of Family Issues* 24:51–73.

Fritsch, Jane. 1996. "Who's Who of Money Moguls in '96 Race." *New York Times*, January 12:A7.

Fuerst, J. S., and Roy Petty. 1992. "Quiet Success: Where Managed School Integration Works." *American Prospect* 10:65–73.

Gagnon, Alain G. 1996. "Quebec: From Its Non-recognition as a Nation qua Distinct Society to Its Quest for a Nation-State." *Regional and Federal Studies* 6:21–29.

Gale, Dennis. 1996. *Understanding Urban Unrest: From Reverend King to Rodney King*. Thousand Oaks, CA: Sage.

Gallup Poll. 1983. *The Gallup Report* (formerly The Gallup Opinion Index) published monthly.

———. 1991. "Annual Gallup–Phi Delta Kappa Poll of Public Attitudes toward the Public Schools," reported in *New York Times*, August 23:A15.

Gamoran, Adam. 1992. "The Variable Effects of High School Tracking." *American Sociological Review* 57:812–828.

Gamoran, Adam, and Robert D. Mare. 1989. "Secondary School Tracking and Educational Inequality: Compensation, Reinforcement, or Neutrality." *American Journal of Sociology* 94(March):1146–1183.

Gamson, William A. 1975. *The Strategy of Social Protest*. Homewood, IL: Dorsey Press.

———. 1995. "Hiroshima, The Holocaust, and the Politics of Exclusion." *American Sociological Review* 60:1–20.

Gans, Herbert J. 1962. The Urban Villagers. New York: Free Press.

Gans, Herbert J. 1979. "Symbolic Ethnicity." In Herbert J, Gans, Nathan Glazer, Joseph R. Gusfield, and Christopher Jencks (eds.), *On the Making of Americans: Essays in Honor of David Riesman*. Philadelphia: University of Pennsylvania Press.

———. 1982. *The Urban Villagers: Group and Class in the Life of Italian-Americans*. Updated and expanded ed. New York: Free Press.

———. 1993. "From 'Underclass' to 'Undercaste': Some Observations about the Future of the Postindustrial Economy and Its Major Victims." *International Journal of Urban and Regional Research* 17:327–335.

———. 1996. *The War Against the Poor: The Underclass and Antipoverty Policy*. New York: Basic Books.

Garfinkel, Harold. 1967. *Studies in Ethnomethodology*. Englewood Cliffs, NJ: Prentice-Hall.

Garrett, Laurie. 2000. "The Return of Infectious Disease." Pp. 340–347 in Jerome H. Skolnick and Elliott Currie (eds.), Crisis in American Institutions. Boston, MA: Allyn and Bacon.

Gartner, Carol B. 1983. *Rachel Carson*. New York: Frederick Ungar.

Gehl, John, and Suzanne Douglas. 2000. "From Movable Type to Data Deluge." Pp. 8–12 in Kathy Schellenberg (ed.), *Computers in Society*. Guilford, CT: Dushkin/McGraw.

Gelb, Joyce, and Vivien Hart. 1999. "Feminist Politics in a Hostile Environment: Obstacles and Opportunities." Pp. 149–181 in Marco Giugni, Doug McAdam, and Charles Tilly, (eds.), *How Social Movements Matter*. Minneapolis: U. of Minnesota Press.

Gelbspan, Ross. 2000. "The Heat is On." Pp. 275–282 in Jerome H. Skolnick and Elliott Currie (eds.), *Crisis in America*. 11th ed. Boston: Allyn & Bacon.

Gelles, Richard. 1979. *Family Violence*. Beverly Hills, CA: Sage.

Gellner, Ernest. 1983. Nations and Nationalism. Ithaca, NY: Cornell University Press.

———. 1998. *Nationalism*. New York: New York University Press.

Gelman, David. 1990. "A Kiss Is Still a Kiss." *Newsweek*, March 5:53.

Georgakas, Dan. 1987. "The Greeks in America." *Journal of the Hellenic Diaspora* 14:5–52.

George, Peter. 1995. "Aboriginal Harvesting in the Moose River Basin: A Historical and Contemporary Analysis." *Canadian Review of Sociology and Anthropology* 32:69–90.

Gerbner, George. 1995. "Television Violence: The Power and the Peril." Pp. 547–557 in Gail Dines and Jean M. Humez (eds.), *Gender, Race, and Class in Media: A Text-Reader*. Thousand Oaks, CA: Sage.

Gershuny, Jonathan. 2000. *Changing Times: Work and Leisure in Post-Industrial Society*. Oxford: University Press.

Gerth, H. H., and C. Wright Mills (eds. and trans.). 1958. *From Max Weber: Essays in Sociology*. New York: Oxford University Press.

Gewertz, Deborah. 1981. "A Historical Reconsideration of Female Dominance Among the Chambri of Papua New Guinea." *American Ethnologist* 8(1):94–106.

Gibbs, John C. 2003. *Moral Development and Reality: Beyond the Theories of Kohlberg and Hoffman*. Thousand Oaks, CA: Sage Publications.

Gibney, Frank, Jr. 1998. "Ending the Culture of Deceit." *Time*, January 26:54.

Gibson, Christina, and George A. Marcodides. 1995. "The Invariance of Leadership Styles Across Four Countries." *Journal of Managerial Issues* 7:176–193.

Giddens, Anthony. 1971. *Capitalism and Modern Social Theory: An Analysis of the Writing of Marx, Durkheim, and Max Weber*. London: Cambridge University Press.

Giddings, Paula. 1996. *When and Where I Enter: The Impact of Black Women on Race and Sex in America*. New York: William Morrow.

Gilbert, Dennis. 1992. The American Class Structure: In an Age of Growing Inequality. New York: Wadsworth.

Gill, Rajesh. 2000. "Cities and Ethnicity: A Case of De-Ethnicazation or Re-Ethnicazation." *Sociological Bulletin* 49:221–228.

Gilligan, Carol. 1993. *In a Different Voice: Psychological Theory and Women's Development*. Cambridge, MA: Harvard University Press.

Giovacchini, Peter L. (1977). "Psychoanalysis." Pp. 15–43 in Raymond Corsini (ed.), *Current Personality Theories*. Itasca, IL: F.E. Peacock Publishers.

Gitlin, Todd. 1995. *The Twilight of Common Dreams*. New York: Metropolitan Books.

Glasberg, Davita S., and Michael Schwartz. 1983. "Ownership and Control of Corporations." *Annual Review of Sociology* 9:311–332.

Glazier, Stephen D. 1996. "New World African Ritual: Genuine and Spurious." *Journal for the Scientific Study of Religion* 35:420–431.

Glick, Paul. 1994. "Living Alone During Middle Adulthood." *Sociological Perspectives* 37:445–457.

Gobetz, Edward. 1987. "Morality, a Neglected Dimension." International Journal of World Peace 4:40–50.

Goffman, Erving. 1959. *The Presentation of the Self in Every Day Life*. New York: Anchor Books.

———. 1961. *Asylums: Essays on the Social Situation of Mental Patients and Other Inmates*. Chicago: Aldine.

———. 1967. Interactional Ritual: Essays on Face to Face Behavior. Garden City, NY: Anchor.

———. 1971. *Relations in Public*. New York: Basic Books.

———. 1977. "Genderisms: An Admittedly Malicious Look at How Advertising Reinforces Sexual Role Stereotypes." *Psychology Today* (August):60–63.

———. 1979. *Gender Advertisements*. New York: Harper & Row.

———. 1986. *Encounters: Two Studies in the Sociology of Interaction*. New York: Macmillan.

Gold, Harry. 2002. *Urban Life and Society*. Upper Saddle River, NJ: Prentice-Hall.

Golden, Tim. 1995. "After a Brief Thaw, Cuba Shows Little Hope for Closer U.S. Ties." *New York Times*, August 7:A1, A3.

Goldring, Ellen B., and C.S. Hausman. 1999. "Reasons for Parental Choice of Urban Schools." *Journal of Educational Policy* 14: 469–490.

Goldschmidt, Walter Rochs. 1990. *The Human Career: The Self in the Symbolic World*. Cambridge, MA: Basil Blackwell.

Goldstone, Jack. 1996. "Gender, Work and Culture: Why the Industrial Revolution Came Early to England but Late to China." *Sociological Perspectives* 39:1–21.

Goldthorpe, John H. 1980. *Social Mobility and Class Structure in Modern Britain*. London: Routledge & Kegan Paul.

Gondolf, F. Edward W. 1997. "Better Programs: What We Know and What We Need to Know." *Journal of Interpersonal Violence* 12:83–98.

Goode, William J. 1982. *The Family*. 2nd ed. Englewood Cliffs, NJ: Prentice-Hall.

Goodland, John L. 1984. *A Place Called School: Prospects for the Future*. New York: McGraw-Hill.

Gordon, David M., Richard C. Edwards, and Michael Reich. 1982. *Segmented Work, Divided Workers*. Cambridge, England: Cambridge University Press.

Gordon, Milton M. 1964. *Assimilation in American Life: The Role of Race, Religion, and National Origins*. New York: Oxford University Press.

Gore, Al. 1992. *Earth in the Balance: Ecology and the Human Spirit*. New York: Houghton Mifflin.

Gottdiener, Mark, and Ray Hutchison. 2000. *The New Urban Sociology*. Boston: McGraw-Hill.

Granovetter, Mark, and Charles Tilly. 1988. "Inequality and Labor Processes." In Neil J. Smelser (ed.), *Handbook of Sociology*. Newbury Park, CA: Sage.

Grant, Carl A. 1978. "Education That Is Multicultural—Isn't That What We Mean?" *Journal of Teacher Education* 29:45–48.

Grant, Nicole J. 1995. "From Margaret Mead's Field Notes: What Counted as 'Sex' in Samoa?" *American Anthropologist* 97: 678–682.

Grebler, Leo, et al. 1970. *The Mexican American People*. New York: Free Press.

Greenhouse, Linda. 1993. "Justices Uphold Stiffer Sentences for Hate Crimes." *New York Times* (June 12):1, 8.

Greeley, Andrew M. 1981. "The Persistence of Diversity." *Antioch Review* 39:141–155.

———. 1989. *Religious Change in America*. Cambridge, MA: Harvard University Press.

———. 1994. "A Religious Revival in Russia?" Journal for the Scientific Study of Religion 33:253–272.

Greeley, Andrew, and Michael Holt. 1999 "Americans' Increasing Belief in Life After Death: Religious Competition and Acculturation." *American Sociological Review* 64: 813–835.

Greenfeld, Karl Taro. 2000. "Giving Billions Isn't Easy." *Time* (July 24):52–53.

Grin, Francois. 1996. "Multiculturalism and Education in Europe." *Journal of Multilingual and Multicultural Development* 17:80–84.

Grosfoguel, Ramon. 1999. "Puerto Ricans in the U.S.A.: A Comparative Approach." *Journal of Ethnic and Migration Studies* 25:233–249.

Gross, Jane. 2000. "Boyhood Tradition is Transformed Into a Moral Battle: Debate Over Policy as Gays Put the Scouts in Turmoil." *New York Times* October 1:56y.

Grossman, Cathy Lynn. 1991a. "Baby Boomers Flock to Full-Service Megachurches." *USA Today*, August 6:1D.

———. 1991b. "Houston's Second Baptist Pursues a King-size Mission." *USA Today*, August 6:4D.

Grover, Mary Beth. 2000. "Lost in Cyberspace." Pp. 23–25 in Kathryn Schellenberg (ed.). Computers in Society. Guilford, CT: Dushkin/McGraw Hill.

Grusky, David, and Robert M. Hauser. 1984. "Comparative Social Mobility Revisited: Models of Convergence and Divergence in 16 Countries." *American Sociological Review* 49:19–38.

Gulalp, Haldun. 1996. "State and Class in Capitalism: Marx and Weber on Modernity." *Current Perspectives in Social Theory* 16:53–70.

Gupta, Kusum. 1993. "Urban Women and Violence: The Life of a Well-to-Do Housewife." *Social Action* 43:183–192.

Gurney, J. N., and K. T. Tierney. 1982. "Relative Deprivation and Social Movements: A Critical Look at Twenty Years of Theory and Research." *Sociological Quarterly* 23:33–47.

Gutman, Herbert. 1976. *The Black Family in Slavery and Freedom: 1750–1925*. New York: Vintage.

Haas, Ain. 1993. "Social Inequality in Aboriginal North America: A Test of Lenski's Theory." *Social Forces* 72:295–313.

Hacker, Andrew. 1995a. *Two Nations: Black and White, Separate, Hostile, Unequal*. New York: Scribner's.

———. 1995b. "Who They Are." *New York Times Magazine*, November 19:70–71.

———. 1998. *Money: Who Has How Much and Why*. New York: Touchstone Books.

Hacker, Jacob S., and Theda Skocpol. 1997. "The New Politics of U.S. Health Care Policy." *Journal of Health Politics, Policy, and Law* 22:315–338.

Hackworth, David H. 1991. "War and the Second Sex." *Newsweek*, August 5:24–29.

Hadaway, C. Kirk, and Wade Clark Roof. 1988. "Apostasy in American Churches: Evidence from National Survey Data." In David G. Bromley (ed.), *Falling from the Faith*. Beverly Hills, CA: Sage.

Hadden, Jeffrey K. 1987. "Religious Broadcasting and the Mobilization of the New Christian Right." *Journal for the Scientific Study of Religion* 26:1–24.

———. 1995. "Religion and the Quest for Meaning and Order: Old Paradigms, New Realities." *Sociological Focus* 28:83–100.

Hafner, Katie. 1995. "Winning the Ivory Tower." *Newsweek*, January 30:62–63.

Hage, Jerald, and Charles H. Powers. 1992. *Post-Industrial Lives: Roles and Relationships in the 21st Century*. Newbury Park, CA: Sage.

Haimes, Erica, and Kate Weiner. 2000. "Everybody's Got a Dad . . . Issues for Lesbian Families in the Management of Donor Insemination." *Sociology of Health and Illness* 22:477–499.

Halebsky, Sandor, and John M. Kirk. 1990. *Transformation and Struggle: Cuba Faces the 1990s*. New York: Praeger.

Hall, Melvin F. 1995. *Poor People's Social Movement Organizations: The Goal Is to Win*. Westport, CT: Praeger.

Hallinan, Maureen T. 1992. "The Organization of Students for Instruction in the Middle School." *Sociology of Education* 65:114–127.

———. 1994. "School Differences in Tracking Effects on Achievement." *Social Forces* 72:799–820.

Hamel, Gary, and Jeff Sampler. 2000. "The e-Corporation: More than Just Web-based, It's Building a New Industrial Order." Pp. 18–22 in Kathryn Schellenberg (ed.) Computers in Society. Guilford, CT.: Dushkin/McGraw Hill.

Hamilton, Charles, and Stokely Carmichael. 1967. *Black Power*. New York: Random House.

Hansen, Niles, and Gilberto Cardenas. 1988. "Immigrant and Native Ethnic Enterprises in Mexican American Neighborhoods: Differing Perceptions of Mexican Immigrant Workers." *International Migration Review* 22:226–242.

Hardin, Michael. 2002. "Altering Masculinities: The Spanish Conquest and the Evolution of the Latin American Machesmo." *International Journal of Sexuality and Gender Studies* 7:1–22

Hare, A. P. 1976. Handbook of Small Group Research. 2nd ed. New York: Free Press.

Hareven, Tamara K. 1994. "Continuity and Change in American Family Life." Pp. 40–41 in Arlene S. Skolnick and Jerome Skolnick (eds.), *Family in Transition*. New York: HarperCollins.

Hargrove, Thomas, and Guido H. Stempel III. 1995. "Those Who Keep on Top of News Get More Involved, Survey Finds." *Columbus Dispatch*, August 9:C6.

Harper, Charles. 2000. *Environment and Society*. Upper Saddle River, NJ: Prentice-Hall.

Harper, Douglas. 1987. *Working Knowledge: Skill and Community in a Small Shop*. Chicago: University of Chicago Press.

Harris, Marvin. 1975. *Cows, Pigs, Wars, and Witches: The Riddle of Culture*. New York: Vintage Books.

Hauser, Philip M., and Otis Dudley Duncan. 1959. *The Study of Population*. Chicago: University of Chicago Press.

Havighurst, Robert J., Bernice Neugarten, and Sheldon S. Tobin. 1968. "Disengagement and Patterns of Aging." In Bernice Neugarten, ed., *Middle Age and Aging*. Chicago: University of Chicago Press.

Hays, Kirsten. 2003. "Probe Could Put Heat on Enron." Associated Press.

Hayward, Derrick Horton, Beverly Lundy Allen, Cedric Herring, and Melvin E. Thomas. 2000. "Lost in the Storm: The Sociology of the Black Working Class, 1850–1990." *American Sociological Review* 65:128–137.

Healey, Joseph F. 1997. *Race, Ethnicity, Gender, and Class: The Sociology of Group Conflict and Change*. Thousand Oaks, CA: Pine Forge Press.

Hedges, Larry V., and Amy Nowell. 1999. "Changes in the Black-White Gap in Achievement Test Scores." *Sociology of Education* 72:111–135.

Heilman, Samuel. 1999. *Synagogue Life: A Study in Symbolic Interaction*. Chicago: University of Chicago Press.

_____. 2000. *The People of the Book: Drama, Fellowship, and Religion*. New York: Transaction Publications.

Heimer, Karen, and Ross L. Matsueda. 1994. "Role-Taking, Role Commitment, and Delinquency: A Theory of Differential Social Control." *American Sociological Review* 59:365–390.

Henig, Jeffrey R. 1989. "Choice, Race, and Public Schools: The Adoption and Implementation of a Magnet Program." *Journal of Urban Affairs* 11:243–259.

Herek, Gregory M., and Erick K. Glunt. 1991. "AIDS-Related Attitudes in the U.S.: A Preliminary Conceptualization." Journal of Sex Research 28:99–123.

Hershey, Robert D. 1989. "The Hand That Shaped America's Poverty Line as the Realistic Index." *New York Times*, August 4:Y11.

Herszenhorn, David M. 1995. "Students Turn to the Internet for Nationwide Protest Planning." *New York Times: Themes of the Times*, Fall:1.

Hertz, Thomas. 1990. "The Professional Class." *Soziale Welt* 7:231–252.

Herzer, Hilda, Maria Mercedes DiVirgilio, Maximo Lanzetta, Carla Maria Rodriguez, and Adriana Redondo. 2000. "The Formation of Social Organizations and Their Attempts to Consolidate Settlements and Neighborhoods Undergoing Transitions in Buenos Aries." *Environment and Urbanization* 12:215–230.

Heuveline, Patrick. 1999. "The Global and Regional Impact of Mortality and Fertility Transitions, 1950–2000." *Population and Development Review* 25:681–702.

Hewitt, John P. 1989. *Dilemmas of the American Self*. Philadelphia: Temple University Press.

_____. 1999. *Self and Society: A Symbolic Interactionist Approach*. New York: Allyn & Bacon.

Hewitt, John P., and Myrna Livingston Hewitt. 1986. *Introducing Sociology: A Symbolic Interactionist Perspective*. Englewood Cliffs, NJ: Prentice-Hall.

Hewlett, Debbie. 1991. "Helicopter Crash Kills Female Pilot." *USA Today*, March 4:4A.

Hiebert, Ray Eldon, Donald F. Ungurait, and Thomas W. Bohn. 1991. Mass Media VI. New York: Longman.

Higher Education Research Institute. 1989. University of California, Los Angeles, California.

Hill, Michael R. and Susan Hoecker Drysdale (Eds.) 2001. *Harriet Martineau: Theoretical and Methodological Perspectives*. New York: Routledge.

Hill, Shirley A., Mary K. Zimmernan, and Michael Fox. 2002. "Rational Choice in Medicaid Managed Care: A Critique." *Journal of Poverty* 6:37–59.

Hilts, Philip J. 1992. "Seeking Limits to a Drug Monopoly." *New York Times*, May 14:C1, C5.

Hinton, Alexander. 1998. " A Head for an Eye: Revenge in Cambodian Genocide" *American Ethnologist* 25:352–377.

Hirsch, E. D. Jr. 1987. *Cultural Literacy: What Every American Needs to Know*. Boston: Houghton Mifflin.

Hirschi, Travis. 1969. *The Causes of Delinquency*. Berkeley, CA: University of California Press.

Hochschild, Arlie, with Anne Machung. 1997. *The Second Shift: Working Parents and the Revolution at Home*. New York: Viking.

Hodson, Randy, and Teresa A. Sullivan. 1990. The Social Organization of Work. Belmont, CA: Wadsworth.

Hoff, Timothy, Winthrop F. Whitcomb, and John R. Nelson. 2002. "Thriving and Surviving in a New Medical Career: The Case of Hospital Physicians." *Journal of Health and Human Behavior* 43:72–91.

Hoffman, Mark S., (ed.). 1991. The World Almanac and Book of Facts. New York: Pharos Books.

Holden, Constance. 2002. "Science Teaching: Georgia County Opens Doors to Creationism" *Science* 298:35–36.

Holmes, Lowell D. 1986. *Quest for the Real Samoa: The Mead/Freeman Controversy and Beyond*. South Hadley, MA: Bergin & Garvey.

Homans, George C. 1950. *The Human Group*. New York: Harcourt, Brace & World.

_____. 1958. "Social Behavior as Exchange." *American Journal of Sociology* 62:597–606.

_____. 1993. *Social Behavior: Its Elementary Forms*. Rev. ed. New York: Harcourt, Brace, Jovanovich.

Hoover's Handbook. 1995. As cited in "After the Mergers: How the Networks Fit." New York Times, August 2:C1.

Horton, Hayward Derrick, Beverly Lundy Allen, Cedric Herring and Melvin Thomas. 2000. "Lost in the Storm: The Sociology of the Black Working Class, 1850–1990." *American Sociological Review* 65:128–137.

Houben, Vincent J. H. 2003. "Southeast Asia and Islam." *Annals of the American Academy of Political and Social Science* 588:149–170.

Howell, James C. 1999. "Youth Gangs. Homicide Alternative." *Review of Crime and Delinquency* 45:208–241.

Hughes, E. C. 1958. *Men and Their Work*. New York: Free Press.

Hughey, Michael W. 1990. "Internal Contradictions of Televangelism: Ethical Quandaries of That Old Time Religion in a Brave New World." *Culture and Society* 4:31–47.

Hummel, Ralph P. 1994. *The Bureaucratic Experience*. 3rd ed. New York: St. Martin's Press.

Humphries, Karin H., and Eddy Van Doorslaer. 2000. "Income-related Health Inequality in Canada." *Social Science and Medicine* 50:663–671.

Hunt, J. C., and L. L. Hunt. 1987. "Here to Play: From Families to Lifestyles." *Journal of Family Issues* 8:440–443.

Hunter, Alfred A., and Jean McKenzie Leiper. 1993. "On Formal Education, Skills, and Earnings: The Role of Educational Certificates in Earnings Determination." *Canadian Journal of Sociology* 18:21–42.

Hunter, James Davidson. 1991. *Culture Wars: The Struggle to Define America*. New York: Basic Books.

Hurlbert, R. T., Hains and Beggs. 2000. "Core Networks and Tie Activation: What Kinds of Routine Network Allocate Resources in Non Routine Situations? *American Sociological Review* 65:597–618.

Hurz, Demie. 1995. *For Richer or Poorer: Mothers Confront Divorce*. New York: Routledge.

Ignatiev, Noel. 1995. *How the Irish Became White*. New York: Routledge.

Ijomah, B. I. C. 2000. Nigeria's Transition From Military To Civilian Rule: An Overview." *Journal of Political and Military Sociology* 28:293–310.

Illich, Ivan D. 1983. *Deschooling Society*. New York: HarperCollins.

Inciardi, James A. 1992. *The War on Drugs II*. Mountain View, CA: Mayfield

Inglehart, Ronald. 1997. *Modernization and Post-modernization: Cultural, Economic, and Political Change in 43 Societies*. Princeton, NJ: Princeton University Press.

Inglehart, Ronald, and Wayne E. Baker. 2000. "Modernization, Culture Change, and the Persistence of Traditional Values." *American Sociological Review* 65:19–51.

Inkeles, Alex, and Smith, D. 1974. *Becoming Modern*. Cambridge, MA: Harvard University Press.

Institute for Social Research. 1994. "Television Violence and Kids: A Public Health Problem?" *ISR Newsletter* 18:5–7.

Jabbra, Joseph G., and Kent Jancaik. 1999. "Challenging Development Issues in a Socialist State, The Case of Cuba." Journal of Developing Studies 15:205–219.

Jacoby, Kerry N. 1998. *Souls, Bodies, and Sports. The Drive to Abolish Abortion Since 1973*. Westport, CT: Praeger.

Jackson, Barbara L., and Bruce S. Cooper. 1989. "Parent Choice and Empowerment: New Roles for Parents." *Urban Education* 24:263–286.

Jackson, Pamela Bradboy and Montenique Finney. 2002. "Negative Life Events and Psychological Distress Among Young Adults." *Social Psychological Quarterly* 65:186–201.

Jakobi, Patricia L. 1990. "Medical Science, Christian Fundamentalism, and the Etiology of AIDS." AIDS and Public Policy Journal 5:89–93.

Jalata, Asafa. 2002. "Revisiting the Black Struggle: Lessons for the 21st Century." *Journal of Black Studies* 33:86–116.

Jamner, Margaret Schneider, and Daniel Stokols (eds.). 2000. *Promoting Human Wellness*. Berkeley, CA: University of California Press.

Jasinski, Janal. 2000 "Beyond High School: An Examination of Hispanic Educational Attainment." *Sociological Quarterly* 81:276–290.

Jecker, Nancy S., and Donnie J. Self. 1991. "Separating Care and Cure: An Analysis of Historical and Contemporary Images of Nursing and Medicine." *Journal of Medicine and Philosophy* 16:285–306.

Jencks, Christopher. 1994. *The Homeless*. Cambridge, MA: Harvard University Press.

Jencks, Christopher, et al. 1979. *Who Gets Ahead? The Determinants of Economic Success in America*. New York: Basic Books.

Jetter, Alexis, Annelise Orieck, and Diana Taylor. 1995. "The War on Poor Women." Pp. 104–120 in George J. Demko and Michael C. Jackson (eds.), *Population at Risk in America: Vulnerable Groups at the End of the 20th Century*. Boulder, CO: Westview Press.

Jimenez, Mary Ann. 1997. "Concepts of Health and National Health Care Policy: A View from American History." *Social Service Review* 71:34–50.

Jiobu, Robert. 1988. "Ethnic Hegemony and the Japanese of California." *American Sociological Review* 53:353–367.

———. 1990. *Ethnicity and Inequality*. Albany, NY: State University of New York Press.

Jiobu, Robert M., and Linda Nishigaya. 1985. "Residential Segregation Among Asians in Honolulu." Presented at the Annual Meeting of the North Central Sociological Association, Cincinnati, Ohio.

Joffee, C. 1971. "Sex Role Socialization and the Nursery School: As the Twig Is Bent." *Journal of Marriage and the Family* 33:467–475.

Johnson, Allan G. 1989. *Human Arrangements: An Introduction to Sociology*. New York: Harcourt Brace Jovanovich.

Johnson, Benton. 1963. "On Church and Sect." *American Sociological Review* 28:539–549.

Johnson, D. 1981. *American Law Enforcement: A History*. St. Louis, MO: Forum Press.

Johnson, Dirk. 1990. "Milwaukee Creating 2 Schools Just for Black Boys." *New York Times*, September 30:1, 18.

Johnson, Otto, (ed.). 1989. *The 1989 Information Please Almanac*. Boston: Houghton Mifflin.

Johnstone, Ronald L. 1996. *Religion in Society: A Sociology of Religion*. Englewood Cliffs, NJ: Prentice-Hall.

Jolidon, Lawrence. 1990. "Females on the Front Lines: No Easy Task." *USA Today*, December 13:5A.

Jonas, Andrew. 1998. "Busing, White Flight, and the Role of Developers in the Continuous Suburbanization of Franklin County, Ohio." *Urban Affairs Review* 34:340–358.

Jones, David H. 1999. *Moral Responsibility in the Holocaust: A Study in the Ethics of Character*. Lanham, Maryland: Rowman and Littlefield Publishers.

Jones, H. James. 1981. *Bad Blood: The Tuskegee Syphilis Experiment*. New York: Free Press.

Jones, James, and Robert T. Carter. 1996. "Racism and White Racial Identity: Merging Realities." Pp. 1–23 in Benjamin P. Bowser and Raymond G. Hunt (eds.), *Impacts of Racism on White Americans*. Thousand Oaks, CA: Sage.

Josephy, Alvin M. Jr. 1994. *500 Nations: An Illustrated History of North American Indians*. New York: Knopf.

Justice Policy Institute 2002. Cellblocks or Classrooms: The Funding of Higher Education and Its Impact on African American Men. Retrieved online December 17, 2003 at http://www.justicepolicy.org/article.php?id=3

Juteau, Danielle. 1994. "Multiple Francophone Minority Communities: Multiple Citizenship." *Sociologie-et-Societies* 26(1):33–45.

Kahera, Akel Ismail. 2002. "Urban Enclaves, Muslim Identity, and the Urban Mosque in America." *Journal of Muslim Minority Affairs* 2:369–380.

Kalish, Carol B. 1988 (May). "International Crime Rates." *Bureau of Justice Statistics Special Report*. Washington, DC: U.S. Government Printing Office.

Kallen, David J. 2002. "Medical Sociology: The Clinical Perspective." Pp. 123–162 in Roger A. Straus (ed.), *Using Sociology: An Introduction from the Applied and Clinical Perspectives*. Lanham, MD: Rowman and Littlefield.

Kallen, Horace M. 1924. *Culture and Democracy in the United States: Studies in the Group Psychology of the American Peoples*. New York: Boni and Liveright.

Kalmuss, Debra. 1984. "The Intergenerational Transmission of Marital Aggression." Journal of Marriage and the Family 46:11–19.

Kalu, W. J. 1993. "Battered Spouses as a Social Concern in Work with Families in Two Semi-Rural Communities of Nigeria." *Journal of Family Violence* 8:361–373.

Kamber, Victor, and Bradley O'Leary. 1996. *Are You a Conservative or a Liberal?: A Fun and Easy Test to Tell Where You Stand on the Political Spectrum*. Austin, TX: Boru Press.

Kammen, Daniel. 1995. "Cookstoves for the Developing World." *Scientific American* (July):72–75.

Kammeyer, Kenneth C. W. 1987. *Marriage and Family*. Boston: Allyn & Bacon.

Kamo, Yoshibori. 2000. "Racial and Ethnic Differences in Extended Family Households." *Sociological Perspectives* 42:211–229.

Kantor, Harvey, and Barbara Brenzel. 1994. "Urban Education and the 'Truly Disadvantaged': The Historical Roots of the Contemporary Crisis." Pp. 393–404 in Jerome H. Skolnick and Elliott Currie (eds.), *Crisis in American Institutions*. New York: HarperCollins.

Kanazawa, Satoshi and Mary C. Still. 1999. "Why Monogamy?" *Social Forces* 78:25–50.

Kaparthy, Zoltan. 1923. *Budapest Nights*. Vienna: Emperor Press.

Kariya, Takehko. 2000. "A Study of Study Hours on Equality of Effort in a Meritocracy." *The Journal of Educational Sociology* 66:213–230.

Katz, Donald, and Kenneth Braley. 1933. "Racial Stereotypes of One Hundred College Students." *Journal of Abnormal Psychology*: 28:280–290.

Keesing, Felix M. 1958. *Cultural Anthropology: The Science of Custom*. New York: Rinehart.

Keister, Lisa A. 2003. "Financial Markets, Money, and Banking." *Annual Review of Sociology* 28:39–61.

Kelly, Dennis. 1990. *USA Today*, September 4:1D, 4D.

Kelly, John R. 1990. *Leisure*. 2nd ed. Englewood Cliffs, NJ: Prentice-Hall.

Kelly, Ron. 2003. "Homelessness Grows as More Live Check-to-Check." USA Today Aug. 12: A1–A2.

Kennedy, Paul. 1993. *Preparing for the Twenty-First Century*. New York: Random House.

Kerewsky, Shoshana Daniel. 1989. "Playing with Cultural Literacy." *English Journal* (January): 18–22.

Kett, Joseph F. 1984. *Rites of Passage: Adolescence in America, 1790 to the Present*. New York: Basic Books.

Khullar, Gurdeep S. and Beverly C. Reynolds. 1990. "Quality of Life and Activity: A Test of the Activity versus Disengagement Theories." *International Review of Modern Sociology* 20:33–68.

Kidd, Bruce. 1995. "Inequality in Sport, the Corporation, and the State: An Agenda for Social Scientists." *Journal of Sport and Social Issues* (19):232–248.

Killingsworth, Maek R. 2002. "Comparable Worth and Pay Equity: Recent Developments in the United States. *Canadian Public Policy Analysis 28*, Supplement:S171–S186.

Kimball, Meredith M. 1986. "Television and Sex-Role Attitudes." In Tannis M. Williams (ed.), *The Impact of Television: A Natural Experiment in Three Communities*. Orlando, FL: Academic Press.

Kimmel, Michael S. 2000. *The Gendered Society*. New York: Oxford University Press.

Kimmel, Michael S., and Michael A. Messner. 1997. *Men's Lives*. New York: Macmillan.

Kinloch, Gram C. 2002. "The Possible Causes and Reduction of Genocide: An Exploration." *International Journal of Contemporary Sociology* 39:131–151.

Kirn, Walter. 2000. "Meet the New Huck." *Time*, July 10:70–72.

Kitano, Harry H. L., and Roger Daniels. 1988. Asian Americans: Emerging Minorities. Englewood Cliffs, NJ: Prentice Hall.

Kitano, Harry H. L., and Wai-tsang Yeung. 1982. "Chinese Interracial Marriage." Pp. 35–48 in Gary A. Cretser and Joseph J. Leon (eds.), *Intermarriage in the United States*. New York: Hayworth Press.

Kitson, Gay C. 1985. "Marital Discord and Marital Separation: A County Survey." *Journal of Marriage and the Family* 47:693–700.

Kivisto, Peter and Georganne Rundblad. 2000. *Multiculturalism in the United States: Current Issues, Contemporary Voices*. Thousand Oaks, CA: Pine Forge Press.

Kleinfield, N. R. 1996. "The Company as Family No More." *New York Times,* March 4:1A, 8A.

Klesius, Michael. 2002. "Search for a Cure." *National Geographic* 201 (2):32–43.

Knapp, Peter. 1994. *One World—Many Worlds*. New York: HarperCollins.

Knight-Ridder Newspapers. 1995. "Packwood to Resign." As reported in Columbus Dispatch, September 8:1A, 2A.

Knipprath, Heidi. 2000. "A Case Study of the Contribution of Tracking to the Reproduction of Social Stratification." *Journal of Educational Sociology* 66:157–175.

Knottnerus, J. David and Frederique Van de Poel-Knottnerus. 1999. *The Social World of Male and Female Children in the Nineteenth Century French Educational System: Youth, Rituals and Elites*. Lewiston, New York: The Edwin Mellen Press.

Knox, George W. 1999. "A Comparison of Gangs and Cults." *Journal of Gang Research* 6:1–39.

Kohlberg, Lawrence. 1966. "A Cognitive-Development Analysis of Children's Sex-Role Concepts and Attitudes." Pp. 82–166 in Eleanor Maccoby (ed.), *The Development of Sex Differences*. Stanford, CA: Stanford University Press.

———. 1975. "The Cognitive-Developmental Approach to Moral Education." *Phi Delta Kappan* 56:670–677.

Kohn, Melvin L., and Carmi Schooler. 1983. *Work and Personality: An Inquiry into the Impact of Social Stratification*. New York: Ablex Press.

Kolatch, Alfred J. 1994. *This Is the Torah*. Middle Village, NY: Jonathan David.

Koomen, Willem, Tom Kniesmeijer, Alice Vos-Panhuijsen, and Aart S. Velthuijsen. 1990. "Social Support and Well-being in Heart Patients: A Longitudinal Study of the Combined Role of Need for Social Support and Perceived Social Support." *Social Behavior* 5:297–306.

Kornblum, William and Julian Joseph, in collaboration with Carolyn D. Smith. 1995. *Social Problems*, Eighth edition. Englewood Cliffs, NJ: Prentice-Hall.

Kornhauser, William. 1959. *The Politics of Mass Society*. New York: Free Press.

Kradin, Nikolay N. 2002. "Nomadism, Evolution, and World Systems: Pastoral Societies in Theories of Historical Development." *Journal of World Systems Research* 8,3 fall.

Krantz, Michael. 1999. "Steve's Two Jobs." Time, July 24:62–68.

Krivo, Lauren J., and Ruth D. Peterson. 2000. "The Structural Context of Homicide: Accounting for Racial Differences in Process." *American Sociological Review* 65:547–559.

———. 1968. *On Death and Dying*. New York: Scribner.

Kubler-Ross, Elisabeth. 1987. *AIDS: The Ultimate Challenge*. New York: Macmillan Publishing Company.

Kubler-Ross, Elisabeth, and David Kessler. 2000. *Life Lessons: Two Experts on Death and Dying Teach Us About the Mysteries of Life and Living*. New York: Scriber.

Kubitschek, Warren N., and Maureen T. Hallinan. 1996. "Race, Gender, and Inequality in Track Assignments." *Research in Sociology of Education and Socialization* 11:121–146.

Kulis, Stephen and Flavio Francisco Marsiglia. 2000. "Gender Labels and Gender Inequality as Predictors of Drug Use Among Ethnically Diverse Middle School Students. Paper presented at the Annual Meeting of the American Sociological Association. Washington, DC. August 12–16.

Kwan, Michael David. 1990. *Broken Portraits: Encounters with Chinese Students*. San Francisco: China Books & Periodicals.

Lacayo, Richard. 1989. "Between Two Worlds." *Time*, March 13:58–68.

———. 1995. "This Land Is Whose Land?" *Time*, October 23:68–71.

LaFollette, Marcel C. 1990. "Daring Steps Are Needed to Increase Women's Role in Science." *Chronicle of Higher Education*. October 3:A56.

LaFree, Gary. 1999. "Declining Violent Crime Rates in the 1990s: Predicting Crime Boom and Busts." *Annual Review of Sociology* 25:145–168.

Lai, Eric Lo Ping and Dennis Arguelles (Eds.) 2003. *The New Face of Asian Pacific America: Numbers, Diversity, Change in the 21st Century*. San Francisco: Asian Week Books.

Lai, Gina and Odalia Wong. 2002. "The Tie Effect on Information Dissemination: The Spread of a Cpmmercial Rumor in Hong Kong." *Social Networks* 24:49–75.

Lamont, Michele. 2002. *The Dignity of Working Men*. New York: Russell Sage Foundation.

Landale, Nancy S. and R. S. Oropesa. 2002. "White, Black, or Puerto Rican: Self-Identification Among Mainland and Island Puerto Ricans." *Social Forces* 81:231–254.

Lane, Katherine E., and Patricia A. Gwartney-Gibbs. 1985. "Violence in the Context of Dating and Sex." *Journal of Family Issues* 6:45–59.

LaPiere, Richard T. 1934. "Attitudes versus Action." *Social Forces* 13:230–237.

Larkin, Maureen. 1999. "Globalization and Health." *Critical Public Health* 9:335–345.

Lasch, Christopher. 1977. *Haven in a Heartless World*. New York: Basic Books.

Lasch, Christopher. 1995. "The Age of Limits," Pp. 227–240 in Arthur M. Melzer, Jerry Weinberger, and M. Richard Zinman (eds.), *History and the Idea of Progress*. Ithaca: Cornell University Press.

———. 1979. The Culture of Narcissism. New York: W. W. Norton.

Latané, Bibb, K. Williams, and S. Harkins. 1979. "Many Hands Make Light the Work: The Causes and Consequences of Social Loafing." *Journal of Personality and Social Psychology* 37:822–832.

Lauer, Robert H. 1991. *Perspectives on Social Change*. 4th ed. Boston: Allyn & Bacon.

Laurence, Leslie, and Beth Weinhouse. 1994. *Outrageous Practices: The Alarming Truth About How Medicine Mistreats Women*. New York: Fawcett Columbine.

———. 1997. *How Gender Bias Threatens Women's Health*. New Brunswick, NJ: Rutgers University Press.

Lauzen, Martha M. and David M. Dozier. 2002. "You Look Mahvelous: An Examination of Gender and Appearance Comments in the 1999–2000 Prime-Time Season." *Sex Roles* 46:429–437.

Lawson, Bill E., (ed.). 1992. *The Underclass Question*. Philadelphia: Temple University Press.

Lawson, Matthew P. 1999. "The Holy Spirit as Collective Conscience." *Sociology of Religion* 60:341–361.

Lawton, Julia. 2003. "Lay Experiences of Health and Illness: Past Research and Future Agendas." *Sociology of Health and Illness* 25:23–40.

LeBlanc, Adrian Nicole. 1995. "Falling." *Esquire*, April:84–100.

LeBon, Gustave. 1895. *The Psychology of the Crowd*. Paris: Alcan.

Lechner, Frank J. 1991. "The Case Against Secularization: A Rebuttal." *Social Forces* 69:1103–1119.

Lee, Felicia R. 1988. "Blacks and Koreans in Brooklyn Forge an Accord." *New York Times*, December 21:28.

Lee. Jennifer. 2003. *Civility in the City: Blacks, Jews, and Koreans in Urban America*. Cambridge: Harvard University Press.

Lee, Jessica. 1992. "Bush Takes Care Plan on the Road." *USA Today*, February 4:4A.

Lemann, Nicholas. 1995a. "The Structure of Success in America." *Atlantic Monthly*, August:41–60.

———. 1995b. "The Great Sorting." *Atlantic Monthly*, September:84–100.

Lemert, Edwin. 1951. Social Pathology. New York: McGraw-Hill.

———, Charles C. Lemmert, and Michael Winter. 2000. *Crime and Deviance*. New York: Rowman & Littlefield.

Lenski, Gerhard. 1954. "Status Crystallization: A Non-Vertical Dimension of Status." *American Sociological Review* 19:405–413.

———. 1956. "Social Participation and Status Crystallization." *American Sociological Review* 21:458–464.

———. 1966. *Power and Privilege: A Theory of Stratification*. New York: McGraw-Hill.

Lenski, Gerhard, Patrick Nolan, and Jean Lenski. 1995. Human Societies: An Introduction to Macrosociology. 5th ed. New York: McGraw-Hill.

Leonard, Karen Isaksen. 1994. *Sociology of an Indian Caste*. Berkeley, CA: University of California Press.

Leonard, Wilbert. 1988. *A Sociological Perspective of Sport*. New York: McMillian.

Levin, Jack and Gordana Rabrenovic. 2001. "Hate Crimes and Ethnic Conflict." *American Behavioral Scientist* 45:574–587.

Levine, Robert. 1987. "Waiting Is a Power Game." *Psychology Today* (April):24–33.

Levinger, George. 1979. "A Social Exchange View on the Dissolution of Pair Relationships." In Robert L. Burgess and Ted L. Huston (eds.), *Social Exchange in Developing Relationships*. New York: Academic Press.

Levinson, D. J. 1978. *The Seasons of a Man's Life*. New York: Knopf.

Lewin, Kurt, Ronald Lippett, and Ralph K. White. 1939. "Patterns of Aggressive Behavior in Experimentally Created 'Social Climates.'" *Journal of Social Psychology* 10:271–299.

Lewin, Tamar. 1994. "Low Pay and Closed Doors Greet Young in Job Market." *New York Times*, March 10:1A, 12A.

Lewis, Martin W. 1992. *Green Delusions*. Durham, NC: Duke University Press.

Lewis, Michael. 1995. "The Rich." *New York Times Magazine*, November 19:65–69.

Lewis, Oscar. 1968. "The Culture of Poverty." Pp. 187–200 in Daniel Patrick Moynihan (ed.), *On Understanding Poverty: Perspectives from the Social Sciences*. New York: Basic Books.

Lieberson, Stanley, Susan Dumais, and Shyon Bauman. 2000. "The Instability of Androgynous Names: The Symbolic Maintenance of Gender Boundaries." *American Journal of Sociology* 105:1249–1287.

Lieberson, Stanley and Greda B. Lynn. 2002. "Barking up the Wrong Branch: Scientific Alternatives to the Correct Model of Social Science." *Annual Review of Sociology* 28:1–19.

Linden, Fabian. 1986. "The Dream Is Alive." *American Demographics* 8:4–6.

Lindesmith, Alfred R., Anselm L. Strauss, and Norman K. Denzin. 1999. *Social Psychology*. Englewood Cliffs, NJ: Prentice-Hall.

Link, Bruce C., and Francis T. Cullen. 1990. "The Labeling of Mental Disorder: A Review of the Evidence." *Research in Community and Mental Health* 6:75–105.

Lipset, Seymour Martin. 1962. "Harriet Martineau's America." Pp. 5–42 in *Society in America* by Harriet Martineau. New York: Anchor Books.

———. 1995. "The Social Requisites of Democracy Revisited." *American Sociological Review* 59 (February 1):1–22.

———. 1996. "Steady Work: An Academic Memoir." *Annual Review of Sociology* 22:1–27.

Lipset, Seymour Martin, and Reinhard Bendix. 1967. *Social Mobility in Industrial Society*. Berkeley, CA: University of California Press.

Livingston, Gretchen and Joan R. Kahn. 2002. "An American Dream Unfulfilled: The Limited Mobility of Mexican Americans." *Social Science Quarterly* 83: 1003–1012

Lockhart, William. 2000. "'We Are One Life', But Not One Gender Ideology: Unity, Ambiguity and the Promise Keepers." *Sociology of Religion* 61:73–92.

Lofland, J., and J. T. Richardson. 1984. "Religious Movement Organization: Elemental Forms and Dynamics." In L. Kriesberg (ed.), *Research in Social Movements, Conflicts, and Change*. Vol. 7. Greenwich, CT: JAI Press.

Lometti, Guy E. 1995. "The Measurement of Television Violence." *Journal of Broadcasting and Electronic Media* 39:292–295.

Longman, Timothy. 1999. "Nation, Race or Class? Defining the Hutu and Tutsi of East Africa." *Research in Politics and Society* 6:103–130.

Looney, Douglas S. 1988. "Bred to Be a Superstar." *Sports Illustrated*, February 22:56.

———. 1990. "The Minefield: For USC Quarterback Todd Marinovich, Fame and Talent May Not Be Enough to See Him Safely Through." Sports Illustrated, September 3:48.

Lopez, Ian F. Hahey. 1996. White Byb Law. The Legal Construction of Race. New York: New York University Press.

Lorber, Judith. 1995. *Paradoxes of Gender*. New Haven, CT: Yale University Press.

Lorch, Donatella. 1995. "Unsafe Abortions Become a Big Problem in Kenya." *New York Times*, June 4:3Y.

Lord, Walter. 1955. *A Night To Remember*. New York: Holt, Rinehart & Winston.

Lovaglia, Michael J. 1999. "Understanding Network Exchange Theory." *Advances in Group Processes* 16:31–59.

Lucas, Samuel R. and Mark Berends. 2002. "Sociodemographic Diversity, Correlated Achievement, and DeFacto Tracking." *Sociology of Education* 75:328–348.

Lutzenhiser, Loren. 2002. "Environmental Sociology: The Very Idea." *Organization and Environment* 15:5–9.

Lynch, Michael. 2002. "Ethnomethodology's Unofficial Journal." *Human Studies* 25: 485–494.

Lynch, Michael. 1999. "Silence in Context: Ethnomethodology and Social Theory." *Human Studies* 22:211–233.

Lynd, Robert S., and Helen Merrel Lynd. 1929. *Middletown: A Study in Contemporary American Culture*. New York: Harcourt, Brace.

Lyon, Larry. 1999. The Community in Urban Society. Philadelphia: Temple University Press.

MacFarquhar, Emily. 1994. "The War Against Women." *U.S. News and World Report*, March 28:42–48.

Macionis, John J. 1996. Society: The Basics. Upper Saddle River, NJ: Prentice Hall.

———. 2004. *Society: The Basics*. 7th ed. Upper Saddle River, NJ: Prentice-Hall.

Macionis, John J. and Vincent N. Parrillo. 2004. Cities and Urban Life. Upper Saddle River, NJ:Prentice Hall.

MacKay, Charles. 1852 [1932]. *Memoirs of Extraordinary Popular Delusions and the Madness of Crowds*. Boston: L. C. Page.

Maguire, E.R., Snipes, J.B., Uchida, C.D., and Townsend, M. 1998. "Counting Cops: Estimating the number of Police Departments and Police Officers in the USA." *Policing: An International Journal of Policing Strategies and Management* 2(1):97–120.

Makepeace, James M. 1981. "Courtship Violence Among College Students." *Family Relations* 35 (January):97–102.

———. 1986. "Gender Differences in Courtship Victimization." *Family Relations* 35 (July):383–388.

Mannon, James M. 1990. *American Gridmark: Why You've Always Suspected that Measuring Up Doesn't Count*. Tuscon: Harbinger House.

Markoff, John. 1995. "Apple Computer Co-Founder Reaps a Billion on Stock Issue." *New York Times*, November 30:1A, 7C.

Marriott, Michael. 1995. "A Bus to the Black March: 31 Men, Hope and History." *New York Times*, October 16:1A, 7A.

Martineau, Harriet. 1962. *Society in America*. New York: Anchor.

Marx, Gary T., and Douglas McAdam. 1994. *Collective Behavior and Social Movements: Process and Structure*. Englewood Cliffs, NJ: Prentice-Hall.

Marx, Karl. 1963 [orig. 1844]. "Estranged Labour-Economic and Philosophic Manuscripts of 1844." In C. Wright Mills (ed.), *Images of Man*. New York: George Braziller.

Marx, Karl, and Friedrich Engels. 1967 [orig. 1848]. *The Communist Manifesto*. London: Penguin.

Masterson, John. 1984. "Divorce as a Health Hazard." *Psychology Today* 18 (October):24.

Matras, Judah. 1984. *Social Inequality, Stratification, and Mobility*. 2nd ed. Englewood Cliffs, NJ: Prentice-Hall.

Mattingly, Cheryl, and Linda Garro. 2000. *Narrative and the Cultural Construction of Illness and Healing*. Berkeley, CA: University of California Press.

May, Tim. 1996. *Situating Social Theory*. Bristol, PA: Open University Press.

Maybury-Lewis, David. 1992. *Millennium: Tribal Wisdom and the Modern World*. New York: Viking.

McAdam, Doug, et al. 1988. "Social Movements." Pp. 695–737 in Neil Smelser (ed.), *Handbook of Sociology*. Newbury Park, CA: Sage.

McCall, George J., and J. L. Simmons. 1978. *Identities and Interactions*. Rev. ed.. New York: Free Press.

McCarthy, John D., and Mayer N. Zald. 1973. *The Trend of Social Movements in America: Professionalism and Resource Mobilization*. Morristown, NJ: General Learning Press.

———. 1977. "Resource Mobilization and Social Movements: A Partial Theory." *American Journal of Sociology* 82:1212–1241.

McCurdy, Jack. 1990. "Cal. Jury Awards $1–Million to Teacher Who Charged Racism in Tenure Denial." *Chronicle of Higher Education*, April 25:A11, A18.

McDonald, Ian. 2003. "Hindu Nationalism, Cultural Space, and Bodily Practices in India." *American Behavioral Scientist* 46:1563–1576.

McDonald, Lynn. 2001. "The Florence Nightingale-Harriet Martineau Collaboration." Pp. 153–167 in Michael R. Hill and Susan Hoecher-Drysdale (eds.). *Harriet Martineu: Theoretical and Methodological Perspectives*. New York: Routledge.

McGarry, Kathleen, and Robert F. Schoen. 2000. "Social Security, Economic Growth, and the Rise in Elderly Widows' Independence in the Twentieth Century." *Demography* 37:221–236.

McGeary, Johanna. 1998. "Clash of Faiths." *Time*, January 26:26–36.

———. 2000. "The End of Milosevic." *Time*, October 16:59–64.

McLaughlin, Paul, and Marwan Khawaja. 2000. "The Organizational Dynamics of the U.S. Environmental Movement: Legitimation, Resource Mobilization, and Political Opportunity." *Rural Sociology* 65:422–439.

McNeill, William H. 1976. *Plagues and Peoples*. Garden City, NY: Anchor Press/Doubleday.

McPhail, Clark. 1991. *The Myth of the Maddening Crowd*. New York: A. de Gruyter.

———. 1997. "Stereotypes of Crowds and Collective Behavior: Looking Backwards, Looking Forward." *Studies in Symbolic Interaction* 3:supplement 35–58.

Mead, George Herbert. 1934. *Mind, Self, and Society*. Chicago: University of Chicago Press.

Mead, Margaret. 1928. *Coming of Age in Samoa: A Psychological Study of Primitive Youth for Western Civilization*. New York: William Morrow.

———. 1935. *Sex and Temperament in Three Primitive Societies*. New York: William Morrow.

———. 1972. *Blackberry Winter: My Early Years*. New York: William Morrow.

Melossi, Dario and Mark Lettiere. 1998. "Punishment in the American Democracy: The Paradoxes of Good Intentions." Pp. 21–59 in Robert P. Weiss and Nigel South (eds), *Comparing Prison Systems: Toward a Comparative and International Penology*. Amsterdam: Gordon and Breach Publishers.

Melton, J. Gordon. 1998. *Encyclopedia of American Religions*. Detroit: Gale Research.

Mendelsohn, Matthew. 2002. "Measuring National Identity and Patterns of Attachment: Quebec and Nationalist Mobilization." *Nationalism and Ethnic Relations* 8:72–94

Merton, Robert K. 1968. *Social Theory and Social Structure*. New York: Free Press.

Messner, Michael A. 1971. "Social Problems and Sociological Theory." In Robert K. Merton (ed.), *Contemporary Social Problems*. 3rd ed. New York: Harcourt, Brace, Jovanovich.

———. 1997. *Politics of Masculinities: Men in Movements*. Thousand Oaks, CA: Sage.

Meyer, Ilan H. 1995. "Minority Stress and Mental Health in Gay Men." *Journal of Health and Social Behavior* 36:38–56.

Meyer, James. 1992. "Nonmainstream Body Modification." *Journal of Contemporary Ethnography* 21 (October):267–306.

Meyer, Josh. 1995. "Staff Shortages Severely Hampering County Health Services, Board Told." *Los Angeles Times*, November 8:12B.

Meyer, Kastherine and Linda Lobao. 2003. "Economic Hardship, Religion. And mental Health During the Midwest Farm Crisis." *Journal of Rural Studies* 19:139–155.

Michels, Robert. 1966 [orig. 1911]. *Political Parties*. New York: Free Press.

Midlarsky, Elizabeth. 1994. *Altruism in Later Life*. Thousand Oaks, CA: Sage.

Milgram, Stanley. 1967. "The Small World Problem." *Psychology Today* 1:61–67.

Miller, David. 1991. "A Vision of Market Socialism." *Dissent* 38 (Summer):406–414.

Miller, Leslie. 1992. "Nursing Research: Caring vs. Curing." *USA Today*, August 4:4D.

Miller, Morris. 1995. "Where Is Globalization Taking Us? Why We Need a New Bretton Woods." *Futures* 7:125–144.

Mills, C. Wright. 1951. *White Collar: The American Middle Classes*. New York: Oxford University Press.

———. 1956. *The Power Elite*. New York: Oxford University Press.

Mills, Kathryn, and Pamela Mills. 2000. *C. Wright Mills: Letters and Autobiographical Writing*. Berkeley, CA: University of California Press.

Mintz, Beth, and Michael Schwartz. 1981a. "The Structure of Intercorporate Unity in American Business." *Social Problems* 29: 87–103.

———. 1981b. "Interlocking Directorates and Interest Group Formation." *American Sociological Review* 46:851–869.

Moghadam, Valentine. 1992. *Development and Patriarchy: The Middle East and North Africa in Economics and Demographic Transition*. Helsinki, Finland: World Institute for Development.

Moore, Joan W. 1991. *Going Down to the Barrio*. Philadelphia: Temple University Press.

Moore, Joan, with Alfredo Cuellar. 1970. *Mexican Americans*. Englewood Cliffs, NJ: Prentice-Hall.

Moore, Joan, and Harry Pachon. 1985. *Hispanics in the United States*. Englewood Cliffs, NJ: Prentice-Hall.

Morgan, Gordon D. 1997. *Toward an American Sociology*. Westport, CT: Greenwood.

Morganthau, Tom. 1994. "The Rise and Fall and Rise and Fall and Fall and Rise of Nixon." *Newsweek*, May 2:24–29.

Morganthau, Tom, Todd Barrett, and Frank Washington. 1993. "Dr. Kevorkian's Death Wish." *Newsweek*, March 8:46–48.

Morley, Rebecca. 1994. "Wife Beating and Modernization: The Case of Papua, New Guinea." *Journal of Comparative Family Studies* 25:25–52.

Morris, Aldon D. 1999. "A Retrospective on the Civil Rights Movement: Political And Intellectual Landmarks." *Annual Review of Sociology* 25:17–53.

Morris, L. D. 1993. "Is There a British Underclass?" *International Journal of Urban and Regional Research* 17:404–412.

Morris, Martina, and Bruce Western. 1999. "Inequality in Earnings at the Close of the Twentieth Century." *Annual Review of Sociology* 25:623–657.

Mortimer, J. T., and R. G. Simmons. 1978. "Adult Socialization." *Annual Review of Sociology* 4:421–54.

Mosley, W. Henry, and Peter Cowley. 1991. "The Challenge of World Health." *Population Bulletin* 46(4).

Moss, Phillip, and Chris Tilly. 2001. *Stories Employees Tell: Race, Skill, and Hiring in America*. New York: Russell Sage Foundation.

Mother Jones. 1996. "The Mother Jones 400." March/April:38–59.

Moynihan, Daniel Patrick. 1965. *The Negro Family: The Case for National Action*. Office of Policy Planning and Research, U.S. Department of Labor. Washington, DC: U.S. Government Printing Office.

Mumford, Lewis. 1961. *The City in History: Its Origins, Its Transformations, and Its Prospects*. New York: Harcourt, Brace & World.

Murdock, George. 1949. *Social Structure*. New York: Free Press.

———. 1956. "How Culture Changes." In Harry L. Shapiro (ed.), *Man, Culture, and Society*. New York: Oxford University Press.

Murdock, George P. 1937. "Comparative Data on the Division of Labor by Sex." *Social Forces* 15:551–553.

Murphy, Michael D. 1985. "Brief Communications." *Human Organization* 44:132–135.

Murphy, Sherry L. 2000. "Death: Final Data for 1998." *National Vital Statistics Report* 48(11):1–105.

Musolf, Gil Richard. 1996. "Interactionism and the Child: Cahill, Corsaro, and Denzin on Childhood Socialization." *Symbolic Interaction* 4:303–321.

Muthvin, Eugene H. 1997. "Mugged by Reality." *Policy Review* (July/August).

Mydans, Seth. 1991. "More Schools Last All Year." *New York Times*, August 18:1, 12.

Myles, John, and Adnan Turegun. 1994. "Comparative Studies in Class Structure." *Annual Review of Sociology* 20:103–124.

Myrdal, Gunnar. 1944. *An American Dilemma: The Negro Problem and Modern Democracy*. New York: Harper & Row.

Nader, Ralph. 2000. The Ralph Nader Reader. New York: Seven Stories Press.

Nabi, Robin L. 2001. "Victims with Voices: How Abused Women Conceptualize the Problem of Spousal Abuse and Implications for Intervention and Prevention." Journal of Family Violence 16: 237–253.

Nabi, Robin L. and Jennifer R. Horner. 2001. "Victims with Voices: How Abused Women Conceptualize the Problems of Spousal Abuse and Implications for Intervention and Prevention." *Journal of Family Violence* 16: 237–253.

Nagel, Joane. 1996. *American Ethnic Renewal: Red Power and the Resurgence of Identity and Culture*. New York: Oxford University Press.

Narasimhan, Sakuntala. 2002. "Gender, class, and Caste Schisms in Affirmative Action Policies: The Curious Case of India's Women's Reservation Bill." *Feminist Economics* 8:183–190.

Narula, Rajneesh, and John H. Dunning. 1999. "Developing Countries vs. Multinational Enterprise in a Globalizing World: The Danger of Falling Behind" *Forum for Development Studies* 2:261–281.

Nasar, Sylvia. 1993. "Why the U.S. Is Indeed Productive." *New York Times*, October 22:1C, 6C.

Nash, J. Madeleine. 2000. "The New Science of Alzheimer's." *Time*, July 19:50–57.

National Center for Health Statistics. 1995. *Health: United States, 1994*. Hyattsville, MD: Public Health Service.

National Commission on Testing and Public Policy. 1990. Reported in *Chronicle of Higher Education*, May 30:A1, A3.

National Institute of Mental Health. 1982. *Television and Behavior: Ten Years of Scientific Progress and Implications for the Eighties*. Washington, DC: U.S. Government Printing Office.

Neto, Felix. 1995. "Conformity and Independence Revisited." *Social Behavior and Personality* 23:217–222.

Neuhouser, Kevin. 1989. "The Radicalization of the Brazilian Catholic Church in Comparative Perspective." *American Sociological Review* 54(April):233–44.

Neumark, David (ed.). 2000. On the Job: Is Long Term Employment a Thing of the Past? New York: Russell Sage Foundation.

New York Times. 1993. "10,000 to Lose Jobs at Xerox." As reported in Columbus Dispatch, December 9:B1.

_____. 1994. "Older College-Educated Men See Paychecks, Earning Potential Shrink." As reported in Columbus Dispatch, February 12:C1.

_____. 1994. "Starving the Poor." November 24:A18.

_____. 2000. September 10:Bu1–14.

Newcomb, James. 2003. "Biology and Borders: SARS and the New Economics of Biosecurity." Bio-Era. May.

Niazi, Tarique. 2002. "The Ecology of Genocide in Rawanda." International Journal of Contemporary Sociology 39: 223–248.

Nieves, Evelyn. 1991. "College Was the Carrot, But Not All Went for It." New York Times, July 12:B10.

Nocera, Joseph. 1995. "The Profit Motive: The Gall of Goldsmith." Gentleman's Quarterly (June):73–76.

Nolan, Patrick, and Gerhard Lenski. 1999. Human Societies: An Introduction to Macrosociology. 8th ed. New York: McGraw-Hill.

NORC (National Opinion Research Center). 1994. General Social Surveys, 1972–1994: Cumulative Codebook. Storrs, CT: Roper Center for Public Opinion Research.

_____. 1996. General Social Surveys, 1972–1996: Cumulative Codebook. Storrs, CT: Roper Center for Public Opinion Research.

_____. 1998. General Social Survey 1998. Storrs, CT: Roper Center for Public Opinion Research.

Novaes, Regina Celia Reyes. 1994. "Pentecostal Identity in Rural Brazil." Social Compass 41:525–535.

Nuruddin, Yusuf. 2002. "Promise and Pitfalls of Reparations." Socialism and Democracy 16:88–114.

Nussbaum, Emily. 2000. "His Only Address Was an e-mail Account." New York Times Magazine, Section 6, September 17: 80–84.

Oaks, Laury. 2003. "Antiabortion Positions and Young Women's Life Plans in Contemporary Ireland." Social Science and Medicine 56:173–198.

Ogburn, William. 1950. Social Changes with Respect to Culture and Original Nature. Revised ed. New York: Viking.

O'Hare, William. 1996. "A New Look at Poverty in America." Population Bulletin 51(2).

Olivera, Rene. 2001. "Suicidal Ideation in Hispanic and Mixed-Ancestry Adolescents." Suicide and Life Threatening Behavior 31:416–427.

Olneck, Michael R. 1993. "Terms of Inclusion: Has Multiculturalism Redefined Equality in American Education?" American Journal of Education 101:234–260.

Organski, Katherine, and A. F. K. Organski. 1961. Population and World Power. New York: Knopf.

Ossowski, Stanislaw. 1983. "Marx's Concept of Class." Pp. 99–102 in T. Bottomore and P. Goode (eds.), Readings in Marxist Sociology. New York: Oxford University Press.

Palen, John J. 1997, 2002. The Urban World. 5th ed. New York: McGraw-Hill.

Palermo, George B. 1994. The Faces of Violence. Springfield, IL: Charles C. Thomas.

Palmer, Colin. 1992. "African Slave Trade: The Cruelest Commerce." National Geographic (September):62–91.

Palmore, Erdman. 1981. Social Patterns in Normal Aging: Findings from the Duke Longitudinal Study. Durham, NC: Duke University Press.

Pampel, Fred. 2000. Sociological Lives and Ideas: An Introduction to Classical Theorists. New York: Wadsworth.

Parelius, Ann Parker, and Robert K. Parelius. 1978. The Sociology of Education. Englewood Cliffs, NJ: Prentice-Hall.

Parfit, Michael. 1995. "Diminishing Returns: Exploiting the Ocean's Bounty." National Geographic, November:2–37.

Park, Robert E., and Earnest W. Burgess. 1921. Introduction to the Science of Sociology. Chicago: University of Chicago Press.

Parker, Laura, 1997. "Bad Blood Still Flows in the Tuskegee Study." USA Today, April 28:6A.

Parrillo, Vincent N. 1996. Diversity in America. Thousand Oaks, CA: Pine Forge Press.

Parsons, Talcott. 1953. "Illness and the Role of the Physician: A Sociological Perspective." Pp. 609–617 in Clyde Kluckhohn and Henry A. Murray (eds.), Personality in Nature, Society, and Culture. 2nd ed. New York: Knopf.

_____. 1966. Societies: Evolutionary and Comparative Perspectives. Englewood Cliffs, NJ: Prentice-Hall.

_____. 1975. "The Sick Role and the Role of the Physician Reconsidered." Milbank Memorial Fund Quarterly/Health and Society 53 (Summer):257–278.

Parsons, Talcott, Robert F. Bales, and Edward A. Shils. 1953. Working Papers in The Theory of Action. Glencoe, IL: Free Press.

Pattillo, Mary. 2003. "Negotiating Blackness, for Richer or Poorer." Ethnography 4:61–93.

Perkins, H. Wesley, and Debra K. DeMeis. 1996. "Gender and Family Effects on the 'Second Shift': Domestic Activities of College-Educated Young Adults." Gender and Society 10:79–93.

Petersen, Anne C., and Jeylan T. Mortimer. 1994. Youth Unemployment and Society.

New York and Cambridge, England: Cambridge University Press.

Petersen, William. 1971. Japanese Americans: Oppression and Success. New York: Random House.

_____. 1998. "A New Look at Malthus." Society 36:60–65.

Peterson, Karen S. 1995. "Battle of the Sexes Starts in the Brain." USA Today, March 14:D1, D2.

Peterson, Richard R. 1996. "A Re-Evaluation of the Economic Consequences of Divorce." American Sociological Review 61:528–536.

_____. 1989. "Stages of Ethnic Identity Development in Minority Group Adolescence." Journal of Early Adolescence 9:34–49.

Phinney, Jean S. 1991. "Ethnic Identity and Self-Esteem: A Review and Integration." Hispanic Journal of Behavioral Sciences 13:193–208.

Phinney, Jean S., and Steve Tarver. 1988. "Ethnic Identity Search and Commitment in Black and White Eighth Graders." Journal of Early Adolescence 8:265–277.

Piaget, J. 1932. The Moral Judgment of the Child. New York: Free Press.

Pickering, W. S. F. 1984. Durkheim's Sociology of Religion. London: Routledge & Kegan Paul.

Pinsof, William M. 2002. "The Death of 'Till Death Do as Part: The Transformation of Pair-Bonding in the 20th Century." Family Process 41:135–157.

Pipes, Richard. 1991. Review of Stalin: Breaker of Nations, by Robert Conquest (New York: Viking) in New York Times Book Review, November 10:14.

Piven, Frances Fox, and Richard A. Cloward. 1989. Why Americans Don't Vote. New York: Pantheon Books.

Pollis, N. P., R. L. Montgomery, and T. G. Smith. 1975. "Autokinetic Paradigms: A Reply to Alexander, Zucker, and Brody." Sociometry 38:358–373.

Popenoe, David. 2000. Sociology. Englewood Cliffs, NJ: Prentice-Hall.

Population Reference Bureau. 1993. 1993 World Population Data Sheet. Washington, DC: Population Reference Bureau.

_____. 1994. 1994 World Population Data Sheet. Washington, DC: Population Reference Bureau.

_____. 1997. 1997 World Population Data Sheet. Washington, DC: Population Reference Bureau.

_____. 2003. 2003 World Population Data Sheet. Washington, DC: Population Reference Bureau.

Portes, Alejandro, and Robert L. Bach. 1985. Latin Journey: Cuban and Mexican Immigrants *in the United States*. Berkeley, CA: University of California Press.

Portes, Alejandro, Juan M. Clark, and Robert D. Manning. 1985. "After Mariel: A Survey of Resettlement Experiences of the 1980 Cuban Refugees in Miami." *Cuban Studies* 15:37–59.

Potter, Harry R. 2000. "Public Awareness of Environmental Issues Prior to Earth Day, 1970". Paper presented at the Annual Meeting of the American Sociological Association, August 12–16, Washington, DC.

Poulin Dubois, Diane and Clara F. Beissel. 2002. "Men Don't Put on Makeup: Toddlers' Knowledge of the Gender Stereotyping of Household Activities." *Social Development* 2:167–181.

Powell, Bill. 1993. "Japan Inc. R.I.P." *Newsweek*, December 13:48–50.

Powers, Jeanne M., and Peter W. Cookson, Jr. 1999. "The Politics of School Choice Research: Fact, Fiction, and Statistics." *Educational Policy* 13:104–122.

Pratap, Anita. 1994. "Master of the Polis." *Time* (America Online, transmitted 6–24–94).

Prose, Francine. 1990. "Confident at 11, Confused at 16." *New York Times Magazine*, January 7:22 ff.

Pryor, Frederic L. 1985. *A Guidebook to the Comparative Study of Economic Systems*. Englewood Cliffs, NJ: Prentice-Hall.

Pugh, Mary JoV., and Daniel Hart. 1999. "Identity Development and Peer Group Participation." *New Directions for Child and Adolescence Development* 84:55–70.

Purdum, Todd S. 1990. "Dinkins Goes to Korean Stores in Defiance of Boycott by Blacks." *New York Times*, September 22:11Y.

Putnam, Robert D. 2000. *Bowling Alone: The Collapse and Revival of American Community*. New York: Simon & Schuster.

Pye, Michael. 1989. "Low Tales of the Highborn." *New York Times Magazine*, November 12:44–46, 48, 113.

Quadagno, Jill. 1987. "Theories of the Welfare State." Pp. 109–128 in W. Richard Scott and James F. Short (eds.), *Annual Review of Sociology. Vol. 13*. Palo Alto, CA: Annual Reviews Inc.

Quinney, Richard. 1977. *Class, State, and Crime: On the Theory and Practice of Criminal Justice*. New York: David McKay.

Rank, Mark. 1994. *Living on the Edge: The Realities of Welfare in America*. New York: Columbia University Press.

Rank, Mark R. and Thomas A. Hirschl. 2001. "Rags or Riches? Estimating the Probability of Poverty and Affluence Across the Adult American Life Span." *Social Science Quarterly* 82:651–669.

Raphael, Dennis, Ivan Brown, Rebecca Renwick, and Irving Rootman. 1997. "Quality of Life: What Are the Implications for Health Promotion?" *American Journal of Health Behavior* 21:118–128.

Raspberry, William. 1995. "War on Poverty a Failure? Don't Believe It." *Columbus Dispatch*, January 13:11A.

Ratnesar, Romesch. 1995. "The Axmen Cometh." *Mother Jones*, November/December:18.

Read, P. P. 1974. *Alive*. New York: Avon.

Reich, Michael. 1977. "The Economics of Racism." Pp. 183–188 in David M. Gordon (ed.), *Problems in Political Economy*. Lexington, MA: D. C. Heath.

———. 1992. "Training a Skilled Work Force: Why U.S. Corporations Neglect Their Workers." *Dissent* 39:42–46.

Reichel, Phillip L. 2002. *Comparative Criminal Justice Systems: A Topical Approach*. 3rd ed. Upper Saddle, NJ: Prentice-Hall.

Reingold, H. L., and K. Cook. 1975. "The Content of Boys' and Girls' Rooms as an Index of Parents' Behavior." *Child Development* 46:459–463.

Reitz, J. 1980. *The Survival of Ethnic Groups*. Toronto: McGraw-Hill.

Renk, Kimberly and Gary Creasey. 2003. "The Relationship of Gender, Gender Identity, and Coping Strategies in Late Adolescents." *Journal of Adolesence* 26:159–168.

Renzetti, Claire M., and Daniel J. Curran. 1998. *Women, Men, and Society*. Boston: Allyn & Bacon.

Reskin, Barbara, and Debra Branch McBrier. 2000. "Why Not Ascription?: Organizations' Employment of Male and Female Managers." *American Sociological Review* 65:210–233.

Reskin, Barbara, and Irene Padavic. 1994. *Women and Men at Work*. Thousand Oaks, CA: Pine Forge Press.

Rest, James R., Darcia Navaez, Muriel J. Bebeau, and Steph Thoma. 1999. *Post Conventional Moral Thinking: A Neo-Kohlbergian Approach*. Mahwah, NJ: Erlbaum Associates.

Richardson, Laurel. 1988. *The Dynamics of Sex and Gender: A Sociological Perspective*. Boston: Houghton Mifflin.

———. 1997. *Fields of Play*. New Brunswick, NJ: Rutgers University Press.

Ridgeway, Cecilia L., and Lynn Smith-Lovin. 1999. "Interaction in the Gender System: Theory and Research." *Annual Review of Sociology* 25:191–216.

———. 1999. "The Gender System and Interaction." *Annual Review of Sociology* 25:191–216.

Riegle, Donald W. Jr. 1982. "The Psychological and Social Effects of Unemployment." *American Psychologist* 37:1113–1115.

Rindfuss, Ronald R., Karin L. Brewster, and Andrew L. Kavee. 1996. "Women, Work and Children: Behavioral and Attitudinal Change in the United States." *Population and Development Review* 22:457–482.

Riska, Elianne, and Ketarina Wegar, (eds.). 1993. *Gender, Work, and Medicine: Women and the Medical Division of Labour*. London: Sage.

Ritzer, George. 1995. Expressing America. Thousand Oaks, CA: Pine Forge Press.

———. 2000. *The McDonaldization of Society*. Thousand Oaks, CA: Pine Forge Press.

Roberts, Sam. 1995. "Women's Work: What's New, What Isn't." *New York Times*, April 27:A12.

Robbins, Alexandra, and Abby Wilner. 2001. *Quarterlife Crisis: The Unique Challenges of Life in Your Twenties*. New York: Parcher/Putnam.

Robin, Ron. 1995. The Barbed-Wire College: Reeducating German POWS on the United States During World War II. Princeton, NJ: Princeton University Press.

Robinson, Fred, and Nicky Gregson. 1992. "The 'Underclass': A Class Apart." *Critical Social Policy* 12:38–51.

Rodwin, Marc A. 1995. *Medicine, Money, and Morals: Physicians' Conflicts of Interest*. New York: Oxford University Press.

Roscigno, Vincent J., and James W. Ainsworth-Darnell. 2000. "Race, Cultural Capital, and Educational Resources: Persistent Inequalities and Achievement Returns." *Sociology of Education* 72:158–178.

Roscow, Irving. 1994. "Lessons from the Museum: Claude Monet and Social Roles." *The Gerontologist* 34:292–298.

Rosenbaum, J. E., and T. Kariya. 1989. "From High School to Work: Market and Institutional Mechanisms in Japan." *American Journal of Sociology* 94:1334–1365.

Rosenberg, Morris. 1979. Conceiving the Self. New York: Basic Books.

Rosenthal, Erich. 1975. "The Equivalence of United States Census Data for Persons of Russian Stock or Descent with American Jews: An Evaluation." *Demography* (May) 12:275–290.

Rosnow, Ralph L., and Gary Alan Fine. 1976. *Rumor and Gossip*. New York: Elsevier.

Ross, Catherine E., and Chia-ling Wu. 1995. "The Links Between Education and Health." *American Sociological Review* 60:719–745.

Ross, E. Mitchell. 2001. "Thorstein Veblen: Pioneer in Environmental Sociology." *Organization and Environment* 14:389–408.

Rossi, Alice S. 1984. "Gender and Parenthood." *American Sociological Review* 49:1–19.

Rossi, Peter H. 1989. *Down and Out in America: The Origins of Homelessness.* Chicago: University of Chicago Press.

Rossides, Daniel W. 1990. *Social Stratification: The American Class System in Comparative Perspective.* Englewood Cliffs, NJ: Prentice-Hall.

Rothberg, Barbara, and David Weinstein. 1996. "A Primer on Lesbian and Gay Families." *Social Services* 4:55–68.

Rothchild, John. 1995. "Wealth: Static Wages, Except for the Rich." *Time* (America Online transmitted 1-22-95).

Roundtree, Pamela Wilox, and Kenneth Land. 1996. "Perceived Risk vs. Fear of Crime: Empirical Evidence of Conceptually Distinct Relations in Survey Data." *Social Forces* 74:1353–1376.

Rowbottom, Anne. 2002. "Following the Queen: The Place of the Royal Family in the Context of Royal Visits and Religion." *Sociological Research On Line,* www.socresonline.org.uk 7,2 Aug.

Ruibal, Sal. 2001. "Marinovich Saga Fails to Go By Script." *USA Today.* Retreived online on December 11, 2003 at http://www.usatoday.com/sports/preps/football/2001-12-26-allusa-marinovich.htm#more

Rutter, Michael. 1979. *Fifteen Thousand Hours: Secondary Schools and Their Effects on Children.* Cambridge, MA: Harvard University Press.

Ryan, William. 1976. *Blaming the Victim.* Rev. ed. New York: Vintage.

Rydell, C. Peter and Susan S. Everingham. 1994. *Controlling Cocaine: Supply versus Demand Programs.* Santa Monica, CA: Rand.

Sadker, Myra. 1995. *Failing at Fairness: How Our Schools Cheat Girls.* New York: Touchstone.

Sadker, Myra P., and David Miller Sadker. 1985. *Effectiveness and Equity in College Teaching: Final Report.* Washington, DC: National Institute of Education.

Sahlins, Marshall. 1978. *Culture and Practical Reason.* Chicago: University of Chicago Press.

St. John, N. 1975. *School Desegregation.* New York: John Wiley.

Sampson, Anthony. 1983. *The Changing Anatomy of Britain.* New York: Random House.

Samuelson, Paul A. 1967. *Economics: An Introductory Analysis.* 7th ed. New York: McGraw-Hill.

Samuelson, Paul A., and William D. Nordhaus. 1998. *Economics.* New York: Richard D. Irwin.

Samuelson, Robert. J. 1990a. "Fears and Fantasies." Newsweek, April 2:25.

———. 1990b. "The Great Pay Game." Newsweek, February 5:49.

———. 1994. "The Rediscovery of the U.S. Economy." Newsweek, February 28:67.

Sanday, Peggy Reeves. 1992. *Fraternity Gang Rape: Sex, Brotherhood, and Privilege on Campus.* New York: New York University Press.

Sanderson, Stephen K. (ed.). 1995. *Civilizations and World Systems: Studying World-Historical Change.* Walnut Creek, CA: Altamira Press.

Sapiro, Virginia. 1994. "Political Socialization During Adulthood: Clarifying the Political Time of Our Lives." *Research in Micropolitics* (4):197–223.

Saporito, Salvatore. 2003. "Private Choices, Public Consequences: Magnet Schools, Choice, and Segregation by Race and Poverty." *Social Problems* 50:181–203.

Sassen, Saskia. 1991. *The Global City: New York, London, Tokyo.* Princeton, NJ: Princeton University Press.

———. 1994. *Cities in a World Economy.* Thousand Oaks, CA: Pine Forge Press.

———. 1996. "Rebuilding the Global City: Economy, Ethnicity, and Space." Pp. 23–42 in Anthony D. King (ed.), *Reshaping the City: Ethnicity, Capital, and Culture in the 21st Century Metropolis.* New York: New York University Press.

Scheffel, David Z. 1999. "The Untouchables of Svinia." *Human Organization* 58:44–53.

Schied, Teresa L. 2003. "Managed Care and the Rationalization of Mental Health Services." *Journal of Health and Social Behavior* 44:142–161.

Schirmer, Jennifer. 1999. "The Guatemalan Politico-Military Project: Legacies of a Violent Peace." *Latin American Perspectives* 26:92–107.

Schnaiberg, Allan. 1980. *The Environment: From Surplus to Scarcity.* New York: Oxford University Press.

Schnaiberg, Allan, and Kenneth Alan Gould. 2000. *Environment and Society.* New York: St. Martin's Press.

Schooler, Carmi. 1996. "Cultural and Social-Structural Explanations of Cross-National Psychological Differences." *Annual Review of Sociology* 22:323–349.

Schorske, Carl E. 1980. *Fin-de-Siecle Vienna.* New York: Knopf.

Schrader, Dawn E., and William Damon, (eds.). 1990. *The Legacy of Lawrence Kohlberg.* New York: Jossey-Bass.

Schrag, Peter. 1994. "The Great American Sell-Off." Pp. 405–413 in Jerome H. Skolnick and Elliott Currie (eds.), *Crisis in American Institutions.* New York: HarperCollins.

Schroeder, Steven A. 2000. "The Medically Uninsured: Will They Always Be With Us?" Pp. 321–327 in Jerome H. Skolnick and Elliott Currie (eds.), *Crisis in American Institutions.* Boston: Allyn & Bacon.

Schwab, William A. 1992. *The Sociology of Cities.* Englewood Cliffs, NJ: Prentice-Hall.

Schulhofer, Stephen J. 1984. "Is Plea Bargaining Inevitable?" *Harvard Law Review* 97:1006–7.

Schwirian, Kent P., and Gustavo S. Mesch. 1993. "Embattled Neighborhoods: The Political Ecology of Neighborhood Change." In Ray Hutchison (ed.), *Research in Urban Sociology: Urban Society in Transition* 3:83–110.

———. 1991/1992. "The Seniors' Lifestyle Inventory: Assessing health Behaviots in Older Adults." *Behavior, Health, and Aging* 2:43–55.

Schwirian, Patricia M. 1998. *Professionalization of Nursing: Current Trends and Issues.* Philadelphia, PA: Lippincott.

Scimecca, Joseph A. 1995. *Society and Freedom.* 2nd ed. Chicago: Nelson-Hall.

Scott, Eugenie C. 1997. "Antievolutionism and Creationism in the United States." *Annual Review of Anthropology* 26:263–289.

Scripps Howard News Service. 1994. "Poverty Report Disputes 'Myth.'" *Columbus Dispatch,* January 31, 1995:3A.

Scully, Diana and Pauline Bart. 2003. "A Funny Thing Happened on the Way to the Oriface: Women in Gynecology Textbooks." *Feminism and Psychology* 13:11–16.

Sculley, J. (with J. A. Byrne). 1987. *Odyssey: Pepsi to Apple . . . A Journey of Adventure, Ideas, and the Future.* New York: Harper & Row.

Scupin, Raymond. 1992. *Cultural Anthropology: A Global Perspective.* Englewood Cliffs, NJ: Prentice-Hall.

Segerstale, Ullica. 1996. "Anti-Antiscience: The Fight for Science and Reason." *Science Studies* 9:5–25.

Seltzer, Judith A. 1994. "Consequences of Marital Dissolution for Children." *Annual Review of Sociology* 20:235–266.

Semrau, Penelope, and Barbara Boyer. 1990. "Examining Visual Components in Educational Software for a Socio-Cultural Perspective." A paper presented at the International Visual Sociology Association Meeting, Whittier College, California.

Seneker, Harold. 1992. "The World's Billionaires." *Forbes,* July 20:148–161.

Sewell, William H. 1971. "Inequality of Opportunity for Higher Education." *American Sociological Review* 36:793–809.

Sewell, William H., and Robert M. Hauser. 1980. "The Wisconsin Longitudinal Study of

Social and Psychological Factors in Aspirations and Achievements." *Research in Sociology of Education and Socialization* 1:59–99.

Shaffer, Martin B. 2000. "Coalition Work Among Environmental Groups: Who Participates?" *Research in Social Movements, Conflict and Change* 22:111–126.

Shakur, Sanyika. 1993. *Monster: The Autobiography of an L.A. Gang Member*. New York: Atlantic Monthly Press.

Shamir, Boas. 1994. "Ideological Position, Leaders' Charisma, and Voting Preferences: Personal vs. Partisan Elections." *Political Behavior* 16(2):265–287.

Shannon, Elaine. 1995. "Crime: Safer Streets, Yet Greater Fear." *Time* (America Online, transmitted 1–22–95).

Shaw, Clifford D., Frederick M. Zorbaugh, Henry D. McKay, and Leon S. Contrell. 1929. *Delinquency Areas*. Chicago: University of Chicago Press.

Sheak, Robert J., and David Dabelko. 1993. *Free Inquiry in Creative Sociology* 21:29–35.

Sherif, C. W. 1976. *Orientations in Social Psychology*. New York: Harper & Row.

Sherif, Muzafer. 1936. *The Psychology of Social Norms*. New York: Harper & Brothers.

———. 1937. "An Experimental Approach to the Study of Attitudes." *Sociometry* 1:90–98.

Shibutani, Tamotsu. 1986. *Social Processes*. Berkeley, CA: University of California Press.

Shields, J. J., Jr. 1989. *Japanese Schooling: Patterns of Socialization, Equality, and Political Control*. University Park, PA: Pennsylvania State University Press.

Shockey, James W. 1989. "Overeducation and Earnings: A Structured Approach to Differential Attainment in the U.S. Labor Force (1970–1982)." *American Sociological Review* 54:856–864.

Short, Samuel D. 1996. "Is Unemployment Pathological? A Review of Current Concepts with Lessons for Policy Planners." *International Journal of Health Services* 26:569–589.

Sibanda, Amson. 1999. "Reproductive Change in Zimbabwe and Kenya: The Role of the Proximate Determinants in Recent Fertility Trends." *Social Biology* 46:82–99.

Siegel, Larry. 2000. *Criminology*, 7th ed. Belmont, CA: Wadsworth.

Sigelman, Lee, and Paul J. Wahlbeck. 1999. "Gender Proportionality in Intercollegiate Athletics: The Mathematics of Title IX Compliances." *Social Science Quarterly* 80:518–538.

Silverstein, Ken. 1998. "The Microsoftnetwork." *Mother Jones* January/February: 30–32.

Simmel, Georg. 1950 [1902]. Pp. 118–169 in Kurt Wolff (ed.), *The Sociology of Georg Simmel*. New York: Free Press.

Simmons, Carolyn H., Alexander von Kolke, and Hideko Shimizu. 1997. "Attitudes Toward Romantic Love Among American, German, and Japanese Students." *Journal of Social Psychology* 126:327–336.

Simon, Robin W., Donna Eder, and Cathy Evans. 1992. "The Development of Feeling Norms Underlying Romantic Love Among Adolescent Females." *Social Psychology Quarterly* 55:29–46.

Simpson, George Eaton, and Milton J. Yinger. 1985. *Racial and Cultural Minorities: An Analysis of Prejudice and Discrimination*. 5th ed. New York: Plenum Press.

Simpson, Ida Harper, and Richard L. Simpson, (eds.). 1995. *Research into the Meaning of Work*. Vol. 5. Greenwich, CT: JAI Press.

Sivard, Ruth Leger. 1986. *World Military and Social Expenditures*. Washington, DC: World Priorities.

———. 1993. *World Military and Social Expenditures*. Washington, DC: World Priorities.

Sjoberg, Gideon. 1960. *The Preindustrial City: Past and Present*. New York: Free Press.

Sklair, Leslie. 1995. *Sociology of the Global System*. Baltimore: Johns Hopkins University Press.

Skolnick, Arlene. 1986. *The Psychology of Human Development*. New York: Harcourt Brace Jovanovich.

Skolnick, Arlene S., and Jerome H. Skolnick. 1998. *Family in Transition*. New York: HarperCollins.

Skrentny, John. 2002. *The Minority Rights Revolution*. Cambridge: Harvard University Press.

Slavin, Barbara. 1998. "Chinese Democracy Leader Freed, Is Flown to USA." *USA Today*, April 20:8A.

Sloan, Allan. 1996. "The Hit Men." *Newsweek*, February 26:44–48.

Small, Mario Luis and Katherine Newman. 2001. "Urban Poverty After the Truly Disadvantaged: The Rediscovery of the Family, Neighborhood, and Culture." *Annual Review of Sociology* 27:23–45.

Smelser, Neil J. 1962. *Theory of Collective Behavior*. New York: Free Press.

———. 1998. "The Rational and the Ambivalent in Two Social Sciences." *American Sociological Review* 63:1–16.

Smith, A. D. 1981. *The Ethnic Revival*. Cambridge, England: Cambridge University Press.

Smith, Adam. 1952 [orig. 1776]. *An Inquiry Into the Nature and Causes of the Wealth of Nations*. Chicago: Encyclopedia Britannica.

Smith, Christian. 2003. (ed.). *The Secular Revolution: Power, Interests, and Conflict in the Secularization of American Public Life*. Berkeley CA: University of California Press.

Smith, Craig S. 2001. "Thananmen's Shadow." *The New York Times Magazine*. February 4, 2001:52–55.

Smith, David Norman. 1995. "The Genesis of Genocide in Rwanda: The Fatal Dialectic of Class and Ethnicity." *Humanity and Society* 19:57–73.

Smith, Douglas A. and Christy A. Visher. 1981. "Street-Level Justice: Situational Determinants of Police Arrest Decisions." *Social Problems* 29(2):167–77.

Smith, F. B. 1982. *Florence Nightingale: Reputation and Power*. London: Croom Helm.

Smock, Pamela J. 2000. "Cohabitation in the U.S.: An Appraisal of Research Themes, Findings and Implications." *Annual Review of Sociology* 26:1–20.

So, Alvin Y., and Stephen W. K. Chiu. 1996. "Modern East Asia in World Systems Analysis." *Sociological Inquiry* 66:471–485.

Sociology Task Force. 1991. "Study in Depth in Sociology." *Liberal Learning and the Sociology Major*. Washington, DC: The Association of American Colleges.

Solomon, Jolie, Peter Annin, and Paul Kandell. 1995. "Are You Anxious? You're Not Alone." *Newsweek*, January 30:42B.

Solomon, Michael. 1987. "Standard Issue." *Psychology Today* 21 (December):30–31.

Soule, Sarah A., Doug McAdam, John McCarthy, and Yang Su. 1999. "Protest Events: Causes or Consequences of State Action? The U.S. Women's Movement and Federal Congressional Action, 1956–1979." *Mobilization* 4:239–255.

South, Scott J., and Kim M. Lloyd. 1995. "Spousal Alternatives and Marital Dissolution." *American Sociological Review* 60:21–35.

Spicer, A. D. 1981. *The Ethnic Revival*. Cambridge, England: Cambridge University Press.

Spielmann, Katherine A., and James F. Eder. 1994. "Hunters and Farmers: Then and Now." *Annual Review of Anthropology* 23:303–324.

Spoeher, Alexander. 1947. Changing Kinship Systems: A Study in the Acculturation of the Creeks, Cherokee, and Choctaw. Anthropology Series, Field Museum of Natural History, Vol. 33.

Sprecher, Susan. 2001. "Equity and Social Exchange in Dating Couples: Associations with Satisfaction, Commitment, and Stability." *Journal of Marriage and the Family* 63:599–613.

Spretnak, C. 1982. "The Christian Right's 'Holy War' Against Feminism." In *The Politics of Women's Spirituality*. New York: Anchor Books.

Srinivas, M. N. 1971. *Social Change in Modern India*. Berkeley, CA: University of California Press.

Stannard, David E. 1992. *American Holocaust: The Conquest of the New World.* New York: Oxford University Press.

Stanton, Marie, Sally Fenn, and Amnesty International U.S.A. 1991. *The Amnesty International Handbook.* Claremont, CA: Hunter House.

Stark, Rodney. 1987. "Religion and Deviance: A New Look." Pp. 111–132 in James M. Day and William S. Laufer (eds.), *Crime, Values, and Religion.* Norwood, NJ: Ablex.

Starkey, Marion L. 1949. *The Devil in Massachusetts: A Modern Inquiry into the Salem Witch Trials.* New York: A.A. Knopf.

———. 1999. "Secularization, RIP." *Sociology of Religion* 60:249–273.

Starr, Paul. 1982. *The Social Transformation of American Medicine.* New York: Basic Books.

Steagall, Jeffrey W., and Ken Jennings. 1996. "Unions, PAC Contributions and the NAFTA Vote." *Journal of Labor Research* 17:512–521.

Stebbins, Robert A. 1987. *Sociology: The Study of Society.* New York: Harper & Row.

Steffensmeier, Darrell, and Cathy Streifel. 1991. "Age, Gender, and Crime Across Three Historical Periods: 1935, 1960, and 1985." *Social Forces* 51:417–426.

Stein, A. 1997. *Sex and Sensibility: Stories of a Lesbian Generation.* Berkeley CA: University of California Press.

Sterngold, James. 1995. "In Japan, the Clamor for Change Runs Headlong into Old Groove." *New York Times,* January 3:A1, A4.

Stets, Jan E., and Peter J. Burke. 2000. "Identity Theory and Social Identity Theory." *Social Psychology Quarterly* 63:224–237.

Stevens, Rosemary. 1998. *American Medicine and the Public Interest.* Berkeley, CA: University of California Press.

Stevenson, H. W. 1989. "The Asian Advantage: The Case of Mathematics." Pp. 85–95 in J. J. Shields, Jr. (ed.), *Japanese Schooling: Patterns of Socialization, Equality, and Political Control.* University Park, PA: Pennsylvania State University Press.

Stinchcombe, Arthur L. 1963. "Some Empirical Consequences of the Davis-Moore Theory of Stratification." *American Sociological Review* 28 (October):805–808.

———. 1994. "Freedom and Oppression of Slaves in the Eighteenth Century." *American Sociological Review* 59:911–929.

Stockwell, Edward G. 1968. *Population and People.* Chicago: Quadrangle Books.

———. 1976. (ed. of condensed edition). Henry S. Shryock, Jacob S. Siegel and Associates. *The Methods and Materials of Demography.* New York: Academic Press.

Stogdill, R. M. 1974. *Handbook of Leadership.* New York: Free Press.

Stokes, G. 1980. *The Beatles.* New York: Rolling Stone Press.

Stouffer, Samuel A. 1950. "Some Observations on Study Design." *American Journal of Sociology,* vol. LV (January):355–391.

Stratton, John. 1996. "Serial Killing and the Transformation of the Social." *Theory, Culture and Society* 13:77–98.

Strube, Michael J., and Linda S. Barbour. 1983. "The Decision to Leave an Abusive Relationship: Economic Dependency and Psychological Commitment." *Journal of Marriage and the Family* 45:785–793.

Subramaniam, Radhika. 1999. "Culture of Suspicion: Riots and Rumor in Bombay, 1992–1993." *Transforming Anthropology* 8:97–110.

Summer, Laura. 1994. "The Escalating Number of Uninsured in the United States." *International Journal of Health and Human Services* 24:409–413.

Summers, Harry G. Jr. 1983. "Lessons: A Soldier's View." *Wilson Quarterly* (Summer): 125–135.

Sumner, William Graham. 1959 [1906]. *Folkways.* New York: Dover.

Sutherland, Edwin, and Donald Cressey. 1978. *Principles of Criminology.* Chicago: Lippincott.

Symposium at the Kobe Institute. 2001. "Immigration Policy in Japan, E.U. and North America" Kobe, Japan.

Tagliabue, John. 1996. "In Europe, a Wave of Layoffs Stuns White-Collar Workers." *New York Times,* June 20:A1, C17.

Takaki, Ronald. 1994. *A Different Mirror: A History of Multicultural America.* Boston: Little, Brown.

Tang, Joyce. 2003. "Women in Mathematics: The Addition of Differences." *Sociological Forum* 18:325–342.

Taylor, Ronald D., Robin Casten, Susanne M. Flickinger, Debra Roberts, and Cecil D. Fulmore. 1994. "Explaining the School Performance of African-American Adolescence." *Journal of Research on Adolescence* 4:21–44.

Taylor, Verta. 1995. Personal communication.

Teaster, Pamela B. 2000. "A Response to the Abuse of Vulnerable Adults: The 2000 Survey of State Adult Protective Services Administrations." Washington, DC: National Center on Elder Abuse. Retrieved online on December 11, 2003 at <http://www.elderabusecenter.org/pdf/research/apsreport030703.pdf>.

Techman, Jay. 2003. "Premarital Sex, Premarital Cohabitation, and the Risk of Subsequent Marital Dissolution Among Women." *Journal of Marriage and the Family* 65:444–455.

Theberge, Nancy. 2000. "No Fear Comes: Adolescent Girls, Ice Hockey, and the Embodiment of Gender." Paper presented at the Annual Meeting of the American Sociological Association. Washington, DC. August 12–16.

Thernstrom, Stephan (ed.). 1980. *Harvard Encyclopedia of American Ethnic Groups.* Cambridge, MA: The Belknap Press of Harvard University Press.

Thernstrom, Stephan, and Abigail Thernstrom. 1998. *America in Black and White: One Nation, Indivisible.* New York: Simon & Schuster.

Thomas, W. I. 1923. *The Unadjusted Girl.* Boston: Little Brown.

———. 1928. *The Child in America: Behavior Problems and Programs.* New York: Knopf.

Thompson, Kenneth. 2002. *Emile Durkheim.* London: Routledge.

Thompson, Martie P., Linda E. Saltzman, and Holly Johnson. 2003. "A Comparison of Risk Factors for Intimate Partner Violence-Related Injury Across Two National Surveys on Violence Against Women." *Violence Against Women* 9:438–457.

Thorne, Barrie. 1993. *Gender Play: Girls and Boys in School.* New Brunswick, NJ: Rutgers University Press.

Thurow, Lester. 1980. *The Zero Sum Society.* New York: Basic Books.

Thurow, Lester C. 1987. "A Surge in Inequality." *Scientific American* 256 (May):30–37.

Tilly, Charles. 1999. *Double Inequality.* Berkeley, CA: University of California Press.

Time. 1991. July 8:12–17.

———. 1994. "The Public Eye: Seeing Stars Over Kelso." (America Online, transmitted 4–29–94).

Tjaden, Patrick, and Nanny Thoennes. 2000. "Prevalence and Consequences of Male-to-Female and Female-to-Male Intimate Partner Violence as Measured by the National Violence Against Women Survey." *Violence Against Women* 6:142–161.

Toennies, Ferdinand. 1963 [orig. 1887]. *Community and Society.* Translated and edited by Charles P. Loomis. New York: Harper and Row.

Toffler, Alvin. 1980. *The Third Wave.* New York: William Morrow.

———. 1990. "Toffler's Next Shock." *World Monitor* (November):33–44.

Tomlinson, Mark. 2003. "Life and Social Class." *European Sociological Review* 19:97–111.

Tonkinson, J. 1974. *The Jigalong Mob: Aboriginal Victors of the Desert Crusade.* Menlo Park, CA: Cummings.

Torres, Arlene, and Norman E. Whitten. 1998. *Blackness in Latin America and the*

Caribbean: Social Dynamics and Transformations. Vol. II: Eastern South America and the Caribbean. Bloomington, IN: University of Indiana Press.

Torres, Sam. 1999. "Hate Crimes Against African Americans: The Extent of the Problem." *Journal of Contemporary Criminal Justice* 15:48–63.

Toynbee, Arnold. 1964. A Study of History. New York: Oxford University Press.

Travis, Russell, and Steven Velasco. 1994. *Social Science Journal* 31:197–207.

Trexler, Richard C. 2002. "Makimg the American Berdache: Choices or Constraint." *Journal of Social History* 35:613–636.

Tripp, Charles 2002. A History of Iraq, 2nd ed. Cambridge: Cambridge University Press.

Troeltsch, Ernst. 1931. *The Social Teachings of the Christian Churches*. New York: Macmillan.

Tropp, Linda R. 2003. "The Psychological Impact of Prejudice: Implications for Intergroup Contact." *Group Processes and Intergroup Contact* 6:131–149.

Tuchman, Gaye. 1988. "Mass Media Institutions." Pp. 601–626 in Neil J. Smelser (ed.), *Handbook of Modern Sociology*. Newbury Park, CA: Sage.

Tully, Carol T. 1994. "To Boldly Go Where No One Has Gone Before: The Legalization of Lesbian and Gay Marriages." *Journal of Gay and Lesbian Social Services* 1:73–87.

Tumin, Melvin, M. 1953a. "Some Principles of Stratification: A Critical Analysis." *American Sociological Review* 18 (August):387–393.

———. 1953b. "Reply to Kingsley Davis." *American Sociological Review* 18:672–673.

Turner, Bryan S., and Colin Samson. 1995. *Medical Power and Social Knowledge*. 2nd ed. Thousand Oaks, CA: Sage.

Turner, Jonathan H., and P.R. Turner 1997. *The Structure of Sociological Theory*. 6th ed. Belmont, CA: Wadsworth.

Turner, Ralph. 1990. "Role Change." *Annual Review of Sociology* 16:87–110.

Turner, Ralph H. 1996. "The Moral Issue in Collective Behavior and Collective Action." *Mobilization* 1:1–15.

Turner, Ralph H., and Lewis M. Killian. 1987. *Collective Behavior*. 3rd ed. Englewood Cliffs, NJ: Prentice-Hall.

Twaddle, Andrew C., and Richard M. Hessler. 1987. A *Sociology of Health*. 2nd ed. New York: Macmillan.

Uchitelle, Louis. 1991. "Trapped in the Impoverished Middle Class." *New York Times*, November 17, 3:1, 10.

———. 1996. "We're Leaner, Meaner, and Going Nowhere Faster." New York Times, May 12:E1, E5.

———. 2000. "Working Families Strain to Live Middle Class Life". *New York Times* Sunday, September 10:1:28.

United Nations. 1991. *The World's Women 1970–1990: Trends and Statistics*. New York: United Nations.

———. 1995. *The World's Women 1995: Trends and Statistics*. New York: United Nations.

United Nations Office on Drugs and Crime. 2002. Global Programme Against Transnational Organized Crime: Results of a Pilot Survey of Forty Selected Organized Criminal Groups in Sixteen Countries. Retrieved online on December 10, 2003 at <http://www.unodc.org/pdf/crime/publications/>.

USA Today. 1991. "A Tribute to Teachers: They've Made a Difference." May 7:6D–7D.

U.S. Bureau of the Census. 1993. *Statistical Abstract of the United States, 1993*. Washington, DC: U.S. Government Printing Office.

———. 1994. *Statistical Abstract of the United States, 1994*. Washington, DC: U.S. Government Printing Office.

———. 1995. *Statistical Abstract of the United States, 1995*. Washington, DC: U.S. Department of Commerce.

———. 1996. *Statistical Abstract of the United States, 1996*. Washington, DC: U.S. Government Printing Office.

———. 1997. *Statistical Abstract of the United States, 1997*. Washington, DC: U.S. Government Printing Office.

———. 2000. *Statistical Abstract of the United States, 1999*. Washington, DC: U.S. Government Printing Office.

———. 2002. *Statistical Abstract of the United States, 1999*. Washington, DC: U.S. Government Printing Office.

U.S. Department of Education. 1990. Reported in *Chronicle of Higher Education*, September 5:22.

U.S. Department of Health, Education, and Welfare. 1976. *The Measure of Poverty: A Report to Congress as Mandated by the Education Amendment of 1974*. Washington, DC: U.S. Government Printing Office.

U.S. Department of Labor. 1986. *Dictionary of Occupational Titles*. 4th ed. Supplement. Washington, DC: U.S. Government Printing Office.

U.S. Federal Bureau of Investigation. 2002. "Crime in the United States." Retrieved online on December 17, 2003 at <http://www.fbi.gov/ucr/cius_02/pdf/0front.pdf>.

Valdez, A. 1997. "In the Hood: Street Gangs Discover White-Collar-Crime." *Police* 5(12): 49–50, 56.

Vande-Berg, L. R., and D. Streckfuss. 1992. "Prime-Time Television's Portrayal of Women and the World of Work: A Demographic Portrayal." *Journal of Broadcasting and Electronic Media* 36:195–208.

Van den Berge, Pierre L. 1967. *Race and Racism*. New York: John Wiley.

Vanderbroeck, Paul J. J. 1987. *Popular Leadership and Collective Behavior in the Late Roman Republic (ca. 80–50 B.C.)*. Amsterdam: J. C. Gieben.

Van Der Lippe, Tanja and Liset Van Dijk. 2002. "Comparative Research on Women's Employment." *Annual Review of Sociology* 28:221–241.

Van Dyke, Nella. 2003. "Crossing Movement Boundaries: Factors that Facilitate Coalition Protests by American College Students, 1930–1990." *Social Problems* 50:226–250.

Vanfossen, B. E., J. D. Jones, and J. Z. Spade. 1987. "Curriculum Tracking and Status Maintenance." *Sociology of Education* 60:104–122.

Veblen, Thorstein. 1899. *The Theory of the Leisure Class*. New York: Viking Press.

———. 1921. *Engineers and the Price System*. New York: Viking.

Veenstra, Gerry. 2000. "Social Capital, SES and Health: An Individual-Level Analysis," *Social Science and Medicine* 50:619–620.

Virtual Jerusalem. 1998. Online <http://www.virtual.co.il/communities/wjcbook/chart map.htm>. "Jewish Communities of the World." [April 3].

Vowell, Paul, and David C. May. 2000. "Another Look at Classic Strain Theory: Poverty Status, Perceived Blocked Opportunity and Group Membership as Predictors of Adolescent Violent Behavior." *Sociological Inquiry* 70:42–60.

Wagner, David. 1993. *Checkerboard Square: Culture and Resistance in a Homeless Community*. Boulder, CO: Westview Press.

Walker, Stephan, and Len Barton. 1983. *Gender, Class, and Education*. London: Falmer Press.

Wallace, Ruth A., and Alison Wolf. 1998. *Contemporary Sociological Theory*. Englewood Cliffs, NJ: Prentice-Hall.

Wallechinsky, David, and Irving Wallace. 1975. *The People's Almanac*. Garden City, NY: Doubleday.

Wallerstein, Immanuel. 1979. The Capitalist World-Economy. New York: Cambridge University Press.

———. 2000. *The Essential Wallerstein*. New York: New Press.

Wallis, Roy. 1975. *Sectarianism: Analyses of Religious and Non-Religious Sects*. New York: John Wiley.

Warner, Lloyd W., with Marchia Meeker, and Kenneth Eells. 1960. *Social Class in America:*

A Manual of Procedure for the Measurement of Social Status. New York: Harper & Row; orig. published in 1949 by Science Research Associates, Inc., Chicago.

Warr, Mark. 1993. "Parents, Peers, and Delinquency." *Social Forces* 72:247–264.

Washington Post. 1995a. "AIDS 'Bomb' Ready to Explode as India Attempts to Modernize." Reported in Columbus Dispatch, August 20:7A.

_____. 1995b. "Parent Company of CBS Buys Six Cigarette Brands." Reported in Columbus Dispatch, December 3:8A.

Waters, Mary C. 1990. *Ethnic Options: Choosing Identities in America*. Berkeley, CA: University of California Press.

Watson, Russell, Daniel Glick, Mark Hosenball, John McCormick, Andrew Murr, Sharon Begley, Susan Miller, Ginny Carroll, and Sherry Keene. 1994. "America's Nuclear Secrets." *Newsweek*, December 27:14–18.

Watson, Russell, et al. 1992. "Ethnic Cleansing." *Newsweek*, August 17:16–20.

Weber, Max. 1922. *Economy and Society*. Translated by Ephraim Fischoff, et al. New York: Bedminster Press.

_____. 1946. From H. H. Gerth and C. Wright Mills (eds.), *Max Weber: Essays in Sociology*. New York: Oxford University Press.

_____. 1947. *The Theory of Social and Political Organization*. Translated by A. M. Henderson and Talcott Parsons. New York: Oxford University Press.

_____. 1958 [orig. 1904]. *The Protestant Ethic and the Spirit of Capitalism*. Translated by Talcott Parsons. New York: Scribner's.

Weeks, John R. 1988. "The Demography of Muslim Nations." *Population Bulletin* 43(4).

Weeks, John R. 2002. *Population: An Introduction to Concepts and Issues* Eighth edition. Belmont, CA: Wadsworth.

_____. 1998. *Population: An Introduction to Concepts and Issues*. Belmont, CA: Wadsworth.

Wehr, Kevin. 1994. "The Power Elite and the Bohemian Grove: Has Anything Changed in the 1990s?" *Critical Sociology* 20(2):121–124.

Weiss, Rick. 2002. "War on Disease" *National Geographic* 201 (No.3):5–31.

Weiss, Robert S. 1975. *Marital Separation*. New York: Basic Books.

Weitzman, Lenore J. 1987. *The Divorce Revolution: The Unexpected Social and Economic Consequences for Women and Children in America*. New York: Free Press.

Wellman, Barry and Caroline Haythornthwaite (Eds.) 2002. *The Internet in Everyday Life*. Oxford, UK: Blackwell.

Wellman, Barry, Janet Salaff, Dimitrina Dimitrova, Laura Garton, Milena Gulia, and Caroline Haythornthwaite. 1996. "Computer Networks as Social Networks: Collaborative Work, Telework, and Virtual Community." *Annual Review of Sociology* 22:213–238.

Welsh, Sandy. 1999. "Gender and Sexual Harassment." *Annual Review of Sociology* 25:169–190.

_____. 2000. "The Multidimensional Nature of Sexual Harassment." *Violence Against Women* 6:118–141.

Wesotowski, Wlodzimierz. 1962. "Some Notes on the Functional Theory of Stratification." *Polish Sociological Bulletin* (3–4):28–38.

Wessel, David. 1986. "More Younger Doctors Shun Private Practice, Work As Employees." *Wall Street Journal*, January 13:503.

Wethington, Elaine. 2000. "Categories of Stress." *Advances in Group Processes* 17:229–253.

Weston, Kath. 1995. "Exiles From Kinship." Pp. 152–160 in David M. Newman (ed.), *Sociology: Exploring the Architecture of Everyday Life Readings*. Thousand Oaks, CA: Pine Forge Press.

Wheatley, Vera. 1957. *The Life and Work of Harriet Martineau*. London: Secker & Warburg.

Whisenant, Warren A., Paul Pedersen, and Bill L. Obenour. 2002. "Success and Gender: Determining the Rate of Advancement For Intercollegiate Athletic Directors." *Sex Roles* 47:485–491.

Whitbeck, Les B., and Danny R. Hoyt. 1994. "Social Prestige and Assortive Mating: A Comparison of Students from 1956 and 1988." *Journal of Social and Personal Relationships* 11:137–145.

White, Ralph K., and Ronald O. Lippett. 1960. *Autocracy and Democracy*. New York: Harper & Row.

Whittier, Nancy. 1995. *Feminist Generations: The Persistence of the Radical Women's Movement*. Philadelphia, PA: Temple University Press.

Whorf, Benjamin L. 1956. *Language, Thought, and Reality*. Cambridge, MA: MIT Press.

Whyte, William Foote. 1943. *Street Corner Society*. Chicago: University of Chicago Press.

_____. 1984. *Learning from the Field*. Newbury Park, CA: Sage.

Wilkinson, Louise C., and Cora B. Marrett, (eds.). 1985. *Gender Influences in Classroom Interaction*. Orlando, FL: Academic Press.

Williams, Alan. 1999. "Economics, Ethics, and the Public Health Care Policy." *International Social Science Journal* 51:297–312.

Williams, Betty Fry. 1992. "Changing Demographics: Challenges for Educators." *Intervention in School and Clinic* 27:157–163.

Williams, L. Susan, Sandra D. Alverez, and Kevin S. Andrade Hauck. 2002. "My Name is Not Maria: Young Latinas Seeking Home in the Heartland." *Social Problems* 49: 563–584.

Williams, Robin M. 1994. "The Sociology of Ethnic Conflicts: Comparative International Perspectives." *Annual Review of Sociology* 20:49–79.

Williams, Robin M., Jr. 1970. *American Society: A Sociological Interpretation*. 3rd ed. New York: Knopf.

Williams, Rhys H., and Robert Benford. 2000. "Two Faces of Collective Action Frames: A Theoretical Consideration." *Current Perspectives in Social Theory* 20:122–151.

Williams, T. B. 1986. *The Impact of Television: A Natural Experiment in Three Communities*. New York: Aldine Press.

Williams, Walter L. 1986. *The Skirt and the Flesh: Sexual Diversity in American Indian Culture*. Boston: Beacon Yount.

Wilson, Clint C., and Félix Gutiérrez. 1995a. *Minorities and the Media*. Newbury Park, CA: Sage.

_____. 1995b. Race, Multiculturalism, and the Media. Newbury Park, CA: Sage.

Wilson, Edward O. 1979. *On Human Nature*. New York: Bantam.

Wilson, James Q. 1983. *Thinking About Crime*. Rev. ed. New York: Vintage.

_____. 1993. *The Moral Sense*. New York: The Free Press.

Wilson, James Q. and George Kelling. 1982. "Broken Windows: The Police and Neighborhood Safety." *Atlantic Monthly* (March): 29–38.

Wilson, Paul E. 1995. *A Time to Lose*. Lawrence, KS: University of Kansas Press.

Wilson, William Julius. 1980. *The Declining Significance of Race: Blacks and Changing American Institutions*. Chicago: University of Chicago Press.

_____. 1987. *The Truly Disadvantaged: The Inner City, the Underclass, and Public Policy*. Chicago: University of Chicago Press.

_____. 1997. *When Work Disappears: The World of the New Urban Poor*. New York: Knopf.

Winship, Janice. 1983. "Handling Sex." *Media, Culture, and Society* 3:25–41.

Wirth, Louis. 1928. *The Ghetto*. Chicago: University of Chicago Press.

_____. 1939. "Urbanism as a Way of Life." *American Journal of Sociology* 49:46–63.

Wissinger, Elizabeth A. 2000. "Marxist Tools for Sociology: Reconsidering Human Nature." Paper presented at the Annual Meeting of the American Sociological Association. August 12–16. Washington, DC.

Wohl, Richard R. 1966. "The 'Rags to Riches' Story: An Episode of Secular Idealism." Pp. 501–506 in Richard Bendix and Seymour Martin Lipset (eds.), *Class, Status, and Power: Social Stratification in Comparative Perspective*, 2nd ed. New York: Free Press.

Wolch, Jennifer, and Michael Dean. 1993. *Malign Neglect: Homelessness in an American City*. San Francisco: Jossey-Bass.

Woolhanler, Steffie, and David Himmelstein. 1997. "Costs of Care and Administration for Profit and Other Hospitals in the United States." *New England Journal of Medicine* 336:769–774.

World Bank. 1984. World Development Report 1984. New York: Oxford University Press.

World Health Organization. 1999. Removing Obstacles to Health Development. Geneva, Switzerland: Altar.

World Health Organization. 2003. *AIDS Epidemic Update*. December

Wren, David J. 1999. "School Culture, Exploring the Hidden Curriculum." *Adolescence* 34:593–596.

Wright, Erik Olin. 1979. *Class Structure and Income Determination*. New York: Academic Press.

Wright, John W., (ed.). 1997. The Universal Almanac. Kansas City: Andrews and McMeel.

Wright, Kelly. 2002. *Homeless in America: How Could It Happen Here?* Detroit: Gale Group.

Wright, Robert E., John C. Palmer, and Joseph C. Miller. 1996. "An Examination of Gender-Based Variations in the Predictive Ability of the SAT." *College Student Journal* 30:81–84.

WuDunn, Sheryl. 1991. "Divorce Rate Soars as Chinese Decide Love Is Part of Marriage." *New York Times*, April 17:B1.

Yamane, David. 1997. "Secularization on Trial: In Defense of a Neosecularization Paradigm." *Journal for the Scientific Study of Religion* 36:109–122.

Young-Eisendrath, Polly. 1995. You're Not What I Expected: Breaking the He Said/She Said Cycle. New York: Simon & Schuster.

Yukawa, Joyce. 1992. "Revaluing the Japanese American Experience: Two Women Writers' Views." *Asian Migrant* 5:33–36.

Zald, Mayer N. and John D. McCarthy. 2002. "The Resource Mobilization Research Program: Progress, Challenge, and Transformation." Pp. 147–171 in Joseph Berger and Morris Zelditch, Jr. (eds.), *New Directions in Contemporary Sociological Theory*. Lanham, MD: Rowman & Littlefield.

Zangwill, Israel. 1921. (orig. 1909). *The Melting Pot*. New York: Macmillan.

Zborowski, Mark. 1969. *People in Pain*. San Francisco: Jossey-Bass.

Zelditch, Morris Jr. 2000. "Legitimacy and the Stability of Authority: A Theoretical Research Program." Cooley-Mead Address presented at the Annual Meeting of the American Sociological Association. August 12–16. Washington, DC.

Zellner, William W. 2001. *Extraordinary Groups: An Examination of Unconventional Lifestyles*. 7th ed. New York: Worth Publishers.

Zhou, Xueguang, Nancy Brandon Tuma, and Phyllis Moen. 1997. "Institutional Change and Job-shift Patterns in Urban China, 1949–1994." *American Sociological Review* 62:339–365.

Zimbardo, Philip, Curtis W. Banks, Craig Handy, and David Jaffe. 1973. "The Mind Is a Formidable Jailer." *New York Times*, April 8.

Zimbardo, Philip, Ebbe B. Ebbesen, and Christine Maslach. 1977. *Influencing Attitudes and Changing Behavior*. Reading, MA: Addison-Wesley.

Zimmerman, Mary K. 2000. "Women's Health and Gender Bias in Medical Education." *Research in the Sociology of Health Care* 17:121–138.

Photo Credits

Chapter 1
Getty Images Inc.—Stone Allstock, 7. Mary Evans Picture Library Ltd, 8. The Granger Collection, 9 (top left, top center, bottom left). Corbis/Bettmann, 9 (top right, bottom right). UPI/Corbis/Bettmann, 9 (bottom center). The Granger Collection, 10. Michael Szulc-Krzyzanowski/The Image Works, 11 (top). Corbis/Bettmann, 11 (margin). The Granger Collection, 12. AP/Wide World Photos, 14. Mark Richards/PhotoEdit, 15. Bill Aron/PhotoEdit, 19. Philip G. Zimbardo, Inc., 22. Lee Snider/The Image Works, 23.

Chapter 2
Eascott-Momatiuk/The Image Works, 34. Michael J. Doolittle/The Image Works, 38. Norman Lightfoot/Photo Researchers, Inc., 39. William M. Rittase/Getty Images Inc.—Hulton Archive Photos, 41 (bottom left). Mitch Kezar/Getty Images Inc.—Stone Allstock, 41 (bottom right). Getty Images Inc.—Hulton Archive Photos, 42. Sunil Malhotra/Getty Images Inc.—Hulton Archive Photos, 43. John Eastcott/Yva Momatiuk/The Image Works, 50. Robert W. Ginn/PhotoEdit, 53.

Chapter 3
David Grossman/The Image Works, 67. Getty Images Inc.—Hulton Archive Photos, 68. Jack Kurtz/The Image Works, 71, Bob Daemmrich/The Image Works, 74, 75. The Norman Rockwell Family Trust, 77. Margot Granitsas/The Image Works, 78. AP/Wide World Photos, 85. John Gapp III/AP/Wide World Photos, 86.

Chapter 4
CORBIS-NY, 97. Roger M. Richards/Getty Images, Inc.—Liaison, 104. Zefa Visual Media-Germany/Index Stock Imagery, Inc., 109. The Cartoon Bank, 111. Bob Daemmrich/The Image Works, 112. Picture Desk, Inc./Kobal Collection, 113. Frank Pedrick/The Image Works, 116.

Chapter 5
Hawkins/Corbis/Sygma, 128. A. Ramey/PhotoEdit, 130. Patricia Agre/Photo Researchers, Inc., 132. Robert Brenner/PhotoEdit, 134. Mark Richards/PhotoEdit, 139.

Mark C. Burnett/Photo Researchers, Inc., 146 (top). Agence France Presse/Corbis/Bettmann, 146 (bottom). Spencer Grant/PhotoEdit, 148.

Chapter 6
William Carter/Photo Researchers, Inc., 161. The Image Works, 162 (left). Anthony Suau/Getty Images, Inc.—Liaison, 162 (right). Getty Images Inc.—Hulton Archive Photos, 166. UPI/Jim Herrmann/Corbis/Bettmann, 173. Tony Freeman/PhotoEdit, 179. Grapes/Michaud/Photo Researchers, Inc., 181. Michael Caulfield/AP/Wide World Photos, 182.

Chapter 7
UPI/Corbis/Bettmann, 200 (top), Frank Siteman/Stock Boston, 200 (bottom). Terry E. Eiler/Stock Boston, 205. The Granger Collection, 206. The Granger Collection, 209 (top). Michael Newman/PhotoEdit, 209 (bottom). Jeff Greenberg/PhotoEdit, 212. Paul Conklin/PhotoEdit, 218.

Chapter 8
Jason Laure/The Image Works, 229. Lawrence Migdale/Pix, 231. Bill Aron/PhotoEdit, 232. Steven Rubin/The Image Works, 240. Michael Newman/PhotoEdit, 244. AP/Wide World Photos, 246.

Chapter 9
Philippe Plailly/Science Photo Library/Photo Researchers, Inc., 254. Getty Images, Inc.—Liaison, 263. Christopher Fitzgerald/The Image Works, 265. Corbis/Bettmann, 270 (left). Robert Sorbo/Corbis/Sygma, 270 (right). Fred R. Conrad/New York Times Pictures, 272.

Chapter 10
Fujifotos/The Image Works, 283. The Granger Collection, 284. Nader/Corbis/Sygma, 285. The Image Works, 287. Topham/The Image Works, 291. AP/Wide World Photos, 298. Mike Luckovich/Creators Syndicate, Inc., 301.

Chapter 11
The Granger Collection, 313 (left). Nubar Alexanian/Stock Boston, 313 (right). Frank Siteman/Stock Boston, 317. Tom Smart/Getty

Images, Inc.—Liaison, 319. Mark Richards/PhotoEdit, 322. David H. Wells/Corbis/Bettmann, 330. Picture Desk, Inc./Kobal Collection, 336.

Chapter 12
Amy Etra/PhotoEdit, 344. Tom Wagner/Corbis/SABA Press Photos, Inc., 351. Michael Newman/PhotoEdit, 352. Ira Wyman/Corbis/Sygma, 353. Michael Newman/PhotoEdit, 355. Scott Cunningham/Merrill Education, 356. G.B. Trudeau/Universal Press Syndicate, 358. Bob Daemmrich/The Image Works, 361. CORBIS-NY, 362. Will Hart/Will Hart, 364. Stock Boston, 367.

Chapter 13
Vivienne della Grotta/Photo Researchers, Inc., 374. Richard Hutchings/PhotoEdit, 376. Chris Lisle/Corbis/Bettmann, 378. DPA/NSR/The Image Works, 380. Mark Chester/Lonely Planet Images/Photo 20-20, 382. UPI/Corbis/Bettmann, 390. Globe Photos, Inc., 393.

Chapter 14
Keith Brofsky/Getty Images, Inc.—Photodisc., 405, Bassano/Camera Press London/Globe Photos, Inc., 406. W.G. Williams/Globe Photos, Inc., 409. Robert Brenner/PhotoEdit, 417. Jonathan Nourok/PhotoEdit, 421.

Chapter 15
George Holton/Photo Researchers, Inc., 430. A. Ramey/PhotoEdit, 436. Corbis/Bettmann, 438. Cary S. Wolinsky/Stock Boston, 440. Michael Siluk/The Image Works, 442. Cahokia Mounds State Historic Site, 444. John Neubauer/PhotoEdit, 446. Randall Hyman/Stock Boston, 453.

Chapter 16
Erik Fowke/PhotoEdit, 465. Beth A. Keiser/AP/Wide World Photos, 466. Ed Andrieski/AP/Wide World Photos, 474. Roger Sandler/Pictor/ImageState/International Stock Photography Ltd., 475. Underwood & Underwood/Corbis/Bettmann, 476. UPI/Corbis/Bettmann, 477. Issei Kato/CORBIS-NY, 478. Corbis/Bettmann, 482. UPI/Corbis/Bettmann, 483.

Name Index

Subject Index

gender inequality, 236
industrialization and, 258–259
inventions and discovery, 54
Tiananmen Square, 461, 483–484
Chinese Americans. *See also*
Asian Americans
assimilation of, 201
from Cuba, 212
discrimination study, 197
ethnicity and, 195
historical records and, 74
inequality and, 214, 220
stereotypes, 198
Chinese Exclusion Act (1882), 214
Cho, Fujio, 478
Cholera, 401
Christianity
born-again Christians, 376, 390
origin of, 284
overview, 379
religion as weapon, 386
social control, 385
in the world, 384
Chronically poor, 171, 220, 325
Chukchee people, 41
Churches
denominations and, 377–378
electronic, 392–393
mega-church, 393–395
religious affiliation, 391
as sacred, 375
separation from state, 387
Churchill, Winston, 416
Cisneros, Alberto, 198
Cities. *See also* Urbanization
agrarian societies and, 41
China and, 43
Gesellschaft and, 450
historical perspective, 444–445
Industrial Revolution and, 7
Native Americans in, 205
refugee influx, 220–221
Sunni Muslims and, 381
of today, 446–450
Citigroup, 260–261
Civil disobedience, 483
Civil law, 111
Civil religion, 389–390
Civil Rights Act (1964), 241
Civil rights movement
1960s and, 207
overview, 473–475
relationships and, 481
role of black women, 74
Civil War
African Americans and, 17, 74
civil rights movement after, 473
slavery and, 207
Class conflict, 271
Class consciousness, 174
Class consistency, 161–162
Class systems, 161. *See also*
Social class
Clausewitz, Carl von, 288
Clijsters, Els, 65
Clijsters, Kim, 65
Clijsters, Leo, 65
Clinton, Bill, 55, 193, 305
Clinton, Hilary Rodham, 235
Cliques, 137–138, 147
Clothing, in gender socialization, 231

Coalitions
environmental movement and, 476
interest groups and, 295
military-industrial complex as, 288, 298
pluralistic model and, 299
political parties and, 294
United Nations and, 289
The Cock Group, 105
Code Napoleon, 111
Coercion, 128, 282
Coercive organizations, 145
Cohabitation, 323, 335
Cohesiveness
conflict and, 16
group dynamics and, 141–142
pluralism and, 202
religion and, 384–385
Cold war
human rights and, 281, 291–292
institutional theory and, 288
socialism and, 258
Coleman, James, 3, 353
Coleman, John, 183–184
Collections, compared with groups, 137
Collective behavior, 463–469
Collective mind, 467–468
Collective social action, 461–463, 469–485
Colleges and universities. *See* Education
Colombus, Christopher, 38
Colonization, 288
Columbus, Christopher, 357
Coming of Age in Samoa (Mead), 68
Commitment-belief bonds, 106–107
Common law, 111
Communal societies
characteristics of, 46
collective social action and, 462
demographic transition and, 437
deviance and crime and, 96
disease and, 402
education in, 344
groups in, 138
industrialization and, 254
overview, 44–45
relationships and, 45, 144
religion and, 374
socialization in, 65–66
social support in, 132
tracking people, 126
view on illness, 402
Communism
human agency and, 53
Marxism and, 9
origins of, 281
religion and, 388
totalitarian states and, 286
Communist Manifesto (Marx), 8
Community and Society (Toennies), 450
Community policing, 112–113
Compadrazgo, 326
Compadres, 326
Comparable worth, 242
Competition, 127
Computers, 57, 139
Comte, Auguste, 7–9, 21
Concentric zone model, 447–449
Condescending chivalry, 147
Conflict. *See also* War
class, 271
in education, 353
groups and, 299

Marx on, 10, 13
in organizations, 15
political parties and, 294
religions and, 379
role, 16, 131
as type of interaction, 127–128
Conflict perspective
on deviance and crime, 108–110
on economy, 269, 271
on education, 361–364
on gender inequality, 244–246
on marriage and family, 333–334
on medicine and health care, 416, 419–420
on political order, 300–301
on racial/ethnic inequality, 217–219
on religion, 385–386
on social change, 15–16, 51–53
on social conflict, 14–15
on socialization, 80
on stratification, 181–182, 185
Conformity
Anglo, 201
group dynamics and, 142–144
internal social controls and, 97
Japan and, 349
labeling and, 108
strain theory and, 105
Confucianism, 383
Confusion (*versus* identity), 82
Conglomerates, 261. *See also* Corporations
Conscious mind, 81
Consciousness of kind, 218
Conservation period, 476
Conservative Jews, 381
Conservatives, 293
Conspicuous consumption, 167
Constitution. *See* U.S. Constitution
Consumerism, industrialization and, 254
Contagion theory, 467–469
Continuity theory, 72
Contraception, 247, 405, 433
Control groups, 20–21
Conventional crowds, 464
Conventional morality, 106–107
Conventional stage, 84
Convergence, economic, 258–260
Convergence theory, 468
Conversation, male dominance in, 234
Cooking methods, 453
Cooley, Charles Horton, 76–77
Cooperation, 127
Core nations, 51
Corning Glass Works, 151
Cornucopian view, 440
Corporate crime, 109
Corporations, 148–149, 260–264, 332
Cosby, Bill, 198
Cosmopolitan magazine, 168
Costs
of childbirth, 440
of health care, 407, 410–411, 423
of secondary education, 366
Courtship, 317
Courts (United States), 113–114
Creationism, 391
Creativity, 57, 66, 141
Credentialism, 347–349
Credit cards, 47–49
Creek Indians, 315
Cree society, 39

Edison, Thomas, 54
Education
    as achieved status, 129
    analysis of, 360–365
    careers and, 349, 351
    civil rights movement, 473
    collective social action and, 481
    defined, 344
    foreign-born students, 349
    future considerations, 365–368
    gender and, 236, 358–359
    Great Social Transformation and, 344
    income and, 239, 348
    in Japan, 345, 349–352
    job loss anxiety and, 268
    life expectancy and, 434
    of medical staff, 405, 420
    minority issues and, 352–360
    modernization theory on, 50
    poverty and, 176, 179
    prestige and, 165
    principle of cumulation and, 220
    race/ethnic groups and, 210–211, 213–216
    service jobs and, 275
    social class and, 161–162, 169, 171
    socialization and, 66
    socioeconomic status and, 163–164
    in United States, 345–350, 352
    voting and, 295
    year-round schooling, 350
Educational inflation, 348–349
Egalitarianism, 163
Ego, 81
Ehrlich, Paul, 452
Eighteenth Amendment, 469
Eisenhower, Dwight D., 284, 297–298
Elder abuse, 99, 101
Elderly, 69–72, 412, 437
Electronic church, 392–393
The Elementary Forms of the Religious Life
        (Durkheim), 384
Elite (class), 166–168, 286
Emergent norm theory, 468–469
Emigration, 435
Endogamy, 317–318
Entrepreneurs, 169, 253–254
Environment. *See also* Ecology
    pluralist model and, 299
    POET model and, 441
    population growth and, 439–443, 452
    pursuit of profit and, 257
    recycling and, 451
    social movements, 476–481
    Union Carbide disaster, 263
Environmental movement, 476–481
Environmental Protection Agency (EPA), 442
Epidemics, 401–402
Epigenic principle, 82
Equal Pay Act (1963), 241
Equal Rights Amendment, 336, 475
Equilibrium, 14, 49
Erikson, Erik, 81–83
Esteem, 165, 167
Ethicalist systems, 383
Ethics, research and, 21–23
Ethnic groups. *See also* Inequality
    analysis of inequality, 216–219
    assimilation of, 199–201
    competition for resources, 301
    defined, 195

discrimination against, 180
    education and, 353
    future considerations, 219–221
    life chances and, 216
    misinterpretation of behavior, 364
    pain and, 420
    pluralism and, 201
    poverty rates by, 176
    structural strains and, 463
    symbolic ethnicity and, 202
    unemployment and, 266
    in United States, 203–216
Ethnic identity, 195, 202
Ethnicity
    as ascribed status, 129–130
    defined, 195
    family forms and, 325–327
    inequality and, 243, 409
    marriage and, 317–318
    population by, 213
    power models and, 299
    race and, 194–196
    social interaction and, 199–203
    social mobility, 173
    socioeconomic status and, 164
Ethnic revival, 202
Ethnocentrism, 37–38, 49
Ethnomethodology, 134–135
Evolution, theory of, 49, 52, 391
Exchange, 127
Exchange theory, 135–136
Exclusion, politics of, 290
Exogamy, 317–318
Experience
    adulthood and, 68
    critical thinking and, 6
    in religion, 376–377, 387
Experimental groups, 20
Experiments, 20, 135, 142–143
Exploitation period, 476
Expressive crowds, 465
Expressive leaders, 140
Expressive movements, 470–471, 478
Expulsion, 202–203
Expulsion and extermination stage, 206
Extended families
    composition of, 314
    marital dissolution in, 328–329
    nuclear family comparison, 316
    race/ethnic groups and, 205, 326
External social controls, 97
Extinction, animal and plant life, 452–453
Exxon Mobil, 260–261

Failure of social control, 463
False consciousness, 174, 245
Family. *See also* Extended families
    as agent of socialization, 73
    alternative forms, 321–324
    analysis of, 332–335
    communal societies and, 138
    defined, 312
    as economic unit, 254
    exogamy and, 318
    future considerations, 335–337
    gangs replacing, 108
    Great Social Transformation and, 312–313
    homelessness and, 170
    issues in, 327–331
    nuclear, 313–316, 329

poverty threshold for, 176
    as primary group, 137–138
    primary socialization and, 66
    race/ethnic groups, 211, 325–327
    roles of women in, 475
    size of, 433
    socialization and, 66, 360
    stratification and, 185
Family of orientation, 313, 315
Family of procreation, 313, 315
Farming, 214–215, 254, 451
Fast societies, 149
Federal Bureau of Investigation (FBI)
    crime and, 95, 99–101
    impression management and, 133–134
    web site, 112
Federal Communications Commission
        (FCC), 393
Federal Economy Act (1932), 241, 475
Federal Express Company (FedEx), 270
Fee for service, 410
Felonies, 114
Female circumcision, 236
The Feminine Mystique, 241
Feminine qualities, 229
Feminism, 240–243, 475
Feminist Majority Foundation, 243
Feminization of poverty, 321–322, 475
Fertility
    demographic transition and, 437
    neo-Malthusians on, 441
    population and, 213, 430, 432–434, 452
Filipinos, 215–216, 435
Flappers, 475
Folkways, 36
Forced assimilation stage, 206
Forcible rape, 99–100, 102
Ford Motor, 260–261
Formal agents of socialization, 273
Formal education, 344
Formal groups, 137
Formal organizational stage, 472
France
    colonies and, 286
    Jewish population, 381
    migration in, 435
    mobility in, 172
    prejudice against, 196
    social stratification in, 182
    total institutions in, 87
Franklin, Benjamin, 403
Freedom of choice, in education, 359
Free-market competition, 255–256, 377–378
French Revolution, 7
Freud, Sigmund, 81
Friedan, Betty, 241
Front region, 133–134
Functionalist perspective
    comparisons, 52
    on deviance and crime, 105–106, 110
    Durkheim and, 12
    on economy, 269–271
    on education, 360–361, 364
    on gender inequality, 244, 246
    on marriage and family, 332–334
    on medicine and health care, 416–418
    on political order, 300
    on racial/ethnical inequality, 217, 219
    on religion, 384–385
    social evolution and, 49–50

Racism, 179, 197–199
Radical ecology, 478
Radical feminists, 242
Random sampling, 20
Rape, 99–100, 102, 333
Rationalization, 12, 45. *See also* Weber, Max
Reagan, Ronald, 71, 198, 284
Rebellion, 106, 284
Reciprocity, norm of, 135–136
Reconstituted families, 313–314
Redistribution, 206, 258
Redlining, 199
Reference groups, 139
Reflective skepticism, 6
Reform Jews, 381
Reform movements, 411, 469
Rehabilitation, 108, 114, 116
Reincarnation, 382, 385
Relationships
    adulthood and, 69
    affinal, 315
    associational society and, 45, 144
    cohesion and, 142
    communal society and, 45, 144
    Confucianism on, 383
    dyads and, 139
    gay and lesbian couples, 322–323
    groups and, 137–138
    interpersonal attachment-involvement
        and, 106
    networks of, 132
    racial/ethnic groups and, 219–221
    religion and, 386
Relative deprivation theory, 471
Relative poverty, 177
Religion
    agrarian societies and, 41
    analysis of, 384–387
    ascribed status and, 129
    charismatic authority and, 284
    in communal society, 45
    defined, 373–374
    diffusion and, 54
    elements of, 375–379
    endogamy and, 318
    future considerations, 392–395
    Great Social Transformation and, 374–375
    social change and, 387–392
    varieties of, 379–384
Religiosity, 391
Religious fundamentalism, 390
Religious law, 111
Replacement level, 433
Representative samples, 19–20
Repression, 81
Republican Party, 284, 294–296, 298
Reputational method, 166
Research methods, 16–23
Residence, marriage and, 319–320
Resistance movements, 470
Resocialization, 86–88
Resource-mobilization theory, 472
Restitution, 96, 112
Retirement, 69–72, 262
Retreatism, strain theory and, 106
Retribution, 114
Revolution
    as change catalyst, 53
    Marx on, 6, 8–10, 181
Revolutionary movements, 283–284,
        469–470

Rewards
    bureaucracies and, 146–147
    Christianity on, 386
    for conformity, 142
    distributive systems theory, 182
    education and, 361–362
    exchange theory and, 136
    gender inequality and, 244
    motivation and, 180
Right practices, 383
Riots, 213, 463, 465–467
Ritual avoidance, 161
Ritual cleansing, 161
Ritualism, strain theory and, 106
Ritual pollution, 161
Rituals
    marriage and, 316
    religion and, 375–376, 384–385
    symbols of nation, 389–390
Ritzer, George, 147
River systems, 444–445
Robber barons, 270
Robbery, 99–100, 102, 110
Robbins, Alexandra, 69
Robertson, Pat, 393
Rockefeller, John D.
    as capitalist, 270
    conglomerates and, 261
    rags-to-riches, 172
    Standard Oil Company, 166
Rockefeller family, 166–167
Rockwell, Norman, 77
Rockwell International, 479
Role conflict, 131
Role making, 334
Role models, 79, 272
Role of the generalized other, 78
Roles
    defined, 130
    example, 129
    families and, 333–334
    formal groups and, 137
    gender, 228–233, 235
    organizations and, 145
    sickness and, 402
    social interaction and, 130–132
    women and, 327, 329, 475
Role strain, 131–132
Role stress, 131–132
Role taking, 78–79, 334
Roman Empire, 377, 445
Romantic love, 311, 316–317, 329
Romero, Oscar Arnulfo, 386
Roosevelt, Franklin, 20
Roosevelt, Theodore, 476
Roosevelt family, 167
Rousseau, Jean-Jacques, 299
Routinizing the violence, 290
Rules
    bureaucracies and, 145–146, 254
    hospitals and, 407
    industrialization and, 183
    legal-rational authority, 283
    social interaction and, 134–135
    socialization and, 66
Ruling class, 166–167, 174, 288
Rumors, 465–467
Russia, 381, 388. *See also* Soviet Union

Sacco, Nicola, 204
Sacred, 375, 385, 389

Saddam Hussein, 285, 291
Salem Witch Trial, 17, 373
Samples, in surveys, 19
Sanger, Margaret, 405
Sanitation, 403, 406
Sapir-Whorf hypothesis, 36
SARS, 55–56, 401
Ibn Saud, 318
Saudi Arabia, 50, 285, 318
Scalping, 97
Scholastic Aptitude Tests (SATs), 199,
        355–356
Schools. *See also* Education
    as agent of socialization, 73–74
    defined, 344
    freedom of choice in, 359
    in gender socialization, 231–232
    magnet, 354
    religion and, 387
    voting in, 297
    year-round, 350
Schuller, Robert H., 393
Science
    defined, 4
    disease and, 416–417
    health care and, 403, 410–411
    population use in, 19
    religion and, 391
    sociology as, 7, 16
Scientific method, 4, 8
Scopes trial, 391
Sculley, John, 253
Seale, Bobby, 474
Secondary groups, 138
Secondary socialization, 66
Second shift, 237
Sector model, 448–449
Sects, 378, 390
Secularization, 388–389
Segregation, 237–238, 353–354. *See also*
        Housing segregation
Selectivity, 349
Self, 76–80
Self-absorption, 82
Self-esteem, 66, 233, 365
Self-fulfilling prophecy, 108, 363
Self-identification method, 166
Semiperiphery nations, 51
Separation stage, 205–206
September 11, 2001
    expressive crowds and, 465
    mobilization due to, 305
    social organization, 125
    terrorism and, 88, 289
Serial monogamy, 321
Services, distribution of, 270, 273–275
Seventh Day Adventists, 378
Severity (punishment), 115
Sex. *See* Gender
Sexism
    defined, 228
    feminism and, 241
    income inequality and, 239
    institutionalized, 236
    poverty and, 179
Sexual harassment, 227–228, 294, 297
Sexuality
    advertising and, 232
    as male property, 333
    Mead's research on, 82
    Mexican Americans and, 326

Shamans
    as leaders, 141
    social control and, 385
    treating illness, 34, 402
Shame, 82, 267, 352
Shaw, George Bernard, 163
Sheldon, Sydney, 71
The Shield, 113
Shifting the blame, 290
Shiite Muslims, 380, 389
Shudra caste, 161
Sick role, 417–418, 421
Siddhartha Gautama, 382
Sierra Club, 476
Sikhs, 376
Silent Spring (Carson), 477
Silicon Valley (California), 253
Simpson, O. J., 109, 193, 215
Single-parent families, 321–322
Six Nations, 286
Size, urban, 450–451
Slash and burn technique, 40
Slavery
    African American family and, 325
    mass education and, 346
    reparations for, 474–475
    trade in, 206–207
Slow societies, 149, 151
Small, Albion, 9
Small-world phenomenon, 132
Smearing the opposition, 128
Smelser, Neil, 463
Smith, Adam, 255–257
Smog, 441–442
Social action. *See* Collective social action
Social bonds, 315
Social bond theory, 106–107
Social capital, 182, 269
Social change
    acting crowds and, 465
    catalysts for, 53–58
    collective social action and, 481–484
    conflict perspective on, 15–16, 51–53
    religion and, 387–392
    resistance to, 483–484
    studying, 4–5
    theories of, 47–52
Social class
    agrarian societies and, 41
    analysis of, 180–185
    ascribed status and, 129
    caste systems and, 160–163
    China and, 43
    education and, 353
    family and, 329, 332–333
    health/health care and, 408–409
    inequality of, 157–160, 185–187, 242–243
    socioeconomic status and, 163–172
    tracking bias, 363
    voting and, 295
Social controls
    community policing, 113
    defined, 97
    failure of, 463
    medicine as, 417
    religion and, 385
    theory of, 106
Social ecology, 478
Social evolution, 49–50
Social identity. *See* Identity
Social institution. *See* Institutions

Social insurance, 259
Social interaction
    analysis of, 133–136
    assimilation, 199–201
    Coleman report, 353
    communal/associational societies
        and, 46
    components of, 128–130
    conflict perspective on, 217
    defined, 4
    deviancy and, 104
    education and, 364
    expulsion and annihilation, 202–203
    future considerations, 149–151
    gender socialization and, 232
    groups and, 126–127
    labeling theory on, 108
    marriage and family, 334
    patriarchy and, 234–235
    physician-patient, 420–421
    pluralism, 201–202
    roles, 130–132
    societies and, 138
    of states, 300
    survival and, 125
    symbolic interactionist theory
        and, 79–80
    types of, 127–128
    urban density and, 451
Socialism
    in Cuba, 258, 292
    defined, 254
    Great Depression and, 259
    wealth and power, 257–258, 270–271
Socialization
    agents of, 73–75
    children and, 313
    culture of poverty, 178
    defined, 65–66
    education and, 360
    functionalist perspective on, 332
    future considerations, 88–89
    of gender roles, 228–233
    Great Social Transformation
        and, 65–66
    internal social controls and, 97
    life course and, 66–76
    moral, 80–86
    of physicians/nurses, 420
    political, 301–302
    primary, 66, 68
    religious identity and, 387
    the self and, 76–80
    total institutions and, 86–88
Social loafing, 143
Social movements
    social theory and, 471–472
    types of, 469–471
    in United States, 473–481
Social organization, 125, 254, 405–406
Social power
    agrarian societies and, 41
    capitalism and, 270
    class system and, 162
    conflict perspective on, 15, 217
    corporations and, 260–262
    defined, 14, 282
    exercise of, 282, 284–292
    family and, 333
    health and, 409
    industrialization and, 183

    male dominance, 234–235
    marriage for, 316
    middle class and, 169
    models of, 297–299
    multinationals and, 263
    patriarchy and, 320
    production of, 270–271
    ruling class and, 174
    surplus and, 183
Social programs
    GEAR UP program, 343
    Head Start, 74, 471
    Medicaid, 414, 423
    Medicare, 177, 412–414
    United Nations Joint Programme, 404
Social relationships. *See* Relationships
Social roles. *See* Roles
Social rules. *See* Rules
Social Security Administration, 177, 259
Social stratification
    analysis of, 180–185
    defined, 157, 160
    gender equality and, 228, 244–245
    race and gender, 171
Social structure
    assimilation and, 201
    cycle of, 217
    defined, 4
    Native Americans and, 206
Social theory, 467–469, 471–472
Societal resources, 182–183
Society
    corporations and, 260–264
    culture and, 33–38
    defined, 34
    demography and, 430
    deviance and crime and, 96
    diffusion and, 54
    Durkheim on, 11
    economy and, 254–260
    education and, 344
    fast/slow, 149
    functionalist perspective on, 14
    gender and, 229, 236, 475
    graying of, 262
    health and, 403–408
    marital dissolution and, 328–329
    Marx on, 9
    medicine and, 417
    pluralism and, 202
    poverty in, 177–179
    power and, 282, 298–299
    racism and, 197–198
    reform movements and, 469
    religion and, 384
    restructuring of, 151
    role of conflict, 16
    role strain and stress, 131
    romantic love, 317
    scripts and, 133
    sexual misconduct in, 227
    social interaction and, 138
    socialization and, 66
    states directing, 300
    status in, 128
    structured mobility and, 173
    types of, 39–44
    unemployment and, 264–267
    urbanization in, 446–447
    war and, 288
Society in America (Martineau), 8